2008

MW00679124

Songwriter's Market®

Ian Bessler, Editor

WRITER'S DIGEST BOOKS
CINCINNATI, OH

If you would like to be considered for a listing in the next edition of *Songwriter's Market*, send a SASE (or SAE and IRC) with your request for a questionnaire to *Songwriter's Market*—QR, 4700 East Galbraith Road, Cincinnati, Ohio 45236. Please indicate which section would like to be included.

Editorial Director, Writer's Digest Books: Jane Friedman
Managing Editor, Writer's Digest Market Books: Alice Pope

Songwriter's Market Web page: www.songwritersmarket.com
Writer's Market Web site: www.writersmarket.com
Writer's Digest Web site: www.writersdigest.com
F + W Publications Bookstore: http://fwpublications.com

2008 Songwriter's Market. Copyright © 2007 by Writer's Digest Books. Published by F + W Publications, 4700 East Galbraith Rd., Cincinnati, Ohio 45236. Printed and bound in the United States of America. All rights reserved. No part of this book may be reproduced in any form or by any electronic or mechanical means including information storage and retrieval systems without written permission from the publisher. Reviewers may quote brief passages to be printed in a magazine or newspaper.

Distributed in Canada by Fraser Direct
100 Armstrong Ave.
Georgetown, ON, Canada L7G 5S4
Tel: (905) 877-4411

Distributed in the U.K. and Europe by David & Charles
Brunel House, Newton Abbot, Devon, TQ12 4PU, England
Tel: (+44) 1626 323200, Fax: (+44) 1626 323319
E-mail: postmaster@davidandcharles.co.uk

Distributed in Australia by Capricorn Link
P.O. Box 704, Windsor, NSW 2756, Australia
Tel: (02) 4577-3555

Distributed in New Zealand by David Bateman Ltd.
P.O. Box 100-242, N.S.M.C., Auckland 1330, New Zealand
Tel: (09) 415-7664, Fax: (09) 415-8892

Distributed in South Africa by Real Books
P.O. Box 1040, Auckland Park 2006, Johannesburg, South Africa
Tel: (011) 837-0643, Fax: (011) 837-0645
E-mail: realbook@global.co.za

ISSN: 0897-9790
ISBN-13: 978-1-58297-502-3
ISBN-10: 1-58297-502-7

Cover design by Josh Roflow
Cover photograph © Purestock/Getty Images
Interior design by Clare Finney
Production coordinated by Kristen Heller and Greg Nock

Attention Booksellers: This is an annual directory of F + W Publications. Return deadline for this edition is December 31, 2008.

Contents

ADVANCED ARTICLES

MARKETS

From the Editor

The more I learn about the world of professional songwriting, the more the same topics and issues keep coming up. Each "revolution" turns out to be just the next logical step in music business history. It's never quite the same each time, but then "history does not repeat, it rhymes"—and a songwriter can surely relate to a good rhyme.

And so, if you're a newbie, here are a few basics you should absorb:

- **Royalty structure.** There is a system in place and a certain way songwriters make money (performance royalties, mechanical royalties, copyright, ASCAP, BMI, SESAC, etc.) Read the **Music Biz Basics** section beginning on page 28. Then read it again.
- **Song structure.** Learn about verses, choruses, bridges, hooks, writing from titles, melody, chords, and how they all fit together. Find a songwriters organization in the **Organizations** section (page 303), start reading books on the topic (see **Publications of Interest**, on page 346), write lots of songs, get them critiqued, and then write some more.
- **Submission etiquette.** Some ways of approaching the industry are better than others. See the **Getting Started** articles beginning on page 5, especially **How Do I Submit My Demo?** on page 15, and **Quiz: Are You Professional?** on page 26.
- **Shark detection and avoidance.** Read **How Do I Avoid the Rip-Offs?** on page 19. Most rip-offs and scams are easy to spot, especially if you already have a good working knowledge of how the legitimate music industry works.
- **Fight for your rights.** Join a songwriters organization—NSAI, ASCAP, BMI, etc.—and join those fighting for the future of songwriting as a profession.

In the **Advanced Articles** this year we have interviews with two acknowledged masters, **Paul Williams** (see pg. 40) and **Ralph Murphy** (page 77), as well as **Kara DioGuardi** (page 44), the latest hot international pop songwriter to break through and ride her own wave of career success. We also have an interview with singer-songwriter **Steve Forbert** (page 73), where he drops hints about success as an independent over the long term.

We have new features on the exploding opportunities on the Internet, licensing music for Film and TV, and the ins and outs of radio promotion. There is a tremendous amount of great knowledge gathered here for you, so check it out.

And don't forget to write a lot of good songs. It helps if you're good.

Ian C. Bessler
songmarket@fwpubs.com
www.songwritersmarket.com

Quick-Start

New to Songwriter's Market?

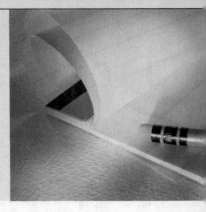

This "Quick-Start" guide is designed to lay it out for you step by step. Each step shows you where to find the information you need in *Songwriter's Market*, from basic to more advanced.

Use this as a guide to launch your songwriting career. Look over the whole list once, then go back and read each article completely. They will show you new facets of the music industry and reinforce what you already know. Good luck!

1. Join a songwriting organization. Connecting with other songwriters and learning from their experience will save you a lot of trouble starting out. Organizations help you learn about the music business, polish your songwriting and help you make contacts who can take you to the next level.

- Organizations, page 303

2. Learn about the music business. Protect yourself with knowledge. Learn how money is really made in the music business and avoid scams. Go to songwriting workshops and music conferences.

- How Do I Avoid the Rip-Offs?, page 19
- Royalties: Where Does the Money Come From?, page 28
- What About Copyright?, page 32
- What About Contracts?, page 36
- Career Songwriting: What Should I Know?, page 34
- Workshops & Conferences, page 325
- Publications of Interest, page 346
- Internet Resources for Songwriters, page 48
- Big Fish Lands TV Song Placements, page 56
- Music for Commercials, page 61
- Radio Promotion Roundtable, page 68
- Starting Your Own Publishing Company, page 81
- Building the Business Team for Today's Market, page 99

3. Develop your songwriting skill. Get letterhead, have your songs critiqued, make contacts and subscribe to songwriting/music magazines. Start building your catalog of songs. If you also perform, start developing your performance skills and build a following.

- Organizations, page 303
- Workshops & Conferences, page 325
- Publications of Interest, page 346
- Web sites of Interest, page 353

4. Choose your best three songs and make a demo recording.

- Demo Recordings: What Should I Know?, page 13

- What About Copyright?, page 32

5. Learn how to spot rip-offs.
- How Do I Avoid the Rip-Offs?, page 19
- What About Copyright?, page 32
- What About Contracts?, page 36

6. Decide which arm(s) of the music business you will submit your songs to.
- Where Should I Send My Songs?, page 9
- Submission Strategies, page 23
- Music Publishers Section Introduction, page 105
- Record Companies Section Introduction, page 158
- Record Producers Section Introduction, page 204
- Managers & Booking Agents Section Introduction, page 225
- Advertising, Audiovisual & Commercial Music Firms Section Introduction, page 257
- Contests & Awards Section Introduction, page 287

7. Find companies open to your style of music and level of experience or use your contacts at Organizations and Performing Rights Organizations (ASCAP, BMI, SESAC) to get a referral and permission to submit. Be picky about where you send your material. Do not waste your time and effort submitting to every company listed in this book without regard to whether they want your style of music.
- Where Should I Send My Songs, page 9
- Openness to Submissions Index, page 389
- Category Indexes, page 366

8. Locate companies in your area.
- Geographic Index, page 397.

9. Read the listings and decide which companies to submit to and whether they are appropriate for you (pay special attention to the Music subhead and also the royalty percentage they pay). Do additional research through trade publications, the Internet and other songwriters.
- Markets, beginning on page 10
- Publications of Interest, page 346
- Web sites of Interest, page 353

10. Find out how to submit. Read information under the How to Contact subhead of each listing. Learn the etiquette involved in contacting companies. Learn how to package your demo in a professional way. Learn how to avoid getting ripped off.
- Songwriter's Market: How Do I Use It?, page 7
- How Do I Submit My Demo?, page 15
- Quiz: Are You Professional?, page 26
- How Do I Avoid the Rip-Offs?, page 19
- Internet Resources for Songwriters, page 48
- Big Fish Lands TV Song Placements, page 56
- Music for Commercials, page 61

11. Call the companies and verify their submission policy has not changed. Also check to make sure the contact person is still there.

12. Send your submission package according to each company's directions. Read the information under the How to Contact subhead in each listing again.
- Quiz: Are You Professional?, page 26
- How Do I Submit My Demo?, page 15
- What About Copyright?, page 32

13. Decide whether to sign with a company.
- Royalties: Where Does the Money Come From?, page 28
- How Do I Avoid the Rip-Offs?, page 19

14. Have an entertainment attorney look over any contract before you sign.

- What About Contracts?, page 36
- How Do I Avoid the Rip-Offs?, page 19
- What About Copyright?, page 32
- Publishing Contracts, page 108
- Record Company Contracts, page 162

15. After signing, how do you get paid?

- Royalties: Where Does the Money Come From?, page 28

Songwriter's Market

How Is It Put Together?

The following articles are for songwriters who have never used this book before and are new to the music industry. This is all important information so don't skip straight to the listings. There's a lot to learn, but it's been rewritten for clarity and simplicity. Taking a little time now to educate yourself can save you from having to learn a lot of things the hard way later on.

How do I use *Songwriter's Market*?

First, take a minute to get to know the book and how it's put together. Here's a rundown of what is in the book:

What you'll find inside this book

Songwriter's Market is a big book and can seem overwhelming at first. But don't worry, it's not that tough to find your way around the book. Here's a quick look at how it's put together.

The book has six basic parts:

1. Articles about the music business and songwriting craft
2. Introductions to each section of listings
3. Listings of music companies and organizations
4. Insider Reports
5. Indexes
6. Lists of Web sites, magazines, books, and other useful extras

Music biz and songwriting articles

These range from articles on the basics of how the music business works—the essentials, laid out in plain English, of how songwriters and artists make money and advance their careers—to articles with more detail and depth on business and creativity, written by music industry insiders with many years of experience in the trenches.

Section intros and listings—the "meat" of the book

There are 11 sections in the book, from Music Publishers and Record Companies to Contests & Awards. Each section begins with an introduction detailing how the different types of companies function—what part of the music industry they work in, how they make money, and what you need to think about when approaching them with your music.

The listings are the heart of *Songwriter's Market*. They are the names, addresses and contact information of music biz companies looking for songs and artists, as well as descriptions of the types of music they are looking for.

What are Insider Reports?

Insider Reports are interviews with songwriters, performers and music industry honchos working at all levels in the music business. By showing how others have achieved success, you learn by example. By peeking behind the curtain of record labels, music publishers and others, you understand more about how the industry works. You learn how the businessmen think, and how to work that to your advantage. Reading these articles gives you an important edge over songwriters and performers who don't. This year, the Insider Reports are all mixed in with the new Advanced Articles. See the Table of Contents.

Songwriter's Market

How Do I Use It?

The quick answer is that you should use the indexes to find companies who are interested in your type of music, then read the listings for details on how they want the music submitted. For support and help of all sorts, join a songwriting or other music industry association. Become a student of the music industry. (Also see the Quick-Start guide on page 2.)

How does *Songwriter's Market* "work"?
The listings in *Songwriter's Market* are packed with a lot of information. It can be intimidating at first, but they are put together in a structured way to make them easy to work with. Take a few minutes to get used to how the listings are organized, and you'll have it down in no time. For more detailed information about how the listings are put together, skip ahead to Where Should I Send My Songs? on page 9.

What are the general rules for working with listings?
Look at A Sample Listing Decoded on page 11 for an example of how a typical listing is put together. The following are general rules about how to use the listings.

1. **Read the entire listing** to decide whether to submit your music! Do not use this book as a mass mailing list! If you blindly mail out demos by the hundreds, you'll waste a lot of money on postage, annoy a lot of people, and your demos will wind up in the trash.
2. **Pay close attention to the "Music" section in each listing.** This will tell you what kind of music the company is looking for. If they want rockabilly only and you write heavy metal, don't submit.
3. **Pay close attention to submission instructions** shown under "How to Contact" and follow them to the letter. A lot of listings are very particular about how they want submissions packaged. Pay close attention. If you do not follow their instructions, they will probably throw your submission in the garbage. You have been warned! If you are confused about their directions, call, e-mail or write to the company for clarification.
4. **If in doubt, contact the company for permission to submit.** This is a good general rule. Many companies don't mind if you send an unsolicited submission, but some will want you to get special prior permission from them. Contacting a company first is also a good way to find out their latest music needs. This is also a chance to briefly make contact on a personal level.
5. **Be courteous, be efficient** and always have a purpose to your personal contact—

DO NOT WASTE THEIR TIME! If you call, always have a reason for making contact—permission to submit, checking on guidelines, following up on a demo, etc. These are solid reasons to make personal contact, but once you have their attention do not wear out your welcome! Always be polite! Always have an upbeat, pleasant attitude when you call (even if you are feeling frustrated or uptight at that particular moment)!

6. **Check for a preferred contact.** A lot of listings have a designated contact person shown after a bolded "**Contact**" in the heading. This is the person you should contact with questions or address your submission to.

7. **Read the "Tips" section.** This part of the listing provides extra information on how to submit or what it might be like to work with the company.

This is just the beginning. For more detailed information about the listings, see Where Should I Send My Songs? on page 9 and the sidebar with the sample listing called A Sample Listing Decoded on page 11. Also see Quiz: Are You Professional? on page 26.

Frequently Asked Questions

1 **How do these companies get listed in the book anyway?** No company pays to be included—all listings are free. The listings come from a combination of research the editor does on the music industry and questionnaires requested by companies who want to be listed (many of them contact us to be included). All questionnaires are screened for known sharks and to make sure they meet our requirements (see How Do I Avoid the Rip-Offs? on page 19 for details of what makes us reject or remove a listing).

2 **Why aren't other companies I know about listed in the book?** We may have sent them a questionnaire, but they did not return it, were removed for complaints, went out of business, specifically asked not to be listed, could not be contacted for an update, etc.

3 **What's the deal with companies that don't take unsolicited submissions?** In the interest of completeness, the editor will sometimes include listings of crucial music companies he thinks you should be aware of. Major labels such as Capitol Records and Warner Bros. fall under this category. You want to at least have some idea of what their policies are, don't you? If a company is closed to unsolicited submissions, you can do either of two things: 1) don't submit to them; or 2) find a way around the roadblock by establishing a relationship or finding a backdoor of some kind (charming them on the phone, through managers, producers, artists, entertainment attorneys, or the fabled Seven Degrees of Separation—i.e., networking like crazy).

4 **A company said in their listing they take unsolicited submissions. My demo came back unopened. What happened?** Some companies' needs change rapidly and may have changed since we contacted them for this edition of the book. This is another reason why it's often a good idea to contact a company before submitting.

Where Should I Send My Songs?

I t depends a lot on whether you write mainly for yourself as a performer, or if you only write and want someone else to pick up your song for their recording (usually the case in country music, for example). *Are you mainly a performing songwriter or a non-performing songwriter*? This is important for figuring out what kind of companies to contact, as well as how you contact them. (For more detail, skip to Submission Strategies on page 23.)

What if I'm a non-performing songwriter?

Many well-known songwriters are not performers in their own right. Some are not skilled instrumentalists or singers, but they understand melody, lyrics and harmony and how they go together. They can write great songs, but they need someone else to bring it to life through skilled musicianship. A non-performing songwriter will usually approach music publishers first for access to artists looking for songs, as well as artists' managers, their producers and their record companies. On the flip side, many incredibly talented musicians can't write to save their lives and need someone else to provide them with good songs to perform. (For more details on the different types of companies and the roles they play for performing songwriters, see the section introductions for Music Publishers on page 105, Record Companies on page 158, Record Producers on page 204, and Managers & Booking Agents on page 225. Also see Submission Strategies on page 23.)

What if I am a performing songwriter?

Many famous songwriters are also famous as performers. They are skilled interpreters of their own material, and they also know how to write to suit their own particular talents as musicians. In this case, their intention is also usually to sell themselves as a performer in hopes of recording and releasing an album, or they have an album and want to find gigs and people who can help guide their careers. They will usually approach record companies or record producers first, on the basis of recording an album. For gigs and career guidance, they talk to booking agents and managers.

A smaller number also approach publishers in hopes of getting others to perform their songs, much like non-performing songwriters. Some music publishers in recent years have also taken on the role of developing artists as both songwriters and performers, or are connected to a major record label, so performing songwriters might go to them for these reasons. (For more details on the different types of companies and the roles they play for performing songwriters, see the section introductions for Music Publishers on page 105, Record Companies on page 158, Record Producers on page 204, and Managers & Booking Agents on page 225. Also see Submission Strategies on page 23.)

Getting Started

Types of Music Companies

- **Music Publishers**—evaluate songs for commercial potential, find artists to record them, finds other uses for the songs such as film or TV, collects income from songs, protects copyrights from infringement

- **Record Companies**—sign artists to their labels, finance recordings, promotion and touring, releases songs/albums to radio and TV

- **Record Producers**—works in the studio and records songs (independently or for a record company), may be affiliated with a particular artist, sometimes develop artists for record labels, locates or co-writes songs if an artist does not write their own

- **Managers & Booking Agents**—works with artists to manage their careers, finds gigs, locates songs to record if the artist does not write their own

How do I use *Songwriter's Market* to narrow my search?

Once you've identified whether you are primarily interested in getting others to perform your songs (non-performing songwriter) or you perform your own songs and want a record deal, etc., there are several steps you can then take:

1. **Identify what kind of music company you wish to approach.** Based on whether you're a performing or non-performing songwriter, do you want to approach a music publisher for a publishing deal? Do you want to approach a record producer because you need somone to help you record an album in the studio? Maybe you want to approach a producer in hopes that an act he's producing needs songs to complete their album. Also see Submission Strategies on page 23 and the Section Introductions for Music Publishers on page 105, Record Companies on page 158, Record Producers on page 204, and Managers & Booking Agents on page 225.

2. **Check for companies based on location.** Maybe you need a manager located close by. Maybe you need to find as many Nashville-based companies as you can because you write country and most country publishers are in Nashville. In this case start with the Geographic Index on page 397. You can also tell Canadian and Foreign listings by the icons in the listing (see A Sample Listing Decoded below and on page 11).

3. **Look for companies based on the type of music they want.** Some companies want country. Some record labels want only punk rock. Check the Category Indexes on page 366 for a list of music companies broken down by the type of music they are interested in.

4. **Look for companies based on how open they are to beginners.** Some companies are more open than others to beginning artists and songwriters. Maybe you are a beginner and it would help to approach these companies first. Some music publishers are hoping to find that wild card hit song and don't care if it comes from an unknown writer. Maybe you are just starting out looking for gigs or record deals, and you need a manager willing to help build your band's career from the ground up. Check the Openness to Submissions Index on page 389.

For more information on how to read the listings, see A Sample Listing Decoded on page 11.

Getting Started

A SAMPLE LISTING DECODED
What do the little symbols at the beginning of the listing mean?
Those are called "icons," and they give you quick information about a listing with one glance. Here is a list of the icons and what they mean:

Openness to submissions
☐ means the company is open to beginners' submissions, regardless of past success

◑ means the company is mostly interested in previously published songwriters/well-established acts*, but will consider beginners

◉ these companies do not want submissions from beginners, only from previously published songwriters/well-established acts*

⊘ companies with this icon only accept material referred by a reputable industry source**

* Well-established acts are those with a following, permanent gigs or previous record deal

** Reputable industry sources include managers, entertainment attorneys, performing rights organizations, etc.

Other icons
✚ means the listing is Canadian

🌐 means the listing is based overseas (Europe, Britain, Australia, etc.)

N indicates a listing is new to this edition

✔ means there has been a change in the contact information: contact name, phone number, fax, e-mail or Web site

$ is for companies who have won an industry award of some sort

🎬 shows a company places songs in films or television shows (excluding commercials)

EASY-TO-USE
REFERENCE
ICONS

DETAILED
SUBMISSION
GUIDELINES

INSIDER
ADVICE

TERMS OF
AGREEMENT

WHAT THEY'RE
LOOKING FOR

N ◑ 🎬 ✔ METAL BLADE RECORDS
2828 Cochran St., Suite 302, Simi Valley CA 93065. (805)522-9111. Fax: (805)522-9380. E-mail: metalblade@metalblade.com. Website: www.metalblade.com. Record company. Estab. 1982. Releases 20 LPs, 2 EPs and 20 CDs/year. Pays negotiable royalty to artists on contract.
How to Contact Submit demo CD by mail. Unsolicited submissions are OK. CD with 3 songs. Does not return material. Responds in 3 months.
Music Mostly **heavy metal** and **industrial**; also **hardcore, gothic** and **noise**. Released "Gallery of Suicide," recorded by Cannibal Corpse; "Voo Doo," recorded by King Diamond; and "A Pleasant Shade of Gray," recorded by Fates Warning, all on Metal Blade Records. Other artists include As I Lay Dying, The Red Chord, The Black Dahlia Murder, and Unearth.
Tips "Metal Blade is known throughout the underground for quality metal-oriented acts."

Getting Started

Additional Resources

For More Info

Songwriter's Market lists music publishers, record companies, producers and managers (as well as advertising firms, play producers and classical performing arts organizations) along with specifications on how to submit your material to each. If you can't find a certain person or company you're interested in, there are other sources of information you can try.

The Recording Industry Sourcebook, an annual directory published by Norris-Whitney Communications, lists record companies, music publishers, producers and managers, as well as attorneys, publicity firms, media, manufacturers, distributors and recording studios around the U.S. Trade publications such as *Billboard* or *Variety*, available at most local libraries and bookstores, are great sources for up-to-date information. These periodicals list new companies as well as the artists, labels, producers and publishers for each song on the charts.

CD booklets and cassette j-cards can also be valuable sources of information, providing the name of the record company, publisher, producer and usually the manager of an artist or group. Use your imagination in your research and be creative—any contacts you make in the industry can only help your career as a songwriter. See Publications of Interest on page 346.

Demo Recordings

What Should I Know?

What is a "demo"?

The demo, shorthand for *demonstration recording*, is the most important part of your submission package. They are meant to give music industry professionals a way to hear all the elements of your song as clearly as possible so they can decide if it has commercial potential.

Should I send a cassette or a CD?

More and more music industry people want CDs, although the cassette is still commonly accepted. A few companies want demos sent on CD only. It's getting cheaper and easier all the time to burn recordings onto CDR ("CD-Recordable"), so it is worth the investment to buy a burner or borrow one. Other formats such as DAT ("Digital Audio Tape") are rarely requested.

What should I send if I'm seeking management?

Some companies want a video of an act performing their songs. Most want VHS format videocassettes. A few ask for video on DVD. Check with the companies for specific requirements.

How many songs should I send, and in what order and length?

Most music industry people agree that three songs is enough. Most music professionals are short on time, and if you can't catch their attention in three songs, your songs probably don't have hit potential. Also, put three *complete songs* on your demo, not just snippets. Make sure to put your best, most commercial song first. An up-tempo number is usually best. If you send a cassette, *put all the songs on one side of the cassette and cue the tape to the beginning of the first song so no time is wasted fast-forwarding or rewinding.*

Should I sing my own songs on my demo?

If you can't sing well, you may want to find someone who can. There are many places to check for singers and musicians, including songwriters organizations, music stores, and songwriting magazines. Some aspiring professional singers will sing on demos in exchange for a copy they can use as a demo to showcase their singing.

Should I use a professional demo service?

Many songwriters find professional demo services convenient if they don't have time or the resources to put together musicians on their own. For a fee, a demo service will produce your songs in their studio using in-house singers and musicians (this is pretty common in

Nashville). Many of these advertise in music magazines, songwriting newsletters and bulletin boards at music stores. Make sure to hear samples of work they've done in the past. Some are mail-order businesses—you send a rough tape of your song or the sheet music, and they produce and record a demo within a month or two. Be sure you find a service that will let you have some control over how the demo is produced, and tell them exactly how you want your song to sound. As with studios, look around for a service that fits your needs and budget. (Some will charge as low as $300 for three songs, while others may go as high as $3,000 and boast a high-quality sound—*shop around and use your best judgment*!)

Should I buy equipment and record demos myself?

If you have the drive and focus to learn good recording technique, yes. If not, it might be easier to have someone else do it. Digital multi-track recorders are now easily available and within reasonable financial reach of many people. For performing songwriters in search of record deals, the actual sound of their recordings can often be an important part of their artistic concept. Having the "means of production" within their grasp can be crucial to artists pursuing the independent route. But, if you don't know how to use the equipment, it may be better to go into a professional studio.

How elaborate and full should the demo production be if I'm a non-performing songwriter?

Many companies in *Songwriter's Market* tell you what they prefer. If in doubt, contact them and ask. In general, country songs and pop ballads can often be demoed with just a vocal plus guitar or piano, although many songwriters in those genres still prefer to get a more complete recording with drums, guitars and other backing instruments. Up-tempo pop, rock and dance demos usually need a more full production.

What kind of production do I need if I'm a performing songwriter?

If you are a band or artist looking for a record deal, you will need a demo that is as fully produced as possible. Many singer/songwriters record their demos as if they were going to be released as an album. That way, if they don't get a deal, they can still release it on their own. Professionally pressed CDs are also now easily within reach of performing songwriters, and many companies offer graphic design services for a professional-looking product.

How Do I Submit
My Demo?

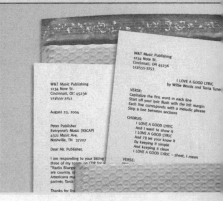

You have three basic options for submitting your songs: submitting by mail, submitting in person and submitting over the Internet (the newest and least widely accepted option at this time).

SUBMITTING BY MAIL

Should I call, write or e-mail first to ask for permission or submission requirements?

This is always a good idea, and many companies ask you to contact them first. If you call, be polite, brief and specific. If you send a letter, make sure it is typed and to the point. Include a typed SASE they can use to reply. If you send an e-mail, again be professional and to the point. Proofread your message before you send it, and then be patient. Give them some time to reply. Do not send out mass e-mails or otherwise spam their e-mail account.

What do I send with my demo?

Most companies have specific requirements, but here are some general pointers:

- Read the listing carefully and submit *exactly* what they ask for, in the exact way they describe. It's also a good idea to call first, just in case they've changed their submission policies.
- Listen to each demo to make sure they sound right and are in the right order (see Demo Recordings: What Should I Know? on page 13).
- If you use cassettes, make sure they are cued up to the beginning of the first song.
- Enclose a *brief,* typed cover letter to introduce yourself. Tell them what songs you are sending and why you are sending them. If you are pitching your songs to a particular artist, say so in the letter. If you are an artist/songwriter looking for a record deal, you should say so. Be specific.
- Include *typed* lyric sheets or lead sheets, if requested. Make sure your name, address and phone number are on each sheet.
- Neatly label each tape or CD with your name, address and phone number, along with the names of the songs in the order they appear on the recording.
- Include a SASE with sufficient postage and large enough to return all your materials. **Warning: Many companies do not return materials, so read each listing carefully!**
- If you submit to companies in other countries, include a self-addressed envelope (SAE) and International Reply Coupon (IRC), available at most post offices. Make sure the envelope is large enough to return all of your materials.
- Pack everything neatly. Neatly type or write the company's address and your return

Submission Mailing Pointers

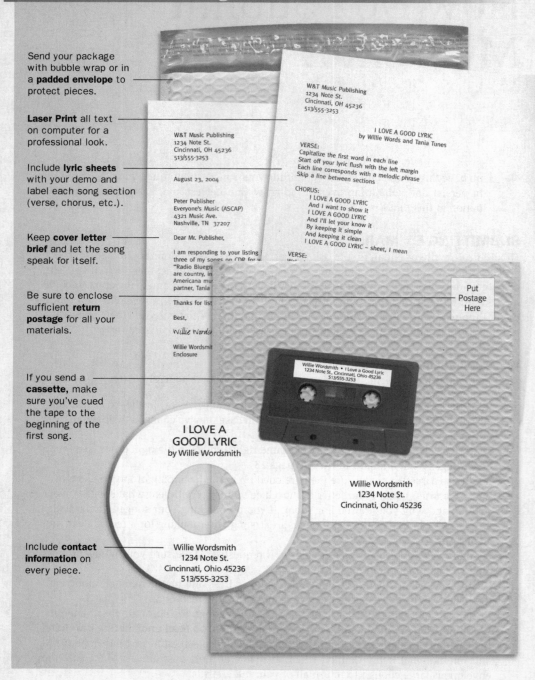

Send your package with bubble wrap or in a **padded envelope** to protect pieces.

Laser Print all text on computer for a professional look.

Include **lyric sheets** with your demo and label each song section (verse, chorus, etc.).

Keep **cover letter brief** and let the song speak for itself.

Be sure to enclose sufficient **return postage** for all your materials.

If you send a **cassette,** make sure you've cued the tape to the beginning of the first song.

Include **contact information** on every piece.

W&T Music Publishing
1234 Note St.
Cincinnati, OH 45236
513/555-3253

August 23, 2004

Peter Publisher
Everyone's Music (ASCAP)
4321 Music Ave.
Nashville, TN 37207

Dear Mr. Publisher,

I am responding to your listing three of my songs on CDR for "Radio Bluegr are country, in Americana mu partner, Tania

Thanks for list

Best,

Willie Words

Willie Wordsmit
Enclosure

W&T Music Publishing
1234 Note St.
Cincinnati, OH 45236
513/555-3253

I LOVE A GOOD LYRIC
by Willie Words and Tania Tunes

VERSE:
Capitalize the first word in each line
Start off your lyric flush with the left margin
Each line corresponds with a melodic phrase
Skip a line between sections

CHORUS:
I LOVE A GOOD LYRIC
And I want to show it
I LOVE A GOOD LYRIC
And I'll let your know it
By keeping it simple
And keeping it clean
I LOVE A GOOD LYRIC ~ sheet, I mean

VERSE:

Put Postage Here

Willie Wordsmith • I Love a Good Lyric
1234 Note St., Cincinnati, Ohio 45236
513/555-3253

I LOVE A
GOOD LYRIC
by Willie Wordsmith

Willie Wordsmith
1234 Note St.
Cincinnati, Ohio 45236

Willie Wordsmith
1234 Note St.
Cincinnati, Ohio 45236
513/555-3253

address so they are clearly visible. Your package is the first impression a company has of you and your songs, so neatness counts!

- Mail first class. Stamp or write "First Class Mail" on the package and the SASE you enclose.
- **Do not use registered or certified mail unless requested!** Most companies will not accept or open demos sent by registered or certified mail for fear of lawsuits.
- Keep records of the dates, songs and companies you submit to.

Is it OK to send demos to more than one person or company at a time?

It is usually acceptable to make simultaneous submissions. One exception is when a publisher, artist or other industry professional asks to put your song "on hold."

What does it mean when a song is "on hold"?

This means they intend to record the song and don't want you to give the song to anyone else. This is not a guarantee, though. Your song may eventually be returned to you, even if it's been on hold for months. Or it may be recorded and included on the album. If either of these happens, you are free to pitch your song to other people again.

How can I protect myself from my song being put "on hold" indefinitely?

You can, and should, protect yourself. Establish a deadline for the person who asks for the hold (for example, "You can put my song on hold for [number of] months."), or modify the hold to specify you will still pitch the song to others but won't sign another deal without allowing the person with the song on hold to make you an offer. Once you sign a contract with a publisher, they have exclusive rights to your song and you may not pitch it to other would-be publishers.

SUBMITTING IN PERSON

Is a visit to New York, Nashville or Los Angeles to submit in person a good idea?

A trip to one of the major music hubs can be valuable if you are organized and prepared to make the most of it. You should have specific goals and set up appointments before you go. Some industry professionals are difficult to see and may not feel meeting out-of-town writers is a high priority. Others are more open and even encourage face-to-face meetings. By taking the time to travel, organize and schedule meetings, you can appear more professional than songwriters who submit blindly through the mail.

What should I take?

Take several copies of your demo and typed lyric sheets of each of your songs. More than one company you visit may ask you to leave a copy for them to review. You can expect occasionally to find a person has cancelled an appointment, but want you to leave a copy of your songs so they may listen and contact you later. (Never give someone the only or last copy of your demo if you absolutely want it returned, though.)

Where should I network while visiting?

Coordinate your trip with a music conference or make plans to visit ASCAP, BMI, or SESAC offices while you are there. For example, the South by Southwest Music Conference in Austin and the NSAI Spring Symposium often feature demo listening sessions, where industry professionals listen to demos submitted by songwriters attending the seminar. ASCAP, BMI, and SESAC also sometimes sponsor seminars or allow aspiring songwriters to make appointments with counselors who can give them solid advice.

How do I deal with rejection?

Many good songs have been rejected simply because they were not what the publisher or record company was looking for at that particular point. Do not take it personally. If few people like your songs, it does not mean they are not good. On the other hand, if you have a clear vision for what your particular songs are trying to get across, specific comments can also teach you a lot about whether your concept is coming across as you intended. If you hear the same criticisms of your songs over and over—for instance, the feel of the melody isn't right or the lyrics need work—give the advice serious thought. Listen carefully and use what the reviewers say constructively to improve your songs.

SUBMITTING OVER THE INTERNET

Is it OK to submit over the Internet?

It can be done, but it's not yet widely accepted. There can still be problems with audio file formats. Although e-mail is more common now if you look through the listings in *Songwriter's Market*, not all music companies are necessarily equipped with computers or Internet access sufficient to make the process easy. But it shows a lot of promise for the future. Web-based companies like Tonos.com or TAXI, among many others are making an effort to connect songwriters and industry professionals over the Internet. The Internet is proving important for networking. Tunesmith.net has extensive bulletin boards and allow members to post audio files of songs for critique. Stay tuned for future developments.

If I want to try submitting over the Internet, what should I do?

First, send an e-mail to confirm whether a music company is equipped to stream or download audio files properly (whether mp3 or real audio, etc.). If they do accept demos online, one strategy becoming common is build a Web site with audio files that can be streamed or downloaded. Then, when you have permission, send an e-mail with links to that Web site or to particular songs. All they have to do is click on the link and it launches their Web browser to the appropriate page. Do not try to send mp3s or other files as attachments. They are often too large for the free online e-mail accounts people commonly use, and they may be mistakenly erased as potential viruses.

How Do I Avoid the Rip-Offs?

The music industry has its share of dishonest, greedy people who will try to rip you off by appealing to your ambition, by stroking your ego, or by claiming special powers to make you successful—for a price, of course. Most of them use similar methods, and you can prevent a lot of heartbreak by learning to spot them and stay away.

What is a "song shark"?

"Song sharks," as they're called, prey on beginners—songwriters unfamiliar with how the music industry works and what the ethical standards are. Two general signs of a song shark are:

- Song sharks will take *any* songs—quality doesn't count.
- They're not concerned with future royalties, since they get their money up front from songwriters who think they're getting a great deal.

What are some of the more blatant rip-offs?

A request for money up front is the most common element. Song sharks may ask for money in the form of submission fees, an outright offer to publish your song for a fee or an offer to re-record your demo for a sometimes hefty price (with the implication that they will make your song wildly successful if you only pay to have it re-demoed in *their studio*). There are many variations on this theme.

If You Write Lyrics, But Not Music

- **You must find a collaborator.** The music business is looking for the complete package: music plus lyrics. If you don't write music, find a collaborator who does. The best way to find a collaborator is through songwriting organizations. Check the Organizations section (page 303) for songwriting groups near you.

- **Don't get ripped-off.** "Music mills" advertise in the back of magazines or solicit you through the mail. For a fee they will set your lyrics or poems to music. The rip-off is that they may use the same melody for hundreds of lyrics and poems, whether it sounds good or not. Publishers recognize one of these melodies as soon as they hear it.

Here is a list of rules that can help you avoid a lot of scams:

- **DO NOT SELL YOUR SONGS OUTRIGHT!** It's unethical for anyone to offer such a proposition. If your song becomes successful after you've sold it outright, you will never get royalties for it.
- **Never pay any sort of "submission fees," "review fees," "service fees," "filing fees," etc.** Reputable companies review material free of charge. If you encounter a company in this book who charges to submit, report them to the editor. If a company charges "only" $15 to submit your song, consider this: *if "only" 100 songwriters pay the $15, this company has made an extra $1,500 just for opening the mail!*
- **Never pay to have your songs published.** A reputable company interested in your songs assumes the responsibility and cost of promoting them, in hopes of realizing a profit once the songs are recorded and released. If they truly believe in your song, they will accept the costs involved.
- **Do not pay a company to pair you with a collaborator.** It's much better to contact a songwriting organization that offers collaboration services to their members.
- **Never pay to have your lyrics or poems set to music.** This is a classic rip-off. "Music mills"—for a price—may use the same melody for hundreds of lyrics and poems, whether it sounds good or not. Publishers recognize one of these melodies as soon as they hear it.
- **Avoid "pay-to-play" CD compilation deals.** It's totally unrealistic to expect this will open doors for you. These are mainly a money-maker for the music company. CDs are cheap to manufacture, so a company that charges $100 to include your recording on a CD is making a killing. They claim they send these CDs to radio stations, producers, etc., but they usually wind up in the trash or as drink coasters. Music industry professionals have no incentive to listen to them. Everybody on the CD paid to be included, so it's not like they were carefully screened for quality.
- **Avoid "songpluggers" who offer to "shop" your song for an upfront fee or retainer.** This practice is not appropriate for *Songwriter's Market* readers, many of whom are beginners and live away from major music centers like Nashville. Professional, established songwriters in Nashville are sometimes known to work on a fee basis with songpluggers they have gotten to know over many years, *but the practice is controversial even for professionals*. Also, the songpluggers used by established professionals are very selective about their clients and have their own reputation to uphold. Companies who offer you these services but barely know you or your work are to be avoided. Also, contracting a songplugger by long distance offers little or no accountability—you have no direct way of knowing what they're doing on your behalf.
- **Avoid paying a fee up front to have a publisher make a demo of your song.** Some publishers may take demo expenses out of your future royalties (a negotiable contract point usually meant to avoid endless demo sessions), but avoid paying up front for demo costs. Avoid situations where it is implied or expressed that a company will publish your song in return for you paying up front to use their demo services.
- **No record company should ask you to pay them or an associated company to make a demo.** The job of a record company is to make records and decide which artists to sign *after* listening to demo submissions.
- **Read all contracts carefully before signing.** And don't sign any contract you're unsure about or that you don't fully understand. It is well worth paying an attorney for the time it takes him to review a contract if you can avoid a bad situation that may cost you thousands of dollars.
- **Before entering a songwriting contest, read the rules carefully.** Be sure what you're

giving up in the way of entry fees, etc., is not more than what you stand to gain by winning the contest. See the Contests & Awards section on page 287.

- **Verify any situation about an individual or company if you have any doubts at all.** Contact the company's Performing Rights Society—ASCAP, BMI, SESAC, or SOCAN (in Canada). Check with the Better Business Bureau in the company's town, or contact the state attorney general's office. Contact professional organizations you're a member of and inquire about the reputation of the company.
- **If a record company or other company asks you to pay expenses up front, be careful.** Record producers commonly charge up front to produce an artist's album. Small indie labels sometimes ask a band to help with recording costs (but seek less control than a major label might). It's up to you to decide to whether or not it is a good idea. Talk to other artists who have signed similar contracts before you sign one yourself. Research companies to find out if they can deliver on their claims, and what kind of distribution they have. Visit their Web site, if they have one. Beware of any company that won't let you know what it has done in the past. If a company has had successes and good working relationships with artists, it should be happy to brag about them.

I noticed record producers charge to produce albums. Is this bad?

Not automatically. Just remember what your goals are. If you write songs, but do not sing or perform, you are looking for publishing opportunities with the producer instead of someone who can help you record an album or CD. If you are a performing artist or band, then you might be in the market to hire a producer, in which case you will most likely pay them up front (and possibly give them a share in royalties or publishing, depending on the specific deal you negotiate). For more information see the Record Producers section introduction on page 204 and Royalties: Where Does the Money Come From? on page 28.

How Do I File a Complaint?

Write to the *Songwriter's Market* editor at: 4700 E. Galbraith Rd., Cincinnati OH 45236. Include:

- A complete description of the situation, as best you can describe it.
- Copies of any materials a company may have sent you that we may keep on file.

If you encounter situations similar to any of the "song shark" scenarios described above, let us know about it.

Will it help me avoid rip-offs if I join a songwriting organization?

Yes. You will have access to a lot of good advice from a lot of experienced people. You will be able to research and compare notes, which will help you avoid a lot of pitfalls.

What should I know about contracts?

Negotiating a fair contract is important. You must protect yourself, and there are specific things you should look for in a contract (see What About Contracts? on page 36).

Are companies that offer demo services automatically bad?

No, but you are not obligated to make use of their services. Many music companies have their own or related recording studios, and with good recording equipment becoming so cheap and easy to use in recent years, a lot of them are struggling to stay afloat. This doesn't mean a company is necessarily trying to rip you off, but use your best judgment. In some cases, a company will submit a listing to *Songwriter's Market* for the wrong reasons—to pitch their demo services instead of finding songs to sign—in which case you should report them to the *Songwriter's Market* editor.

Submission Strategies

NON-PERFORMING SONGWRITERS

Here's a short list of avenues non-performing songwriters can pursue when submitting songs:

1. Submit to a music publisher. This is the obvious one. Look at the information under "Music" in the listing to see examples of a publisher's songs and the artists they've found cuts with. Do you recognize the songs? Have you heard of the artists? Who are the writers? Do they have cuts with artists you would like to get a song to?

2. Submit to a record company. Are the bands and artists on the record company's roster familiar? Do they tend to use outside songs on their albums? When pursuing this angle, it often helps to contact the record company first. Ask if they have a group or artist in development who needs material.

3. Submit to a record producer. Do the producer's credits in the listings show songs written by songwriters other than the artist? Does he produce name artists known for using outside material? Be aware that producers themselves often write with the artists, so your song might also be competing against the producer's songwriting.

4. Submit to an artist's manager. If an artist needs songs, their manager is a prime gateway for your song. Contact the manager and ask if he has an act in need of material.

5. Join a songwriting organization. Songwriting organizations are a good way to make contacts. You'll discover opportunities through the contacts you make that others might not hear about. Some organizations can put you in direct contact with publishers for song critique sessions. You can increase your chances of a hit by co-writing with other songwriters. Your songs will get better because of the feedback from other members.

6. Approach Performing Rights Organizations (PROs). PROs like ASCAP and BMI have writer relations representatives who can sometimes (if they think you're ready) give you a reference to a music company. This is one of the favored routes to success in the Nashville music scene.

PERFORMING SONGWRITERS

This is a bit more complicated, because there are a lot of different avenues available.

Finding a record deal.

This is often a performing songwriter's primary goal—to get a record deal and release an album. Here are some possible ways to approach it:

1. Approach a record company for a record deal. This is another obvious one. Independent labels will be a lot more approachable than major labels, who are usually deluged with demos. Independent labels give you more artistic freedom, while major labels will demand more compromise, especially if you do not have a previous track record. A compromise between the two is to approach one of the "fake indie" labels owned by a major. You'll get more of the benefits of an indie, but with more of the resources and connections of a major label.

2. Approach a record producer for a development deal. Some producers sign artists, produce their album and develop them like a record company, and then approach major labels for distribution deals. This has advantages and drawbacks. For example, the producer gives you guidance and connections, but it can also be harder to get paid because you are signed to the producer and not the label.

3. Get a manager with connections. The right manager with the right connections can make all the difference in getting a record deal.

4. Ask a music publisher. Publishers are taking on more and more of a role of developing performing songwriters as artists. Many major publishers are sister companies to record labels and can shop you for a deal when they think you're ready. They do this in hopes of participating in the mechanical royalties from an album release, and these monies can be substantial when it's a major label release.

5. Approach an entertainment attorney. Entertainment attorneys are a must when it comes to negotiating record contracts, and some moonlight by helping artists make connections for record deals (they will get their cut, of course).

6. Approach PROs. ASCAP and BMI can counsel you on your career and possibly make a referral. They also commonly put on performance showcases where A&R ("artist and repertoire") people from record labels attend to check out new artists.

Finding a producer to help with your album

Independently minded performing songwriters often find they need help navigating the studio when it comes time to produce their own album. In this case, the producer often works for an upfront fee from the artist, for a percentage of the royalty when the album is released and sold (referred to as "points," as in "percentage points"), or a combination of both.

Things to keep in mind when submitting a demo to a producer on this basis:

1. Is the producer known for a particular genre or "sound"? Many producers have a signature sound to their studio productions and are often connected to specific genres. Phil Spector had the "Wall of Sound." Bob Rock pioneered a glossy metal sound for Metallica and The Cult. Daniel Lanois and Brian Eno are famous for the atmospheres they created on albums by U2. Look at your favorite CDs to see who produced. Use these as touchstones when approaching producers to see if they are on your wavelength.

2. What role does a particular producer like to take in the studio? The "Tips" section of *Songwriter's Market* Record Producers listings often have notes from the producer about how they like to work with performing songwriters in the studio. Some work closely as a partner with the artist on developing arrangements and coaching performances. Some prefer final authority on creative decisions. Think carefully about what kind of working relationship you want.

Finding a manager

Many performing songwriters eventually find it necessary to find a manager to help with developing their careers and finding gigs. Some things to keep in mind when looking:

1. Does the manager work with artists in my genre of music? A manager who typically works with punk rock bands may not have as many connections useful to an aspiring country singer-songwriter. A manager who mainly works with gospel artists might not know what to do with a hedonistic rock band.

2. How big is the manager's agency? If a manager is working with multiple acts, but has a small (or no) staff, you might not get the attention you want. Some of the listings have information in the heading about the agency's staff size.

3. Does the manager work with acts from my region? You can check the Geographic Index on page 397 to check for management agencies located near your area. Many of the listings also have information in their headings provided by the companies describing whether they work with regional acts only or artists from any region.

4. Does the manager work with name acts? A manager with famous clients could work wonders for your career. Or you could get lost in the shuffle. Use your best judgment when sizing up a potential manager and be clear with yourself about the kind of relationship you would like to have and the level of attention you want for your career.

5. If I'm a beginner, will the manager work with me? Look in the Openness to Submissions Index on page 389 to find companies open to beginners. Some may suggest extensive changes to your music or image. On the other hand, you may have a strong vision of what you want to do and need a manager who will work with you to achieve that vision instead of changing you around. Decide for yourself how much you are willing to compromise in good faith.

Remember that a relationship between you and a manager is a two-way street. You will have to earn each other's trust and be clear about your goals for mutual success.

Quiz: Are You Professional?

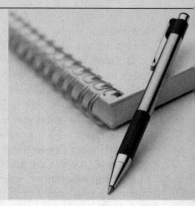

Okay, everybody! Take out your submission package and let's take a look. Hmm . . . very interesting. I think you're well on your way, but you should probably change a few things.

We asked record companies, music publishers and record producers, "What do songwriters do in correspondence with your company (by phone, mail or demo) that screams 'amateur' "? Take this quiz and find out how professional you appear to those on the receiving end of your submission. The following are common mistakes songwriters make all the time. They may seem petty, but, really, do you want to give someone an excuse not to listen to your demo? Check off the transgressions you have committed.

BY MAIL YOU SENT:

☑ anything handwritten (lyrics, cover letters, labels for cassettes). Today there is no excuse for handwritten materials. Take advantage of your local library's typewriters or businesses that charge by the hour to use a computer. And don't even think about using notebook paper.

☑ materials without a contact name *and* phone number. Put this information on *everything*.

☑ lyrics only. Music companies want music and words. See the If You Write Lyrics, But Not Music sidebar on page 19.

☑ insufficient return postage, an envelope too small to return materials, no SASE at all, or a "certified mail" package. If you want materials returned, don't expect the company to send it back on their dime with their envelope—give them what they need. Certified mail is unnecessary and annoying; first class will suffice.

☑ long-winded, over-hyped cover letters, or no cover letter at all. Companies don't need (or want) to hear your life story, how many instruments you play, how many songs you've written, how talented you are or how all your songs are sure-fire hits. Briefly explain why you are sending the songs (e.g., your desire to have them published) and let the songs speak for themselves. Double check your spelling too.

☑ over-packaged materials. Do not use paper towels, napkins, foil or a mountain of tape to package your submission. Make the investment in bubble wrap or padded envelopes.

☑ photos of your parents or children. As much as you love them, your family's pictures or letters of recommendation won't increase your chances of success (unless your family is employed by a major music company).

☑ songs in the style the company doesn't want. Do not "shotgun" your submissions. Read the listings carefully to see if they want your style of music.

YOU CALLED THE CONTACT PERSON:

☑ to check on the submission only a couple days after it was received. Read the listings to see how soon (or if) they report back on submissions. Call them only after that time has elapsed. If they are interested, they will find a way to contact you.

☑ excessively. It's important to be proactive, but check yourself. Make sure you have given them enough time to respond before you call again. Calling every week is inappropriate.

☑ armed with an angry or aggressive tone of voice. A bad attitude will get you nowhere.

WITH THE DEMO YOU PROVIDED:

☑ no lyric sheet. A typed sheet of lyrics for each song is required.

☑ poor vocals and instrumentation. Spending a little extra for professionals can make all the difference.

☑ a poor-quality cassette. The tape should be new and have a brand name.

☑ long intros. Don't waste time—get to the heart of the song.

☑ buried vocals. Those vocals should be out front and clear as a bell.

☑ recordings of sneezes or coughs. Yuck.

SCORING

If you checked 1-3: Congratulations! You're well within the professional parameters. Remedy the unprofessional deeds you're guilty of and send out more packages.

If you checked 4 or more: Whoa! Overhaul your package, let someone check it over, and then fire away with those impeccably professional submissions!

Royalties

Where Does the Money Come From?

NON-PERFORMING SONGWRITERS
How do songwriters make money?
The quick answer is that songwriters make money through rights available to them through the copyright laws. For more details, keep reading and see the article What About Copyright? on page 32.

What specific rights make money for songwriters?
There are two primary ways songwriters earn money on their songs: Performance Royalties and Mechanical Royalties.

What is a performance royalty?
When you hear a song on the radio, on television, in the elevator, in a restaurant, etc. the songwriter receives royalties, called "Performance Royalties." Performing Rights Organizations (ASCAP, BMI and SESAC in the U.S.A.) collect payment from radio stations, television, etc. and distribute those payments to songwriters (see below).

What is a mechanical royalty?
When a record company puts a song onto a CD, cassette, etc. and distributes copies for sale, they owe a royalty payment to the songwriter for each copy they press of the album. It is called a "mechanical royalty" because of the mechanical process used to mass produce a copy of a CD, cassette or sheet music. The payment is small per song (see the "Royalty Provisions" subhead of the Basic Song Contract Pointers sidebar on page 38), but the earnings can add up and reach massive proportions for songs appearing on successful major label albums. ****Note: This royalty is totally different from the artist royalty on the retail price of the album.****

Who collects the money for performance and mechanical royalties?
Performing Rights Organizations collect performance royalties. There are three organizations that collect performance royalties: ASCAP, BMI and SESAC. These organizations arose many years ago when songwriters and music publishers gathered together to press for their rights and improve their ability to collect fees for the use of their songs. ASCAP, BMI and SESAC collect fees for the use of songs and then pass along the money to their member songwriters and music publishers.

Mechanical rights organizations collect mechanical royalties. There are three organizations that collect mechanical royalties: The Harry Fox Agency (HFA), The American Mechanical Rights Agency (AMRA) and The Songwriters Guild of America (SGA). These three organizations collect mechanical royalties from record companies of all sizes—major labels, mid-size and independents—and pass the royalties along to member music publishers and songwriters.

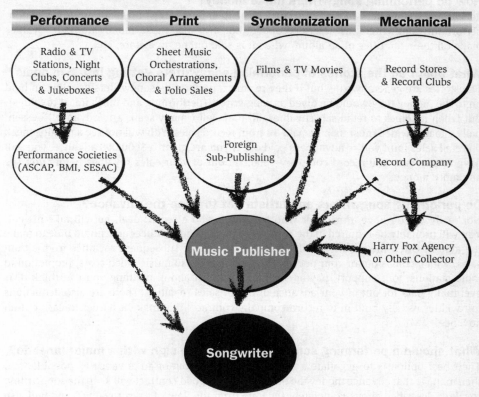

Music Publishing Royalties

How do songwriters hook up with this system to earn royalties?

For **Performance Royalties**, individual songwriters **affiliate** with a Performing Rights Organization of their choice, and register their songs in the PRO database. Each PRO has a slightly different method of calculating payment, different ownership, and different membership structure, so choosing a PRO is an individual choice. Once a songwriter is affiliated and has registered their songs, the PROs then collect fees as described above and issue a check to the songwriter.

For **Mechanical Royalties**, three different things can happen:

1. The songwriter is signed to a publisher that is affiliated with The Harry Fox Agency. The Harry Fox Agency collects the mechanical royalties and passes them along to the publisher. The publisher then passes these along to the songwriter within 30 days. This case usually happens when a songwriter is signed to a major publisher and has a song on a major label album release.

2. The songwriter is not signed to a publisher and owns exclusive rights to his songs, and so works with AMRA or The Songwriters Guild of America, who cut a check directly to the songwriter instead of passing them to the publisher first.

3. They are signed to a publisher, but the songs are being released on albums by independent labels. In this case, the songwriter often works with AMRA since they have a focus on the independent music publishing market.

PERFORMING SONGWRITERS/ARTISTS
How do performing songwriters make money?

Performing songwriters and artists (if they write their own songs) make money just like non-performing songwriters, as described above, but they also make money through royalties made on the retail price of an album when it is sold online, in a store, etc.

What about all the stories of performing songwriters getting into bad deals?

The stories are generally true, but if they're smart, performing songwriters usually can hold on to the money they would be owed as songwriters (performing and mechanical royalties). But when it comes to retail sale royalties, all they will usually see is an "advance"—essentially a loan—which must then be paid off from record sales. You will not see a royalty check on retail sales until you're advance is paid off. If you are given a $600,000 advance, you will have to pay back the record company $600,000 out of your sales royalties before you see any more money.

Do performing songwriters and artists get to keep the advance?

Not really. If you have a manager who has gotten you a record deal, he will take his cut. You will probably be required in the contract to pay for the producer and studio time to make the album. Often the producer will take a percentage of subsequent royalties from album sales, which comes out of your pocket. Then there are also music video costs, promotion to radio stations, tour support, paying sidemen, etc. Just about anything you can think of is eventually paid for out of your advance or out of sales royalties. There are also deductions to royalties usually built in to record company contracts that make it harder to earn out an advance.

What should a performing songwriter wanting to sign with a major label do?

Their best option is to negotiate a fair contract, get as big of an advance as possible, and then manage that advance money the best they can. A good contract will keep the songwriting royalties described above completely separate from the flow of sales royalties, and will also cut down on the number of royalty deductions the record company builds into the contract. And because of the difficulty in earning out any size advance or auditing the record company, it makes sense to get as much cash up front as you can, then to manage that as best you can. You will need a good lawyer.

RECORD COMPANIES, PRODUCERS AND MANAGERS & BOOKING AGENTS
How do music publishers make money?

A publisher works as a songwriter's agent, looks for profitable commercial uses for the songs he represents, and then takes a percentage of the profits. This is typically 50% of all earning from a particular song—often referred to as the *publisher's share*. A successful publisher stays in contact with several A&R reps, finding out what upcoming projects are in need of new material, and whether any songs he represents will be appropriate.

How do record companies make money?

Record companies primarily make their money from profits made selling CDs, cassettes, DVDs, etc. Record companies keep most of the profit after subtracting manufacturing costs, royalties to recording artists, distribution fees and the costs of promoting songs to radio (which for major labels can reach up to $300,000 per song). Record companies also usually have music publishing divisions that make money performing all the functions of publishers.

How do record producers make money?

Producers mostly make their money by charging a flat fee up front to helm a recording project, by sharing in the royalties from album sales, or both. A small independent producer might charge $10,000 (or sometimes less) up front to produce a small indie band, while a "name" producer such as Bob Rock, who regularly works with major label bands, might charge $300,000. Either of these might also take a share in sales royalties, referred to as "points"— as in "percentage points." A producer might say, "I'll produce you for $10,000 and 2 points." If an artist is getting a 15% royalty an album sales, then two of those percentage points will go to the producer instead. Producers also make money by co-writing with the artists to get publishing royalties, or they may ask for part of the publishing from songs written by outside songwriters.

How do managers make money?

Most managers make money by taking a percentage commission of their clients' income, usually 10-25%. If a touring band finishes a show and makes a $2,000 profit, a manager on 15% commission would get $300. If an artist gets a $40,000 advance from a mid-size label, the manager would get $6,000. Whether an artist's songwriting income is included in the manager's commission comes down to negotiation. *The commission should give the manager incentive to make things happen for your career, so avoid paying flat fees up front.*

Music Biz Basics

What About Copyright?

How am I protected by the copyright laws?

Copyright protection applies to your songs the instant you put them down in fixed form—a recording, sheet music, lead sheet, etc. This protection lasts for your lifetime plus 70 years (or the lifetime of the last surviving writer, if you co-wrote the song with somebody else). When you prepare demos, place notification of copyright on all copies of your song—the lyric sheets, lead sheets and labels for cassettes, CDs, etc. The notice is simply the word "copyright" or the symbol © followed by the year the song was created (or published) and your name: © 2005 by John Q. Songwriter.

What parts of a song are protected by copyright?

Traditionally, only the melody line and the lyrics are eligible for copyright. Period. Chords and rhythm are virtually never protected. An incredibly original arrangement can sometimes qualify, but the original copyright owner of the song must agree to it (and they usually don't). Sound recordings can also be copyrighted, but this applies strictly to the actual sounds on the recording, not the song itself (this copyright is usually owned by record companies).

What songs are not protected?

Song titles or mere ideas for music and lyrics cannot be copyrighted. Very old songs in the "public domain" are not protected. You could quote a melody from a Bach piece, but you could not then stop someone else from quoting the same melody in their song.

When would I lose or have to share the copyright?

If you *collaborate* with other writers, they are assumed to have equal interests unless you state some other arrangement, in writing. If you write under a *work-for-hire* arrangement, the company or person who hired you to write the song then owns the copyright. Sometimes your spouse may automatically be granted an interest in your copyright as part of their *spousal rights*, which might then become important if you got divorced.

Should I register my copyright?

Registering you copyright with the Library of Congress gives the best possible protection. Registration establishes a public record of your copyright—even though a song is legally protected whether or not it is registered—and could prove useful in any future court cases involving the song. Registration also entitles you to a potentially greater settlement in a copyright infringement lawsuit.

How do I register my song?

To register your song, request government form PA from the Copyright Office. Call the 24-hour hotline at (202)707-9100 and leave your name and address on the messaging system. Once you receive the PA form, you must return it, along with a registration fee and a CD (or tape) and lead sheet of your song. Send these to the Register of Copyrights, Copyright Office, Library of Congress, Washington DC 20559. It may take several months to receive your certificate of registration from the Copyright Office, but your songs are protected from the date of creation (the date of registration will reflect the date you applied). For more information, call the Copyright Office's Public Information Office at (202)707-3000 or visit their Web site at www.copyright.gov.

Government Resources

For More Info

The Library of Congress's copyright Web site is your best source for current, complete information on the subject of copyright. Not only can you learn all you could possibly wish to know about intellectual property rights and U.S. copyright law (the section of the U.S. Code dealing with copyright is reprinted there in its entirety), but you can also download copyright forms directly from the site. The site also includes links to other copyright-related web pages, many of which will be of interest to songwriters, including ASCAP, BMI, SESAC, and the Harry Fox Agency. Check it out at **www.copyright.gov.**

Music Biz Basics

How likely is it that someone will try to steal my song?

Copyright infringement is very rare. But, if you ever feel that one of your songs has been stolen—that someone has unlawfully infringed on your copyright—you must prove that you created the work and that the person you are suing had access to your song. Copyright registration is the best proof of a date of creation. You *must* have your copyright registered in order to file a lawsuit. Also, it's helpful if you keep your rough drafts and revisions of songs, either on paper or on tape.

Why did song sharks begin soliciting me after I registered my song?

This is one potential, unintended consequence of registering your song with the Library of Congress. The copyright indexes are a public record of your songwriting, and song sharks often search the copyright indexes and mail solicitations to songwriters who live out away from major music centers such as Nashville. They figure these songwriters don't know any better and are easy prey. *Do not allow this possibility to stop you from registering your songs!* Just be aware, educate yourself, and then throw the song sharks' mailings in the trash.

What if I mail a tape to myself to get a postmark date on a sealed envelope?

The "poor man's copyright" has not stood up in court, and is not an acceptable substitute for registering your song. If you feel it's important to shore up your copyright, register it with the Library of Congress.

Career Songwriting

What Should I Know?

What career options are open to songwriters who do not perform?

The possibilities range from a beginning songwriter living away from a music center like Nashville who lands an occasional single-song publishing deal, to a staff songwriter signed to a major publishing company. And then there are songwriters like Desmond Child who operate independently, have developed a lot of connections, work with numerous artists, and have set up their own independent publishing operations.

What is "single-song" songwriting about?

In this case, a songwriter submits songs to many different companies. One or two songs gain interest from different publishers, and the songwriter signs separate contracts for each song with each publisher. The songwriter can then pitch other songs to other publishers. In Nashville, for instance, a single-song contract is usually the first taste of success for an aspiring songwriter on his way up the ladder. Success of this sort can induce a songwriter to move to a music center like Nashville (if they haven't already), and is a big boost for a struggling songwriter already living there. A series of single-song contracts often signals a songwriters' maturing skill and marketability.

What is a "staff songwriter"?

A staff songwriter usually works for a major publisher and receives a monthly stipend as an advance against the royalties he is likely to earn for the publisher. The music publisher has exclusive rights to everything the songwriter writes while signed to the company. The publisher also works actively on the writer's behalf to hook him or her up with co-writers and other opportunities. A staff songwriting position is highly treasured by many because it offers a steady income, and in Nashville is a sign the songwriter has "arrived."

What comes after the staff songwriting position?

Songwriters who go to the next level have a significant reputation for their ability to write hit songs. Famous artists seek them out, and they often write actively in several markets at once. They often write on assignment for film and television, and commonly keep their own publishing companies to maximize their income.

As my career grows what should I do about keeping track of expenses, etc.?

You should keep a ledger or notebook with records on all financial transactions related to your songwriting—royalty checks, demo costs, office supplies, postage, travel expenses, dues to organizations, class and workshop fees, plus any publications you purchase pertaining to songwriting. You may also want a separate checking account devoted to your songwriting activities. This will make record keeping easier and help to establish your identity as a business for tax purposes.

What should I know about taxes related to songwriting income?

Any royalties you receive will not reflect taxes or any other mandatory deductions. It is your responsibility to keep track of income and file the correct tax forms. For specific information, contact the IRS or talk to an accountant who serves music industry clients.

Music Biz Basics

What About Contracts?

CO-WRITING

What kind of agreements do I need with co-writers?

You may need to sign a legal agreement between you and a co-writer to establish percentages you will each receive of the writer's royalties. You will also have to iron out what you will do if another person, such as an artist, wants to change your song and receive credit as a cowriter. For example, in the event, a major artist wants to cut your song for her album—but also wants to rewrite some lyrics and take a share of the publishing—you and your co-writer need to agree whether it is better to get a song on an album that might sell millions (and make a lot of money) or pass on it because you don't want to give up credit. The situation could be uncomfortable if you are not in sync on the issue.

When do I need a lawyer to look over agreements?

When it comes to doing business with a publisher, producer, or record company, you should always have the contract reviewed by a knowledgeable entertainment attorney. As long as the issues at stake are simple, the co-writers respect each other, and they discuss their business philosophies before writing a song together, they can probably write up an agreement without the aid of a lawyer.

SINGLE-SONG CONTRACTS

What is a single-song contract?

A music publisher offers a single-song contract when he wants to sign one or more of your songs, but doesn't want to hire you as a staff songwriter. You assign your rights to a particular song to the publisher for an agreed-upon number of years, so that he may represent the song and find uses profitable for both of you. This is a common contract and will probably be the first you encounter in your songwriting career.

What basic elements should every single-song contract contain?

Every contract should have the publisher's name, the writer's name, the song's title, the date, and the purpose of the agreement. The songwriter also declares the song is a original work and he is creator of the work. The contract *must* specify the royalties the songwriter will earn from various uses of the song, including performance, mechanical, print and synchronization royalties.

How should the royalties usually be divided in the contract?

The songwriter should receive no less than 50% of the income his song generates. That means the songwriter and publisher split the total royalties 50/50. The songwriter's half is

When Does 50% Equal 100%?

Tip

NOTE: the publisher's and songwriter's share of the income are sometimes referred to as each being 100%—for 200% total! You might hear someone say, "I'll take 100% of the publisher's share." **Do not be needlessly confused!** If the numbers confuse you, ask for the terms to be clarified.

called the "writer's share" and the publisher's half is called the "publisher's share." If there is more than one songwriter, the songwriters split the writer's share. Sometimes, successful songwriters will bargain for a percentage of the publisher's share, negotiating what is basically a co-publishing agreement. For a visual explanation of how royalties are collected and flow to the songwriter, see the chart called Music Publishing Royalties on page 29.

What should the contract say about a "reversion clause"?

Songwriters should always negotiate for a "reversion clause," which returns all rights back to the songwriter if some provision of the contract is not met. Most reversion clauses give a publisher a set amount of time (usually one or two years) to work the song and make money with it. If the publisher can't get the song recorded and released during the agreed-upon time period, the songwriter can then take his song to another publisher. The danger of *not* getting some sort of reversion clause is that you could wind up with a publisher sitting on your song for the entire life-plus-70-years term of the copyright—which may as well be forever.

Is a reversion clause difficult to get?

Some publishers agree to it, and figure if they can't get any action with the song in the first year or two, they're not likely to ever have much luck with it. Other publishers may be reluctant to agree to a reversion clause. They may invest a lot of time and money in demoing and pitching a song to artists and want to keep working at it for a longer period of time. Or, for example, a producer might put a song on hold for a while and then go into a lengthy recording project. A year can easily go by before the artist or producer decides which songs to release as singles. This means you may have to agree to a longer time period, be flexible and trust the publisher has your best mutual interests in mind. Use your best judgment.

What other basic issues should be covered by a single-song contract?

The contract should also address these issues:

- will an advance be paid, and if so, how much will the advance be?
- when will royalties be paid (annually or semiannually)?
- who will pay for demos—the publisher, songwriter or both?
- how will lawsuits against copyright infringement be handled, including the cost of lawsuits?
- will the publisher have the right to sell its interest in the song to another publisher without the songwriter's consent?
- does the publisher have the right to make changes in a song, or approve changes by someone else, without the songwriter's consent?
- the songwriter should have the right to audit the publisher's books if he feels it is necessary and gives the publisher reasonable notice.

Basic Song Contract Pointers

Tips

The following list, taken from a Songwriters Guild of America publication, enumerates the basic features of an acceptable songwriting contract:

1 **Work for Hire.** When you receive a contract covering just one composition, you should make sure the phrases "employment for hire" and "exclusive writer agreement" are *not* included. Also, there should be no options for future songs.

2 **Performing Rights Affiliation.** If you previously signed publishing contracts, you should be affiliated with either ASCAP, BMI, or SESAC. All performance royalties must be received directly by you from your performing rights organization and this should be written into your contract.

3 **Reversion Clause.** The contract should include a provision that if the publisher does not secure a release of a commercial sound recording within a specified time (one year, two years, etc.), the contract can be terminated by you.

4 **Changes in the Composition.** If the contract includes a provision that the publisher can change the title, lyrics or music, this should be amended so that only with your consent can such changes be made.

5 **Royalty Provisions.** You should receive fifty percent (50%) of all publisher's income on all licenses issued. If the publisher prints and sells his own sheet music, your royalty should be ten percent (10%) of the wholesale selling price. The royalty should not be stated in the contract as a flat rate ($.05, $.07, etc.).

6 **Negotiable Deductions.** Ideally, demos and all other expenses of publication should be paid 100% by the publisher. The only allowable fee is for the Harry Fox Agency collection fee, whereby the writer pays one half of the amount charged to the publisher for mechanical rights. The current mechanical royalty collected by the Harry Fox Agency is 9.1 cents per cut for songs under 5 minutes; and 1.75 cents per minute for songs over 5 minutes.

7 **Royalty Statements and Audit Provision.** Once the song is recorded, you are entitled to receive royalty statements at least once every six months. In addition, an audit provision with no time restriction should be included in every contract.

8 **Writer's Credit.** The publisher should make sure that you receive proper credit on all uses of the composition.

9 **Arbitration.** In order to avoid large legal fees in case of a dispute with your publisher, the contract should include an arbitration clause.

10 **Future Uses.** Any use not specifically covered by the contract should flbe retained by the writer to be negotiated as it comes up.

Music Biz Basics

Where else can I go for advice on contracts?

The Songwriters Guild of America has drawn up a Popular Songwriter's Contract which it believes to be the best minimum songwriter contract available (see the Ten Basic Points Your Contract Should Include sidebar above). The Guild will send a copy of the contract at no charge to any interested songwriter upon request (see the Songwriters Guild of America listing in the Organizations section on page 303). SGA will also review—free of charge—any contract offered to its members, and will check it for fairness and completeness. Also see these two books published by Writer's Digest Books: *The Craft and Business of Songwriting, 3rd Edition,* by John Braheny and *The New Songwriter's Guide to Music Publishing, 3rd Edition,* by Randy Poe.

Paul Williams

Connected to the Creative Rainbow

by Dan Kimpel

An Oscar, a Grammy, enshrinement in the Songwriters Hall of Fame and a star on fabled Hollywood Boulevard: Paul Williams' illustrious career is highlighted by awards, kudos and successes across a expansive swath of popular media, from hit songs to films, television, and theater. Conceivably, at this career juncture, Williams could be resting on his laurels and reclining on a beach somewhere. Instead, the 60-something songwriter has been co-writing with Jake Shears and Baby Daddy for their band, Scissor Sisters, merits a credit on Dizzee Rascal and Lily Allen's "Wanna Be" (thanks to a sample from his score to *Bugsy Malone*) and is writing and composing for a number of upcoming stage projects including *Happy Days*, a theatrical version of the famous television show as conceived by the series' producer, Garry Marshall. He also maintains a steady touring sched-ule and performs in concert venues and for numerous charitable events. Paul is also a board member of the American Society of Composer, Authors and Publishers (ASCAP).

As a songwriter, Paul's beloved catalog of hits includes such perennial favorites as: "We've Only Just Begun," "An Old Fashioned Love Song," "Evergreen," "Rainy Days and Mondays," "I Won't Last a Day Without You," "You and Me Against the World," "The Rainbow Connection," "*The Love Boat* Theme," "You're Gone," "Let Me Be the One," "Nice to Be Around," "Out in the Country," "Family of Man," "Cried Like a Baby," "Love Dance," "My Fair Share." Williams scored the films: *Bugsy Malone*, *Phantom of the Paradise*, *The Muppet Movie*, *A Muppet Christmas Carol*, *One on One*, *Ishtar*, *Cinderella Liberty*, *A Star Is Born*, and *The End*. Elvis, Sinatra, Streisand, Ella Fitzgerald and Ray Charles are among the legendary singers who have performed Williams' work.

Unlike many songwriters who appear uncomfortable in the spotlight, Williams effectively parlayed his personality into a parallel career in the '70s, as an actor in films including the cult classic *Phantom of the Paradise*, a favorite talk show guest and an irreverent regular on the daytime television show *Hollywood Squares*.

ON THE LOT AT A&M

In the '60s, Los Angeles was at the center of the music that mirrored tumultuous times, but Paul Williams explains that he was more influenced by The Great American Songbook than

DAN KIMPEL has interviewed Leonard Cohen, Sheryl Crow, and Rosanne Cash for United Airlines' in-flight United Enter-tainment Network, and also conducted on-camera interviews for ASCAP's commemorative 90th Anniversary video with Randy Newman, Hal David, Quincy Jones, Jimmy Jam, and Terry Lewis. He is the author of the book *Networking in the Music Business* and also writes and edits the biweekly "Song Biz" column for *Music Connection* magazine.

the psychedelic sounds of the Sunset Strip. "I loved Stephen Stills, Moody Blues, and the Beatles, but what was inside me was maybe music from the '40s: Rodgers and Hammerstein; Rodgers and Hart; the Gershwins; Cole Porter; Sinatra's *Only the Lonely* and *Songs for Swinging Lovers,* the Gordon Jenkins arrangements; and Mickey Rooney movies I watched as a kid, all gave me a basis for the craft of songwriting.''

Many songwriters struggle with their craft and endure years of rejection and anonymity, but Williams' rise was dramatic and virtually immediate. First signed to a company in Los Angeles called White Whale (home to '60s pop group The Turtles, among others) he was released by the company only months into his contract with the dictum that he might not have a future as a songwriter. "I've always said that in my life, 'no' is a gift and a great example is my songwriting. I started out to be an actor, and when the acting dried up—very quickly—I was left with nothing to do, no money to go to the movies, and a chest full of emotion. Before I made a living at writing songs, I got a life from songwriting, and the life I got was an emotional healing, sitting down to write about this stuff that was going on in the center of my chest. In a sense it was a healing and a self-discovery process, dealing with the emotions in a way that I didn't even realize I was dealing with them. Songwriting became a kind of journaling process for me. I hadn't done any analysis, or spent any time on the couch, I wasn't aware I was doing that, but the first real gift of songwriting was that it put me in touch with who I was. The interesting thing for me was that with songwriting, almost immediately, I found myself being given the opportunity to do it for a living, through a couple of chance meetings with other songwriters who led me to A&M Records.''

Williams says he doesn't believe that our destinies are totally planned out by the universe but he notes the power of his path. "I'm a big believer in the power of intention. An unchecked fantasy about what a fabulous life you're going to have, not weighted down with the reality of circumstance—for people who don't end up in the asylum—often ends up with billionaires and huge successes. I think what we dwell on, and think about, we manifest. I feel like more of an active participant in my life today, but I look back on it, and I realize that I was being led. I think that there were elements at work in my life that I see as an absolute gift now, that I was led to where I needed to be. And once again, 'no' began a navigational nudge—it put me in the direction I needed to be going.''

COLLECTIVE COLLABORATION

"I use to joke that I arrived at A&M in a stolen car," laughs Williams. "I was unemployed and unemployable. But [music publisher] Chuck Kaye had been looking for a lyricist for this brilliant composer, Roger Nichols for years. Roger and I, physical opposites, seemed to have a commonality of spirit about the way we lived our lives. Sitting in the same office with Roger Nichols for three or four years was truly my music school. My labor, the craft of songwriting—you build a building from the ground up, and that was my foundation as a songwriter. It seemed everything we wrote from the beginning was recorded. We never thought we'd hear it on the air, but we were the providers of album cuts and B-sides—until The Carpenters.''

It was "We've Only Just Begun," originally penned by Williams and Nichols for a Crocker Bank commercial, that elevated the pair into the pop stratosphere. "We sat down in an afternoon and wrote the commercial, then strung it together into a song in case anyone was interested. I sang it in the commercial, but the first recorded version was by Mark Lindsay, who'd heard the commercial. It was on its way up the charts when The Carpenters recorded it. It changed my life.''

Williams shares that he was inspired by his mother to create "Rainy Days and Mondays," another classic Carpenters' song. "My mother used to talk to herself, she'd walk through the room mumbling, especially as she got older, and she cussed. You couldn't catch the words but you knew it was basic sailor talk. I'd say, 'What's the matter?' and she'd say, 'I feel ancient.' So the line, 'Talking to myself and feeling old,' came out of my mother. My philosophy of life is in the bridge, the positive place, when it says, 'Funny but it seems I always end up here with you.' "

HOLLYWOOD HITS

Williams and Kenny Ascher wrote most of the songs for the Barbra Streisand/Kris Kristofferson film, *A Star is Born*; "Evergreen," co-written by Williams and Streisand, won an Academy Award. "It was a challenge, writing songs for two icons. People ask, 'Weren't you intimidated to write songs for Barbra Streisand?' And I say, 'Can you imagine how it felt to sing songs to Kris Kristofferson?' I wrote all those songs in seven weeks, it was a tight schedule. Barbara has a phenomenal sense of what works."

Also co-written with Kenny Ascher, "The Rainbow Connection" has become a modern day pop standard, sung by everyone from Kermit the Frog to Willie Nelson. "I can't think of two sweeter souls in the world to work with than Willie and Kermit," Williams notes. " 'Rainbow Connection' was written for *The Muppet Movie*. To have the sweetest, easiest experience on the world making a motion picture you have to go back in time and do a picture with Jim Henson; it was the most giving, flexible enjoyable experience I'd ever had. We sat down with Jerry Juhl, the screenwriter, Jim, Kenny and I, and said, 'What are we going to do?' We were doing basically a road picture of the Muppets getting together. And we start with Kermit, sitting in the swamp, sitting on a Lily pad with a banjo, and he's going to sing something but he has to sing something that shows you he's a 'thoughty' guy, he has an inner life, he's everyman, that he wonders big things. What does he have to work with? He has sky, water, mist that is mystical—ah, it's going to create a rainbow! And what we loved was the culture—Kermit has awareness; he's seen *The Wizard of Oz*."

THE OTHER SIDE

Paul Williams has been very open in speaking about his personal history as a recovering alcoholic with 17 sober years to his credit, and his subsequent experience as a certified drug and alcohol counselor. "I think that there is that whiplash experience of going from anonymity into the glare of the spotlight for many people in the music business. Also the whiplash of being told, 'You're different' to being told 'You're special.' There's a larger gulf between those two words: 'different' and 'special' that any other two words I can think of that have affected my life. We're all special. That's the gift of our recovery. At this point in my life I'm a classic example of the Lazarus principle at work. I was given my life back when I became sober. Everything in my life relates to that moment, that gift of being reborn. I've heard people joke about how an alcoholic can read the same book twice and enjoy it more the second time; in the same way I think there is perspective on the gifts of my life that I can see in this day and age that I couldn't see then. I find myself being overwhelmed with gratitude for things that happened 35 years ago. It's an interesting process."

He relates that there was period in his life when he didn't write, but when he returned it was with a renewed perspective. "The big part of the writing process I've become aware of is how much of it I do in my unconscious. When I became sober I didn't know if I'd ever be passionate about writing again, so I waited a long time. One of the first things I did, and I had maybe been sober for a year, I wrote the songs for *The Muppet Christmas Carol*. What I did was a great lesson. I'd look at the script, 'Now Disney wants a song about Scrooge. We're seeing his feet as he goes by, and little rats and things are even colder.' There's an expression, 'I don't know how to do this, but something inside me does.' And that's essentially what I was saying. In my collective experience, in my unconscious, in the gifts that I've been given is the ability to write this song. So I'm not even going to think about it," he says.

"I picked up a murder mystery by Lawrence Block and got as far away from *A Christmas Carol* as I could get. I had the original script, I knew what was needed, and I ignored it. I started reading. Within the hour it popped in my head. I set down the book and wrote, 'When the wind blows it chills you, chills you to the bone/But there's nothing in nature that freezes your heart like years of being alone.' I know it came out of my process and out of my own mentality. But I didn't work at it. I trusted my own instincts and add to that the ability to play at writing rather than working at it, that's the successful mix for me as a writer."

THE GIFT

"There is an energy, a joy of writing and the element of sitting down with a stranger for three hours and sharing your bad ideas, and trusting that if God is in the mood, you're going to write a song that day," says Williams. "More than anything else I connect with the inherent gift of sitting down with a stranger and collaborating. And it is something I take to the rest of my life. At this point it's all a gift—my wife says she's going to put that on my headstone."

Kara DioGuardi

Platinum Power

by Dan Kimpel

With her colossal list of cuts, Kara DioGuardi is undeniably the current queen of the pop songwriting cosmos. Named BMI Songwriter of the Year at the Society's 2007 Award ceremonies, DioGuardi contributed to multiple songs for Christina Aguilera's *Back to Basics* including the smash single "Ain't No Other Man." The list of artists who have recorded her songs includes: Celine Dion, Anastacia, Britney Spears, Enrique Iglesias, Ricky Martin, Ashlee Simpson ("Pieces of Me"), Kelly Clarkson, Kylie Minogue, Hilary Duff, Marc Anthony, Pussycat Dolls, Jewel, Gwen Stefani ("Rich Girl"), Bo Bice, Clay Aiken, Santana, Jessica Simpson, Lindsay Lohan and Paris Hilton. Recent tracks with Avril Lavigne, Kelly Clarkson and Faith Hill continue to enrich this eye-popping discography.

WRITER AS PUBLISHER

If she were simply a songwriter, DioGuardi would be a formidable industry force, but she's much more: a stunning vocalist, an accomplished producer, and the founder of Arthouse Entertainment, a music publishing firm that also provides corporate branding, management for artists, writers and producers, and an interface with film and television productions and record labels. "Business can overshadow many things. Even though you're running a business—and business is business—you have to be very careful because your main commodity is your creativity," she says. "It always has to come from the song, it has to come from a point of truth, it has to be the best you can make it and it has to have integrity. Once you start selling those things out your business is going to go down. I have to protect my gift at all costs, whether it costs me money or not."

DioGuardi is proud to note that a recent *Billboard* airplay chart of music publishers listed Arthouse Entertainment at number eight. "We're right below (a company) that employs 60 or 70 people. I have a little office with two people. It's not about money or lunches; it's about people who work. It's an incredible amount of effort creating and writing, making sure a certain song goes to the right artist, and then following up after the song is done. Each song is like a mini corporation." Work is a mantra for DioGuardi, and as a woman in a clearly male-dominated field, she is keenly aware of the challenges and opportunities as she notes, "Growing up, there weren't a lot of role models for women and what I wanted to do."

DAN KIMPEL has interviewed Leonard Cohen, Sheryl Crow, and Rosanne Cash for United Airlines' in-flight United Entertainment Network, and also conducted on-camera interviews for ASCAP's commemorative 90th Anniversary video with Randy Newman, Hal David, Quincy Jones, Jimmy Jam, and Terry Lewis. He is the author of the book *Networking in the Music Business* and also writes and edits the biweekly "Song Biz" column for *Music Connection* magazine.

DRIVE AND FOCUS

DioGuardi confides that when she was younger, dressing up dolls wasn't a part of her experience. "I played in my dad's basement, writing my own scripts and putting on musicals; dreaming of my corner office and being the boss." She was supposed to go to law school. That's what her family—including her father Joseph, a former Congressman—expected when she graduated from Duke University. Instead, she began waitressing and singing with a garage band in New York. When a college friend landed a job with *Billboard* magazine, but was offered another position for more money, DioGuardi slid into her gig. The magazine's Larry Flick was an early believer. "He used to call me 'Runway' because I'd walk up and down the hallway, delegating all of my work so that I could write," she recalls. "About three or four months into our relationship I thought, 'I've got to get his opinion on my stuff, but I can't tell him it's me. He'll feel forced to listen to it and if he doesn't like it he'll say he likes it anyway.' I gave him a tape and said, 'This is my friend, and she's been bugging me.' He rushed over after listening and said, "Oh my God, who is this girl?' I said, 'It's me.' He introduced me to Clyde Lieberman (BMG Music Publishing) and that started my career."

Working with *Billboard's* legendary editor, Timothy White, gave DioGuardi deeper insight into her own creative past and future. "As a kid I felt very lonely. I don't think my family understood I was creative. I was a circle in a square. Timothy had this thing where he felt that great art came from pain. And a lot of his favorites were artists who'd had rocky childhoods and misfortunes. I never understood that until I began doing my own writing. I think he helped me. He was a kind, great man who loved music."

DioGuardi credits her academic background with instilling a strong sense of discipline. "When you're trying to be a writer or an artist you'd better know how to structure a life or you'll fall into a deep depression. It's about staying in the game. I don't necessarily believe the people who are in the music business are the most talented people; the most talented people are in a bed somewhere, curled up. And that's because the GM of some business who is at a label and doesn't know anything about music said, 'I'm not sure I hear the hit,' and the kid went home and hasn't spoken for a year. True creatives can't always take that kind of rejection. To be a great artist or writer you've got to be that sensitive. And you've got to have pain, or joy, and to feel really deeply."

SENSITIVE COLLABORATION

The sensitivity to which DioGuardi alludes is a crucial component in all of her collaborative relationships. "I'm very careful who I surround myself with, co-writers, or who works in my office. I cannot be in a room where anything is affecting me in the sense that my gift is compromised. I tell that to writers: they have to put themselves in situations where they're the best they can be. Never go into a room with someone who makes you doubt or feel bad about yourself. You need to be in a place where you feel that you're open, and you can touch on themes that are really true to you."

DioGuardi says multiplicity of endeavors fuels her songwriting process. In her creative mode, she needs to be somewhat distracted in order for inspiration to hit. "If I'm staring at my co-writer nothing is going to happen. I'm always doing three things at once and when I'm inspired my focus shifts over. The fact of just sitting and looking at somebody, and knowing we have to create this song out of thin air is kind of scary. I'd rather just wait until something moves me. The perfect song is where the craft meets the inspiration. Songwriting is an act of faith. Every time I walk into a room I don't know what I'm going to do."

One of DioGuardi's gifts is being able to work with young artists to help them interpret their emotions via songs. That said, she says that the lyrics should be taken at face value and not over-analyzed. "It's dangerous for people to read too far into songs; they're really moments in time. It's difficult when you have an artist that comes out with a hate song, or something that powerfully negative, because they don't realize they have to carry that for years. I always caution people I'm working with to be careful what they want to put out into the ether.''

DioGuardi, who makes her home in the fabled Hollywood Hills, has been making frequent jaunts to Nashville for writing sessions. She notes the fundamental differences between L.A.—quite notably a project town—and Nashville, where the songs rule. ''In Nashville you can express yourself in a broader way and it's much more lyrically driven. I've enjoyed going to Nashville, working with incredible musicians and people who have another take on words and how to use them in songs. Pop music is more personality driven while country lyrics are more universal. But talent doesn't have boundaries; it crosses boundaries. And if you believe that it's coming from a truly creative place, you'll infuse your music with that and it has a better chance of traveling in many different ways as opposed to one specific genre.''

Writing with Christina Aguilera was an especially valuable experience according to DioGuardi. ''I love Christina Aguilera. I don't usually tell people, 'You are so talented and great.' It's not in my personality, kissing someone's ass. But I had to tell her. At her age, to be that focused and talented and driven? People said, 'She's going to be difficult.' She was the easiest woman I've ever worked with because she knew what she wanted. That's easy. I'm much prefer to work with someone who knows who they are as opposed to someone who says, 'Yes,' and then the next day, 'I'm not so sure.' We're great writing team. What I love is when artists are really open about their lives. That's how it was with Christina. That's a gift when someone lets you share her life with you. That's what music is about.''

GHOST IN THE MACHINE

''There is a spiritual component in what I do in that I have to be true to myself and to the people out there,'' DioGuardi continues. ''I made those mistakes in my career sometimes, 'I wish I hadn't put that lyric in that song,' because it's bigger than me. And you don't realize that when you're coming up; you think it's small, just what's happening in the room, but when it starts going out into the universe you can't control it. If there's a lyric that's kind of racy for kids for example, now I feel like I have more responsibility. What do I want to express, but how can it be positive for the world, too? What I'm writing personally is my responsibility. When I'm co-writing with an artist or a co-writer I have them to consider. So I'm not infusing the room only with what I want. So that's why I've been able to do this for so long. I don't feel like it's my record—I'm helping the artist.''

''When she has an idea, she can sell that idea not only lyrically but physically,'' hit producer and songwriter John Shanks told the *Los Angeles Times* about his frequent collaborator. DioGuardi relates this example. ''I got on L.A. Reid's desk and started dancing to a song I'd written. It was the song 'Screwed' and he wanted Pink to cut it. He asked me, 'How would you sing the song?' I got on the desk. They asked me to get down because the candles on it were shaking, and the room almost caught fire. Then I went home and stayed in bed for a day.''

As a collaborator, DioGuardi is always aware of rising artists and writers. ''The perfect song is where the craft meets inspiration. I'm at a place where craft takes care of itself, but I need to be constantly inspired as a writer or artist.'' Among her favorite collaborators are will.i.am of Black Eyed Peas, and Atlanta's Lil Jon. ''(Jon) is so generous, so fun, creative and hard working. So is will.i.am; they're cut from the same thread—generous and open—no ego! I love that.''

While other songwriters might express their ideas through the guitar or piano, DioGuardi, uses her expressive voice as an instrument. A world-class singer, she is also adept at producing vocals for the artists for whom she writes although she is becoming much more selective. ''When I do the demo I do it like a record. Most of the time they take my voice off and put

Advanced Articles

someone else's on. I don't want to produce too many vocals anymore—it's very time intensive unless I feel like it's something I need to do. I much prefer creating, and I find I'm a happier person when I'm not producing, with more time to live life, take in things I can then put out into songs. It's important to me, as I grow older, not to work as intensely. I used to be about being in the studio 12-18 hours a day; it's not as fun as it used to be."

After almost 15 years in ascent to the highest echelons of the songwriting world, DioGuardi reflects that a key to her success has been in projecting an aura of unshakeable confidence. "You've got to believe in yourself. If you don't, pretend. Half the time I didn't believe. The producer would say, 'Cut the vocals.' And I'd better know what I was doing because Enrique Iglesias was going to walk in. A lot of it is assuming the role. Assume your ability matches up to your balls. Then you're in the golden spot and nobody can get at you."

Internet Resources for Songwriters

by Brian Austin Whitney

Writing an article on Internet Resources can be dangerous territory. Major changes are around nearly every corner and it's difficult to know which of the "next big things" out there will take off or tank. Rather than list all the names of sites you might check out, I am taking the approach of choosing some examples and explaining why the concept of their services and resources might be worth checking out. Though I will use examples that have great reputations and in some cases very long track records, it's very important for you to check out all the options carefully before spending a lot of time or money with any service or site. It's a brave new world on the Internet, and the most tumultuous part of that world is music. With a little planning, a little research and a little common sense, you have access to more tools and opportunities than any previous generation of songwriters in history. Take advantage!

EDUCATIONAL SITES

When starting your songwriting career, it's really important to get the right information. The Internet is filled with misinformation, partial truths, and even traps set by scam artists. Fortunately there are some very trusted places to learn about songwriting and get your questions answered by folks you can trust.

For a school-like educational experience, here are the two places you should start your search:

Song U (www.songu.com)

This is perhaps the best educational Web site ever placed online for songwriting. It's been built from scratch by two excellent songwriting teachers, Sara Light and Danny Arena. Both have been staff writers at Curb Magnatone, both are Tony Nominated and Light had a huge hit song for John Michael Montgomery called "Home To You." Arena is a long-time educator on the college level, and the site he and Sara have built is truly a marvel. You can take classes and do it in a warm, friendly, collegiate-type environment with a wide variety of educators and guest lecturers. Their rates are reasonable, and the feedback we've heard from their members has been universally glowing.

BRIAN AUSTIN WHITNEY founded the Just Plain Folks Music Organization (JPF) in 1998 with 60 members and has seen it grow to become the largest music organization in the world. JPF offers member networking opportunities, educational support and a real life community both online and face-to-face around the world. They also host the largest music awards in the world. Visit them at www.justplainfolks.org.

Berklee Online (www.berkleemusic.com)

For an actual accredited online music school experience, check out Berklee School of Music's online courses. They feature both songwriting and production classes which qualify as actual college credits. It's a little pricey compared to any other resource we're covering here, but far more affordable than moving to Boston and enrolling full time at the college. You'll get classes created and taught by the same faculty and you can do it from your own home.

For a more informal approach, try one of these Internet communities and organizations:

Muses Muse (www.musesmuse.com)

This is perhaps the oldest active songwriting resource on the Internet. It is still run by creator Jodi Krangle and offers a wide variety of resource links, articles and a friendly message board where songwriters hang out, exchange critiques and a warm community vibe. Membership is free and Jodi offers regular raffles where she gives away books, DVD's, and other items reviewed in her newsletter.

Just Plain Folks (www.justplainfolks.org)

JPF is the largest music organization in the world and supports both songwriters and artists equally. They offer a very busy message board for networking and educational help, have a large mentor staff to answer questions and offer advice, conduct the world largest music awards which are free to enter, and boast local chapters around the world where members meet face-to-face in a variety of activities. The group also travels around North America and Europe and sets up networking showcases where members from the area can come out, play a song or two, and network. There's a monthly e-mail newsletter that includes articles and essays to boost your spirit and keep you up-to-date on issues affecting the community. Membership is free.

Nashville Songwriters Association International (www.nashvillesongwriters.com)

This is a long-established music organization with local chapters throughout North America. Their Web site offers a variety of features and information, but it's only available to paid members. Check their site for current fees and chapter locations.

For a one-on-one teacher approach, try these:

John Braheny (www.johnbraheny.com)

John Braheny is often considered the Grandfather of the organized songwriting education world. His book *The Craft and Business of Songwriting* is considered a must-read for all songwriters who seriously want to pursue a career. He also offers one-on-one critiques and mentoring via his Web site.

Harriet Schock (www.harrietschock.com)

Harriet Schock is a hit songwriter, successful composer and author, and award-winning performer. She has both online courses as well as local classes in Southern California. She's also available for one-on-one mentoring.

Jason Blume (www.jasonblume.com)

Jason Blume is one of the few songwriters to ever achieve the distinction of having his songs on *Billboard*'s Pop, R&B, and Country charts all at the same time! His book *This Business of Songwriting* is essential reading. His site has articles, resources, and critique services.

Barbara Cloyd (www.barbaracloyd.com)

Barbara Cloyd is a Nashville icon. She's hosted the Monday Open Mic and booked the

Advanced Articles

early shows at the Bluebird Cafe for many years. She's a hit writer and runs successful writer nights in many clubs in town. She offers a variety of educational services including critiques on her site.

NETWORKING SITES

Big public networking and entertainment sites like MySpace and YouTube have sprung up in mega proportions. There will inevitably be many others popping up on the radar screen, but right now these two companies are changing the way people reach fans and promote their work. A low budget but clever video on YouTube can literally make an unknown writer or artist a household buzz word. A concerted effort to reach fans via MySpace can quickly build a massive fan list for even non-performing songwriters with great demos of their work.

Like all tools, you need to understand how to use networking sites to get the most out them. Here are a few tips on how to best use these types of mass media sites.

1. Have a hook: A page on one of these massive sites needs to stand out and catch people's attention. You need a hook, which is similar to a hook in a song. Give them a reason to be interested in you and your page. It takes more than just a photo, though that is very important. It also takes a backstory, or a gimmick. Make people laugh and you're golden. Make them laugh so hard they forward you to all their friends, and you might catch on like wild fire. But even if humor is not your thing, you have to reach out through cyberspace and make them care enough to notice. Great music alone won't do the trick. Become a real-life interesting person and people will want to know more.

2. Follow up: Once you have someone's interest, interact and follow up with them. Don't just add "friends" to build up large numbers—find out who they really are. Even for non-performing songwriters, these fans can help you in ways you can never predict. One of them may be the uncle of an up-and-coming artist who would be perfect for your song. Another might run a venue in a town you really need a gig in. Someone else could work for a publisher and might send a link to your page to someone who can put your writing career in the fast track. But you'll never know any of this unless you take the time to get to know your fan base and friends. Even for an artist, 5,000 fans can support you for life. Using the tools available today on these media networking sites, you can build that type of fan base quickly.

3. Network: Take the time to network with other artists and writers on these sites. For a songwriter, there's nothing more valuable than keeping your finger on the pulse of what is up-and-coming and new. These sites are incubators for new talent, and you should be using time each day to surf around and look for new artists who might record your type of songs, or simply making friends with those who are rising through the ranks now, before they are famous. You can't have too many talented friends, and these sites are swarming with them.

PERFORMING RIGHTS ORGANIZATIONS

The Performing Rights Organizations are often under-utilized resources for songwriters. They are there to help songwriters make a living from their music, so take full advantage of their knowledge and help. For any non-U.S. readers, you likely have similar PROs in your country. There are three U.S. Performance Rights Organizations. For musicians in the U.S., there is a new PRO for musician's royalties called SoundExchange. You should familiarize yourself with all four organizations.

ASCAP (www.ascap.com)
BMI (www.bmi.com)
SESAC (www.sesac.com)
SoundExchange (www.soundexchange.com)

SONG PLACEMENT/LICENSING SITES, COMPANIES, AND RESOURCES

Song placement sites and companies are springing up everywhere. Some are worthless and run by complete novices who may mean well, but have no practical ability or connections to do anything for you. Others are run by knowledgeable professionals with track records, but even then, they have a big hill to climb with far more songs than opportunities. Then there are complete scam artists who exist solely to rip you off. It's quite a minefield, but here are a few things to consider when navigating through them.

1. Quality control: Sites that don't filter for quality are likely to be a waste of time. This means that if they will accept and post any music from any source as long as they are willing to pay a fee of some type, you should seriously consider not joining. If a site is crammed full of really bad recordings and poorly written songs, why would any serious industry professional go to that site to look for good music? There's not enough time in the day.

2. Exclusive versus non-exclusive: There are two schools of thought on this issue. First, all things being equal, signing a non-exclusive deal is a great thing. That means you are free to also offer your songs up for licensing to any other site at the same time. Conventional wisdom has been that this will give you the most wide range of opportunities. One dissenting opinion which has recently surfaced is that some Music Supervisors prefer to avoid sites with non-exclusive licensing because they don't want to risk having multiple sites claim they should get the fees and the headaches that might involve. If in doubt, it's always safest to go with a non-exclusive company. If you do decide to sign an exclusive deal, make sure the company gives you a reasonable "out" that will allow you to leave their service and go elsewhere in a reasonable amount of time and at no penalty to you. That way you won't get stuck somewhere should that company not deliver on their promises or if a better or brand new opportunity comes up for your songs.

3. Fees: Avoid sites that charge large fees up front. Most online licensing sites should be making their money from getting placement deals and then taking their percentage from that business. If they are going to charge a fee up front, then their fees on the back end should be smaller than their competitors, or they should be able to demonstrate and produce superior results than the other sites. When in doubt, avoid sites that charge you on both ends (i.e. an up-front fee and a percentage of your license deal).

4. Placement options: Make sure the site allows you to opt out of certain types of placements. For example, if you don't want your song to be used in something you consider offensive, make sure there are ways to avoid having your music used in those types of media (for example, an adult film, or a politically offensive cause). At the very least, make sure you understand up front what types of things your songs can be used for so you can make an informed decision. If a site allows you to veto a placement, that would be a positive, but don't expect it because part of what makes a licensing site useful is that the music is pre-cleared, meaning you can pay a fee and use it without hesitation for the purpose agreed to.

5. Payment policy: Make sure you understand how you will be paid and how quickly. Some sites are not very good at paying you in a reasonable time and you should expect, in writing, a policy that details how quickly you will receive payment. Some sites allow you to set minimums for licensing. Make sure you check out this policy and only offer up your songs for amounts that are acceptable to you. Do some research on what fair rates are for the types of placements available to help you set that number. If they don't allow you to set your own levels, ask for their pricing levels in writing in advance and do some comparison shopping.

Many companies have come and gone in this general field, but one remains the clear leader in the industry for placements and opportunities: TAXI. This isn't simply an online site hosting songs for licensing opportunities. It's much more. TAXI is an independent A&R

company that's been around since the early '90s. Most songwriters, especially those just getting started, have no real industry contacts and very little perspective on how well their songs stack up to other commercially viable songs. TAXI can help you with both problems.

For those just getting started, they'll help you write better songs and learn how to target the songs you do write well for the right opportunities. Because they have successfully connected themselves to nearly every major and independent record label, publisher and film/TV supervisor, they have access to opportunities for your music that you'd never be able to make on your own. Not everyone can move to a music center and spend day and night pounding on doors, sitting in music clubs and hanging out at the local industry haunts for years to make direct industry contacts. TAXI allows you to submit your music for a wide variety of opportunities with the knowledge that if your music is good enough and on target for the listing, your song will get heard directly by the person making the final decision. If your song isn't quite good enough, the experts at TAXI will give you feedback on what needs to be improved and they'll also let you know if you sent the wrong type of song. There are other companies out there who make claims to do the same type of work, so definitely do some research on what is available and how they stack up to TAXI. The best part of TAXI is they offer a money back guarantee so there's really no risk. Most of the others don't make that offer.

TAXI (www.taxi.com)

INTERNET RADIO

Internet radio is exploding in listener numbers. There's also some turmoil over rights and royalties. When it's all worked out, this may be the best possible medium for songwriters to get their recorded music out to an audience directly. All stations and broadcasters have their own submission policies so check directly with them to learn how to get your songs included. Generally your recordings will have to be "radio ready" which means a quality vocal and instrument performance and a recording that is sonically acceptable for radio broadcast. If you use union musicians, be sure that your recordings are "masters" and not "demos." It may cost more, but a responsible writer will duly compensate the musicians playing on their recordings if they are to be used for airplay.

At the time of this writing, the two leading examples in the grassroots Internet radio world are Pandora and Live 365. Pandora is a company who specializes in playing songs similar to songs you request and allows you to create stations based on your own musical tastes. Live 365 is a collective of small Internet radio stations of all genres and sizes. Once you check these two out, do some searches for many more that are out there.

Pandora (www.pandora.com)
Live 365 (www.live365.com)

ONLINE MUSIC CHARTS

With the advent of music sites has also come a somewhat nefarious number of "charts" which are supposed to represent popularity of various songs on those sites. Though we should never say "never," it is clear that most of the time, charts on Web sites mean little or nothing at all. Think of it this way, if a site measures the ranking on a chart by the number of times someone clicks a link to play a song, that has nothing to do at all with the quality of the song once they click it. The song could be a listener's least favorite ever, yet it still gets credit for their click. The only thing most charts might indicate is the popularity of your song title, or the interest the rest of your page might have to someone browsing in. The truth about most charts are that they are simply tools that sites and companies use to stroke your ego enough to keep you coming back, or worse, spending money with their site or company.

For most practical purposes, there's really one, granddaddy chart that always means something across all genres of music: *Billboard*. If you make it onto a *Billboard* chart, that means you have real sales, real radio airplay or both. Even their Internet charts have a level of validity that most others do not. The print version is a crucial resource and tool for songwriters and artists looking to break into the commercial music scene. Their online Web site is equally useful and includes even more than their print version. The downside is that it's not inexpensive. But in this case, you get what you pay for.

Billboard (**www.billboard.com**)

ONLINE RECORDING AND DEMO RESOURCES

There are a lot of tools and services that you can use to record, release and sell your own CD.

For recording, it's all about two things: quality and price.

Always do some homework before hiring anyone to record your music. If you're an artist as well as a songwriter, you can likely save a lot of money by performing much or all of the music yourself. There's amazing recording gear available today that surpasses anything available to anyone just a decade ago. If you decide you'd like someone else to handle the recording and performances for you, you can go to a local recording studio, or, with some research, you can find a reliable and affordable company online to do it.

First, compare prices among several recommended recording service sites. The cheapest price won't always be the best option, nor will the most expensive. Find a range of prices and make sure you're talking to the ones who fall somewhere in the middle. Next, ask for examples of their most recent five projects. With the ease of mp3 files, they should be able to e-mail you samples right away. Ask for the contact info for the clients as well to do follow up referencing. Also make sure they are still using the same engineers and producers from those samples. Then listen to the samples to see which companies have the sound quality you're after that also fall within your budget. Remember that you should usually get a better rate the more songs you record. If a company doesn't want to give you examples and references, move on to the next one. It's a buyers market and they need your business a lot more than you need their services. Always remember you are the boss. Anyone who tries to pressure you is simply showing their hand and the fact that they know if you really take a hard look at them you'll go elsewhere. Never impulsively close a deal. Always give yourself time to consider options and sleep on it first.

Note: There's a long, ongoing debate about simple demos versus full blown demos. Let me make this perfectly clear. In either case, you *must* have a strong vocal performance and a solid instrumental performance. *If you don't have that, you're making a grave mistake.* Anyone who tells you a recording with a warbling, off key vocal is good enough and they can "hear past it" is likely trying to get money from you for something. It may have been true in the past, but with the inexpensive recording gear available to anyone today, it's simply no longer acceptable to send out a recording with a bad vocal, weak guitar or piano performance or poor overall sound quality. The business is far too competitive to put yourself into that kind of disadvantage and expect to find success. Your competition will be submitting top notch recordings of top notch songs for every opportunity. Don't miss a chance of a lifetime because you believe some old wives tale that a terrible demo is OK.

You can spend as much as $1,000 for a song demo at the absolute highest end or as little as $50 on the low end. Listen to examples of both to see the differences. If you can't afford the quality you want, wait to record and save more money. It's better to pay a little too much for a great final product than too little on a terrible one. In one case you waste a little extra but get a great result and in the other you wasted it all and have nothing usable to show for it. Never pay an amount outrageously high. *Never!* There are too many good studios that do great work for a fair price you can use instead. Just because some famous (or supposedly famous) name is attached doesn't mean you should pay an outrageous amount. It's not worth it.

Though there are literally thousands of options out there, here are two companies I would set as a measuring stick to start your research. They both do excellent work, have a lot of experienced and successful musicians on staff and if you have a little extra in the budget, Session Players can even offer world famous musicians (who cost a premium) to perform on your recording. Waymo Music has a successful track record with producing music for TV, Film and some top name artists as well.

Session Players (www.sessionplayers.com)
Waymo Music (www.waymomusic.com)

CD DUPLICATION/REPLICATION

Once you have your project recorded and you want to put it onto CD or DVD, there are two companies that have the lion's share of the market—and for good reason. Both do excellent work for competitive prices. Both offer a lot of extras and both are big supporters of the independent artist and songwriter communities. I could write an entire article on how great these companies are. Check them out and see for yourself.

Disc Makers (www.discmakers.com)
Oasis (www.oasisduplication)

ONLINE DISTRIBUTION

So now that you have your songs recorded, and you've got your CDs in hand, the next step is to get your discs online to sell. You'll also want to get those songs placed on all the digital sites like iTunes.com, Rhapsody, Yahoo, etc. Fortunately for you, there's a clear cut, no-brainer, one-stop-shop option for you.

CD Baby is not only the best place to sell independent music, it's also your gateway to get your music into every major digital sales site in one fell swoop. For a $35 dollar fee and five copies of your project for their warehouse, you're in business. CD Baby has over 200,000 other artists already on their site and they got that large by taking care of one artist at a time. Their customer service, for both the artists involved as well as those buying CDs, is first class. They pay weekly and only take $4 dollars per CD sold and only 9% (an industry low) of your digital download sales. They can also set up and host your own domain name and Web site via their outstanding web hosting site Hostbaby.

CD Baby (www.cdbaby.com)
Hostbaby (www.hostbaby.com)

Now that you've learned how to write songs from online educators, learned how the business works from expert teachers, made a lot of friends and business contacts via networking and music organization sites, found places to post and submit your music for use in film and TV and for major label artist opportunities, found online Internet radio stations to play your songs, found people to record your music, put your music on CD, placed it up for sale on the Net and on all the digital sales sites and even found a place to host your Web site, what's left?

PROTECT YOUR RIGHTS

The Future of Music Coalition is a hard working collection of advocates for grassroots artists and songwriters in many important political issues that deeply affect our community now and in the future. They've fought and won epic battles to protect and promote the little guys and gals in the music industry in ways that will affect us for decades to come. The issues

Advanced Articles

are always changing but their vision and passion never waivers. You owe it to yourself and future songwriters and musicians to get involved in your own future before someone else makes all the decisions for you. The Future of Music Coalition is the best resource to do that. It's free to join!

Future of Music Coalition (www.futureofmusic.org)

A CAUTIONARY WARNING

The Internet is teaming with scam artists on a level never before seen in the music industry. There are bogus contests, bogus Web sites, and bogus record label frauds offering bogus record deals that *cost you money* instead of *paying* you. (Never pay to get a record or publishing deal. *Never!*) If you get contacted by e-mail by a company you've never heard of expressing interest in your music, be very cautious because most of the time it's a scam. Sometimes it's an honest company just trying to drum up business. Almost never is it a legit contact out of the blue from a real industry person who can actually do something for your career. *If it is a legitimate contact, they will never ask you for money.* Please understand that. Real publishing, licensing, record, or other deals don't start by you paying anyone a dime. If someone contacts you out of nowhere, ask for a name and phone number you can call. Then before calling, do some research by searching the companies name on Google. You'll be amazed at how often you'll immediately find hundreds of pages exposing them as a fraud. In cases where nothing comes up, go to a friendly message board and ask around. People will fill you in quickly. There are a lot of wonderful and honest companies doing business on the web. We've named some above. Scam artists are great at telling you exactly what you hope to hear. The old cliché usually applies. If it sounds too good to be true, it is.

Be careful out there. And remember one golden rule that will make your entire career much more successful: Give credit where credit is due and say thank you to everyone at everyone level who helps you 100% of the time. If you do that one thing, you'll be miles ahead of your peers in no time.

Advanced Articles

Big Fish Lands TV Song Placements

by Ian Bessler

Chuck Tennin, CEO of Big Fish Music™ in Los Angeles, has had a long and varied career in the music business extending back to 1968 when he began work as Production Assistant and 2nd Engineer to legendary engineer/producer Ray Thompson (with 450 albums to his credit). During this period, Tennin participated in numerous recording projects, both live and studio, with legendary artists such as Neil Young, Aretha Franklin, Steppenwolf, Elvis Presley, Procol Harum, CSNY, Jimi Hendrix, Little Feat, George Benson, Peter Frampton, and many others.

Following this period, he embarked on a long journey through multiple niches within the music industry, including artist manager, club promoter, album art director, and record producer. He also spent four years working for Hollywood-based H.D.M. Records/Murrell Music as a professional music manager; joined the Country Music Association (CMA) and Academy of Country Music (ACM); served as a song contest judge for the American Song Festival until its close in 1984, as well as three years judging for the Colgate Country Showdown (a country version of *American Idol* on radio stations across the country); and conducted workshops for the National Academy of Songwriters (NAS), Northern California Songwriters Association (NCSA), and Los Angeles Songwriters Showcase (LASS).

Tennin formed his own BMI publishing company in 1975, and he named the company Big Fish Music after a suggestion by the late Lowell George of Little Feat (followed by a sister ASCAP company, California Sun Music™). Big Fish publishes and licenses music to all outlets—including recording artists, motion picture producers, and other users of music, as well as artist and songwriter development projects—but has developed a specialized focus in background and theme music for television. Over the years Big Fish has placed numerous songs with NBC's *Passions* television show, as well as with ABC's *General Hospital* and *All My Children* on CBS.

So, what does a songwriter interested in breaking in to television music licensing need to know? When asked, Tennin begins with the Master License Agreement and the Synchronization License. "[The television show's producers] have to have a Master License Agreement, and that allows the TV station or show to use the master recording that contains the song. The song itself is different. The song comes under a Synchronization License, which allows them to use the song."

IAN BESSLER has been editor of *Songwriter's Market* since the 2001 edition.

So, if the show's producers must actually pay two different fees to use the song—one for the recording, and another for the "underlying composition"— how exactly are these two fees paid out?

One is an immediate [fee] paid by the licensee for the right to use the master recording that embodies the song, and then there's the performance rights from airing in different countries and so on. All the major networks—NBC, CBS, and ABC—pay a blanket licensing fee at the beginning of the year. They pay this money into an account, and then ASCAP and BMI use that money to pay the royalties, but each time a song is used, it's required by law that the networks have to log the air date, and they send what they call cue sheets into BMI and ASCAP, and that's how writers and publishers are paid for the performance use. The master license is something negotiated by the publisher with whomever uses the music.

How much can you get for the Synch License fee?

If it's a movie, it could be a $30,000 fee or a $10,000 fee. A fee for *Passions* could be $1,000 or $2,000 or $3,000, and that's paid in advance of any [performance] royalties that come from airing it. They pay that directly, and the publisher splits that with the writer. So the publisher will pay the writer in that case. But the two have to go hand in hand.

And it's all done on a one-time basis, meaning if, for example, on *Passions* if they want to use the same song three times on the same show, they have to have clearance from a master recording license agreement that allows them to use the recording that embodies the song. They pay the publisher for the master rights use—and the publisher splits that fee with the writer—and then they have the performance royalties that go through ASCAP and BMI that are collected for every time that show is aired on the station.

What about songwriters marketing a recording where someone else is singing?

If a songwriter has a song used on TV where they didn't sing it, but they had another singer, they need to pay [the singer] and get a release. But there are times when they'll use an artist on a record label, and then they have to negotiate with the record label to get another fee or to get permission to use that artist's voice on the recording, and it complicates things.

How do a show's producers usually use the music they license?

Sometimes they'll use it in a major part, and sometimes they'll use it as a theme. It all depends on what show, what network, what company, and the time of the day, because they have "prime time" and "down time." We do a lot of music on the soaps, which are considered prime time during the day. BMI and ASCAP have a formula for performance rights, and that could be *the amount of stations × the amount of use of the song × the time of the day*.

Or, they'll take a song that's three minutes long, and they might dissect it and take one minute of a section to insert in part of a show or scene or episode where it fits. They might use one minute and 20 seconds and not use the whole song. NBC and ABC, what they'll do is, if they have a song in their library that's four minutes long, they can dissect sections of that many times over and use parts of the same song. They keep that in their library indefinitely, and so you could have ten different segments of a song that are used for different things.

How does all of this dissecting and bit-by-bit use of the song affect royalty payments?

Anything that is used under 30 seconds gets one rate, while anything over a minute gets another rate. If they use the song on a show three different times, they'll pay a master license fee for the first-time use—maybe it's $1,000—then the second time will be $1,000, the third time will be $500, and I think it goes down to $350.

So, on that particular use, the first two times the rate would be the same, and then it

Advanced Articles

changes. But then if they use it again on a different episode, it starts at the top rate, and if they use the song six times, the sixth time would get less than the first time. But, say they use two minutes the first time—that would be a substantial performance rate—and maybe the sixth time they use the whole song even though the fee was lower, but the royalty rate will be very high because it all has to do with how they use it.

Anything used over 30 seconds is considered a real good use, because with *Passions*, for example, if they shoot three times a week and they do a one-hour episode, they have their theme song that is played over and over, but in that one hour they're inserting a lot of music. Some could be 30 seconds. Some could be a minute. It depends on where the music is needed. But they might have 50 different pieces of music in one episode.

How long does it typically take to receive a check from a song placement?

The one good thing about TV is that the payments for the master license fee are paid generally within a very reasonable time, at the most maybe several months. But that's very quick to receive monies for the use of a song, and if a songwriter made a couple thousand dollars or two or three thousand dollars, well the majority, how often do they get two or three thousand dollars from BMI and ASCAP?

How long does it then usually take for performance royalties to come in from ASCAP or BMI?

BMI and ASCAP pay by quarters, four quarters a year, and they're generally maybe three quarters behind. It's a funny thing, because writers will say, "Wow, I didn't get anything in a surveyed performance." Well, the thing is if a show uses a song, and they have a big workload, they may not send the cue sheet in for a month, and then when it goes in to BMI and ASCAP, they're behind by three quarters, so it could be six or nine months later.

But, in the foreign market, it can take two or three years. Generally three years. And they'll say, "Well, I didn't get anything from it airing." It might be Australia, it might be Canada, it might be France, it might be wherever, but BMI and ASCAP have no control over or ability to police those countries. All they have is a sheet they'll send the publisher, which will tell the expected time frame of when these countries pay the royalties on it. Some of them do it one time a year, some of them do it every year, some of them do it a couple times a year, and if you get a country that does it one time a year, and you missed it, well then you have to wait another year. And ASCAP and BMI cannot pay songwriters or publishers until they actually get the monies in, and they can't go and tell these people when to do it. They all have their own set schedules, and unfortunately in foreign countries it's just the way it is. It can take two or three years.

When people submit music to you, is it useful to have several different mixes of the same song, maybe even one without vocals?

A lot of times it could be a plus to have mixes of the music tracks, in addition to the vocals and the music, the whole thing. And in this case, the thought is the song could be used at the beginning, or be at the end, and the music can be extracted to be used throughout the film. And it might be where they want the vocals to really cut through. A lot of people put the vocals closer to the music, as if you were trying to sell a band. But sometimes, and it's happened many times, they want the vocals out a little bit further. It's not necessarily that they're trying to sell the song and the lyrics, but they don't want people to have to reach to hear what they're singing.

Then it pays to have other mixes. When we do mixes in the studio in song development, we'll do it with the vocal "in the pocket," in the middle, and then we'll have it high, and that way you've covered yourself in all ways. They can say, "I like this one. This one works the best. That's the one I want." They have choices.

When you're there [at mixdown], you might as well try and get them all, because when you go back at some other time, you have to start over, take the tracks and start mixing, and you may never get the same thing again. You probably won't.

What do you mean exactly by "in the pocket"?

It's arrangement. It's equalization. It's a number of things. It's building around the vocalist. It's complementing the vocalist. It's building the music around and with the vocal. It just makes vocals richer, easier to work with, because then you can mix them closer or you can pull it out more, or you can do a medium one, and then you've got choices. You can find the one that fits the best, where you can get the quality of the vocalist and all the lyrics, and you're not reaching. It's not conflicting or drowned out or swept up in there.

We get submissions all the time where vocals are drowned out because they're not in the pocket. They're mixed into the tracks so that it's distracting, it's distorting, and it's not complementing the singer. There's a conflict. If you're selling the song, then people need to hear the words. If you're selling the artist, they need to hear the artist.

Do most of the songs you place come from performing songwriters? How often do you place songs by "pure" writers who do not perform?

I would say it's running as much 70% where the songwriter used another vocalist. But, a lot of times a songwriter will submit a really good song, but they submit it where they are doing the vocals and for different reasons. A lot of times, when they do it—the songwriter does it—they're saving money or they're doing it because they think they can do it, but they don't always know because they're not on the other end where people are listening to it. That's a bad reason, but we get a lot of submissions, and you can tell right off that [the songwriter] is the singer. A songwriter has to put a value on the song, because people are overloaded, and people are listening all the time. You have to do something to make it a cut above. You're trying to take their song further and put it out on the marketplace.

When they use a singer that fits, the difference can be great. But a listener has to believe the singer, and has to feel the song, and the lyrics have to capture them. For that moment, for the time that they're singing, that singer should in reality believe what they're singing and feel it, because whoever listens to it, they need to believe it, and they need to feel it.

Others that want to go a little further and take it another step, because naturally they want their song listened to, and they want somebody to like their song, and they want to get it used. But in concept, that song has to cut through to the listener on the first listen because people generally want to run with something. They don't want to fix things up.

How important is the choice of demo singer?

Putting the right vocal on there is so important, because it's vocally got to cut through, and those lyrics and those words and the song, they've got to cut through, the first time around, the first time, on the first listen, because you may not get another chance. And maybe somebody just doesn't listen to a complete song a hundred percent, but if there is something that catches their ear, and they like it, whether it's a line in the song, or the singer, or whatever, then they'll generally take that song, and at another time when they're really listening, they'll listen to it to see what their feelings are.

Is it best to invest in the highest-quality demo you can afford?

A lot of the songwriting organizations would say, "Hey, we've got a studio here. $100 and we'll do you a demo." Well, my feelings were, if they did ten songs for $1,000, I'd rather take $1,000 and take my *best song* or the one that felt strongest and put it into that. When they listen, it's essentially that they either like it or they don't like it, and you don't want other things to interfere—that it wasn't the right vocalist, or it drags, or it does this or that. It's got to be shoved in their face, and it's no different than somebody painting the Mona Lisa, where they take a charcoal rendering or a pencil drawing and say, "Hey, here it is! When it's done it's going to have all these colors or whatever." Most people can't grasp that, and truthfully, most people can't hear music.

You at least want a quality demo, not cutting off your arm to cut a master, like you're going to put it out, but you've got to go beyond a basic thing, because these people want to run with something. These people only have so much listening time, and they know what they want. At worst they're going to tell you, "I like the song" or "I don't like the song." That's what you really want to hear. Or, "I can use it" or "I can't use it." Because they're not going to say, "I can't hear the words." If they have to reach with their ears, you're done. You need to put it right to them, and they've got to hear all the elements.

What steps can songwriters take to make sure their songs are worthy before they spend that money? Should they seek critiques through songwriters organizations?

The good thing about those organizations—because I did workshops and critiquing and seminars for many years—and the good thing for a lot of those songwriters, is that because they were a member they could sit down with somebody in the industry. They had different people every week or every month, and they would listen to the songs critique them, and they'd answer questions. And that was very helpful if somebody took the fine points or the important points out of that and followed that. It would help them.

But sadly a lot of people don't do it. As I found out from presidents of songwriting organizations, they'll have members who are still there five years later and are wondering why nothing happened, because they're expecting that organization to do it all for them. It's a stepping stone or a guide to help you with your craft to get some kind of database or foundation to help you, whether it's collaborating with others, meeting different people, or doing your demos and having a vocal bank, or having someone you can go to.

What other areas is Big Fish Music currently exploring?

Especially with a songwriter or new artist, there isn't any question I can't answer. We're involved in all areas of marketing songs. One new thing we're doing is that we're engaged in a new avenue of testing songs on radio with Loggins Promotions to see how they would do on radio. On the basis of our screening, we'll send them a song, and they'll take a song and get testing on radio and score it. Paul Loggins will test it for us free of charge on some stations and get a rating. Then if you want to go forth and market it, he'll help set up a campaign for it. If it doesn't rate well, he'll recommend you not go forward. He has a good longstanding relationship as a promoter with radio stations, and it's a way even independent songwriters, if they choose to go that way, can find out how well their song could perform commercially. In the case of a songwriter who does not perform and didn't sing on their own recording, we wouldn't run a campaign, but this radio rating could be useful in other areas to open doors. It shows that you're doing something interesting, and it can be used as a tool in moving further along and securing some other deal, like with a recording artist. Also, if I was writing songs and got tons of rejections, if I got a good test with radio I would know I was still on the right track. But if people tell me they don't like it *and* radio doesn't like it, then I should go back to the drawing board.

Advanced Articles

Music for Commercials

by John Braheny

The marketplace for music in commercials has undergone a major change in just the past few years and a sea change from when I had my own commercial jingle company in the 1970s. The philosophy then was that no self-respecting artist would ever consider selling out to corporate sponsors by allowing his music to be used in commercials. There were special clauses they demanded in their contracts that prevented it, and their managers realized the artists could lose a major part of their fan-base if they were presented in this way. Now, despite holdouts among revered artists like Bruce Springsteen, Tom Waits, and The Doors (well, Jim Morrison anyway, even though the band had vowed to stick together), others including The Rolling Stones, Paul McCartney, and Bob Dylan went for it. Who knows why—did they really need the money? My attitude in those cases, after the initial shock, was. "I think they've earned the right to do whatever they want. If I don't like it, that's *my* problem."

Unknown indie bands and artists slogging it out on the road with families to feed can get a lot more pragmatic and it's not hard to see why they'd go for a good paycheck. Young idealistic fans often get disillusioned by that move, though, so it can be a risky proposition for some bands, even when they see the possibilities of mass exposure. The risk is softened in many cases by some of the ways current commercials use music:

1. Hit songs with a hook that becomes a perfect fit for an ad slogan: Bob Seger's "Like a Rock" for Chevy, Billy Steinberg and Paul Kelly's "True Colors" for Kodak.

2. Song that crafts a message specifically written for the product: Squeak E. Clean's "Hello Tomorrow" for Adidas.

3. Song creates a mood, much as its used in TV or film: Gorillaz's "Feel Good Inc." for Apple's iPod and Sting's "Desert Rose" for Jaguar. All of the tracks from Moby's *Play* album are used in a variety of commercials.

4. Lifestyle background music, a presentation of what someone in the ad might be listening to: Volkswagen ads by Stereolab and Spiritualized.

The last two categories are ones that some bands and artists feel more comfortable with since they seem less like an endorsement of the product and more like the music *they* listen to.

For artists who have yet to experience mass exposure, commercials can be a career boost.

Excerpted from *The Craft & Business of Songwriting, 3rd Edition* ©2007 by **JOHN BRAHENY**. Used with permission of Writer's Digest Books, an imprint of F+W Publications, Inc. Visit your local bookseller or call (800)754-2912 to obtain your copy.

Sony's PlayStation Portable ad introduced Franz Ferdinand to a mass audience with "Take Me Out." Same thing with the Concretes' "Say Something New" for Target.

PROS AND CONS

Artists with major hits who are approached to use them in commercials need to carefully consider several important issues before deciding to do it.

Will it negatively affect the future market of the song? Sometimes overexposure can make people not want to hear it anymore. Or it can actually corrupt the "nostalgia factor" by too much association with the product. High blood pressure pills being advertised by the song you fell in love to in high school might be a bad idea. On the upside, if a listener hasn't heard it in years it could rekindle the "nostalgia factor" in a positive way—again, depending on the product.

Another positive effect might be that once people in film, TV, video games, and ringtones hear the song again, they may want to use it in their own media. This is a common effect for unknown bands, too.

Positive or negative, big money talks and huge corporations have it to spend on advertising. For established hits on a year-long ad campaign, selling to a commercial can be worth over $1 million.

THE APPEAL OF THE INDIE ARTIST TO AD AGENCIES

It's all about smarter marketing and economics. Ad agencies who create the campaigns and individual commercials realized that, for certain youth-oriented products, using contemporary music was a more effective and less expensive approach. It helps their clients become, in effect, part of the *tribe* they're selling the product to. The 30-something creative staff of the ad agencies is part of that musical culture, so when they think of music to use in their ads they think about music *they* like. It conveniently happens that some of their favorite bands and artists are independent artists or signed to small record labels who make their livings primarily by touring and sales of merchandise and CDs. From the agencies point of view, they give the bands national exposure—and at a fraction of what it usually cost their clients for music in commercials.

So, the lines are blurring between the shame of selling out and the hipness of buying in. Not that there aren't still artists who feel they'll lose their fan base, autonomy and dignity by doing commercials—just a lot fewer of them.

If you're a band or solo artist who writes your own music and own the rights to it (you haven't assigned your publishing rights to another publisher), and you also own your own masters (you haven't signed a record deal in which the record company owns your master recordings), you make it easy for an agency to license your song for use in a commercial. (Obviously you need to be a very good band!) You'll get a few hundred to a few thousand dollars depending on the budget of the client, whether the ad is local or national, radio or TV, and how long they want to use it, If it's renewed past the original contract period, you get an additional payment. You'll get most of the income from the up-front synchronization fee and master-use fee. You'll get some, but not much, from your performing rights organization as they all pay just a fraction for commercials of what you'd get for use in film or TV shows.

MAKING IT HAPPEN

To pursue the scenario, get in touch with song placement companies or services like TAXI (www.taxi.com) or SongCatalog (www.songcatalog.com) or other Online Pitch Services.

Call major ad agencies, tell them your situation, and ask if there are placement services they work with that you can contact. This gives them a way to politely turn you away knowing that if you're worth hearing there's someone they trust who will prescreen. Just in case they're intrigued though, it also helps if you have a Web site to refer them to, or another place they can hear your music online.

They also use Production Music Libraries to supply them with underscore music if they don't want to hire someone to create custom tracks for them.

YOUR OWN JINGLE PRODUCTION COMPANY

You may already be producing film and TV music or library music and want to branch out. If you decide you want to start your own jingle company, you'll need to have very good production skills or to partner with someone who does. You need to own or have access to excellent recording facilities, musicians, engineers, arrangers, and an attorney. Because most ad agencies are signatories to American Federation of Musicians (AFM), American Federation of Television and Radio Artists for singers and actors (AFTRA), and Screen Actors Guild (SAG), your company should also be a signatory to their agreements. This allows you, as a union member, to play on your own sessions and for you and the other musicians and singers to collect residual payments for every thirteen-week period the ad is used after the initial period. Check with your local union to set that up and learn how to do the reports or the union reps can refer you to someone who can do it for you. Go to AFM (www.afm.org), AFTRA (www.aftra.org) and SAG (www.sag.org) and search for ''commercials.'' A thirty-second commercial can bring you $5,000 to $50,000 for the combined production costs and creative fee depending on whether it's local or national and how long it is used.

The agency will always want this to be a work-for-hire and will want to own all rights to what you create for them. If possible, try to retain rights to receive performance royalties from your performing rights organization (ASCAP, BMI, or SESAC) or if it's a song, to receive any writer's share of royalties that might come from other uses: film, TV series, or ringtones. Chances are you won't be able to negotiate that, but it's worth a shot.

DEALING WITH AD AGENCIES

Large ad agencies may have multi-million dollar accounts and with the stakes so high, they can't afford to gamble. If they choose music that sounds less than professional and appropriate, they risk losing an account and their jobs. So a composer not only needs to understand the advertising medium and be thoroughly professional, but must be a kind of psychologist, instilling confidence in his abilities and making agency personnel feel secure in their musical choices.

They'll usually want to hire you because of something else they heard from you. If not and you're just pitching them your music cold, you'll need to develop a musical and personal rapport with the creative exec you'll be working with. You'll need a musical frame of reference, much like a music supervisor does with a film or TV director, since the agency people may not have a technical knowledge of music. Good communication will save you lots of time and error.

When you start a project, they'll have a storyboard already worked out—a series of drawings or a simple animation depicting the way they see the commercial from beginning to end. Each section is timed with a script that shows where the voiceover (VO) goes.

They may want you to create the lyric yourself or more likely give you a lyric or slogan to work from. (If you're lucky, the lyric is actually singable!)

You and several other producers will usually be asked to come up with demos to play for the client. They may give a minimal budget to cover demo costs, but occasionally you'll be asked to do the demos on spec (your money). Digital demos are usually not hard to put together for a maximum sixty-second spot and not hard to adapt and change quickly. It's a good idea to come up with more than one to give them a choice. If you get something they like, you can ultimately just embellish the tracks you have or arrange it for live musicians.

Ad agencies prefer to do business with music producers with whom they have good rapport, who are professional, who understand their needs, and who deliver the goods at an equal or better price than anyone else. They also like to deal with people who are personable and even charismatic, because they can depend on them to impress their clients. It won't do to have the client come to your session and have the ad executive who hired you have to apologize for your bad attitude. That's not the way business is done at that level. He wants the client to have confidence in you and compliment him on his good taste. A great personality will never substitute for competence in this business, but in this case at least it can provide a competitive edge.

NEGOTIATING YOUR CREATIVE FEE

Just as it is in any other business, negotiating your fee depends on clout and chutzpah. It takes a lot of nerve to ask for twice what you think you can get and negotiate from there. At any rate, figuring out what to ask for is one of the most difficult parts of the business. You don't want to downgrade yourself by asking too little or price yourself out of business by asking too much. Get all the information you can ahead of time about the client's needs, the target demographic, and whether it's a national or regional campaign. A union representative may be able to give you guidance on what other producers charge as creative fees. They'll also be helpful in planning your recording budget if you're using live musicians. There are some general principles to remember that I learned by trial and error.

I once bid against two competitors on a job that was to be a series of thirty-second spots, variations on a basic theme. My bid was based on my figuring out a low-cost way to do the variations. (This was in the dark ages before digital software.) I lost the bid, and it wasn't until two years later that the agency representative would tell me why. The spots had gone for nearly twice my figure, because the other two bids were in the same neighborhood and the client decided that if my competitors, both well-known pros, were charging that much, he didn't see how I could possibly deliver for half that amount. The agency exec, who I'd done other projects for, tried to convince the client, but the psychology of "If it costs more, it must be better" worked against me. After that I changed my negotiating tactics.

Bid high, and let them tell you it's too steep. You can then say, "Well, let me see if I can figure out some shortcuts without compromising the quality." You get back to them with something like, "I made a good deal with a new studio so I can knock off a couple hundred," or "I can use three singers instead of six," etc. If you have a solid relationship with the ad agency, they may hint at what sort of ballpark figure they're thinking about, but they'd rather not. Obviously, if you're talking about Coca-Cola, you're dealing with a company that annually spends billions on advertising, as opposed to a local jewelry store that spends thousands.

THE AUDITION DEMO

Because this field is very competitive, having a first-rate demo that shows your skill and versatility is essential. Collect up to ten pieces (no more) in no more than five minutes of music. If you've already got legitimate credits, include them. If not, don't be intimidated. The agencies are always looking for new talent because some composers, after a few years, get too expensive or their style gets old. Agencies look for fresh ideas and very contemporary styles, particularly for youth market products. Put a sample of whatever you do best first on the demo. Do a piece of atmospheric background on it. Create some jingles for imaginary products. Show them some different moods in both vocal jingles and instrumental underscore in different styles.

Many commercials only identify the product on screen and not in the jingle. Create a couple of evocative jingles with lyrics that express some emotional comment on life in general. Print a label and CD insert with your logo so you'll look like a pro. Print some credits or other self-promotion on the insert, don't forget your address, phone number, e-mail address, and Web site. If you have a site devoted to your business with samples of other commercials you've done, you're ahead of the game, but you also want them to have an actual CD (or a DVD with a video collection of past work) and résumé that they can keep on file and put their hands on quickly.

MAKING CONTACT

Try to make personal contact by setting up a meeting, especially if you tend to make a good impression in person. If you have an impressive studio, try to get them there for the meeting. When you get a meeting at their office, take copies of your audio/visuals, After the meeting, send a card to thank them for their time. On a file card or database, keep track of your meetings, listing:

1. Their contact information
2. Their clients (always subject to change)
3. Who you met there
4. Their comments on your presentation
5. The names of their secretaries and assistants
6. A date and time to call back (ask them before you leave the meeting)

You'll probably make several calls before you talk to your main contact, but you'll make friends with the secretary or assistants who also will be able to give you valuable information on upcoming projects. Continue to update your data file every time you call, noting the date. All this is important because after your first twenty appointments (or sooner) you'll start to lose track of who's where.

Most major jingle activity is in New York, Chicago, Dallas, and Los Angeles, so if you don't live near those cities you need to pursue some other options. Among those options is to establish an Internet presence with a great looking Web site. Make that your online office. Since audio files can be sent anywhere and since any ad agency worth approaching these days has a high speed Internet connection, you can do a lot of business that way.

Here are some other suggestions for finding work as an independent jingle producer:

- Place ads in advertising and production trade magazines such a:
  Adweek (www.adweek.com)
  Advertising Age (www.adage.com)
  Millimeter (www.digitalcontentproducer.com): More on the video/film post-production tech side.
  Adtunes.com (www.adtunes.com): Just for fun and to update yourself on popular music used in commercials.
- Contact your state film commission and try to get listed as a music resource in the catalogue they send to companies to solicit film projects in your state. These catalogues are also sent to companies within the state. Search the Internet under "film commission."
- It may cost you $1,000 for the CD-ROM edition, but the *Advertising Redbooks* (www.red books.com) have all the information on major ad agencies, their personnel, contact information, and client lists. Before you spend the money though, call your local library and see if they have a reference copy.
- Most major cities have an ad club whose members include ad agencies, media professionals, clients, and music producers in that region. They also have newsletters in which you can advertise. The American Advertising Federation is a national organization for

advertising professionals. They have periodic conventions in various cities that provide valuable opportunities to show your wares and make contacts. Get information on membership and schedules from:

American Advertising Federation
1101 Vermont Avenue, NW Suite 500
Washington, DC 20005-6306
Phone: (202)898-0089
Fax: (202)898-0159
E-mail: aaf@aaf.org
Web site: www.aaf.org

Western Region Office
251 Post St., Suite 302, San Francisco, CA 94108.
Phone (415)421-6867
Fax: (415)421-0512

PURSUING SMALL LOCAL AD ACCOUNTS

Yet another possibility is to form your own small-scale ad agency and music production company dealing with small local accounts. It's a good idea to start small. It's possible to build a business on small local accounts and progress into bigger accounts. This works best if you live in a small town outside large metro areas where you don't have as much competition and know people on a more personal basis. Take advantage of the fact that you know business people from school, church, and work. It requires less research when you already know your potential clients. But even in big cities there are lots of potential customers. Check out local restaurants, clubs, hotels, tourist attractions, car dealerships, and similar businesses to see if they already do or will do radio ads. If you have a good home studio, put together a catchy jingle for some of them. Write a sample script, get a voiceover actor to read it, and present your potential clients with a thirty-second version of the whole thing. If it sounds professional, you'll be surprised at how positively people react to hearing their very own commercial jingle. They may even want to do the voiceovers for their own commercials (an approach that can either be wonderful or a disaster!).

Research the various businesses to see how they're promoting themselves currently—local radio spots without music or stock library music underscore, print ads only, etc. Record several styles of music for various businesses—Latin for Mexican restaurants, country for a Western clothing store, some solid pop or rock tracks for any kind of business. Spend some creative time coming up with something special after you've made note of their business slogans or whatever means they've used to distinguish themselves in their market.

Your competition for local radio ads are the radio stations themselves, whose salesmen sell businesses package deals that include their staff announcers writing and reading the ad copy. A good plan is to form alliances with the ad sales people at the stations and help them put together those packages. Your advantage is that you can provide the client with an original jingle and likely can do it cheaper than a jingle house, which has more overhead. You would sell the jingle to the client and have the station's announcer write and read additional copy.

A drawback to this approach is that, in order to give the client an inexpensive deal, you'd pretty much have to do it without union help. When you do non-union spots and play on them yourself, you do not receive residuals. You charge a one-time "buyout" fee that includes your creative fee and covers your production cost. You'll hope to create a lasting relationship with the client and periodically create new jingles for him.

Advanced Articles

Check out Jingle Course (www.jinglebiz.com). They have a list of resources and offer a reasonably priced course in starting your own jingle business.

All of the above can be applied to television ads as well. Find a video production company to partner with and come up with some creative concepts together.

WORKING FOR A JINGLE PRODUCTION COMPANY

If you're not interested in being in business for yourself, another alternative is to hook up with a jingle music production company or "jingle house." These are established businesses that usually represent several composers. You may not have the potential to make as much money if you choose this route, but you wouldn't have as many expenses and headaches, either. Find them in the Yellow Pages and on the Internet, usually under "music arrangers and composers," "music producers," "jingle production," or "commercial music production." Also, check out the local recording studios and find out if any jingle production is done there and who is doing it. Compile a demo of your best work and play it for them.

What if you have a jingle idea for a major product?

If you think up an outstanding jingle or concept for a particular product, can you sell it to an agency? Your odds are not good. Remember, ad agencies who represent those products pay a lot of money to copywriters in their company to come up with those ideas. There's a good chance they don't want to hear yours. If they do, you risk that they'll borrow your idea or some important aspects of it without paying you. Ideas are not copyrightable. What you *can* copyright is an actual slogan or jingle (song), but unless it's compatible with the product image already planned by the agency, the odds are against the company using it no matter how clever the idea. Having said that, if you believe enough in your idea you should give it a shot anyway. Your best strategy is to find out which ad agency represents the product, present them a finished product, get your ego out of the way, and allow one of the creative execs at the company to take credit for it. Always consider that, in this kind of situation, you need to join power, not fight it.

Radio Promotion Roundtable

by Aaron J. Poehler

The role of the radio promoter has always been somewhat murky and mysterious. It's not uncommon for even experienced songwriters to be unclear on just what a radio promoter can do to aid—or impede—a song's success. But, just as no two songwriters are the same, radio promoters have different approaches, angles, and areas of specialization. Further, as the traditional radio industry splinters into terrestrial radio, satellite radio, Internet radio, and other online venues, does the traditional belief that radio play is absolutely necessary still hold true?

To shed some light on this corner of the music industry, I asked several prominent radio promoters to talk a little bit about what they do to help their clients' music get on the airwaves—and what songwriters can do to help make the process go a little more smoothly.

Karen Lee is President and Founder of Evolution Promotion, a full-service artist development company specializing in radio promotion, tour promotion, online marketing, music publishing, and consulting in all areas of the music business. Evolution's roster includes Blow Up Hollywood, AIR, The White Stripes, Porcupine Tree, Brian Eno, Moby, Craig Armstrong, Jane Siberry, and William Orbit. Evolution Promotion handles daily promotion operations for various major and independent record labels.

Adam Lewis is one of the co-owners of the Planetary Group, an artist development and promotions firm based out of Boston. Planetary has worked with such acts as The Decemberists; Bloc Party; Peter, Bjorn & John; Apples In Stereo; Kings of Leon; and The Lemonheads. Lewis also currently handles all publicity, promotion and media buying for Great Northeast Productions.

Paul Loggins is the CEO and founder of Loggins Promotion, a firm that specializes in radio promotion & marketing, consulting and management, with clients including Queen, Mariah Carey, Boyz II Men, Gwen Stefani, Dave Matthews, and of course, cousin Kenny Loggins. Loggins also founded and developed Backstage Entertainment, a management firm which specializes in working with independent and unsigned artists and independent labels.

Steve Theo co-founded Pirate! in Jan 2004 with Douglas Blake. Steve spent many years in the radio department at The Planetary Group, previously ran the College/Metal radio department at Columbia Records, was a DJ and Music Director at WBTY in Massachusetts, and still spins records for WFNX in Boston.

AARON POEHLER is a musician, songwriter, and freelance writer. He has produced a wide range of writing, including music journalism, fiction, and technical documentation. He offers technical writing, professional editing, proofreading, co-writing, and ghostwriting services (see www.aaronpoehler.com). He is not related to Amy Poehler of SNL.

Bill Wence opened Bill Wence Promotions in 1980 after the success he had with four self-penned, self-produced and self-promoted *Billboard* singles led people to ask him, "Hey, can you do that for me?" Clients have included Collin Raye, Jerry Jeff Walker, Blackhawk, Randy Travis, James Talley, Paul Stookey, Mary Gauthier, Red Meat, Mare Winningham, Ruthie and the Wranglers, Tom T. Hall, The Outlaws, Bobby Bare, The Amazing Rhythm Aces, and Orleans. Additionally, Bill was one of the 30 founding members of the Americana Music Association.

As you'll see, our roundtable participants' views sometimes differ radically, so remember: if you decide to pursue radio promotion for your music, choosing the right person to help promote your music can be just as important as selecting the right producer and engineer to record it.

What basics should all songwriters know about independent radio promotion?

Steve Theo: They are hiring professionals who know the ins and outs of several hundred radio stations. We know who to target with their music and why, as well as who and when to call. Often artists try to do this themselves—and then come to us when they realize it takes a whole radio department to get the job done.

Adam Lewis: Artists should always consider hiring someone to help them get the word out. This does not mean hiring a huge company to go after commercial radio—college and non-commercial radio are, in general, very supportive to new and independent artists. There are 600-plus stations out there that are reporting their playlists to *CMJ* and that are run, for the most part, by music fans looking for new music to program. Obviously, you can do the work yourself: service the stations, do the mailings, and make all the follow-up calls and e-mails. However, this is an incredibly time-consuming process. Realize that you need to call these stations *every single week*. As an artist, if you are doing this, then you will not be doing much else, like writing, playing, or practicing. That is where a professional can come in and really help you.

Paul Loggins: No promoter [equals] no radio airplay, at least at the stations that matter in the industry. Any and all airplay is great, but there are only certain stations that will help your career blossom. A radio promoter is the key ingredient in exposing your music: they are the ones with the contacts you need, and they are the ones that get you in the front door. Radio is the only way to fully expose your music to the masses. Independent artists seem to be coming out of every corner of the world these days, and with the overwhelming demand for radio airplay, independent radio promotion will get stronger every step of the way.

Karen Lee: Hire an expert. Radio folks will never take a call directly from the artist unless they already know them. Part of this is because they are already strapped for time and have a full slate of professional promotion representatives who call on them at the same time each week.

Know your audience. If you write and perform R&B, don't expect your local rock station to take a shot at playing your song. Knowing where to go with your music is a job for a pro who is in the trenches, who knows the radio stations and the target demographic of your audience. Taking blind shots at the wrong stations is like trying to win the lottery. Find a professional who works in that given arena.

Make sure to send a CD to your performing rights society prior to starting your radio campaign so you can get your royalties. Also, don't forget to sign up at SoundExchange (www.soundexchange.com) in addition to your performing rights society so the performers on the recording can get their royalties.

Bill Wence: The quality of their songs and production must meet some rigid standards in today's marketplace. I'm just amazed at how good the competition is for radio airplay. Technology has played an important role but also the songs are just getting better than ever.

What about non-performing songwriters?

Wence: The same thing applies here but you're going to need a great artist to record your material.

Advanced Articles

Loggins: It is important that non-performing songwriters work with performing artists to get their music recorded so that they are able to get some substance behind their product. Shopping around music and lyric sheets is a thing of the past.

Lee: Non-performing songwriters can—and should—seek radio play. They should try to make themselves available for radio interviews and try to work up their songs acoustically so that they can play live in that setting. They should also seek music placements in film and television to create awareness. However, to have a comprehensive career as an artist, a songwriter must perform live. There is no better representative of their music than themselves.

Lewis: If an artist is performing live or not does not really come into play with college and non-commercial radio. As long as the CD and songs are good, that is all that truly matters at that format.

Theo: I haven't dealt with any non-performing songwriters.

Do you promote solely to terrestrial broadcast radio? What about satellite radio, or Internet radio?

Wence: I work all of the above. Satellite and Internet radio are becoming more important by the day.

Lee: We promote to FM terrestrial radio, XM and Sirius satellite radio, Internet radio, cable delivered (such as Music Choice), and nationally syndicated radio programs. We also promote to music supervisors for film and television music placements.

Theo: We cover Sirius, XM, Music Choice, and dozens of Internet stations like WOXY.COM.

Lewis: We promote to all formats, as long as they report to *CMJ*. We cover college, non-commercial radio, and Web-based radio, as they all report to *CMJ*, generally. We also cover satellite and commercial specialty.

Loggins: We promote to terrestrial radio in addition to Internet, syndicated radio shows, satellite radio, and podcasts. Although terrestrial radio is where an artist will receive the maximum success, we believe that all radio airplay is good visibility.

Some non-performing songwriters produce high-quality demos and are able to get these recordings of their songs placed in TV or film. Would these songwriters get any benefit from a radio campaign? What if the song hasn't been placed?

Lee: If a non-performing songwriter has a high-profile placement of their song on television or in a popular film, it would be an excellent time to actively promote the music to radio, concurrent with the television or film's marketing campaign. This can significantly boost awareness of a song or a band. However, it is important to note that while television and independent films will potentially make use of a high-quality demo, radio stations will not. If the song has not been placed, it would be important to mix and master the demo and package it up for servicing to radio. I would also suggest that non-performing songwriters work with their publishers to try to place their songs with established artists who might potentially record and release them. This is a solid way to raise substantial royalties that can further fund their career—we had a client last year who made about $12,000 on a marginally successful radio hit that an established artist covered.

Loggins: Having a song placed in a TV show or film helps to create a story at radio. Any buzz or hype an artist can create will inevitably help during their campaign at radio. This strategy may also be effective by creating your story at radio and then shopping for a TV or film deal.

Lewis: If placed, that can help a great deal. Even if not placed, if the music is strong, we can get play. However, college/non-commercial radio is an album-based format, so you would need to have at least an EP's worth of material. A full-length is preferred, though—you cannot really work a single to this format.

Theo: I see them as totally unrelated. It may be a nice talking point to say, "Hey, this band was in this show," but overall the songs are what matter.

Wence: I don't think I'd put a demo out to radio. You certainly want to log whatever you do with ASCAP, BMI, or SESAC, but demos are to pitch to publishers and artists, not radio.

When it comes to convincing you to come on board to run a campaign, do MySpace/iTunes downloads or plays on Internet radio help in piquing your interest?

Theo: Nope. Again, for us, it's the songs that are important. Plays, downloads, views, and number of "friends" can all be easily inflated with readily available software.

Lewis: Not really. For us, it is really all about the sound of the act. If the CD is strong, we can get it played.

Loggins: It's always nice to see an artist dedicated and excited about their venture into the music industry. An artist who has taken their career seriously by networking their product with iTunes and MySpace shows us that they are ready to seriously move forward with a radio campaign.

Wence: I think they are starting to be a big part of the game, but all the traditional methods still need to be followed too.

Lee: Generally, we work with artists whose music we like and on whose career we feel we can make a positive impact. Those are our only criteria. That said, the first place that I check out a band is on MySpace. Because of its templated layout, it is simple to navigate and I can usually sample four songs and get a general vibe about the artist or band. We are always especially interested if the band is touring and proactively promoting themselves.

What do you think is the most common misconception about radio promotion?

Theo: That it isn't worthwhile. Every bit of promotion—press, radio, online, retail, etc.—helps build a foundation for the band to increase fanbase and awareness.

Lee: That music will get airplay simply by servicing it. Radio promotion requires strategy, planning, and execution.

Wence: I think some artists think that the minute you mail the music, the airplay begins. It's a really slow-moving process and takes months, not weeks.

Loggins: Too many artists believe that radio airplay generated is based on how good their music is. Unfortunately, this is far from the truth—a successful radio airplay campaign is 75% based upon the promotion and marketing behind an artist's song, not the song itself.

Any myths that need to be dispelled?

Lewis: Some of the myths about college radio are that it leads to CD sales—it doesn't, it builds fanbase—and that college kids on campus are all listening to the campus stations. Often college stations have larger community listening audiences than on-campus listeners.

Another big one is that college radio shuts down for the summer. While many stations do shut down, these tend to be the smaller stations. The larger, more community-based stations are on year-round, and these are the ones you should truly be concerned with. Often summer can be a great time to reach these programmers, because they are not as busy at that time of year. The reverse applies to the fall. Many acts want to hold their release until the fall since all the students are back, but this time of year is so busy that for a new act to try and compete at this time of year is really tough.

Loggins: That an artist must have major label distribution in order to secure radio airplay. This misconception was put to bed decades ago with the growth of independent labels, the

Advanced Articles

explosion of the Internet, and most recently with the new FCC ruling stating that the major conglomerates of radio must supply radio time to artists who are *not* signed to the major labels.

Wence: That you're going to make a lot of airplay money. Oh, that's possible, but not likely with a first release.

Theo: That just doing a radio campaign will catapult a band to success. Along with radio, many things are required to make it happen—press, online, touring, and hard work.

Contact Information

Evolution Promotion
Karen Lee, President/Founder
info@evolutionpromotion.com
(978)658-3357.
Clients: Blow Up Hollywood, AIR, The White Stripes, Porcupine Tree, Brian Eno, Moby, Craig Armstrong, Jane Siberry, and William Orbit

Planetary Group
Adam Lewis, co-owner
580 Harrison Avenue, 4th Floor
Boston, MA 02118
(617)275-7665
www.planetarygroup.com.
Clients: The Decemberists; Bloc Party; Peter, Bjorn & John; Apples In Stereo; Kings of Leon; The Lemonheads; and Great Northeast Productions

Loggins Promotion/Backstage Entertainment
Paul Loggins, CEO/founder
(888)325-2901
www.logginspromotion.com
www.backstageentertainment.net
Clients: Queen, Mariah Carey, Boyz II Men, Gwen Stefani, Dave Matthews, and Kenny Loggins

Pirate!
Steve Theo, co-founder with Douglas Blake
(617)354-5200
steve@piratepirate.com
http://piratepirate.com

Bill Wence Promotions
Bill Wence
billwencepro@earthlink.net
www.billwencepromotions.com
Clients: Collin Raye, Jerry Jeff Walker, Blackhawk, Randy Travis, James Talley, Paul Stookey, Mary Gauthier, Red Meat, Mare Winningham, Ruthie and the Wranglers, Tom T. Hall, The Outlaws, Bobby Bare, The Amazing Rhythm Aces, and Orleans.

Advanced Articles

Steve Forbert

Go for Word on the Street and the Big Break

by Robin Renée

Steve Forbert's latest CD, *Strange Names & New Sensations* (429 Records), is a solid mix of new songs that balance on love, maturity, humor, and politics. The smooth folk rock arrangements and raspy-melodic vocals for which the veteran songwriter has long been known are present, and some tracks—"Middle Age," "The Baghdad Dream," and "Strange Names (North Jersey's Got 'em)"—are already familiar to those who attend his frequent live shows. Also familiar is the song that ends the CD, "Romeo's Tune," an updated version of the Forbert's 1979 hit from the album *Jackrabbit Slim*.

Born and raised in Meridian, Mississippi, Forbert performed in his home state before moving on to the clubs and cafes of New York City at age 21. His debut, *Alive on Arrival*, with its well-known song "Goin' Down to Laurel," hit the airwaves in 1978. In the mid-1980's Forbert moved to Nashville to connect with its emerging singer/songwriter scene. Though the Nashville sound shifted away from that rootsy direction, Forbert and his family remained, happy to stay in a city still full of music and convenient for travel to and from performances. He has released consistently acclaimed albums ever since.

In October 2006, Forbert was inducted into the Mississippi Musicians Hall of Fame. In 2007, the original versions of "Romeo's Tune" and "Goin' Down to Laurel" were licensed for use in *Margot at the Wedding*, a movie starring Nicole Kidman and Jack Black. For Forbert, the help of early fame, diligent touring, current CD sales, and occasional song licensing pay off with a rewarding career.

How did "Romeo's Tune" and "Goin' Down to Laurel" come to be used in the *Margot at the Wedding* soundtrack?

Those things seem to be just luck. As I understand it, the director liked the songs in college. But now he's all grown up and directing movies with Nicole Kidman. I guess he said, "One day I'm going to use a Steve Forbert song or two in one of my movies," and he meant it. So that was that. I think most of those things happen because people really like Elton John's "Tiny Dancer" or Alice Cooper's "Eighteen" or whatever, so they use it.

Do you own the publishing and the masters for those songs?

Well, Brad Hunt is my manager. He had to facilitate between the owner of the master tapes— a guy named Nat Weiss—and there are a few different publishers involved, just through

---

Performing songwriter and freelance writer **ROBIN RENÉE** has contributed to *Curve, Elmore Magazine, WeirdoMusic.com*, and many other publications. Her CDs include *In Progress, All Six Senses*, and the latest, *Live Devotion*. Visit www.robinrenee.com and www.myspace.com/robinrenee.

Advanced Articles

different things that have happened over the years. So Brad had to sort of get all of these people on the same page.

Have you ever re-recorded a song to avoid the master recording issue?

No, no, because that's just too tall of an order. You could do some tricks, but to me, it would just be an exercise in futility. You probably have a 20% chance of fooling anybody, you know. The one remake I've heard that really will fool you was ? and the Mysterians' "96 Tears." They remade it about ten years ago.

Do you think that those interested in licensing really only want the original? How did you come to remake "Romeo's Tune" for the new CD?

Yeah, that's where your magic is, on the thing that's a hit. The new "Romeo's Tune" is a key lower. It's a slower tempo. We didn't make any attempt to re-create the original. Tim Coats, my co-producer, and I made the recording because the record company said, "We want to re-establish you and there are a lot of people out there that, let's face it, they only know 'Romeo's Tune.' " If we had a new version of it, it could be a good calling card. At first I thought it was crazy, but then I said, if it turns out good they might be right. And now I just think it turned out to be a good way to end the album because the mood of it is good.

Is 429 Records a true indie label, or does it have major distribution?

They are distributed through Warner Bros., and EMI in England.

What do you think will be the role of major labels going into the future of music? Some people say they still provide a level of publicity that you can't get in any other way. Do you think that's still true?

Yeah, I think it is. Madonna could have a big tour and a big career on her own with her people and her organization, but that wouldn't be why people would pay attention. It'd be because she became a megastar with Sire Records in the early '80s. I know about break-throughs on YouTube and all, and I think you can do a lot with touring and you can develop a following, but after that to reach the ordinary person, I think you're going to need the help of a record company. There are also large management companies that just control the whole picture for a certain artist. They handle the recordings, publicity, the merchandise sales, and they might own the publishing, so they would develop the artist and own a major piece of the action. That wouldn't be a record company per se, but would be involved in everything— T-shirts, you name it. Actually, that's not a lot different from the situation The Rolling Stones had in the beginning with Andrew Loog Oldham and Eric Easton!

Do you think that's too all-encompassing?

You know, if someone's thinks they're getting a chance to break through, they'll probably be interested. You can make a really good record on your own, possibly in your house these days, but it takes some really deep pockets to let the general public know about it. So yeah, I think there'll be a future for that.

So would you say that initial blast of publicity is the lasting benefit of your early label deals?

Absolutely. There's a lot of people having their own label now and doing pretty well, but aside from Ani DiFranco, they all got a start with a major label. And then through the decades, they could work from that initial exposure that they could never have achieved on their own.

You seem to really love what you do. I've met other artists who feel bitter about having an early big hit and not a lot of chart action after that. Do you have a philosophy or a way of seeing your career that keeps you connected to what you're doing now?

I've been doing it since I was 10, so I like it. The odds become smaller all the time with record stores closing and a lot of music magazines struggling, but I always like to think that there might be a record I could do that would somehow, through some energy of its own, strike a chord and reach a lot of people. I find feeling that way certainly doesn't hurt, and it helps me to keep trying to make the best—what I think are competitive—recordings of these songs that I can make. So I think I'm still in the game. It doesn't hurt if I'm right or wrong.

How do you feel about really sticking to your guns artistically, with well-made recordings in the folk rock genre? Other artists try to alter their productions or change with the times.

I really don't have time to make up different guises and concepts, you know? With the traveling that I do and trying to play these shows that I do, I don't have extra time to say I'd like to be Buster Poindexter. What I do, I don't have to get rid of it every now and then. It's a durable thing. People come along, and they still come along. It's not at the top of the charts, but it's still a workable thing. It's about the songs—it's folk rock or Americana, or whatever people call it.

What are your words of wisdom to singer/songwriters starting out today?

The main thing to me is always the playing. I played everywhere I could in Mississippi, and when the time came I went to New York because I wanted to play. If I had to I'd sing in the streets, and I did have to. There were all the folk clubs and the CBGB's, and different things that you could get to on the subway. If you're good you'll develop a following and the rest will take care of itself. Then people will come to you because something's going on and they'll want to find out what it is.

So getting the buzz on the street is the way to go.

Yes, and besides, you'll be improving what you do, because you'll be a person who can really sing, really show up on time, and do a show that people will want to talk about. To me, that's the way it's done.

Advanced Articles

ADVANCED ARTICLES

Ralph Murphy

Making History in Nashville

by Jim Melko

Whenever an aspiring songwriter first visits Nashville, the name "Ralph Murphy" soon pops up. As ASCAP Vice President International & Domestic Membership Group, Murphy is regularly involved in the ASCAP seminars, is the continuing author of an often-cited ASCAP column called "Murphy's Law," is an active campaigner for songwriter rights in legislative issues, and is a frequent instructor for the Nashville Songwriters Association International (NSAI) Song Camps. He is known among songwriters for offering some of the toughest song critiques in the industry, and he insists that if songwriters want to have partnerships with publishers and the industry, they must move to Nashville.

Naturally, aspiring songwriters often ask where he gets his authority and expertise. The answer is simple: he shaped his career by going where the action was, developing great songwriters, and writing, picking and promoting great songs—even when the market was at its weakest. Murphy knows exactly what he is talking about.

THE YOUNG FOLKY

Ralph Murphy was born in Saffron, Walden, southeast of London, England, in 1944. In 1950, he moved with his mother to Salt Spring Island on the west coast of Canada; they then worked back across the prairies to Ontario.

Murphy formed his first band at 11 and by age 14, he was performing songs from the radio— Everly Brothers, Marty Robbins, Ray Price, Eddie Arnold, Little Jimmie Dickens, etc. He played whatever was easiest to play, forming an early appreciation for songs with simple progressions. In the early '60s, Murphy went to L.A.'s Manhattan Beach, playing the coffeehouses in Hermosa Beach by the lighthouse. "It was folky. You played 'Puff the Magic Dragon' and 'Michael, Row Your Boat' and all that stuff. The old songs had big stories but were simple to play. I could add some of my own songs and they fared pretty well against the others. People would ask, 'Oh, who wrote that one?' 'Well, I did!' 'Oh, man, that's so cool!' "

He first heard the Beatles while working as a ship's night cook on an ocean-going dredge working the St. Lawrence Seaway. "The Beatles stuff was like two and a half, three minutes max, and it jumped out of the speakers at you! The harmonies were cool because they didn't fill in the blanks on the upper harmony, which invited you in. They did the under-harmony, left open the top harmony, and yahoo, I knew my part! It was so alive! I just had to go to Liverpool."

JIM MELKO was a staff writer for Chris Keaton Productions in Nashville and was a co-coordinator from 1993-2006 for the Songwriter's Workshop at Southbrook, the Dayton/Cincinnati chapter of NSAI (Nashville Songwriters Association International), and still teaches there. See the NSAI listing in the Organizations section of this book.

ACROSS THE POND

Murphy and Jack Klaeysen, his musical partner, bought one-way tickets from New York to Liverpool on February 14, 1965. While on ship, they played in steerage. Word spread, and they were invited to first class. An agent on board gave them a referral to Joe Collins—father and early manager of Joan Collins—with a big agency in London. "I said, 'Yeah, sure, pal,' stuck the card in my sock and kept playing for free drinks and carrying on with the actresses," Murphy recalls.

In Liverpool, they performed at the Birdcage, but the scene was "pretty bleak." By that time, Liverpool was nearly tapped out for musical talent. One night, Gerry and the Pacemakers came and heard them. "They said, 'Hey, man, you guys are really good! What are you doing in Liverpool?' We said, 'Hey, this is where it's at!' 'No, it's not! You need to go to London!' "

The equipment van was leaving for London at 4 a.m. and they were offered a ride. "We all loaded into this old van with no heater and headed out in a snowstorm. About 10 miles out of Liverpool, the windshield shattered into a million pieces. We kept on, stopping every 10 minutes for hot cups of tea. They dropped us off in Trafalgar Square in the middle of a white-out. I remember shouting over the howling wind, 'Jack, we made it!' He yelled back, 'Ralph! You're an asshole!' "

As Canadians coming to England while British acts were "invading" the U.S., Murphy and Klaeysen were a novelty in London. They played at the New Theatre Oxford, opening for the Ivy League, the Bachelors, the Pretty Things, the Byrds, and Martha and the Vandellas.

Within four months, Joe Collins brokered a record deal for them with Tony Hatch, the already legendary producer and writer for Petula Clark, under his label Pye Records. While auditioning for a publishing deal with Tony Hiller of Mills Music (later Belwin Mills Publishing), "Roger Cook stumbled in, heard us playing and told Tony, 'You're gonna sign them, right?' " That encounter began a long and productive relationship between Murphy and Cook.

Jack and Ralph's first album, a folk effort, was as the Guardsmen. They went pop as the Slade Brothers for their second album, cutting two originals and a Roger Greenway/Roger Cook song called "What a Crazy Life" that became a radio hit in early 1966.

A year earlier in the fall of 1965, a song by Murphy and Klaeysen with Mills Music—"Call My Name"—became a hit for James Royal. "It was earth-shaking, everything I wanted it to be. I was addicted," recalls Murphy. "All I ever wanted was to have everyone record my songs and play them on the radio. I was ready—bring it on!"

RECORD PRODUCTION

That recording also introduced Murphy to record production. Although Tony Hatch never directly mentored him, "you watch, and you learn," Murphy noted. "When they were recording 'Call My Name,' I got called in. The producer was fumbling and said, 'If you help me, I'll put you in on everything.' I saw they had Roger Coulam from the demo playing the Hammond B3. I walked over and said, 'Hey, Roger . . . remember that sound you got on the demo?' 'Oh, yeah,' he said, and began jamming things in and kicking things over. He began playing and everyone said, 'Oh man, Ralph, you're a genius!' "

Murphy began working as a producer throughout town, including CBS, Decca, and Phillips. He cut lots of records but made little money. "We didn't need much. I played lots of gigs, including some for the mob—the Kray twins—and they took care of us musicians."

Murphy also encountered the British tax system that plagued other British rockers: "the more you made, the more you got screwed," he recalls. He received several offers to produce acts in New York, so he moved in the spring of 1969. As a producer, he soon earned the reputation of "getting stuff done—on budget, on time, even if I had to lock the doors—whatever it took."

Advanced Articles

That fall, Brian Chater in Toronto called him. "Ralph, I need a favor. I've got this band April Wine and this song I want them to cut, and I need it done." "You Could Have Been a Lady" had been a hit earlier for Hot Chocolate in England. "I dressed it up, changed the tempo, put more 'na-na's' in the middle, and suddenly it was on Big Tree Records. The song and the album [*On Record*] were huge, and so was the next [*Electric Jewels*]." The song hit #1 on Canadian stations and stayed in the U.S. Billboard Top 30 for 11 weeks [http://www.aprilwine.ca/history.html].

NASHVILLE CALLING

In 1972, Murphy wrote "Good Enough to Be Your Wife" and played it for his girlfriend in his New York office. A producer heard it and cut it with Janet Lawson, a jazz singer. It was released as a single, but wasn't a hit. Then, a few months later, Shelby Singleton called: "Hey, man, I just cut your song, it's gonna be a smash!" Murphy was stunned when Jeanie C. Riley's recording became his first country hit.

Murphy made his first visit to Nashville to accept his award. "There is a funny picture of me at the ASCAP Awards with hair down to my ass with all these conservative-looking people around me." Murphy became convinced that Nashville was the place to be, but he still had obligations in New York with Double M Records (with London Records) and GRT.

By 1976, however, Murphy wanted out of New York because of his kids, and Roger Cook wanted out of England. Together they moved to Nashville, opening a publishing company called Pic-a-Lic Music. With some experience as publisher, pitcher, and plugger for Bellwin Mills, Murphy now moved into full-time publishing. "I had done production, the label thing, and I have a low threshold of boredom. Once I've done something successfully, I'm not into repeating it."

Murphy and Cook began with songwriters Bobby Wood, Charles Cochran, and themselves. Pic-a-Lic's first big hit was Wood and Cook's "Talking in Your Sleep," 1977's Song of the Year. Murphy co-wrote "Half the Way" and "He Got You" with Wood. He remembers fondly hearing and pitching the song "I Believe in You" to Garth Fundis, who immediately cut it with Don Williams. Other songs took much longer—"Eighteen Wheels and a Dozen Roses" took four years from inception to hit. Over the years, every writer but one had at least one #1 hit through Pic-a-Lic, totaling more than twenty.

THE *URBAN COWBOY* ERA

Pic-a-Lic emerged during the *Urban Cowboy* period, when country moved into mainstream pop. "It was great because pop writers were valid and valued. We dealt with loss and romance and such, but we didn't deal in honky-tonks and trucks. 'Half the Way' and 'Talking in Your Sleep' were pop songs." Murphy notes, "The deregulation of radio allowed big companies to use their own jingles, produced in Chicago, New York or L.A. and sounding like Bon Jovi or Mötley Crüe. When a Don Williams record went into 'Mötley Crüe', it sounded weird. Jingles are what's important to radio, so they looked for records that sounded like the jingles. It wasn't the demographics or market, it was the radio sound. Rock producers came in from L.A. and New York making country records that sounded like the jingles while young producers from the South, raised on rock, had a field day."

The *Urban Cowboy* period attracted producers and record companies from New York and L.A., but traditional country listeners were alienated. The new "light" country didn't play well in traditional country culture. "What we did didn't have a lot of depth. It worked great for radio, but at 10 o'clock at night when you needed a drinking song, you went to George Jones. You didn't go to the 'lighter side.' Also, Mothers Against Drunk Drivers (MADD) convinced people to stay home rather than go drinking in the honky tonks, so listeners were tuning in more at 7 a.m. than 10 p.m."

The *Urban Cowboy* momentum turned into a bust, the New York and L.A. opportunists retreated, and country music floundered until Randy Travis tied the traditional and the new together again in the late '80s. When Soundscan changed the radio charting landscape in 1991, Garth Brooks led a revolution. "Suddenly country markets jumped from 30,000 to 2 million with 18 records on the pop charts. L.A. and New York said, 'Oh, there *is* money there!' They came slamming back! It was a new era."

Pic-a-Lic survived the lean years and rode into the new market, but renegotiations with the writers hurt them. "We'd have success, but when the writers came in to regenotiate, we hadn't yet recouped what we'd spent, which came out of our pockets. They'd say, 'OK, I want co-publishing, etc.,' and we'd say, 'Well, we haven't recovered our original investment yet. Can you hold on till we at least get even?' They'd say, 'Well, Warner Brothers offered me this, and I can go with them and still get all my money from you.' We understood that completely, but then we'd have to start new writers from scratch and get them on the charts. We'd meet every day to get them grounded in the craft and find co-writers to complement what they did. That cost money!"

This was when Murphy really began to analyze the elements of the craft. "That focused me. It's called survival. When your butt is on the line, when you could lose your house, when every penny comes out of your pocket and you have to move that writer from ground zero to the charts quickly, you do whatever it takes."

SUPPORTING THE SONGWRITER

Meanwhile, Murphy and Cook had been supporting Nashville Songwriters Association International (NSAI) fundraisers. Murphy began serving on the board and became more involved in leadership. He helped organize seminars and other events, and in 1987 he was elected President of NSAI, a year after serving as President of the National Academy of Recording Arts and Sciences. In these roles he first learned "the value of songwriters speaking with one voice." Murphy recalls, "The business community suddenly recognized that we were eminently qualified to raise money, go to Washington, be vocal and have a coherent message. Now they rely on us—'What is NSAI's position on this issue?' It's great!"

Selling Pic-a-Lic to EMI in the early '90s was heartbreaking for Murphy, but financially Murphy and Cook had no other options. "It felt like selling one of my children and was one of the nightmares of my life." Murphy started another publishing company, Kersha Music, with scattered success—"Crime of the Century" with Shania Twain in the movie *Red Rock West*, "Seeds" with Kathy Mattea, "I'm Still Here, You're Still Gone" with Randy Travis, and the title song of the movie *The Thing Called Love*—but in the Murphy tradition, publishing was something he'd already done successfully. It was time for the next big thing.

In 1994, Murphy was offered the position of Vice President with ASCAP by Connie Bradley—and turned it down. Pat Alger, Henry Gross, Richard Leigh and others kept after him to reconsider. He talked to them over some beers and by the second beer had second thoughts. He explains, "I just follow my heart. One of the terms ASCAP gave me was to be vocal. If I didn't understand something, or if something didn't work the way I thought it should, I could question it. When they explained it to me, if it still didn't make sense, then I could still challenge it. So I took the position."

Today Murphy is a featured speaker or guest at most Music Row events, including the annual NSAI symposium. New writers visiting Nashville may find themselves meeting directly with him or with one of his staff. He is often involved in ASCAP seminars and other educational programs, and leads legislative efforts by the music industry to protect songwriter income and copyrights.

Murphy used to worry that his voice could be compromised because songwriters might perceive him as just a paid employee of ASCAP. But Murphy's voice always conveys authentic and sincere passion. "ASCAP allows me to go out and meet with songwriter groups and be involved in the educational programs here. My boredom threshold is minimized now because my duties are divided between international and domestic. Because of the number of years I've been doing this, I think I still have a valid message." No words could be truer than those.

Advanced Articles

Starting Your Own Publishing Company

by Randy Poe

Music publishing is a *business*. If you have a relatively good head for business—or even a marginally good head for business—you will want to seriously consider having your own publishing company at some point in your songwriting career (preferably sooner rather than later). It's hard for me to understand why a songwriter would want to give 100 percent of the publisher's share of his song to an outside publisher when some, most, or even all of the publisher's share could belong to the songwriter's own publishing company.

However, I've almost always been on the business end of the music business, so I can't claim to know what it's like to actually be a professional songwriter and have a songwriter's point of view of music publishing. But I have known an awful lot of songwriters over the years—almost all of whom ended up forming their own publishing companies—and I can safely say that I've yet to find a single songwriter who regretted the decision to step into the business world.

Since you are reading this article, it's apparent that you are interested enough in publishing that you will probably want to have your own publishing company some day—if not at the beginning of your career, then as soon as possible after the hits start coming.

The bottom line is this: If you write a song and allow me to be your sole publisher, I will get half of all the royalties your song earns. If you allow me to co-publish a song with your publishing company, and the publisher's share is split fifty-fifty between our companies, then I will get 25 percent of all the income your song makes. If you want me to administer your publishing company at a rate of 15 percent of the gross income, then I will get 15 percent of all of the royalties for the duration of the administration agreement.

If you have your own publishing company and you administer that company yourself, then I will get nothing and you will get 100 percent of the publisher's share and 100 percent of the songwriter's share (assuming, of course, that you wrote the song by yourself). However, there is a lot of work involved in administering a publishing company, and enough expenses involved that you may be better off allowing someone else to administer your company for you.

Unless your attitude is that you just don't want to be bothered with business details at all, the time will come when you should form your own publishing company, even if you

Excerpted from *The New Songwriter's Guide to Music Publishing, 3rd Edition* © 2006 by **RANDY POE**. Used with permission of Writer's Digest Books, an imprint of F + W Publications, Inc. Visit your local bookseller or call (800) 754-2912 to obtain your copy.

still split your songs with another publisher or rely on outside administration. After all, a professional administrator or an administering co-publisher will take care of most of the important publishing business for you, leaving you more time to write songs. And whatever the administrator's fee or co-publisher's percentage may be, you won't have as much money coming out of your pocket as you would if you signed all of the publishing away to an outside company.

As I said earlier, I have known a lot of songwriters and have met very few successful ones who didn't have a publishing company of their own. Granted, many of these songwriters' biggest hits were signed away to outside publishers early in their careers. It was usually this "live and learn" aspect of their lives that caused them eventually to start their own companies in the first place.

Jerry Leiber and Mike Stoller—inductees into both the Rock and Roll Hall of Fame and the Songwriters Hall of Fame—are among the most successful songwriting teams of all time. They learned early on the importance of owning their own publishing company. One of Leiber and Stoller's first hits was the original recording of "Hound Dog" by Big Mama Thornton. (Her version predated Elvis's by three years.) Mike Stoller recalls, "We had this number-one hit by Big Mama Thornton on Peacock Records, but after resolving some problems in getting songwriter royalties from Don Robey—who owned the record label and the publishing rights to 'Hound Dog'—he left town and stopped payment on the check. Not getting paid on a million-selling record sparked the idea that we could have our own publishing company. Simply, the idea was that Jerry and I shouldn't end up being screwed out of our royalties again."

Rupert Holmes is one successful writer who determined that self-publishing was right for him. "I had a record deal and I was producing my own albums," he says. "I didn't know anyone who was going to do anything great for my songs that I couldn't do myself. It made more sense for me to keep the publishing until someone could show me that it made more sense for *them* to acquire the publishing. And the only time it made more sense was when a publisher offered to give me a great deal of money and split the publishing so that I got to keep half of it. For half of the publishing, they would also do the administration, which was a lot of paperwork I didn't want to do myself."

Songwriter and record producer Kevin Bowe shares the opinion that writers should publish their own songs:

> There are many legitimate business reasons for starting your own publishing company, but I believe that *emotionally* it is a good thing to do as well. The more you can put yourself in the position of being responsible for your own career, the better off you'll be. Almost every writer I've ever met has been frustrated by their publisher promising to do things that didn't get done. After all, if you look realistically at any publishing deal, the bottom line is this: If the songs don't get cut because the writer does a bad job—the writer gets dropped. If the songs don't get cut because the publisher does a bad job—the writer gets dropped! Although it's a little more work, I think most writers are better off—if they can make it without the advance—to take care of their own publishing.
>
> In my case, after three publishing deals in which I was responsible for generating much more money than any of my publishers were, I started running all my new songs solely through my own publishing company. I hired an administrator and several song pluggers, and the company is now generating serious revenue.

If you are still doubtful about the importance of having your own company, find a successful songwriter who doesn't own or co-own the publishing on her biggest hit and ask her if she wishes she had the publishing on that song, or if she's happy about having it published by an outside company—particularly if that outside company now owns hundreds of thousands of other copyrights.

THE BIG CATCH-22

If you've never had a song recorded, it may seem there is a major catch-22 involved in forming your own publishing company. Almost all of us who applied for our very first job sat across the desk from a prospective employer who told us, "You can't get a job without some experience," to which we replied, "But how can I have had any experience if I haven't had a job before?" Right now you might be thinking, *How can I have a publishing company if I don't have a song recorded? And if I'm going to have a song recorded, how is that possible without going to an outside publisher?*

As I said before, you, as a songwriter, always have options. A couple of those major options are co-publishing your song with an established publisher or allowing an outside publisher or independent administrator to administer your publishing company for you.

I'll be the first to admit that, at the beginning of your songwriting career, it might be very difficult to get your first song cut by a major artist on a major label and still walk away with 100 percent of the publishing. However, it's not impossible. If your song is good enough, and an artist wants to record it badly enough, you're in a powerful position.

Should you by some stroke of luck reach that position, you might be tempted with a single-song agreement offering a massive advance against future royalties; a staff writer deal; a co-publishing agreement; or a host of other wonderful things that might seem impossible to pass up. But that big advance might turn out to be no more than a loan of a sum of money that you would be entitled to anyway should your song become a hit; you might not want to be tied down to a staff writer deal; and a co-publishing agreement will still usually take away more than an administrator's fee would.

"But wait," you say. "How will my song get into the hands of that major artist without a publisher?" The answer is: *You* will be the publisher. Acting as your own music publisher cuts out the middleman that many songwriters wrongly believe is an absolute requisite to becoming a successful songwriter. Of course, I don't want to imply that going out and getting your own songs recorded by superstars (or anyone else) is a simple task. In fact, one of the main advantages of being signed to an established publishing company is having access to the creative department's contacts in the recording and film industries. I'm only trying to point out that, should you begin to develop contacts in those industries, you might find yourself in a position to plug your songs and not have to sign away part or all of the publishing.

THE SONGWRITER/PERFORMER

If you sign a recording contract (or your band does), it is almost essential that you have your own publishing company. Why sign a publishing agreement if you are the one responsible for getting your songs recorded in the first place?

One of the main functions of a publisher is to exploit your songs. If you are a recording artist, you are exploiting your own songs when you record them yourself. If your songs are signed to an outside publisher, you don't really want her to be trying to get your songs cut by other acts right away. If she does, you may find yourself competing against another act who's trying to get a hit with the song you wish to take up the charts yourself. So, in this case, what's the point of having an outside publisher? Do you really need her to collect your money and keep part of it, when you've done all the legwork necessary to get the songs cut?

Even worse is the idea of signing a publishing agreement with a publishing company affiliated with the record company. The main function of a record company is to make and sell records. In many cases, their publishing company is merely collecting money from the record company across town, or across the hall (or across the room).

THE *CONTROLLED COMPOSITION* CLAUSE

Songwriter/performers who control the publishing to their owns songs avoid losing the publisher's share of royalties from those songs, but they must watch out for another potential drain on royalties: the *controlled composition* clause. Controlled compositions are songs owned and controlled by the songwriter/performer. Generally this means songs written by the songwriter/performer and not signed to an outside publisher. A controlled composition clause in the recording contract of a songwriter/performer states that the record company will pay a reduced rate on the titles controlled by the artist.

This means that if a song on the album is written by an outside party, that song will earn more for the outside party than a song written by the recording artist will earn the artist as a songwriter. The only exception to this rule is when the publisher of an outside song—usually in an effort to curry favor with the record label—agrees to go along with the terms of the controlled composition clause. (Of course, this isn't particularly helpful to the outside songwriter, since his or her royalties will be diminished as well.) Although the songwriter/performer may find it difficult (or near impossible) to achieve, it is in her best interest to have any controlled composition clause removed from her contract before signing with a record company.

Some controlled composition clauses allow the record company to pay a reduced mechanical rate on a maximum number of songs in an album. (In music business parlance, this maximum number of songs is known as the *cap.*) In other words, if the clause says that the record company will pay 75 percent of the statutory rate on a cap of twelve songs, the artist may have to take a serious cut in songwriter pay if any outside (noncontrolled) songs are included on the CD.

Here's how it would work: Joe is a singer/songwriter who has a controlled composition clause in his contract that says the record company will pay 75 percent of stat (the statutory rate) with the cap at twelve songs. Joe records six songs he wrote himself and six songs written by other songwriters. Unfortunately for Joe, the publishers of the six outside songs refuse to grant a reduced rate for the use of their songs.

The statutory rate is 8.5 cents, but the maximum amount the record company will agree to pay for each of the songs on the album is 6.375 cents (a total of 76.5 cents for the twelve songs). Meanwhile, the outside publishers are demanding 8.5 cents for each of their songs, for a total of 51 cents for their six songs. This means Joe is only going to receive 25.5 cents for his own six songs (76.5 cents minus 51 cents)—the equivalent of only 4.25 cents per song.

To carry this concept another step, imagine an album of twelve songs filled with samples. On top of the controlled composition that allows the artist to receive only 75 percent of the statutory rate on twelve songs, there are all the outside songs to be considered which were sampled in the first place. It is entirely conceivable that the sampled songs could not only use up the entire allowance for mechanical royalties that the record company has granted to the artist, but also cut into the performer's artist royalties.

For example, let's say that an artist writes and records twelve new songs, but samples twenty-four other songs over the course of those twelve. (To keep this simple, we'll say that each of the artist's new songs includes two samples of outside songs.) Then let's say that all of the publishers of those twenty-four outside songs demand that their share of the new songs the artist created be 50 percent of the mechanical royalties. At this point, assuming the outside publishers agree to be bound by the artist's controlled composition clause, each of the artist's new songs now has an effective mechanical royalty of zero (each song contains two samples, and each sample earns its publisher 50 percent of the mechanical royalties, for a total of 100 percent).

But what happens if all twenty-four publishers want to charge the statutory rate for their 50 percent? Each outside publisher will get 4.25 cents per album, and their total mechanical royalties for the album will be $1.02 (4.25 cents times twenty-four). Since the record company will only pay a total of 76.5 cents in mechanical royalties for the album, the artist is suddenly in the hole for 25.5 cents ($1.02 minus 76.5 cents). Let's hope he's getting a good royalty as an artist, or this album is going to cost him money every time he sells a copy!

This scenario might be an exaggeration, but only a slight one. Imagine if the artist had a controlled composition clause with a cap of twelve songs, but decided to record sixteen songs, with each track containing a couple of samples. Hopefully, for the sake of the artist, the outside publishers won't ask for such high percentages. Otherwise, that artist will need to sell a lot of concert tickets and T-shirts just to make ends meet.

WHEN SHOULD YOU YIELD TO TEMPTATION?

By now I may have convinced you that you should strongly consider self-publishing. But, in the music business, there are very few absolutes. If self-publishing seems such an obvious route to take, why doesn't everyone start her own publishing company and publish 100 percent of everything she writes?

Some songwriters sign with music publishing companies because they prefer not to deal with the business aspect of music publishing. This reason isn't good enough by itself, however, because the business aspect of songwriting is impossible to avoid entirely. Successful songwriting generates a great deal of business-related activities—unless you write for the sheer pleasure of writing, with no intention of having your songs recorded. For instance, you will need to learn how to read royalty statements. You will have to hire an accountant and a lawyer. The accountant will require you to keep track of your expenses and receipts, while your lawyer will take up your time (while you pay for hers) advising you about contracts and other legal details of the songwriting life. There is always much paperwork to do and much time to be consumed by things that aren't nearly as creative or enjoyable as songwriting itself. You can't avoid business-related activities entirely by signing with a music publisher.

But there are other strong reasons for going with an outside publisher. If a publisher hears your song and offers you a large advance, she is offering you something your own publishing company can't. The advance is why many songwriters decide to throw the concept of self-publishing out the window.

If a publisher tells you that Britney Superseller is her best friend and that Ms. Superseller is in the studio right now but will only record your song if the publisher delivers it to her by hand (and, by the way, here's a $50,000 advance), and you've never had a song recorded by anybody before—you may find your hand has separated itself from the rest of your body and has signed on the dotted line without your being able to stop it.

Then there is the matter of the record deal. If you are a songwriter/performer and you have been turned down by several record companies, you might be offered a recording contract by a label if—and only if—you agree to sign a publishing or co-publishing deal with the record label's sister publishing company.

It's not always easy (and sometimes it might not even be wise) to insist on controlling 100 percent of the publishing on every song you write. Every case is different, and your decision should depend on the situation and circumstances. One thing is certain, though: You don't want to give away the publishing if you don't have to. So, it's best to be ready for the moment when luck is on your side—when a record producer you know is in the studio and desperate for one more song, or when it turns out that the drunk guy you drove home

Advanced Articles

from a bar last night is actually a major recording artist who now owes you his life and is looking for new songs for his next album.

Whatever the scenario, if you can keep some or all of the publishing in a particular situation, you should be prepared to do so—if not by already having your own company, then at least by having the knowledge necessary to set up a publishing company.

You may wonder why, if I'm so gung ho about self-publishing, I have written the first chapters of this book. One reason is fairly obvious: You, like most songwriters (especially the nonperforming type), are probably going to find yourself dealing with outside publishers for some time as a necessary means of achieving success. A staff writer earning a thousand dollars or more a week as an advance against future royalties can live comfortably, with a feeling of security. Also, if you find yourself facing an offer too good to refuse, you should know from what you've learned in this book what some of your options are. Another reason I've written so much about working with music publishers is to give you the kind of knowledge that I hope will be of help to you if you set up your own company.

The information that follows should provide a starting point for learning how to form and run your own company. I have even tried to give you pointers on some of the aspects of handling your own administration, if you should be so inclined.

SETTING UP SHOP

Becoming a music publisher doesn't have to be terribly difficult or expensive. Unlike businesses that require the actual manufacturing of a product, music publishing is largely a business of intangibles. But, like all businesses, your publishing company has to exist somewhere. I would recommend that you begin with that basic tool of most small businesses— the kitchen table. If you're lucky enough to have a spare room in your house or apartment, that's a fine workstation too.

There are generally three business structures in this country: the sole proprietorship, the partnership, and the corporation. Once you have made the decision to form your own publishing company, you should speak with a lawyer and/or an accountant about which of these three types of business arrangements makes the most sense for you from a legal and financial standpoint.

The most common form of small business is the sole proprietorship. If you want to start your company on a small scale, the sole proprietorship is usually the best avenue to take— at least at the beginning. However, everyone's financial circumstances are different, so you really should speak to an attorney or an accountant you trust so that she can let you know if your particular financial status would make forming a partnership or corporation more appropriate for you.

To set up a sole proprietorship in most parts of the country, you must file a DBA form at your city hall or county clerk's office (DBA stands for "doing business as"). You can find standard DBA forms at almost any stationery store or on the Internet. One of the purposes of filing a DBA form is to officially inform your local government of the name of your business venture. Coming up with a name for your publishing company is an important step in becoming a publisher. Before you can choose a name, you will have to decide which performing rights society your company is going to be affiliated with. If you are already affiliated with a society as a songwriter, your publishing company must be affiliated with the same society.

Assuming you are not already affiliated with a performing rights society as a songwriter, the decision of which society you affiliate with as a writer and self-publisher should not be made lightly. You've read about all three organizations (ASCAP, BMI, and SESAC) in chapter four of this book. If you haven't already made contact with any of the societies at this point in your career, now is the time. Write, e-mail, or call all three societies and ask them to send you information about their organizations, as well as applications for writer and publisher membership. Read the literature, then talk to other affiliated songwriters or publishers you know and get their opinions on the societies they belong to. All three societies have informative Web sites that provide a wealth of information about how they operate.

I would also strongly urge you to talk to representatives of each society on the phone. Are they friendly? Are they helpful? Do they sound like they're interested in having you affiliated with them? Once you've done your preliminary research, call them all back again. Can you get them on the phone right away? If not, do they return your calls promptly? The reason I'm putting an emphasis on this aspect of your business is that your performance royalty income is extremely important. If you have questions about whether you are being paid properly by your performing rights society, you don't want to have to wait days, weeks, or months for an answer.

Having run several publishing companies, I have dealt with both BMI and ASCAP frequently. Some of the companies I have run have had several hundred songwriters signed to them. On more than one occasion, I've discovered that an outside songwriter with the same name as one of my writers was getting money that was supposed to be going to my writer. I've also had cases in which the songwriters' percentages (for songs with two or more writers) were being split improperly. On the publishing end, I've dealt with situations in which royalties due for a song transferred to one of my publishing companies were still being paid to the previous publisher. The number of things that can go wrong in the publishing business is almost unbelievable.

I discovered a long time ago that the only way to get these problems corrected is to make contacts at the societies and hound them until things get fixed. Since you will be starting from scratch and operating on a small level at the beginning, you're not as likely to encounter the same kinds of problems as would a publisher with thousands of copyrights. However, it's good to make those initial contacts and find out who you will be best able to work with before you lock yourself in to a society for an extended period of time.

Once you have decided which society is good enough (and fortunate enough) to be the performing rights society for you and your publishing company, you will have to fill out the songwriter and publisher affiliation applications. It is at this point that you will have to pick a name for your company (plus a few options, in case the name you've chosen is already in use or is too similar to another publishing company's name). There are thousands of music publishing companies in the world. The name of yours has to be completely unique, so don't be surprised if it takes a while to come up with a name somebody hasn't already thought of.

The performing rights society will check the names of all other existing publishing companies and will inform you which of your name choices is available. If you've come up with the perfect name for your company and you're anxious to get it on the books, you might want to call your contact at the performing rights society you've chosen and see if that name is available even before you fill out the publisher affiliation application. If it is, ask them to reserve the name for you. Remember that your company name is going to represent *you*, so choose something that is appropriate and that will look good on your stationery, business cards, and Web site, and in small type on CDs, sheet music, etc. Once your name has been approved, it's time to fill out your DBA form and file your business name in the manner required by your local government.

You should also check with your bank to find out what information it requires for your business checking account. Once you have a company name, a bank account in your company name, and a performing rights society affiliation, you're officially in business. Your state or county may require more on your part (especially in the area of business taxes), and your accountant or lawyer will be able to provide you with more information about that topic.

THE COMPANY IMAGE

Your music publishing company will need to have a professional image. Since much of your business will involve correspondence, your stationery should complement that image. A sheet of plain white paper won't do. Even though most of your correspondence will probably be via e-mail and fax, you're still going to need professional-looking letterhead and envelopes from time to time, whether you create them on your computer or have them printed up for you by your local copy shop or stationer.

You might want to start by looking at the stationery of other publishing companies. If you've sent CDs out to publishers and have gotten rejection letters back (and if you didn't throw them out in a fit of anger), take a look at them now. Most publishers' stationery I've seen looks pretty conservative. But if most of your songs are novelty tunes, you might want to create stationery more consistent with the nature of your catalog. Just keep in mind that your stationery and business cards are representing you and the songs in your publishing company, as is your company name. The information on your letterhead should include your company name, address, phone and fax numbers, and e-mail address.

YOUR PUBLISHING OFFICE

By day I work in a large office with a high-backed black leather chair, a dramatic glass-top desk, gold and platinum albums on one wall, original artwork on another, and a handmade wall unit that holds all of my audio equipment. The wall behind my desk is a giant window that faces the Hollywood Hills. Outside my office is a large waiting room where a receptionist sits, keeping an eye on who's coming in and going out all day. The office is on Sunset Boulevard in Los Angeles, in the heart of the music industry of that city. Overall, it's a pretty impressive setup.

By night, however, if I'm not out attending one of the many music industry functions that take place pretty frequently in this town, I work in a spare room in my house. There are no gold records or expensive paintings in this room. Since writers don't have frequent visitors to their places of business, I'm not out to impress anyone with my workspace.

As a self-publisher, you don't need to impress anyone with a fancy office. Most of your work will be done on the phone, via e-mail, over a fax machine, through regular old-fashioned mail, or in person. But people won't be coming to see you—you'll be going to them. Always keep in mind that you are running a small home business that should remain small until enough money comes rolling in to justify an actual office with a secretary, a high-backed leather chair, and all of those other accoutrements that come with a large, successful enterprise.

So, what will your home office need and how much expense will be involved? You probably already have much of what you need. If you've been sending your songs out to publishers, then you've been printing copies of your lyrics on your computer. Two more items essential to your operation are a telephone and an answering machine. Along with your written correspondence, your phone is your contact to the outside world. You will need an answering machine or voice mail service because you can't possibly be where your phone is at all times. Most likely you have school or a day job that will keep you away from your phone when important calls are coming in. If you have a cell phone, you could use it as your business phone. (In that case, you *can* be where your phone is all the time, but you will still need a voice mail account on your cell phone just in case. Most cell phone plans include voice mail.) Or, you can include your cell phone number as part of your outgoing message on your home answering machine (or voice mail service) so people who need to can reach you right away.

One other thought about answering machines: Make your outgoing message as brief and professional as you can. If someone is taking the time to call your place of business, she doesn't want to sit through bad jokes, thirty seconds of your latest composition, or anything else that distracts from the reason she is calling you. The only exception to this advice is if

Advanced Articles

your image is off-the-wall in the first place. If all you write are hilarious novelty tunes, feel free to have a field day with your answering machine message. If you deal only in serious ballads, my advice is to stick to the basics. I realize this may seem like a small point to dwell on, but more than one person has missed out on a serious opportunity when I hung up on thirty seconds of answering-machine gibberish that I didn't have time to listen to.

Since you're a songwriter, your remaining major purchase—whatever device you choose to record your songs with—is probably already in your home. If you have your own home recording studio and a CD burner, you've got everything you need in the way of recording equipment—at least until the next wave of technology makes your current equipment outdated.

When you are beginning a small publishing company, you have to keep in mind that professional-sounding demos are very important. There are professional publishers all around you using the latest technologies available. When I speak at songwriting seminars and workshops, I always remind those in attendance that they are not only competing against the other songwriters at their level, they are also competing against the person who wrote the song sitting at the top of the various *Billboard* charts this week.

The same applies to you as a publisher. You're in competition with Warner/Chappell, EMI, Universal, Sony/ATV, and every other large and small publisher in the business today. You're even in competition with me! So, although your publishing empire might be in one corner of your bedroom, you have to give the outward appearance of being a professional enterprise.

One of your best options for establishing a professional presence in the worldwide market-place is creating a Web site for your company. Granted, you don't want to spend the kind of fortune on yours that many large publishers have on theirs. However, you might want to seriously consider having an inexpensive—but professional-looking—page or two on the Internet. Even if the site contains just your company name and contact information—and perhaps a few audio files of some of your songs—at least you'll have a Web address to give people if they should ask. The ability to e-mail audio files of your songs is invaluable. It's quicker, easier, and cheaper than sending CDs by messenger or through the post office or a shipping company.

One more essential item for your publishing company is a subscription to *Billboard*, the most popular trade journal in the music business. The subscription rate is pretty high, so be prepared to lay out some serious money. If you have a songwriting partner or a friend who's in need of a subscription as well, perhaps the two of you can subscribe to it together. *Billboard* will provide you with the news and information you need to make contacts, to see what acts are on the charts, to find out the latest changes in the publishing business, etc. *Hits* magazine is another trade publication with a large following. *Hits* also has one of the most entertaining Web sites in the entertainment business (HitsDailyDouble.com).

Before we discuss the business aspects of operating a small-scale publishing company, let's review everything you're going to need to get started.

1. First, you'll require a space to operate in. In the beginning, that space can be the size of a kitchen table or a desk.
2. Next you'll need to find out what type of business structure is best for you: a sole proprietorship, a partnership, or a corporation.
3. Then you will need to create a name for your company (with a few options in case your first choice is already taken).
4. Once you have chosen your name, you will need to apply for affiliation with the performing rights society that you have decided upon—a decision you shouldn't make until you've done your own research and have found the society that works best for you.

5. Once your name has been approved by the performing rights society, you must file the documents required by your local government to set up your business.

6. You will need to create (or have someone else create) your company's professional stationery and business cards.

7. For printed and e-mail correspondence (and generally keeping track of your operation), you will need a computer. You will also need a phone, a fax machine, and an answering machine or voice mail service (even if your cell phone is going to also act as your business phone).

8. You will need the latest high-quality equipment for making demos and creating recordings. The songs on your demos are the product that your business is manufacturing and selling. (I know that sounds impersonal, but it is the ultimate reality of music publishing.) Therefore, your product must be excellent if you want to compete with the other publishers who are marketing their product to the same buyers you are trying to reach.

9. If it's in your budget, you should have a Web site so that your publishing company has a presence around the world just like other music publishers do.

10. And, you'll need a subscription to *Billboard* (and possibly other trade journals) to keep you abreast of everything that's happening in the music business.

DAY-TO-DAY OPERATION

As a self-publisher, you must either handle all of the departments and functions of a full-scale publishing company yourself, or hire an administrator. (The latter may not be necessary until you get a song or two recorded and released.) Since your main goal is to get your songs recorded and released, your primary function is to act as the creative director of your company. In other words, you must make contacts in the music industry and choose which of your songs goes to which contacts. If you live in or near one of the major music centers (such as New York City, Nashville, or Los Angeles), the time has come to start shoving your foot in the door by meeting artists' managers, record producers, recording artists, A&R people, booking agents, and anyone else who might be able to help you.

Everyone's experience in acquiring contacts is different, which makes it very difficult for anyone to say, ''Here's the proper way to get to know people in the music business.'' My personal method was so strange that it would be almost impossible for anyone to duplicate (although perhaps not quite as strange as when a young Kris Kristofferson got Johnny Cash's attention by landing a helicopter on his lawn). The short version of my story goes like this: I quit my job as a small-town disk jockey; took a bus from Florence, Alabama, to New York City; and quickly began trying to figure out how I was going to survive. My first gig was as an assistant to the general manager of a well-known print publishing firm. After about a year with no movement upward in the company, I got a job in a museum called the Songwriters Hall of Fame, where I met some of the top songwriters in the business.

Not long after I went to work there, the gentleman who hired me left the organization. Since I had been his assistant (although for less than three months), the board of directors promoted me to his position. I'll be the first to admit it was pure luck.

Among other things, it was my job to coordinate the annual Songwriters Hall of Fame awards dinners. One of the board members who showed some personal interest in me told me it was important that I get to know everyone I could if I wanted to move up in the music business. At the annual awards dinners, I met an amazing array of the biggest names in the entertainment world.

As fate would have it, we lost our lease on the space where the museum was housed. When we were offered space for a small office in a building on West 57th Street in Manhattan, I ended up working on a floor that also contained the offices of a record company. As you

Advanced Articles

might have guessed, I went to work for the record company, eventually running its affiliated publishing company. Meanwhile, I was elected to the board of directors of the Songwriters Hall of Fame, which allowed me to continue to meet more and more people in the industry at each function the Hall of Fame held.

Always realizing the importance of keeping my name and face in the public eye, I made friends with the trade press who attended the same functions I was attending. I also made friends with a photographer—who I made sure was standing nearby with camera in hand when I was chatting with Michael Douglas, Willie Nelson, Chuck Berry, Henry Mancini, Carole King, Dick Clark, and a host of others.

With a minimal amount of begging, I managed to get my photos with some of these famous people into *Billboard*, newspapers, and the occasional magazine. Since all of the people I needed to know in the music business were subscribers to *Billboard*, I managed to become a semi-familiar name and face to them.

Granted, I'm not as well known as the presidents of the major record companies (or even some of the vice presidents, for that matter), but I have made enough contacts over the years that I can get the attention of almost anyone I need to speak to or get a song to. If I don't know the record producer of a hot act I have a song for, it's almost a sure thing that I know someone who does. With a little networking, I will get the song heard.

As you can see from my own story, there is no set way to get to know the people you need to know. Just keep in mind that making contacts is not an impossible task—new song-writers and publishers are managing to get their songs cut all the time. If they can do it—and if your songs are as good as or better than theirs—then you can do it too.

Acting as the creative director of your own publishing company, you will have to learn to hustle. In case you're thinking that you'd rather not be your own publisher if it means having to be brave enough to go out and meet high-powered music executives, let me remind you that it takes an awful lot of work and effort to go out and meet music publishers. If your songs are going to be heard, you're going to have to start making contacts sooner or later.

But the question remains, how do you meet these seemingly elusive music industry types? To me, the most obvious method is to attend the various workshops and seminars where music executives are speaking.

In major music industry cities like New York, Nashville, and Los Angeles, there are semi-nars going on all the time that are sponsored by ASCAP, BMI, the National Academy of Popular Music, the Songwriters Guild of America, and other music organizations. Get on the phone, call these organizations, and find out when and where their next function is taking place. Some seminars are free; others have fees attached. As a publisher, you will probably be able to write off these types of fees as business expenses (tax laws, like the Copyright Act, are always changing, so check with your accountant for details).

If you're lucky at these seminars, you might learn something about the business that you didn't already know. The main reason for being there, though, is to meet the speakers who can do you some good, as well as other music executives who might be in attendance.

Don't go to these functions unprepared. This is where your subscription to *Billboard* is worth its annual rate. Once you're signed up to attend a specific seminar and you know who the speakers will be, check through your issues of *Billboard* to see if you can get some detailed information about what these speakers have accomplished lately. Look them up on the In-ternet too. Does that record producer have a big hit on the charts? Did that A&R person just get a big promotion? Did that manager just sign a performer who uses outside material and sings the kind of songs you write? Get to know these people before you ever meet them in person.

Most importantly, follow up! I can't tell you the number of people who've come up to me at seminars where I've spoken, introduced themselves to me, shoved a CD in my hand, and then disappeared into the ether. Just like everybody else in the music business, I tend to be a tad busy. If somebody has given me a CD, she should call me and remind me about it. She should (nicely) encourage me to listen to it. She should try to squeeze my e-mail address out of me so she can correspond with me and keep reminding me she exists. (By the way, don't do this just to me. Do it to everybody in the business that you meet. If you're thinking this sounds obnoxious or overbearing, just remember that most of us in the industry got where we are by being obnoxious and overbearing!)

When my son was very young, he learned that the more persistent he was, the better his chances of getting what he wanted. For some reason, a lot of people seem to lose this talent as they get older. They make one phone call and then give up. Remember, when you're wearing your publishing hat, your job is to be as persistent as a kid wanting the latest toy.

PUTTING IT ALL TOGETHER

If your songs are good, if you make enough contacts, if you refuse to give up, and if luck is on your side, then the day will finally come when someone somewhere will record one of your songs. At that point, you will need to either apply the information you've learned from this book to your own publishing business, or allow an outside administrator to do the detail work for you (and then your job will be to monitor the administrator's work based on all you now know).

If you should decide to try your hand at administration, you will have to put on your licensing department hat. The party releasing the initial recording of your song will require a mechanical license from you. Since this is the first recording of a particular work, the copyright law says you have the right to determine whether you want this first recording to be made and distributed, as well as the right to determine the royalty rate.

Realistically, though, unless the initial recording is so bad that you want to prevent its release, you are obviously going to give permission for the recording at the current statutory mechanical rate. (Although it is allowed by law, I'm not aware of anyone who has actually charged more than statutory.) You may even find yourself granting a reduced rate if circumstances require it. In fact, the label releasing the initial recording of your song may have agreed to do so only if you would grant a three-quarter rate, or allow yourself to be bound by the artist's controlled composition clause.

But to issue a mechanical license, you need to know how the license should read. If you prefer to have your licensing handled through the Harry Fox Agency, this would be the time to contact them about representing you.

When royalties are due from the record company that has released a recording of your song, you will need to keep track of the royalties you receive. If your mechanical license calls for royalty payments to be due within 45 days of each calendar quarter, you will probably get paid on or very close to the 45th day. (You probably won't get the money any earlier. Why? One of the primary ways record companies make money is by earning interest on the vast amounts of money they hold prior to making payments to artists and publishers. Record companies have historically taken full advantage of this 45-day clause, so there's no real reason to expect money to show up any earlier than the record company is contractually obligated to send it.)

Once the 45 days are up, however, you should receive royalties on records sold during the preceding quarter. Assuming payment is made (and reputable record companies will usually pay on time), it's your job as the royalty department of your publishing company to make sure the amount of money received equals the number of copies reported on the statement times the mechanical rate agreed to in your mechanical license. If it is, congratulations. If it's not, it's time for you to get on the phone and contact the royalty department of the record company. If there is a discrepancy, it's your responsibility to get it corrected.

Unless you happen to be a combination songwriter/publisher/lawyer, though, you can't be your own legal department. If a record company still refuses to pay you even 30 or more days after, you most likely have grounds for a breach-of-contract suit. (If the breach is determined by the court to be material, you could then claim that the agreement is terminated and that further acts of manufacturing and distribution constitute copyright infringement.)

However, before you start accruing legal fees, it's best to decide if the money you're not being paid by the record company is substantially more than the amount of money your lawyer is going to charge to recover it. If the answer is no, make your best effort to recover the money yourself by hounding the record company and threatening legal action. You could also choose a lawyer willing to work on a contingency basis, in which case the lawyer's fee would be a percentage of the money recovered.

Once "distribution of . . . phonorecords . . . to the public by sale" has taken place, your composition qualifies as having been published. As your own copyright department, you will need to inform your performing rights society that your song has been released so that the society will be able to properly account to you.

If your song is a hit, it's likely that you will be approached by print publishers for the right to release your song in sheet music and folio form. Although you will probably be able to negotiate the basic points of the agreement (amount of advance, royalty per copy, etc.) yourself, it would be a good idea to have a lawyer look over the agreement to make suggestions or implement changes she feels are necessary.

Since the recording of your song will probably be released in foreign territories, you will need to start making subpublishing deals. Acting as your own foreign department, you will have to decide which of the subpublishing options is best for your company. Obviously, you won't want to go around setting up your own foreign corporations, but you will need to get involved with subpublishers on some level, because serious money can be made in the international market.

This is the point at which you'll find out one of the advantages of having an e-mail account and owning a fax machine. You probably prefer not to do business in the middle of the night. While you're sleeping, your subpublisher—in another time zone halfway around the world— can be faxing or e-mailing you information about what is happening with your song there.

A hit song often prompts other types of uses, as I have pointed out in other sections of this book. It is possible you'll get calls requesting use of the song in commercials, movies, or TV shows. In these situations, you will have to don your licensing department hat once again to negotiate a fair price for these uses.

As a self-publisher, then, you will at least have to be your own creative department. If you decide to delve into administration, you will have to act as the licensing, royalty, copyright, and international departments as well. The legal and print departments, of course, will be handled out-of-house by others qualified in those areas.

As more of your songs are recorded, your publishing company may find it needs a real office with a part- or full-time assistant/secretary/receptionist. If your success rate becomes high enough, you may find yourself turning into a larger publishing company, taking on additional writers and bringing in large sums of money.

On the other hand, the success of your publishing business can frequently leave you buried in business details, with little time for the more creative endeavors of being a songwriter. To avoid this situation, you can either try to keep the company small enough for you to handle alone (most likely by using an outside administrator) or hire someone to act as an in-house administrator. Before you decide to hire personnel, make sure that your company is active enough and financially successful enough to justify such expenses.

Advanced Articles

ADVANCED ARTICLES

Songwriting Wrongs & How to Right Them

by Pat and Pete Luboff

Editor's Note: Pat and Pete Luboff are releasing a new edition of their classic book on songwriting, *101 Songwriting Wrongs & How to Right Them* (Writer's Digest Books), which should be available in major bookstores by Chrismas of 2007. The book covers a lot of crucial songwriting topics, from creativity and craft to the business of songwriting. What follows are four chapters from the book combined into a single article.

SENDING MONEY DOWN THE DEMO HOLE
Make the best of mail-order demos

We've heard from songwriters who have sent off 10 or 20 songs to a mail-order demo service, along with a great big check, only to receive a great big disappointment in the mail a couple of weeks later.

Making demos of your songs is an important part of learning the songwriting process. We recommend that you participate personally in the process. If you think that's impossible because you live far away from any recording facilities or because you feel you are not technically inclined enough to do your own recording at home, think again.

There is probably a recording studio near you no matter where you live. An Internet search for "recording studios in [Your Town]" will yield a number of possibilities.

Wherever there is a radio station, there is recording equipment. Some local cable TV stations make their facilities available for free to the public. You can also approach your local radio station about using their audio recording facilities.

Networking and collaborating with other songwriters can put you in touch with people who do not operate official recording studio businesses, but are willing to help you record your project. The proliferation of easy-to-use, in-home recording studio equipment has made the process possible for just about anyone. With a little money and a little more experimentation, you can record your own demos—at least your own rough demos.

If, after researching your possibilities, you still feel you want to go the mail-order demo route, you're going to need that rough demo. When you order a demo by mail, you are not there to give any input during the process. Therefore, you need to make your up-front input as clear as possible. Making a rough demo with at least an indication of the feel and the parts you want included will go a long way toward ensuring the final product is something you can live with.

Excerpted from *101 Songwriting Wrongs & How to Right Them* © 2007 by **PAT & PETE LUBOFF**. Used with permission of Writer's Digest Books, an imprint of F + W Publications, Inc. Visit your local bookseller or call (800)754-2912.

How do you find a mail-order demo studio? Call your nearest songwriters' organization for recommendations. You can search online, but don't confuse a legitimate mail-order demo service with a song shark. A legitimate mail-order demo service will *not* charge you an exorbitant fee or promise to make you a star or release a record of your song.

Legitimate mail-order demo services will have sites with contact information for a specific person, usually the studio owner. You'll be able to call her up, talk with her about your ideas for the demo, and discuss your choice of instrumentation. The more instruments you want, the more the demo will cost. Many times, legitimate mail-order demo sites will have samples of previous productions you can listen to online.

When you've found a couple of likely studios, e-mail or call them. If they are legit, they will gladly furnish you with information about their recording equipment, instruments, services available, and what they cost. Some demo studios specialize in certain styles, such as country. Ask the demo producers what styles of music they do best. Check with them about what information they need from you.

When you have made your studio choice, send as much information as possible about your song and how you want it demoed. The more you communicate, the better your chances are of getting what you want. Your package should include:

- a rough demo of the song
- a neatly typed lyric sheet
- a chord sheet or a number chart—a lead sheet is not necessary
- instructions about the feel you want in the demo including references to recognizable songs and possibly a recording of a song that you want your demo to sound like
- your choice of male or female lead vocal
- your choice of instrumentation
- a money order or credit card number for the cost of recording the demo (Projects paid for by personal checks are not recorded until after the checks clear the bank.)

If you're sending a cassette or CD through snail mail, use delivery confirmation or certified mail (no return receipt) so you can track it. Never send your only copy of a song. Alternately, the whole process can be transacted online. Using mp3 files, you can e-mail the studio your rough demo and get the finished product back to burn to a CD.

We recommend that you try a mail-order demo service on only one song at first. If you don't like the product, you can change to another service for the next song. If you send a bunch of songs at once, you may be stuck with a bunch of demos you don't like.

When you're deciding which song to try first, keep this is mind: It's a rare song that will impress the professional listener with just a piano or guitar vocal demo. That's because most professional listeners have no imagination. They want the finished product, or as close as you can get to it, handed to them on a silver platter. If you do have to go with a simple guitar or piano demo, you absolutely have to have a dynamite singer to do the lead vocal. A big, soulful ballad is your best choice when a guitar- or piano-vocal demo is all you can do. Save up for a bigger production on your grooving up-tempo rocker.

WHAT THEY DON'T KNOW WILL HURT YOU
Register a song that is getting airplay with your performance rights organization

Getting a song recorded is the songwriter's dream come true. It's especially dreamy when you make the connection yourself with the artist, which makes you the publisher. The record company will ask you to issue a mechanical license, so you will do some research and deliver the appropriate piece of paper to them. You're already a member of a performance rights organization, so you've got your bases covered.

Advanced Articles

Sorry, but you're way off base. Membership in a performance rights organization and five bucks will get you a cup of coffee. Your performance rights organization is not a guardian angel who watches over you and notes your successes on a golden scroll. If you don't tell them about your recording, they will never know. They won't look for it in their survey, and you won't get paid. But since no one will ask you to do this the way a record company asks for a mechanical license, you may not know that registering your song with your performance rights organization is a prerequisite to getting paid for any airplay.

Ask your performance rights organization how to register your song when airplay is imminent. All the PROs (ASCAP, BMI, and SESAC) have online title registration. Please note that this administrative work with the record company and the performance rights society needs to be done by you only if you do not have a publisher representing you on the song.

How about that mechanical license? Is there anyone you should inform about it? It is possible to have the record company pay you directly for sales of records. However, we recommend that you let the Harry Fox Agency in New York City collect mechanical royalties for you. Harry Fox, which is related to the National Music Publishers Association, collects mechanical royalties for many of the largest publishers in the world. They charge a small percentage of the royalties for the service and it is well worth it. When a recording you have made the connection for is about to be released, contact the Harry Fox Agency (www.harryfox.com).

After all you've been through to get this recording, don't keep it a secret from the organizations that are the conduits for your income stream from the song. In the end, the glamorous music business comes down to filling out forms, shuffling papers, and accounting for figures in a column. But the check won't be in the mail unless you let someone know they should be sending it.

NO PAPER TRAIL
Don't lose those contracts!

Congratulations! You pitched a song to a major publisher, were offered a contract and, after some negotiations to make the contract work for you, signed it. Not only that, the publisher actually succeeded in securing a commercially recorded release of your song with a somewhat successful artist. You actually start getting some checks in the mail from the publisher. How great is that?!

Life goes on and the checks stop coming. Then you hear about a re-release of the song on a "Best of . . ." CD and you look forward to more checks. They don't come. Now what do you do? Some songwriters who are members of the Songwriters Guild will go to Rick Carnes, the Guild's first president from Nashville, and ask for help.

Rick says:

> The first thing I ask is, "Do you have the contract under which you were supposed to be paid so we can look at what the remedies are in that contract?" The songwriters never, never have the contract. It makes it impossible for us to go after the publishers. It does no good to fight, fight, fight to negotiate the right contract and then lose the contract. But that is what 99.999 percent of all songwriters will do. Don't lose your contract! Keep it in a lock box that will survive World War III.

Many songwriters don't know that 35 to 40 years after you sign a song to a publisher, you have the right to terminate the contract. That is true even if the contract appears to be binding forever. There are complicated windows of time when you have to give notice and when you can reclaim the copyright, which are best handled by an expert in the field. But what you need to know is, time flies when you're having fun being a songwriter. Termination time will be here before you know it. And when it comes, you're going to need that contract to get your song back.

You're not only going to need that contract, you're going to need the signatures of all your collaborators. Rick advises:

> When you co-write a song, get some way of identifying your co-writer that will allow you to find her 40 years from the day that you're writing. People are loath to give out their Social Security numbers now, because of identity theft. But that number may be your only way of locating the writer in the far future. Put it on the lyric sheet when you file the lyric sheet away. Don't lose it. Because 35 or 40 years from now, when you try to reclaim that song, you have to contact all the writers on the song and everybody has to sign on the same paper. It's particularly hard to find females when they've changed their names four times. Males are little bit easier but not that much easier.
>
> Anybody trying to find Rick Carnes 30 years from now isn't going to find me because that isn't my legal name. Finding me personally or my heirs is going to be very difficult if they don't have my Social Security number.

Those pieces of paper you signed can mean many more pieces of paper (money, that is) in your bank account. Don't put them in your recycling, or your shredder, or line your birdcage with them. File them so you can find them.

ONCE IS NOT ENOUGH
Join your PRO twice if you're self-publishing

When we had our first success with a song that we pitched directly to an artist, we made a mistake that cost us a substantial sum of money. We take solace in the fact that we can pass what we learned onto you so you will not make the same mistake. Since we had made the connection with the artist, we were the publishers of the song. We were already members of a performing rights organization, so we notified them of the recording. We figured we had done all we needed to do.

Ignorance is not bliss, we discovered. We did receive songwriting royalties from ASCAP in due time, a year to eighteen months after the release. But a couple of years later the light dawned: We saw we had not received royalties as the publishers of the song. We called ASCAP and explained that we had neglected to join as publishers and to notify them we were the publishers on the song, a process called title registration. Unfortunately, the recording was too old for them to make any payment on the performances. The result was that we had collected *half* of the performance royalties possible on that song.

If reading this makes you realize you have made the same mistake, it is possible to retrieve some back performance royalties. ASCAP will go back nine months from the current quarter. BMI is not obligated by its contract with its songwriter members to go back at all. However, as a courtesy to the writer and depending on the situation, they may go back as far as nine months from the current quarter. SESAC will go back a year. Any royalties from further back in time are lost.

It is not necessary, or advisable, to join a performance rights organization as a publisher unless you expect a song of yours to be recorded, released, and played on a substantial number of radio stations or on television. ASCAP doesn't charge any fees. BMI charges publishing members a one-time processing fee of $150 for individually owned publishing companies, or $250 for partnerships, corporations, and limited liability companies (LLCs). Both organizations require proof of your status as an active publisher with songs that qualify for performance income. Unlike the other two PROs, you can't just join SESAC. You have to apply and be accepted by a "selective process."

Advanced Articles

When the time is right, the first step in the process is to choose which organization you want to join. This is a major decision, and again, we recommend you research the organizations to see which will pay the best for the uses your songs are most likely to have. Each organization has its own way of determining payments for various uses. Ask specific questions; for example, "My album is going to have airplay on college stations across the country. Does your survey cover those stations?" or "What are your rates of payment for television show theme songs?" The publishing company must be in the same PRO as the songwriter. If you choose to be an ASCAP songwriter, then you will be an ASCAP publisher. In other words, you cannot choose to be an ASCAP writer and have your songs published by a BMI company.

Generally speaking, radio performance royalties are paid on the basis of a statistical survey. You are not paid every time your song is played, because no one can keep track of all that information. There are over 9,000 radio stations in the United States. If you figure that each station plays 15 songs an hour, 24 hours a day, that's 3,240,000 airplays to keep track of every day. Systems being developed for use in the future can track airplay exactly. For now, they find out what's being played at X number of stations and then extrapolate mathematically from the sample to determine their payment for radio airplay for the whole country.

Television music is reported more accurately and is paid for according to different formulas that depend on a number of variables, such as whether the music is featured—that is, a singer is center stage singing it—or just playing in the background. The amount of payment also depends on the length of time the song is heard during the television show. Performance royalties are not paid by movie theaters in the United States, but they are in Europe.

The next step is to choose a company name. First you will have to come up with three or four names and submit them to your chosen performance rights organization. They will tell you which names are available. (Check out the names you're thinking of on the three PROs' Web sites. All have search features for publisher names which you can use to eliminate from your wish list names that are already in use. Not all names are on the sites, so not finding it in the search is not a guarantee that the name is free. We had to go through eight names before we found one that wasn't already taken.) Then, each time you make the connection that means airplay for your songs, notify your performance royalty organization—twice.

We don't want you to have to learn this lesson the hard way, like we did.

Building the Business Team for Today's Market

by Scott Mathews

L et's say you are a budding performer who writes good songs, and you are expressing yourself through music and having a ton of fun. That, my friend, is success! Don't ever lose what you have found.

Now, let's say as your songs get better, people acknowledge you are in fact gifted, and you gain momentum to the point where you realize music is not just another crazy dream, but something you wish to pursue as a career. I hereby pronounce you a professional artist! You may now kiss yourself.

Wow, a real bona fide artist—wait, that means you have a real job! Yes, you are among the blessed in that you have wisely chosen a field of endeavor you are passionate about— but a job is a job nonetheless. It doesn't take long to find that a career doing what you love may involve more tasks and details than you can handle alone. It may be time to build a support team—usually some combination of producers, lawyers and managers—to handle business tasks on your behalf and help grow that facet of your career, while you focus on letting the artistic juices flow.

The first step in building your team is assessing your current strengths and weaknesses in areas outside of performing and writing. Do you want to record an album but are clueless about how to work in a studio? Are you overwhelmed with phone calls organizing gigs and rehearsals? Are you long on talent but short on industry connections? Is a record company or publisher waving contracts in your face, but you're scared of the legalese and want to make sure it's a fair deal? Are you just plain clueless about what your next step should be?

Set goals for where you want your career to go and make a checklist of everything you need to get done to move toward those goals. We live in a "do it yourself" time with little or no development or direction coming from record companies. Artists must now develop their own act well before deals are done, so it's up to them to get ready for the big time. Figure out what kind of helping hand you need most to help guide the masses to your music. Who should you turn to first?

SCOTT MATHEWS of Hit or Myth Productions has produced, recorded, or performed with a range of artists including John Hiatt, Van Morrison, Keith Richards, and John Lee Hooker. His songs have been cut by artists such as Barbra Streisand and Dave Edmunds. See the Hit or Myth Productions listing in the Record Producers section. "Not affiliated with scottmathewsmusic.com or scottmathewsproductions.com." E-mail him at hitormyth@aol.com.

PRODUCERS, PROGRESS & PROCEEDS

One major hurdle to get over in the music business is the need to present your work in a fully-realized form so that everyone who hears "gets it." This means documenting your music the best you can, usually in a recording studio. Recorded music can travel places you can't go, be heard by many different people, and present your music to interested ears when you can't be there in person to perform it live. It can also make money for you through your own sales efforts or from licensing it to an interested label. So, it needs to be as good as you can make it—great songs, great sound, and great performances.

In my experience, when you prove you can deliver a killer, marketable record, that's the time good managers, attorneys and record execs will come out of the woodwork seeking you—and you then end up with a much better deal because hold the goods and you don't need a record company's expensive money to complete the project. Plus, the all-important "creative control" is built into a situation where you have proven your own commercial potential on the front end.

Sound advice for the new music industry

With today's digital recording technology, you can make a great record for a fraction of the hundreds of thousands of dollars big labels like to throw at recording projects. And at the end, you own the masters and keep the profits. But, it's not always as easy as it might seem. For the amount of money you spend buying your own recording equipment and learning to use it, you could hire a producer and save a lot of time by making use of his or her expertise and musical knowledge to get what you want.

Making a truly great record requires technical expertise in recording, arranging skills, and a lot of knowledge about how people tick, especially temperamental artists. An inexperienced artist who tries to self-produce may well find herself staring into a microphone, frustrated and stuck, while precious studio time burns away her budget. An artist in this situation needs a producer to guide her through the process of recording and help her get the best bang for her buck in terms of performance and time spent in the studio.

The right producer can also be a great long-term creative partner, and help you make great strides in developing your sound, either as an individual singer/songwriter or a band, even before you go into the studio. Good producers understand how instruments blend, support one another, and in turn support the vocal and lyrics, which is the real focus of any effective arrangement.

If you are a band, a good producer can be an objective sounding board, hear the overall picture of your sound, and point out aspects of how you play together as a group that can be tightened up. This will save you time, both as a performing group and in the studio. The version of yourself a good producer can conjure in the studio will also help you see the big picture for yourself and help you move forward on your sound with new direction and focus.

For singer/songwriters, the right producer can frame their songs in new and startling ways they may not have considered and open up whole new vistas of sound for them to explore. Since the artist and producer are not trying to capture a particular band sound, there is actually *more* freedom to explore styles or radical sounds.

A good producer can also help artists hone their songs to absolute perfection before they go in the studio, and open artists up to whole new areas of songwriting they may not have considered. A good producer can suggest ways for bands to rethink the basic outlines of verse and chorus, or take a singer/songwriter's basic vocal and melody and suggest small changes in phrasing that take it to the next level (or even take the basic vocal and build completely new chords and rhythms around it).

Beware of Big Promises

You must understand there are absolutely no guarantees for success after the record is made. The moment a producer (or anyone else) makes such guarantees, you know you are working with an excitable amateur or a scam artist. There are simply too many variables to consider, and every creative/business endeavor is unique. Good fortune comes from many sources—contacts, determination, quality, timing, and yes, plain old good luck. You can only lay plans, make your best efforts, and hope for the best.

When hiring a producer, you should first seek a person with complementary creative drives who can help you make the best possible record. He or she should then also have reasonable contacts in the industry and a plan to help the record get the recognition it deserves. Not all producers can actually offer all of this, but that doesn't stop many from representing themselves as people who can practically guarantee quick-and-easy record deals and instant rock stardom (for a price). As a producer, I strive to make successful records and careers, but I also demand that reality and honest expectations are weighed out and realized by all parties.

MANAGERS, MOMENTUM & MONEY

I began in the music *business*, now it's called the music *industry*. Anyone can start a business but it takes several large corporations to start an industry. Frankly, I prefer to treat music like a business and fit into the industry while remaining independent. I encourage any self-respecting artist to follow that logic. It's healthy to know how one fits into the overall industry (and how they get paid!), but staying true to your artistic vision is key. Who will be able to share that vision and help you in your day-to-day duties as a business? A great manager can.

An effective artist manager can help lead you where you need to be and keep you on track once you get there. A manager often handles all of the "office-related" work your business conducts such as bookkeeping, booking appearances, publishing and recording deals, press, etc., not to mention being a good friend and confidante (much like your producer should be).

The right manager will understand your artistic vision and help you achieve your goals. A good manager can provide useful advice, draw upon industry connections you do not possess, represent you in business negotiations (in some cases playing the bad cop, so you can be the good guy), and take the load of day-to-day business chores off your back so you have more time to write, practice, and rehearse.

Yes, there is a lengthy laundry list of activities a good manager handles, but be warned— a bad manger can hang you out to dry, *so make sure you choose carefully based on your goals and make sure this business relationship is fulfilling a bona fide need for your career*. The entertainment field is rife with managers who have amassed huge sums of money by being world-class ambulance chasers. This type tends to watch for when an artist or band has generated enough heat on their own, and then pounces on them with their charm and smarm. This school of manager is usually cheesy enough to promise the moon. If they time it right, it can be a quick way for them to step in and collect a full commission on all the years of hard labor an artist has put in. When there are hundreds of thousands of dollars at stake, that 15 or 20% is one fat payday for the heat-seeking missile type of management.

There are countless heartbreaking stories to be told of artists being overly eager to sign any deal. They sign away a large percentage to the wrong party and then find themselves

Advanced Articles

dirt poor. Ouch! So, when inking a management deal, I suggest every artist negotiate a fair percentage accurately reflecting what has been earned, by whom and when. You might even ask a manager to work with you on a trial basis before signing formally. Let them earn their keep and prove they can enhance your career.

LAWYERS, GUNS AND MONEY

You will need an established entertainment attorney if people are throwing contracts at you. Shop around and find someone with the knowledge to know what's up and the honesty to keep your costs down.

Sometimes I feel I have single-handedly paid for at least one of the two towers in Century City where so many of the L.A.-based entertainment law firms operate. Okay, that is an absurd stretch of the truth, but early in my career, I spent much of the money I earned on attorney's fees. I don't mean to bash lawyers—heaven knows, there have been a ton of overpaid producers in the record business!—but, I've concluded the only thing worse than learning from expensive lessons is not learning from expensive lessons.

I still see my fair share of lawyer bills—can't live without them—but there are strategies I've found for making every dollar you spend on legal fees more effective:

- **Be cautious about paying attorneys on a retainer basis when starting out.** It's better not to set lawyers up on extra long retainers and let them run amuck. Pay for their services only when you need them for specific, limited issues. You will save money, and the lawyer will not be tempted to exceed his authority and meddle with your career.
- **Hire specialists for specific needs.** I commonly hire a person who is an expert in whatever area of concern for which I am in need of advice. A certain lawyer whose expertise is publishing is who I will talk to regarding a situation involving my songs. An attorney who deals in accounting might be who I'd call when there is a dispute over royalties. (That would never happen in this industry—right?)
- **Watch and learn.** After many years in the business, I began to see a pattern of entertainment lawyers negotiating record production deals in pretty much the same fashion from one deal to the next. I paid attention, asked a lot of questions and therefore learned a whole lot from my attorneys (and I still do). When I discovered I could apply much of that information to new agreements myself, I took a more active role in the process and set up my own system. Now my company can deal directly in certain areas in which we're well-versed.

Most of the lawyers I have used proved to be smart—some brilliant. I learned from the best and the cost of that education was worth every penny. Still, in the overall scheme of

Don't Knock Before You Rock

Even if you are currently capable of running the entire show yourself, without the aid (or expense) of your own team of "people," be aware that most high-powered industry mucky-mucks do not have an open door policy towards new talent. Due to the sheer volume of solicitations, a "gatekeeper" system is in place, and only known managers, producers or attorneys are allowed to present the case for a new artist. However, it is my experience that there is simply no reason to bring a lawyer into play until your act is developed enough that you are ready to be shopped. You only knock when you are ready to rock!

things, I believe the people who make the music should share in the monetary proceeds more than the people who don't make the music.

In the end, it comes down to the old saying that "knowledge is power." If you know the game, you will be able not only to talk to your attorney about what your needs are (and understand your attorney, which can be no small feat) but also be empowered to deal directly with many concerns that involve your day-to-day dealings.

A NEW VISION AND APPROACH

Above and beyond all this talk about putting together a team of players to work the music industry system to your advantage, I think we need to look at the larger picture and lay some groundwork for the future. There is a whole new model for success waiting in the wings, and you can begin planning for that and shaping your strategy right now.

As we know, the music industry is changing and changing rapidly. Digital technology is changing how music is recorded and distributed, and the days of the old-model major record labels are fading. The balance of power between artists and record companies is changing in the artists' favor.

Past standard agreements between labels and artists were mainly to finance recording and provide distribution of the product. Today the record that used to cost $1,000,000 is $100,000 and the $100,000 budget of yesteryear is now roughly $10,000 to $20,000 (or less). So the need for the big guns 'bank' to record projects is indeed gone. So is the 90/10 ratio of what I'll laughingly refer to as royalties.

Same is true for distribution. The old model called for hard copies being shipped to brick and mortar stores around the world and with Tower Records shutting their doors, my point is clear on this subject. Online distribution is way of the future and the future is now. Yes, hard copies are needed to but in less numbers as the sales of said decrease daily.

Viral marketing techniques are working wonders and ownership of a much larger chunk is affording artists the chance to make a living with relatively small fan bases (compared to when you had to sell "Gold" or better to recoup not long ago).

I can expand a lot but the general resources and services an artist needs and a good new company must be willing to tackle are:

- **A&R** (it doesn't happen anymore as people are signed on their MySpace numbers alone)
- **record budgets** (smaller but still a factor)
- **publishing** (finding outside sources for the songs and working the catalog)
- **marketing** (new online strategies as well as good old PR and press)
- **tour support** (artists need to be in front of their audience—it's costly but effective if done right)
- **merchandise** (provide all kinds of merch for the artist—again costly but high profit margin)

If these job descriptions (and more) are provided and truly delivered to the artist from the company, in a sense everyone on all sides of the deal are performers. It's no about longer throwing stuff against the wall to see what sticks and then work the hits, it's belief and follow through with a firm commitment in the deal and everybody working towards the same goal and reaping the rewards of their performance.

This is a brief overview but I hope you can see where it's going. I now have a pile of contracts from every kind of label, and I am now in discussions to build a new company that can be one of the most helpful and realistic partners to artists and their careers.

The "Entertainment Company"

In a nutshell, today's artist should focus on allying with a wide-ranging *entertainment company* that can cover a wide range of roles, rather than a *record company* built on the standard major label model. The *nature of the relationship* makes the difference, meaning a move from *exploitation* of the artist to *partnership* between the artist and the company.

The change of wording represents a change of focus and responsibility toward the artist, the product, and its success. It's a subtle distinction, and the outlines of this new paradigm are still emerging, but right now is the time when you can begin thinking in a different way about your goals as an artist and how you believe they can be achieved.

Beware of the Spec Deal

A word of caution regarding finding the right producer and development deal: beware the "spec" offer that provides free studio time but commits you to giving away publishing rights or other valuable assets. As a recording artist, the publishing generated by your songs will likely represent the first royalties you see and will continue to be a main source of income as long as you control the copyrights. Most record company accounting techniques can be frustrating to say the least but your songs are earning money (your writer's and publishing share) in a fair and equitable way. That's why I chose "Hang On To Your Publishing" as the name for my own music publishing company—that says it all.

QUICK RESULTS? YOU MUST CONSULT

It isn't always the right move to hand over all the reins of your business concerns. But, there may be specific help available in the form of consultants you access on an "as needed" basis as opposed to hiring them full-time.

Due to huge industry layoffs, many qualified people are deciding they don't want to work for giant corporations. Some of the most talented that have done great work for various labels now offer their services as consultants. They can be hired to help emerging artists answer big and small questions along the way. The guidance and advice from someone who has been in the industry long enough to know what to look out for and at the same time is current enough to keep an eye on new developments can be a fantastic guiding light to an up-and-comer.

So, do you smell team spirit? Go out and assemble the best you can find, based on your needs. This is no time to be shy . . . wrong business for that. Search out who can help you and present yourself in a professional and ambitious way.

Music Publishers

Music publishers find songs and then get them recorded. In return for a share of the money made from your songs, they work as an agent for you by plugging your songs to recording artists, taking care of paperwork and accounting, setting you up with co-writers (recording artists or other songwriters), and so on.

HOW DO MUSIC PUBLISHERS MAKE MONEY FROM SONGS?

Music publishers make money by getting songs recorded onto albums, Film and TV sound-tracks, commericals, etc. and other areas. While this is their primary function, music publishers also handle administrative tasks such as copyrighting songs; collecting royalties for the songwriter; negotiating and issuing synchronization licenses for use of music in films, television programs and commercials; arranging and administering foreign rights; auditing record companies and other music users; suing infringers; and producing new demos of new songs. In a small, independent publishing company, one or two people may handle all these jobs. Larger publishing companies are more likely to be divided into the following departments: creative (or professional), copyright, licensing, legal affairs, business affairs, royalty, accounting and foreign.

HOW DO MUSIC PUBLISHERS FIND SONGS?

The *creative department* is responsible for finding talented writers and signing them to the company. Once a writer is signed, it is up to the creative department to develop and nurture the writer so he will write songs that create income for the company. Staff members often put writers together to form collaborative teams. And, perhaps most important, the creative department is responsible for securing commercial recordings of songs and pitching them for use in film and other media. The head of the creative department—usually called the ''professional manager''—is charged with locating talented writers for the company.

HOW DO MUSIC PUBLISHERS GET SONGS RECORDED?

Once a writer is signed, the professional manager arranges for a demo to be made of the writer's songs. Even though a writer may already have recorded his own demo, the publisher will often re-demo the songs using established studio musicians in an effort to produce the highest-quality demo possible.

Once a demo is produced, the professional manager begins shopping the song to various outlets. He may try to get the song recorded by a top artist on his or her next album or get the song used in an upcoming film. The professional manager uses all the contacts and leads he has to get the writer's songs recorded by as many artists as possible. Therefore, he must be able to deal efficiently and effectively with people in other segments of the music industry, including A&R personnel, recording artists, producers, distributors, managers and lawyers. Through these contacts, he can find out what artists are looking for new material, and who may be interested in recording one of the writer's songs.

HOW IS A PUBLISHING COMPANY ORGANIZED?

After a writer's songs are recorded, the other departments at the publishing company come into play.

- The *licensing and copyright departments* are responsible for issuing any licenses for use of the writer's songs in film or TV and for filing various forms with the copyright office.
- The *legal affairs department and business affairs department* works with the professional department in negotiating contracts with its writers.
- The *royalty and accounting departments* are responsible for making sure that users of music are paying correct royalties to the publisher and ensuring the writer is receiving the proper royalty rate as specified in the contract and that statements are mailed to the writer promptly.
- Finally, the *foreign department*'s role is to oversee any publishing activities outside of the United States, to notify sub-publishers of the proper writer and ownership information of songs in the catalogue and update all activity and new releases, and to make sure a writer is being paid for any uses of his material in foreign countries.

LOCATING A MUSIC PUBLISHER

How do you go about finding a music publisher that will work well for you? First, you must find a publisher suited to the type of music you write. If a particular publisher works mostly with alternative music and you're a country songwriter, the contacts he has within the industry will hardly be beneficial to you.

Each listing in this section details, in order of importance, the type of music that publisher is most interested in; the music types appear in **boldface** to make them easier to locate. It's also very important to submit only to companies interested in your level of experience (see A Sample Listing Decoded on page 11). You will also want to refer to the Category Indexes on page 366, which list companies by the type of music they work with. Publishers placing music in film or TV will be proceded by a ▨ (see the Film & TV Index on page 396 for a complete list of these companies).

Do your research!

It's important to study the market and do research to identify which companies to submit to.

- Many record producers have publishing companies or have joint ventures with major publishers who fund the signing of songwriters and who provide administration services. Since producers have an influence over what is recorded in a session, targeting the producer/publisher can be a useful avenue.
- Since most publishers don't open unsolicited material, try to meet the publishing representative in person (at conferences, speaking engagements, etc.) or try to have an intermediary intercede on your behalf (for example, an entertainment attorney; a manager, an agent, etc.).
- As to demos, submit no more than 3 songs.
- As to publishing deals, co-publishing deals (where a writer owns part of the publishing share through his or her own company) are relatively common if the writer has a well-established track record.

- Are you targeting a specific artist to sing your songs? If so, find out if that artist even considers outside material. Get a copy of the artist's latest album, and see who wrote most of the songs. If they were all written by the artist, he's probably not interested in hearing material from outside writers. If the songs were written by a variety of different writers, however, he may be open to hearing new songs.
- Check the album liner notes, which will list the names of the publishers of each writer. These publishers obviously have had luck pitching songs to the artist, and they may be able to get your songs to that artist as well.
- If the artist you're interested in has a recent hit on the *Billboard* charts, the publisher of that song will be listed in the "Hot 100 A-Z" index. Carefully choosing which publishers will work best for the material you write may take time, but it will only increase your chances of getting your songs heard. "Shotgunning" your demo packages (sending out many packages without regard for music preference or submission policy) is a waste of time and money and will hurt, rather than help, your songwriting career.

Once you've found some companies that may be interested in your work, learn what songs have been successfully handled by those publishers. Most publishers are happy to provide you with this information in order to attract high-quality material. As you're researching music publishers, keep in mind how you get along with them personally. If you can't work with a publisher on a personal level, chances are your material won't be represented as you would like it to be. A publisher can become your most valuable connection to all other segments of the music industry, so it's important to find someone you can trust and feel comfortable with.

Independent or major company?

Also consider the size of the publishing company. The publishing affiliates of the major music conglomerates are huge, handling catalogs of thousands of songs by hundreds of songwriters. Unless you are an established songwriter, your songs probably won't receive enough attention from such large companies. Smaller, independent publishers offer several advantages. First, independent music publishers are located all over the country, making it easier for you to work face-to-face rather than by mail or phone. Smaller companies usually aren't affiliated with a particular record company and are therefore able to pitch your songs to many different labels and acts. Independent music publishers are usually interested in a smaller range of music, allowing you to target your submissions more accurately. The most obvious advantage to working with a smaller publisher is the personal attention they can bring to you and your songs. With a smaller roster of artists to work with, the independent music publisher is able to concentrate more time and effort on each particular project.

SUBMITTING MATERIAL TO PUBLISHERS

When submitting material to a publisher, always keep in mind that a professional, courteous manner goes a long way in making a good impression. When you submit a demo through the mail, make sure your package is neat and meets the particular needs of the publisher. Review each publisher's submission policy carefully, and follow it to the letter. Disregarding this information will only make you look like an amateur in the eyes of the company you're submitting to.

Listings of companies in Canada are preceded by a ⬙, and international markets are designated with a ⊕. You will find an alphabetical list of these companies at the back of the book, along with an index of publishers by state in the Geographic Index (see page 397).

Icons

For More Info

For more instructional information on the listings in this book, including explanations of symbols (☒ ✔ ☟ ☞ ☜ 🌐 ◯ ⬭ ⬮ ⬭), read the article *Songwriter's Market: How Do I Use It?* on page 7.

PUBLISHING CONTRACTS

Once you've located a publisher you like and he's interested in shopping your work, it's time to consider the publishing contract—an agreement in which a songwriter grants certain rights to a publisher for one or more songs. The contract specifies any advances offered to the writer, the rights that will be transferred to the publisher, the royalties a songwriter is to receive and the length of time the contract is valid.

- When a contract is signed, a publisher will ask for a 50-50 split with the writer. *This is standard industry practice*; the publisher is taking that 50% to cover the overhead costs of running his business and for the work he's doing to get your songs recorded.
- It is always a good idea to have a publishing contract (or any music business contract) reviewed by a competent entertainment lawyer.
- There is no "standard" publishing contract, and each company offers different provisions for their writers.

Make sure you ask questions about anything you don't understand, especially if you're new in the business. Songwriter organizations such as the Songwriters Guild of America (SGA) provide contract review services, and can help you learn about music business language and what constitutes a fair music publishing contract. Be sure to read What About Contracts? on page 36 for more information on contracts. See the Organizations section, beginning on page 303 of this book, for more information on the SGA and other songwriting groups.

When signing a contract, it's important to be aware of the music industry's unethical practitioners. The "song shark," as he's called, makes his living by asking a songwriter to pay to have a song published. The shark will ask for money to demo a song and promote it to radio stations; he may also ask for more than the standard 50% publisher's share or ask you to give up all rights to a song in order to have it published. Although none of these practices is illegal, it's certainly not ethical, and no successful publisher uses these methods. *Songwriter's Market* works to list only honest companies interested in hearing new material. (For more on "song sharks," see How Do I Avoid the Rip-Offs? on page 19.)

ADDITIONAL PUBLISHERS

There are **more publishers** located in other sections of the book! On page 156 use the list of Additional Publishers to find listings within other sections who are also music publishers.

◢ ABALORN MUSIC (ASCAP)

P.O. Box 5537, Kreole Station, Moss Point MS 39563-1537. (601)914-9413. "No collect calls." Estab. 1974. **Contact:** Joe F. Mitchell, executive vice president/general manager. First Vice President: Justin F. Mitchell. Second Vice President: Jayvean F. Mitchell. Music publisher and record company (Missile Records).

- Also see the listing for Bay Ridge Publishing in this section and the listing for Missile Records in the Record Companies section.

Affiliate(s) Bay Ridge Publishing Co. (BMI).

How to Contact *"Please don't send us anything until you contact us by phone or in writing and receive submission instructions. You must present your songs the correct way to get a reply.* **No registered mail—no exceptions! Standing in line to sign for your package wastes our time. Tracking your package is a service you can get by asking for it at your Post Office.** Always whenever you write to us, be sure you include a #10 business-size envelope addressed back to you with a first class USA postage stamp on the envelope. We reply back to you from the SASE you send to us. All songs sent for review must include sufficient return postage. No reply made back to you without SASE or return of material without sufficient return postage. **Absolutely no reply postcards—only SASE.** If you only write lyrics, do not submit. We only accept completed songs, so you must find a collaborator. We are not interested in reviewing homemade recordings." Prefers CD (first choice) or cassette with 3-8 songs and lyrics to songs submitted. Responds in 2 months. "A good quality demo recording will always get preference over a poor recording."

Music All types and styles of songs. "Mixed Up Love Affair," "Sweet Sexy Lady," and "My Love Just Fell Again" (singles) from *album title TBD* (album), written and recorded by Herb Lacy (blues); "Hello Heartbreak" and "You Owe Some Back to Me" (singles by Joe F. Mitchell), recorded by Ann Black (country); and "Rose Up On a Stem" (single by Joe F. Mitchell) from *My Kind of Country* (album), recorded by Jerry Piper (modern country), all released on Missile Records.

Tips "Songwriters and singers, we are in business to serve you. Our doors are open to you. If you want experience and know-how on your side to work with you, then we are who you are looking for. We go that extra mile for you. Working with the right people helps you to be successful by getting on the right track. Let us show you what we can do. Give us a call or write us today. Your professionally recorded album or 10-12 well-produced and well-written songs, that you have ready for radio, may have a chance to be placed with our contacts in the U.S.A. and foreign record companies or released on our label. We have gotten record deals for some recording artists previously that you have read about in the 2005, 2006 and 2007 issues of *Songwriter's Market*. Here are some of the current recording artists we have gotten record deals for: Karen Frazier (pop) of Ren & T (mother/daughter act) from Hyattsville, MD on Mr. Wonderful Productions of Louisville, KY; and Bernard Williams (gospel) from Lanett, AL, also on Mr. Wonderful Productions of Louisville, KY. Missile Records, Abalorn Music (ASCAP) and Bay Ridge Publishing Co. (BMI) are listed in some well-known publications such as the *Billboard International Buyer's Guide*, *Mix Master Directory*, *Industrial Source Book*, *Pollstar*, *Yellow Pages of Rock* and other publications. Some well-known recording artists born and raised in Mississippi include Elvis Presley, Conway Twitty, B.B. King and Faith Hill. The Moss Point, MS area music scene is also home to nationally-known rock group Three Doors Down, who sold more than 10 million of their CD albums and singles. Singers and songwriters thinking about doing professional recording, give us a call before you make that move. We can save you money, time, headaches, heartaches and troubles you may run into. We know what to do and how to do it to benefit you and get the best results."

◢ ABEAR PUBLISHING (BMI)/SONGTOWN PUBLISHING (ASCAP)

323 N. Walnut St., Murfreesboro TN 37130. (615)890-1878. Fax: (615)890-3771. E-mail: hebert@gmail.com. Web site: www.songtownpub.com. **Contact:** Ron Hebert, publisher. Estab. 2000. Pays standard royalty.

How to Contact Submit demo by mail. Unsolicited submissions are OK. Prefers CD of 5 songs with lyric sheets. "Finished demos only, please." Does not return material. Responds in 2 weeks if interested.

Music Mostly **country**, **country/pop**, **pop**, **dance**, and **Christian**.

▨ ◐ ▧ ACKEAN MUSIC PUBLISHING/PROMOTION/CRITIQUE (SOCAN)

5454 198th St., Suite 208, Langley BC V3A 1G2.(604)532-9203. E-mail: pamelaroyal47@shaw.ca. Web site: www.ackeanmusic.net. **Contact:** Pamela Royal, professional manager (country). Professional Managers: Kim McLeod (traditional country); Cristine Royal (instrumental country). Music publisher and Promotion/Critique. Estab. 2005. Publishes 6 songs/year. Publishes 3 new songwriters/year. Staff size: 2. Pays standard royalty of 50%.

Affiliate(s) Crowe Entertainment. "Crowe Entertainment is our co-publisher in Nashville"

How to Contact *Write first and obtain permission to submit a demo.*Prefers CD with 3 songs with lyric sheets and cover letter. Include SASE or SAE and IRC for outside United States. "Please include SASE, cover letter, and clean typed lyric sheets." Responds in 2 months.

Film & TV Places 2 songs/year in film. Music Supervisor: Joe Lenders (Minnot Lenters Music, Florida). Recently selected "Someone Like You" and "Heart on the Line" (singles by Angie Bull), recorded by Marie Willson, in *Terror Within* (film).

Music Mostly **country**, **traditional country**, and **instrumental country**; also **instrumental music for film**. Published "Someone Like You" and "The Cheater's Out of Town" (single by Angie Bull) from *Rock Hard Lovin'* (album), recorded by Marie Willson (traditional country), released independently in 2006; "Where My Truck Stops" (single) from *Where My Truck Stops* (album), written and recorded by Wolfe Milestone(country), released in 1999.

Tips "Professional demos only, best one to three songs, great voice. Keep the hook exciting. First impression is important. Serious writers only, please. We also pitch songs to TV/film/movie companies, so music should be broadcast quality. Interested also in instrumental music for film productions. Please have songs registered and copyrighted. Ackean Music is a new company and will work hard for the songwriters and artists we publish and promote. We also offer a critique service."

◐ ACUFF-ROSE MUSIC (BMI)

- Acuff-Rose Music has been sold to Sony Music and is not accepting submissions.

▧ ◌ ALEXANDER SR. MUSIC (BMI)

PMB 364, 7100 Lockwood Blvd., Boardman OH 44512. (330)726-8737. Fax: (330)726-8747. E-mail: dap@netdotcom.com. Web site: www.dapentertainment.com. **Contact:** Darryl Alexander, owner. Music publisher, record company (DAP Entertainment), music consulting, distribution and promotional services and record producer. Estab. 1992. Publishes 12-22 songs/year; publishes 2-4 new songwriters/year. Staff size: 3. Pays standard royalty.

- Also see the listing for DAP Entertainment in the Record Producers section of this book.

How to Contact *Write first and obtain permission to submit.* Prefers CD with 4 songs and lyric sheet. "We will accept finished masters (CD) for review." Include SASE. Responds in 2 months. "No phone calls or faxes please."

Film & TV Places 2 songs in TV/year. Music Supervisor: Darryl Alexander. Recently published "Love Never Fails in Saturday Night Live" (through DSM); "Material has been licensed for television and e-television."

Music Mostly **contemporary jazz** and **urban gospel**; also **R&B**. Does not want rock, gangsta rap, heavy metal or country. Published "Plumb Line" (single by Herb McMullan/Darryl Alexander) from *Diamond In The Sky* (album), recorded by Darryl Alexander (contemporary jazz); "3rd Eye" and "Too Late For Love" (singles) from *Diamond In The Sky* (album), written and recorded by Darryl Alexander (contemporary jazz), all released 2004 on DAP Entertainment.

Tips "Send only music in styles that we review. Submit your best songs and follow submission guidelines. Finished masters open up additional possibilities. Lead sheets may be requested for material we are interested in. Must have SASE if you wish to have CD returned. No phone calls, please. We have licensed music through the Brazilian Performance Rights Society."

☑ ☐ ALIAS JOHN HENRY TUNES (BMI)

11 Music Square E., Suite 607, Nashville TN 37203. (615)582-1782. E-mail: bobbyjohnhenry@gmail .com. **Contact:** Bobby John Henry, owner. Music publisher and record producer. Publishes 3 songs/ year; publishes 1 new songwriter/year. Staff size: 3. Pays standard royalty.

How to Contact Send by mail. Prefers cassette or CD with 3 songs and lyric sheet. Does not return material. Responds in 6 months only if interested.

Music Mostly **country**, **rock** and **alternative**; also **inspirational**, **gospel**, **Christian** and **jazz**. Does not want rap. Published *Mr. Right Now* (album by Kari Jorgensen), recorded by "Hieke" on Warner Bros. (rock); and *Nothing to Me* (album by B.J. Henry), recorded by Millie Jackson on Spring.

Tips "Focus and rewrite, rewrite, rewrite. We are looking into inspirational material, any style, also gospel and Christian music, any style. I like when the story is so good you don't even realize it's a spiritual or inspirational song. I'm not crazy about the 'glory be, glory be'type of song. I'm all gloried out! I'm also interested in hearing jazz standard types of songs that might be done with a big band. I don't know what I'll do with them, but if you have them, let me hear them. I don't know if anyone knows what to do with them, but I know some great singers that are singing new material in the Cole Porter/Johnny Mercer tradition. What have ya got?"

▣ ◨ ALPHA MUSIC INC. (BMI)

747 Chestnut Ridge Rd., Chestnut Ridge NY 10977. (845)356-0800. Fax: (845)356-0895. E-mail: alpha@trfmusic.com. Web site: www.trfmusic.com. **Contact:** Michael Nurko. Music publisher. Estab. 1931. Pays standard royalty.

Affiliate(s) Dorian Music Publishers, Inc. (ASCAP) and TRF Music Inc.

• Also see listing for TRF Production Music Libraries in the Advertising, Audiovisual & Commercial Music Firms section of this book.

How to Contact "We accept submissions of new compositions. Submissions are not returnable."

Music All categories, mainly **instrumental** and **acoustic** suitable for use as **production music**, including **theme and background music for television and film**. "Have published over 50,000 titles since 1931."

◨ AMERICATONE INTERNATIONAL (ASCAP)

1817 Loch Lomond Way, Las Vegas NV 89102-4437. (702)384-0030. Fax: (702)382-1926. E-mail: jjj@americatone.com. Web site: www.americatone.com. President: Joe Jan Jaros. Estab. 1975. Publishes 25 songs/year. Pays variable royalty.

Affiliate(s) Americatone Records International, Christy Records International USA, Rambolt Music International (ASCAP).

• Also see the listing for Americatone Records International in the Record Companies section of this book.

How to Contact Submit demo by mail. Unsolicited submissions OK. Prefers CDs, "studio production with top sound recordings." Include SASE. Responds in 1 month.

Music Mostly **country**, **R&B**, **Spanish** and **classic ballads**. Published *Explosion* (album), recorded by Sam Trippe; *A New Life Start* (album), by Gabriel Oscar Rosati; *Many Ways to Go* (album), by Bill Perkins; and *Jazz in the Rain* (album), by the Rain Jazz Band; all on Americatone International Records.

☐ ANTELOPE PUBLISHING INC. (BMI)

P.O. Box 55, Rowayton CT 06853. **Contact:** Tony LaVorgna, owner/president. Music publisher. Estab. 1982. Publishes 5-10 new songs/year; publishes 3-5 new songwriters/year. Pays standard royalty.

How to Contact Submit demo by mail. Unsolicited submissions are OK. Prefers cassette with lead sheet. Does not return material. Responds in 1 month "only if interested."

Music Only **bebop** and **1940s swing**. Does not want anything electronic. Published "Somewhere Near" (single by Tony LaVorgna) from *Just For My Friends* (album), recorded by Jeri Brown (easy listening); "Cookie Monster" and "The Lady From Mars" (singles by Tony LaVorgna) from *Just For My Friends* (album), recorded by Tony LaVorgna (jazz/easy listening), released 2007 on Antelope.

Tips "Put your best song first with a short intro."

☐ AUDIO MUSIC PUBLISHERS (ASCAP)

449 N. Vista St., Los Angeles CA 90036. (818)362-9853. Fax: (323)653-7670. E-mail: parlirec@aol.com. Web site: www.parliamentrecords.com. **Contact:** Len Weisman, professional manager. Owner: Ben Weisman. Music publisher, record company and record producer (The Weisman Production Group). Estab. 1962. Publishes 25 songs/year; publishes 10-15 new songwriters/year. Staff size: 10. Pays standard royalty.

• Also see the listings for Queen Esther Music Publishers in the Music Publishers section of this book; the Weisman Production Group in the Record Producers section of this book and Parliament Records in the Record Companies section of this book.

How to Contact Submit demo by mail. Unsolicited submissions are OK. "No permission needed." Prefers CD with 3-10 songs and lyric sheet. "We do not return unsolicited material without SASE. Don't query first; just send CD." Responds in 6 weeks. "We listen; we don't write back. If we like your material we will telephone you."

Music Mostly **pop** and **R&B**; also **dance**, **funk**, **soul** and **gospel**. Does not want heavy metal. "Crazy About You" (single) and *Where Is Love* (album), both written by Curtis Womack; and *Don't Make Me Walk Away* (album by Debe Gunn), all recorded by Valerie (R&B) on Kon Kord. Other artists include Jewel With Love (gospel), Chosen Recovery Ministry (gospel), Rapture 7 (gospel), Winds of Faith (gospel), and E'Mory (R&B).

🅽 ☑ AVI 39563 MUSIC (ASCAP)

P.O. Box 5537, Kreole Station, Moss Point MS 39563-1537. (601)914-9413 or (228)235-8092 (cell). "No collect calls, please." **Contact:** Jemiah F. Mitchell, president/owner. Estab. 2003. Music publisher and record company (Avitor Music International Records).Releases 10 singles and 5 LPs/year. Pays negotable royalty to artists on contract; statutory rate to publisher per song on record. "Avitor Music has National and International distribution."

• Also see the listing for Avitor Music International in the Record Companies section of this book.

Affiliate(s) AVI 39563 Music (ASCAP).

How to Contact *Write or call first for submission instructions.* " Always whenever you write, be sure you include a #10 business-size envelope addressed back to yourself with a first-class USA postage stamp on the envelope. A reply will come back to you using the SASE you include in your mailing when you write. *Absolutely no reply postcards—only SASE.* If you only write lyrics, do not submit; only complete songs reviewed, so you must find a collaborator. Not interested in reviewing homemade recordings." Prefers CD (first choice) or cassette with 3-10 songs along with lyrics to songs submitted. Responds in 2 months.

Music Mostly singers and songwriters of **country**, **modern country today**, **mainstream**, **rock**, **Americana**, **hip-hop**, **rap**, **R&B**, **bluegrass**, **hot A/C**, **adult A/C**, **urban**, **jazz**, **blues**, **teen**, **pop**, **gospel**, **top 40**, **Spanish**, **Spanish R&B**, **Spanish pop**, **Spanish hip-hop**, and **world music**. "We will review traditional country. If there is a convincing market for your music, then we are basically open to all genres.'' Released ''6 O'Clock,'' ''Cowboy Mix,'' and ''Second Chance'' (singles) from *Aron Dees* (album), written and recorded by Aron Dees (modern country), released on Avitor. ''On July 4, 2007, Aron Dees played as opening act for Universal Records recording artist Keith Anderson before a crowd of 6,500 people at the University of Wyoming. Aron Dees' Web site is www.arondees.com.''

Tips ''We work with artists on trying to get financial support through creative means. Artists submitting material that is accepted must be ready and willing to work together with us to create a buzz. We are looking for serious-minded artists who are talented and want to make a career for themselves. If you are a team player and know what you want to accomplish, then by all means, give us a call or write us today. You matter to us and we will respond ASAP.''

◖ BAIRD MUSIC GROUP (BMI)

P.O. Box 42, 1 Main St., Ellsworth PA 15331. **Contact:** Ron Baird, president. Music publisher, record company (La Ron Ltd. Records), record producer (Ron Baird Enterprises). Estab. 1999. Publishes 5-12 songs/year. Pays standard royalty.

Affiliate(s) Baird Family Music (ASCAP).

- Also see the listing for Ron Baird Enterprises in the Record Producers section of this book.

How to Contact Submit demo tape by mail. Unsolicited submissions are OK. ''No certified mail.'' Prefers cassette only with 2-4 songs and lyric sheet. Does not return submissions. Responds only if interested.

Music Mostly **country** and **country rock**. Does not want hip-hop, gospel/religious or R&B.

Tips ''Don't give up!''

◖ BAITSTRING MUSIC (ASCAP)

2622 Kirtland Rd., Brewton AL 36426. (251)867-2228. **Contact:** Roy Edwards, president. Music publisher and record company (Bolivia Records). Estab. 1972. Publishes 20 songs/year; publishes 10 new songwriters/year. Hires staff songwriters. Pays standard royalty.

Affiliate(s) Cheavoria Music Co. (BMI).

- Also the listings for Cheavroia Music in this section, Bolivia Records in the Record Companies section, and Known Artist Productions in the Record Producers section of this book.

How to Contact Submit demo by mail. Unsolicited submissions are OK. Prefers CD with 3 songs and lyric sheet. Does not return material. Responds in 1 month.

Music Mostly **R&B**, **pop** and **easy listening**; also **country** and **gospel**. Published ''Forever and Always,'' written and recorded by Jim Portwood (pop); and ''Make Me Forget'' (by Horace Linsley) and ''Never Let Me Go'' (by Cheavoria Edwards), both recorded by Bobbie Roberson (country), all on Bolivia Records.

Tips ''We need some good gospel.''

◻ BARKIN' FOE THE MASTER'S BONE (ASCAP)

405 Broadway St. Suite 900, Cincinnati OH 45202-3329. (513)241-6489. Fax: (513)241-9226. E-mail: autoredcurtis@aol.com. Web site: www.1stbook.com. Company Owner (rock, R&B): Kevin Curtis. Professional Managers: Shonda Barr (country, jazz, pop, rap); Betty Barr (gospel, soul, soft rock). Music publisher. Estab. 1989. Publishes 4 songs/year; publishes 1 new songwriter/year. Staff size: 4. Pays standard royalty.

Affiliate(s) Beat Box Music (ASCAP) and Feltstar (BMI).

How to Contact Submit demo by mail. Unsolicited submissions are OK. Prefers CD (or VHS videocassette) with 3 songs. Include SASE. Responds in 2 weeks.

Music Mostly **top 40** and **pop**; also **soul**, **gospel**, **rap** and **jazz**. Does not want classical. Published ''Lover, Lover'' (single by J Tea/Jay B./Skylar) from The Time Has Come (album), recorded by J-Trey (rap), released 2003 on East Side Records; ''Been A Long Time'' (single by J Tea/Jay B./

Skylar), from The Time Has Come (album), recorded by J-Trey (rap), released 2003 on East Side Records; ''No Worries'' (single by Mejestic/7-Starr/D-Smooy/Hardhead), from Home Grown (album), recorded by Low Down Boyz (rap), released 2002 on Untamed Records.

◪ BAY RIDGE PUBLISHING CO. (BMI)

P.O. Box 5537, Kreole Station, Moss Point MS 39563-1537. (601)914-9413. ''No collect calls.'' Estab. 1974. **Contact**: Joe F. Mitchell, executive vice president/general manager. First Vice President: Justin F. Mitchell. Second Vice President: Jayvean F. Mitchell. Music publisher and record company (Missile Records).

- Also see the listing for Abalorn Music in this section and the listing for Missile Records in the Record Companies section of this book.

Affiliate(s) Abalorn Music (ASCAP).

How to Contact ''*Please don't send us anything until you contact us by phone or in writing and receive submission instructions. You must present your songs the correct way to get a reply.* **No registered mail—no exceptions! Standing in line to sign for your package wastes our time. Tracking your package is a service you can get by asking for it at your Post Office.** Always whenever you write to us, be sure you include a #10 business-size envelope addressed back to you with a first class USA postage stamp on the envelope. We reply back to you from the SASE you send to us. All songs sent for review must include sufficient return postage. No reply made back to you without SASE or return of material without sufficient return postage. **Absolutely no reply postcards—only SASE.** If you only write lyrics, do not submit. We only accept completed songs, so you must find a collaborator. We are not interested in reviewing homemade recordings.'' Prefers CD (first choice) or cassette with 3-8 songs and lyrics to songs submitted. Responds in 2 months. ''A good quality demo recording will always get preference over a poor recording.''

Music All types and styles of songs. ''Mixed Up Love Affair,'' ''Sweet Sexy Lady,'' and ''My Love Just Fell Again'' (singles) from *album title TBD* (album), written and recorded by Herb Lacy (blues); ''Hello Heartbreak'' and ''You Owe Some Back to Me'' (singles by Joe F. Mitchell), recorded by Ann Black (country); and ''Rose Up On a Stem'' (single by Joe F. Mitchell) from *My Kind of Country* (album), recorded by Jerry Piper (modern country), all released on Missile Records.

Tips ''Songwriters and singers, we are in business to serve you. Our doors are open to you. If you want experience and know-how on your side to work with you, then we are who you are looking for. We go that extra mile for you. Working with the right people helps you to be successful by getting on the right track. Let us show you what we can do. Give us a call or write us today. Your professionally recorded album or 10-12 well-produced and well-written songs, that you have ready for radio, may have a chance to be placed with our contacts in the U.S.A. and foreign record companies or released on our label. We have gotten record deals for some recording artists previously that you have read about in the 2005, 2006 and 2007 issues of *Songwriter's Market*. Here are some of the current recording artists we have gotten record deals for: Karen Frazier (pop) of Ren & T (mother/daughter act) from Hyattsville, MD on Mr. Wonderful Productions of Louisville, KY; and Bernard Williams (gospel) from Lanett, AL, also on Mr. Wonderful Productions of Louisville, KY. Missile Records, Abalorn Music (ASCAP) and Bay Ridge Publishing Co. (BMI) are listed in some well-known publications such as the *Billboard International Buyer's Guide*, *Mix Master Directory*, *Industrial Source Book*, *Pollstar*, *Yellow Pages of Rock* and other publications. Some well-known recording artists born and raised in Mississippi include Elvis Presley, Conway Twitty, B.B. King and Faith Hill. The Moss Point, MS area music scene is also home to nationally-known rock group Three Doors Down, who sold more than 10 million of their CD albums and singles. Singers and songwriters thinking about doing professional recording, give us a call before you make that move. We can save you money, time, headaches, heartaches and troubles you may run into. We know what to do and how to do it to benefit you and get the best results.''

◨ ◪ BIG FISH MUSIC PUBLISHING GROUP (ASCAP, BMI)

11927 Magnolia Blvd., Suite 3, N. Hollywood CA 91607. (818)984-0377. President, CEO and Music Publisher: Chuck Tennin. Producer: Gary Black (country, pop, adult contemporary, rock, crossover songs, other styles). Professional Music Manager: Lora Sprague (jazz, New Age, instrumental, pop rock, R&B). Professional Music Manager: B.J. (pop, TV, film and special projects). Professional Music & Vocal Consultant: Zell Black (country, pop, gospel, rock, blues). Producer Independent Artists: Darryl Harrelson—Major Label Entertainment (country, pop and other genres). Nashville Music Associate: Ron Hebert (Abear/Songtown Publishing). Songwriter/Consultant: Jerry Zanandrea (Z Best Muzic). Music publisher, record company (California Sun Records) and production company. Estab. 1971. Publishes 10-20 songs/year; publishes 5-10 new songwriters/year. Staff size: 7. Pays standard royalty. "We also license songs and music copyrights to users of music, especially TV and film."

Affiliate(s) Big Fish Music (BMI) and California Sun Music (ASCAP).

How to Contact *Write first and obtain permission to submit.* Include SASE for reply. *"Please do not call.* After permission to submit is confirmed, we will assign and forward to you a submission code number allowing you to submit up to 4 songs maximum, preferably on CD or cassette. Include a properly addressed cover letter, signed and dated, with your source of referral (*Songwriter's Market*) with your assigned submission code number and SASE for reply and/or return of material. Include lyrics. *Unsolicited material will not be accepted.* That is our Submission Policy to review outside and new material." Responds in 2 weeks.

Film & TV Places 6 songs in TV/year. Recently published "Even the Angels Knew" (by Cathy Carlson/Craig Lackey/Marty Axelrod); "Stop Before We Start" (by J.D. Grieco); "Oh Santa" (by Christine Bridges/John Deaver), all recorded by The Black River Girls in *Passions* (NBC); licensed "A Christmas Wish" (by Ed Fry/Eddie Max), used in *Passions* (NBC); "Girls Will Be Girls" (by Cathy Carlson/John LeGrande), recorded by The Black River Girls, used in *All My Children* (ABC); "The Way You're Drivin' Me" and "Ain't No Love 'Round Here" (by Jerry Zanandrea), both recorded by The Black River Girls, used in *Passions* (NBC); "Since You Stole My Heart" (by Rick Coimbra/Jamey Whiting), used in *Passions* (NBC); "Good Time To Fly," "All I Need Is A Highway," and "Eyes Of The Children" (by Wendy Martin), used in *Passions* (NBC); "It's An Almost Perfect Christmas" (by Michael Martin), used in *Passions* (NBC).

Music Country, including **country pop**, **country A/C** and **country crossover** with a cutting edge; also **pop**, **pop ballads**, **adult contemporary**, **uplifting**, **praise**, **worship**, **spiritual**, and **inspirational adult contemporary gospel** with a powerful message, **instrumental background and theme music** for TV & films, **New Age/instrumental jazz** and **novelty**, **orchestral classical**, **R&B** and **Children's music** for all kinds of commercial use. Published "If Wishes Were Horses" (single by Billy O'Hara); "Purple Bunny Honey" (single by Robert Lloyd/Jim Love); "Leavin' You For Me" (single by J.D. Grieco); "Move That Train" (single by Robert Porter); "Happy Landing" (by T. Brawley/B. Woodrich); "Girls Will Be Girls" (single by Cathy Carlson/John LeGrande); "You Should Be Here With Me" (single by Ken McMeans); "Stop Before We Start" (single by J.D. Grieco); "The Way You're Drivin' Me" and "Ain't No Love 'Round Here" (singles by Jerry Zanandrea), all recorded by Black River Girls on California Sun Records; "Let Go and Let God" and "There's A Power in Prayer" (singles by Corinne Porter/Molly Finkle), recorded by Molly Pasutti, released on California Sun Records; "Good Time To Fly," "All I Need Is A Highway," and "Eyes Of The Children" (singles by Wendy Martin); "Don't Give Up," "Sinner's Prayer," and "I'm Living A Brand New Life" (singles) from *Now Is The Time For Living A Brand New Life* (album), written and recorded by Zell Black.

Tips "Demo should be professional, high quality, clean, simple, dynamic, and must get the song across on the first listen. Good clear vocals, a nice melody, a good musical feel, good musical arrangement, strong lyrics and chorus—a unique, catchy, clever song that sticks with you. Looking for unique country and pop songs with a different edge that can crossover to the mainstream market for ongoing Nashville music projects and songs for a hot female country trio that crosses over to adult contemporary and pop with great lush, warm harmonies that reach out to middle America and baby boomers and their grown up children (25 to 65). Also, catchy up-tempo songs with an attitude, meaningful lyrics (Shania Twain style), and unique pop songs (Celine Dion style) for upcoming album projects and song pitches. Also, soundtrack music of all types (melodic, uplifting, moody, mystique, orchestral, mind soothing, pretty, action packed, etc.) for new film production company and upcoming film and TV projects. Demo should be broadcast quality.''

◙ BMG MUSIC PUBLISHING (ASCAP)

245 5th Ave. 8th Floor, New York NY 10016. (212)287-1300. Fax: (212)930-4263. Web site: www.b mgmusicsearch.com. **Contact:** Adam Epstein (pop/rock). **Beverly Hills office:** 8750 Wilshire Blvd., Beverly Hills CA 90211. (310)358-4700. Fax: (310)358-4727. **Contact:** Monti Olson (pop/rock), Brad Aarons (pop/rock), or Derrick Thompson (urban). **Nashville office:** 1600 Division St. Suite 225, Nashville TN 37203. (615)687-5800. Fax: (615)687-5839. Music publisher.
How to Contact *BMG Music Publishing does not accept unsolicited submissions.*
Music Published works by Maroon 5, Christina Aguilera, Coldplay, Nelly, Britney Spears, Keane, R. Kelly, Ne-Yo, and The All-American Rejects.

◙ BOURNE CO. MUSIC PUBLISHERS (ASCAP)

5 W. 37th St., New York NY 10018. (212)391-4300. Fax: (212)391-4306. E-mail: bourne@bournemu sic.com. Web site: www.bournemusic.com. **Contact:** Professional Manager. Music publisher. Estab. 1919. Publishes educational material and popular music.
Affiliate(s) ABC Music, Ben Bloom, Better Half, Bogat, Burke & Van Heusen, Goldmine, Harborn, Lady Mac and Murbo Music.
How to Contact *Does not accept unsolicited submissions.*
Music Piano/vocal, **band pieces** and **choral pieces**. Published ''Amen'' and ''Mary's Little Boy Child'' (singles by Hairston); ''When You Wish Upon a Star'' (single by Washington/Harline); and ''San Antonio Rose'' (single by Bob Willis, arranged John Cacavas).

◻ ALLAN BRADLEY MUSIC (BMI)

835 E. Buckeyewood Ave., Orange CA 92865. (714)685-9958. E-mail: melodi4ever@earthlink.net. Web site: www.ablmusic.com. **Contact:** Allan Licht, owner. Music publisher, record company (ABL Records) and record producer. Estab. 1993. Publishes 10 songs/year; publishes 5 new songwriters/year. Staff size: 2. Pays standard royalty.
Affiliate(s) Lichtenfeld Music (ASCAP).
   • Also see the listing for ABL Records in the Record Companies section of this book.
How to Contact Submit demo by mail. Unsolicited submissions are OK. Prefers CD with 3 songs and lyric sheet. ''Send only unpublished works.'' Does not return material. Responds in 2 weeks only if interested.
Music Mostly **A/C**, **pop** and **R&B**; also **country** and **Christian contemporary**. Does not want hard rock. Published *Time to Go* (album), written and recorded by Alan Douglass; *The Sun that Follows the Rain* (album by R.K. Holler/Rob Driggers), recorded by Michael Cavanaugh (pop), released 1999; *Only In My Mind* (album by Jonathon Hansen), recorded by Allan Licht, all on ABL Records.
Tips ''Be open to suggestions from well-established publishers. Please send only songs that have Top 10 potential. Only serious writers are encouraged to submit.''

◻ BRANDON HILLS MUSIC, LLC (BMI)/HEATH BROWN MUSIC (ASCAP)

N. 3425 Searle County Line Rd., Brandon WI 53919. (920)398-3279 or (cell) (920)570-1076. E-mail: marta@dotnet.com. **Contact:** Mike Heath, vice president. Music publishers. Estab. 2005. Publishes 4 new songwriters/year. Staff size: 2. Pays standard royalty of 50%.

How to Contact Submit demo package by mail. Unsolicited submissions are OK. Prefers CD with 1-4 songs and cover letter. Does not return submissions. Responds only if interested.

Music Mostly **country (traditional, modern, country rock)**, **contemporary Christian**, **blues**; also **children's** and **bluegrass**. Does not want rap or hip-hop.

Tips "We prefer studio-produced CDs. The lyrics and the CD must match. Cover letter, lyrics, and CD should have a professional look. Demos should have vocals up front and every word should be distinguishable. Please make sure your lyrics match your song. Submit only your best. The better the demo, the better of chance of getting your music published and recorded."

BRANSON COUNTRY MUSIC PUBLISHING (BMI)

P.O. Box 2527, Broken Arrow OK 74013. (918)455-9442. Fax: (918)451-1965. E-mail: bransoncm@aol.com. **Contact:** Betty Branson, A&R. Music publisher. Estab. 1997. Publishes 5 songs/year; publishes 4-5 new songwriters/year. Pays standard royalty.

Affiliate(s) High Lonesome Country (ASCAP).

How to Contact Submit demo package by mail with lyric sheet. Unsolicited submissions are OK. Prefers CD or cassette with 3-5 songs and lyric sheet. Does not return material. Responds in 3 weeks only if interested.

Music Mostly **traditional country** and **upbeat country**. Published "Sharin Sharon" (CD single), written and recorded by Roger Wayne Manard (country), released 2001; "Odds Are" (video single by Dale Ray/Allison Rae), recorded by Chris Lowther and the Sidewinder Band (country), released 2004; "Toy Soldier" (CD single by Teena Eaton), recorded by Carol Shull (country), released 2004; "Happy Mother's Day, Momma" (CD single), written and recorded by Jerry James, released 2006; and "Sharin' the Love," "She Goes Out," and "Miss Wonderful" (singles), written and recorded by Jackson Ray; "But I Did" (CD single), written and recorded by Robert Presley.

Tips "Send good quality demo capable of competing with airplay top 40. Put your 'attention getter' up front and build from that point as the listener will give you about 10-15 seconds to continue listening or turn you off. Use a good hook and keep coming back to it."

BSW RECORDS (BMI)

P.O. Box 2297, Universal City TX 78148. (210)653-3989. E-mail: bswr18@wmconnect.com. Web site: bsw-records.com. **Contact:** Frank Willson, president. Music publisher, record company and record producer (Frank Willson). Estab. 1987. Publishes 26 songs/year; publishes 14 new songwriters/year. Staff size: 5. Pays standard royalty.

Affiliate(s) WillTex Music and Universal Music Marketing (BMI).

• This company has been named Record Label of the Year ('94-'01) by the Country Music Association of America. Also see the listings for BSW Records in the Record Companies section, Frank Wilson in the Record Producers section, and Universal Music Marketing in the Managers & Booking Agents section of this book.

How to Contact Submit demo package by mail. Unsolicited submissions are OK. Prefers CD with 3 songs, lyric sheet and cover letter. Include SASE. Responds in 2 months.

Film & TV Places 2 songs in film/year.

Music Mostly **country**, **blues**, and **soft rock**. Does not want rap. Published *These Four Walls* (album), written and recorded by Dan Kimmel (country); and *I Cried My Last Tear* (album by T. Toliver), recorded by Candeeland (country), both released 1999 on BSW Records. "Visit our Web site for an up-to-date listing of releases."

BUCKEYE MUSIC GROUP (ASCAP)

5695 Cherokee Rd., Cleveland OH 44124-3047. (440)442-7777. Fax: (440)442-1904. **Contact:** John J. Selvaggio (country) or Joseph R. Silver (rock and roll). Music publisher. Estab. 1998. Publishes 1 song/year. Staff size: 4. Pays standard royalty.

How to Contact Submit demo package by mail. Unsolicited submissions are OK. Prefers cassette or CD/CDR along with VHS videocassette. "Send your best three songs with a lead sheet." Include SASE. Responds in 3 weeks.

Music Mostly **country**, **rock** and **R&B**; also **jingles** and **ballads**.

Tips "Write from the heart, not from the head. Strive to be different."

⊘ BUG MUSIC, INC. (ASCAP, BMI)

7750 Sunset Blvd., Los Angeles CA 90046. (323)969-0988. Fax: (323)969-0968. E-mail: buginfo@bu gmusic.com. Web site: www.bugmusic.com. Vice President of Creative: Eddie Gomez. Creative Manager: Mara Schwartz. Creative Assistant: Nissa Pedraza. **Nashville:** 1910 Acklen Ave., Nashville TN 37212. (615)279-0180. Fax: (615)279-0184. Creative Director: John Allen; Creative Manager: Drew Hale. **New York:** 347 W. 36th St., Suite 1203, New York NY 10018. (212)643-0925. Fax: (212)643-0897. Senior Vice President: Garry Valletri. Music publisher. Estab. 1975. "We handle administration."

Affiliate(s) Bughouse (ASCAP).

How to Contact *Does not accept unsolicited submissions.*

Music All genres. Published "You Were Mine" (by E. Erwin/M. Seidel), recorded by Dixie Chicks on Monument.

☐ BURIED TREASURE MUSIC (ASCAP)

524 Doral Country Dr., Nashville TN 37221. **Contact:** Scott Turner, owner/manager. Music publisher and record producer (Aberdeen Productions). Estab. 1972. Publishes 30-50 songs/year; publishes 3-10 new songwriters/year. Pays standard royalty.

Affiliate(s) Captain Kidd Music (BMI).

- Also see the listing for Aberdeen Productions in the Record Producers section of this book.

How to Contact Submit demo by mail. Unsolicited submissions are OK. Prefers cassette or VHS videocassette with 1-4 songs and lyric sheet. Responds in 2 weeks. "Always enclose SASE if answer is expected."

Music Mostly **country**, **country/pop** and **MOR**. Does not want rap, hard rock, metal, hip-hop or alternative. Published "I Still Can't Say Goodbye" (single by Bunn/Moore) from *Chicago Wind* (album), recorded by Merle Haggard (country), released 2005 on Capitol; "Please Mr. Music Man" (single by Scott Turner/Audie Murphy) and "My Baby's Coming Home" (Scott Turner/Buddy Holly/Harry Nilsson) from *Hollywood Dreamer* (album), recorded by Harry Nilsson (rock/pop), released 2006 on E-Music.

Tips *"DO NOT* send songs in envelopes that are 15×20, or by registered mail. The post office will not accept tapes in regular business-size envelopes. Also, always enclose a SASE. Submission without same aren't answered because of the wealth of tapes that come in."

☐ CALIFORNIA COUNTRY MUSIC (BMI)

112 Widmar Pl., Clayton CA 94517. (925)833-4680. **Contact:** Edgar J. Brincat, owner. Music publisher and record company (Roll On Records). Estab. 1985. Staff size: 1. Pays standard royalty. Affiliate(s) Sweet Inspirations Music (ASCAP).

- Also see the listing for Roll On Records in the Record Companies section of this book.

How to Contact Submit demo by mail. Unsolicited submissions are OK. "Do not call or write. Any calls will be returned collect to caller." Prefers CD or cassette with 3 songs and lyric sheet. Include SASE. Responds in 6 weeks.

Music Mostly **MOR**, **contemporary country** and **pop**. Does not want rap, metal or rock. Published *For Realities Sake* (album by F.L. Pittman/R. Barretta) and *Maddy* (album by F.L. Pittman/M. Weeks), both recorded by Ron Banks & L.J. Reynolds on Life & Bellmark Records; and *Quarter Past Love* (album by Irwin Rubinsky/Janet Fisher), recorded by Darcy Dawson on NNP Records.

N ⊘ CHEAVORIA MUSIC CO. (BMI)

2622 Kirtland Rd., Brewton AL 36426. (251)867-2228. **Contact:** Roy Edwards, president. Music publisher, record company (Bolivia Records) and record producer (Known Artist Production). Estab. 1972. Publishes 20 new songwriters/year. Pays standard royalty.
Affiliate(s) Baitstring Music (ASCAP).
  • Also see the listings for Baitstring Music in this section, Bolivia Records in the Record Companies section, and Known Artists Productions in the record Producers sections of this book.
How to Contact Write first and obtain permission to submit. Prefers CD with 3 songs and lyric sheet. Does not return material. Responds in 1 month.
Music Mostly **R&B**, **pop** and **country**; also **ballads** and **gospel**. Published ''Forever and Always'' (single), written and recorded by Jim Portwood on Bolivia Records (country).
Tips ''We need some good gospel.''

⊘ CHRISTMAS & HOLIDAY MUSIC (BMI)

24351 Grass St., Lake Forest CA 92630. (949)859-1615. E-mail: justinwilde@christmassongs.com. Web site: www.christmassongs.com. **Contact:** Justin Wilde, president. Music publisher. Estab. 1980. Publishes 8-12 songs/year; publishes 8-12 new songwriters/year. Staff size: 1. ''All submissions must be complete songs (i.e., music and lyrics).'' Pays standard royalty.
Affiliate(s) Songcastle Music (ASCAP).
How to Contact Submit demo CD or cassette by mail. Unsolicited submissions are OK. *Do not call. Do not send unsolicited mp3s or links to Web sites.* See Web site for submission guidelines. ''First class mail only. Registered or certified mail not accepted.'' Prefers CD or cassette with no more than 3 songs with lyric sheets. Do not send lead sheets or promotional material, bios, etc.'' Include SASE but does not return material out of the US. Responds only if interested.
Film & TV Places 4-5 songs in TV/year. Published ''Mr. Santa Claus'' in *Casper's Haunted Christmas*.
Music Strictly **Christmas**, **Halloween**, **Hanukkah**, **Mother's Day**, **Thanksgiving**, **Father's Day** and **New Year's Eve music** in every style imaginable: easy listening, rock, R&B, pop, blues, jazz, country, reggae, rap, children's secular or religious. *Please do not send anything that isn't a holiday song.* Published ''It Must Have Been the Mistletoe'' (single by Justin Wilde/Doug Konecky) from *Christmas Memories* (album), recorded by Barbra Streisand (pop Christmas), released 2001 by Columbia; ''What Made the Baby Cry?'' (single by Toby Keith) and ''You've Just Missed Christmas'' (single by Penny Lea/Buzz Smith/Bonnie Miller) from *The Vikki Carr Christmas Album* (album), recorded by Vikki Carr (holiday/Christmas), released 2000 on Delta; and ''Mr. Santa Claus'' (single by James Golseth) from *Casper's Haunted Christmas* soundtrack (album), recorded by Scotty Blevins (Christmas), released 2000 on Koch International.
Tips ''We only sign one out of every 200 submissions. Please be selective. If a stranger can hum your melody back to you after hearing it twice, it has 'standard' potential. Couple that with a lyric filled with unique, inventive imagery, that stands on its own, even without music. Combine the two elements, and workshop the finished result thoroughly to identify weak points. Submit to us only when the song is polished to perfection. Submit positive lyrics only. Avoid negative themes like 'Blue Christmas'.''

⊘ CHRYSALIS MUSIC GROUP (ASCAP, BMI)

8500 Melrose Ave., Suite 207, Los Angeles CA 90069. (310)652-0066. Fax: (310)652-5428. Web site: www.chrysalismusic.com. **Contact:** Mark Friedman, vice president of A&R. Music publisher. Estab. 1968.
How to Contact *Chrysalis Music does not accept any submissions.*
Music Published ''Sum 41'' (single), written and recorded by OutKast; ''Light Ladder'' (single), written and recorded by David Gray. Administer, David Lee Roth, Andrea Boccelli, Velvet Revolver, and Johnta Austin.

◪ COAL HARBOR MUSIC (BMI)

P.O. Box 148027, Nashville TN 37214-8027. (616)883-2020. E-mail: info@coalharborbmusic.com. Web site: www.coalharbormusic.com. **Contact:** Jerry Ray Wells, president. Music publisher, Record company (Coal Harbor Music), Record producer (Jerry Ray Wells), also recording studio, demo services, sheet music, number charts, management and booking services, artist development. Estab. 1990. Publishes 28 songs/year; publishes 3 new songwriters/year. Staff size: 2. Pays standard royalty.

- Also see the listing for Coal Harbor Music in the Record Companies Record section of this book.

How to Contact *Contact first via e-mail to obtain permission to submit a demo.* Send CD and SASE with lyric sheet and cover letter. Does not return submissions. Only responds if interested.

Music Mostly **country**, **gospel** and **bluegrass**; also **contemporary Christian**, **Christmas**, **patriotic**, **comedy** and **pop/rock**. Does not want heavy metal, rap, hard rock/grunge. Released "Forever True" (single) written by Ogie De Guzman, recorded by Back on Track (contemporary Christian) released 2005 on Tribute Family Corporation label; "So Good to Know" (single) from *All I Need* (album), written and recorded by Damon Westfaul (country Gospel), released 2004 on Coal Harbor/Shoreline Music; "You" (single) from *Unraveled* (album), written and recorded by Anne Borgen (contemporary Christian), released 2004 on Coal Harbor.

Tips "Write from the heart—the listener knows. Join songwriter organizations, go to seminars, co-write, etc. When submitting material send everything on one cassette or CD. Don't send two CDs and one cassette and tell us what song or track numbers to listen to. We don't have time. Put your best song first, even if it is a ballad. Keep writing; we ARE looking for GREAT songs!"

◪ COME ALIVE COMMUNICATIONS, INC. (ASCAP)

348 Valley Rd., Suite A, P.O. Box 436, West Grove PA 19390-0436. (610)869-3660. Fax: (610)869-3660. E-mail: info@comealivemusic.com. Web site: www.comealivemusic.com. Professional Managers: Joseph L. Hooker (pop, rock, jazz); Bridget G. Hylak (spiritual, country, classical). Music publisher, record producer and record company. Estab. 1985. Publishes 4 singles/year. Staff: 7. Pays standard royalty of 50%.

- Come Alive Communications received a IHS Ministries Award in 1996, John Lennon Songwriting Contest winnter, 2003.

How to Contact *Call first to obtain permission to submit a demo.* For song publishing submissions, prefers CD with 3 songs, lyric sheet, and cover letter. Does not return submissions. Responds only if interested.

Music Mostly **pop**, **easy listening**, **contemporary Christian**, and **patriotic**; also **country** and **spiritual**. Does not want obscene, suggestive, violent, or morally offensive lyrics. Produced "In Search of America" (single) from *Long Road to Freedom* (album), written and recorded by J. Hooker (patriotic), released 2003 on ComeAliveMusic.com.

◪ COPPERFIELD MUSIC GROUP/PENNY ANNIE MUSIC (BMI)/TOP BRASS MUSIC (ASCAP)/BIDDY BABY MUSIC (SESAC)

1400 South St., Nashville TN 37212. (615)726-3100. E-mail: ken@copperfieldmusic.com. Web site: www.copperfieldmusic.com. **Contact:** Ken Biddy, president/CEO.

How to Contact Contact first and obtain permission to submit a demo. Does not return submissions. Responds only if interested.

Music Mostly **country**; also **pop**, and **modern bluegrass**. Does not want rap or heavy/metal/rock. Recently published "Daddy Won't Sell the Farm" from *Tattoos and Scars* (album), recorded by Montgomery Gentry (country).

✅ 🔲 CORELLI MUSIC GROUP (BMI/ASCAP)

P.O. Box 2314, Tacoma WA 98401-2314. (253)536-6751. E-mail: JerryCorelli@CorelliMusicGroup.c om. Web site: www.CorelliMusicGroup.com. **Contact:** Jerry Corelli, owner. Music publisher, record company (Omega III Records), record producer (Jerry Corelli/Angels Dance Studio) and booking agency (Tone Deaf Booking). Estab. 1996. Publishes 12 songs/year; publishes 6 new songwriters/ year. Staff size: 3. Pays standard royalty.

Affiliate(s) My Angel's Songs (ASCAP); Corelli's Music Box (BMI).

How to Contact Submit demo by mail. Unsolicited submissions are OK. "No phone calls, e-mails, or letters asking to submit." Prefers CD with 3 songs, lyric sheet and cover letter. *"We DO NOT accept mp3s vie e-mail.* We want songs with a message and overtly Christian. Make sure all material is copyrighted. *You MUST include SASE or we DO NOT respond!"* Responds in 2 months.

Music Mostly **contemporary Christian**, **Christian soft rock** and **Christmas**; also **love songs**, **ballads** and **new country**. Does not want rap, hip-hop, southern gospel or songs without lyrics. Published "Did You See Him" (single by Rich Green), "Jesus Is His Name" (single by Carolyn Swayze), and "All He Ever Wanted" (single by Rich Green/Jerry Corelli), all from *Righteous Man* (album), released 2006 on Omega III Records.

Tips "Success is obtained when opportunity meets preparation! If a SASE is not sent with demo, we don't even listen to the demo. Be willing to do a rewrite. Don't send mat erial expecting us to place it with a Top Ten artist. Be practical. Do your songs say what's always been said, except differently? Don't take rejection personally."

✅ THE CORNELIUS COMPANIES (BMI, ASCAP, SESAC)

Dept. SM, 1710 Grand Ave., Nashville TN 37212. (615)321-5333. E-mail: corneliuscomps@bellsout h.net. Web site: www.gatewayentertainment.com. **Contact:** Ron Cornelius, owner/president. Music publisher and record producer (Ron Cornelius). Estab. 1986. Publishes 60-80 songs/year; publishes 2-3 new songwriters/year. Occasionally hires staff writers. Pays standard royalty.

Affiliate(s) RobinSparrow Music (BMI), Strummin' Bird Music (ASCAP) and Bridgeway Music (SESAC).

How to Contact *Contact by e-mail or call for permission to submit material.* Submit demo package by mail. Unsolicited submissions are OK. "Send demo on CD format only with 2-3 songs." Include SASE. Responds in 2 months.

Music Mostly **country** and **pop**; also **positive country**, **gospel** and **alternative**. Published songs by Confederate Railroad, Faith Hill, David Allen Coe, Alabama and over 50 radio singles in the positive Christian/country format.

Tips "Looking for material suitable for film."

Ⓝ ✅ 🔲 CUPIT MUSIC GROUP (ASCAP, BMI)

P.O. Box 121904, Nashville TN 37212. (615)731-0100. Fax: (615)731-3005. E-mail: info@cupitmusi c.com. Web site: www.cupitmusic.com. **Contact:** Publishing Division. Music publisher, record producer, record company, entertainment division and recording studio. Estab. 1986. Staff size: 8. Pays standard royalty.

Affiliate(s) Cupit Memaries (ASCAP) and Cupit Music (BMI).

- ● Also see the listing for Jerry Cupit Productions in the Record Producers section. Cupit Music's "Jukebox Junkie" won BMI Millionair Award.

How to Contact *Please visit cupitmusic.com for our submission policy.* Prefers CD with lyric sheet. "We will return a response card." Include SASE. Usually responds in 2 months.

Music Mostly **country**, **bluegrass**, **blues**, **pop**, **gospel** and **instrumental**. Does not want rap, hard rock or metal. Published "He'll Never Be A Lawyer Cause He Can't Pass the Bar" (single), recorded by Mustang (country), released 2007 on Cupit Records; "Your Love Reaches Me" (single), recorded by Kevin Sharp (country), released 2007 on Cupit Records; "I Bought the Shoes (That Just Walked

Out On Me)'' (single) from *Dierks Bentley* (album), recorded by Dierks Bentley (country), released 2005 on Cupit Records; and ''I Know What You Got Up Your Sleeve'' (single) from *Maverick* (album), recorded by Hank Williams, Jr. (country), released 2001 on Curb Records.

☑ CURB MUSIC (ASCAP, BMI, SESAC)
48 Music Square East, Nashville TN 37203. Web site: www.curb.com.
Affiliates Mike Curb Music (BMI); Curb Songs (ASCAP); and Curb Congregation Songs (SESAC).
  • *Curb Music only accepts submissions through reputable industry sources and does not accept unsolicited demos.*

☑ JOF DAVE MUSIC (ASCAP)
1055 Kimball Ave., Kansas City KS 66104. (913)593-3180. **Contact:** David Johnson, CEO. Music publisher, record company (Cymbal Records). Estab. 1984. Publishes 30 songs/year; publishes 12 new songwriters/year. Pays standard royalty.
How to Contact *Contact first and obtain permission to submit.* Prefers CD. Include SASE. Responds in 1 month.
Music Mostly **gospel** and **R&B**. Published ''The Woman I Love'' (single) from *Sugar Bowl* (album), written and recorded by King Alex, released 2001 on Cymbal Records; and ''Booty Clap'' (single by Johnny Jones) from *Gotta Move On* (album), recorded by Jacuzé, released 2005 on Cymbal Records.

☑ ☒ ☑ THE EDWARD DE MILES MUSIC COMPANY (BMI)
10573 W. Pico Blvd., #352, Los Angeles CA 90064-2348. Phone: (310)948-9652. Fax: (310)474-7705. E-mail: info@edmsahara.com. Web site: www.edmsahara.com. **Contact:** Professional Manager. Music publisher, record company (Sahara Records), record producer, management, bookings and promotions. Estab. 1984. Publishes 50-75 songs/year; publishes 5 new songwriters/year. Hires staff songwriters. Pays standard royalty.
  • Also see the listings for Edward De Miles in the Record Producers and Managers & Booking Agents sections, and Sahara Records And Filmworks Entertainment in the Record Companies section of this book.
How to Contact *Write first and obtain permission to submit.* Prefers CD with 1-3 songs and lyric sheet. Does not return material. Reponds in 1 month.
Music Mostly **top 40 pop/rock**, **R&B/dance** and **country**; also **musical scores for TV, radio, films** and **jingles**. Published ''Dance Wit Me'' and ''Moments'' (singles), written and recorded by Steve Lynn on Sahara Records (R&B).
Tips ''Copyright all songs before submitting to us.''

☑ DELEV MUSIC COMPANY (ASCAP, BMI)
7231 Mansfield Ave., Philadelphia PA 19138-1620. (215)276-8861. Fax: (215)276-4509. E-mail: delevmusic@msn.com. President/CEO: William L. Lucas. A&R: Darryl Lucas. Music publisher. Publishes 6-10 songs/year; publishes 6-10 new songwriters/year. Pays standard royalty.
Affiliate(s) Sign of the Ram Music (ASCAP) and Delev Music (BMI).
How to Contact *Does not accept unsolicited material. Write or call first to obtain permission to submit.* Prefers CD format only—no cassettes—with 1-8 songs and lyric sheet. ''We will not accept certified mail or SASE.'' Does not return material. Responds in 1-2 months.
Music Mostly **R&B ballads** and **dance-oriented**; also **pop ballads**, **christian/gospel**, **crossover** and **country/western**. No gangsta rap. Published ''Angel Love'' (single by Barbara Heston/Geraldine Fernandez) from *The Silky Sounds of Debbie G* (album), recorded by Debbie G (light R&B/easy listening), released 2000 on Blizzard Records; *Variety* (album), produced by Barbara Heston and Carment Lindsay, released on Luvya Records; and ''Ever Again'' by Bernie Williams, released 2003 on SunDazed Records.

Tips "Persevere regardless if it is sent to our company or any other company. Most of all, no matter what happens, believe in yourself."

ⓝ 🖸 DIAMONDS SEVEN MUSIC (BMI)

P.O. Box 10528, Parker FL 32404-1528. (850)896-5965. E-mail: diamonds_seven@yahoo.com. **Contact:** Clinton Wade, publisher/owner. Music publisher. Estab. 2007. Staff size: 2.

How to Contact Submit demo package by mail. Unsolicited submissions are OK. Prefers CD or cassette with 1-4 songs and lyric sheet, cover letter. Responds in 1 months.

Music Mostly **pop**, **country**, and **alternative**; also **rock**, **Americana**, and **blues**.

✔ ⊘ DISNEY MUSIC PUBLISHING (ASCAP, BMI)

500 S. Buena Vista St., Burbank CA 91521-6182. (818)567-5069. **Contact:** Ashley Saunig, DMP creative department.

Affiliate(s) Seven Peaks Music and Seven Summits Music.

How to Contact "*We cannot accept any unsolicited material.*"

🖸 DREAM SEEKERS PUBLISHING (BMI)

21 Coachlight Dr., Danville IL 61832-8240. (615)822-1160. President: Sally Sidman. Music publisher. Estab. 1993. Publishes 25-50 songs/year; publishes 15-20 new songwriters/year. Pays standard royalty.

Affiliate(s) Dream Builders Publishing (ASCAP).

How to Contact Submit demo by mail. Unsolicited submissions are OK. "Please do not call to request permission—just submit your material. There are no code words. We listen to everything." Prefers cassette or CD with 2 songs and lyric sheet. "If one of your songs is selected for publishing, we prefer to have it available on CD for dubbing off copies to pitch to artist." Include SASE. Responds in 6 weeks.

Music Mostly **country**. "All types of **country** material, but mostly in need of up-tempo songs, preferably with positive lyrics." Does not want rap, jazz, classical, children's, hard rock, instrumental or blues. Published "Hang On Tight" (single by Germain Brunet) from *Fantasy* (album), recorded by Cheryl K. Warner (country), released 2007 on CKW Records; "Burn Your Memory Down" (single by Jeff Moxcey/Catharine Haver) from *Who Am I to You* (album), recorded by Jennifer LeMoss (country), released 2007 on Vision Way Records; and "80 Mile from Memphis" (single by Mark Collie) from *Rose Covered Garden* (album), recorded by Mark Collie (country), released 2006 on Sixteen Ton.

Tips "Be willing to work hard to learn the craft of songwriting. Be persistent. Nobody is born a hit songwriter. It often takes years to achieve that status."

⊘ DREAMWORKS SKG MUSIC PUBLISHING

331 N. Maple Dr., Suite 300, Beverly Hills CA 90210. Web site: www.dreamworkspublishing.com. Music publisher and record company (DreamWorks Records).

- Dreamworks SKG Music Publishing has been bought out by Universal Music Publishing.

🖸 DUANE MUSIC, INC. (BMI)

382 Clarence Ave., Sunnyvale CA 94086. (408)739-6133. **Contact:** Garrie Thompson, President. Music publisher and record producer. Publishes 10-20 songs/year; publishes 1 new songwriter/year. Pays standard royalty.

Affiliate(s) Morhits Publishing (BMI).

How to Contact Submit demo by mail. Unsolicited submissions are OK. Prefers CD with 1-2 songs. Include SASE. Responds in 2 months.

Music Mostly **blues**, **country**, **disco** and easy listening; also **rock**, **soul** and **top 40/pop**. Published

"Little Girl" (single), recorded by The Syndicate of Sound & Ban (rock); "Warm Tender Love" (single), recorded by Percy Sledge (soul); and "My Adorable One" (single), recorded by Joe Simon (blues).

✷ EARITATING MUSIC PUBLISHING (BMI)

P.O. Box 1101, Gresham OR 97030. Music publisher. Estab. 1979. Pays individual per song contract, usually greater than 50% to writer.

How to Contact Submit demo package by mail. Unsolicited submissions are OK. Prefers CD with lyric sheet. "Submissions should be copyrighted by the author. We will deal for rights if interested." Does not return material. Responds only if interested.

Music Mostly **rock**, **country** and **folk**. Does not want rap.

Tips "Melody is most important, lyrics second. Style and performance take a back seat to these. A good song will stand with just one voice and one instrument. Also, don't use staples on your mailers."

✷ EARTHSCREAM MUSIC PUBLISHING CO. (BMI)

8377 Westview Dr., Houston TX 77055. (713)464-GOLD. E-mail: sarsjef@aol.com. Web site: www.s oundartsrecording.com. **Contact:** Jeff Wells; Peter Verkerk. Music publisher, record company and record producer. Estab. 1975. Publishes 12 songs/year; publishes 4 new songwriters/year. Pays standard royalty.

- Also see the listings for Surface Records in the Record Companies section and Sound Arts Recording Studio in the Record Producers section of this book.

Affiliate(s) Reach For The Sky Music Publishing (ASCAP).

How to Contact Submit demo by mail. Unsolicited submissions are OK. Prefers CD or videocassette with 2-5 songs and lyric sheet. Does not return material. Responds in 6 weeks.

Music Mostly **new rock**, **country**, **blues** and **top 40/pop**. Published "Baby Never Cries" (single by Carlos DeLeon), recorded by Jinkies on Surface Records (pop); "Telephone Road" (single), written and recorded by Mark May(blues) on Icehouse Records; "Do You Remember'" (single by Barbara Pennington), recorded by Perfect Strangers on Earth Records (rock), and "Sheryl Crow" (single), recorded by Dr. Jeff and the Painkillers (pop); "Going Backwards" (single), written and recorded by Tony Vega (Gulf swamp blues), released on Red Onion Records.

Ⓝ ✷ EAST MADISON MUSIC PUBLISHING (BMI)

9 Music Square South, #143, Nashville TN 37203.(615)838-4171. E-mail: eastmadisonmusic@chart er.net. Web site: www.emmrecords.net. **Contact:** Dean Holmen, publisher. Music publisher, record company (East Madison Music Records), and record producer (Dean Holmen). Estab. 2003 Published 6 songs/year; publishes 3 new songwriters/year. Staff size: 2. Pays standard royalty.

- East Madison Music Publishing received a First Place Award in 2005 for "If Teardrops Played the Juke Box" and First Place in 2006 for "I Should Get 30 Years" from Songwriters of Wisconsin.

Affiliate(s) Ricki Lynn Publishing (BMI).

How to Contact Submit demo by mail. Unsolicited submissions are OK. Prefers CD with 1-3 songs with lyric sheet and cover letter. Does not return submissions. Responds only if interested.

Music Mostly **traditional country** and **gospel**; does not want rock or hip-hop. Published "Weekend Willie Nelson," "I Gave My Heart Away," and "Don't Ever Leave Me" (singles by Tim Schweeberger) from *Heartaches & Honky Tonks*, recorded by Dean Holmen (traditional country), released 2006 on EMM Records.

Tips "Please follow submission guidelines. If you follow our guidelines, your song will be reviewed. If not, it will be disregarded. Don't overlook the independent artist. Most songs cut today are cut by them."

✒ ELECTRIC MULE PUBLISHING COMPANY (BMI)/NEON MULE MUSIC (ASCAP)

1500 Clifton Ln., Nashville TN 37215. E-mail: emuleme@aol.com. **Contact:** Jeff Moseley, President.

◖ EMANDELL TUNES (ASCAP, BMI, SESAC)

10220 Glade Ave., Chatsworth CA 91311. (818)341-2264. Fax: (818)341-1008. E-mail: epa4music@s bcglobal.net. **Contact:** Leroy C. Lovett, Jr., president/administrator. Music Publisher. Estab. 1979. Publishes 6-12 songs/year; publishes 3-4 new songwriters/year. Pays standard royalty.
Affiliate(s) Ben-Lee Music (BMI), Birthright Music (ASCAP), Em-Jay Music (ASCAP), Northworth Songs, Chinwah Songs, Gertrude Music (all SESAC), Andrask Music, Australia (BMI), Nadine Music, Switzerland.
How to Contact *Write first and obtain permission to submit.* Prefers CD with 4-5 songs and lead or lyric sheet. Include bio of writer, singer or group. Include SASE. Responds in 6 weeks.
Music Mostly **inspirational**, **contemporary gospel**, and **choral**; also **strong country** and **light top 40**. Published "Under My Skin" and "Colorada River" (singles by Diana/Kim Fowley), recorded by Diana, released 2001 on WFL Records; and "Runaway Love" (single by Gil Askey), recorded by Linda Clifford (new gospel), released 2001 on Sony Records.
Tips "We suggest you listen to current songs. Imagine how that song would sound if done by some other artist. Keep your ear tuned to new groups, bands, singers. Try to analyze what made them different, was it the sound? Was it the song? Was it the production? Ask yourself these questions: Do they have that 'hit' feeling? Do you like what they are doing?"

✒ EMI CHRISTIAN MUSIC PUBLISHING (ASCAP, BMI, SESAC)

P.O. Box 5085, Brentwood TN 37024. (615)371-6800. Web site: www.emicmg.com. Music publisher. Publishes 100 songs/year; publishes 2 new songwriters/year. Hires staff songwriters. Pays standard royalty.
Affiliate(s) Birdwing Music (ASCAP), Sparrow Song (BMI), His Eye Music (SESAC), Ariose Music (ASCAP), Straightway Music (ASCAP), Shepherd's Fold Music (BMI), Songs of Promise (SESAC), Dawn Treader Music (SESAC), Meadowgreen Music Company (ASCAP), River Oaks Music Company (BMI), Stonebrook Music Company (SESAC), Bud John Songs, Inc. (ASCAP), Bud John Music, Inc. (BMI), Bud John Tunes, Inc. (SESAC).
How to Contact *"We do not accept unsolicited submissions."*
Music Published "Concert of the Age" (by Jeffrey Benward), recorded by Phillips, Craig & Dean; "God Is In Control," written and recorded by Twila Paris, both on StarSong Records; and "Faith, Hope and Love" (by Ty Lacy), recorded by Point of Grace on Word Records.
Tips "Come to Nashville and be a part of the fastest growing industry. It's nearly impossible to get a publisher's attention unless you know someone in the industry that is willing to help you."

✒ EMI MUSIC PUBLISHING

1290 Avenue of the Americas, 42nd Floor, New York NY 10104. (212)492-1200. Web site: www.emi musicpub.com. Music publisher.
How to Contact *EMI does not accept unsolicited material.*
Music Published "All Night Long" (by F. Evans/R. Lawrence/S. Combs), recorded by Faith Evans featuring Puff Daddy on Bad Boy; "You" (by C. Roland/J. Powell), recorded by Jesse Powell on Silas; and "I Was" (by C. Black/P. Vassar), recorded by Neal McCoy on Atlantic.
Tips "Don't bury your songs. Less is more—we will ask for more if we need it. Put your strongest song first."

✒ EMSTONE MUSIC PUBLISHING (BMI)

Box 398, Hallandale FL 33008. (305)936-0412. E-mail: webmaster@emstonemusicpublishing.com. **Contact:** Michael Gary, creative director. President: Mitchell Stone. Vice President: Madeline Stone. Music publisher. Estab. 1997. Pays standard royalty.

How to Contact Submit demo CD by mail with any number of songs. Unsolicited submissions are OK. Does not return material. Responds only if interested.

Music Everything except classical and opera. Published "www.history" (single by Tim Eatman) and "Gonna Recall My Heart" (single by Dan Jury) from *No Tears* (album), recorded by Cole Seaver and Tammie Darlene, released on CountryStock Records; and "I Love What I've Got" (single by Heather and Paul Turner) from *The Best of Talented Kids* (compilation album) recorded by Gypsy.

Tips "We only offer publishing contracts to writers whose songs exhibit a spark of genius. Anything less can't compete in the music industry."

FAMOUS MUSIC PUBLISHING LLC (ASCAP, BMI)

10635 Santa Monica Blvd., Suite 300, Los Angeles CA 90025. (310)441-1300. Fax: (310)441-4722. President: Ira Jaffe. Vice President, Film and TV: Stacey Palm. Senior Creative Director: Carol Spencer (rock/pop/alternative). Senior Creative Director/Latin: Claribell Cuevas. **New York office:** 1633 Broadway, 11th Floor, New York NY 10019. (212)654-7433. Fax: (212)654-4748. Chairman and CEO: Irwin Z. Robinson. Executive Vice President, Finance and Administration: Margaret Johnson. Vice President Catalogue Development: Mary Beth Roberts. Creative Director: Britt Morgan-Saks. **Nashville office:** 65 Music Square East, Nashville TN 37212. (615)329-0500. Fax: (615)321-4121. Senior Creative Director: Curtis Green. Music Publisher. Estab. 1929.

Affiliate(s) Famous Music (ASCAP) and Ensign Music (BMI).

How to Contact *Famous Music does not accept unsolicited submissions.*

Film & TV Famous Music is a Paramount Pictures' company. Music Supervisor: Stacey Palm.

FIFTH AVENUE MEDIA, LTD. (ASCAP)

1208 W. Broadway, Hewlett NY 11557. (212)691-5630. Fax: (212)645-5038. E-mail: thefirm@thefirm.com. Web site: www.thefirm.com. Professional Managers: Bruce E. Colfin(rootsy bluesy rock/reggae, Jam Bands/alternative rock/heavy metal); Jeffrey E. Jacobson (hip-hop/R&B/dance). Music publisher and record company (Fifth Avenue Media, Ltd.). Estab. 1995. Publishes 2 songs/year. Staff size: 4. Pays standard royalty.

Music Published "Analog" (single by Paul Byrne) from Paul Byrne & the Bleeders (album), recorded by Paul Byrne (pop rock), released 2001 on Independent.

FIRST TIME MUSIC (PUBLISHING) U.K. (PRS, MCPS)

Sovereign House, 12 Trewartha Road, Praa Sands, Penzance, Cornwall TR20 9ST United Kingdom. (01736)762826. Fax: (01736)763328. E-mail: panamus@aol.com. Web site: www.panamamusic.co.uk. **Contact:** Roderick G. Jones, managing director. Music publisher, record company (Rainy Day Records, Mohock Records, Pure Gold Records). Estab. 1986. Publishes 500-750 songs/year; 20-50 new songwriters/year. Staff size: 6. Hires staff writers. Pays standard royalty; "50-60% to established and up-and-coming writers with the right attitude."

Affiliate(s) Scamp Music Publishing, Panama Music Library, Musik Image Library, Caribbean Music Library, Psi Music Library, ADN Creation Music Library, Promo Sonor International, Eventide Music, Melody First Music Library, Piano Bar Music Library, Corelia Music Library, Panama Music Ltd.

How to Contact Submit demo package by mail. Unsolicited submissions are OK. Submit on CD only, "of professional quality" with unlimited number of songs and lyric or lead sheets. Responds in 1 month. SAE and IRC required for reply.

Film & TV Places 200 songs in film and TV/year. "Copyrights and phonographic rights of Panama Music Limited and its associated catalogue idents have been used and subsist in various productions broadcasts and adverts produced by major and independent production companies, television, film/video companies, radio broadcasters (not just in the UK, but in various countries world-wide) and by commercial record companies for general release and sale. In the UK & Republic of Ireland they include the BBC networks of national/regional television and radio, ITV network programs and promotions (Channel 4, Border TV, Granada TV, Tyne Tees TV, Scottish TV, Yorkshire TV, HTV, Central TV, Channel TV, LWT, Meridian TV, Grampian TV, GMTV, Ulster TV, Westcountry TV, Channel TV, Carlton TV, Anglia TV, TV3, RTE (Ireland), Planet TV, Rapido TV, VT4 TV, BBC Worldwide, etc.), independent radio stations, satellite Sky Television (BskyB), Discovery Channel, Learning Channel, National Geographic, Living Channel, Sony, Trouble TV, UK Style Channel, Hon Cyf, CSI, etc., and cable companies, GWR Creative, Premier, Spectrum FM, Local Radio Partnership, Fox, Manx, Swansea Sound, Mercury, 2CRFM, Broadland, BBC Radio Collection, etc. Some credits include copyrights in programs, films/videos, broadcasts, trailers and promotions such as *Desmond's*, *One Foot in the Grave*, *EastEnders*, *Hale* and *Pace*, *Holidays from Hell*, *A Touch of Frost*, *999 International*, and *Get Away*."

Music All styles. Published "Still the One" recorded by United in Dance (album track & single - hardcore dance) released by Universal; *Helter Skelter Hardcore Euphoria* (album), also by Warner Music: *Clubland X-Treme Hardcore* (album) also by Resit Music: *Hardcore Till I Die 2* (album), *Bonkers 13* (album), *Hardcore Horror Show* (album), also by Power Records; *Wigan Pier # 42* (album) also by Essential Platinum Records; *12" Vinyl Club release* (album), also by Raver Baby Records; *12" Vinyl Club release* (album), also by Nukleuz/Warner; *Hardcore Nation Classics* (album); "Going my own sweet way" (single) from *My Heart Would Know* (album), recorded by Charlie Landsborough (country), released 2006 on Rosette Records; "Peace of Mind" (single) from *Zena James—Tell Me More* (album), recorded by Zena James (jazz), released 2007 on Jazzizit Records; "Remembrance Day" (jazz) from *The Drums of Childhood Dreams* (album) recorded by Pete Arnold (folk), released 2007 on Digimix Records.

Tips "Have a professional approach—present well produced demos. First impressions are important and may be the only chance you get. Writers are advised to join the Guild of International Songwriters and Composers in the United Kingdom (www.songwriters-guild.co.uk)."

☑ FRICON MUSIC COMPANY (BMI)

1050 S. Ogden Dr., Los Angeles CA 90019. (323)931-7323. Fax: (323)938-2030. E-mail: fricon@comcast.net. President: Terri Fricon. **Contact:** Madge Benson, professional manager. Music publisher. **Tennessee Office:** 134 Bluegrass Circle, Hendersonville TN 37075. (615)826-2288. **Contact:** Jan Morales. Estab. 1981. Publishes 25 songs/year; publishes 1-2 new songwriters/year. Staff size: 6. Pays standard royalty.

Affiliate(s) Fricout Music Company (ASCAP) and Now and Forever Songs (SESAC).

How to Contact *Contact first and obtain permission to submit.* Prefers CD with 3-4 songs and lyric or lead sheet. "Prior permission must be obtained or packages will be returned." Include SASE. Responds in 2 months.

Music Mostly **country**.

☑ G MAJOR MUSIC (BMI)

P.O. Box 3331, Fort Smith AR 72913-3331. E-mail: JerryGlidewell@juno.com. Web site: www.GMajorPublishing.com. Owner: Jerry Glidewell. Professional Managers: Alex Hoover. Music publisher. Estab. 1992. Publishes 10 songs/year; publishes 2 new songwriters/year. Staff size: 2. Pays standard royalty.

How to Contact *No unsolicited submissions.* Submit inquiry by mail with SASE. Prefers CD or mp3. Submit up to 3 songs with lyrics. Include SASE. Responds in 3 weeks.

Music Mostly **country** and **contemporary Christian**. Published *Set The Captives Free* (album by Chad Little/Jeff Pitzer/Ben Storie), recorded by Sweeter Rain (contemporary Christian), for Cornerstone Television; "Hopes and Dreams" (single by Jerry Glidewell), recorded by Carrie Underwood (country), released on Star Rise; and "Dreamer" (single by Chad Little/Bryan Morse/Jerry Glidewell), recorded CO3 (contemporary Christian), released on Flagship Records.

Tips "We are looking for 'smash hits' to pitch to the Country and Christian markets."

☑ ☐ GLAD MUSIC CO. (ASCAP, BMI, SESAC)

14340 Torrey Chase, Suite 380, Houston TX 77014. (281)397-7300. Fax: (281)397-6206. E-mail: hwesdaily@gladmusicco.com. Web site: www.gladmusicco.com. **Contact:** Wes Daily, A&R Director (country). Music publisher, record company and record producer. Estab. 1958. Publishes 10 songs/year; publishes 10 new songwriters/year. Staff size: 4. Pays standard royalty.

Affiliate(s) Bud-Don (ASCAP) and Rayde (SESAC).

How to Contact *Write first and obtain permission to submit.* Prefers CD with 3 songs, lyric sheet and cover letter. Does not return material. Responds in 6 weeks. SASE or e-mail address for reply.

Music Mostly **country**. Does not want weak songs. Published **Love Bug** (album by C. Wayne/W. Kemp), recorded by George Strait, released 1995 on MCA; *Walk Through This World With Me* (album), written and recorded by George Jones; and *Race Is On* (album by D. Rollins), recorded by George Jones, both released 1999 on Asylum.

Ⓝ ☐ L.J. GOOD PUBLISHING (ASCAP)

P.O. Box 1696, Omak WA 98841.(509)422-1400. Fax: (509)267-8611. E-mail: ljgood@wingsforchrist.com. Web site: www.wingsforchrist.com. **Contact:** Lonnie Good, president. Music publisher. Estab. 2006. Publishes 5 songs/year. Publishes 1 new songwriters/year. Staff size: 1. Pays standard royalty of 50%.

Affiliate(s) L.J. Good Publishing (ASCAP).

How to Contact *Contact first and obtain permission to submit a demo.* Prefers CD or mp3 with 3 songs and lyric sheet, cover letter. Does not return submissions.

Music Mostly **country**, **blues**, and **folk**; also **soft rock**.

▣ ☑ GOODNIGHT KISS MUSIC (BMI, ASCAP)

10153½ Riverside Dr. #239, Toluca Lake CA 91602. (831)479-9993. Web site: www.goodnightkiss.com. **Contact:** Janet Fisher, managing director. Music publisher, record company and record producer. Estab. 1986. Publishes 6-8 songs/year; publishes 4-5 new songwriters/year. Pays standard royalty.

• Goodnight Kiss Music specializes in placing music in movies and TV.

Affiliate(s) Scene Stealer Music (ASCAP).

How to Contact "Check our Web site or subscribe to newsletter (www.goodnightkiss.com) to see what we are looking for and to obtain codes. Packages must have proper submission codes, or they are discarded." Only accepts material that is requested on the Web site. Does not return material. Responds in 6 months.

Film & TV Places 3-5 songs in film/year. Published "I Do, I Do, Love You" (by Joe David Curtis), recorded by Ricky Kershaw in Road Ends; "Bee Charmer's Charmer" (by Marc Tilson) for the MTV movie *Love Song*; "Right When I Left" (by B. Turner/J. Fisher) in the movie *Knight Club*.

Music All modern styles. Published and produced Addiction: *Highs & Lows* (CD), written and recorded by various artists (all styles), released 2004; *Tall Tales of Osama Bin Laden* (CD), written and recorded by various artists (all styles parody), released 2004; and *Rythm of Honor* (CD), written and recorded by various artists (all styles), slated release 2005, all on Goodnight Kiss Records.

Tips "The absolute best way to keep apprised of the company's needs is to subscribe to the online newsletter. Only specifically requested material is accepted, as listed in the newsletter (what the industry calls us for is what we request from writers). We basically use an SGA contract, and there are never fees to be considered for specific projects or albums. However, we are a real music company, and the competition is just as fierce as with the majors."

☐ RL HAMMEL ASSOCIATES, INC. (ASCAP/BMI)

"Consultants to the Music, Recording & Entertainment Industries," P.O. Box 531, Alexandria IN 46001-0531. E-mail: info@rlhammel.com. Web site: www.rlhammel.com. **Contact:** A&R Department. President: Randal L. Hammel. Music publisher, record producer and consultant. Estab. 1974. Staff size: 3-5. Pays standard royalty.

Affiliate(s) LADNAR Music (ASCAP) and LEMMAH Music (BMI).

How to Contact Submit demo package and brief bio by mail. Unsolicited submissions are OK. Prefers CD, DAT or VHS/8mm videocassette with a maximum of 3 songs and typed lyric sheets. ''Please notate three (3) best songs—no time to listen to a full project.'' Does not return material. Responds ASAP. ''No fixed timeline.''

Music Mostly **pop**, **R&B** and **Christian**; also **MOR**, **light rock**, **pop country** and **feature film title cuts**. Produced/arranged *The Wedding Collection Series* for WORD Records. Published *Lessons For Life* (album by Kelly Hubbell/Jim Boedicker) and *I Just Want Jesus* (album by Mark Condon), both recorded by Kelly Connor, released on iMPACT Records.

HICKORY LANE PUBLISHING AND RECORDING (ASCAP, SOCAN)

2713 Oakridge Crescent, Prince George BC V2K 3Y2 Canada. (250)962-5135. E-mail: urbanski2008 @aol.com. **Contact:** Chris Urbanski, president. Music publisher, record company and record producer. Estab. 1988. Hires staff writers. Publishes 30 songs/year; publishes 5 new songwriters/year. Pays standard royalty.

How to Contact *Does not accept unsolicited submissions.*

Music Mostly **country** and **country rock**. Published ''Just Living For Today'' (single by Chris Urbanski), recorded by Chris Michaels (country), released 2005 on Hickory Lane Records; ''This is My Sons'' (single by Tyson Avery/Chris Urbanski/Alex Bradshaw), recorded by Chris Michaels (country), released 2005 on Hickory Lane Records; ''Stubborn Love'' (single by Owen Davies/Chris Urbanski/John Middleton), recorded by Chris Michaels (country), released 2005 on Hickory Lane Records.

Tips ''Send us a professional quality demo with the vocals upfront. We are looking for hits, and so are the major record labels we deal with. Be original in your approach, don't send us a cover tune.''

HIS POWER PRODUCTIONS AND PUBLISHING (ASCAP, BMI)

1304 Canyon, Plainview TX 79072-4740. (806)296-7073. E-mail: dcarter@hispower.net. Web site: www.powerproductions.org. Professional Managers: T.D. (Darryl) Carter (R&B, gospel, country rock, jazz, pop, new rock, classic rock) . Music publisher, record company (Lion and Lamb), record producer, artist and song development, agent for placement and representation (End-Time Management & Booking Agency). Estab. 1995. Publishes 0-3 songs/year; publishes 0-3 new songwriters/year. Staff size: 3. May hire staff songwriters. Pays negotiable royalty.

Affiliate(s) Love Story Publishing (BMI).

• The song ''Heal Me,'' published by His Power, was awarded ASCAP Popular Award from 1998-2005.

How to Contact *E-mail or call first and obtain permission to submit.* Prefers mp3, CD or DAT with 1-4 songs and lyric sheet. ''No material returned. send copies only.'' Responds if interested.

Music Mostly **gospel**, **pop**, **inspirational**, **black**, **new rock**, **classic rock**, **country rock gospel** and **adult contemporary gospel**; also **R&B**, **jazz**, **Christ-oriented Christmas music**, **pro-life** and **family**. Looking for unconventional styles and structure. Does not want negative-based lyrics of any kind. Published ''It's His Life'' (single) and ''Bible Thumper Blues'' (single), written and recorded by Mike Burchfield (country gospel), released on Lion and Lamb Records, produced by T.D. Carter.

Tips ''Be serious. We are only interested in those who have meaning and substance behind what is created. Music is an avenue to change the world. Submit what comes from the heart. Don't be in a hurry. Good music has no time limits. And yet, time will reward the desire you put into it. Be willing to embark on newly designed challenges that will meet a new century of opportunity and needs never before obtainable through conventional music companies.''

☐ HITSBURGH MUSIC CO. (BMI)

P.O. Box 1431, 233 N. Electra, Gallatin TN 37066. (615)452-0324. Promotional Director: Kimolin Crutcher. A&R Director: K'leetha Gilbert. Executive Vice President: Kenneth Gilbert. Contact: Harold Gilbert, president/ general manager. Music publisher. Estab. 1964. Publishes 12 songs/year. Staff size: 4. Pays standard royalty.

Affiliate(s) 7th Day Music (BMI).

How to Contact Submit demo by mail. Unsolicited submissions are OK. Prefers cassette or quality videocassette with 2-4 songs and lead sheet. Prefers studio produced demos. Include SASE. Responds in 6 weeks.

Music Mostly **country gospel** and **MOR**. Published "That Kind'a Love" (single by Kimolin Crutchet and Dan Serafini), from *Here's Cissy* (album), recorded by Cissy Crutcher (MOR), released 2005 on Vivaton; "Disorder at the Border" (single), written and recorded by Donald Layne, released 2001 on Southern City; and "Blue Tears" (single by Harold Gilbert/Elaine Harmon), recorded by Hal, released 2006 (reissue) on Southern City.

☐ HOME TOWN HERO'S PUBLISHING (BMI)

112 West Houston, Leonard TX 75452. **Contact:** Tammy Wood, owner. Music publisher. Estab. 2003. Staff size: 2. Pays standard royalty.

How to Contact Submit demo by mail. Unsolicited submissions are OK. Prefers cassette or CD with 3-6 songs, lyric sheet, and cover letter. Does not return submissions. Responds only if interested.

Music Mostly **country (all styles)**, **pop**, **Southern rock**; also **ballads**, **gospel**, and **blues**. Does not want heavy metal and rap.

Tips "Most of all, believe in yourself. The best songs come from the heart. Don't get discouraged, be tough, keep writing, and always think positive. Songwriters, no calls please. I will contact you if interested. Send me your best."

⊕ ☑ INSIDE RECORDS/OK SONGS

St.-Jacobsmarkt 72, Antwerp 6 2000 Belgium. (32) + 3 + 226-77-19. Fax: (32) + 3 + 226-78-05. **Contact**: Jean Ney, MD. Music publisher and record company. Estab. 1989. Publishes 50 songs/year; publishes 30-40 new songwriters/year. Hires staff writers. Royalty varies "depending on teamwork."

How to Contact Submit demo by mail. Unsolicited submissions are OK. Prefers cassette with complete name, address, telephone and fax number. SAE and IRC. Responds in 2 months.

Music Mostly **dance**, **pop** and **MOR contemporary**; also **country**, **reggae** and **Latin**. Published *Fiesta De Bautiza* (album by Andres Manzana); *I'm Freaky* (album by Maes-Predu'homme-Robinson); and *Heaven* (album by KC One-King Naomi), all on Inside Records.

⊕ 🖂 ☑ INTOXYGENE SARL

283 Fbg St. Antoine, Paris 75011 France. 011(33)1 43485151. Fax: 011(33)1 43485753. E-mail: infos@intoxygene.com. Web site: www.intoxygene.com or www.intoxygene.net. **Contact:** Patrick Jammes, managing director. Music publisher and record company. Estab. 1990. Staff size: 1. Publishes 30 songs/year. Pays 50% royalty.

How to Contact *Does not accept unsolicited submissions.*

Film & TV Places 3/5 songs in film and in TV/year.

Music Mostly **new industrial** and **metal**, **lounge**, **electronic**, and **ambient**. Publisher for Peeping Tom (trip-hop), Djaimin (house), Missa Furiosa by Thierry Zaboitzeff (progressive), and The Young Gods (alternative) amongst others.

Ⓝ ⊕ ☐ ISLAND CULTURE MUSIC PUBLISHERS (BMI)

7005 Bordeaux, St. John 00830-9510. U.S. Virgin Islands. E-mail: L_monsanto@hotmail.com. Web site: www.IslandKingRecords.com. **Contact:** Liston Monsanto, Jr., president. Music publisher and record company (Island King Records). Estab. 1996. Publishes 10 songs/year; publishes 3 new songwriters/year. Hires staff songwriters. Staff size: 3. Pays standard royalty.

How to Contact Submit demo package by mail. Unsolicited submissions are OK. Prefers CD with 8 songs and lyric sheet. Send bio and 8×10 glossy. Does not return material. Responds in 1 month.

Music Mostly **reggae**, **calypso**, and **zouk**; also **house**. Published *De Paris a Bohicon* (album), recorded by Rasbawa (reggae), released 2006 on Island King Records; "Jah Give Me Life" (single by Chubby) from *Best of Island King* (album), recorded by Chubby (reggae), released 2003 on Island King Records; "When People Mix Up" (single by Lady Lex/L. Monsanto/Chubby) and "I Am Real" (single by L. Monsanto) from *Best of Island King* (album), recorded by Lady Lex (reggae), released 2003 on Island King Records.

◯ IVORY PEN ENTERTAINMENT (ASCAP)

P.O. Box 1097, Laurel MD 20725. (301)490-4418. Fax: (301)490-4635. E-mail: ivorypen@comcast.n et. Web site: www.ivorypen.com. Professional Managers: Steven Lewis (R&B, pop/rock, inspirational); Sonya Lewis (AC/dance/jazz). Music publisher. Estab. 2003. Publishes 10 songs/year. Staff size: 4. Pays standard royalty.

How to Contact Submit demo package by mail. Unsolicited submissions are OK. Prefers CD with 3-5 songs and cover letter. Include SASE. Does not return material. Responds in 3 months. "Don't forget contact info with e-mail address for faster response! Always be professional when you submit your work to any company."

Music Mostly **R&B**, **pop/rock**, and **inspirational/gospel**; also **jazz**, **adult contemporary**, and **dance**. Published *Wandaliz Colon* (album), written and recorded by Wandaliz Colon (reggaeton/pop/rock), released on Ivory Pen Entertainment; and "All Healed" (single), by Angel Demone, on Vox Angel Inc./Ivory Pen Entertainment.

Tips "Learn your craft. Always deliver high quality demos. *Remember, if you don't invest in yourself don't expect others to invest in you.* Ivory Pen Entertainment is a music publishing company that caters to the new songwriter, producer, and aspiring artist. We also place music tracks (no vocals) with artists for release."

⊕ ◯ JA/NEIN MUSIKVERLAG GMBH (GEMA)

Oberstr. 14 A, D - 20144, Hamburg Germany. Fax: (49)(40)448 850. E-mail: janeinmv@aol.com. General Manager: Mary Dostal. Music publisher, record company and record producer. Member of GEMA. Publishes 50 songs/year; publishes 5 new songwriters/year. Staff size: 3. Pays 50-66% royalty.

Affiliate(s) Pinorrekk Mv., Star-Club Mv. (GEMA).

How to Contact Submit audio (visual) carrier by mail. Unsolicited submissions are OK. Prefers CD or DVD (if CS, leave three seconds between tracks). Enclose e-mail address. Responds in maximum 2 months.

Music Mostly **jazz**, **klezmer**, **pop**, **rap** and **rock**.

Tips "We do not return submitted material. Send your best A-Side works only, please. Indicate all rights owners, like possible co-composer/lyricist, publisher, sample owner. Write what you expect from collaboration. If artist, enclose photo. Enclose lyrics. Be extraordinary! Be fantastic!"

N ◯ JANA JAE MUSIC (BMI)

P.O. Box 35726, Tulsa OK 74153. (918)786-8896. Fax: (918)786-8897. E-mail: janajae@janajae.com. Web site: www.janajae.com. **Contact:** Kathleen Pixley, secretary. Music publisher, record company (Lark Record Productions, Inc.) and record producer (Lark Talent and Advertising). Estab. 1980. Publishes 5-10 songs/year; publishes 1-2 new songwriters/year. Staff size: 8. Pays standard royalty.

How to Contact Submit demo by mail. Unsolicited submissions are OK. Prefers CD or VHS videocassette with 3-4 songs and typed lyric and lead sheet if possible. Does not return material. Responds only if accepted for use.

Music Mostly **country**, **bluegrass**, **jazz** and **instrumentals** (**classical** or **country**). Published *Mayonnaise* (album by Steve Upfold), recorded by Jana Jae; and *Let the Bible Be Your Roadmap* (album by Irene Elliot), recorded by Jana Jae, both on Lark Records.

☑ ⊘ QUINCY JONES MUSIC (ASCAP)

6671 Sunset Blvd., #1574A, Los Angeles CA 90028. (323)957-6601. E-mail: info@quincyjonesmusic. com. Music publisher.
How to Contact *Quincy Jones Music does not accept unsolicited submissions*.

☐ JPMC MUSIC INC. (BMI, ASCAP)

P.O. Box 526, Burlington VT 05402. (802)860-7110. Fax: (802)860-7112. E-mail: music@jpmc.com. Web site: www.jpmc.com. **Contact:** Jane Peterer, president. Music publisher, record company (JPMC Records) and book publisher. Estab. 1989. Publishes 20 songs/year; publishes 10 new songwriters/year. Pays standard royalty.
Affiliate(s) GlobeSound Publishing (ASCAP) and GlobeArt Publishing Inc. .
How to Contact Submit a demo by mail. Unsolicited submissions are OK. Prefers ''professional'' CD, cassette, or DAT with 3 songs and lyric sheet. ''If submitting a CD, indicate which three tracks to consider, otherwise only the first three will be considered.'' Include SASE. Responds in 2 months. See Web site for complete guidelines.
Music Mostly **pop/R&B**, **jazz** and **gospel**; also **country** and **instrumental**. Published ''Ode to Ireland'' (single by Breschi), recorded by Breschi/Cassidy on Pick Records (instrumental); and ''Ici Paris'' (single), written and recorded by Michael Ganian.
Tips ''We are in constant communication with record and film producers and will administer your work on a worldwide basis. We also publish songbooks for musicians and fans, as well as educational and method books for students and teachers.''

⊘ JUKE MUSIC (BMI)

P.O. Box 120277, Nashville TN 37212. **Contact:** Becky Gibson, songwriter coordinator. Music publisher. Estab. 1987. Publishes 60-150 songs/year; publishes 3-25 new songwriters/year. Pays standard royalty.
How to Contact Submit demo by mail. Unsolicited submissions are OK. Prefers CD with 3 songs and lyric sheet. ''Send only radio-friendly material.'' Does not return material. Responds only if interested.
Music Mostly **country/pop** and **rock**; also **alternative adult** and **Christian**. Does not want theatrical, improperly structured, change tempo and feel, poor or no hook. Published ''Cross on the Highway'' (single) from *Sumner Country Drive Inn* (album), written and recorded by Ronnie McDowell, released 2001 on Portland; ''Wichita Woman'' (single), written and recorded by Buddy Jewell (country), released 2006 on Sony; ''Living the American Dream'' (single) from *Kansas Storm* (album), written and recorded by Dave Parks (country), released 2006 on DayDreamer.
Tips ''Do your homework, craft the song, be sure you're willing to gamble your songwriting integrity on this song or songs you're sending. We recommend songwriters attend workshops or conferences before submitting material. Help us cut through the junk. Send positive, up -tempo, new country for best results. It seems most of our submitters read what we do not want and send that! Please listen to country radio.''

Ⓝ ☐ KAUPPS & ROBERT PUBLISHING CO. (BMI)

P.O. Box 5474, Stockton CA 95205. (209)948-8186. Fax: (209)942-2163. Web site: www.makingmus ic4u.com. **Contact:** Melissa Glenn, A&R coordinator (all styles). Production Manager (country, pop, rock): Rick Webb. Professional Manager (country, pop, rock): Bruce Boun. President: Nancy L. Merrihew. Music publisher, record company (Kaupp Records), manager and booking agent (Merri-

Music Publishers

Webb Productions and Most Wanted Bookings). Estab. 1990. Publishes 15-20 songs/year; publishes 5 new songwriters/year. Pays standard royalty.

How to Contact *Write first and obtain permission to submit.* Prefers cassette or VHS videocassette (if available) with 3 songs maximum and lyric sheet. "If artist, send PR package." Include SASE. Responds in 6 months.

Music Mostly **country**, **R&B** and **A/C rock**; also **pop**, **rock** and **gospel**. Published "Prisoner of Love" (single by N. Merrihew/Rick Webb), recorded by Nanci Lynn (country/rock/pop); "Excuse Me, But That Ain't Country," "I Thank You Father," and "On the Other Side" (singles by N. Merrihew/B. Bolin), recorded by Bruce Bolin (country/rock/pop); and "Did You Think That I Thought That You Liked Me" (single by N. Merrihew/B. Bolin), recorded by Nanci Lynn (country/rock/pop) and Cheryl (country/rock/pop), all released on Kaupp Records.

Tips "Know what you want, set a goal, focus in on your goals, be open to constructive criticism, polish tunes and keep polishing."

✒ LAKE TRANSFER PRODUCTIONS & MUSIC (ASCAP, BMI)
11300 Hartland St., North Hollywood CA 91605. (818)508-7158. **Contact:** Jim Holvay, professional manager (pop, R&B, soul); Tina Antoine (hip-hop, rap); Steve Barri Cohen (alternative rock, R&B). Music publisher and record producer (Steve Barri Cohen). Estab. 1989. Publishes 11 songs/year; publishes 3 new songwriters/year. Staff size: 6. Pay "depends on agreement, usually 50% split."

Affiliate(s) Lake Transfer Music (ASCAP) and Transfer Lake Music (BMI).

How to Contact Accepting unsolicited submissions through mid-2008.

Music Mostly **alternative pop**, **R&B/hip-hop** and **dance**. Does not want country & western, classical, New Age, jazz or swing. Published "Tu Sabes Que Te Amo (Will You Still Be There)" (single by Steve Barri Cohen/Rico) from *Rico: The Movement II* (album), recorded by Rico (rap/hip-hop), released 2004 on Lost Empire/Epic-Sony; "When Water Flows" (single by Steve Barri Cohen/Sheree Brown/Terry Dennis) from *Sheree Brown "83"* (album), recorded by Sheree Brown (urban pop), released 2004 on BBEG Records (a division of Saravels, LLC); and "Fair Game" (single by LaTocha Scott/Steve Barri Cohen) *Soundtrack from the movie Fair Game* (album), recorded by LaTocha Scott (R&B/hip-hop), released 2004 on Raw Deal Records, College Park, Georgia. "All our staff are songwriters/producers. Jim Holvay has written hits like 'Kind of a Drag' and 'Hey Baby They're Playin our Song' for the Buckinghams. Steve Barri Cohen has worked with every one from Evelyn 'Champagne' King (RCA), Phantom Planets (Epic), Meredith Brooks (Capitol) and Dre (Aftermath/Interscope)."

Tips "Trends change, but it's still about the song. Make sure your music and lyrics have a strong (POV) point of view."

✒ LARI-JON PUBLISHING (BMI)
P.O. Box 216, Rising City NE 68658. (402)542-2336. **Contact:** Larry Good, owner. Music publisher, record company (Lari-Jon Records), management firm (Lari-Jon Promotions) and record producer (Lari-Jon Productions). Estab. 1967. Publishes 20 songs/year; publishes 2-3 new songwriters/year. Staff size: 1. Pays standard royalty.

How to Contact Submit demo by mail. Unsolicited submissions are OK. Prefers CD with 5 songs and lyric sheet. "Be professional." Include SASE. Responds in 2 months.

Music Mostly **country**, **Southern gospel** and **'50s rock**. Does not want rock, hip-hop, pop or heavy metal. Published "Bluegrass Blues" and "Carolina Morning" (singles by Larry Good) from *Carolina Morning* (album), recorded by Blue Persuasion (country), released 2002 by Bullseye; "Those Rolling Hills of Glenwood" (single by Tom Campbell) from *Single* (album), recorded by Tom Campbell (country), released 2001 by Jeffs-Room-Productions.

◫ ▨ ◲ LILLY MUSIC PUBLISHING (SOCAN)

61 Euphrasia Dr., Toronto ON M6B 3V8 Canada. (416)782-5768. Fax: (416)782-7170. E-mail: panfilo @sympatico.ca. **Contact:** Panfilo Di Matteo, president. Music publisher and record company (P. & N. Records). Estab. 1992. Publishes 20 songs/year; publishes 8 new songwriters/year. Staff size: 3. Pays standard royalty.

Affiliate(s) San Martino Music Publishing and Paglieta Music Publishing (CMRRA).

How to Contact Submit demo by mail. Unsolicited submissions are OK. Prefers CD (or videocassette if available) with 3 songs and lyric and lead sheets. "We will contact you only if we are interested in the material." Responds in 1 month.

Film & TV Places 12 songs in film/year.

Music Mostly **dance**, **ballads** and **rock**; also **country**. Published "I'd Give It All" (single by Glenna J. Sparkes), recorded by Suzanne Michelle (country crossover), released 2005 on Lilly Records.

◪ LINEAGE PUBLISHING CO. (BMI)

P.O. Box 211, East Prairie MO 63845. (573)649-2211. **Contact:** Tommy Loomas, professional manager. Staff: Alan Carter and Joe Silver. Music publisher, record producer, management firm (Staircase Promotions) and record company (Capstan Record Production). Pays standard royalty.

How to Contact Submit demo by mail. Unsolicited submissions are OK. Prefers cassette with 2-4 songs and lyric sheet; include bio and photo if possible. Include SASE. Responds in 2 months.

Music Mostly **country**, **easy listening**, **MOR**, **country rock** and **top 40/pop**. Published "Let It Rain" (single by Roberta Boyle), recorded by Vicarie Arcoleo on Treasure Coast Records; "Country Boy" (single), written and recorded by Roger Lambert; and "Boot Jack Shuffle" (single by Zachary Taylor), recorded by Skid Row Joe, both on Capstan Records.

◲ LITA MUSIC (ASCAP)

2831 Dogwood Place, Nashville TN 37204. (615)269-8682. Fax: (615)269-8929. Web site: http:// songsfortheplanet.com. **Contact:** Justin Peters, president. Music publisher. Estab. 1980.

Affiliate(s) Justin Peters Music, Platinum Planet Music and Tourmaline (BMI).

How to Contact Submit demo package by mail. Unsolicited submissions are OK. Prefers CD with 5 songs and lyric sheet. Does not return material. "Place code '2007' on each envelope submission."

Music Mostly **Southern gospel/Christian**, **country**, **classic rock** and **worship songs**. Published "No Less Than Faithful" (single by Don Pardoe/Joel Lyndsey), recorded by Ann Downing on Daywind Records, Jim Bullard on Genesis Records and Melody Beizer (#1 song) on Covenant Records; "No Other Like You" (single by Mark Comden/Paula Carpenter), recorded by Twila Paris and Tony Melendez (#5 song) on Starsong Records; "Making A New Start" and "Invincible Faith" (singles by Gayle Cox), recorded by Kingdom Heirs on Sonlite Records; and "I Don't Want To Go Back" (single by Gayle Cox), recorded by Greater Vision on Benson Records; "Lost In The Shadow of the Cross" (single by James Elliott and Steven Curtis Chapman) recorded by Steven Curtis Chapman on Spawn Records.

◲ M & T WALDOCH PUBLISHING, INC. (BMI)

4803 S. Seventh St., Milwaukee WI 53221. (414)482-2194. VP, Creative Management (rockabilly, pop, country): Timothy J. Waldoch. Professional Manager (country, top 40): Mark T. Waldoch. Music publisher. Estab. 1990. Publishes 2-3 songs/year; publishes 2-3 new songwriters/year. Staff size: 2. Pays standard royalty.

How to Contact Submit demo package by mail. Unsolicited submissions are OK. Prefers CD with 3-6 songs and lyric or lead sheet. "We prefer a studio produced demo tape." Include SASE. Responds in 3 months.

Music Mostly **country/pop**, **rock**, **top 40 pop**; also **melodic metal**, **dance**, **R&B**. Does not want rap. Published "It's Only Me" and "Let Peace Rule the World" (by Kenny LePrix), recorded by Brigade on SBD Records (rock).

Tips "Study the classic pop songs from the 1950s through the present time. There is a reason why good songs stand the test of time. Today's hits will be tomorrow's classics. Send your best well-crafted, polished song material."

🎵 🎶 MANUITI L.A. (ASCAP)

℅ Rosen Music Corp. (310)230-6040. Fax: (310)230-4074. E-mail: assistant@rosenmusiccorp.com. **Contact:** Steven Rosen, president. Music publisher and record producer. "The exclusive music publishing company for writer/producer Guy Roche."

How to Contact *Does not accept unsolicited material.*

Film & TV Recently published "Connected," recorded by Sara Paxton in *Aquamarine*; "As If," recorded by Blaque in *Bring It On*; "Turn the Page," recorded by Aaliyah in *Music of the Heart*; and "While You Were Gone," recorded by Kelly Price in *Blue Streak*.

Music All genres. Published "What A Girl Wants" (single), recorded by Christina Aguilera (pop); "Almost Doesn't Count" (single), recorded by Brandy (R&B) on Atlantic; "Beauty" (single), recorded by Dru Hill (R&B) on Island; and "Under My Tree" (single), recorded by *NSync on RCA.

Tips "Do your homework on who you are contacting and what they do. Don't waste yours or their time by not having that information."

🎵 🎶 MANY LIVES MUSIC PUBLISHERS (SOCAN)

RR #1, Kensington PE COB 1MO Canada. (902)836-4571 (studio). E-mail: paul.milner@summerside .ca. **Contact:** Paul C. Milner, publisher. Music publisher. Estab. 1997. Pays standard royalty.

- Chucky Danger's *Colour* album was named Winner Best Pop Recording at the East Coast Music Awards 2006, "Sweet Symphony" was nominated for Single of the Year, and Chucky Danger was nominated for Best New Group. The *Temptation* album won a SOCAN #1 award.

How to Contact Submit demo by mail. Unsolicited submissions are OK. Prefers CD and lyric sheet (lead sheet if available). Does not return material. Responds in 3 months if interested.

Music All styles. Released *Temptation* (album by various writers), arrangement by Paul Milner, Patrizia, Dan Cutrona (rock/opera), released 2003 on United One Records; *Six Pack EP* and *Colour* (album), written and recorded by Chucky Danger (Pop/Rock), released 2005 on Landwash Entertainment; *The Edge Of Emotion* (album by various writers), arrangement by Paul Milner, Patrizia, Dan Cutrona (rock/opera), released 2006 on Nuff entertainment /United One Records.

🎶 JOHN WELLER MARVIN PUBLISHING (ASCAP)

P.O. Box 513, Akron OH 44309. (330)733-8585. Fax: (330)733-8595. E-mail: stephanie.arble@jwmp ublishing.net. Web site: www.jwmpublishing.net. **Contact:** Stephanie Arble, president. Music Publisher. Estab. 1996. Pays standard royalty.

How to Contact Submit demo by mail. Unsolicited submissions are OK. Prefers cassette, CD or VHS and lyric or lead sheet. Responds in 6 weeks.

Music All genres, mostly **pop**, **R&B**, **rap**; also **rock**, and **country**. Published "Downloading Files" (single by S. Arble/R. Scott), recorded by Ameritech Celebration Choir (corporate promotional). "We work with a promoter, Nuff entertainment /United One Records."

🎶 MATERIAL WORTH PUBLISHING (ASCAP)

46 First St., Walden NY 12586. (845) 283-0795. E-mail: franksardella@materialwothpublishing.c om. Web site: www.materialworthpublishing.com. **Contact:** Frank Sardella, owner. Music publisher. Estab. 2003. Staff size: 3. Pays standard royalty of 50%.

How to Contact *Call first and obtain permission to submit a demo.* Prefers CD and lyric sheet, lead sheet, cover letter. Does not return submissions. Responds in 1 week.

Music Mostly **pop**, **adult contemporary**, and **country**. Also **alternative**, **rock**, and **female singer-songwriter**.

🖉 MAUI ARTS & MUSIC ASSOCIATION/SURVIVOR RECORDS/TEN OF DIAMONDS MUSIC (BMI)

PMB 208, P.O. Box 79-1540, Paia HI 96779. (808)874-5900. E-mail: mamamaui@mac.com. Web site: www.dreammaui.com. Professional Manager: Greta Warren (pop). Director: Jason Schwartz. Music publisher and record producer. Estab. 1974. Publishes 1-2 artists/year. Staff size: 2. Pays standard royalty.

How to Contact *Prefers that submitters send a sound file submission via e-mail, maximum of 5 minutes in length.*

Music Mostly **pop**, **country**, **R&B**, and **New Age**. Does not want rock. Published "In the Morning Light" (by Jack Warren), recorded by Jason (pop ballad); "Before the Rain" (by Giles Feldscher), recorded by Jason (pop ballad), both on Survivor; and "Then I Do" (single), written and recorded by Lono, released on Ono Music.

Tips "Looking for a great single only!"

🖉 MAVERICK MUSIC (ASCAP)

3300 Warner Blvd., Burbank CA 91505. (310)385-7800. Web site: www.maverick.com. Music publisher and record company (Maverick).

How to Contact *Maverick Music does not accept unsolicited submissions.*

🖾 🖳 ◯ MAYFAIR MUSIC (BMI)

2600 John St., Unit 203, Markham ON L3R 3W3 Canada. (905)475-1848. Fax: (905)474-9870. **Contact:** John Loweth, A&R director. Music publisher, record company (MBD Records), music print publisher (Mayfairmusic), record producer and distributor. Member CMPA, CIRPA, CRIA. Estab. 1979. Pays standard royalty.

How to Contact Submit demo by mail. Unsolicited submissions are OK. Prefers CD/CDR with 2-5 songs. Does not return material. Responds in 3 weeks.

Music Mostly **instrumental**.

Tips "Strong melodic choruses and original-sounding music receive top consideration."

🖉 MCA MUSIC PUBLISHING

● MCA music has been taken over by Universal, now functions only as a catalog of past music, and does not publish new material any longer.

🖉 MCCLURE & TROWBRIDGE PUBLISHING, LTD (ASCAP, BMI)

P.O. Box 70403, Nashville TN 37207. (615)902-0509. Web site: www.TrowbridgePlanetEarth.com. Contact: Miig Miniger, director of marketing. Music publisher, and record label (JIP Records) and production company (George McClure, producer). Estab. 1983. Publishes 25 songs/year. Publishes 5 new songwriters/year. Staff size: 8. Pays standard royalty of 50%.

How to Contact *Follow directions ONLINE ONLY—obtain Control Number to submit a demo.* Requires CD with 1-5 songs, lyric sheet, and cover letter. Does not return submissions. Responds in 3 weeks if interested.

Music Pop, **country**, **gospel**, **Latin** and **swing**. "We are very open-minded as far as genres. If it's good music, we like it!" Published "You're One In A Million" (single), recorded by Layni Kooper (R&B/pop), released 2007 on JIP Records; "Little Miss Santa Claus" (Christmas single), released 2006 on JIP Records; "My Way or Hit the Highway" (single), written and recorded by Jacqui Watson (Americana), released 2005 on Artist Choice CD; and "I'm A Wild One" (single), recorded by Veronica Leigh, released 2006 on Artist Choice CD.

🖾 🖉 MIDI TRACK PUBLISHING (BMI)/ALLRS MUSIC PUBLISHING CO. (ASCAP)

P.O. Box 1545, Smithtown NY 11787. (718)767-8995. E-mail: allrsmusic@aol.com. Web site: www.geocities.com/allrsmusic or www.myspace.com/allrsmusic or www.myspace.com/miditrackrecords.

Contact: Renee Silvestri, president. Music publisher, record company (MIDI Track Records), music consultant, artist management. Voting member of NARAS (The Grammy Awards), CMA, SGMA, SGA. Estab. 1994. Staff size: 5. Publishes 3 songs/year; publishes 2 new songwriters/year. Pays standard royalty.

Affiliate(s) Midi-Track Publishing Co. (BMI).

How to Contact *Write or e-mail first to obtain a Log number and permission to submit. "We do not accept unsolicited submissions."* Prefers CD or cassette with 3 songs, lyric sheet and cover letter. "Make sure your CD or cassette tape is labeled with your name, mailing address, telephone number, and e-mail address. We do not return material." Responds via e-mail in 6 months.

Film & TV Places 1 song in film/year. Published "Why Can't You Hear My Prayer" (single by F. John Silvestri/Leslie Silvestri), recorded by Iliana Medina in a documentary by Silvermine Films.

Music Mostly **country**, **gospel**, **top 40**, **R&B**, **MOR** and **pop**. Does not want showtunes, jazz, classical or rap. Published "Why Can't You Hear My Prayer" (single by F. John Silvestri/Leslie Silvestri), recorded by eight-time Grammy nominee Huey Dunbar of the group DLG (Dark Latin Groove), released on Trend Records (other multiple releases, also recorded by Iliana Medina and released 2002 on MIDI Track Records); "Chasing Rainbows" (single by F. John Silvestri/Leslie Silvestri), recorded by Tommy Cash (country), released on MMT Records (including other multiple releases); "Because of You" (single by F. John Silvestri/Leslie Silvestri), recorded by Iliana Medina, released 2002 on MIDI Track Records, also recorded by three-time Grammy nominee Terri Williams, released on KMA Records; also recorded by Grand Ole Opry member Ernie Ashworth, released 2004 on KMA Records; "My Coney Island" (single by F. John Silvestri/Leslie Silvestri), recorded by eight-time Grammy nominee Huey Dunbar, released 2005 on MIDI Track Records.

Tips "Attend workshops, seminars, and join songwriters organizations. Write, write, write, and re-write, re-write, re-write, and you will achieve your goal."

⛏ ◯ MONTINA MUSIC (SOCAN)

Box 702, Snowdon Station, Montreal QC H3X 3X8 Canada. **Contact:** David P. Leonard, professional manager. Music publisher and record company (Monticana Records). Estab. 1963. Pays negotiable royalty.

Affiliate(s) Saber-T Music (SOCAN).

How to Contact Unsolicited submissions are OK. Prefers CD. SAE and IRC. Responds in 3 months.

Music Mostly **top 40**; also **bluegrass**, **blues**, **country**, **dance-oriented**, **easy listening**, **folk**, **gospel**, **jazz**, **MOR**, **progressive**, **R&B**, **rock** and **soul**. Does not want heavy metal, hard rock, jazz, classical or New Age.

Tips "Maintain awareness of styles and trends of your peers who have succeeded professionally. Understand the markets to which you are pitching your material. Persevere at marketing your talents. Develop a network of industry contacts, first locally, then regionally, nationally and internationally."

◯ THE MUSIC ROOM PUBLISHING GROUP (ASCAP)/MRP MUSIC (BMI)

P.O. Box 219, Redondo Beach CA 90277. (310)316-4551. E-mail: mrp@aol.com. Web site: www.MusicRoomOnline.com and www.Hollywood2You.tv (editorial site). **Contact:** John Reed, president/owner. Music publisher and record producer. Estab. 1982. Pays standard royalty.

Affiliate(s) MRP Music (BMI).

How to Contact *Not accepting unsolicited material.*

Music Mostly **pop/rock/R&B** and **crossover**. Published "That Little Tattoo," "Mona Lisa" and "Sleepin' with an Angel" (singles by John E. Reed) from *Rock With An Attitude* (album), recorded by Rawk Dawg (rock), released 2002; "Over the Rainbow" and "Are You Still My Lover" (singles) from *We Only Came to Rock* (album), recorded by Rawk Dawg, released 2004 on Music Room Productions®.

🎵 ⊘ NAKED JAIN RECORDS (ASCAP)

P.O. Box 4132, Palm Springs CA 92263-4132. (760)325-8663. Fax: (760)320-4305. E-mail: info@nak
edjainrecords.com. Web site: www.nakedjainrecords.com. **Contact:** Dena Banes, vice president/
A&R. Music publisher, record company and record producer (Dey Martin). Estab. 1991. Publishes
40 songs/year; publishes 2 new songwriters/year. Staff size: 5. Pays standard royalty.
Affiliate(s) Aven Deja Music (ASCAP).
How to Contact "Submit online at www.mtraks.com."
Film & TV Places 10 songs in TV/year. Music Supervisors: Dey Martin (alternative). Recently pub-
lished "Yea Right" (single), written and recorded by Lung Cookie in Fox Sports TV; "Just Ain't
Me" (single), written and recorded by Lung Cookie in ESPN-TV; and "Speak Easy" (single), written
and recorded by Lung Cookie in ESPN-TV.
Music Mostly **alternative rock**. Does not want country.
Tips "Write a good song."

🎵 A NEW RAP JAM PUBLISHING (BMI)

P.O. Box 683, Lima OH 45802. E-mail: just_chilling_2002@yahoo.com. Professional Managers:
William Roach (rap, clean); James Milligan (country, 70s music, pop). **Contact:** A&R Dept. Music
publisher and record company (New Experience/Faze 4 Records, Pump It Up Records, and Rough
Edge Records). Estab. 1989. Publishes 40 songs/year; publishes 2-3 new songwriters/year. Hires
staff songwriters. Staff size: 6. Pays standard royalty.
Affiliate(s) Party House Publishing (BMI), Creative Star Management, and Rough Edge Records.
Distribution through Sonic Wave International (SONY/BMG/SMD).
How to Contact *Write first to arrange personal interview or submit demo CD by mail.* Unsolicited
submissions are OK. Prefers CD with 3-5 songs and lyric or lead sheet. Include SASE. Responds in
6-8 weeks weeks. "Visit www.NewExperienceRecords.com for more information."
Music Mostly **R&B**, **pop**, **blues** and **rock/rap**; also **contemporary**, **gospel**, **country** and **soul**.
Published "Lets Go Dancing" (single by Dion Mikel), recorded and released 2006 on Faze 4 Re-
cords/New Experience Records; "The Broken Hearted" (single) from *The Final Chapter* (album),
recorded by T.M.C. the milligan conection (R&B/gospel), released 2003/2007 on New Experience/
Pump It Up Records. Other artists include singer-songwriter James, Jr. on Faze 4 Records/Sonic
Wave International.
Tips "We are seeking hit artists of the 1970s and 1980s who would like to be re-signed, as well as
new talent and female solo artists. Send any available information supporting the group or act. We
are a label that does not promote violence, drugs or anything that we feel is a bad example for our
youth. Establish music industry contacts, write and keep writing and most of all believe in yourself.
Use a good recording studio but be very professional. Just take your time and produce the best
music possible. Sometimes you only get one chance. Make sure you place your best song on your
demo first. This will increase your chances greatly. If you're the owner of your own small label
and have a finished product, please send it. And if there is interest we will contact you. Also be
on the lookout for new artists on Rough Edge Records. Sonic Wave International now reviewing
material. Please be aware of the new sampling laws and laws for digital downloading. It is against
the law. People are being jailed and fined for this act. Do your homework. Read the new digital
downloading contracts carefully or seek legal help if need be. Good luck and thanks for considering
our company for your musical needs. We have had a wonderful 22 years. God bless you. Let's
continue to support our troops that they may have a happy return trip home."

✅ ⊘ NEWBRAUGH BROTHERS MUSIC (ASCAP, BMI)

228 Morgan Lane, Berkeley Springs WV 25411-3475. (304)261-0228. E-mail: Nbtoys@verizon.net.
Contact: John S. Newbraugh, owner. Music publisher, record company (NBT Records, BMI/AS-

CAP). Estab. 1967. Publishes 124 songs/year. Publishes 14 new songwriters/year. Staff size: 1. Pays standard royalty.

Affiliate(s) NBT Music (ASCAP) and Newbraugh Brothers Music (BMI).

How to Contact Submit demo by mail. Unsolicited submissions are OK. Prefers cassette or CD with any amount of songs, a lyric sheet and a cover letter. Include SASE. Responds in 6 weeks. "Please don't call for permission to submit. Your materials are welcomed."

Music Mostly **rockabilly, hillbilly, folk** and **bluegrass**; also **rock**, **country**, and **gospel**. "We will accept all genres of music except songs with vulgar language." Published "Blink Of An Eye" (single), by Steve Osheyack, released 2005; *Malcolm Arthur and the Knights* (album, from Australia), released 2005. "We also released and published many of the songs for *Ride The Train—Vol #20* in 2007, which brings the total of train/railroad related song issued on this NBT series to 420 songs, with writers and artists from over half the states in the U.S.A., Canada, several countries in Europe, and Australia.

Tips "Find out if a publisher/record company has any special interest. NBT, for instance, is always hunting 'original' train songs. Our 'registered' trademark is a train and from time to time we release a compilation album of all train songs. We welcome all genres of music for this project."

⊘ ORCHID PUBLISHING (BMI)

Bouquet-Orchid Enterprises, P.O. Box 1335, Norcross GA 30091. Phone/fax: (770)339-9088. **Contact:** Bill Bohannon, president. Music publisher, record company, record producer (Bouquet-Orchid Enterprises) and artist management. Member: CMA, AFM. Publishes 10-12 songs/year; publishes 3 new songwriters/year. Pays standard royalty.

How to Contact Submit demo by mail. Unsolicited submissions are OK. Prefers cassette or CD with 3-5 songs and lyric sheet. "Send biographical information if possible—even a photo helps." Include SASE. Responds in 1 month.

Music Mostly **religious** ("Amy Grant, etc., contemporary gospel"); **country** ("Garth Brooks, Trisha Yearwood-type material"); and **top 100/pop** ("Bryan Adams, Whitney Houston-type material"). Published "Blue As Your Eyes" (single), written and recorded by Adam Day; "Spare My Feelings" (single by Clayton Russ), recorded by Terri Palmer; and "Trying to Get By" (single by Tom Sparks), recorded by Bandoleers, all on Bouquet Records.

⊘ PEERMUSIC (ASCAP, BMI)

5358 Melrose Ave., Suite 400, Los Angeles CA 90038. (323)960-3400. Fax: (323)960-3410. Web site: www.peermusic.com. Music publisher and artist development promotional label. Estab. 1928. Hires staff songwriters. "All deals negotiable."

Affiliate(s) Songs of Peer Ltd. (ASCAP) and Peermusic III Ltd. (BMI).

How to Contact "We do NOT accept unsolicited submissions. We only accept material through agents, attorneys and managers." Prefers CD and lyric sheet. Does not return material.

Music Mostly **pop**, **rock** and **R&B**. Published music by David Foster (writer/producer, pop); Andrew Williams (writer/producer, pop); Christopher "Tricky" Stewart (R&B, writer/producer).

⊘ PERLA MUSIC (ASCAP)

122 Oldwick Rd., Whitehouse Station NJ 08889-5014. (908)439-9118. Fax: (908)439-9119. E-mail: PerlaMusic@PMRecords.org. Web site: www.PMRecords.org. **Contact:** Gene Perla (jazz). Music publisher, record company (PMRecords.org), record producer (Perla.org), studio production (TheSystemMSP.com) and Internet Design (CCINYC.com). Estab. 1971. Publishes 5 songs/year. Staff size: 5. Pays 75%/25% royalty.

How to Contact *E-mail first and obtain permission to submit.*

Music Mostly **jazz** and **rock**.

❏ JUSTIN PETERS MUSIC (BMI)

P.O. Box 40251, Nashville TN 37204. (615)269-8682. Fax: (615)269-8929. Web site: www.songsfort heplanet.com. **Contact:** Justin Peters, president. Music publisher. Estab. 1981.
Affiliate(s) Platinum Planet Music(BMI), Tourmaline (BMI) and LITA Music (ASCAP).
How to Contact Submit demo package by mail. Unsolicited submissions are OK. Prefers CD with 5 songs and lyric sheet. Does not return material. "Place code '2008' on each envelope submission."
Music Mostly **pop**, **reggae**, **country** and **comedy**. Published "Saved By Love" (single), recorded by Amy Grant on A&M Records; "Nothing Can Separate Us", recorded by Al Denson; "A Gift That She Don't Want" (single), recorded by Bill Engvall on Warner Brother Records; and "I Wanna Be That Man" (single), recorded by McKameys on Pamplin Records, all written by Justin Peters; "Heaven's Got to Help Me Shake These Blues" (single), recorded by B.J. Thomas; "It's Christmas Time Again" (single by Constance Peters/Justin Peters), recorded by Jimmy Fortune.

❷ PHOEBOB MUSIC (BMI)

5181 Regent Dr., Nashville TN 37220. (615)832-4199. **Contact:** Phoebe Binkley.
How to Contact "We do not want unsolicited submissions."
Music Mostly **country**, **Christian**, and **theatre**.

❏ PIANO PRESS (ASCAP)

P.O. Box 85, Del Mar CA 92014-0085. (619)884-1401. Fax: (858)755-1104. E-mail: pianopress@pian opress.com. Web site: www.pianopress.com. **Contact:** Elizabeth C. Axford, M.A., owner. Music publisher and distributor. Publishes songbooks & CD's for music students and teachers. Estab. 1998. Licenses 32-100 songs/year; publishes 1-24 new songwriters/year. Staff size: 5. Pays standard print music and/or mechanical royalty; songwriter retains rights to songs.
How to Contact *E-mail first to obtain permission to submit.* Prefers CD with 1-3 songs, lyric and lead sheet, cover letter and sheet music/piano arrangements. "Looking for children's songs for young piano students and arrangements of public domain folk songs of any nationality." Currently accepting submissions for various projects. Include SASE. Responds in 2-3 months.
Music Mostly **children's songs**, **folk songs** and **holiday songs**; also **teaching pieces**, **piano arrangements**, **lead sheets with melody, chords and lyrics** and **songbooks**. Does not want commercial pop, R&B, etc. Published My Halloween Fun Songbook and CD and My Christmas Fun Songbook series. "I Can" (single by Tom Gardner) from Kidtunes (album), recorded by The Uncle Brothers (children's), released 2002 by Piano Press; "Rock & Roll Teachers" (single by Bob King) from Kidtunes (album), recorded by Bob King & Friends (children's), released 2002 by Piano Press; and "It Really Isn't Garbage" (single by Danny Einbender) from Kidtunes (album), recorded by Danny Eibende/Pete Seeger/et al. (children's), released 2002 by Piano Press.
Tips "Songs should be simple, melodic and memorable. Lyrics should be for a juvenile audience and well-crafted."

❏ PLATINUM PLANET MUSIC, INC. (BMI)

2831 Dogwood Place, Nashville TN 37204. (615)269-8682. Fax: (615)269-8929. Web site: www.son gsfortheplanet.com. **Contact:** Justin Peters, president. Music publisher. Estab. 1997.
Affiliate(s) Justin Peters Music (BMI), Tourmaline (BMI) and LITA Music (ASCAP).
How to Contact Submit demo package by mail. Unsolicited submissions are OK. Prefers CD with 5 songs and lyric sheet. Does not return material. "Place code '2008' on each envelope submission."
Music Mostly **R&B**, **dance** and **country**; also represents many **Christian** artists/writers. Published "Happy Face" (single by Dez Dickerson/Jordan Dickerson), recorded by Squirt on Absolute Records; "Welcome To My Love" (single by Mike Hunter), recorded by Kyndl on PPMI; "Love's Not A Game" (single), written and recorded by Kashief Lindo on Heavybeat Records; "Dancing Singing" (single by A. Craig/Justin Peters) recorded by Dan Burda on Independent; and "Loud" (single), written and recorded by These Five Down on Absolute Records.

❷ POLLYBYRD PUBLICATIONS LIMITED (ASCAP, BMI, SESAC)

P.O. Box 261488, Encino CA 91426. (818)506-8533. Fax: (818)506-8534. E-mail: pplzmi@aol.com. Web site: www.pplzmi.com. Branch office: 468 N. Camden Drive Suite 200, Beverly Hills CA 90210. **Contact:** Dakota Hawk, vice president. Professional Managers: Cisco Blue (country, pop, rock); Tedford Steele (hip-hop, R&B). Music publisher, record company (PPL Entertainment) and Management firm (Sa'mall Management). Estab. 1979. Publishes 100 songs/year; publishes 25-40 new songwriters/year. Hires staff writers. Pays standard royalty.

Affiliate(s) Kellijai Music (ASCAP), Pollyann Music (ASCAP), Ja'Nikki Songs (BMI), Velma Songs International (BMI), Lonnvanness Songs (SESAC), PPL Music (ASCAP), Zettitalia Music, Butternut Music (BMI), Zett Two Music (ASCAP), Plus Publishing and Zett One Songs (BMI).

How to Contact *Write first and obtain permission to submit.* No phone calls. Prefers CD, cassette, or videocassette with 4 songs and lyric and lead sheet. Include SASE. Responds in 2 months.

Music Published "Return of the Players" (album) by Juz-Cuz 2004 on PPL; "Believe" (single by J. Jarrett/S. Cuseo) from *Time* (album), recorded by Lejenz (pop), released 2001 on PRL/Credence; *Rainbow Gypsy Child* (album), written and recorded by Riki Hendrix (rock), released 2001 on PRL/Sony; and "What's Up With That" (single by Brandon James/Patrick Bouvier) from *Outcast* (album), recorded by Condottieré; (hip-hop), released 2001 on Bouvier.

Tips "Make those decisions—are you really a songwriter? Are you prepared to starve for your craft? Do you believe in delayed gratification? Are you commercial or do you write only for yourself? Can you take rejection? Do you want to be the best? If so, contact us—if not, keep your day job."

❷ PORTAGE MUSIC (BMI)

16634 Gannon Ave. W., Rosemount MN 55068. (952)432-5737. E-mail: olrivers@earthlink.net. President: Larry LaPole. Music publisher. Publishes 0-5 songs/year. Pays standard royalty.

How to Contact *Call or e-mail first for permission to submit.*

Music Mostly **country** and **country rock**. Published "Lost Angel," "Think It Over" and "Congratulations to Me" (by L. Lapole), all recorded by Trashmen on Sundazed.

Tips "Keep songs short, simple and upbeat with positive theme."

☑ ▣ ◯ QUARK, INC.

P.O. Box 771, New City NY 10956-0771. (917)687-9988. E-mail: quarkent@aol.com. **Contact:** Curtis Urbina, manager. Music publisher, record company (Quark Records) and record producer (Curtis Urbina). Estab. 1984. Publishes 12 songs/year; 2 new songwriters/year. Staff size: 4. Pays standard royalty.

Affiliate(s) Quarkette Music (BMI), Freedurb Music (ASCAP), and Quark Records.

How to Contact Prefers CD only with 2 songs. No cassettes. Include SASE. Responds in 2 months.

Film & TV Places 10 songs in film/year. Music Supervisor: Curtis Urbina.

Music House music only. Does not want anything short of a hit. Published [new credits in mid-July]

❷ QUEEN ESTHER MUSIC PUBLISHERS (ASCAP)

449 N. Vista St., Los Angeles CA 90036. (323)653-0693. E-mail: unclelenny@aol.com. Web site: www.parlirec.com. **Contact:** Len Weisman, owner. Record producer, personal manager, music publisher. Estab. 1980. Publishes 30-50 songs/year.

• Also see the listings for Audio Music Publishers in the Music Publishers section of this book; Parliament Records in the Record Companies section and The Weisman Production Group in this section of this book.

How to Contact Send demo CD with 3-10 songs. Include SASE. We only return in prepaid large envelopes.

Music Mostly **R&B**, **soul**, **blues** and **2nd gospel**. Just finished *E'morey* (album); *Jus van* (album); *Jewel With Love* (album); and *Chosen Rapture Ministry* (album).

☑ 🌐 ◻ R.T.L. MUSIC

Perthy Farm, The Perthy, Shropshire SY12 9HR United Kingdom. (01691)623173. **Contact:** Tanya Woof, international A&R manager. Professional Managers: Ron Dickson (rock/rock 'n roll); Katrine LeMatt (MOR/dance); Xavier Lee (heavy metal); Tanya Lee (classical/other types). Music publisher, record company (Le Matt Music) and record producer. Estab. 1971. Publishes approximately 30 songs/year. Pays standard royalty.

Affiliate(s) Lee Music (publishing), Swoop Records, Grenouille Records, Check Records, Zarg Records, Pogo Records, R.T.F.M. (all independent companies).

How to Contact Submit demo by mail. Unsolicited submissions are OK. Prefers CD, cassette, MDisc or DVD (also VHS 625/PAL system videocassette) with 1-3 songs and lyric and lead sheets; include still photos and bios. "Make sure name and address are on CD or cassette." Send IRC. Responds in 6 weeks.

Music All types. Published "The Old Days" (single by Ron Dickson) from *Groucho* (album), recorded by Groucho (pop); "Orphan in the Storm" (single by M.J. Lawson) from *Emmit Till* (album), recorded by Emmit Till (blues); "Donna" (single by Mike Sheriden) from *Donna* (album), recorded by Mike Sheriden (pop), all released 2006 on Swoop.

◻ ⊘ RAINBOW MUSIC CORP. (ASCAP)

45 E. 66 St., New York NY 10021. (212)988-4619. Fax: (212)861-9079. E-mail: fscam45@aol.com. **Contact:** Fred Stuart, vice president. Music publisher. Estab. 1990. Publishes 25 songs/year. Staff size: 2. Pays standard royalty.

Affiliate(s) Tri-Circle (ASCAP).

How to Contact *Only accepts material referred by a reputable industry source.* Prefers CD with 2 songs and lyric sheet. Include SASE. Responds in 1 week.

Film & TV Published "You Wouldn't Lie To An Angel, Would Ya?" (single by Diane Lampert/Paul Overstreet) from Lady of the Evening (album), recorded by Ben te Boe (country), released 2003 on Mega International Records; "Gonna Give Lovin' A Try" (single by Cannonball Adderley/Diane Lampert/Nat Adderley) from The Axelrod Chronicles (album), recorded by Randy Crawford (jazz), released 2003 on Fantasy Records; "Breaking Bread" (single by Diane Lampert/Paul Overstreet) from Unearthed (album), recorded by Johnny Cash (country), released 2003 on Lost Highway Records; "Gonna Give Lovin' A Try" (single by Cannonball Adderley/Diane Lampert/Nat Adderley) from Day Dreamin' (album), recorded by Laverne Butler (jazz), released 2002 on Chesky Records; "Nothin' Shakin' (But the Leaves on the Trees)" (single by Diane Lampert;John Gluck, Jr./Eddie Fontaine/Cirino Colcrai) recorded by the Beatles, from *Live at the BBC* (album).

Music Mostly **pop**, **R&B** and **country**; also **jazz**. Published "Break It To Me Gently" (single by Diane Lampert/Joe Seneca) from *TIME/LIFE* compilations *Queens of Country* (2004), *Classic Country* (2003), and *Glory Days of Rock 'N Roll* (2002), recorded by Brenda Lee.

◻ RED SUNDOWN MUSIC (BMI)

P.O. Box 609, Pleasant View TN 37146. (615)746-0844. E-mail: rsdr@bellsouth.net. Web site: www.redsundown.com. **Contact:** Ruby Perry.

How to Contact *Does not accept unsolicited submissions.* Submit CD and cover letter. Does not return submissions.

Music Country, **rock**, and **pop**. Does not want rap or hip-hop. Published "Take A Heart" (single by Kyle Pierce) from *Take Me With You* (album), recorded by Tammy Lee (country) released in 1998 on Red Sundown Records.

⚓ ⊘ REN ZONE MUSIC (ASCAP)

P.O. Box 3153, Huntington Beach CA 92605. (714)596-6582. Fax: (714)596-6577. E-mail: renzone@ socal.rr.com. **Contact:** Renah Wolzinger, president. Music publisher. Estab. 1998. Publishes 14 songs/year; publishes 2 new songwriters/year. Staff size: 2. Pays standard royalty.

• This company won a Parents Choice 1998 Silver Honor Shield.

How to Contact *Does not accept unsolicited submissions.*

Music Mostly **world music** and **children's**. Published *Tumble-n-Tunes*, *Elementary My Friend*, *Songs from the Sea to the Shore*, *Pourings from the Heart*, *Classic American Klezmer*, *Klezmer Coast to Coast*, and *Yiddish America* (albums)

Tips ''Submit well-written lyrics that convey important concepts to kids on good quality demos with easy to understand vocals.''

⊘ RHINESTONE COWBOY MUSIC (ASCAP)

P.O. Box 22971, Nashville TN 37202. (615)554-3400.

How to Contact *Contact first and obtain permission to submit a demo.* Submit demo CD with 5 songs. Responds only if interested.

Ⓝ ⊘ ROCK SOLID ENTERTAINMENT (ASCAP)

P.O. Box 5537, Moss Point MS 39563. E-mail: jmitch7@student.mgccc.edu. Web site: www.solidasa rock.net. **Contact:** Justin Mitchell, owner. Music Publisher, Record Company, Rock Solid: Engineers, Radio, Magazine & Solidasarock.net

Affiliate(s) Force Tha Fitt Musik (ASCAP).

How to Contact *''Request permission before you send music.* We accept music & creative video. No permission needed to send creative video. Send permission request to: jmitch7@student.mgccc.edu.''

Music Looking for **rap**, **techno**, **bass**, **jungle**, **IDM**, **R&B**, **experimental music**, and **instrumental music**. We also are looking for creative videos for our online radio station (Rock Solid Radio).

Tips ''Your sound quality has to be just as good as what you hear on the radio. Check for more tips on our site www.solidasarock.net. Maybe some people can do everything themselves. Stop at engineering. Please find a good engineer to shape, chisel, and smooth out your sound.''

⊘ ROCKFORD MUSIC CO. (ASCAP, BMI)

150 West End Ave., Suite 6-D, New York NY 10023. **Contact:** Danny Darrow, manager. Music publisher, record company (Mighty Records), record and video tape producer (Danny Darrow). Publishes 1-3 songs/year; publishes 1-3 new songwriters/year. Staff size: 3. Pays standard royalty.

Affiliate(s) Corporate Music Publishing Company (ASCAP), Stateside Music Company (BMI), and Rockford Music Co. (BMI).

How to Contact Submit demo by mail. Unsolicited submissions are OK. ''No phone calls and do not write for permission to submit.'' Prefers cassette with 3 songs and lyric sheet. Does not return material. Responds in 2 weeks.

Music Mostly **MOR** and **top 40/pop**; also **adult pop**, **country**, **adult rock**, **dance-oriented**, **easy listening**, **folk** and **jazz**. Does not want rap. Published ''Look to the Wind'' (single by Peggy Stewart/Danny Darrow) from *Falling in Love* (album), recorded by Danny Darrow (movie theme); ''Doomsday'' (single by Robert Lee Lowery/Danny Darrow) from *Doomsday* (album), recorded by Danny Darrow (euro jazz), all released 2004 on Mighty Records;and ''Telephones'' (single Robert Lee Lowery/Danny Darrow) from *Telephones* (album), and ''Love to Dance'' (single by Robert Lee Lowery/Danny Darrow) from *Love to Dance* (album), both recorded by Danny Darrow (trance dance), released 2006 on Mighty Records.

Tips ''Listen to Top 40 and write current lyrics and music.''

⊘ RONDOR MUSIC INTERNATIONAL/ALMO/IRVING MUSIC, A UNIVERSAL MUSIC GROUP COMPANY (ASCAP,BMI)

2440 Sepulveda Blvd., Suite 119, Los Angeles CA 90064. (310)235-4800. Fax: (310)235-4801. Web site: www.universalmusicpublishing.com. **Contact:** Creative Staff Assistant. Nashville office: 1904 Adelicia St., Nashville TN 37212. (615)321-0820. Fax: (615)329-1018. Music publisher. Estab. 1965. **Affiliates** Almo Music Corp. (ASCAP) and Irving Music, Inc. (BMI).

How to Contact *Does not accept unsolicited submissions.*

▢ RUSTIC RECORDS, INC. PUBLISHING (ASCAP, BMI, SESAC)

6337 Murray Lane, Brentwood TN 37027. (615)371-0646. Fax: (615)370-0353. E-mail: info@countr yalbums.com. Web site: www.countryalbums.com. **Contact:** Jack Schneider, president. Vice President: Claude Southall. Office Manager: Nell Tolson. Music publisher, record company (Rustic Records Inc.) and record producer. Estab. 1984. Publishes 20 songs/year. Pays standard royalty.

Affiliate(s) Covered Bridge Music (BMI), Town Square Music (SESAC), Iron Skillet Music (ASCAP). How to Contact Submit demo by mail. Unsolicited submissions are OK. Prefers CD with 3-4 songs and lyric sheet. Include SASE. Responds in 3 months.

Music Mostly **country**. Published "In Their Eyes" (single by Jamie Champa); "Take Me As I Am" (single by Bambi Barrett/Paul Huffman); and "Yesterday's Memories" (single by Jack Schneider), recorded by Colte Bradley (country), released 2003.

Tips "Send three or four traditional country songs, novelty songs 'foot-tapping, hand-clapping' gospel songs with strong hook for male or female artist of duet. Enclose SASE (manilla envelope)."

▢ RUSTRON MUSIC PUBLISHERS (BMI)/WHIMSONG MUSIC (ASCAP)

1156 Park Lane, West Palm Beach FL 33417-5957. (561)686-1354. E-mail: rmp_wmp@bellsouth.n et. **Contact:** Sheelah Adams, office administrator (for current submission guidelines). Professional Managers: Rusty Gordon (adult contemporary, acoustic-electric, New Age instrumentals, folk fusions, children's, blues, cabaret, soft vocal & instrumental jazz fusions, soft rock, women's music, world music); Ron Caruso (all styles); Davilyn Whims (folk fusions, country, R&B). Music publisher, record company, management firm and record producer (Rustron Music Productions). Estab. 1972. Publishes 100-150 songs/year; publishes 10-20 new songwriters/year. Staff size: 9. Pays standard royalty.

Affiliate(s) Whimsong Publishing (ASCAP).

How to Contact Submit demo by mail. Cover letter should explain reason for submitting and what songwriter needs from Rustron-Whimsong. Unsolicited submissions are OK. Current submission guidelines will be sent by e-mail upon request. If requesting by snail mail, include SASE. All songs submitted must be Copyrighted by the songwriter(s) on Form PA with the U.S. Library of Congress prior to submitting. For freelance songwriters we prefer CD with up to 10 songs or cassette with 1-3 songs and typed lyric sheets (1 sheet for each song). For performing songwriters we prefer CD with up to 15 songs. A typed lyric sheet for each song submitted is required. "Clearly label your tape container or jewel box. We don't review songs on Web sites." SASE or International Reply Coupon (IRC) required for all correspondence. No exceptions. Responds in 4 months.

Music Mostly **pop** (ballads, blues, theatrical, cabaret), **progressive country** and **folk/rock**; also **R&B**, **New Age** (instrumental fusions with classical, jazz or pop themes), **women's music**, **children's music** and **world music**. Does not publish Youth Music—rap, hip-hop, new wave, hard rock, heavy metal or punk. Published "White House Worries" (single) from *Whitehouse Worries* (album), written and recorded by The Ramifications (progressive country-folk/socio-political-topical), released 2007 on Rustron Records; "Sanibel-Captiva and the Gulf of Mexico" (single—historical song) from *Song of Longboat Key* (album), recorded by Florida Rank & File (Florida folk); "Take the High Road" (single) from *Voting for Democracy* (album), recorded by The Panama City Pioneers (progressive-political-folk), released 2007 on Whimsong Records.

Tips "Accepting performing and freelance songwriter's CD for full "Body of Work" product review of all songs on CD. Write strong hooks. For single-song marketing, songs should have definitive verse melody. Keep song length 3-3½ minutes or less. Avoid predictability—create original and unique lyric themes. Tell a story. Develop a strong chorus with well-planned phrasing that can build into song titles and/or tags. Tune in to the trends and fusions indicative of commercially viable new music for the new millennium. All songs reviewed for single-song marketing must be very carefully crafted. Album cuts can be eclectic."

S.M.C.L. PRODUCTIONS, INC.

P.O. Box 84, Boucherville QC J4B 5E6 Canada. (450)641-2266. **Contact:** Christian Lefort, president. Music publisher and record company. SOCAN. Estab. 1968. Publishes 25 songs/year. Pays standard royalty.

Affiliate(s) A.Q.E.M. Ltee, Bag Music, C.F. Music, Big Bazaar Music, Sunrise Music, Stage One Music, L.M.S. Music, ITT Music, Machine Music, Dynamite Music, Cimafilm, Coincidence Music, Music and Music, Cinemusic Inc., Cinafilm, Editions La Fete Inc., Groupe Concept Musique, Editions Dorimen, C.C.H. Music (PRO/SDE) and Lavagot Music.

How to Contact *Write first and obtain permission to submit.* Prefers CD with 4-12 songs and lead sheet. SAE and IRC. Responds in 3 months.

Film & TV Places songs in film and TV. Recently published songs in French-Canadian TV series and films, including *Young Ivanhoe, Twist of Terror, More Tales of the City, Art of War, Lance & Comte (Nouvelle Generation), Turtle Island* (TV series), *Being Dorothy, The Hidden Fortress, Lance et Compte:La Revanche* (TV series), and *A Vos Marques, Party* (film).

Music Mostly **dance**, **easy listening** and **MOR**; also **top 40/pop** and **TV and movie soundtracks**. Published *Always and Forever* (album by Maurice Jarre/Nathalie Carien), recorded by N. Carsen on BMG Records (ballad); *Au Nom De La Passion* (album), written and recorded by Alex Stanke on Select Records.

SADDLESTONE PUBLISHING (BMI, SOCAN)

556 Amess St., New Westminster BC V3L 4A9 Canada. (604)523-9309. Fax: (604)523-9310. E-mail: saddlestone@shaw.ca. Web site: www.saddlestone.net. **Contact:** Candice James (country), CEO. President: Grant Lucas (rock). Professional Manager: Sharla Cuthbertson (pop, R&B). Music publisher, record company (Saddlestone) and record producer (Silver Bow Productions). Estab. 1988. Publishes 100 songs/year; publishes 12-30 new songwriters/year. Pays standard royalty.

Affiliate(s) Silver Bow Publishing (SOCAN, ASCAP).

How to Contact Submit demo by mail. Unsolicited submissions are OK. Prefers CD with any amount of songs and lyric sheet. "Make sure vocal is clear." Does not return material. Responds in 3 months.

Film & TV Places 1 song in film and 2 songs in TV/year. Music Supervisors: Janet York; John McCullough. Recently published "Midnite Ride" (by Cam Wagner), recorded by 5 Star Hillbillies in *North of Pittsburgh*.

Music Mostly **country**, **rock** and **pop**; also **gospel** and **R&B**. Published *That's Real Love* (album), written and recorded by Darrell Meyers (country), released 2000; "Silent River" (single by John Reilly), album recorded by Wolfe Milestone.

Tips "Submit clear demos, good hooks and avoid long intros or instrumentals. Have a great singer do vocals."

SALT WORKS MUSIC (ASCAP, BMI)

80 Highland Dr., Jackson OH 45640-2074. (740)286-1514 or (740)286-6561. Professional Managers: Jeff Elliott(country/gospel); Mike Morgan (country). Music publisher and record producer (Mike Morgan). Staff size: 2. Pays standard royalty.

Affiliate(s) Salt Creek Music (ASCAP) and Sojourner Music (BMI).

How to Contact Submit demo package by mail. Unsolicited submissions are OK. Prefers cassette or CD. Include SASE. Responds in 2 weeks.

Music Mostly **country**, **gospel** and **pop**. Does not want rock, jazz or classical. Published "The Tracks You Left On Me" (single by Ed Bruce/Jeff Elliott/MikeMorgan) and "Truth Is I'm A Liar" (single by Jeff Elliott/Mike Morgan) from This Old Hat (album), recorded by Ed Bruce (country), released 2002 on Sony/Music Row Talent.

☐ SANDALPHON MUSIC PUBLISHING (BMI)

P.O. Box 29110, Portland OR 97296. (503)957-3929. E-mail: jackrabbit01@sprintpcs.com. **Contact:** Ruth Otey, president. Music publisher, record company (Sandalphon Records), and management agency (Sandalphon Management). Estab. 2005. Staff size: 2. Pays standard royalty of 50%.

How to Contact Submit demo by mail. Unsolicited submissions are OK. Prefers cassette or CD with 1-5 songs, lyric sheet, and cover letter. Include SASE or SAE and IRC for outside United States. Responds in 1 month.

Music Mostly **rock**, **country**, and **alternative**; also **pop**, **blues**, and **gospel**.

☑ SDB MUSIC GROUP

● *SDB Music Group only accepts music through reputable industry sources.*

Music Mostly **country**. SDB has had cuts with artists including John Michael Montgomery, Leann Rimes, Don Williams, Steve Holy, and Trace Adkins.

☑ SHAWNEE PRESS, INC.

1221 17th Avenue S., Nashville TN 37212. (615)320-5300. Fax: (615)320-7306. E-mail: shawnee-info@shawneepress.com. Web site: www.ShawneePress.com. **Contact:** Director of Church Music Publications (sacred choral music): Joseph M. Martin. Director of School Music Publications (secular choral music): Greg Gilpin. Music publisher. Estab. 1939. Publishes 150 songs/year. Staff size: 12. Pays negotiable royalty.

Affiliate(s) GlorySound, Harold Flammer Music, Mark Foster Music, Wide World Music, Concert Works.

How to Contact Submit manuscript. Unsolicited submissions are OK. See Web site for guidelines. Prefers manuscript; recording required for instrumental submissions. Include SASE. Responds in 4 months. "No unsolicited musicals or cantatas."

Music Mostly **church/liturgical**, **educational choral** and **instrumental**.

Tips "Submission guidelines appear on our Web site."

☒ ☒ ☑ SHU'BABY MONTEZ MUSIC

P.O. Box 28816, Philadelphia PA 19151. (215)473-5527. E-mail: schubaby@verizon.net. Web site: http://www.smm.indiegroup.com. **Contact:** Leroy Schuler, president. Music publisher. Estab. 1986. Publishes 25 songs/year; publishes 10 new songwriters/year. Pays standard royalty.

● Also see the listing for Shu'Baby Montez Music in the Record Producers section of this book.

How to Contact *Contact first and obtain permission to submit.* Prefers CD with 3 songs and lyric sheet. Include SASE. Responds in 5 weeks.

Film & TV Places 3 songs in film/year.

Music Mostly **R&B**, **dance**, **hip-hop** and **pop**. Does not want country. Published "Every Day," recorded by Tom White; "Rainbow," recorded by Dr. Faye (Christian); "Play Me Out" and "They Love It When I Floss," recorded by Mallygeez (hip-hop).

Tips "Keep the music simple, but with nice changes. Don't be afraid to use altered chords."

☐ SILICON MUSIC PUBLISHING CO. (BMI)

222 Tulane St., Garland TX 75043-2239. President: Gene Summers. Vice President: Deanna L. Summers. Public Relations: Steve Summers. Music publisher and record company (Front Row Records). Estab. 1965. Publishes 10-20 songs/year; publishes 2-3 new songwriters/year. Pays standard royalty.

- Also see the listing for Front Row Records in the Record Companies section of this book.

How to Contact Submit demo package by mail. Unsolicited submissions are OK. Prefers cassette with 1-2 songs. Does not return material. Responds ASAP.

Music Mostly **rockabilly** and **'50s material**; also **old-time blues/country** and **MOR**. Published "Rockaboogie Shake" (single by James McClung) from *Rebels and More* (album), recorded by Lennerockers (rockabilly), released 2002 on Lenne (Germany); "Be-Bop City" (single by Dan Edwards), "So" (single by Dea Summers/Gene Summers), and "Little Lu Ann" (single by James McClung) from *Do Right Daddy* (album), recorded by Gene Summers (rockabilly/'50s rock and roll), released 2004 on Enviken (Sweden).

Tips "We are very interested in '50s rock and rockabilly original masters for release through overseas affiliates. If you are the owner of any '50s masters, contact us first! We have releases in Holland, Switzerland, United Kingdom, Belgium, France, Sweden, Norway and Australia. We have the market if you have the tapes! Our staff writers include James McClung, Gary Mears (original Casuals), Robert Clark, Dea Summers, Shawn Summers, Joe Hardin Brown, Bill Becker and Dan Edwards."

☒ ⊘ SILVER BLUE MUSIC/OCEANS BLUE MUSIC (ASCAP, BMI)

3940 Laurel Canyon Blvd., Suite 441, Studio City CA 91604. (818)980-9588. E-mail: jdiamond20@aol.com. **Contact:** Joel Diamond, president. Music publisher and record producer (Joel Diamond Entertainment). Estab. 1971. Publishes 50 songs/year. Pays standard royalty.

How to Contact *Does not accept unsolicited material.* "No tapes returned."

Film & TV Places 4 songs in film and 6 songs in TV/year.

Music Mostly **pop** and **R&B**; also **rap** and **classical**. Does not want country or jazz. Published "After the Lovin" (by Bernstein/Adams), recorded by Engelbert Humperdinck; "This Moment in Time" (by Alan Bernstein/Ritchie Adams), recorded by Engelbert Humperdinck. Other artists include David Hasselhoff, Kaci (Curb Records), Ike Turner, Andrew Dice Clay, Gloria Gaynor, Tony Orlando, Katie Cassidy, and Vaneza.

⊕ ⊘ ☒ SINUS MUSIK PRODUKTION, ULLI WEIGEL

Geitnerweg 30a, D-12209, Berlin Germany. +49-30-7159050. Fax: +49-30-71590522. E-mail: ulli.weigel@arcor.de. Web site: www.ulli-weigel.de. **Contact:** Ulli Weigel, owner. Music publisher, record producer and screenwriter. Wrote German lyrics for more than 500 records. Member: GEMA, GVL. Estab. 1976. Publishes 20 songs/year; publishes 6 new songwriters/year. Staff size: 3. Pays standard royalty.

Affiliate(s) Sinus Musikverlag H.U. Weigel GmbH.

How to Contact Submit demo package by mail. Unsolicited submissions are OK. Prefers CD or cassette with up to 10 songs and lyric sheets. Responds in 2 months by e-mail. "If material should be returned, please send 2 International Reply Coupons (IRC) for cassettes and 3 for a CD. No stamps."

Music Mostly **rock**, **pop** and **New Age**; also **background music for movies**. Published "Simple Story" (single), recorded by MAANAM on RCA (Polish rock); *Die Musik Maschine* (album by Klaus Lage), recorded by CWN Productions on Hansa Records (pop/German), "Villa Woodstock" (film music/comedy) Gebrueder Blattschuss, Juergen Von Der Lippe, Hans Werner Olm (2005).

Tips "Take more time working on the melody than on the instrumentation. I am also looking for master-quality recordings for non-exclusive release on my label (and to use them as soundtracks for multimedia projects, TV and movie scripts I am working on)."

◪ SIZEMORE MUSIC (BMI)

P.O. Box 210314, Nashville TN 37221. (615)356-3453. E-mail: gary@sizemoremusic.com. Web site: www.sizemoremusic.com. Contact: Gail Rhine. Music publisher, record company (Willowind) and record producer (G.L. Rhine). Estab. 1960. Publishes 5 songs/year; 1 new songwriter/year. Pays standard royalty.

How to Contact Submit demo by mail. Unsolicited submissions are OK. Prefers CD with 2 songs and lyric sheets. Does not return material. Responds in 3 months.

Music Mostly **hip-hop**, **soul**, **blues**, and **country**. Published "Liquor and Wine" and "The Wind," written and recorded by K. Shackleford (country), released on Heart Records.

◪ SME PUBLISHING GROUP (ASCAP,BMI)

P.O. Box 1150, Tuttle OK 73089. (405)381-3754. Fax: (405)381-3754. E-mail: smemusic@juno.com. Web site: www.smepublishinggroup.com. Professional Managers: Cliff Shelder (southern gospel); Sharon Kinard (country gospel). Music publisher. Estab. 1994. Publishes 6 songs/year; publishes 2 new songwriters/year. Staff size: 2. Pays standard royalty.

Affiliates Touch of Heaven Music (ASCAP) and SME Music (BMI).

How to Contact Submit demo package by mail. Unsolicited submissions are OK. Prefers CD with 3 songs and lyric sheet. Make sure tapes and CDs are labeled and include song title, writer's name and phone number. Does not return material. Responds only if interested.

Music Mostly **Southern gospel**, **country gospel** and **Christian country**. Does not want Christian rap, rock and roll, and hard-core country. Released "Come See A Man" (single by Mike Spanhanks) from *God Writes Our Story* (album), recorded by The Jody Brown Indian Family (southern gospel) on Crossroads Records; and "I Love You Son" (single by Quint Randle, Patricia Smith and Jeff Hinton) from *Here I Come Again* (album) recorded by Jackie Cox (Christian country), released 2005 on Stonghouse Records.

Tips "Always submit good quality demos. Never give up."

◙ SONY/ATV MUSIC PUBLISHING (ASCAP, BMI, SESAC)

8 Music Square W., Nashville TN 37203. (615)726-8300. Fax: (615)242-3441. Web site: www.sonyat v.com. **Santa Monica:** 2100 Colorado Ave., Santa Monica CA 90404. (310)449-2100. **New York:** 550 Madison Ave., 5th Floor, New York NY 10022. (212)833-8000.

How to Contact *Sony/ATV Music does not accept unsolicited submissions.*

◪ SOUND CELLAR MUSIC (BMI)

703 N. Brinton Ave., Dixon IL 61021. (815)288-2900. E-mail: president@cellarrecords.com. Web site: www.cellarrecords.com. **Contact:** Todd Joos (country, pop, Christian), president. Professional Managers: James Miller (folk, adult contemporary); Mike Thompson (metal, hard rock, alternative). Music publisher, record company (Sound Cellar Records), record producer and recording studio. Estab. 1987. Publishes 15-25 songs/year. Publishes 5 or 6 new songwriters/year. Staff size: 7. Pays standard royalty.

How to Contact Submit demo by mail. Unsolicited submissions are OK. Prefers CD with 3 or 4 songs and lyric sheet. Does not return material. "We contact by phone in 3-4 weeks only if we want to work with the artist."

Music Mostly **metal**, **country** and **rock**; also **pop** and **blues**. Published "Problem of Pain" (single by Shane Sowers) from *Before the Machine* (album), recorded by Junker Jorg (alternative metal/rock), released 2000; "Vaya Baby" (single by Joel Ramirez) from *It's About Time* (album), recorded by Joel Ramirez and the All-Stars (latin/R&B), released 2000; and "X" (single by Jon Pomplin) from *Project 814* (album), recorded by Project 814 (progressive rock), released 2001, all on Cellar Records. "Vist our Web site for up-to-date releases."

⊠ ⊘ STILL WORKING MUSIC GROUP (ASCAP, BMI, SESAC)

1625 Broadway, Stuie 200, Nashville TN 37203. (615)242-4201. Fax: (615)242-4202. Web site: www.stillworkingmusic.com. **Owner:** Barbara Orbison. Music publisher and record company (Orby Records, Inc.). Estab. 1994.

Affiliate(s) Still Working for the Woman Music (ASCAP), Still Working for the Man Music (BMI) and Still Working for All Music (SESAC).

How to Contact *Does not accept unsolicited submissions.*

Film & TV Published "First Noel," recorded by The Kelions in Felicity.

Music Mostly **rock**, **country** and **pop**; also **dance** and **R&B**. Published "If You See Him/If You See Her" (by Tommy Lee James), recorded by Reba McIntire/Brooks & Dunn; "Round About Way" (by Wil Nance), recorded by George Strait on MCA; and "Wrong Again" (by Tommy Lee James), recorded by Martina McBride on RCA (country).

Tips "If you want to be a country songwriter you need to be in Nashville where the business is. Write what is in your heart."

⊘ SUPREME ENTERPRISES INT'L CORP. (ASCAP, BMI)

12304 Santa Monica Blvd., 3rd Floor, Los Angeles CA 90025. (818)707-3481. Fax: (818)707-3482. E-mail: supreme2@earthlink.net. **Contact:** Lisa Lew, general manager copyrights. Music publisher, record company and record producer. Estab. 1979. Publishes 20-30 songs/year; publishes 2-6 new songwriters/year. Pays standard royalty.

Affiliate(s) Fuerte Suerte Music (BMI), Bigh Daddy G. Music (ASCAP).

How to Contact *No phone calls.* Submit demo by mail. Unsolicited submissions are OK. Prefers CD. Does not return material and you must include an e-mail address for a response. **Mail Demos To:** P.O. Box 1373, Agoura Hills CA 91376. "Please copyright material before submitting and include e-mail." Responds in 12-16 weeks if interested.

Music Mostly **reggae**, **rap**, and **dance**. Published "Paso La Vida Pensando," recorded by Jose Feliciano on Motown Records; "Cucu Bam Bam" (single by David Choy), recorded by Kathy on Polydor Records (reggae/pop); and "Mineaita" (single), recorded by Gaby on SEI Records.

Tips "A good melody is a hit in any language."

⊘ T.C. PRODUCTIONS/ETUDE PUBLISHING CO. (BMI)

121 Meadowbrook Dr., Hillsborough NJ 08844. (908)359-5110. Fax: (908)359-1962. E-mail: tcproductions@patmedia.net. Web site: www.tcproductions2005.com. President: Tony Camillo. Music publisher and record producer. Estab. 1992. Publishes 25-50 songs/year; publishes 3-6 new songwriters/year. Pays negotiable royalty.

Affiliate(s) We Iz It Music Publishing (ASCAP), Etude Publishing (BMI), and We B Records (BMI).

How to Contact *Write or call first and obtain permission to submit.* Prefers CD or cassette with 3-4 songs and lyric sheet. Include SASE. Responds in 1 month.

Music Mostly **R&B** and **dance**; also **country** and **outstanding pop ballads**. Published "I Just Want To Be Your Everything" (single) from *A Breath of Fresh Air* (album), recorded by Michelle Parto (spiritual),released 2006 on Chancellor Records; and New Jersey Jazz (album).

Tips "Michelle Parto will soon be appearing in the film musical Sing Out, directed by Nick Castle and written by Kent Berhard."

⊠ ◯ THISTLE HILL (BMI)

P.O. Box 707, Hermitage TN 37076. (615)320-6071. E-mail: acemusicgroup@hotmail.com. **Contact:** Arden Miller.

How to Contact Submit demo by mail. Unsolicited submissions OK. Prefers CD with 3-10 songs. *No* lyric sheets. Responds only if interested.

Music Country, **pop**, and **rock**; also **songs for film/TV**. Published "Angry Heart " (single) from *See What You Wanna See* (album), recorded by Radney Foster (Americana); and "I Wanna be Free" (single) from *I Wanna be Free* (album), recorded by Jordon MyCoskie (Americana), released 2003 on Ah! Records; "Que Vamos Hacer" (single) from *Rachel Rodriguez* (album), recorded by Rachel Rodriguez.

N ☐ TIKI ENTERPRISES, INC. (ASCAP, BMI)

195 S. 26th St., San Jose CA 95116. (408)286-9840. E-mail: onealproduction@juno.com. Web site: www.onealprod.com. **Contact**: Gradie O'Neal, president. Professional Manager: Jeannine O'Neil. Music publisher, record company (Rowena Records) and record producer (Jeannine O'Neal and Gradie O'Neal). Estab. 1967. Publishes 40 songs/year; publishes 12 new songwriters/year. Staff size: 3. Pays standard royalty.

Affiliate(s) Tooter Scooter Music (BMI), Janell Music (BMI) and O'Neal & Friend (ASCAP).

How to Contact Submit demo by mail. Unsolicited submissions are OK. Prefers CD with 3 songs and lyric or lead sheets. Include SASE. Responds in 2 weeks.

Music Mostly **country**, **Mexican**, **rock/pop**, **gospel**, **R&B** and **New Age**. Does not want atonal music. Published "You're Looking Good To Me" (single) from *A Rock 'N' Roll Love Story* (album), written and recorded by Warren R. Spalding (rock 'n' roll), released 2003-2004; "I Am Healed" (single) from *Faith On The Front Lines* (album), written and recorded by Jeannine O'Neal (praise music), released 2003-2004; and "It Amazes Me" (single by David Davis/Jeannine O'Neal) from *The Forgiven Project* (album), recorded by David Davis and Amber Littlefield, released 2003, all on Rowena Records.

Tips "For up-to-date published titles, review our Web site. Keep writing and sending songs in. Never give up—the next hit may be just around the bend."

☑ TOURMALINE MUSIC, INC. (BMI)

2831 Dogwood Place, Nashville TN 37204. (615)269-8682. Fax: (615)269-8929. Web site: www.songsfortheplanet.com. **Contact:** Justin Peters, president. Music publisher. Estab. 1980.

Affiliate(s) Justin Peters Music (BMI), LITA Music (ASCAP) and Platinum Planet Music (BMI).

How to Contact Submit demo package by mail. Unsolicited submissions are OK. Prefers CD with 5 songs and lyric sheet. Does not return material. "Place code '2008' on each envelope submissions."

Music Mostly **rock and roll**, **classy alternative**, **adult contemporary**, **classic rock**, **country**, **Spanish gospel**, and some **Christmas music**. Published "Santa Can You Bring My Daddy Home" (single by D. Mattarosa); "The Hurt Is Worth The Chance" (single by Justin Peters/Billy Simon), recorded by Gary Chapman on RCA/BMG Records; and "For So Long" (single by Monroe Jones/Chris McCollum), recorded by GLAD on Benson Records; "Love is Catching On" (single by Enoch Rich/Marcell Macarthy), recorded by Mighty Clouds of Joy, released on Word Entertainment.

☑ ☒ ☑ TOWER MUSIC GROUP (ASCAP, BMI)

30 Music Square W., Suite 103, Nashville TN 37203. (615)401-7111. Fax: (615)401-7119. E-mail: castlerecords@castlerecords.com. Web site: www.castlerecords.com. **Contact:** Dave Sullivan, A&R Director. Professional Managers: Ed Russell; Eddie Bishop. Music publisher, record company (Castle Records) and record producer. Estab. 1969. Publishes 50 songs/year; publishes 10 new songwriters/year. Staff size: 15. Pays standard royalty.

Affiliate(s) Cat's Alley Music (ASCAP) and Alley Roads Music (BMI).

How to Contact See submission policy on Web site. Prefers CD with 3 songs and lyric sheet. Does not return material. "You may follow up via e-mail." Responds in 3 months only if interested.

Film & TV Places 2 songs in film and 26 songs in TV/year. Published "Run Little Girl" (by J.R. Jones/Eddie Ray), recorded by J.R. Jones in Roadside Prey.

Music Mostly **country** and **R&B**; also **blues**, **pop** and **gospel**. Published "If You Broke My Heart" (single by Condrone) from *If You Broke My Heart* (album), recorded by Kimberly Simon (country); "I Wonder Who's Holding My Angel Tonight" (single) from Up Above (album), recorded by Carl Butler (country); and "Psychedelic Fantasy" (single by Paul Sullivan/Priege) from *The Hip Hoods* (album), recorded by The Hip Hoods (power/metal/y2k), all released 2001 on Castle Records. "Visit our Web site for an up-to-date listing of published songs."
Tips "Please contact us via e-mail with any other demo submission questions."

☑ ◯ ▨ TRANSITION MUSIC CORPORATION (ASCAP, BMI, SESAC)

P.O. Box 2586, Toluca Lake CA 91610. (323)860-7074. Fax: (323)860-7986. E-mail: onestopmus@aol.com. Web site: www.transitionmusic.com. Creative Director: Todd Johnson. Chief Administrator: Mike Dobson. Music publisher. Estab. 1988. Publishes 250 songs/year; publishes 20 new songwriters/year. Variable royalty based on song placement and writer.
Affiliate(s) Pushy Publishing (ASCAP), Creative Entertainment Music (BMI) and One Stop Shop Music (SESAC).
How to Contact Address submissions to: New Submissions Dept. Submit demo by mail. Unsolicited submissions are OK. Prefers CD with no more than 3 songs. Include SASE. Responds in 5 weeks.
Film & TV "TMC provides music for all forms of visual media, mainly TV."
Music All styles.
Tips "Supply master quality material with great songs."

☑ ◎ TRIO PRODUCTIONS (BMI, ASCAP)

1026 15th Ave. S., Nashville TN 37212. (615)726-5810. E-mail: info@trioproductions.com. Web site: www.trioproductions.com. **Contact:** Robyn Taylor-Drake.
Affiliate(s) Birdseye Ranch Music (ASCAP), Unframed Music (ASCAP), and Whiskey Gap Music (BMI).
How to Contact *Contact first by e-mail to obtain permission to submit demo. Unsolicited material will not be listened to or returned.* Submit CD with 3-4 songs and lyric sheet. "We do not return submissions."
Music Country, **Americana**, and **bluegrass**.

☑ ◎ TWIN TOWERS PUBLISHING CO. (ASCAP)

8455 Beverly Blvd., Suite 400, Los Angeles CA 90048. (323)655-5007. Web site: www.HarmonyArtists.com. President: Michael Dixon. Music publisher and booking agency (Harmony Artists, Inc.). Publishes 24 songs/year. Pays standard royalty.
How to Contact *Call first and get permission to submit.* Prefers CD's with 3 songs and lyric sheet. Include SASE. Responds only if interested.
Music Mostly **pop**, **rock**, and **R&B**. Published "Magic," from Ghostbusters soundtrack on Arista Records; and "Kiss Me Deadly" (by Lita Ford) on RCA Records.

◎ UNIVERSAL MUSIC PUBLISHING (ASCAP, BMI, SESAC)

2440 Sepulveda Blvd., Suite 100, Los Angeles CA 90064. (310)235-4700. **New York:** 1755 Broadway, 3rd Floor, New York NY 10019. (212)841-8000. **Tennessee:** 1904 Adelicia St., Nashville TN 37212. (615)340-5400. Web site: www.umusicpub.com or www.synchexpress.com.
  • In 1999, MCA Music Publishing and PolyGram Music Publishing merged into Universal Music Publishing.
How to Contact *Does not accept unsolicited submissions.*

◎ VAAM MUSIC GROUP (BMI)

P.O. Box 29550, Hollywood CA 90029-0550. E-mail: pmarti3636@aol.com. Web site: www.VaamMusic.com. **Contact:** Pete Martin, president. Music publisher and record producer (Pete Martin/Vaam Productions). Estab. 1967. Publishes 9-24 new songs/year. Pays standard royalty.

Affiliate(s) Pete Martin Music (ASCAP).

• Also see the listings for Blue Gem Records in the Record Companies section of this book and Pete Martin/Vaam Music Productions in the record Producers section of this book.

How to Contact Send CD or cassette with 2 songs and lyric sheet. Include SASE. Responds in 1 month. "Small packages only."

Music Mostly **top 40/pop**, **country**, and **R&B**. "Submitted material must have potential of reaching top 5 on charts."

Tips "Study the top 10 charts in the style you write. Stay current and up-to-date with today's market."

☑ ☑ VINE CREEK MUSIC (ASCAP)

P.O. Box 171143, Nashville TN 37217. (615)366-1326. Fax: (615)367-1073. E-mail: vinecreek1@aol.com. Contact: Darlene Austin, Brenda Madden. Administration: Jayne Negri. Creative Director: Brenda Madden.

How to Contact *Vine Creek Music does not accept unsolicited submissions.* "Only send material of good competitive quality. We do not return tapes/CDs unless SASE is enclosed."

☑ WALKER PUBLISHING CO. L.L.C. (ASCAP/BMI)

P.O. Box 11084, Birmingham AL 35202-1084. (205)601-4420. E-mail: superior_marketing@msn.com. Web site: www.walkerpublishingco.com or www.myspace.com/personaltouchmusic. **Contact:** Gary Walker, owner. Professional Managers: Gary Walker (pop/R&B/ country), Charlie Craig (country/new country). Music Publisher, record producer (Charlie Craig Productions). Estab. 2000. Publishes 10 new songs/year; publishes 3 new songwriters/year. Staff size: 3. Hires staff songwriters. Pays standard royalty.

• Also see the listing for Charlie Craig Productions in the Record Producers section of this book.

Affiliate(s) Cryptogram Music (ASCAP) and Star Alliance Music (BMI).

How to Contact Submit demo package by mail. Unsolicited submissions are OK. Prefers CD with 3 songs, lyric sheet and writer's e-mail address. Does not return material. Responds in 6 weeks if interested, via e-mail only. "Submit only professional studio quality demos."

Music Mostly **country** and **new country**. Does not want rap, hard rock or metal. Published "Dallas Didn't Do It" (single by Craig/Wilkinson/Crosby), recorded by The Wilkinsons (country); "Tin Can" (single by Charlie Craig/Jerry Cupid) from debut album recorded by Brad & Shelly (country), released on Cupid Records; "Tranquilizers and Prayer" (single) and "For Your Love" (single), recorded by Jim Van Fleet, released on Navibar Records.

Tips "Walker Publishing Co. L.L.C. has partnered with Charlie Craig Productions, owned by legendary writer/producer Charlie Craig—his writing credits include Alan Jackson's 'Wanted'; Travis Tritt's 'Between an Old Memory and Me'; Dolly Parton's 'Chicken Every Sunday'; and Johnny Cash's 'I Would Like to See You Again.' See www.charliecraig.com."

☑ ☐ WALKERBOUT MUSIC GROUP (ASCAP, BMI, SESAC)

(formerly The Goodland Music Group, Inc.), P.O. Box 24454, Nashville TN 37202. (615)269-7071. Fax: (615)269-0131. E-mail: info@walkerboutmusic.com. Web site: www.walkerboutmusic.com. **Contact:** Matt Watkins, publishing coordinator. Estab. 1988. Publishes 50 songs/year; 5-10 new songwriters/year. Pays standard royalty.

Affiliate(s) Goodland Publishing Company (ASCAP), Marc Isle Music (BMI), Gulf Bay Publishing (SESAC), Con Brio Music (BMI), Wiljex Publishing (ASCAP), Concorde Publishing (SESAC).

How to Contact "Please see Web site for submission information."

Music Mostly **country/Christian** and **adult contemporary**.

🎵⊘ WARNER/CHAPPELL MUSIC, INC.

10585 Santa Monica Blvd., Third Floor, Los Angeles CA 90025. (310)441-8600. Fax: (310)470-3232.
New York: 1290 Avenue of the Americas, 23rd floor, New York NY 10104. (212)707-2600. Fax:
(212)405-5428. **Nashville:** 20 Music Square E., Nashville TN 37203. (615)733-1880. Fax: (615)733-
1885. Web site: www.warnerchappell.com. Music publisher.
How to Contact *Warner/Chappell does not accept unsolicited material.*

🎵 WEAVER OF WORDS MUSIC (BMI)

(administered by Bug Music), P.O. Box 803, Tazewell VA 24651. (276)988-6267. E-mail: cooksong
@verizon.net. Web site: www.weaverofwordsmusic.com. **Contact:** H.R. Cook, president. Music
publisher and record company (Fireball Records). Estab. 1978. Publishes 12 songs/year. Pays stan-
dard royalty.
Affiliate(s) Weaver of Melodies Music (ASCAP).
How to Contact Submit demo by mail. Unsolicited submissions are OK. Prefers CD with 3 songs
and lyric or lead sheets. "We prefer CD submissions but will accept submissions on cassette."
Include SASE. Responds in 3 weeks.
Music Mostly **country**, **pop**, **bluegrass**, **R&B**, **film and television** and **rock**. Published "Zero To
Love" (single by H. Cook/Brian James Deskins/Rick Tiger) from *It's Just The Night* (album), recorded by Del McCoury Band (bluegrass), released 2003 on McCoury Music; "Muddy Water"
(single by Alan Johnston) from *The Midnight Call* (album), recorded by Don Rigsby (bluegrass),
released 2003 on Sugar Hill; "Ol Brown Suitcase" (single by H.R. Cook) from *Lonesome Highway*
(album), recorded by Josh Williams (bluegrass), released 2004 on Pinecastle; and "Mansions of
Kings" (single by Pat Kramer) from *Cherry Holmes II* (album), recorded by IBMA 2005 Entertainer
of the Year Cherry Holmes (bluegrass), released 2007 on Skaggs Family Records.

🎵 ANGELA BAKER WELLS MUSIC (ASCAP)

P.O. Box 148027, Nashville TN 37214-8027. (615)883-2020. E-mail: angie@coalharbormusic.com.
Web site: www.coalharbormusic.com. **Contact:** Angela Baker Wells, president/owner. Music publisher. Estab. 2004. Publishes 25 songs/year. Publishes 2 new songwriters/year. Staff size: 2. Pays
standard royalty of 50%.
How to Contact *Contact first and obtain permission to submit a demo.* Prefers CD with 3-5 songs
and cover letter. "Put 'ATTN: Publ.' on submissions. Include SASE or stamped reply card for reply
to submission" Does not return submissions. Responds only if interested.
Music Mostly **Christian country**, **contemporary Christian**, **Southern gospel**; also **gospel (all
forms)**, **country**, and **bluegrass**. Does not want heavy metal, hard rock, rap, grunge, or punk.
Published "They Never Had You" (single) from *Coal Harbor Gospel, Vol. 2*, written and recorded
by Don Freeman (country/Christian country/AC); "Storms of Life" (single by Angela Renee Wells)
from *Coal Harbor Gospel, Vol. 2*, recorded by Angela Baker Wells (Christian country/Southern
gospel); "The Anointing" (single), written and recorded by Ray Holland (Southern gospel/inspira-
tional), all released 2004 on Coal Harbor Music.
Tips "We are actively seeking great songs to pitch to Christian and country artists. We are also
interested in Christmas, patriotic, and children's songs. Please put all contact info on your cover
letter, and include your name, phone, and e-mail on your CD. Do not send certified or registered
mail!"

🌐 ▢ BERTHOLD WENGERT (MUSIKVERLAG)

Hauptstrasse 36, Pfinztal-Söllingen, D-76327 Germany. **Contact:** Berthold Wengert. Music pub-
lisher. Pays standard GEMA royalty.
How to Contact Prefers cassette and complete score for piano. SAE and IRC. Responds in 1 month.
"No cassette returns!"
Music Mostly **light music** and **pop**.

✪ WILCOM PUBLISHING (ASCAP)

Box 913, Cherokee Village AR 72525. (870)847-1721. Fax: (870)847-1721. E-mail: william@wilcom publishing.com. **Contact:** William Clark, owner. Music publisher. Estab. 1989. Publishes 10-15 songs/year; publishes 1-2 new songwriters/year. Staff size: 2. Pays standard royalty.

How to Contact *Write or call first and obtain permission to submit.* Prefers CD with 1-2 songs and lyric sheet. Include SASE. Responds in 3 weeks.

Music Mostly **R&B**, **pop** and **rock**; also **country**. Does not want rap. Published ''Girl Can't Help It'' (single by W. Clark/D. Walsh/P. Oland), recorded by Stage 1 on Rockit Records (top 40). Also produced a cover of ''D'yer M'aker'' by Mylo Bigsby on MGL Records.

✪ ✪ WINSTON & HOFFMAN HOUSE MUSIC PUBLISHERS (ASCAP, BMI)

P.O. Box 1415, Burbank CA 91507-1415. E-mail: sixties1@aol.com. **Contact:** Lynne Robin Green, president. Music publisher. Estab. 1958. Publishes 25 songs/year. Staff size: 2. Pays standard royalty.

Affiliate(s) Lansdowne Music Publishers (ASCAP), Bloor Music (BMI) and Ben Ross Music (ASCAP), ''also administers 30 other publishing firms.''

How to Contact Submit demo package by mail. Unsolicited submissions are OK. ''Do not query first. Do not call. Do not send lyrics without completed music (or CD without lyric sheets).'' Prefers cassette or CD with 3 songs maximum and lyric sheet. ''Must include SASE or e-mail, or no reply!'' Responds in 1 month.

Film & TV Places 45 songs in film and 25 songs in TV/year. Recently published ''Dooley'' (by Dillard/Jayne) in *Baby Blues*; ''Closer Walk With Thee'' (by Craver/Henderson) in Smiling Fish and Goat on Fire; and ''Born to Jump'' (by Larry Dunn) in Olympics 2000, as well as songs placed in *Alias*, *Six Feet Under*, and on MTV, as well as Starz promo spot, *Los Tres Magos* DVD and soundtrack, *Saturday Night Live*, Comedy Central's *100 Greatest Comedy Moments*, *Malcolm in the Middle*, CMT's *20 Greatest Country Stars* and *Greatest Road Trips*, *The Best of Etta James*, and more.

Music Mostly **R&B**, **pop**, **ballads**, **hip-hop**, **vocal jazz**, **alternative rock**, and **R&B**; also **bluegrass**, **Spanish pop**, and **pop ballads**.

Tips ''Be very selective in what you send. 'A' side hit quality single songs only. For film or TV submissions you must specify you own all the master rights yourself! Be interesting lyrically and strikingly original melodically. No metal or hard rock. No vague lyrics. No alternative, New Age, violent, or sexist lyrics. No novelty, kids' music, or holiday songs. We don't work with lyrics only. No instrumental score-type synthy music, please. Independent artist's album material most welcome.''

✪ YOUR BEST SONGS PUBLISHING (ASCAP)

1402 Auburn Way N, Suite 396, Auburn WA 98002. (877)672-2520. **Contact:** John Markovich, general manager. Music publisher. Estab. 1988. Publishes 1-5 songs/year; publishes 1-3 new songwriters/year. Query for royalty terms.

How to Contact *Write first and obtain permission to submit.* Prefers CD or cassette with 1-3 songs and lyric sheet. ''Submit your 1-3 best songs per type of music. Use separate CDs or cassettes per music type and indicate music type on each CD or cassette.'' Include SASE. Responds in 3 months.

Music Mostly **country**, **rock/blues**, and **pop/rock**; also **progressive**, **A/C**, some **heavy metal** and **New Age**. Published ''Sea of Dreams,'' written and recorded by J.C. Mark on Cybervoc Productions, Inc. (New Age).

Tips ''We just require good lyrics, good melodies and good rhythm in a song. We absolutely do not want music without a decent melodic structure. We do not want lyrics with foul language or lyrics that do not inspire some form of imaginative thought.''

☑ ☑ ZETTITALIA MUSIC INTERNATIONAL (ASCAP, BMI)

P.O. Box 261488, Encino CA 91426. (818)506-8533. Fax: (818)506-8534. E-mail: zettworks@aol.c om. Web site: www.pplzmi.com. **Contact:** Cheyenne Phoenix, A&R. Assistant . A&R: Kaitland Diamond. Music publisher. Estab. 1995. Publishes 40 songs/year; publishes 2 new songwriters/ year. Staff size: 2. Hires staff songwriters. Pays standard royalty.

Affiliate(s) Zett One Songs (ASCAP) and Zett Two Music (BMI).

How to Contact *E-mail or write to obtain permission to submit.* No phone calls. "Include SASE or e-mail." Prefers CD or cassette with 3 songs. Include SASE. Responds in 6 weeks.

Film & TV Places 2 songs in film and 4 songs in TV/year.

Music Mostly **pop**, **film music**, **country**, **instrumental** and **R&B**.

Tips "In art, be a good student and stay true to your instincts. In business, be thorough, realistic, flexible and straightforward. Finally, The Golden Rule rules."

☑ ZOMBA MUSIC PUBLISHING (ASCAP, BMI)

245 Fifth Avenue., 8th Floor, New York NY 10001. (212)727-0016. Web site: www.zomba.com. **Contact:** Jennifer Blakeman (pop/rock), Peter Visvardis (pop/rock), or Tanya Brown (urban). **Beverly Hills:** 8750 Wilshire Blvd., Beverly Hills CA 90211. (310)358-4200. **Contact:** Andrea Torchia (pop/rock). Music publisher. Publishes 5,000 songs/year.

Affiliate(s) Zomba Enterprises, Inc. (ASCAP); Zomba Songs, Inc. (BMI).

How to Contact *Zomba Music Publishing does not accept unsolicited material.* "Contact us through management or an attorney."

Music Mostly **R&B**, **pop**, and **rap**; also **rock** and **alternative**. Published ". . . Baby One More Time" (single by M. Martin), recorded by Britney Spears on Jive; "Home Alone" (single by R. Kelly/K. Price/K. Murray), recorded by R. Kelly featuring Keith Murray on Jive; and "Taking Everything" (single by G. Levert/D. Allamby/L. Browder/A. Roberson), recorded by Gerald Levert on EastWest.

ADDITIONAL MUSIC PUBLISHERS

The following companies are also music publishers, but their listings are found in other sections of the book. Read the listings for submission information.

A
A.A.M.I. Music Group 163
ACR Productions 206
Apodaca Promotions Inc. 229
Arkadia Entertainment Corp. 165
Atlan-Dec/Grooveline Records 166
Avita Records 167

B
Banana Records 168
Blues Alley Records 207

C
Cacophony Productions 207
Cambria Records & Publishing 169
Chattahoochee Records 171
Circuit Rider Talent & Management Co. 231
Cosmotone Records 172
CPA Records 172

D
DaVinci's Notebook Records 209
DreamWorks Records 174

E
Ellis International Talent Agency, The 236

F
Final Mix Inc. 210

G
Generic Records, Inc. 175
Gig Records 176

H
Hardison International Entertainment Corporation 238
Heads Up Int., Ltd. 177

Heart Consort Music 210
Heart Music, Inc. 178
Hi-Bias Records Inc. 178

J
J & V Management 240

K
Knight Agency, Bob 241
Kuper Personal Management/Recovery Recordings 241

L
L.A. Entertainment, Inc. 211
Levy Management, Rick 242
Lucifer Records, Inc. 180

M
Mac-Attack Productions 212

O
Only New Age Music, Inc. 185

P
Panama Music Group of Companies, The 186
Philly Breakdown Recording Co. 216
Pierce, Jim 216
PM Music Group 245

R
Red Onion Records 188
Riohcat Music 247
RN'D Distribution, LLC 217
Robbins Entertainment LLC 189

S
Serge Entertainment Group 249
Sound Works Entertainment Productions Inc. 219

Record Companies

Record companies release and distribute records, cassettes and CDs—the tangible products of the music industry. They sign artists to recording contracts, decide what songs those artists will record, and determine which songs to release. They are also responsible for providing recording facilities, securing producers and musicians, and overseeing the manufacture, distribution and promotion of new releases.

MAJOR LABELS & INDEPENDENT LABELS

Major labels and independent labels—what's the difference between the two?

The majors

As of this writing, there are four major record labels, commonly referred to as the "Big 4":

- **The EMI Group** (Capitol Music Group, Angel Music Group, Astralwerks, Chrysalis Records, etc.)
- **Sony BMG** (Columbia Records, Epic Records, RCA Records, Arista Records, J Records, Provident Label Group, etc.)
- **Universal Music Group** (Universal Records, Interscope/Geffen/A&M, Island/Def Jam, Dreamworks Records, MCA Nashville Records, Verve Music Group, etc.)
- **Warner Music Group** (Atlantic Records, Bad Boy, Asylum Records, Warner Bros. Records, Maverick Records, Sub Pop, etc.)

Each of the "Big 4" is a large publicly-traded corporation beholden to shareholders and quarterly profit expectations. This means the major labels have greater financial resources and promotional muscle than a smaller "indie" label, but it's also harder to get signed to a major. A big major label may also expect more contractual control over an artist or band's sound and image.

As shown in the above list, they also each act as umbrella organizations for numerous other well-known labels—former major labels in their own right, well-respected former independent/boutique labels, as well as subsidiary "vanity" labels fronted by successful major label recording artists. Each major label also has its own related worldwide product distribution system, and many independent labels will contract with the majors for distribution into stores.

If a label is distributed by one of these major companies, you can be assured any release coming out on that label has a large distribution network behind it. It will most likely be sent to most major retail stores in the United States.

The independents

Independent labels go through smaller distribution companies to distribute their product. They usually don't have the ability to deliver records in massive quantities as the major distributors do. However, that doesn't mean independent labels aren't able to have hit records just like their major counterparts. A record label's distributors are found in the listings after the **Distributed by** heading.

Which do I submit to?

Many of the companies listed in this section are independent labels. They are usually the most receptive to receiving material from new artists. Major labels spend more money than most other segments of the music industry; the music publisher, for instance, pays only for items such as salaries and the costs of making demos. Record companies, at great financial risk, pay for many more services, including production, manufacturing and promotion. Therefore, they must be very selective when signing new talent. Also, the continuing fear of copyright infringement suits has closed avenues to getting new material heard by the majors. Most don't listen to unsolicited submissions, period. Only songs recommended by attorneys, managers and producers who record company employees trust and respect are being heard by A&R people at major labels (companies with a referral policy have a ⊘ preceding their listing). But that doesn't mean all major labels are closed to new artists. With a combination of a strong local following, success on an independent label (or strong sales of an independently produced and released album) and the right connections, you could conceivably get an attentive audience at a major label.

But the competition is fierce at the majors, so you shouldn't overlook independent labels. Since they're located all over the country, indie labels are easier to contact and can be important in building a local base of support for your music (consult the Geographic Index at the back of the book to find out which companies are located near you). Independent labels usually concentrate on a specific type of music, which will help you target those companies your submissions should be sent to. And since the staff at an indie label is smaller, there are fewer channels to go through to get your music heard by the decision makers in the company.

HOW RECORD COMPANIES WORK

Independent record labels can run on a small staff, with only a handful of people running the day-to-day business. Major record labels are more likely to be divided into the following departments: A&R, sales, marketing, promotion, product management, artist development, production, finance, business/legal and international.

- The *A&R department* is staffed with A&R representatives who search out new talent. They go out and see new bands, listen to demo tapes, and decide which artists to sign. They also look for new material for already signed acts, match producers with artists and oversee recording projects. Once an artist is signed by an A&R rep and a record is recorded, the rest of the departments at the company come into play.
- The *sales department* is responsible for getting a record into stores. They make sure record stores and other outlets receive enough copies of a record to meet consumer demand.
- The *marketing department* is in charge of publicity, advertising in magazines and other media, promotional videos, album cover artwork, in-store displays, and any other means of getting the name and image of an artist to the public.
- The *promotion department*'s main objective is to get songs from a new album played on the radio. They work with radio programmers to make sure a product gets airplay.
- The *product management department* is the ringmaster of the sales, marketing and

Record Companies

The Case for Independents

Tip

If you're interested in getting a major label deal, it makes sense to look to independent record labels to get your start. Independent labels are seen by many as a stepping stone to a major recording contract. Very few artists are signed to a major label at the start of their careers; usually, they've had a few independent releases that helped build their reputation in the industry. Major labels watch independent labels closely to locate up-and-coming bands and new trends. In the current economic atmosphere at major labels—with extremely high overhead costs for developing new bands and the fact that only 10% of acts on major labels actually make any profit—they're not willing to risk everything on an unknown act. Most major labels won't even consider signing a new act that hasn't had some indie success.

But independents aren't just farming grounds for future major label acts; many bands have long term relationships with indies, and prefer it that way. While they may not be able to provide the extensive distribution and promotion that a major label can (though there are exceptions), indie labels can help an artist become a regional success, and may even help the performer to see a profit as well. With the lower overhead and smaller production costs an independent label operates on, it's much easier to ''succeed'' on an indie label than on a major.

promotion departments, assuring that they're all going in the same direction when promoting a new release.

- The *artist development department* is responsible for taking care of things while an artist is on tour, such as setting up promotional opportunities in cities where an act is performing.
- The *production department* handles the actual manufacturing and pressing of the record and makes sure it gets shipped to distributors in a timely manner.
- People in the *finance department* compute and distribute royalties, as well as keep track of expenses and income at the company.
- The *business/legal department* takes care of contracts, not only between the record company and artists but with foreign distributors, record clubs, etc.
- And finally, the *international department* is responsible for working with international companies for the release of records in other countries.

LOCATING A RECORD LABEL

With the abundance of record labels out there, how do you go about finding one that's right for the music you create? First, it helps to know exactly what kind of music a record label releases. Become familiar with the records a company has released, and see if they fit in with what you're doing. Each listing in this section details the type of music a particular record company is interested in releasing. You will want to refer to the Category Index on page 373 to help you find those companies most receptive to the type of music you write. You should only approach companies open to your level of experience (see A Sample Listing Decoded on page 11). Visiting a company's website can also provide valuable information about a company's philosophy, the artists on the label and the music they work with.

Networking

Recommendations by key music industry people are an important part of making contacts with record companies. Songwriters must remember that talent alone does not guarantee success in the music business. You must be recognized through contacts, and the only way to make contacts is through networking. Networking is the process of building an interconnecting web of acquaintances within the music business. The more industry people you meet, the larger your contact base becomes, and the better are your chances of meeting someone with the clout to get your demo into the hands of the right people. If you want to get your music heard by key A&R representatives, networking is imperative.

Networking opportunities can be found anywhere industry people gather. A good place to meet key industry people is at regional and national music conferences and workshops. There are many held all over the country for all types of music (see the Workshops and Conferences section for more information). You should try to attend at least one or two of these events each year; it's a great way to increase the number and quality of your music industry contacts.

Creating a buzz

Another good way to attract A&R people is to make a name for yourself as an artist. By starting your career on a local level and building it from there, you can start to cultivate a following and prove to labels that you can be a success. A&R people figure if an act can be successful locally, there's a good chance they could be successful nationally. Start getting booked at local clubs, and start a mailing list of fans and local media. Once you gain some success on a local level, branch out. All this attention you're slowly gathering, this "buzz" you're generating, will not only get to your fans but to influential people in the music industry as well.

SUBMITTING TO RECORD COMPANIES

When submitting to a record company, major or independent, a professional attitude is imperative. Be specific about what you are submitting and what your goals are. If you are strictly a songwriter and the label carries a band you believe would properly present your song, state that in your cover letter. If you are an artist looking for a contract, showcase your strong points as a performer. Whatever your goals are, follow submission guidelines closely, be as neat as possible and include a top-notch demo. If you need more information concerning a company's requirements, write or call for more details. (For more information on submitting your material, see the article Where Should I Send My Songs? on page 9, Demo Recordings: What Should I Know? on page 13 and Quiz: Are You Professional? on page 26.)

Icons

For More Info

For more instructional information on the listings in this book, including explanations of symbols ([N] ✓ ▽ ☒ ✿ ⊕ ○ ⊘ ⊙ ⊘), read the article *Songwriter's Market: How Do I Use It?* on page 7.

RECORD COMPANY CONTRACTS

Once you've found a record company that is interested in your work, the next step is signing a contract. Independent label contracts are usually not as long and complicated as major label ones, but they are still binding, legal contracts. Make sure the terms are in the best interest of both you and the label. Avoid anything in your contract that you feel is too restrictive. It's important to have your contract reviewed by a competent entertainment lawyer. A basic recording contract can run from 40-100 pages, and you need a lawyer to help you understand it. A lawyer will also be essential in helping you negotiate a deal that is in your best interest.

Recording contracts cover many areas, and just a few of the things you will be asked to consider will be: What royalty rate is the record label willing to pay you? What kind of advance are they offering? How many records will the company commit to? Will they offer tour support? Will they provide a budget for video? What sort of a recording budget are they offering? Are they asking you to give up any publishing rights? Are they offering you a publishing advance? These are only a few of the complex issues raised by a recording contract, so it's vital to have an entertainment lawyer at your side as you negotiate.

ADDITIONAL RECORD COMPANIES

There are **more record companies** located in other sections of the book! On page 202 use the list of Additional Record Companies to find listings within other sections who are also record companies.

⊕ ◐ A.A.M.I. MUSIC GROUP

Maarschalklaan 47, 3417 SE Montfoort, The Netherlands. Fax: 31-384-471214. E-mail: aamimus@w xs.nl. Release Manager: Joop Gerrits; manager (dance, rap): Carlo Bonti. Labels include Associated Artists, Disco-Dance Records and Italo. Record company, music publisher (Hilversum Happy Music/BUMA-STEMRA, Intermedlodie/BUMA-STEMRA and Hollands Glorie Productions), record producer (Associated Artists Productions) and TV promotions. Estab. 1975. Releases 10 singles, 25 12″ singles, 6 LPs and 6 CDs/year. Pays 14% royalty to artists on contract; variable amount to publishers.

How to Contact Submit demo package by mail. Unsolicited submissions are OK. Prefers CD or DVD with any number of songs and lyric or lead sheets. Records also accepted. SAE and IRC. Responds in 6 weeks.

Music Mostly **dance**, **pop**, **house**, **hip-hop**, and **rock**. Released ''Black Is Black'' (single by Gibbons/Hayes), recorded by Belle Epoque (dance); ''Pocket Full of Whishes'' (single by Robert Jones), recorded by Assault Team (dance), both on Movin' Novelties; and ''Let Me Be Free'' (single), written and recorded by Samantha Fox on LLP (pop). Other artists include Robert Ward, Yemisi, F.R. David and Black Nuss.

Tips ''We invite producers and independent record labels to send us their material for their entry on the European market. Mark all parcels as 'no commercial value—for demonstration only.' We license productions to record companies in all countries of Europe and South Africa. Submit good demos or masters.''

◖ ABL RECORDS

835 E. Buckeywood Ave., Orange CA 92865. (714)685-9958. E-mail: melodi4ever@earthlink.net. Web site: www.ABLmusic.com. **Contact:** Allan Licht, owner. Record company and music publisher (Allan Bradley Music/BMI and Lichtenfeld Music/ASCAP). Estab. 1993. Staff size: 2. Releases 10 singles/year. Pays 50% royalty to artists on contract; statutory rate to publisher per song on record.

 • Also see the listing for Allan Bradley Music in the Music Publishers section of this book.

How to Contact Submit demo package by mail. Unsolicited submissions are OK. Prefers CD with 3 songs and lyric sheet. Does not return material. Responds in 1 month.

Music Mostly **A/C**, **pop**, and **R&B**; also **country** and **Christian contemporary**. Released I'll Keep the Change (by Betty Kay Miller/Marcia McCaslin), recorded by Dakota Brad (country), released 1999 on ABL Records; ''22 Years Old'' (single), recorded by Donny Goldberg (pop/rock); ''I Trusted You'' (single), by Bree Noble/Linda Barbarino (A/C); ''Center of my Heart'' (single) by Tony Rooney (A/C); ''Impossibly Beautiful'' (single) by Daniel Goodman (A/C); ''His Own Hall of Fame'' (single) by Scott Ward/Chris Bradshaw (country); ''He Rolled The Stone Away'' (single) and ''A Dad Who Took The Time'' (single) by Jeff Knapp (Christian/country). Other artists include Tracy Todd, Sam Morrison, Donna West, Jill J. Switzer, Tony Rooney, Donny Goldberg, and Michael Cavanaugh.

Tips ''Submit top-notch material with great demos.''

ℕ ◐ ⊠ ALLIGATOR RECORDS

Attn: New Material, P.O. Box 60234, Chicago IL 60660.(773)973-7736. Fax: (773)973-2088. E-mail: info@allig.com. Web site: www.alligator.com. Contact: Estab. 1971.

 • With a catalog of over 200 titles, Alligator Records is the largest independent blues label in the world. Its recordings have won more awards than any other contemporary blues label, including a total of 34 Grammy nominations (two wins), 18 Indie Awards from the Association For Independent Music (AFIM) and three Grand Prix du Disque awards. Alligator and its artists have won a total of 70 W.C. Handy Blues Awards, the blues community's highest honor.

How to Contact Submit demo package by mail. *''We do not visit artist Web sites or listen to e-mail* *submissions. DO NOT SEND DIGITAL FILES BY E-MAIL!"* Prefers CD with no more than 4 songs. "If we like what we hear, we will ask for more." Responds in 7 months. *"Alligator will NOT accept inquiries or phone calls regarding the receipt or status of submissions.* All submissions will be responded to by mail. If no legible address is on the demo material, there will be no response.

Music Mostly **blues**; also **roots rock**. Released *Old School* (album), recorded by Koko Taylor (blues); *Moment of Truth* (album), recorded by Tinsley Ellis (blues); *Black Cat Bone* (album), recorded by Lee Rocker (rockabilly); *Have A Little Faith* (album), recorded by Mavis Staples (gospel/soul). Other artists include Shemekia Copeland, Roomful of Blues, Guitar Shorty, and W.C. Clark.

N ☑ ALTERNATIVE TENTACLES

P.O. Box 419092, San Francisco CA 94141.(510)596-8981. Fax: (510)596-8982. E-mail: press@altern ativetentacles.com. Web site: www.alternativetentacles.com. **Contact:** Jello Biafra. Estab. 1979. Staff size: 4. Releases 15-20 albums/year.

Distributed by Lumberjack/Mordam Records.

How to Contact Unsolicited submissions OK. Prefers CD or cassette. Does not return material. Responds only if interested. *" We accept demos by postal mail ONLY! We do not accept mp3s sent to us.* We will not go out and listen to your mp3s on Web sites. If you are interested in having ATR hear your music, you need to send us a CD, tape or vinyl. We cannot return your demos either, so please don't send us your originals or ask us to send them back. Sometimes Jello replies to people submitting demos; sometimes he doesn't. There is no way for us to check on your 'status', so please don't ask us."

Music Mostly **punk rock**, **spoken word**, **Brazilian hardcore**, **bent pop**, **faux-country**, and **assorted rock & roll**. Released *It's Not the Eat, It's the Humidity* (album), recorded by the Eat (punk); *Fuck World Trade* (album), recorded by Leftover Crack (punk); *Live from the Armed Madhouse* (album), recorded by Greg Palast (spoken word); *Dash Rip Rock* (album), recorded by Hee Haw Hell (southern country punk); *Homem Inimigo Do Homem* (album), recorded by Ratos De Parao (Brazilian hardcore). Other artists include Jello Biafra, The (International) Noise Conspiracy, Akimbo, Robert Fisk, Subhumans, Blowfly, Ludicra, The Heads, Fleshies, Fish Karma, Bloodhag, Nausea, Tarantella, and Melvins.

☑ AMERICAN RECORDINGS

8920 Sunset Blvd., 2nd Floor, W. Hollywood CA 90069. (310)288-5300. Web site: www.americanrec ordings.com. A&R: Dino Paredes, George Drakoulias, Antony Bland, Brendon Mendoza. Labels include Too Pure, Infinite Zero, UBL, Venture and Onion. Record company.

• American Recordings is a subsidiary of Sony BMG, one of the "Big 4" major labels.

Distributed by Sony.

How to Contact Submit demo by mail. Unsolicited submissions are OK. Prefers CD, cassette or videocassette with lyric and lead sheet.

Music Released *Unchained*, recorded by Johnny Cash on American Recordings. Other artists include Slayer, System of a Down, The Jayhawks, Rahat Feteh Ali Khan, Paloalto, Noise Ratchet, and The (International) Noise Conspiracy.

☑ AMERICATONE RECORDS INTERNATIONAL USA

1817 Loch Lomond Way, Las Vegas NV 89102-4437. (702)384-0030. Fax: (702)382-1926. E-mail: jjjamericatone@aol.com. Web site: www.americatone.com. Estab. 1985. **Contact:** A&R Director. Labels include The Rambolt Music International (ASCAP), Americatone Publishers (BMI) and Christy Records International. Record company, producer and music publisher. Releases 4-5 CDs and cassettes/year. Pays 10% royalty.

Distributed by Big Band Dist., Otter Music, North County, General, Harbor Export, International Dist., Twinbrook Dist., Gibson Dist.

How to Contact Submit demo by mail. Unsolicited submissions are OK. Prefers CD. Include SASE. Responds in 1 month.

Music Jazz and **Spanish jazz** only. Artists include Raoul Romero and His Jazz Stars Orchestra, Mark Masters and His Jazz Orchestra, Dick Shearer and His Stan Kenton Spirits, Sam Trippe and His Jazz Orchestra, Ladd McIntosh and His Orchestra, Caribbean Jazz, Jazz in the Rain Quintet, Brad Saunders and His Quintet, Bill Perkins and His Jazz Quintet, and the Eugene Shapiro Jazz Quintet. Americatone International USA is also a publisher of piano music and orchestrations.

⬛ ☑ AMP RECORDS & MUSIC

Box BM F.A.M.E., London WC1N 3XX United Kingdom. E-mail: markjenkins@beeb.net. Web site: www.markjenkins.net or www.myspace.com/markjenkinsmusic. **Contact:** Mark Jenkins, A&R (New Age, instrumental, ambient, progressive rock). Record company. Estab. 1985. Staff size: 10. Releases 12 CDs/year. Pays negotiable royalty to artists on contract; negotiable rate to publisher per song on record.

Distributed by Shellshock (UK), Eurock/ZNR/NSA (USA), MP (Italy) and Crystal Lake (France).

How to Contact *"Your must be in the styles released by the label! You are strongly advised to e-mail us first, without any attachments. Singer-songwriter, R&B, soul, indie guitar rock, country, all go straight in the trash unplayed!"* Does not return material. Responds in 2 months.

Music Mostly **New Age**, **instrumental** and **ambient**; also **progressive rock**, **synthesizer** and **ambient dance**. Does not want ballads, country or AOR. Released *Changing States* (album), recorded by Keith Emerson (progressive rock); *Tyranny of Beauty* (album), written and recorded by Tangerine Dream (synthesizer); and *Spirit of Christmas* (album), written and recorded by various artists (instrumental compilation), all on AMP Records.

Tips "See what we're about from our Web site before wasting your money sending irrelevant styles of music."

☑ ANGEL RECORDS

150 Fifth Ave., 6th Floor, New York NY 10011. (212)786-8600. Web site: www.angelrecords.com. Record company. Labels include EMI Classics, Manhattan Records, and Virgin Classics.

• Angel Records is a subsidiary of the EMI Group, one of the "Big 4" major labels. EMI is a British-based company.

Distributed by EMI Music Distribution.

How to Contact *Angel/EMI Records does not accept unsolicited submissions.*

Music Artists include Sarah Brightman, Paul McCartney, and Bernadette Peters.

☑ ARISTA RECORDS

888 7th Ave., New York NY 10019. (212)489-7400. Fax: (212)977-9843. Web site: www.arista.com. Beverly Hills office: 8750 Wilshire Blvd., 3rd Floor, Beverly Hills CA 90211. (310)358-4600. Nashville office: 7 Music Circle North, Nashville TN 37203. (615)846-9100. Fax: (615)846-9192. Labels include Bad Boy Records, Arista Nashville and Time Bomb Recordings. Record company.

• Arista Records is a subsidiary of Sony BMG, one of the "Big 4" major labels.

Distributed by BMG.

How to Contact *Does not accept unsolicited material.*

Music Artists include Outkast, Dido, Pink, Usher, Avril Lavigne, Babyface, and Sarah McLachlan.

☑ ARKADIA ENTERTAINMENT CORP.

34 E. 23rd St., New York NY 10010. (212)533-0007. Fax: (212)979-0266. E-mail: info@arkadiarecords.com. Web site: www.arkadiarecords.com. **Contact:** A&R Song Submissions. Labels include Arkadia Jazz, Arkadia Classical, Arkadia Now and Arkadia Allworld. Record company, music publisher (Arkadia Music), record producer (Arkadia Productions) and Arkadia Video. Estab. 1995.

How to Contact *Write or call first and obtain permission to submit.*

Music Mostly **jazz**, **classical**, and **pop/R&B**; also **world**.

☑ ☺ ASTRALWERKS

Attn: A&R Dept., 101 Avenue of the Americas, 4th Floor, New York NY 10013. E-mail: A&R@astralw erks.net. Web site: www.astralwerks.com/demo.html. **Contact:** A&R. Record company. Estab. 1979. Releases 10-12 12″ singles and 100 CDs/year. Pays varying royalty to artists on contract; statutory rate to publisher per song.

- Astralwerks is a subsidiary of the EMI Group, one of the "Big 4" major labels. EMI is a British-based company.

How to Contact Send submissions to: "A&R Dept." to address above. No unsolicited phone calls please. Prefers CD. "Please include any pertinent information, including your group name, track titles, names of members, bio, background, successes, and any contact info. Do not send e-mail attachments."

Music Mostly **alternative/indie/electronic**. Artists include VHS or BETA, Badly Drawn boy, The Beta Band, Chemical Brothers, Turin Breaks, and Fatboy Slim.

Tips "We are open to artists of unique quality and enjoy developing artists from the ground up. We listen to all types of 'alternative' music regardless of genre. It's about the aesthetic and artistic quality first. We send out rejection letters so do not call to find out what's happening with your demo."

☐ ATLAN-DEC/GROOVELINE RECORDS

2529 Green Forest Court, Snellville GA 30078-4183. (770)985-1686. Fax: (877)751-5169. E-mail: atlandec@prodigy.net. Web site: www.ATLAN-DEC.com. President/Senior A&R Rep: James Hatcher. A&R Rep: Wiletta J. Hatcher. Record company, music publisher and record producer. Estab. 1994. Staff size: 2. Releases 3-4 singles, 3-4 LPs and 3-4 CDs/year. Pays 10-25% royalty to artists on contract; statutory rate to publisher per song on record.

Distributed by C.E.D. Entertainment Dist.

How to Contact Submit demo package by mail. Unsolicited submissions are OK. Prefers CD with lyric sheet. Does not return material. Responds in 3 months.

Music Mostly **R&B/urban**, **hip-hop/rap**, and **contemporary jazz**; also **soft rock**, **gospel**, **dance**, and **new country**. Released "Temptation" by Shawree, released 2004 on Atlan-Dec/Grooveline Records; *Enemy of the State* (album), recorded by Lowlife (rap/hip-hop); *I'm The Definition* (album), recorded by L.S. (rap/hip-hop), released 2007; "AHHW" (single), recorded by LeTebony Simmons (R&B), released 2007. Other artists include Furious D (rap/hip-hop), and Mark Cocker (new country).

☑ ∅ ATLANTIC RECORDS

1290 Avenue of the Americas, New York NY 10104. (212)707-2000. Fax: (212)581-6414. Web site: www.atlanticrecords.com. **New York:** 1290 Avenue of the Americas, New York, NY 10104. **Los Angeles:** 3400 W. Olive Ave., 3rd Floor, Burbank CA 91505. (818)238-6800 Fax: (310)205-7411. **Nashville:** 20 Music Square East, Nashville TN 37203. (615)272-7990. Labels include Big Beat Records, LAVA, Nonesuch Records, Atlantic Classics, and Rhino Records. Record company. Pays negotiable royalty to artists on contract; negotiable rate to publisher per song on record.

- Atlantic Records is a subsidiary of Warner Music Group, one of the "Big 4" major labels.

Distributed by WEA.

How to Contact *Does not accept unsolicited material.* "No phone calls please."

Music Artists include Matchbox Twenty, Jewel, Sugar Ray, Kid Rock, Luna, P.O.D., The Darkness, and The Corrs.

◉ AVITA RECORDS

P.O. Box 764, Hendersonville TN 37077-0764. (615)824-9313. Fax: (615)824-0797. E-mail: tachoir@ bellsouth.net. Web site: www.tachoir.com. **Contact:** Robert Kayre, manager. Record company, music publisher (Riohcat Music, BMI) and record producer (Jerry Tachoir). Estab. 1976. Staff size: 8. Releases 2 LPs and 2 CDs/year. Pays negotiable royalty to artists on contract; statutory rate to publisher per song on record.

• Also see the listing for Riohcat Music in the Managers & Booking Agents section of this book.

How to Contact *Contact first and obtain permission to submit.* We only accept material referred to us by a reputable industry source. Prefers CD, cassette, or DAT. Does not return materials. Responds only if interested.

Music Mostly **jazz**. Released *Improvised Thoughts* (album by Marlene Tachoir/Jerry Tachoir/Van Manakas), recorded by Jerry Tachoir and Van Manakas (jazz), released 2001 on Avita Records. Other artists include Van Manakas.

☑ ◉ AVITOR MUSIC INTERNATIONAL

P.O. Box 5537, Kreole Station, Moss Point MS 39563-1537. (601)914-9413 or (228)235-8092 (cell). "No collect calls, please." **Contact:** Jemiah F. Mitchell, president/owner. Estab. 2003. Music publisher and record company (Avitor Music International Records).Releases 10 singles and 5 LPs/ year. Pays negotiable royalty to artists on contract; statutory rate to publisher per song on record. "Avitor Music has National and International distribution."

• Also see the listing for AVI 39563 Music in the Music Publishers section of this book.

Distributed by Select-O-Hits, CD Baby, and Amazon.Com.

How to Contact *Write or call first for submission instructions.* " Always whenever you write, be sure you include a #10 business-size envelope addressed back to yourself with a first-class USA postage stamp on the envelope. A reply will come back to you using the SASE you include in your mailing when you write. *Absolutely no reply postcards—only SASE.* If you only write lyrics, do not submit; only complete songs reviewed, so you must find a collaborator. Not interested in reviewing homemade recordings." Prefers CD (first choice) or cassette with 3-10 songs along with lyrics to songs submitted. Responds in 2 months.

Music Mostly singers and songwriters of **country**, **modern country today**, **mainstream**, **rock**, **Americana**, **hip-hop**, **rap**, **R&B**, **bluegrass**, **hot A/C**, **adult A/C**, **urban**, **jazz**, **blues**, **teen**, **pop**, **gospel**, **top 40**, **Spanish**, **Spanish R&B**, **Spanish pop**, **Spanish hip-hop**, and **world music**. "We will review traditional country. If there is a convincing market for your music, then we are basically open to all genres." Released "6 O'Clock," "Cowboy Mix," and "Second Chance" (singles) from *Aron Dees* (album), written and recorded by Aron Dees (modern country), released on Avitor. "On July 4, 2007, Aron Dees played as opening act for Universal Records recording artist Keith Anderson before a crowd of 6,500 people at the University of Wyoming. Aron Dees' Web site is: www.arondee s.com."

Tips "We work with artists on trying to get financial support through creative means. Artists submitting material that is accepted must be ready and willing to work together with us to create a buzz. We are looking for serious-minded artists who are talented and want to make a career for themselves. If you are a team player and know what you want to accomplish, then by all means, give us a call or write us today. You matter to us and we will respond ASAP."

☑ ◉ AWARE RECORDS

624 Davis St., 2nd Floor, Evanston IL 60201. (874)424-2000. E-mail: info@awaremusic.com. Web site: www.awaremusic.com. A&R: Steve Smith. President: Gregg Latterman. Record company. Estab. 1993. Staff size: 7. Releases 5 LPs, 1 EP and 3 CD/year. Pays negotiable royalty to artists on contract; statutory rate to publisher per song on record.

Distributed by Sony/Columbia.

How to Contact *Does not accept unsolicited submissions.*

Music Mostly **rock/pop**. Artists include John Mayer, Five for Fighting, Kyle Riabko, and Mat Kearney.

◐ BANANA RECORDS

3115 Hiss Ave., Baltimore MD 21234. (410)663-5915. E-mail: theunholythree@yahoo.com. **Contact:** Ron Brown, President. Record company, music publisher (Infinite Publishing) and record producer (Ronald Brown). Estab. 1990. Releases 30 singles, 20 LPs and 20 CDs/year. Pays standard royalty to artists on contract; statutory rate to publisher per song on record.

How to Contact Submit demo by mail. Unsolicited submissions are OK. Prefers CD with 3 songs and lyric sheet. Include SASE. Responds in 3 weeks.

Music Mostly **top 40/commercial**, **pop/ballads** and **alternative**. Released "Crack of the Universe," written and recorded by Jesse Brown (pop) on Global; *The Unholy Three* (album), written and recorded by Ronnie B. (commercial), released 2002 on Banana Records.

Tips "A good singer works hard at his craft. A hit song has good punch and a lot of talent."

ℕ ◙ BLACKHEART RECORDS

636 Broadway, Suite 1210, New York NY 10012.(212)353-9600. Fax: (212)353-8300. E-mail: ar@blackheart.com. Web site: www.blackheart.com. **Contact:** Zander Wolff, a&r. Record label. Estab. 1982.

How to Contact Unsolicited submissions are OK. Prefers CD with 1-3 songs and lyric sheets. Include SASE. Responds only if interested.

Music Mostly **rock**. Artists include Joan Jett & the Blackhearts, The Dollyrots, The Vacancies, Girl In A Coma, and The Eyeliners.

◑ BLUE GEM RECORDS

P.O. Box 29550, Hollywood CA 90029. (323)664-7765. E-mail: pmarti3636@aol.com. Web site: www.VaamMusic.com. **Contact:** Pete Martin. Record company, music publisher (Vaam Music Group) and record producer (Pete Martin/Vaam Productions). Estab. 1981. Pays 6-15% royalty to artists on contract; statutory rate to publisher per song on record.

> • Also see the listings for Vaam Music Group in the Music Publishers section of this book and Pete Martin/Vaam Music Productions in the Record Producers section of this book.

How to Contact Submit demo by mail. Unsolicited submissions are OK. Prefers CD or cassette with 2 songs. Include SASE. Responds in 3 weeks.

Music Mostly **country** and **R&B**; also **pop/top 40** and **rock**.

◙ BOLIVIA RECORDS

2622 Kirtland Rd., Brewton AL 36246. (251)867-2228. **Contact:** Roy Edwards, president. Labels include Known Artist Records. Record company, record producer (Known Artist Productions) and music publisher (Cheavoria Music Co.). Estab. 1972. Releases 10 singles and 3 LPs/year. Pays 5% royalty to artists on contract; statutory rate to publishers for each record sold.

> • Also see ths listings for Baitstring Music and Chearovia Music in the Music Publishers section and Known Artist Productions in the Record Producers section of this book.

How to Contact Submit demo by mail. Unsolicited submissions are OK. Prefers CD with 3 songs and lyric sheet. Include SASE for reply. All tapes will be kept on file. Responds in 1 month.

Music Mostly **R&B**, **country** and **pop**; also **easy listening**, **MOR**, **soul** and **gospel**. Released "If You Only Knew" (single by Horace Linsley), recorded by Roy Edwards; "Make Me Forget" (single by Horace Linsley), recorded by Bobbie Roberson, both on Bolivia Records; and "We Make Our Reality" (single), written and recorded by Brad Smiley on Known Artist Records. Other artists include Jim Portwood.

Tips "We need some good gospel."

☑ ◑ BOUQUET RECORDS

Bouquet-Orchid Enterprises, P.O. Box 1335, Norcross GA 30091. Phone/fax: (770)339-9088. **Contact:** Bill Bohannon, president. Record company, music publisher (Orchid Publishing/BMI), record producer (Bouquet-Orchid Enterprises) and management firm (Bouquet-Orchid Enterprises). Releases 3-4 singles and 2 LPs/year. Pays 5-8% royalty to artists on contract; pays statutory rate to publishers for each record sold.

How to Contact Submit demo by mail. Unsolicited submissions are OK. Prefers cassette or CD with 3-5 songs and lyric sheet. Include SASE. Responds in 1 month.

Music Mostly **religious** (contemporary or country-gospel, Amy Grant, etc.), **country** ("the type suitable for Kenny Chesney, George Strait, Carrie Underwood, Patty Loveless, etc." and **top 100** ("the type suitable for Billy Joel, Whitney Houston, R.E.M., etc."; also **rock**, and **MOR**. Released *Blue As Your Eyes* (by Bill Bohannon), recorded by Adam Day (country); *Take Care of My World* (by Bob Freeman), recorded by Bandoleers (top 40); and *Making Plans* (by John Harris), recorded by Susan Spencer (country), all on Bouquet Records.

Tips "Submit 3-5 songs on a cassette tape or CD with lyric sheets. Include a short biography and perhaps a photo. Enclose SASE."

☑ ◑ BSW RECORDS

P.O. Box 2297, Universal City TX 78148. (210)653-3989. E-mail: bswr18@wmconnect.com. Web site: www.bsw-records.com. President: Frank Willson. Vice Presidents: Frank Weatherly (country, jazz); Regina Willson (blues). Record company, music publisher (BSW Records/BMI), management firm (Universal Music Marketing) and record producer (Frank Willson). Estab. 1987. Staff size: 5. Releases 18 albums/year. Pays standard royalty to artists on contract; statutory rate to publisher per song on record.

- Also see the listings for BSW Records in the Music Publishers section, Frank Wilson in the Record Producers section and Universal Music Marketing in the Managers & Booking Agents section of this book.

How to Contact Submit demo package by mail. Unsolicited submissions are OK. Prefers CD (or ¾" videocassette) with 3 songs and lyric sheet. Include SASE. Responds in 6 weeks.

Music Mostly **country**, **rock**, and **blues**. Released *Memories of Hank Williams, Sr.* (album), recorded by Larry Butler and Willie Nelson. Other artists include Candee Land, Crea Beal, John Wayne, Sonny Marshall, and Bobby Mountain. "Visit our Web site for an up-to-date listing of releases."

◑ CAMBRIA RECORDS & PUBLISHING

P.O. Box 374, Lomita CA 90717. (310)831-1322. Fax: (310)833-7442. E-mail: admin@cambriamus.c om. **Contact:** Lance Bowling, director of recording operations. Labels include Charade Records. Record company and music publisher. Estab. 1979. Staff size: 3. Pays 5-8% royalty to artists on contract; statutory rate to publisher for each record sold.

Distributed by Albany Distribution.

How to Contact *Write first and obtain permission to submit.* Prefers cassette. Include SASE. Responds in 1 month.

Music Mostly **classical**. Released *Songs of Elinor Remick Warren* (album) on Cambria Records. Other artists include Marie Gibson (soprano), Leonard Pennario (piano), Thomas Hampson (voice), Mischa Leftkowitz (violin), Leigh Kaplan (piano), North Wind Quintet, and Sierra Wind Quintet.

⦿ ◑ CANTILENA RECORDS

1925 5th Ave., Sacramento CA 95818. (916)600-2424. E-mail: llzz@aol.com. Web site: www.cantile narecords.com. A&R: Laurel Zucker, owner. A&R: B. Houseman. Record company. Estab. 1993. Releases 5 CDs/year. Pays Harry Fox standard royalty to artists on contract; statutory rate to publishers per song on record.

How to Contact *Write first and obtain permission to submit or to arrange personal interview.* Prefers CD. Does not return material.

Music Classical, **jazz**, **world music**. Released "Caliente!" (single by Christopher Caliendo) from *Caliente! World Music for Flute & Guitar* (album), recorded by Laurel Zucker and Christopher Caliendo! (world crossover); *Suites No. 1 & 2 For Flute & Jazz Piano Trio* (album by Claude Bolling), recorded by Laurel Zucker, Joe Gilman, David Rokeach, Jeff Neighbor (jazz); and *HOPE! Music for Flute, Soprano, Guitar* (album by Daniel Akiva, Astor Piazzolla, Haim Permont, Villa-Lobos) (classical/world), recorded by Laurel Zucker, Ronit Widmann-Levy, Daniel Akiva, all released in 2004 by Cantilena Records. Other artists include Tim Gorman, Prairie Prince, Dave Margen, Israel Philharmonic, Erkel Chamber Orchestra, Samuel Magill, Renee Siebert, Robin Sutherland, and Gerald Ranch.

🅾 CAPITOL RECORDS

1750 N. Vine St., Hollywood CA 90028-5274. (323)462-6252. Fax: (323)469-4542. Web site: www.hollywoodandvine.com. **Nashville:** 3322 West End Ave., 11th Floor, Nashville TN 37203. (615)269-2000. Labels include Blue Note Records, Grand Royal Records, Pangaea Records, The Right Stuff Records and Capitol Nashville Records. Record company.

• Capitol Records is a subsidiary of the EMI Group, one of the "Big 4" major labels.

Distributed by EMD.

How to Contact *Capitol Records does not accept unsolicited submissions.*

Music Artists include Coldplay, Beastie Boys, Liz Phair, and Auf der Maur.

🖾 🅾 CAPP RECORDS

P.O. Box 150871, San Rafael CA 94915-0871. Phone/fax: (415)457-8617. E-mail: manus@capprecords.com. Web site: www.capprecords.com. CEO/International Manager: Dominique Toulon (pop, dance, New Age); Creative Manager/A&R: Manus Buchart (dance, techno). President: Rudolf Stember. Vice President/Publisher: Radi Tamimi (tamimi@capprecords.com); Public Relations/A&R: Michael Oliva (oliva@capprecords.com). Music publisher (Cappster music/ASCAP and CIDC Music/BMI) and record company. Member: NARAS, NCSA, Songwriter's Guild of America. Estab. 1993. Publishes 100 songs/year; publishes 25 new songwriters/year. Staff size: 8. Pays standard royalty.

Affiliate(s) Cary August Publishing Co./CAPP Company (Germany)/Capp Company (Japan).

How to Contact Submit demo package by mail. Unsolicited submissions are OK. Prefers CD or NTSC videocassette with 3 songs and cover letter. "E-mail us in advance for submissions, if possible." Include SASE. Only responds if interested.

Film & TV Places 20 songs in film and 7 songs in TV/year. Music Supervisors: Dominique Toulon (pop, dance, New Age). "Currently doing music placement for television—*MTV, VH1, Oprah, A&E Network,* and *Discovery Channel.*"

Music Mostly **pop**, **dance**, and **techno**; also **New Age**. Does not want country. Released "It's Not a Dream" (single by Cary August/Andre Pessis), recorded by Cary August on CAPP Records (dance). "Visit our Web site for new releases."

🅾 CAPSTAN RECORD PRODUCTION

P.O. Box 211, East Prairie MO 63845. (575)649-2211. **Contact:** Joe Silver or Tommy Loomas. Labels include Octagon and Capstan Records. Record company, music publisher (Lineage Publishing Co.), management firm (Staircase Promotion) and record producer (Silver-Loomas Productions). Pays 3-5% royalty to artists on contract.

How to Contact Unsolicited submissions are OK. Prefers cassette or VHS videocassette with 2-4 songs and lyric sheet. "Send photo and bio." Include SASE. Responds in 1 month.

Music Mostly **country**, **easy listening**, **MOR**, **country rock**, and **top 40/pop**. Released "Country

Boy'' (single by Alden Lambert); and "Yesterday's Teardrops" (single) and "Round & Round" (single), written and recorded by The Burchetts. Other artists include Bobby Lee Morgan, Skidrow Joe, Vicarie Arcole, and Fleming and Scarlett Britoni.

◙ CELLAR RECORDS
703 N. Brinton Ave., Dixon IL 61021. (866)287-4997. E-mail: president@cellarrecords.com. Web site: www.cellarrecords.com. **Contact:** Todd Joos, president. A&R Department: Bob Brady, Albert Hurst, Jim Miller, Mark Summers, Jon Pomplin. Record company, music publisher (Sound Cellar Music/BMI) and record producer (Todd Joos). Estab. 1987. Staff size: 6. Releases 6-8 CDs/year. Pays 15-100% royalty to artists on contract; statutory rate to publisher per song on record. Charges in advance "if you use our studio to record."
Distributed by "We now service retail and online (Apple iTunes, etc. direct from Cellar Records."
How to Contact Submit demo package by mail. Unsolicited submissions are OK. Prefers CD with 3-4 songs and lyric sheet. Does not return material. Responds in 1 month only if interested. "If we like it we will call you."
Music Mostly **metal**, **country**, **rock**, **pop**, and **blues**. "No rap." Released "With Any Luck at All" (single by Tony Stampley/Randy Boudreaux/Joe Stampley) from *With Any Luck At All* (album), recorded by Cal Stage (pop/country); "Sleeping With a Smile" (single by Tony Stampley/Melissa Lyons/Tommy Barnes) from *With Any Luck At All* (album), recorded by Cal Stage (pop/country); and "Speed of My Life" (single by Jon Pomplin/Todd Joos) from *Declassified* (album), recorded by Project 814 (rock), all released 2001 on Cellar Records. "Visit our Web site for upcoming releases." Other artists include Eric Topper, Snap Judgment, Ballistic, Dago Red, Sea of Monsters, Rogue, Kings, James Miller, Vehement, Noopy Wilson, Dual Exhaust, Junker Jorg, The Unknown, Joel Ramirez & the Allstars, Tracylyn, Junk Poet, Cajun Anger, Roman, Flesh Pilgrims, LYZ, and Justice4.
Tips "Make sure that you understand your band is a business and you must be willing to self-invest time, effort and money just like any other new business. We can help you, but you must also be willing to help yourself."

◻ CHATTAHOOCHEE RECORDS
2544 Roscomare Rd., Los Angeles CA 90077. (818)788-6863. Fax: (310)471-2089. E-mail: cyardum @prodigy.net. **Contact:** Robyn Meyers, Music Director/A&R. Music Director: Chris Yardum. Record company and music publisher (Etnoc/Conte). Member NARAS. Releases 4 singles/year. Pays negotiable royalty to artists on contract.
How to Contact Submit demo by mail. Unsolicited submissions are OK. Prefers CD with 2-6 songs and lyric sheet. Does not return material. Responds in 2 months only if interested.
Music Mostly **rock**. Released *Don't Touch It Let It Drip* (album), recorded by Cream House (hard rock), released 2000 on Chattahoochee Records. Artists include DNA, Noctrnl, and Vator.

◙ CLEOPATRA RECORDS
11041 Santa Monica Blvd., PMB 703, Los Angeles CA 90025. (310)477-4000. Fax: (310)312-5653. E-mail: cleoinfo@cleorecs.com. Web site: www.cleorecs.com. **Contact:** Ali Ohta, A&R. Labels include Hypnotic, Deadline, X-Ray, Cult, Stardust and Purple Pyramid. Record company. Estab. 1991. Releases 5 singles, 10 LPs, 5 EPs and 100 CDs/year. Pays 10-14% royalty to artists on contract; negotiable rate to publisher per song on record.
How to Contact *E-mail first for permission to submit material.* Prefers CD with 3 songs. Does not return material. Responds in 1 month.
Music Mostly **industrial**, **gothic** and **trance**; also **heavy metal**, **space rock** and **electronic**.

⊘ COLUMBIA RECORDS

550 Madison Ave., 24th Floor, New York NY 10022. (212)833-4000. Fax: (212)833-4389. E-mail: sonymusiconline@sonymusic.com. Web site: www.columbiarecords.com. **Santa Monica:** 2100 Colorado Ave., Santa Monica CA 90404. (310)449-2100. Fax: (310)449-2743. **Nashville:** 34 Music Square E., Nashville TN 37203. (615)742-4321. Fax: (615)244-2549. Labels include So So Def Records and Ruffhouse Records. Record company.

• Columbia Records is a subsidiary of Sony BMG, one of the "Big 4" major labels.

Distributed by Sony.

How to Contact *Columbia Records does not accept unsolicited submissions.*

Music Artists include Aerosmith, Marc Anthony, Beyonce, Bob Dylan, and Patti Smith.

☑ ⊘ COMPADRE RECORDS

1505 Hadley St., Houston TX 77002. (713)772-5175. Fax: (713)289-5777. E-mail: info@compadrerec ords.com. Web site: www.compadrerecords.com. **Contact:** Brad Turcotte, president. Record company. Subsidiary of Music World Entertainment. Estab. 2001.

Distributed by Fontana/Universal.

How to Contact *E-mail first for permission to submit. We do not accept unsolicited submissions.*

Music Mostly **Americana**. Released *The Real Deal* (album), recorded by Billy Joe Shaver (Americana); and *Childish Things* (album), recorded by James McMurtry (Americana), both released 2005 on Compadre. Other artist included Julie Lee and Honeybrowne.

⊘ COSMOTONE RECORDS

2951 Marina Bay Dr., League City TX 77573-2733. E-mail: marianland@earthlink.net. Web site: www.marianland.com/music.html. Record company, music publisher (Cosmotone Music, ASCAP) and record producer (Rafael Brom). Estab. 1984.

Distributed by marianland.com.

How to Contact "We do not accept material at this time." Does not return materials.

Music Mostly **Christian pop/rock**. Released *Dance for Padre Pio*, *Peace of Heart*, *Music for Peace of Mind*, *The Sounds of Heaven*, *The Christmas Songs*, *Angelophany*, *The True Measure of Love*, *All My Love to You Jesus* (albums), and *Rafael Brom Unplugged* (live concert DVD), by Rafael Brom.

◉ CPA RECORDS

15104 Golden Eagle Way, Tampa FL 33625-1545. (813)920-4605. Fax: (813)926-0846. E-mail: al@cp arecords.com. Web site: www.cparecords.com. **Contact:** Al McDaniel, president. Labels include Coffee's Productions and Associates. Record company and music publisher (CPA Music Publishing). Estab. 1999. Staff size: 5. Releases 3 singles and 2 albums/year. Pays negotiable royalty to artists on contract; negotiable royalty to publisher per song on record.

How to Contact *Write or call first and obtain permission to submit a demo.* Does not accept unsolicited submissions. Does not return unsolicited materials. Guidelines given when permission to submit granted. Responds in 2 weeks.

Music Mostly **R&B** and **jazz**; also **pop**. Does not want country. Released *A Shoe is a Shoe* (album), *A Special Blend* (album), and *Blues in my Shoes* (album), recorded by Al "Coffee" McDaniel. Other artists include Project Necessary, Blusion, Sax Kari, Anthony "Big Lou" McDaniel, and Mike and Anita.

Tips "Be marketable, creative, committed to achieving success, and willing to work hard to accomplish your goals."

◻ CREATIVE IMPROVISED MUSIC PROJECTS (CIMP) RECORDS

CIMP LTD, Cadence Building, Redwood NY 13679. (315)287-2852. Fax: (315)287-2860. E-mail: cimp@cadencebuilding.com. Web site: www.cimprecords.com. **Contact:** Bob Rusch, producer.

Labels include Cadence Jazz Records. Record company and record producer (Robert D. Rusch). Estab. 1980. Releases 25-30 CDs/year. Pays negotiable royalty to artists on contract; pays statutory rate to publisher per song on record.

Distributed by North Country Distributors.

● CIMP specializes in jazz and creative improvised music.

How to Contact Submit demo by mail. Unsolicited submissions are OK. Prefers cassette or CD. ''We are not looking for songwriters but recording artists.'' Include SASE. Responds in 1 week.

Music Mostly **jazz** and **creative improvised music**. Released *The Redwood Session* (album), recorded by Evan Parker, Barry Guy, Paul Lytton, and Joe McPhee; *Sarah's Theme* (album), recorded by the Ernie Krivda Trio, Bob Fraser, and Jeff Halsey; and *Human Flowers* (album), recorded by the Bobby Zankel Trio, Marily Crispell, and Newman Baker, all released on CIMP (improvised jazz). Other artists include Arthur Blythe, Joe McPhee, David Prentice, Anthony Braxton, Roswell Rudd, Paul Smoker, Khan Jamal, Odean Pope, etc.

Tips ''CIMP Records are produced to provide music to reward repeated and in-depth listenings. They are recorded live to two-track which captures the full dynamic range one would experience in a live concert. There is no compression, homogenization, eq-ing, post-recording splicing, mixing, or electronic fiddling with the performance. Digital recording allows for a vanishingly low noise floor and tremendous dynamic range. This compression of the dynamic range is what limits the 'air' and life of many recordings. Our recordings capture the dynamic intended by the musicians. In this regard these recordings are demanding. Treat the recording as your private concert. Give it your undivided attention and it will reward you. CIMP Records are not intended to be background music. This method is demanding not only on the listener but on the performer as well. Musicians must be able to play together in real time. They must understand the dynamics of their instrument and how it relates to the others around them. There is no fix-it-in-the-mix safety; either it works or it doesn't. What you hear is exactly what was played. Our main concern is music not marketing.''

⊘ CURB RECORDS

47 Music Square E., Nashville TN 37203. (615)321-5080. Fax: (615)327-1964. Web site: www.curb.com. **Contact:** John Ozler, A&R coordinator. Record company.

How to Contact Curb Records does not accept unsolicited submissions; accepts previously published material only. *Do not submit without permission.*

Music Released *Everywhere* (album), recorded by Tim McGraw; *Sittin' On Top of the World* (album), recorded by LeAnn Rimes; and *I'm Alright* (album), recorded by Jo Dee Messina, all on Curb Records. Other artists include Mary Black, Merle Haggard, Kal Ketchum, David Kersh, Lyle Lovett, Tim McGraw, Wynonna, and Sawyer Brown.

◻ DEEP SOUTH ENTERTAINMENT

P.O. Box 17737, Raleigh NC 27619-7737. (919)844-1515. Fax: (919)847-5922. E-mail: info@deepsou thentertainment.com. Web site: www.deepsouthentertainment.com. Director of Artist Relations: Kali Bryan. Manager: Amy Cox. Record company and management company. Estab. 1996. Staff size: 10. Pays negotiable royalty to artists on contract; statutory rate to publisher per song on record.

Distributed by Redeye Distribution, Valley, Select-O-Hits, City Hall, AEC/Bassin, Northeast One Stop, Pollstar, and Koch International.

How to Contact Submit demo by mail. Unsolicited submissions are OK. Prefers cassette or CD with 3 songs, cover letter, and press clippings. Does not return material. Responds only if interested.

Music Mostly **pop**, **modern rock**, and **alternative**; also **swing**, **rockabilly**, and **heavy rock**. Does not want rap or R&B. Artists include Bruce Hornsby, Little Feat, Mike Daly, SR-71, Stretch Princess, Darden Smith, and Vienna Teng.

Record Companies

☐ DENTAL RECORDS

P.O. Box 20058, New York NY 10017. E-mail: info@dentalrecords.com. Web site: www.dentalrecor ds.com. **Contact:** Rick Sanford, owner. Record company. Estab. 1981. Staff size: 2. Releases 1-2 CDs/year. Pays negotiable royalty to artists on contract; statutory rate to publisher per song on record.

Distributed by Dutch East India Trading.

How to Contact *Not currently accepting unsolicited submissions.* Prefers CD with any number of songs, lyric sheet, and cover letter. "Check our Web site to see if your material is appropriate." Include SASE. Responds only if interested.

Music Pop-derived structures, **jazz-derived harmonies**, and **neo-classic-wannabee-pretenses**. Does not want urban, heavy metal, or hard core. Released *Perspectivism* (album), written and recorded by Rick Sanford (instrumental), released 2003 on Dental Records. Other artists include Les Izmor.

🔲 ⊘ DREAMWORKS RECORDS

2220 Colorado Ave., Santa Monica CA 90404. (310)865-1000. Fax: (310)865-8059. Web site: www.d reamworksrecords.com. **Nashville:** 60 Music Sq. E., Nashville TN 37203. (615)463-4600 Fax: (615)463-4601. Record company and music publisher (DreamWorks SKG Music Publishing). Labels include Interscope, Geffen, and A&M.

• Dreamworks Records is a subsidiary of Universal Music Group, one of the "Big 4" major labels.

How to Contact Material must be submitted through an agent or attorney. *Does not accept unsolicited submissions.*

⊘ DRUMBEAT INDIAN ARTS, INC.

4143 N. 16th St., Suite 1, Phoenix AZ 85016. (602)266-4823. Web site: www.DrumbeatIndianArts.c om. **Contact:** Bob Nuss, president. Record company and distributor of American Indian recordings. Estab. 1984. Staff size: 8. Releases 100 CDs/year. Royalty varies with project.

• Note that Drumbeat Indian Arts is a very specialized label, and only wants to receive submissions by Native American artists.

How to Contact *Call first and obtain permission to submit.* Include SASE. Responds in 2 months.

Music Music by American Indians—any style (must be enrolled tribal members). Does not want New Age "Indian style" material. Released Pearl Moon (album), written and recorded by Xavier (native Amerindian). Other artists include Black Lodge Singers, R. Carlos Nakai, Lite Foot, and Joanne Shenandoah.

Tips "We deal only with American Indian performers. We do not accept material from others. Please include tribal affiliation."

⊘ ELEKTRA RECORDS

75 Rockefeller Plaza, 17th Floor, New York NY 10019. Web site: www.elektra.com. Labels include Elektra Records, Eastwest Records, and Asylum Records. Record company.

• Elektra Records is a subsidiary of Warner Music Group, one of the "Big 4" major labels.

Distributed by WEA.

How to Contact *Elektra does not accept unsolicited submissions.*

Music Mostly **alternative/modern rock**. Artists include Phish, Jason Mraz, Bjork, Busta Rhymes, and Metallica.

⊘ EPIC RECORDS

550 Madison Ave., 21st Floor, New York NY 10022. (212)833-8000. Fax: (212)833-4054. Web site: www.epicrecords.com. Senior Vice Presidents A&R: Ben Goldman, Rose Noone. **Santa Monica:**

2100 Colorado Ave., Santa Monica CA 90404. (310)449-2100 Fax: (310)449-2848. A&R: Pete Giberga, Mike Flynn. Labels include Epic Soundtrax, LV Records, Immortal Records, and Word Records. Record company.

- Epic Records is a subsidiary of Sony BMG, one of the "Big 4" major labels.

Distributed by Sony Music Distribution.

How to Contact *Write or call first and obtain permission to submit* (New York office only). Does not return material. Responds only if interested. *Santa Monica and Nashville offices do not accept unsolicited submissions.*

Music Artists include Celine Dion, Macy Gray, Modest Mouse, Audioslave, Fuel, Jennifer Lopez, B2K, Incubus, Ben Folds.

Tips "Do an internship if you don't have experience or work as someone's assistant. Learn the business and work hard while you figure out what your talents are and where you fit in. Once you figure out which area of the record company you're suited for, focus on that, work hard at it and it shall be yours."

☐ FRONT ROW RECORDS

Ridgewood Park Estates, 222 Tulane St., Garland TX 75043. **Contact:** Gene or Dea Summers. Public Relations/Artist and Fan Club Coordinator: Steve Summers. A&R: Shawn Summers. Labels include Juan Records. Record company and music publisher (Silicon Music/BMI). Estab. 1968. Releases 5-6 singles and 2-3 LPs/year. Pays negotiable royalty to artists on contract; standard royalty to songwriters on contract.

Distributed by Crystal Clear Records.

- Also see the listing for Silicon Music Publishing Co. in the Music Publishers section of this book.

How to Contact Submit demo by mail. Unsolicited submissions are OK. Prefers cassette or VHS videocassette with 1-3 songs. "We request a photo and bio with material submission." Does not return material. Responds ASAP.

Music Mostly **'50s rock/rockabilly**; also **country**, **bluegrass**, **old-time blues**, and **R&B**. Released "Domino" (single), recorded by Gene Summers on Pollytone Records (rockabilly); "Goodbye Priscilla" and "Cool Baby" (singles), both recorded by Gene Summers on Collectables Records.

Tips "If you own masters of 1950s rock and rockabilly, contact us first! We will work with you on a percentage basis for overseas release. We have active releases in Holland, Switzerland, Belgium, Australia, England, France, Sweden, Norway, and the US at the present. We need original masters. You must be able to prove ownership of tapes before we can accept a deal. We're looking for little-known, obscure recordings. We have the market if you have the tapes! We are also interested in country and rockabilly artists who have not recorded for awhile but still have the voice and appeal to sell overseas."

☐ GENERIC RECORDS, INC.

433 Limestone Rd., Ridgefield CT 06877. (203)438-9811. Fax: (203)431-3204. E-mail: hifiadd@aol.com. President (pop, alternative, rock): Gary Lefkowith. A&R (pop, dance, adult contemporary): Bill Jerome. Labels include Outback, GLYN. Record company, music publisher (Sotto Music/BMI) and record producer. Estab. 1976. Staff size: 2. Releases 6 singles and 2 CDs/year. Pays 15% royalty to artists on contract; statutory rate to publisher per song on record.

Distributed by Dutch East India.

How to Contact Submit demo package by mail. Unsolicited submissions are OK. Prefers CD or cassette with 2-3 songs. Include SASE. Responds in 2 weeks.

Music Mostly **alternative rock**, **rock**, and **pop**; also **country** and **rap**. Released "Young Girls" (by Eric Della Penna/Dean Sharenow), recorded by Henry Sugar (alternative/pop); "Rock It," written and recorded by David Ruskay (rock/pop); and Tyrus, written and recorded by Tyrus (alternative),

all on Generic Records, Inc. Other artists include Hifi, Honest, Loose Change, and John Fantasia.
Tips "Love what you're doing. The music comes first."

☑ GIG RECORDS

520 Butler Ave., Point Pleasant NJ 08742. E-mail: lenny@gigrecords.com. Web site: www.gigrecord
s.com. **Contact:** Lenny Hip, A&R. Labels include AMPED. Record company and music publisher
(Gig Music). Estab. 1998. Staff size: 8. Releases 2 singles, 2 EPs and 15 CDs/year. Pays negotiable
royalty to artists on contract; statutory rate to publisher per song on record.
Distributed by Amazon, E-Music, CD Now, Nail, and Sumthing.
How to Contact Submit demo package by mail. Unsolicited submissions are OK. Prefers CD or
DVD with lyric sheet and cover letter. Does not return materials, "but will respond if SASE is
included." Responds ASAP if interested.
Music Mostly **rock** and **electronic**; also **drum & bass**, **trip-hop**, and **hip-hop**. Does not want
country. Released *Hungry* (album), recorded by Gum Parker (electronico), released 2003 on Gig
Records; *Waiting For You* (album), recorded by Nick Clemons Band (alternative rock/pop), released
2003 on Groove Entertainment; and a new release to come from Fight of Your Life. Other artists
include Ned's Atomic Dustbin, Virginia, The Vibrators, Groundswell UK, Nebula Nine, The Youth
Ahead, Dryer, Red Engine Nine, Michael Ferentino, Amazing Meet Project, and Love in Reverse.
Tips "No egos."

☐ GOLDWAX RECORD CORPORATION

P.O. Box 54700, Atlanta GA 30308-0700. (770)316-7454. Fax: (770)454-8088. E-mail: goldwaxrec@
aol.com. Web site: www.goldwax.com. **Contact:** Jimmy McClendon, A&R. Labels include Abec,
Bandstand USA, Urban Assault, and Beale Street USA. Record company and music publisher (Stellar
Music Industries). Estab. 1963. Staff size: 4. Releases 15 singles, 12 LPs, 4 EPs and 2 CDs/year.
Pays negotiable royalty to artists on contract; statutory rate to publisher per song on record.
Distributed by City Hall Records, Goldwax Distributing.
How to Contact *Write or call first and obtain permission to submit.* Prefers CD or DVD with 4 songs
and lyric sheet. Include SASE. Responds in 6 weeks.
Music Mostly **R&B/hip-hop**, **pop/rock** and **jazz**; also **blues**, **contemporary country** and **contem-
porary gospel**. Released *Clifford & Co.* (album) (soul) on Beale Street Records; and *Double Deuce*
(album), recorded by Double Deuce (rap) on Urban Assault Records. Other artists include Elvin
Spenser and Margie Alexander.
Tips "Songwriters need to provide great melodies; artists need to have commercial appeal."

☑ ☐ GONZO! RECORDS INC.

5757 E. Erin Ave., Fresno CA 93727. (559)269-2244. Fax: (559)452-9694. E-mail: gonzorcrd2@aol.c
om. Web site: members.aol.com/gonzorcrds. **Contact:** Jeffrey Gonzalez, president. Record company. Estab. 1993. Staff size: 3. Releases 3 singles and 1-6 CDs/year. Pays negotiable royalty to
artists on contract; statutory rate to publisher per song on record.
 • Gonzo! Records was awarded Best Indie Label, and Full Frequency was awarded Best Techno/
   Industrial Band at the 1999 Los Angeles Music Awards.
How to Contact Submit demo package by mail. Unsolicited submissions are OK. Prefers cassette
or CD. "When submitting, please specify that you got the listing from Songwriter's Market." Does
not return material. Responds in 6 weeks.
Music Mostly **commercial industrial**, **dance** and **techno**; also **commercial alternative** and **synth
pop**. Released *Hate Breeds Hate* (album), written and recorded by BOL (hard industrial); *Momentum*
(album), written and recorded by Full Frequency (commerical industrial); and *Ruth in Alien Corn*
(album), written and recorded by Pinch Point (alternative pop), all on Gonzo! Records. Other artists
include Turning Keys.

Tips "If you're going to submit music to me, it must be because you love to write music, not because you want to be a rock star. That will eventually happen with a lot of hard work."

☑ ◖ GOTHAM RECORDS

Attn: A&R, P.O. Box 237067, New York NY 10023. E-mail: ar@gothamrecords.com. Web site: www.gothamrecords.com. Record company. Estab. 1994. Staff size: 3. Releases 8 LPs and 8 CDs/ year. Pays negotiable royalty to artists on contract; statutory rate to publisher per song on record. **Distributed by** KOCH Distribution and Sony RED.

How to Contact Submit demo by mail "in a padded mailer or similar package." Unsolicited submissions are OK. Prefers cassette or CD and bios, pictures, and touring information. Does not return material. Responds in 6 weeks.

Music Mostly **rock**, **pop**, **alternative**, and **AAA**. Released *Nineteenth Soul*, recorded by Liquid Gang (rock); *Supafuzz*, written and recorded by Supafuzz (rock); and *Oh God! Help Our Fans!*, written and recorded by The Loose Nuts (ska), all on Gotham Records. Other artists include Love Huskies, Flybanger, and The Booda Velvets.

Tips "Send all submissions in regular packaging. Spend your money on production and basics, not on fancy packaging and gift wrap."

◖ HACIENDA RECORDS & RECORDING STUDIO

1236 S. Staples St., Corpus Christi TX 78404. (361)882-7066. E-mail: info@haciendarecords.com. Web site: www.haciendarecords.com. **Contact:** Rick Garcia, executive vice president. Founder/ CEO: Roland Garcia. Record company, music publisher, and record producer. Estab. 1979. Staff size: 10. Releases 12 singles and 15 CDs/year. Pays negotiable royalty to artists on contract; negotiable rate to publisher per song on record.

How to Contact Submit demo package by mail. Unsolicited submissions are OK. Prefers CD with cover letter. Does not return material. Responds in 6 weeks.

Music Mostly **tejano**, **regional Mexican**, **country** (Spanish or English), and **pop**. Released "Chica Bonita" (single), recorded by Albert Zamora and D.J. Cubanito, released 2001 on Hacienda Records; "Si Quieres Verme Llorar" (single) from *Lisa Lopez con Mariachi* (album), recorded by Lisa Lopez (mariachi), released 2002 on Hacienda; "Tartamudo" (single) from *Una Vez Mas* (album), recorded by Peligro (norteno); and "Miento" (single) from *Si Tu Te Vas* (album), recorded by Traizion (tejano), both released 2001 on Hacienda. Other artists include Ricky Naramzo, Gary Hobbs, Steve Jordan, Grammy Award nominees Mingo Saldivar and David Lee Garza, Michelle, Victoria Y Sus Chikos, La Traizion.

◖ HEADS UP INT., LTD.

23309 Commerce Park Dr., Cleveland OH 44122. (216)765-7381. Fax: (216)464-6037. E-mail: dave @headsup.com. Web site: www.headsup.com. **Contact:** Dave Love, president. Record company, music publisher (Heads Up Int., Buntz Music, Musica de Amor), and record producer (Dave Love). Estab. 1980. Staff size: 57. Releases 10 LPs/year. Pays negotiable royalty to artists on contract. **Distributed by** Universal Fontana (domestically).

How to Contact Submit demo by mail. Unsolicited submissions are OK. Prefers CD. Does not return material. Responds in one month.

Music Mostly **jazz**, **R&B**, **pop** and **world**. Does not want anything else. Released *Long Walk to Freedom* (album), recorded by Ladysmith Black Mambazo (world); *Pilgrimage* (album), recorded by Michael Brecker (contemporary jazz); *Rizing Sun* (album), recorded by Najee (contemporary jazz). Other artists include Philip Bailey, Joe McBride, Richard Smith, Roberto Perera, Spyro Gyra, Pieces of a Dream, Andy Narell, Zap Mama, Marion Meadows, Chuck Loeb, Candy Dulfer, Stanley Clarke, Gerald Veasley, Yellowjackets, Mike Stern, Doc Powell, and Nestor Torres.

ⓃⓄ HEART MUSIC, INC.

P.O. Box 160326, Austin TX 78716-0326. (512)795-2375. E-mail: info@heartmusic.com. Web site: www.heartmusic.com. **Contact:** Tab Bartling, president. Record company and music publisher (Coolhot Music). "Studio available for artists." Estab. 1989. Staff size: 2. Releases 1-2 CDs/year. Pays statutory rate to publisher per song on record.

How to Contact *Not interested in new material at this time.* Does not return material. Responds only if interested.

Music Mostly **rock**, **pop**, and **jazz**; also **blues** and **contemporary folk**. Released *The Fisherman* (album), recorded by Darin Layne; In the City of Lost Things (jazz), recorded by joe LoCascio, both released in 2007; *Collaborations* (album), recorded by Will Taylor and Strings Attached (folk rock), featuring Eliza Gilkyson, Shawn Colvin, Patrice Pike, Ian Moore, Guy Forsyth, Ruthie Foster, Libby Kirkpatrick, Jimmy LaFave, Slaid Cleaves, and Barbara K., released 2006; *Goodnight Venus* (album), recorded by Libby Kirkpatrick, released in 2003, and Be Cool Be Kind (album), recorded by Carla Helmbrecht (jazz), released January 2001.

🎵 ✓ ◻ HI-BIAS RECORDS INC.

Attn: A&R Dept., 20 Hudson Dr. (side entrance), Maple ON L6A 1X3 Canada. (905)303-9611. Fax: (905)303-6611. E-mail: info@hibias.ca. Web site: www.hibias.ca. **Contact:** Nick Fiorucci, director. Labels include Tilt, Riff, Toronto Underground, Remedy, and Club Culture. Record company, music publisher (Bend 60 Music/SOCAN), and record producer (Nick Fiorucci). Estab. 1990. Staff size: 5. Releases 20-30 singles and 2-5 CDs/year. Pays negotiable royalty to artists on contract; statutory rate to publisher per song on record.

Distributed by EMI.

How to Contact Submit demo by mail. Unsolicited submissions are OK. Prefers cassette or DAT with 3 songs and lyric sheet. Does not return material. Responds in 6 weeks.

Music Mostly **dance**, **house**, **club**, **pop**, and **R&B**. Released "Hands of Time" (single by N. Fiorucci/B. Cosgrove), recorded by Temperance; "Now That I Found You" (single by B. Farrinco/Cleopatra), recorded by YBZ; and "Lift Me Up" (single), written and recorded by Red 5, all on Hi-Bias (dance/pop). Other artists include DJ's Rule.

Ⓞ IDOL RECORDS PUBLISHING

P.O. Box 720043, Dallas TX 75372. (214)321-8890. E-mail: info@idolrecords.com. Web site: www.IdolRecords.com. **Contact:** Erv Karwelis, president. Record company. Estab. 1992. Releases 30 singles, 80 LPs, 20 EPs and 10-15 CDs/year. Pays negotiable royalty to artists on contract; negotiable rate to publisher per song on record.

Distributed by Navarre.

How to Contact See Web site at www.IdolRecords.com for submission policy. No phone calls or e-mail follow-ups.

Music Mostly **rock**, **pop**, and **alternative**; also some **hip-hop**. Released *The Man* (album), recorded by Sponge (alternative); *Movements* (album), recorded by Black Tie Dynasty (alternative); In Between Days (album), recorded by Glen Reynolds (rock), all released 2006/2006 on Idol Records. Other artists include Flickerstick, the Fags, DARYL, Centro-matic, The Deathray Davies, and GBH.

Ⓝ ◻ IMAGINARY RECORDS

P.O. Box 66, Whites Creek TN 37189-0066. E-mail: jazz@imaginaryrecords.com. Web site: www.imaginaryrecords.com. **Contact:** Lloyd Townsend, proprietor. Labels include Imaginary Records, Imaginary Jazz Records. Record company. Estab. 1981. Staff size: 1. Releases 1-3 CDs/year. Pays negotiable royalty to artists on contract; statutory rate to publisher per song on record.

Distributed by North Country, Harbor Record Export and Imaginary Distribution.

How to Contact *Write first to obtain permission to submit.* "We do not act as a publisher placing songs with artists.'' Prefers CD with 3-5 songs (or full-length album), cover letter, and press clippings. Include SASE. Responds in 4 months if interested.

Music Mostly **mainstream jazz**, **swing jazz**, and **classical**. Does not want country, rap, hip-hop or metal. Released *Fifth House* (album), recorded by New York Trio Project (mainstream jazz), released 2001; *Triologue* (album), recorded by Stevens, Siegel, and Ferguson (mainstream jazz), released 2001; and *Perspectives* (album), written and recorded by the Tom Dempsey/Tim Ferguson Quartet (jazz), released 2003.

Tips ''Be patient, I'm slow. I'm primarily considering mainstream jazz or classical—other genre submissions are much less likely to get a response.''

INTERSCOPE/GEFFEN/A&M RECORDS

2220 Colorado Ave., Santa Monica CA 90404. (310)865-1000. Fax: (310)865-7908. Web site: www.i nterscoperecords.com. Labels include Death Row Records, Nothing Records, Rock Land, Almo Sounds, Aftermath Records, and Trauma Records. Record company.

- Interscope/Geffen/A&M is a subsidiary of Universal Music Group, one of the ''Big 4'' major labels.

How to Contact *Does not accept unsolicited submissions.*

Music Released *Worlds Apart*, recorded by . . . And You Will Know Us By The Trail Of Dead; and *Guero*, recorded by Beck. Other artists include U2, M.I.A, Keane, and Marilyn Manson.

ISLAND/DEF JAM MUSIC GROUP

825 Eighth Ave., 29th Floor, New York NY 10019. (212)333-8000. Fax: (212)603-7654. Web site: www.islanddefjam.com. **Los Angeles:** 8920 Sunset Blvd, 2nd Floor, Los Angeles CA 90069. (310)276-4500. Fax: (310)242-7023. Executive A&R: Paul Pontius. Labels include Mouth Almighty Records, Worldly/Triloka Records, Blackheart Records, Private Records, Slipdisc Records, Thirsty Ear, Blue Gorilla, Dubbly, Little Dog Records, Rounder, and Capricorn Records. Record company.

- Island/Def Jam is a subsidiary of Universal Music Group, one of the ''Big 4'' major labels.

How to Contact *Island/Def Jam Music Group* does not accept unsolicited submissions. Do not send material unless requested.

Music Artists include Bon Jovi, Ja Rule, Jay-Z, and Ludacris.

KAUPP RECORDS

P.O. Box 5474, Stockton CA 95205. (209)948-8186. **Contact:** Melissa Glenn. Record company, music publisher (Kaupps and Robert Publishing Co./BMI), management firm (Merri-Webb Productions) and record producer (Merri-Webb Productions). Estab. 1990. Releases 1 single and 4 LPs/year. Pays standard royalty to artists on contract; statutory rate to publisher per song on record.

Distributed by Merri-Webb Productions and Cal-Centron Distributing Co.

How to Contact *Write first and obtain permission to submit or to arrange personal interview.* Prefers cassette or VHS videocassette with 3 songs. Include SASE. Responds in 3 months.

Music Mostly **country**, **R&B**, and **A/C rock**; also **pop**, **rock**, and **gospel**. Released ''I Thank You Father'' and ''On the Other Side (singles by N. Merrihew/B. Bolin), recorded by Bruce Bolen; and ''Did You Think That I Thought That You Liked Me'' (single by N. Merrihew/B. Bolin), recorded by Cheryl, all on Kaupp Records.

KILL ROCK STARS

120 N.E. State #418, Olympia WA 98501. E-mail: krs@killrockstars.com. Web site: www.killrocksta rs.com. **Contact:** Slim Moon, CEO, or Maggie Vail, VP of A&R. Record company. Estab. 1991. Releases 4 singles, 10 LPs, 4-6 EPs and 35 CDs/year. Pays 50% of net profit to artists on contract; negotiated rate to publisher per song on record.

Distributed by Touch and Go.

Record Companies

How to Contact *Write first and obtain permission to submit.* Prefers link to Web page or EPK. Does not return material.

Music Mostly **punk rock**, **neo-folk** or **anti-folk** and **spoken word**. Artists include Deerhoof, Xiu Xiu, Mary Timony, The Gossip, Erase Errata, and Two Ton Boa.

Tips "Send a self-released CD or link. NEVER EVER send unsolicited mp3s. We will not listen. We will only work with touring acts, so let us know if you are playing Olympia, Seattle or Portland. Particularly interested in young artists with indie-rock background."

☑ LARI-JON RECORDS

P.O. Box 216, Rising City NE 68658. (402)542-2336. **Contact:** Larry Good, owner. Record company, management firm (Lari-Jon Promotions), music publisher (Lari-Jon Publishing/BMI) and record producer (Lari-Jon Productions). Estab. 1967. Staff size: 1. Releases 15 singles and 5 LPs/year. Pays varying royalty to artists on contract.

How to Contact Submit demo by mail. Unsolicited submissions are OK. Prefers CD with 5 songs and lyric sheet. Include SASE. Responds in 2 months.

Music Mostly **country**, **Southern gospel** and **'50s rock**. Released "Glory Bound Train" (single), written and recorded by Tom Campbell; *The Best of Larry Good* (album), written and recorded by Larry Good (country); and *Her Favorite Songs* (album), written and recorded by Johnny Nace (country), all on Lari-Jon Records. Other artists include Kent Thompson and Brenda Allen.

ℕ ☑ LARK RECORD PRODUCTIONS, INC.

P.O. Box 35726, Tulsa OK 74153. (918)786-8896. Fax: (918)786-8897. E-mail: janajae@janajae.com. Web site: www.janajae.com. **Contact:** Kathleen Pixley, vice president. Record company, music publisher (Jana Jae Music/BMI), management firm (Jana Jae Enterprises) and record producer (Lark Talent and Advertising). Estab. 1980. Staff size: 8. Pays negotiable royalty to artists on contract; statutory rate to publisher per song on record.

How to Contact Submit demo by mail. Unsolicited submissions are OK. Prefers CD or VHS videocassette with 3 songs and lead sheets. Does not return material. Responds only if interested.

Music Mostly **country**, **bluegrass**, and **classical**; also **instrumentals**. Released "Fiddlestix" (single by Jana Jae); "Mayonnaise" (single by Steve Upfold); and "Flyin' South" (single by Cindy Walker), all recorded by Jana Jae on Lark Records (country). Other artists include Sydni, Hotwire, and Matt Greif.

◗ LUCIFER RECORDS, INC.

P.O. Box 263, Brigantine NJ 08203-0263. (609)266-2623. Fax: (609)266-4870. **Contact:** Ron Luciano, president. Labels include TVA Records. Record company, music publisher (Ciano Publishing and Legz Music), record producer (Pete Fragale and Tony Vallo), management firm and booking agency (Ron Luciano Music Co. and TVA Productions). "Lucifer Records has offices in South Jersey; Palm Beach, Florida; and Las Vegas, Nevada."

How to Contact *Call or write to arrange personal interview.* Prefers cassette with 4-8 songs. Include SASE. Responds in 3 weeks.

Music Mostly **dance**, **easy listening**, **MOR**, **rock**, **soul**, and **top 40/pop**. Released "I Who Have Nothing," (single), by Spit-N-Image (rock); "Lucky" (single), by Legz (rock); and "Love's a Crazy Game" (single), by Voyage (disco/ballad). Other artists include Bobby Fisher, Jerry Denton, FM, Zeke's Choice, Al Caz, Joe Vee, and Dana Nicole.

ℕ ☑ MAGNA CARTA RECORDS

208 E. 51st St., PMB 1820, New York NY 10022. (585)381-5224. Fax: (585)381-0658. E-mail: magcart @aol.com. Web site: www.magnacarta.net. **Contact:** Pete Morticelli. Record label.

How to Contact Contact first and obtain permission to submit. No unsolicited material.

Music Mostly progressive metal, progressive rock, and progressive jazz. Released The Ereyn Chronicles, Part 1 (album), recorded by Anthropia (progressive metal); Last Day in Paradise (album), recorded by The Alex Skolnick Trio (progressive jazz); The Journey (album), recorded by Khallice (progressive metal), all released 2007. Other artists include Tony Levin, Ozric Tentacles, Mike Portnoy, Kansas, Steve Morse, Tony Hymas, Billy Sheehan, Bozzio, The Fareed Haque Group, Liquid Tension Experiment, Niacin, World Trade, and Vapourspace.

☑ ⦿ MAKOCHE RECORDING COMPANY

208 N. Fourth St., Bismarck ND 58501. (701)223-7316. Fax: (701)255-8287. E-mail: info@makoche. com. Web site: www.makoche.com. **Contact:** Chelsea Farnco, A&R assistant. Labels include Makoche and Chairmaker's Rush. Record company and recording studio. Estab. 1995. Staff size: 5. Releases 4 CDs/year. Pays negotiable royalty to artists on contract; statutory rate to publisher per song on record.

Distributed by DNA, Music Design, Four Winds Trading, Zango Music, and New Leaf Distribution.
 • Makoche is noted for releasing quality music based in the Native American tradition. Recognized by the Grammys, Nammys, New Age Voice Music Awards, Indian Summer Music Awards, and C.O.V.R. Music Awards.

How to Contact *Call first and obtain permission to submit.* "Please submit only fiddle and American Indian-influenced music." Include SASE. Responds in 2 months.

Music Mostly **Native American**, **flute** and **fiddle**. Released *Edge of America* (album), written and recorded by Annie Humphrey (folk), released 2004 on Makoche; and *Togo* (album), written and recorded by Andrew Vasquez (Native American flute), released on Makoche 2004; *Way of Life* (album), recorded by Lakota Thunder (drum group), released on Makoche 2004. Other artists include Gary Stroutsos, Bryan Akipa, Keith Bear, Andrew Vasquez, Lakota Thunder, Sissy Goodhouse, and Kevin Locke.

Tips "We are a small label with a dedication to quality."

☑ ⦿ MAVERICK RECORDS

9348 Civic Center Dr., Beverly Hills CA 90210. Web site: www.maverick.com. CEO/Head of A&R: Guy Oseary. A&R: Russ Rieger, Jason Bentley, Danny Strick, Berko Weber, Michael Goldberg. Record company.
 • Maverick Records is a subsidiary of Warner Music Group, one of the "Big 4" major labels.

Distributed by WEA.

Music Released *Under Rug Swept* (album); *Supposed Former Infatuation Junkie* (album) and *Jagged Little Pill* (album), both recorded by Alanis Morissette; *The Spirit Room* (album), recorded by Michelle Branch; *Tantric* (album), recorded by Tantric; and *Ray of Light* (album), recorded by Madonna. Other artists include Deftones, Home Town Hero, Mest, Michael Lee, Me'shell Ndegeocello, Muse, Onesidezero, Prodigy and Paul Oakenfold.

Ⓝ ☑ ⦿ MAYFAIR MUSIC

2600 John St., Unit 203, Markham ON L3R 3W3 Canada. (905)475-1848. **Contact:** John Loweth, A&R. Record company, music publisher (MBD Records). Estab. 1979. Pays 10% royalty to artists on contract; statutory rate to publisher per song on record.
 • Mayfair Music is also listed in the Music Publishers section.

How to Contact Submit demo by mail. Unsolicited submissions are OK. Prefers CD/CDR only with 4 songs. Does not return material. Responds in 3 weeks.

Music Mostly **instrumental**. Current acts include Frank Mills and Paul Saulnier.

☑ ⦿ MCA NASHVILLE

60 Music Square E., Nashville TN 37203. (615)244-8944. Fax: (615)880-7447. Web site: www.mca-nashville.com. Record company and music publisher (MCA Music).

• MCA Nashville is a subsidiary of Universal Music Group, one of the "Big 4" major labels.

How to Contact MCA Nashville cannot accept unsolicited submissions.

Music Artists include Tracy Byrd, George Strait, Vince Gill, The Mavericks, and Trisha Yearwood.

☐ MEGAFORCE RECORDS

P.O. Box 63584, Philadelphia PA 19147. New York office: P.O. Box 1955, New York NY 10113. (212)741-8861. Fax: (509)757-8602. E-mail: gregaforce@aol.com. Web site: www.megaforcerecords.com. **Contact:** Robert John, President. General Manager: Missi Callazzo. Record company. Estab. 1983. Staff size: 5. Releases 6 CDs/year. Pays various royalties to artists on contract; ¾ statutory rate to publisher per song on record.

Distributed by Red/Sony Distribution.

How to Contact *Contact first and obtain permission to submit.* Submissions go to the Philadelphia office.

Music Mostly **rock**. Artists include Ministry, Clutch, S.O.D., and Blackfire Revelation.

☑ METAL BLADE RECORDS

2828 Cochran St., Suite 302, Simi Valley CA 93065. (805)522-9111. Fax: (805)522-9380. E-mail: metalblade@metalblade.com. Web site: www.metalblade.com. **Contact:** A&R. Record company. Estab. 1982. Releases 20 LPs, 2 EPs and 20 CDs/year. Pays negotiable royalty to artists on contract.

How to Contact Submit demo by mail. Unsolicited submissions are OK. Prefers CD with 3 songs. Does not return material. Responds in 3 months.

Music Mostly **heavy metal** and **industrial**; also **hardcore**, **gothic** and **noise**. Released "Gallery of Suicide," recorded by Cannibal Corpse; "Voo Doo," recorded by King Diamond; and "A Pleasant Shade of Gray," recorded by Fates Warning, all on Metal Blade Records. Other artists include As I Lay Dying, The Red Chord, The Black Dahlia Murder, and Unearth.

Tips "Metal Blade is known throughout the underground for quality metal-oriented acts."

Ⓝ ☑ MIGHTY RECORDS

150 West End, Suite 6-D, New York NY 10023. Manager: Danny Darrow. Labels include Mighty Sounds & Filmworks. Record company, music publisher (Rockford Music Co./BMI, Stateside Music Co./BMI and Corporate Music Publishing Co./ASCAP) and record producer (Danny Darrow). Estab. 1958. Releases 1-2 singles, 1-2 12" singles and 1-2 LPs/year. Pays standard royalty to artists on contract; statutory rate to publisher per song on record.

Distributed by Amazon.com and CDBaby.com.

How to Contact Submit demo package by mail. Unsolicited submissions are OK. "No phone calls." Prefers cassette or CD with 2 songs and lyric sheet. Does not return material. Responds in 1 month only if interested.

Music Mostly **pop**, **country** and **dance**; also **jazz**. Released "Look to the Wind" (single by Peggy Stewart/Danny Darrow) from *Falling in Love* (album), recorded by Danny Darrow (movie theme); "Doomsday" (single by Robert Lee Lowery/Danny Darrow) from *Doomsday* (album), recorded by Danny Darrow (euro jazz), all released 2004 on Mighty Records; "Telephones" (single Robert Lee Lowery/Danny Darrow) from *Telephones* (album), and "Love to Dance" (single by Robert Lee Lowery/Danny Darrow) from *Love to Dance* (album), both recorded by Danny Darrow (trance dance), released 2006 on Mighty Records.

☑ MINOTAUR RECORDS

P.O. Box 620, Redwood Estates CA 95044.Estab. 1987. (408)353-1006. E-mail: dminotaur@hotmail.com. **Contact:** A&R. Record company. Estab. 1987. Staff size: 2. Releases 2 CDs/year. Pays statutory royalty to publishers per song on record. Distributed by CDbaby.com. Member of BMI, ASCAP, NARAS, TAXI.

How to Contact *We only accept material referred to us by a reputable industry source (manager, entertainment attorney, etc.).* Does not return submissions. Responds only if interested.

Music Mostly **adult contemporary**, **country**, **dance**. Also **easy rock**, **pop**. Does not want rap, heavy metal, jazz, hip-hop, hard rock and instrumentals. "Maybe Love" written by D. Baumgartner and Steven Worthy,from the *Dancing in the Dark* (album) recorded by Andrew Ceglio (pop/dance); "That Was A Great Affair" written by Tab Morales and Ron Dean Tomich, from *This Side of Heaven* (album), recorded by Doug Magpiong (adult contemporary); "Baby Blue Eyes and Tight Levis" written by Ron Dean Tomich, from *This Side of Nashville* (album) recorded by Candy Chase (country).

☑ MISSILE RECORDS

P.O. Box 5537, Kreole Station, Moss Point MS 39563-1537. (601)914-9413. "No collect calls!" Estab. 1974. **Contact:** Joe F. Mitchell, executive vice president/general manager. First Vice President: Justin F. Mitchell. Second Vice President: Jayvean F. Mitchell. Record company and music publisher (Abalorn Music/ASCAP, Bay Ridge Publishing/BMI) and record producer. Releases 28 singles and 10 LPs/year. Pays "negotiable royalty to new artists on contract"; statutory rate to publisher for each record sold. "Missile Records has National and International Distribution."

- Also see the listing for Bay Ridge Publishing and Abalorn Music in the Music Publishers section.

Distributed by Star Sound Music Distributors, Hits Unlimited, Action Music Sales, Inc., Allegro Corp., Big Easy Distributing, Select-O-Hits, Total Music Distributors, Music Network, Impact Music, Universal Record Distributing Corporation, Dixie Rak Records & Tapes, Navaree Corporation, Curtis Wood Distributors, Big Daddy Music Distribution Co., ATM Distributors, HL Distribution, Bayside Distribution, Blue Sky Distribution, Alamo Record Distributors and MDI Distribution.

How to Contact *"Please don't send us anything until you contact us by phone or in writing and receive submission instructions. You must present your songs the correct way to get a reply.* **No registered mail—no exceptions! Standing in line to sign for your package wastes our time. Tracking your package is a service you can get by asking for it at your Post Office.** Always whenever you write to us, be sure you include a #10 business-size envelope addressed back to you with a first class USA postage stamp on the envelope. We reply back to you from the SASE. All songs sent for review must include sufficient return postage. No reply made back to you without SASE or return of material without sufficient return postage. **Absolutely no reply postcards—only SASE.** If you only write lyrics, do not submit. We only accept completed songs, so you must find a collaborator. We are not interested in reviewing homemade recordings." Prefers CD (first choice) or cassette with 3-8 songs and lyrics to songs submitted. Responds in 2 months. A good quality demo recording will always get preference over a poor recording.

Music All types and styles of songs. Released "Mixed Up Love Affair," "Sweet Sexy Lady," and "My Love Just Fell Again" (singles) from *album title TBD* (album), written and recorded by Herb Lacy (blues); "Excuse Me Lady" and "When She Left Me" (singles by Rich Wilson); "Everyone Gets A Chance (To Lose In Romance)" and "I'm So Glad We Found Each Other" (singles by Joe F. Mitchell), from Excuse Me Lady (album), recorded by Rich Wilson (country/western); "Hello Heartbreak" and "You Owe Some Back to Me" (singles by Joe F. Mitchell), recorded by Ann Black (country); and "Rose Up On a Stem" (single by Joe F. Mitchell) from *My Kind of Country* (album), recorded by Jerry Piper (modern country); "Southern Born" and "Old Folks Know" (singles by Christian Ramsey); "Innocent Little One" (single by Bob Levy), "Pretty Lady Come Closer" (single by David L. Resler) and "She Was Sittin' Pretty" (single by Jim Hendricks) all from If *It Takes All Night* (album), recorded by Christian Ramsey (modern pop country), all released on Missile Records. Other artists include Moto (reggae), Jackie Lambarella (country pop), Sarah Cooper (pop/R&B), Della Reed (contemporary Christian), Metellica (heavy metal), Coco Hodge (alternative) and Lady Love (rap).

Tips "Songwriters and singers, we are in business to serve you. Our doors are open to you. If you want experience and know-how on your side to work with you, then we are who you are looking for. We go that extra mile for you. Working with the right people helps you to be successful by getting on the right track. Let us show you what we can do. Give us a call or write us today. Your professionally recorded album or 10-12 well-produced and well-written songs, that you have ready for radio, may have a chance to be placed with our contacts in the U.S.A. and foreign record companies or released on our label. We have gotten record deals for some recording artists previously that you have read about in the 2005, 2006, and 2007 issues of *Songwriter's Market*. Here are some of the current recording artists we have gotten record deals for: Karen Frazier (pop) of Ren & T (mother/daughter act) from Hyattsville, MD on Mr. Wonderful Productions of Louisville, KY; and Bernard Williams (gospel) from Lanett, AL, also on Mr. Wonderful Productions of Louisville, KY. Missile Records, Abalorn Music (ASCAP) and Bay Ridge Publishing Co. (BMI) are listed in some well-known publications such as the *Billboard International Buyer's Guide*, *Mix Master Directory*, *Industrial Source Book*, *Pollstar*, *Yellow Pages of Rock* and other publications. Some well-known recording artists born and raised in Mississippi include Elvis Presley, Conway Twitty, B.B. King and Faith Hill. The Moss Point, MS area music scene is also home to nationally-known rock group Three Doors Down, who sold more than 10 million of their CD albums and singles. Singers and songwriters thinking about doing professional recording, give us a call before you make that move. We can save you money, time, headaches, heartaches and troubles you may run into. We know what to do and how to do it to benefit you and get the best results''

☐ MODAL MUSIC, INC.™

P.O. Box 6473, Evanston IL 60204-6473. (847)864-1022. E-mail: info@modalmusic.com. Web site: www.modalmusic.com. President: Terran Doehrer. Assistant: J. Distler. Record company and agent. Estab. 1988. Staff size: 2. Releases 1-2 LPs/year. Pays negotiable royalty to artists on contract; negotiable rate to publisher per song on record.

How to Contact Submit demo package by mail. Unsolicited submissions are OK. Prefers CD with bio, PR, brochures, any info about artist and music. Does not return material. Responds in 4 months.

Music Mostly **ethnic** and **world**. Released ''St. James Vet Clinic'' (single by T. Doehrer/Z. Doehrer) from *Wolfpak Den Recordings* (album), recorded by Wolfpak, released 2005; ''Dance The Night Away'' (single by T. Doehrer) from *Dance The Night Away* (album), recorded by Balkan Rhythm Band™; ''Sid Beckerman's Rumanian'' (single by D. Jacobs) from *Meet Your Neighbor's Folk Music*™ (album), recorded by Jutta & The Hi-Dukes™; and *Hold Whatcha Got* (album), recorded by Razzem-etazz™, all on Modal Music Records. Other artists include Ensemble M'chaiya™, Nordland Band™ and Terran's Greek Band™.

Tips ''Please note our focus is primarily traditional and traditionally-based ethnic which is a very limited, non-mainstream market niche. You waste your time and money by sending us any other type of music. If you are unsure of your music fitting our focus, please call us before sending anything. Put your name and contact info on every item you send!''

☒ ☑ MONTICANA RECORDS

P.O. Box 702, Snowdon Station, Montreal QC H3X 3X8 Canada. **Contact:** David P. Leonard, general manager. Record company, record producer (Monticana Productions) and music publisher (Montina Music/SOCAN). Estab. 1963. Staff size: 1. Pays negotiable royalty to artists on contract.

How to Contact Submit demo package by mail. Unsolicited submissions are OK. Prefers CD. Include SASE.

Music Mostly **top 40**, **blues**, **country**, **dance-oriented**, **easy listening**, **folk** and **gospel**; also **jazz**, **MOR**, **progressive**, **R&B**, **rock** and **soul**.

Tips ''Be excited and passionate about what you do. Be professional.''

☑ ◯ NBT RECORDS

228 Morgan Lane, Berkeley Springs WV 25411-3475.(304)261-0228. E-mail: nbtoys@verizon.net. **Contact:** John S. Newbraugh, owner. Record company, music publisher (Newbraugh Brothers Music/BMI, NBT Music/ASCAP). Estab. 1967. Staff size: 1. Releases 4 singles and 52 CDs/year. Pays negotiable royalty to artists on contract; statutory royalty to publishers per song on record.
Distributed by "Distribution depends on the genre of the release. Our biggest distributor is perhaps the artists themselves, for the most part, depending on the genre of the release. We do have product in some stores and on the Internet as well."
How to Contact Submit demo package by mail. Unsolicited submissions are OK. Prefers CD or cassette with any amount of songs, lyric sheet and cover letter. Include SASE. Responds in 4-6 weeks. "Please don't call for permission to submit. Your materials are welcomed."
Music Mostly **rockabilly**, **hillbilly**, **folk** and **bluegrass**; also **rock**, **country** and **gospel**. Does not want any music with vulgar lyrics. "We will accept all genres of music except songs that contain vulgar language." Released *Sailing Down the River of Memories* (album), recorded by the Sanders Sisters, released 2006; *I'll Be Home for Christmas* (album), by Shelly Champion released 2006. "We also released and published many of the songs for *Ride The Train-Vol #20* in 2007, which brings the total of train/railroad related song issued on this NBT series to 420 songs, with writers and artists from over half the states in the U.S.A., Canada, several countries in Europe, and Australia.
Tips "We are best known for our rockabilly releases. Reviews of our records can be found on both the American and European rockabilly Web sites. Our 'registered' trademark is a train. From time to time, we put out a CD with various artists featuring original songs that use trains as part of their theme. We use all genres of music for our train releases. We have received train songs from various parts of the world. All submissions on this topic are welcomed."

☑ NEURODISC RECORDS, INC.

3801 N. University Dr., Suite 403, Ft. Lauderdale FL 33351. (954)572-0289. Fax: (954)572-2874. E-mail: info@neurodisc.com. Web site: www.neurodisc.com or www.myspace.com/neurodiscrecords. President: Tom O'Keefe. Business Affairs Manager: Emilie Kennedy. Record company and music publisher. Estab. 1992. Releases 6 singles and 10 CDs/year. Pays negotiable royalty to artists on contract.
Distributed by Koch Entertainment.
How to Contact Submit demo package by mail. Unsolicited submissions are OK. Prefers CD, mp3 or DVD. Include SASE and contact information. Responds only if interested.
Music Mostly **electronic**, **chillout in lounge**, **down tempo**, **New Age**, and **electro-bass**. Released albums from Sleepthief, Blue Stone, Peplab, Etro Anime, Deviations Project, Ryan Farish & Amethystium, as well as Bass Lo-Ryders and Bass Crunk. Other artists include Eric Hansen, Bella Sonus and NuSound as well as DJ Vicious Vic, DJ Andy Hughes and DJ Scott Stubbs.

◯ ONLY NEW AGE MUSIC, INC.

8033 Sunset Blvd. #472, Hollywood CA 90046. (323)851-3355. Fax: (323)851-7981. E-mail: info@newagemusic.com. Web site: www.newagemusic.com or www.newageuniverse.com. **Contact:** Suzanne Doucet, president. Record company, music publisher and consulting firm. Estab. 1987.
How to Contact *Call first and obtain permission to submit*. Does not return material.
Music Mostly *New Age*; also **world music**.
Tips "You should have a marketing strategy and at least a small budget for marketing your product."

☑ ◪ OUTSTANDING RECORDS

P.O. Box 2111, Huntington Beach CA 92647. (714)377-7447 E-mail: beecher@outstandingmusic.com. Web site: www.outstandingmusic.com. **Contact:** Earl Beecher, owner. Labels include Morrhythm (mainstream/commercial), School Band (educational/charity), Church Choir (religious charity), and Empowerment (educational CDs and DVDs). Record company, music publisher (Earl Beecher Publishing/BMI and Beecher Music Publishing/ASCAP) and record producer (Earl Beecher). Estab. 1968. Staff size: 1. Releases 100 CDs/year. Pays $2/CD royalty to artists on contract; statutory rate to publisher per song on record.

Distributed by Sites on the Internet and "through distribution companies who contact me directly, especially from overseas."

How to Contact Submit demo by mail. Unsolicited submissions are OK. Prefers CD (full albums), lyric sheet, photo and cover letter. Include SASE. Responds in 3 weeks.

Music Mostly **jazz**, **rock** and **country**; also **everything else especially Latin**. Does not want music with negative, anti-social or immoral messages. "View our Web site for a listing of all current releases."

Tips "We prefer to receive full CDs, rather than just three numbers. A lot of submitters suggest we release their song in the form of singles, but we just can't bother with singles at the present time. Especially looking for performers who want to release their material on my labels. Some songwriters are pairing up with performers and putting out CDs with a 'Writer Presents the Performer' concept. No dirty language. Do not encourage listeners to use drugs, alcohol or engage in immoral behavior. I'm especially looking for upbeat, happy, danceable music."

P. & N. RECORDS

61 Euphrasia Dr., Toronto ON M6B 3V8 Canada. (416)782-5768. Fax: (416)782-7170. E-mail: panfilo @sympatico.ca. **Contact:** Panfilo Di Matteo, president, A&R. Record company, record producer and music publisher (Lilly Music Publishing). Estab. 1993. Staff size: 2. Releases 10 singles, 20 12" singles, 15 LPs, 20 EPs and 15 CDs/year. Pays 25-35% royalty to artists on contract; statutory rate to publisher per song on record.

How to Contact Submit demo by mail. Unsolicited submissions are OK. Prefers CD or videocassette with 3 songs and lyric or lead sheet. Does not return material. Responds in 1 month only if interested.

Music Mostly **dance**, **ballads** and **rock**. Released *Only This Way* (album), written and recorded by Angelica Castro; *The End of Us* (album), written and recorded by Putz, both on P. & N. Records (dance); and "Lovers" (single by Marc Singer), recorded by Silvana (dance), released 2001 on P. and N. Records.

THE PANAMA MUSIC GROUP OF COMPANIES

(formerly Audio-Visual Media Productions), Sovereign House, 12 Trewartha Rd., Praa Sands, Penzance, Cornwall TR20 9ST England. (17)(36)762-826. Fax: (17)(36)763-328. E-mail: panamus@aol. com. Web site: www.songwriters-guild.co.uk and www.panamamusic.co.uk. **Contact:** Roderick G. Jones, managing director A&R. Labels include Pure Gold Records, Panama Music Library, Rainy Day Records, Panama Records, Mohock Records. Registered members of Phonographic Performance Ltd. (PPL). Record company, music publisher (Panama Music Library, Melody First Music Library, Eventide Music Library, Musik Image Music Library, Promo Sonor International Music Library, Caribbean Music Library, ADN Creation Music Library, Piano Bar Music Library, Corelia Music Library, PSI Music Library, Scamp Music, First Time Music Publishing U.K.), registered members of the Mechanical Copyright Protection Society (MCPS) and the Performing Right Society (PRS), management firm and record producer (First Time Management & Production Co.). Estab. 1986. Staff size: 6. Pays variable royalty to artists on contract; statutory rate to publisher per song on record subject to deal.

Distributed by Media U.K. Distributors.

How to Contact Submit demo package by mail. Unsolicited submissions are OK. Prefers CD with unlimited number of songs and lyric or lead sheets. SAE and IRC. Responds in 3 months.

Music All styles. Published by Scamp Music: "Hot Looking Babes" (single), recorded by Dougal & Gammer (hardcore/dance track) on *Clubland: X:Treme Hardcore Volume 3* (album), released 2006 on Universal Records; "Going My Own Sweet Way" (single) from *My Heart Would Know* (album), recorded by Charlie Landsborough, released 2006 on Rosette Records; "Thanks" (single) from *Someone From Somewhere* (album), recorded by P.J. Proby (pop), released 2007 on Digimix Records (www.digimixrecords.com). Published by Panama Music Library: "Salsa Rico" by Arthur Howell for BBC Drama production TV series *Dalziel & Pascoe*; "In the News" by Stephen James for BBC light entertainment TV series *One Foot in The Grave*; "Chinese Way" for UK Independent television (ITV1) documentary *Art Attack*.

◙ PARLIAMENT RECORDS

449 N. Vista St., Los Angeles CA 90036. (323)653-0693. E-mail: parlirec@aol.com. Web site: www.parlirec.com. **Contact:** Ben Weisman, owner. Record company, record producer (Weisman Production Group) and music publisher (Audio Music Publishers, Queen Esther Music Publishing). Estab. 1965. Produces 30 singles/year. Fee derived from sales royalty when song or artist is recorded.

- Also see the listings for Audio Music Publishers and Queen Esther Music Publishing in the Music Publishers section and Weisman Production Group in the Record Producer section.

How to Contact Submit demo package by mail. Unsolicited submissions are OK. Prefers CD with 3-10 songs and lyric sheet. Include SASE. "Mention Songwriter's Market. Please make return envelope the same size as the envelopes you send material in, otherwise we cannot send everything back." Responds in 6 weeks.

Music Mostly **R&B**, **soul**, **dance**, and **top 40/pop**; also **gospel** and **blues**. Arists include Rapture 7 (gospel), Wisdom (male gospel singers), and Chosen Recovery Ministry (female gospel group).

Tips "Parliament Records will also listen to 'tracks' only. If you send tracks, please include a letter stating what equipment you record on—ADAT, Protools or Roland VS recorders."

◙ PPL ENTERTAINMENT GROUP

P.O. Box 261488, Encino, CA 91426. (818)506-8533. Fax: (818)506-8534. E-mail: a&r/labels@pplzmi.com. Web site: www.pplentertainmentgroup.com. **Contact:** Cisco Crowe, vice president A&R. Vice President A&R: Dakota Kelly. Vice President, A&R: Kaitland Diamond. General Manager: Jim Sellavain. President, Creative: Suzette Cuseo. Labels include Bouvier, Credence and JBK. Record company, music publisher (Pollybyrd Publications), management firm (Sa'mall Management) and distributor (Malibu Trading Company). Estab. 1979. Staff size: 15. Releases 10-30 singles, 12 12" singles, 6 LPs and 6 CDs/year. Pays 10-15% royalty to artists on contract; statutory rate to publisher per song on record.

Distributed by Sony and The Malibu Trading Company.

How to Contact *E-mail and obtain permission to submit.* "Only interested in professional full-time artists who tour and have fan bases. No weekend warriors, please." Prefers CD, cassette, or videocassette with 3 songs. Include SASE. Responds in 6 weeks.

Music Released *The Return of the Players* (album) by Juz-Cuz on PPL2004; "Bigg Leggeded Woman" (single by Buddy Wright) from *Destiny* (album), recorded by Buddy Wright (blues), released 2003 on PPL; *Ghost* (album), recorded by The Band AKA, written and produced by J. James Jarrett; "Step Aside" (single by Gary Johnson) from *Step Aside* (album), recorded by Gary J., released 2003 on PPL/Sony. Other artists include Phuntaine, Condottiere and Gary J.

☑ ◙ QUARK RECORDS

P.O. Box 771, New York NY 10956-0771. (917)687-9988. E-mail: quarkent@aol.com. **Contact:** Curtis Urbina. Record company and music publisher (Quarkette Music/BMI and Freedurb Music/ASCAP). Estab. 1984. Releases 3 singles and 3 LPs/year. Pays negotiable royalty to artists on contract; ¾ statutory rate to publisher per song on record.

How to Contact Prefers CD with 2 songs (max). Include SASE. "Must be an absolute 'hit' song!" Responds in 6 weeks.

Music House music only.

☐ RADICAL RECORDS

77 Bleecker St., Suite C2-21, New York NY 10012. (212)475-1111. Fax: (212)475-3676. E-mail: info@radicalrecords.com. Web site: www.radicalrecords.com. **Contact:** Bryan Mechutan. Record company. Estab. 1986. Staff size: 4. Releases 1 single and 6 CDs/year. Pays 14% royalty to artists on contract; statutory rate to publisher per song on record.

Distributed by City Hall, Revelation, Select-O-Hits, Choke, Southern, Carrot Top, and other indie distributors.

How to Contact *E-mail first for permission to submit demo.* Prefers CD. Does not return material. Responds in 1 month.

Music Mostly **punk**, **hardcore**, **glam** and **rock**. Released *New York City Rock N Roll* (compilation album featuring 22 NYC bands); *Too Legit for the Pit-Hardcore Takes the Rap* (compilation album), recorded by various; *Punk's Not Dead - A Tribute to the Exploited* (compilation album), recorded by various; *East Coast of Oi!* (compilation album), recorded by various; *Ramones Forever* (compilation album), recorded by various; *Sex Pistols Tribute - Never Mind The Sex Pistols, Here's The Tribute* (compilation album), recorded by various; and 3 volumes of OI!/Skampilation (compilation albums, recorded by various shi and oi! punk bands). Artists include Sex Slaves, 5¢ Deposit, Blanks 77,Speadealer, The Agents, Inspector 7 and ICU.

Tips "Create the best possible demos you can and show a past of excellent self-promotion."

⊘ RAZOR & TIE ENTERTAINMENT

214 Sullivan St., Suite 4A, New York NY 10012. (212)473-9173. E-mail: info@razorandtie.com. Web site: www.razorandtie.com. Record company.

How to Contact *Does not accept unsolicited material.*

Music Released *The Beauty of the Rain* (album) by Dar Williams; *The Sweetheart Collection* by Frankie & The Knockouts; *Everybody's Normal But Me* by Stuttering John; and *Marigold* (album) by Marty Lloyd, all on Razor & Tie Entertainment. Other artists include Graham Parker, Marshall Crenshaw, Sam Champion and Toshi Reagon.

🎜 ⊘ RCA RECORDS

1540 Broadway, 36th Floor, New York NY 10036. (212)930-4936. Fax: (212)930-4447. Web site: www.rcarecords.com. A&R: Donna Pearce. **Beverly Hills:** 8750 Wilshire Blvd., Beverly Hills CA 90211. (310)358-4105 Fax: (310)358-4127. Senior Vice President of A&R: Jeff Blue. **Nashville:** 1400 18th Ave. S., Nashville TN 37212. A&R Director: Jim Catino. Labels include Loud Records, Deconstruction Records and Judgment/RCA Records. Record company.

- RCA Records is a subsidiary of Sony BMG, one of the "Big 4" major labels.

Distributed by BMG.

How to Contact *RCA Records does not accept unsolicited submissions.*

Music Artists include The Strokes, Dave Matthews Band, Clay Aiken, Christina Aguilera, and Velvet Revolver.

🅽 ⦿ RED ONION RECORDS

8377 Westview, Houston TX 77055. (713)464-4653. Fax: (713)464-2622. E-mail: jeffwells@soundar tsrecording.com. Web site: www.soundartsrecording.com. **Contact:** Jeff Wells, president. A&R: Peter Verkerk. Record company, music publisher (Reach for the Sky Music Publishing/ASCAP; Earthscream Music Publishing Co./BMI) and record producer (Jeff Wells). Estab. 2007. Releases 4 CDs/year. Pays negotiable royalty to artists on contract; statutory rate to publisher per song on record.

Distributed by Earth Records.

How to Contact Submit demo by mail. Unsolicited submissions are OK. Prefers CD with 4 songs and lyric sheet. Does not return material. Responds in 6 weeks.

Music Mostly **country**, **blues** and **pop/rock**. Released *Glory Baby* (album), recorded by Tony Vega Band (blues); *Two For Tuesday* (album), recorded by Dr. Jeff and the Painkilllers (blues), all released 2007 on Red Onion Records.

☐ REDEMPTION RECORDS

P.O. Box 10238, Beverly Hills CA 90213. E-mail: info@redemption.net. Web site: www.redemption. net. A&R Czar: Ryan D. Kuper (indie rock, power pop, rock, etc.). Record company. Estab. 1990. Staff size: varies. Releases 2-3 (various)/year. "We typically engage in profit splits with signed artists.

Distributed by IRIS Distribution (digital).

How to Contact Submit digital linky by e-mail. "Include band's or artist's goals." Responds only if interested.

Music Mostly **indie rock** and **power pop**. Artists include Vicious Vicious, The Working Title, Race For Titles, Schatzi, Motion City Soundtrack, Nolan, and the Redemption Versus Series featuring indie rock bands from different geographical locations.

Tips "Be prepared to tour to support the release. Make sure the current line-up is secure."

☑ REPRISE RECORDS

3300 Warner Blvd., 4th Floor, Burbank CA 91505. (818)846-9090. Fax: (818)840-2389. Web site: www.repriserecords.com. Labels include Duck and Sire. Record company.

- Reprise Records is a subsidiary of Warner Music Group, one of the "Big 4" major labels.

Distributed by WEA.

How to Contact *Reprise Records does not accept unsolicited submissions*.

Music Artists include Eric Clapton, Guster, Josh Groban, The Distillers, and Neil Young.

☑ ROBBINS ENTERTAINMENT LLC

159 W. 25th St., 4th Floor, New York NY 10001. (212)675-4321. Fax: (212)675-4441. E-mail: info@r obbinsent.com. Web site: www.robbinsent.com. **Contact:** John Parker, vice president, A&R/dance promotion. Record company and music publisher (Rocks, No Salt). Estab. 1996. Staff size: 10. Releases 25 singles and 12-14 CDs/year. Pays negotiable royalty to artists on contract; statutory rate to publisher per song on record.

Distributed by Sony/BMG.

How to Contact Accepts unsolicited demos as long as it's dance music. Prefers CD with 2 songs or less. "Make sure everything is labeled with the song title information and your contact information. This is important in case the CD and the jewel case get separated. Do not call us and ask if you can send your package. The answer is yes."

Music Commercial **dance** only. Released top 10 pop smashes, "Heaven" (single), recorded by DJ Sammy; "Everytime We Touch" (single), recorded by Cascada; "Listen To Your Heart" (single), recored by DHT; as well as Hot 100 records from Rockell, Lasgo, Reina and K5. Other artists include Ian Van Dahl, September, Andain, Judy Torres, Jenna Drey, Marly, Dee Dee, Milky, Kreo and many others.

Tips "Do not send your package 'Supreme-Overnight-Before-You-Wake-Up' delivery. Save yourself some money. Do not send material if you are going to state in your letter that, 'If I had more (fill in the blank) it would sound better.' We are interested in hearing your best and only your best. Do not call us and ask if you can send your package. The answer is yes. We are looking for dance music with crossover potential."

❑ ROLL ON RECORDS

112 Widmar Pl., Clayton CA 94517. (925)833-4680. E-mail: rollonrecords@aol.com. **Contact:** Edgar J. Brincat, owner. Record company and music publisher (California Country Music). Estab. 1985. Pays 10% royalty to artists on contract; statutory rate to publisher per song on record. Member of Harry Fox Agency.

Distributed by Tower.

How to Contact Submit demo package by mail. Unsolicited submissions are OK. "Do not call or write for permission to submit, if you do you will be rejected." Prefers CD or cassette with 3 songs and lyric sheet. Include SASE and phone number. Responds in 6 weeks.

Music Mostly **contemporary/country** and **modern gospel**. Released "Broken Record" (single by Horace Linsley/Dianne Baumgartner), recorded by Edee Gordon on Roll On Records; Maddy and For Realities Sake (albums both by F.L. Pittman/Madonna Weeks), recorded by Ron Banks/L.J. Reynolds on Life Records/Bellmark Records.

Tips "Be patient and prepare to be in it for the long haul. A successful songwriter does not happen overnight. It's rare to write a song today and have a hit tomorrow. If you give us your song and want it back, then don't give it to us to begin with."

Ⓝ ❑ ROWENA RECORDS

195 S. 26th St., San Jose CA 95116. (408)286-9840. E-mail: onealproduction@juno.com. Web site: www.onealprod.com. Owner/A&R (country, Mexican, gospel): Gradie O'Neal. A&R (all styles): Jeannine O'Neal. Record company and music publisher (Tiki Enterprises). Estab. 1967. Staff size: 3. Releases 8-12 LPs and 8-12 CDs/year. Pays negotiable royalty to artists on contract; pays statutory rate to publisher per song on record.

• Also see the listing for Tiki Enterprises Inc. in the Music Publishers section of this book.

How to Contact Submit demo by mail. Unsolicited submissions are OK. Prefers CD with 2 songs and lyric sheet. Include SASE. Responds in 2 weeks.

Music Mostly **gospel**, **country** and **pop**; also **Mexican** and **R&B**. Released "It Amazes Me" (single by David Davis/Jeannine O'Neal) from *Forgiven* (album), recorded by Amber Littlefield/David Davis (Christian), released 2003-2004; "I'm Healed" (single by Jeannine O'Neal) from *Faith On the Front Lines* (album), recorded by Jeannine O'Neal, released 2004; and "You're Looking Good to Me" (single by Warren R. Spalding) from *A Rock 'N' Roll Love Story* (album), recorded by Warren R. Spalding, released 2003-2004, all on Rowena Records.

Tips "For up-to-date releases, view our Web site."

❑ RUSTIC RECORDS

6337 Murray Lane, Brentwood TN 37027. (615)371-0646. Fax: (615)370-0353. E-mail: rusticrecordsinc@aol.com. Web site: www.rusticrecordsinc.com. President: Jack Schneider. Executive VP & Operations Manager: Nell Schneider. VP Publishing, Catalog Manager, and In-house Engineer: Amanda Mark. VP Marketing, Promotions, and Artist Development: Carol-Lynn Daigle. Independent traditional country music record label and music publisher (Iron Skillet Music/ASCAP, Covered Bridge/ BMI, Town Square/SESAC). Estab. 1979. Staff size: 4. Releases 2-3 albums/year. Pays negotiable royalty to artists on contract; statutory royalty to publisher per song on record.

Distributed by CDBaby.com, BathtubMusic.com and available on iTunes, MSN Music, Rhapsody, and more.

How to Contact Submit professional demo package by mail. Unsolicited submissions are OK. CD only; no mp3s or e-mails. Include no more than 4 songs with corresponding lyric sheets and cover letter. Include appropriately-sized SASE. Responds in 4 weeks.

Music Mostly **traditional country**, **redneck novelty**, and **country gospel**. Released *Takin' it South* (debut album), recorded by Lloyd Knight (country), released 2006; "Drankin' Business" (single), recorded by Colte Bradley; "Love Don't Even Know My Name" (single), recorded by Beckey Burr, both released 2005.

Tips "Professional demo preferred."

☑ ◻ RUSTRON/WHIMSONG MUSIC PRODUCTIONS

1156 Park Lane, West Palm Beach FL 33417-5957. (561)686-1354. E-mail: rmp_wmp@bellsouth.n et. **Contact:** Sheelah Adams, office administrator. Executive Director: Rusty Gordon (folk fusions, blues, women's music, adult contemporary, electric-acoustic, New Age instrumentals, children's, cabaret, pop ballads). Director A&R: Ron Caruso (all styles). Associate Director of A&R: Kevin Reeves (pop, country, blues, R&B, jazz, folk). Labels include Rustron Records and Whimsong Records. "Rustron administers 20 independent labels for publishing and marketing." Record company, record producer, management firm and music publisher (Whimsong Music Publishing/ASCAP and Rustron Music Publishing/BMI). Estab. 1970. Releases 5-10 CDs/year. Pays variable royalty to artists on contract. "Artists with history of product sales get higher percent than those with no sales track record." Pays statutory rate to publisher.

How to Contact *Songwriters may write or call first to discuss your submission.* You may send a snail-mail request for current submission guidelines. Include a SASE or International Response Coupon (IRC) for all correspondence, including sending submissions. No Exceptions. E-mail gets the quickest response. Song submissions should include a cover letter that explains why you are submitting and what type of review you want. You may want a combined publishing and record company review. If your songs are already published, let us know what publishing company you signed with. Tell us about your intentions for the future and if you are a performing or a freelance songwriter. Tell us if you are collaborating on some or all of your songs. All songwriters who creatively contributed to a song must sign the cover letter authorizing the review. Copyrighting the songs in your submission with The U.S. Library of Congress is essential before sending them to us. We do not review uncopyrighted original songs. Songwriter's must officially own the exclusive rights to their songs by copyrighting them. As soon as you have mailed the Copyright Form PA to the Library of Congress, the songs are "Copyright Pending," and you can send them. Submit 1 CD or several CDs, requesting a "body of work review" by snail-mail. You may present up to 15 songs on each CD you submit. Unsolicited submissions are OK. We prefer a CD with up to 15 songs and typed 8 1/2 X 11 lyric sheets, one song per sheet. Cassettes are limited to 3 songs. Responds in 4 months.

Music Mostly **mainstream** and **women's music**, **adult contemporary electric-acoustic**, **pop (cabaret, blues)** and **blues (R&B, country and folk)**; also **soft rock** (ballads), **New Age fusions** (instrumentals), **modern folk fusions** (environmental, socio-political), **children's music** and **light jazz**. Released "White House Worries" (single) from *Whitehouse Worries* (album), written and recorded by The Ramifications (progressive country-folk/socio-political-topical), released 2007 on Rustron Records; "Sanibel-Captiva and the Gulf of Mexico" (single—historical song) from *Song of Longboat Key* (album), recorded by Florida Rank & File (Florida folk); "Take the High Road" (single) from *Voting for Democracy* (album), recorded by The Panama City Pioneers (progressive-political-folk), released 2007 on Whimsong Records.

Tips "Find your own unique style; write well crafted songs with unpredictable concepts, strong hooks and definitive verse melody. New Age composers: evolve your themes and add multi-cultural diversity with instruments. Don't be predictable. Don't over-produce your demos and don't drown vocals. Carefully craft songs for single-song marketing. An album can have nine eclectic songs that are loosely crafted and not very commercially viable individually. It takes only one carefully crafted 'radio ready' song with the right arrangement to get your album the exposure it needs."

N ◻ SAFIRE RECORDS

5617 W. Melvina, Milwaukee WI 53216. (414)444-3385. **Contact:** Darnell Ellis, president. A&R Representatives: Darrien Kingston (country, pop); Reggie Rodriqez (world, Latin, Irish). Record

Record Companies

company, music publisher (Ellis Island Music/ASCAP), record producer (Darnell Ellis) and management firm (The Ellis International Talent Agency). Estab. 1997. Staff size: 2. Releases 3 singles, 3 LPs, 1 EP and 3 CDs/year. Pays negotiable royalty to artists on contract; statutory rate to publisher per song on record.

• Also see the listing for The Ellis International Talent Agency in the Managers & Booking Agents section of this book.

How to Contact Submit demo by mail. Unsolicited submissions are OK. Prefers cassette or CD with 3-4 songs. Does not return material. Responds in 2 months. "We will respond only if we are interested."

Music Mostly **country, pop, mainstream pop, rock** (all styles)—emphasis on female acts—and anything else except rap or hip-hop. Artists include Tracy Beck. Released *Into The Sun* (album), recorded by Tracy Beck (blues, alt. country/acoustic/roots), released 2004 on Safire Records.

Tips "We emphasize female acts. Songwriters need to get back to the basics of songwriting: great hooklines, strong melodies. We would love to hear from artists and songwriters from all over the world. And remember, just because someone passes on a song it doesn't mean that it's a bad song. Maybe it's a song that the label is not able to market or the timing is just bad."

☑ ▨ ⊘ SAHARA RECORDS AND FILMWORKS ENTERTAINMENT

10573 W. Pico Blvd., #352, Los Angeles CA 90064-2348. Phone: (310)948-9652. Fax: (310)474-7705. E-mail: info@edmsahara.com. Web site: www.edmsahara.com. **Contact:** Edward De Miles, president. Record company, music publisher (EDM Music/BMI, Edward De Miles Music Company) and record producer (Edward De Miles). Estab. 1981. Releases 15-20 CD singles and 5-10 CDs/year. Pays 9½-11% royalty to artists on contract; statutory rate to publishers per song on record.

How to Contact *Does not accept unsolicited submissions.*

Music Mostly **R&B/dance, top 40 pop/rock** and **contemporary jazz**; also **TV-film themes, musical scores and jingles**. Released "Hooked on U," "Dance Wit Me" and "Moments" (singles), written and recorded by Steve Lynn (R&B) on Sahara Records. Other artists include Lost in Wonder, Devon Edwards and Multiple Choice.

Tips "We're looking for strong mainstream material. Lyrics and melodies with good hooks that grab people's attention."

☑ ⊘ SALEXO MUSIC

P.O. Box 1513, Hillsborough NC 27278. (919)245-0681. E-mail: salexo@bellsouth.net. **Contact:** Samuel OBie, president. Record company. Estab. 1992. Releases 1 CD/year.

How to Contact *Write first and obtain permission to submit.*

Music Mostly **contemporary gospel** and **jazz**. Released *A Joyful Noise* (album), recorded by Samuel Obie with J.H. Walker Unity Choir (gospel), released 2003, Macedonia Baptist Church; "Favor" (single) from *Favor* (album), written and recorded by Samuel Obie (contemporary gospel), released 2004 on Salexo Music; "Hillsborough (NC) USA" (single), from TRAGEDY (album), written recorded by Samuel OBie (R&B), released 2006 ("Samuel's new solo project that covers 9/11 subject matter to R&B sounds, including "Hillsborough (NC) USA," a country-sounding story of Samuel's early family life in the '70s. Definitely the one to listen to."

Tips "Make initial investment in the best production."

☐ SANDALPHON RECORDS

P.O. Box 29110, Portland OR 97296. (503)957-3929. E-mail: jackrabbit01@sprintpcs.com. **Contact:** Ruth Otey, president. Record company, music publisher (Sandalphon Music/BMI), and management agency (Sandalphon Management). Estab. 2005. Staff size: 2. Pays negotiable royalty to artists on contract; statutory royalty to publisher per song on record.

Distributed by "We are currently negotiating for distribution."

How to Contact Submit demo packageby mail. Unsolicited submissions are OK. Prefers cassette or CD with 1-5 songs with lyric sheet and cover letter. Returns submissions if accompanied by a SASE or SAE and IRC for outside the United States. Responds in 1 month.

Music Mostly **rock**, **country**, and **alternative**; also **pop**, **gospel**, and **blues**.

☑ ◢ SHERIDAN SQUARE ENTERTAINMENT INC.

(formerly Compendia Music), 210 25th Ave. N., Suite 1200, Nashville TN 37203. (615)277-1800. Web site: www.SheridanSquareMusic.com. Vice President/General Manager, Compendia Label & Intersound: Mick Lloyd (country/rock; contemporary jazz); Vice President/General Manager, Light Records: Phillip White (black gospel). Record company. Labels include Sheridan Square Records, Light, V2, and Intersound. Pays negotiable royalty to artists on contract; negotiable rate to publisher per song on record.

How to Contact *Write or call first and obtain permission to submit.* Prefers CD with 3 songs. "We will contact the songwriter when we are interested in the material." Does not return material. Responds only if interested.

Music Mostly **country**, **rock**, **gospel**, and **classical**. Artists include Joan Osborne, Mighty Clouds of Joy, Moby, and Susan Tedeschi.

◢ SILVER WAVE RECORDS

P.O. Box 7943, Boulder CO 80306. (303)443-5617. Fax: (303)443-0877. E-mail: info@silverwave.com. Web site: www.silverwave.com. **Contact:** James Marienthal. Record company. Estab. 1986. Releases 3-4 CDs/year. Pays varying royalty to artists on contract and to publisher per song on record.

How to Contact *Call first and obtain permission to submit.* Prefers CD. Include SASE. Responds only if interested.

Music Mostly **Native American** and **world**.

☑ ◢ SILVERTONE RECORDS

137-139 W. 25th St., New York NY 10001. (212)727-0016. Fax: (212)337-0990. Label Director: Michael Tedesco. Labels include Essential Records. Record company. Distributed by BMG.

How to Contact *Does not accept unsolicited materials.* "Contact us through management or an attorney."

Music Released *Jars of Clay* (album), recorded by Jars of Clay on Essential Records. Other artists include Chris Duarte, Buddy Guy, Hed, Livingstone, John Mayall, Metal Molly, and Solar Race.

◢ SMALL STONE RECORDS

P.O. Box 02007, Detroit MI 48202. (248)219-2613. Fax: (248)541-6536 E-mail: sstone@smallstone.com. Web site: www.smallstone.com. Owner: Scott Hamilton. Record company. Estab. 1995. Staff size: 1. Releases 2 singles, 2 EPs and 10 CDs/year. Pays negotiable royalty to artists on contract; statutory rate to publisher per song on record.

Distributed by AEC, Allegro/Nail.

How to Contact Submit CD/CD Rom by mail. Unsolicited submissions are OK. Does not return material. Responds in 2 months.

Music Mostly **alternative**, **rock** and **blues**; also **funk (not R&B)**. Released *Fat Black Pussy Cat*, written and recorded by Five Horse Johnson (rock/blues); *Wrecked & Remixed*, written and recorded by Morsel (indie rock, electronica); and *Only One Division*, written and recorded by Soul Clique (electronica), all on Small Stone Records. Other artists include Acid King, Perplexa, and Novadriver.

Tips "Looking for esoteric music along the lines of Bill Laswell to Touch & Go/Thrill Jockey records material. Only send along material if it makes sense with what we do. Perhaps owning some of our records would help."

☑ ◯ SOLANA RECORDS

4225 ½ Avocado St., Los Angeles CA 90027. E-mail: info@solanarecords.com. Web site: www.sola narecords.com or www.ericfriedmann.com or www.myspace.com/ericfriedmann. **Contact:** Eric Friedmann, president. Record company, record producer (Eric Friedmann), and music publisher (Neato Bandito Music). Estab. 1992.

How to Contact "Please, *you must request permission to submit first via e-mail only*, and a myspace and/or Web site link is always appreciated, as are EPKs. Your request doesn't have to come from a manager or lawyer, but any and all unsolicited snail-mail submissions, not pre-approved via e-mail and given the Special Super-Secret Handshake, will be heartily chucked into the Los Angeles River, a fate worse than death (not really a river in the traditional sense, so much as a long concrete glorified storm drain sliming its way through the city, past my office, out to my beautiful Pacific Ocean). Next stop for your demo, the shores of Honolulu. But not before we rip open your package with our teeth and tack your picture up on The Wall Of Shame. No joke." Prefers CD with 3-5 of your very best songs, a great non-cheezy photo, and brief cover letter. Include return email and contact info on everything. Responds in roughly 1 month.

Music Mostly any kind of **guitar/vocal-based rock/pop** and **country**. Does not want rap, hip-hop. or metal. Released *Break Up The Skies* (by Emily Hickey), recorded by Emily Hickey Band (singer/ songwriter, pop), "Spacious" (single by Valerie Moorhead), recorded by Enda (alternative rock); "Livin' the High Life" (single by James Cook), recorded by The Wags (yardcore); "The Grain" (single by Rick Ordin), recorded by The Grain (progressive rock); *Delectric* (album), recorded by Delectric (Skiffle). Other artists include The Detonators, Eric Friedmann and the Lucky Rubes, The Mudkats, Doormouse, Five Times Fast, and Suenteus Po.

Tips "Just be honest and genuine. Know how to write a good song, know how to sing it, and record it to the best of your ability. A sense of whimsy is always welcome. Don't send along your resume or life story, please. Put your very best foot forward always. Hint: my name is mentioned many times above, and spelled correctly. Please do not address me as 'To Whom It May Concern' in your letter. Let your music speak for itself. Big bonus points for Telecaster players. We respond well to red wine bribes. No porn please; we're already up to our eyeballs in it."

☒ ◯ SONIC UNYON RECORDS CANADA

P.O. Box 57347, Jackson Station, Hamilton ON L8P 4X2 Canada. (905)777-1223. Fax: (905)777-1161. E-mail: jerks@sonicunyon.com. Web site: www.sonicunyon.com. Co-owners: Tim Potocic; Mark Milne. Record company. Estab. 1992. Releases 2 singles, 2 EPs and 6-10 CDs/year. Pays negotiable royalty to artists on contract; statutory rate to publisher per song on record.

Distributed by Caroline Distribution.

How to Contact *Call first and obtain permission to submit.* Prefers CD or cassette. "Research our company before you send your demo. We are small; don't waste my time and your money." Does not return material. Responds in 4 months.

Music Mostly **rock**, **heavy rock** and **pop rock**. Released *Doberman* (album), written and recorded by Kittens (heavy rock); *What A Life* (album), written and recorded by Smoother; and *New Grand* (album), written and recorded by New Grand on sonic unyon records (pop/rock). Other artists include A Northern Chorus, Ad Astra Per Aspera, Wooden Stars, The Ghost is Dancing, The Nein, Simply Saucer, Raising the Fawn, and Aereogramme.

Tips "Know what we are about. Research us. Know we are a small company. Know signing to us doesn't mean that everything will fall into your lap. We are only the beginning of an artist's career."

☑ SONY BMG

550 Madison Ave., New York NY 10022. Web site: www.sonymusic.com.
- Sony BMG is one of the primary "Big 4" major labels.

How to Contact *For specific contact information see the listings in this section for Sony subsidiaries Columbia Records, Epic Records, Sony Nashville, RCA Records, Arista Records, and American Recordings.*

☑ SONY MUSIC NASHVILLE

1400 18th Ave. South, Nashville TN 37212-2809. Labels include Columbia, Epic, Lucky Dog Records, Monument.
- Sony Music Nashville is a subsidiary of Sony BMG, one of the "Big 4" major labels.

How to Contact *Sony Music Nashville does not accept unsolicited submissions.*

☑ SPOONFED MUZIK/HELAPHAT ENTERTAINMENT

(formerly CKB Records/Helaphat Entertainment), 527 Larry Court, Irving TX 75060. (214)223-5181. E-mail: spoonfedmuzik@yahoo.com. **Contact:** Tony Briggs, CEO. Record company, production company, artist management, and record distribution. Estab. 1999. Staff size: 6. Pays negotiable royalty to artists on contract.

Distributed by CKB Records.

How to Contact Submit demo package by mail. Unsolicited submissions are OK. Prefers CD with 4 songs, cover letter and press clippings. Does not return materials. Responds only if interested.

Music Exclusively **rap**, **hip-hop**, and **R&B**. Released "Dirrty 3rd" (single), recorded by T-SPOON aka NAP (rap/hip-hop), released 2003 on CKB Records; "Sippin' & Creepin' (featuring Squeekie Loc)" (single) from *OZAPHIdE—Tha 40 Oz. CliQue Vol. 1 compilation* (album), written and recorded by Tha 40 Clique and various artists (rap), released 2007 on Ozaphide Musik/Spoonfed Muzik. Other artists include Baby Tek, Lil' Droop, royal Jonez, Deuce Loc, Tre Loc, and Daylight and Forty.

Tips "Be professional and be about your business."

Ⓝ ☑ SUGAR HILL RECORDS

P.O. Box 55300, Durham NC 27717-5300. E-mail: info@sugarhillrecords.com. Record company. Estab. 1978.
- Welk Music Group acquired Sugar Hill Records in 1998.

How to Contact *No unsolicited submissions.* "If you are interested in having your music heard by Sugar Hill Records or the Welk Music Group, we suggest you establish a relationship with a manager, publisher, or attorney that has an ongoing relationship with our company. We do not have a list of such entities."

Music Mostly **Americana**, **bluegrass**, and **country**. Artists include Nickel Creek, Allison Moorer, The Duhks, Sonny Landreth, Scott Miller, Reckless Kelly, Tim O'Brien, The Gibson Brothers, and more.

☑ SURFACE RECORDS

8377 Westview, Houston TX 77055. (713)464-4653. Fax: (713)464-2622. E-mail: jeffwells@soundartsrecording.com. Web site: www.soundartsrecording.com. **Contact:** Jeff Wells, president. A&R: Peter Verkerk. Record company, music publisher (Earthscream Music Publishing Co./BMI) and record producer (Jeff Wells). Estab. 1996. Releases 4 CDs/year. Pays negotiable royalty to artists on contract; statutory rate to publisher per song on record.

Distributed by Earth Records.

How to Contact Submit demo by mail. Unsolicited submissions are OK. Prefers CD with 4 songs and lyric sheet. Does not return material. Responds in 6 weeks.

Music Mostly **country**, **blues** and **pop/rock**. Released *Everest* (album), recorded by The Jinkies; *Joe "King" Carrasco* (album), recorded by Joe "King" Carrasco; *Perfect Strangers* (album), recorded by Perfect Strangers, all on Surface Records (pop); and "Sheryl Crow" (single) recorded by Dr. Jeff and the Painkillers. Other artists include Rosebud.

☐ TANGENT® RECORDS

P.O. Box 383, Reynoldsburg OH 43068-0383. (614)751-1962. Fax: (614)751-6414. E-mail: info@tang entrecords.com. Web site: www.tangentrecords.com. **Contact:** Andrew Batchelor, president. Director of Marketing: Elisa Batchelor. Record company and music publisher (ArcTangent Music/BMI). Estab. 1986. Staff size: 3. Releases 10-12 CDs/year. Pays negotiable royalty to artists on contract; statutory rate to publisher per song on record.

How to Contact Submit demo package by mail. Unsolicited submissions are OK. Prefers CD, with minimum of 3 songs and lead sheet if available. "Please include a brief biography/history of artist(s) and/or band, including musical training/education, performance experience, recording studio experience, discography and photos (if available)." Does not return material. Responds in 3 months.

Music Mostly **artrock** and **contemporary instrumental/rock instrumental**; also **contemporary classical**, **world beat**, **jazz/rock**, **ambient**, **electronic**, and **New Age**.

Tips "Take the time to pull together a quality CD or cassette demo with package/portfolio, including such relevant information as experience (on stage and in studio, etc.), education/training, biography, career goals, discography, photos, etc. Should be typed. We are not interested in generic sounding or 'straight ahead' music. We are seeking music that is innovative, pioneering and eclectic with a fresh, unique sound."

☑ TEXAS ROSE RECORDS

2002 Platinum St., Garland TX 75042. (972)272-3131. Fax: (972)272-3155. E-mail: txrr1@aol.com. Web site: www.texasroserecords.com. **Contact:** Nancy Baxendale, president. Record company, music publisher (Yellow Rose of Texas Publishing) and record producer (Nancy Baxendale). Estab. 1994. Staff size: 3. Releases 3 CDs/year. Pays negotiable royalty to artists on contract; statutory rate to publisher per song on record.

Distributed by Self distribution.

How to Contact *Call, write or e-mail first for permission to submit.* Submit maximum of 2 songs on CD and lyrics. Does not return material. Responds only if interested.

Music Mostly **country**, **soft rock** and **blues**; also **pop** and **gospel**. Does not want hip-hop, rap, heavy metal. Released *Flyin' High Over Texas* (album), recorded by Dusty Martin (country); *High On The Hog* (album), recorded by Steve Harr (country); *Time For Time to Pay* (album), recorded by Jeff Elliot (country); and *Pendulum Dream* (album), written and recorded by Maureen Kelly (alternative/americana), and "Cowboy Super Hero" (single) written and recorded by Robert Mauldin.

Tips "We are interested in songs written for today's market with a strong hook. Always use a good vocalist."

⧈ ⧆ ☐ THIRD WAVE PRODUCTIONS LTD.

P.O. Box 563, Gander NL A1V 2E1 Canada. (709)256-8009. Fax: (709)256-7411. Web site: www.bud dywasisname.com. Manager: Wayne Pittman. President: Arch Bonnell. Labels include Street Legal Records. Record company, music publisher, distributor and agent. Estab. 1986. Releases 2 singles, 2 LPs and 2 CDs/year. Pays negotiable royalty to artists on contract; statutory rate to publisher per song on record.

How to Contact Submit demo by mail. Unsolicited submissions are OK. Prefers CD or cassette, and lyric sheet. Include SASE. Responds in 2 months.

Music Mostly **folk/traditional**, **bluegrass** and **country**; also **pop**, **Irish** and **Christmas**. Released

Record Companies

Salt Beef Junkie (album), written and recorded by Buddy Wasisname and Other Fellers (folk/traditional); *Newfoundland Bluegrass* (album), written and recorded by Crooked Stovepipe (bluegrass); and *Nobody Never Told Me* (album), written and recorded by The Psychobilly Cadillacs (rockabilly/country), all on Third Wave Productions. Other artists include Lee Vaughn.
Tips "We are not really looking for songs but are always open to take on new artists who are interested in recording/producing an album. We market and distribute as well as produce albums. Not much need for 'songs' per se, except maybe country and rock/pop."

☑ TOMMY BOY ENTERTAINMENT LLC
120 Fifth Avenue, 7th Floor, New York NY 10011. (212)388-8300. Fax: (212)388-8431. E-mail: info@tommyboy.com. Web site: www.tommyboy.com. Record company. Labels include Penalty Recordings, Outcaste Records, Timber and Tommy Boy Gospel.
Distributed by WEA.
How to Contact *Call to obtain current demo submission policy.*
Music Artists include Chavela Vargas, Afrika Bambaataa, Biz Markie, Kool Keith, and INXS.

☐ TON RECORDS
4474 Rosewood Ave., Los Angeles CA 90004. E-mail: tonmusic@earthlink.net. Web site: www.tonrecords.com or www.myspace.com/tonrecords. Vice President: Jay Vasquez. Labels include 7″ collectors series and Ton Special Projects. Record company and record producer (RJ Vasquez). Estab. 1992. Releases 6-9 LPs, 1-2 EPs and 10-11 CDs/year. Pays negotiable royalty to artists on contract; statutory rate to publisher per song on record.
Distributed by MS, Com Four, Rotz, Subterranean, Revelation, Get Hip, Impact, Page Canada and Disco Dial.
How to Contact Submit demo package by mail. Unsolicited submissions are OK. Prefers CD or cassette. Include SASE. Responds in 1 month.
Music Mostly **new music**; also **hard new music**. Released *Intoxicated Birthday Lies* (album), recorded by shoegazer (punk rock); *The Good Times R Killing Me* (album), recorded by Top Jimmy (blues); and *Beyond Repair* (album), recorded by Vasoline Tuner (space rock), all on Ton Records. Other artists include Why? Things Burn, Hungry 5, and the Ramblers.
Tips "Work as hard as we do."

☑ TOPCAT RECORDS
P.O. Box 670234, Dallas TX 75367. (972)484-4141. Fax: (972)620-8333. E-mail: info@topcatrecords.com. Web site: www.topcatrecords.com or www.myspace.com/topcatrecords. President: Richard Chalk. Record company and record producer. Estab. 1991. Staff size: 3. Releases 4-6 CDs/year. Pays 10-15% royalty to artists on contract; statutory rate to publisher per song on record.
Distributed by City Hall.
How to Contact *Call first and obtain permission to submit.* Prefers CD. Does not return material. Responds in 1 month.
Music Mostly **blues**, **swing**, **rockabilly**, **Americana**, **Texana** and **R&B**. Released *If You Need Me* (album), written and recorded by Robert Ealey (blues); *Texas Blueswomen* (album by 3 Female Singers), recorded by various (blues/R&B); and *Jungle Jane* (album), written and recorded by Holland K. Smith (blues/swing), all on Topcat. Released CDs: *Jim Suhler & Alan Haynes—Live*; Bob Kirkpatrick *Drive Across Texas*; *Rock My Blues to Sleep* by Johnny Nicholas; *Walking Heart Attack*, by Holland K. Smith; *Dirt Road* (album), recorded by Jim Suhler; *Josh Alan Band* (album), recorded by Josh Alan; *Bust Out* (album), recorded by Robin Sylar. Other artists include Grant Cook, Muddy Waters, Big Mama Thornton, Big Joe Turner, Geo. "Harmonica" Smith, J.B. Hutto and Bee Houston. "View our Web site for an up-to-date listing of releases."
Tips "Send me blues (fast, slow, happy, sad, etc.) or good blues oriented R&B. No pop, hip-hop, or rap."

✔ TRANSDREAMER RECORDS

P.O. Box 1955, New York NY 10113. (212)741-8861. E-mail: gregaforce@aol.com. Web site: www.transdreamer.com. **Contact:** Greg Caputo, marketing savant. President: Robert John. Record company. Estab. 2002. Staff size: 5. Released 4 CDs/year. Pays negotiable rate to artists on contract; 3/4 statutory rate to publisher per song on record.

• Also see the listing for Megaforce in this section of the book.

Distributed by Red/Sony.

How to Contact *Contact first and obtain permission to submit.*

Music Mostly **alternative/rock**. Artists include The Delgados, Arab Strap, Dressy Bessy, Bill Richini, and Wellwater Conspiracy.

✔ TVT RECORDS

A&R Dept. 23 E. Fourth St., 3rd Floor, New York NY 10003. Web site: www.tvtrecords.com. **Contact:** A&R. Labels include Tee Vee Toons, TVT Soundtrax, 1001 Sundays. Record company and music publisher (TVT Music). Estab. 1986. Releases 25 singles, 20 12″ singles, 40 LPs, 5 EPs and 40 CDs/year. Pays varying royalty to artists on contract; statutory rate to publisher per song on record.

How to Contact Send e-mail to demo-help@tvtrecords.com to receive information on how to submit your demo.

Music Mostly **alternative rock**, **rap** and **techno**; also **jazz/R&B**. Released *Home*, recorded by Sevendust; *Hoopla*, recorded by Speeches; and *Retarder*, recorded by The Unband.

Tips "We look for seminal, ground breaking, genre-defining artists of all types with compelling live presentation. Our quest is not for hit singles but for enduring important artists."

✔ ◯ 28 RECORDS

P.O. Box 88456., Los Angeles CA 90009-8456. E-mail: rec28@aol.com. Web site: www.28records.com. **Contact:** Eric Diaz, president/CEO/A&R. Record company. Estab. 1994. Staff size: 1. Releases 2 LPs and 4 CDs/year. Pays 12% royalty to artists on contract; statutory rate to publisher per song on record.

Distributed by Rock Bottom-USA.

How to Contact *Contact first and obtain permission to submit.* Submit demo package by mail. Unsolicited submissions are OK. Prefers cassette, VHS videocassette or CD (if already released on own label for possible distribution or licensing deals). If possible send promo pack and photo. "Please put ATTN: A&R on packages." Does not return material. Responds in 6 weeks.

Music Mostly **hard rock/modern rock**, **metal** and **alternative**; also **punk** and **death metal**. Released *Julian Day* (album), recorded by Helltown's Infamous Vandal (modern/hard rock); *Fractured Fairy Tales* (album), written and recorded by Eric Knight (modern/hard rock); and *Mantra* (album), recorded by Derek Cintron (modern rock), all on 28 Records.

Tips "Be patient and ready for the long haul. We strongly believe in nurturing you, the artist/songwriter. If you're willing to do what it takes, and have what it takes, we will do whatever it takes to get you to the next level. We are looking for artists to develop. We are a very small label but we are giving the attention that is a must for a new band as well as developed and established acts. Give us a call."

✔ ✔ UNIVERSAL RECORDS

1755 Broadway, 7th Floor, New York NY 10019. (212)841-8000. Fax: (212)331-2580. Web site: www.universalrecords.com. Universal City office: 70 Universal City Plaza, 3rd Floor, Universal City CA 91608. (818)777-1000. Vice Presidents A&R: Bruce Carbone, Tse Williams. Labels include Uptown Records, Mojo Records, Republic Records, Bystorm Records and Gut Reaction Records. Record company.

• Universal Records is a subsidiary of Universal Music Group, one of the "Big 4" major labels.
How to Contact *Universal Records in California does not accept unsolicited submissions*. The New York office *only* allows you to call first and obtain permission to submit.
Music Artists include India Arie, Erykah Bad, Godsmack, Kaiser Chiefs, and Lindsey Lohan.

VALTEC PRODUCTIONS

721 E. main St., #206, Santa Maria CA 93454. (805)928-8559. E-mail: info@valtec.net. Web site: www.valtec.net. **Contact:** J. Andersonand J. Valenta, owner/producers. Record company and record producer (Joe Valenta). Estab. 1986. Releases 20 singles, 15 LPs and 10 CDs/year. Pays negotiable royalty to artists on contract; statutory rate to publisher per song on record.
How to Contact Submit demo by mail. Unsolicited submissions are OK. Prefers DAT with 4 songs and lyric sheet. Does not return material. Responds in 2 months.
Music Mostly **country**, **top 40** and **A/C**; also **rock**. Released *Just Me* (album by Joe Valenta) and *Hold On* (album by Joe Valenta/J. Anderson), both recorded by Joe Valenta (top 40); and *Time Out (For Love)* (album by Joe Valenta), recorded by Marty K. (country), all on Valtec Records.

THE VERVE MUSIC GROUP

1755 Broadway, 3rd Floor, New York NY 10019. (212)331-2000. Fax: (212)331-2064. Web site: www.vervemusicgroup.com. A&R Director: Dahlia Ambach. A&R Coordinator: Heather Buchanan. **Los Angeles**: 100 N. First St., Burbank CA 91502. (818)729-4804 Fax: (818)845-2564. Vice President A&R: Bud Harner. A&R Assistant: Heather Buchanan. Record company. Labels include Verve, GRP, Blue Thumb and Impulse! Records.
• Verve Music Group is a subsidiary of Universal Music Group, one of the "Big 4" major labels.
How to Contact *The Verve Music Group* does not accept unsolicited submissions.
Music Artists include Roy Hargrove, Diana Krall, George Benson, Al Jarreau, John Scofield, Natalie Cole, David Sanborn.

VIRGIN RECORDS

5750 Wilshire Blvd., Los Angeles CA 90036. (323)692-1100. Fax: (310)278-6231. Web site: www.virginrecords.com. New York office: 150 5th Ave., 3rd Floor, New York NY 10016. (212)786-8200 Fax:(212)786-8343. Labels include Rap-A-Lot Records, Pointblank Records, SoulPower Records, AWOL Records, Astralwerks Records, Cheeba Sounds and Noo Trybe Records. Record company.
• Virgin Records is a subsidiary of the EMI Group, one of the "Big 4" major labels.
Distributed by EMD.
How to Contact Virgin Records does not accept recorded material or lyrics unless submitted by a reputable industry source. "If your act has received positive press or airplay on prior independent releases, we welcome your written query. Send a letter of introduction accompanied by all pertinent artist information. Do not send a tape until requested. All unsolicited materials will be returned unopened." Artists include Lenny Kravitz, Janet Jackson, Mick Jagger, Nikka Costa, Ben Harper, and Boz Scaggs.

WAREHOUSE CREEK RECORDING CORP.

P.O. Box 102, Franktown, VA 23354. (757)442-6883. E-mail: warehousecreek@verizon.net. Web site: www.warehousecreek.com. President: Billy Sturgis. Record company, music publisher (Bayford Dock Music) and record producer (Billy Sturgis). Estab. 1993. Staff size: 1. Releases 11 singles and 1 CD/year. Pays negotiable royalty to artists on contract; statutory rate to publisher per song on record.
Distributed by City Hall Records.
How to Contact Submit demo by mail. Unsolicited submissions are OK. Prefers cassette, CD, or VHS videocassette with lyric sheet. Does not return material.

Music Mostly **R&B, blues** and **gospel**. Released *Nothin' Nice* (album), recorded by Guitar Slim, Jr. (blues); *Frank Town Blues* (album), recorded by the Crudup Brothers (blues); *Hi-Fi Baby* (album), recorded by Greg "Fingers" Taylor (blues), all released on Warehouse Creek Records.

⚡ ⊘ WARNER BROS. RECORDS

3300 Warner Blvd., 3rd Floor, Burbank CA 91505. (818)846-9090. Fax: (818)953-3423. Web site: www.wbr.com. **New York:** 75 Rockefeller Plaza, New York NY 10019. (212)275-4500 Fax:(212)275-4596. A&R: James Dowdall, Karl Rybacki. **Nashville:** 20 Music Square E., Nashville TN 37203. (615)748-8000 Fax:(615)214-1567. Labels include American Recordings, Eternal Records, Imago Records, Mute Records, Giant Records and Maverick Records. Record company.
- Warner Bros. Records is a subsidiary of Warner Music Group, one of the "Big 4" major labels.

Distributed by WEA.

How to Contact *Warner Bros. Records does not accept unsolicited material.* All unsolicited material will be returned unopened. Those interested in having their tapes heard should establish a relationship with a manager, publisher or attorney that has an ongoing relationship with Warner Bros. Records.

Music Released *Van Halen 3* (album), recorded by Van Halen; *Evita* (soundtrack); and *Dizzy Up the Girl* (album), recorded by Goo Goo Dolls, both on Warner Bros. Records. Other artists include Faith Hill, Tom Petty & the Heartbreakers, Jeff Foxworthy, Porno For Pyros, Travis Tritt, Yellowjackets, Bela Fleck and the Flecktones, Al Jarreau, Joshua Redmond, Little Texas and Curtis Mayfield.

⊘ WATERDOG MUSIC

(a.k.a. Waterdog Records), 329 W. 18th St., #313, Chicago IL 60616-1120. (312)421-7499. Fax: (312)421-1848. E-mail: waterdog@waterdogmusic.com. Web site: www.waterdogmusic.com. **Contact:** Rob Gillis, label manager. Labels include Whitehouse Records. Record company. Estab. 1991. Staff size: 2. Releases 2 CDs/year. Pays negotiable royalty to artists on contract; statutory rate to publisher per song on record.

Distributed by Big Daddy Music.

How to Contact "Not accepting unsolicited materials, demos at this time. If submission policy changes, it will be posted on our Web site."

Music Mostly **rock** and **pop**. Released *Good Examples of Bad Examples: The Best of Ralph Covert & The Bad Examples, Vol. 2* (album), released 2005. Other artists have included Middle 8, Al Rose & The Transcendos, Kat Parsons, Torben Floor (Carey Ott), MysteryDriver, Joel Frankel, Dean Goldstein & Coin, and Matt Tiegler.

Tips "Ralph Covert's children's music (Ralph's World) is released in Disney Sound. We are not looking for any other children's music performers or composers."

⊘ WIND-UP ENTERTAINMENT

79 Madison Ave., 7th Floor, New York NY 10016. (212)895-3100. Web site: www.winduprecords.c om. **Contact:** A&R. Record company. Estab. 1997. Releases 6-7 CDs/year. Pays negotiable royalty to artists on contract; statutory rate to publisher per song on record.

Distributed by BMG.

How to Contact *Write first and obtain permission to submit.* Prefers CD or DVD. Does not return material or respond to submissions.

Music Mostly **rock, folk** and **hard rock**. Artists include Seether, Scott Stapp, Evanescence, and People In Planes.

Tips "We rarely look for songwriters as opposed to bands, so writing a big hit single would be the rule of the day."

🌐 ❑ X.R.L. RECORDS/MUSIC

Perthy Farm, The Perthy, Shropshire SY12 9HR United Kingdom. (01691)623173. **Contact:** Xavier Lee, International A&R Manager. A&R: Tanya Woof. UK A&R Manager: Cathrine Lee. Labels include Swoop, Zarg Records, Genouille, Pogo and Check Records. Record company, record producer and music publisher (Le Matt Music, Lee Music, R.T.F.M. and Pogo Records). Member MPA, PPL, PRS, MCPS, V.P.L. Estab. 1972. Staff size: 11. Releases 30 12″ singles, 20 LPs and 20 CDs/year. Pays negotiable royalty to artists on contract; negotiable rate to publisher for each record sold. Royalties paid to US songwriters and artists through US publishing or recording affiliate.

Distributed by Lematt Music.

How to Contact Submit demo package by mail. Unsolicited submissions are OK. Prefers CD, cassette, MD, DVD, or VHS 625 PAL standard videocassette with 1-3 songs and lyric sheet. Include bio and still photos. IRC only. Responds in 6 weeks.

Music Mostly **pop/top 40**; also **bluegrass**, **blues**, **country**, **dance-oriented**, **easy listening**, **MOR**, **progressive**, **R&B**, **'50s rock**, **disco**, **new wave**, **rock** and **soul**. Released "Oh Carol" (single) from *The Best of Johnny Moon* (album), written and recorded by Johnny Moon (pop), released 2007 on X.R.L; "One Night" (single by Gary Piper) from *One Night* (album), recorded by Sight 'N' Sound (rock), released 2007 on Pogo; "Dead Fish" (single by P. Robson) from *It's All Over Now* (album), recorded by The Hush (rock), released 2007 on Zarg. Other artists include Orphan, The Chromatics, Mike Sheriden and the Nightriders, Johnny Moon, and Emmitt Till.

Tips "Be original."

❑ XEMU RECORDS

19 W. 21st St., Suite 503, New York NY 10010. (212)807-0290. Fax: (212)807-0583. E-mail: xemu@xemu.com. Web site: www.xemu.com. **Contact:** Dr. Claw, vice president A&R. Record company. Estab. 1992. Staff size: 4. Releases 4 CDs/year. Pays negotiable royalty to artists on contract; statutory rate to publisher per song on record.

Distributed by Redeye Distribution.

How to Contact *Write first and obtain permission to submit.* Prefers CD with 3 songs. Does not return material. Responds in 2 months.

Music Mostly **alternative**. Released *Happy Suicide, Jim!* (album) by The Love Kills Theory (alternative rock); *Howls From The Hills* (album) by Dead Meadow; *The Fall* (album), recorded by Mikki James (alternative rock); *A is for Alpha* (album), recorded by Alpha Bitch (alternative rock); *Hold the Mayo* (album), recorded by Death Sandwich (alternative rock); *Stockholm Syndrome* (album), recorded by Trigger Happy (alternative rock) all released on Xemu Records. Other artists include Malvert P. Redd, The Fifth Dementia, and the Neanderthal Spongecake.

ADDITIONAL RECORD COMPANIES

The following companies are also record companies, but their listings are found in other sections of the book. Read the listings for submission information.

Record Producers

The independent producer can best be described as a creative coordinator. He's often the one with the most creative control over a recording project and is ultimately responsible for the finished product. Some record companies have in-house producers who work with the acts on that label (although, in more recent years, such producer-label relationships are often non-exclusive). Today, most record companies contract out-of-house, independent record producers on a project-by-project basis.

WHAT RECORD PRODUCERS DO

Producers play a large role in deciding what songs will be recorded for a particular project and are always on the lookout for new songs for their clients. They can be valuable contacts for songwriters because they work so closely with the artists whose records they produce. They usually have a lot more freedom than others in executive positions and are known for having a good ear for potential hit songs. Many producers are songwriters and musicians themselves. Since they wield a great deal of influence, a good song in the hands of the right producer at the right time stands a good chance of being cut. And even if a producer is not working on a specific project, he is well-acquainted with record company executives and artists and can often get material through doors not open to you.

SUBMITTING MATERIAL TO PRODUCERS

It can be difficult to get your tapes to the right producer at the right time. Many producers write their own songs and even if they don't write, they may be involved in their own publishing companies so they have instant access to all the songs in their catalogs. Also, some genres are more dependent on finding outside songs than others. A producer working with a rock group or a singer-songwriter will rarely take outside songs.

It's important to understand the intricacies of the producer/publisher situation. If you pitch your song directly to a producer first, before another publishing company publishes the song, the producer may ask you for the publishing rights (or a percentage thereof) to your song. You must decide whether the producer is really an active publisher who will try to get the song recorded again and again or whether he merely wants the publishing because it means extra income for him from the current recording project. You may be able to work out a co-publishing deal, where you and the producer split the publishing of the song. That means he will still receive his percentage of the publishing income, even if you secure a cover recording of the song by other artists in the future. Even though you would be giving up a little bit initially, you may benefit in the future.

Some producers will offer to sign artists and songwriters to "development deals." These can range from a situation where a producer auditions singers and musicians with the intention of building a group from the ground up, to development deals where a producer signs a band or singer-songwriter to his production company with the intention of developing the act and producing an album to shop to labels (sometimes referred to as a "baby record deal").

You must carefully consider whether such a deal is right for you. In some cases, such a deal can open doors and propel an act to the next level. In other worst-case scenarios, such a deal can result in loss of artistic and career control, with some acts held in contractual bondage for years at a time. Before you consider any such deal, be clear about your goals, the producer's reputation, and the sort of compromises you are willing to make to reach those goals. If you have any reservations whatsoever, don't do it.

The listings that follow outline which aspects of the music industry each producer is involved in, what type of music he is looking for, and what records and artists he's recently produced. Study the listings carefully, noting the artists each producer works with, and consider if any of your songs might fit a particular artist's or producer's style. Then determine whether they are open to your level of experience (see the A Sample Listing Decoded on page 11).

Consult the Category Index on page 378 to find producers who work with the type of music you write, and the Geographic Index at the back of the book to locate producers in your area.

Icons

For More Info

For more instructional information on the listings in this book, including explanations of symbols (N ✔ ❦ ⛰ ❧ 🌐 ◯ ◗ ◉ ⊘), read the article *Songwriter's Market: How Do I Use It?* on page 7.

ADDITIONAL RECORD PRODUCERS

There are **more record producers** located in other sections of the book! On page 223 use the list of Additional Record Producers to find listings within other sections who are also record producers.

⬥ ☑ ◧ "A" MAJOR SOUND CORPORATION

RR #1, Kensington PE COB 1MO Canada. (902)836-4571. E-mail: info@amajorsound.com. Web site: www.amajorsound.com. **Contact:** Paul C. Milner, producer. Record producer and music publisher. Estab. 1989. Produces 8 CDs/year. Fee derived in part from sales royalty when song or artist is recorded, and/or outright fee from recording artist or record company, or investors.

How to Contact Submit demo package by mail. Unsolicited submissions are OK. Prefers CD with 5 songs and lyric sheet (lead sheet if available). Does not return material. Responds only if interested in 3 months.

Music Mostly **rock, A/C, alternative** and **pop**; also **Christian** and **R&B**. Produced *COLOUR* (album written by J. MacPhee/R. MacPhee/C. Buchanan/D. MacDonald), recorded by The Chucky Danger Band (pop/rock), released 2006; *Rock Classics* (album, by various writers), recorded by Phe Cullen with Randy Waldman Trio (jazz), released 2002 on United One Records; *Jazz Standards* (album, by various writers), recorded by Phe Cullen with the Norm Amadio Trio (jazz), to be released in 2003 on United One Records; "Temptation" (single by Verdi, Paul Milner and Patrizia Pomeroy) from *Edge of Emotion* (album), recorded by Patrizia, released 2005 on Nuff Entertainment; and *Fury* (album, adapted from public domain), recorded by Patricia Pomeroy, Paul Milner and Dan Cutrona, released 2003 on B&B/Edel/Nuff Entertainment.

☑ ◻ ACR PRODUCTIONS

P.O. Box 5636, Midland TX 79704. (432)687-2702. E-mail: dwainethomas@sbcglobal.net. **Contact:** Dwaine Thomas, owner. Record producer, music publisher (Joranda Music/BMI) and record company (ACR Records). Estab. 1986. Produces 120 singles, 8-15 12" singles, 25 LPs, 25 EPs and 25 CDs/year. Fee derived from sales royalty when song or artist is recorded. "We charge for in-house recording only. Remainder is derived from royalties."

How to Contact Submit demo package by mail. Unsolicited submissions are OK. Prefers CD/DVD with 5 songs and lyric sheet. Does not return material. Responds in 6 weeks if interested.

Music Mostly **country swing, pop,** and **rock**; also **R&B** and **gospel**. Produced *Bottle's Almost Gone* (album) and "Black Gold" (single), written and recorded by Mike Nelson (country), both released 1999 on ACR Records; and *Nashville Series* (album), written and recorded by various (country), released 1998 on ProJam Music.

Tips "Be professional. No living room tapes!"

☑ ◙ ADR STUDIOS

(formerly Stuart J. Allyn), 250 Taxter Rd., Irvington NY 10533. (212)486-0856. Fax: (914)591-5617. E-mail: adrstudios@adrinc.org. Web site: www.adrinc.org. Associate: Jack Walker. **Contact:** Jack Davis, general manager. President: Stuart J. Allyn. Record producer. Estab. 1972. Produces 6 singles and 3-6 CDs/year. Fee derived from sales royalty and outright fee from recording artist and record company.

How to Contact *Does not accept unsolicited submissions.*

Music Mostly **pop, rock, jazz,** and **theatrical**; also **R&B** and **country**. Produced *Thad Jones Legacy* (album), recorded by Vanquard Jazz Orchestra (jazz), released 2000 on New World Records. Other artists include Billy Joel, Aerosmith, Carole Demas, Michael Garin, The Magic Garden, Bob Stewart, The Dixie Peppers, Nora York, Buddy Barnes and various video and film scores.

◙ AUDIO 911

(formerly Steve Wytas Productions), P.O. Box 212, Haddam CT 06438. (860)345-3300. E-mail: songwritersmarket@audio911.com. Web site: www.audio911.com. **Contact:** Steven J. Wytas. Record producer. Estab. 1984. Produces 4-8 singles, 3 LPs, 3 EPs and 4 CDs/year. Fee derived from outright fee from recording artist or record company.

How to Contact Submit demo by mail. Unsolicited submissions are OK. Prefers CD or VHS videocassette with several songs and lyric or lead sheet. "Include live material if possible." Does not return material. Responds in 3 months.

Music Mostly **rock**, **pop**, **top 40** and **country/acoustic**. Produced *Already Home* (album), recorded by Hannah Cranna on Big Deal Records (rock); *Under the Rose* (album), recorded by Under the Rose on Utter Records (rock); and *Sickness & Health* (album), recorded by Legs Akimbo on Joyful Noise Records (rock). Other artists include King Hop!, The Shells, The Gravel Pit, G'nu Fuz, Tuesday Welders and Toxic Field Mice.

☐ BLUES ALLEY RECORDS

Rt. 1, Box 288, Clarksburg WV 26301. (304)598-2583. Web site: www.bluesalleymusic.com. **Contact:** Joshua Swiger, producer. Record producer, record company and music publisher (Blues Alley Publishing/BMI). New Christian record label (Joshua Tree Records/BMI). Produces 4-6 LPs and 2 EPs/year. Fee derived from sales royalty when song or artist is recorded.

How to Contact Submit demo package by mail. Unsolicited submissions are OK. Prefers CD with 4 songs and lyric and lead sheets. Does not return material. Responds in 6 weeks.

Music Mostly **Christian**, **alternative** and **pop**. Produced *Songs Your Radio Wants to Hear* (album), recorded by The New Relics (acoustic rock), released 2006; *Sons of Sirens* (album), recorded by Amity (rock), released 2004; and *It's No Secret* (album), recorded by Samantha Caley (pop country), released 2004, all on Blues Alley Records.

☑ CACOPHONY PRODUCTIONS

2400 Vasanta Way, Los Angeles CA 90068. (917)856-8532. Producer: Steven Miller. Record producer and music publisher (In Your Face Music). Estab. 1981. Fee derived from sales royalty when song or artist is recorded, or outright fee from recording artist or record company.

How to Contact *Call first and obtain permission to submit.* Prefers 3 songs and lyric sheet. "Send a cover letter of no more than three paragraphs giving some background on yourself and the music. Also explain specifically what you are looking for Cacophony Productions to do." Does not return material. Responds only if interested.

Music Mostly **progressive pop/rock**, **singer/songwriter** and **progressive country**. Produced Dar Williams, Suzanne Vega, John Gorka, Michael Hedges, Juliana Hatfield, Toad the Wet Sprocket, and Medeski-Martin & Wood.

☐ COACHOUSE MUSIC

P.O. Box 1308, Barrington IL 60011. (847)382-7631. Fax: (847)382-7651. E-mail: coachouse1@aol.com. **Contact:** Michael Freeman, president. Record producer. Estab. 1984. Produces 6-8 CDs/year. Fee derived from sales royalty when song or artist is recorded.

How to Contact *Write or e-mail first and obtain permission to submit.* Prefers CD with 3-5 songs and lyric sheet. Include SASE. Responds in 6 weeks.

Music Mostly **rock**, **pop** and **blues**; also **alternative rock** and **country/Americana/roots**. Produced *Casque Nu* (album), written and recorded by Charlelie Couture on Chrysalis EMI France (contemporary pop); *Time Will Tell* (album), recorded by Studebaker John on Blind Pig Records (blues); *Where Blue Begins* (album by various/D. Coleman), recorded by Deborah Coleman on Blind Pig Records (contemporary blues); *A Man Amongst Men* (album), recorded by Bo Diddley (blues); and *Voodoo Menz* (album), recorded by Corey Harris and Henry Butler. Other artists include Paul Chastain, Candi Station, Eleventh Dream Day, Magic Slim, The Tantrums, The Pranks, The Bad Examples, Mississippi Heat and Sherri Williams.

Tips "Be honest, be committed, strive for excellence."

Record Producers

☑ CHARLIE CRAIG PRODUCTIONS

P.O. Box 1448, Mt. Juliet TN 37121-1448. Web site: www.charliecraig.com or www.myspace.com/songwritercharliecraig. **Contact:** Charlie Craig, producer. Record producer and music publisher (Song Machine/BMI, Walker Publishing Co. L.L.C./ASCAP/BMI). Estab. 2001. Produces 5 singles and 5 CDs/year. Fee derived from sales royalty and/or outright fee from recording artist.

• Charlie Craig Productions received a Grammy nomination in 1991 and Song of the Year nominations in 1986 and 1991. Was inducted into the South Carolina Entertainment Hall of Fame in 1998.

How to Contact *Write or call first to arrange personal interview.* For song publishing submissions, prefers CD with 3 songs, lyric sheet and lead sheet. "Include e-mail address for response." Does not return submissions. Responds in 3 weeks via e-mail only.

Music Mostly **traditional country**, **new country** and **country pop**. Co-produced *The Nashville Super Pickers* (album), recorded by The Nashville Super Pickers Band (country), released 1972 on Royal American Records; and *Headlights on the Highway* (album), recorded by Rebecca Lindsey (country), released 2007 on Rebecca Lindsey LLC. "First Nashville writer to work with Alan Jackson. Extensively involved in getting a record deal for the Wilkinsons with Giant Records."

Tips "Be prepared to record only the best songs, even if it takes an extended length of time. We won't go into the studio until we have great songs. Vocals should be memorized before going into the studio. You need to express as much emotion as possible. Suggestions are welcome from artists and musicians, but final decisions are made by the Producer. We will make sure the vocals are perfect no matter how many takes are necessary. Be prepared to work."

Ⓝ ☑ JERRY CUPIT PRODUCTIONS

Box 121904, Nashville TN 37212. (615)731-0100. Fax: (615)731-3005. E-mail: dan@cupitmusic.com. Web site: www.cupitrecords.com. **Contact:** Elizabeth Howe, creative assistant. Record producer and music publisher (Cupit Music). Estab. 1984. Fee derived from sales royalty when song or artist is recorded or outright fee from artist.

• Also see the listing for Cupit Music Group in the Music Publishers section of this book.

How to Contact *Visit Web site for policy.* Prefers CD with bio and photo. Include SASE. Responds in 2 months.

Music Mostly **traditional and contemporary uptempo country**, **Southern rock** and **gospel**. Produced "Make A wish" (single) from *Kevin Sharp* (album), recorded by Kevin Sharp (country), released 2007 on Cupit Records; "Working for the Weekend" (single) from *Ken Mellons* (album), recorded by Ken Mellons, released 1994 on Sony. Other artists include Memarie and Mustang Creek.

Tips "Be prepared to work hard and be able to take constructive/professional criticism."

☐ DAP ENTERTAINMENT

PMB 364, 7100 Lockwood Blvd., Boardman OH 44512. (330)726-8737. Fax: (330)726-8747. Web site: www.dapentertainment.com. **Contact:** Darryl Alexander, producer. Record Producer and music publisher (Alexander Sr. Music, BMI). Estab. 1997. Produces 12 singles and 2-4 CDs/year. Fee derived from sales royalty (producer points) when song or artist is recorded or outright fee from recording artist or record company.

• Also see the listing for Alexander Sr. Music in the Music Publishers section of this book.

How to Contact *Write first and obtain permission to submit.* Prefers CD with 2-4 songs and lyric sheet. Include SASE. Responds in 1 month. "No phone calls or faxes will be accepted."

Music Mostly **contemporary jazz**, **urban contemporary gospel**; also **R&B**. Produced "Plumb Line" (single by Herb McMullen/Darryl Alexander), "Cafe Rio," (single) and "Garden of My Heart" (single) from *Diamond In the Sky* (album), recorded by Darryl Alexander (contemporary jazz), all released 2004 on DAP Entertainment. Other artists include Kathryn Williams.

⚡ ◪ DAVINCI'S NOTEBOOK RECORDS

10070 Willoughby Dr., Niagara Falls, ON L2E 6S6 Canada. E-mail: admin@davincismusic.com. Web site: www.davincismusic.com. Owner: Kevin Richard. Record producer, record company, music publisher, distributor and recording studio (The Sound Kitchen). Estab. 1992. Produces 1 CD/year. Fee derived from outright fee from artist or commission on sales. "Distribution is on consignment basis. Artist is responsible for all shipping, taxes, and import/export duties."

How to Contact *"E-mail first for postal details then submit demo CD by mail."* Unsolicited submissions are OK. Prefers CD and bio. Does not return material. Responds in 6 weeks.

Music Mostly **rock**, **instrumental rock**, **New Age** and **progressive-alternative**; also **R&B**, **pop** and **jazz**. Produced *Windows* (album by Kevin Hotte/Andy Smith), recorded by Musicom on DaVinci's Notebook Records (power New Age); *Inventing Fire, Illumination, A Different Drum* (albums) written and recorded by Kevin Richard on DNR/Independent (instrumental rock); and *The Cunninghams* (album), written and recorded by The Cunninghams on Independent (gospel).

Tips "DNR is an artist-run label. Local bands and performers will receive priority. You should be more interested in getting a-foot-in-the-door exposure as opposed to making a fortune. Be satisfied with conquering the world using 'baby steps.' Indie labels don't have large corporate budgets for artist development. For non-local artists, we are more about online distribution than artist development. Being a local act means that you can perform live to promote your releases. For indie artist, selling from the stage is probably going to bring you the biggest volume of sales."

☑ 🖼 ◪ EDWARD DE MILES

10573 W. Pico Blvd., #352, Los Angeles CA 90064-2348. Phone: (310)948-9652. Fax: (310)474-7705. E-mail: info@edmsahara.com. Web site: www.edmsahara.com. **Contact:** Edward De Miles, president. Record producer, music publisher (Edward De Miles Music Co./BMI) and record company (Sahara Records and Filmworks Entertainment). Estab. 1981. Produces 5-10 CDs/year. Fee derived from sales royalty when song or artist is recorded.

- Also see the listing for Edward De Miles in the Music Publishers and Managers & Booking Agents sections, as well as Sahara Records and Filmworks Entertainment in the Record Companies section of this book.

How to Contact Does not accept unsolicited submissions.

Music Mostly **R&B/dance**, **top 40 pop/rock** and **contemporary jazz**; also **country**, **TV and film themes—songs and jingles**. **Produced** "Moments" and "Dance Wit Me" (singles) (dance), both written and recorded by Steve Lynn; and "Games" (single), written and recorded by D'von Edwards (jazz), all on Sahara Records. Other artists include Multiple Choice.

Tips "Copyright all material before submitting. Equipment and showmanship a must."

⚡ ◪ AL DELORY AND MUSIC MAKERS

E-mail: aldelory@mn.rr.com. Web site: www.aldelory.com. **Contact:** Al DeLory, president. Record producer and career consultant (MUSIC MAKERS/ASCAP). Estab. 1987. Fee derived from outright fee from recording artist.

- Al DeLory has won two Grammy Awards and has been nominated five times.

How to Contact *E-mail first and obtain permission to submit.* Prefers CD. Include SASE. Responds in 2-3 months only if interested.

Music Mostly **pop** and **Latin**. Produced "Gentle On My Mind" (single), "By the Time I Get to Phoenix" (single) and "Wichita Lineman" (single), all recorded by Glen Campbell. Other artists include Lettermen, Wayne Newton, Bobbie Gentry, and Anne Murray.

Tips "Seek advice and council only with professionals with a track record and get the money up front."

JOEL DIAMOND ENTERTAINMENT

Dept. SM, 3940 Laurel Canyon Blvd., Suite 441, Studio City CA 91604. (818)980-9588. Fax: (818)980-9422. E-mail: jdiamond20@aol.com. Web site: www.joeldiamond.com. **Contact:** Joel Diamond. Record producer, music publisher and manager. Fee derived from sales royalty when song is recorded or outright fee from recording artist or record company.

- Also see the listing for Silver Blue Music/Oceans Blue Music in the Music Publishers section of this book.

How to Contact Does not return material. Responds only if interested.

Music Mostly **dance**, **R&B**, **soul** and **top 40/pop**. Produced "One Night In Bangkok" (single by Robey); "I Think I Love You," recorded by Katie Cassidy (daughter of David Cassidy) on Artemis Records; "After the Loving" (single), recorded by E. Humperdinck; "Forever Friends," recorded by Vaneza (featured on Nickelodeon's *The Brothers Garcia*); and "Paradise" (single), recorded by Kaci.

FINAL MIX INC.

(formerly Final Mix Music), 2219 W. Olive Ave., Suite 102, Burbank CA 91506. (818)970-8717. E-mail: finalmix@aol.com. **Contact:** Theresa Frank, A&R. Record producer/remixer/mix engineer, independent label (3.6 Music, Inc.) and music publisher (Ximlanif Music Publishing). Estab. 1989. Releases 12 singles and 3-5 LPs and CDs/year. Fee derived from sales royalty when song or artist is recorded.

How to Contact *Does not accept unsolicited submissions.*

Music Mostly **pop**, **rock**, **dance**, **R&B** and **rap**. Produced Hilary Duff, Jesse McCartney, Christina Aguilera, American Idol, Rach Charles, Quincy Jones, Michael Bolton, K-Ci and Jo Jo (of Jodeci), Will Smith, and/or mixer/remixer for Janet Jackson, Ice Cube, Queen Latifah, Jennifer Paige, and The Corrs.

HEART CONSORT MUSIC

410 First St. SW., Mt. Vernon IA 52314. E-mail: mail@heartconsortmusic.com. Web site: www.heartconsortmusic.com. **Contact:** Catherine Lawson, manager. Record producer, record company and music publisher. Estab. 1980. Produces 2-3 CDs/year. Fee derived from sales royalty when song or artist is recorded.

How to Contact Submit demo package by mail. Unsolicited submissions are OK. Prefers CD or cassette with 3 songs and 3 lyric sheets. Include SASE. Responds in 3 months.

Music Mostly **jazz**, **New Age** and **contemporary**. Produced *New Faces* (album), written and recorded by James Kennedy on Heart Consort Music (world/jazz).

Tips "We are interested in jazz/New Age artists with quality demos and original ideas. We aim for an international audience."

INTEGRATED ENTERTAINMENT

1815 JFK Blvd., #1612, Philadelphia PA 19103. (215)563-7147. E-mail: gelboni@aol.com. **Contact:** Gelboni, president. Record producer. Estab. 1991. Produces 6 EPs and 6 CDs/year. Fee derived from sales royalty when song or artist is recorded or outright fee from recording artist or record company.

How to Contact Submit demo package by mail. Solicited submissions only. CD only with 3 songs. "Draw a guitar on the outside of envelope so we'll know it's from a songwriter." Responds in 2 months.

Music Mostly **rock** and **pop**. Produced *Gold Record* (album), written and recorded by Dash Rip Rock (rock) on Ichiban Records; *Virus* (album), written and recorded by Margin of Error (modern rock) on Treehouse Records; and *I Divide* (album), written and recorded by Amy Carr (AAA) on Evil Twin Records. Other artists include Land of the Blind, Gatlin, Ash Wednesday, Playing for Audrey, Three Miles Out, and others.

🌐 ✅ 🔊 JUNE PRODUCTIONS LTD.

The White House, 6 Beechwood Lane, Warlingham, Surrey CR6 9LT England. Phone: 44(0) 1883 622411. Fax: 44(0)1883 652457. E-mail: david@mackay99.plus.com. **Contact:** David Mackay, producer. Record producer and music producer (Sabre Music). Estab. 1970. Produces singles, CDs, and live stage show recordings. Fee derived from sales royalty.

How to Contact Submit demo CD or mp3 by mail. Unsolicited submissions are OK. Prefers CD or cassette with 1-2 songs and lyric sheet. SAE and IRC. Responds in 2 months.

Music Mostly **MOR**, **rock** and **top 40/pop**. Produced *Web of Love* (by various), recorded by Sarah Jory on Ritz Records (country rock). Other artists include Bonnie Tyler, Cliff Richard, Frankie Miller, Johnny Hallyday, Dusty Springfield, Charlotte Henry and Barry Humphries.

Tips "I am currently producing the music for the America 2007 celebrtions and two new musicals. I am happy to review songs, but on the understanding that it is less likely I can deliver cuts based on the fact I am currently rarely recording for single releases."

🔊 KAREN KANE PRODUCER/ENGINEER

(910)681-0220. E-mail: mixmama@total.net. Web site: www.mixmama.com. **Contact:** Karen Kane, producer/engineer. Record producer and recording engineer. Estab. 1978. Produces 3-5 CDs/year. Fee derived from sales royalty when song or artist is recorded or outright fee from recording artist or record company.

How to Contact *E-mail first and obtain permission to submit. Unsolicited submissions are not OK.* "Please note: I am not a song publisher. My expertise is in album production." Does not return material. Responds in 1 week.

Music Mostly **acoustic music of any kind**, **rock**, **blues**, **pop**, **alternative**, **R&B/reggae**, **country**, and **bluegrass**. Produced *Independence Meal* (album), recorded by Alix Olson (blues), released on Subtle Sister Records; Topless (Juno-nominated album), recorded by Big Daddy G, released on Reggie's Records; *Mixed Wise and Otherwise* (Juno-nominated album), recorded by Harry Manx (blues). Other artists include Tracy Chapman (her first demo), Chad Mitchell, Ember Swift, Laura Bird, Wishing Chair, Blue Mule, Barenaked Ladies (live recording for a TV special), and Ron Wiseman.

Tips "Get proper funding to be able to make a competitive, marketable product."

📋 🔊 KNOWN ARTIST PRODUCTIONS

2622 Kirtland Rd., Brewton AL 36426. (251)867-2228. **Contact:** Roy Edwards, president. Record producer, music publisher (Cheavoria Music Co./BMI, Baitstring Music/ASCAP) and record company (Bolivia Records, Known Artist Records). Estab. 1972. Produces 10 singles and 3 LPs/year. Fee derived from sales royalty when song or artist is recorded.

• Also see the listings for Baitstring Music and Cheavoria Music in the Music Publishers section of this book, and Bolivia Records in the Record Companies section of this book.

How to Contact *Write first and obtain permission to submit.* Prefers CD with 3 songs and lyric sheet. Responds in 1 month. "All tapes will be kept on file."

Music Mostly **R&B**, **pop** and **country**; also **easy listening**, **MOR**, **soul** and **gospel**. Produced "Got To Let You Know," "You Are My Sunshine" and "You Make My Life So Wonderful" (singles), all written and recorded by Roy Edwards on Bolivia Records (R&B). Other artists include Jim Portwood, Bobbie Roberson and Brad Smiley.

Tips "We need some good gospel."

🔲 L.A. ENTERTAINMENT, INC.

7095 Hollywood Blvd., #826, Hollywood CA 90028. 1-800-579-9157. Fax: (323)924-1095. E-mail: info@warriorrecords.com. Web site: www.WarriorRecords.com. **Contact:** Jim Ervin, A&R. Record producer, record company (Warrior Records) and music publisher (New Entity Music/ASCAP, New

Record Producers

Copyright Music/BMI, New Euphonic Music/SESAC). Estab. 1988. Fee derived from sales royalty when song or artist is recorded.

How to Contact Submit demo package by mail. Unsolicited submissions are OK. Prefers CD and/or videocassette with original songs, lyric and lead sheet if available. "We do not review Internet sites. Do not send MP3s, unless requested. All written submitted materials (e.g., lyric sheets, letter, etc.) should be typed." Does not return material unless SASE is included. Responds in 2 months only via e-mail or SASE.

Music All styles. "All genres are utilized with our music supervision company for Film & TV, but our original focus is on **alternative rock** and **urban genres** (e.g., **R&B**, **rap**, **gospel**).

LARI-JON PRODUCTIONS

P.O. Box 216, Rising City NE 68658. (402)542-2336. **Contact:** Larry Good, owner. Record producer, music publisher (Lari-Jon Publishing/BMI), management firm (Lari-Jon Promotions) and record company (Lari-Jon Records). Estab. 1967. Produces 10 singles and 5 LPs/year. Fee derived from sales royalty when song or artist is recorded.

- Also see the listings for other Lari-Jon companies in the Music Publishers, Record Companies, and Managers & Booking Agents sections of this book.

How to Contact Submit demo CD by mail. Unsolicited submissions are OK. "Must be a professional demo." Include SASE. Responds in 2 months.

Music Mostly **country**, **Southern gospel** and **'50s rock**. Produced *Jesus is my Hero* (album), written and recorded by Larry Good on Lari-Jon Records (gospel). Other artists include Brenda Allen, Tom Campbell, and Tom Johnson.

LARK TALENT & ADVERTISING

P.O. Box 35726, Tulsa OK 74153. (918)786-8896. Fax: (918)786-8897. E-mail: janajae@janajae.com. Web site: www.janajae.com. **Contact:** Kathleen Pixley, vice president. Owner: Jana Jae. Record producer, music publisher (Jana Jae Music/BMI) and record company (Lark Record Productions, Inc.). Estab. 1980. Fee derived from sales royalty when song or artist is recorded.

- Also see the listings for Jana Jae Music in the Music Publishers section, Lark Record Productions in the Record Companies section, and Jana Jae Enterprises in the Managers & Booking Agents section of this book.

How to Contact Submit demo by mail. Unsolicited submissions are OK. Prefers CD or VHS videocassette with 3 songs and lead sheet. Does not return material. Responds in 1 month only if interested.

Music Mostly **country**, **bluegrass** and **classical**; also **instrumentals**. Produced "Bussin' Ditty" (single by Steve Upfold); "Mayonnaise" (single by Steve Upfold); and "Flyin' South" (single by Cindy Walker), all recorded by Jana Jae on Lark Records (country). Other artists include Sydni, Hotwire and Matt Greif.

MAC-ATTACK PRODUCTIONS

868 NE 81st St., Miami FL 33138. (305)949-1422. E-mail: GoMacster@aol.com. **Contact:** Michael McNamee, engineer/producer. Record producer and music publisher (Mac-Attack Publishing/ASCAP). Estab. 1986. Fee derived from outright fee from recording artist or record company.

How to Contact Submit demo by mail. Unsolicited submissions are OK. Prefers CD or cassette or VHS videocassette with 3-5 songs, lyric sheet and bio. Does not return material. Responds in up to 3 months.

Music Mostly **pop**, **alternative rock** and **dance**. Engineered Compositions (album), written and recorded by Paul Martin (experimental), released 2006 on PMR Music. Produced and engineered *Tuscan Tongue* (album by Caution Automatic), recorded by Caution Automatic (rock), released 2005 on C.A. Records; Produced and engineered "Never Gonna Let You Go" (single by Bruce Jordan/John Link/Michael McNamee), recorded by Bruce Jordan (pop), released 2002 on H.M.S.

Records. Other artists include Blowfly, Tally Tal, Nina Llopis, The Lead, Girl Talk, Tyranny of Shaw, and Jacobs Ladder.

✉ COOKIE MARENCO

P.O. Box 874, Belmont CA 94002. E-mail: cojemamusic@yahoo.com. (650)591-6857. Record producer/engineer. "Over 20 years experience, 5 Grammy nominations, 2 gold records, proprietary surround recording technique. Estab. 1981. Produces 10 CDs/year. $2,000 per day payable in advance.

How to Contact *Contact only if interested in production. Does not accept unsolicited material.*

Music Mostly **alternative modern rock**, **country**, **folk**, **rap**, **ethnic** and **avante-garde**; also **classical**, **pop** and **jazz**. Produced *Winter Solstice II* (album), written and recorded by various artists; *Heresay* (album by Paul McCandless); and *Deep At Night* (album by Alex DeGrassi), all on Windham Hill Records (instrumental). Other artists include Tony Furtado Band, Praxis, Oregon, Mary Chapin Carpenter, Max Roach and Charle Haden & Quartet West.

Tips "If you're looking for Beat Detective and Autotune, please call someone else. We still believe in analog recording and great musicianship."

✉ PETE MARTIN/VAAM MUSIC PRODUCTIONS

P.O. Box 29550, Hollywood CA 90029-0550. (323)664-7765. E-mail: pmarti3636@aol.com. Web site: www.VaamMusic.com. **Contact:** Pete Martin, president. Record producer, music publisher (Vaam Music/BMI and Pete Martin Music/ASCAP) and record company (Blue Gem Records). Estab. 1982.

- Also see the listings for Vaam Music Group in the Music Publishers section of this book and Blue Gem Records in the Record Companies section of this book.

How to Contact Send CD or cassette with 2 songs and a lyric sheet. Send small packages only. Include SASE. Responds in 1 month.

Music Mostly **top 40/pop**, **country** and **R&B**.

Tips "Study the market in the style that you write. Songs must be capable of reaching top 5 on charts."

⚈ ⬜ SCOTT MATHEWS, D/B/A HIT OR MYTH PRODUCTIONS INC.

246 Almonte Blvd., Mill Valley CA 94941. Fax: (415)389-9682. E-mail: hitormyth@aol.com. Web site: www.ScottMathews.com. **Contact:** Mary Ezzell, A&R Director. President: Scott Mathews. Assistant: Tom Luekens. Record producer, song doctor, studio owner and music publisher (Hang On to Your Publishing/BMI). Estab. 1990. Produces 6-9 CDs/year. Fee derived from recording artist or record company (with royalty points).

- Scott Mathews has several gold and platinum awards for sales of over 13 million records. He has worked with more than 60 Rock & Roll Hall of Fame inductees and on several Grammy and Oscar-winning releases. In 2007, a "Box Set / Best of" package called Everything You Wanted to Know about The Rubinoos was released on Castle Music, featuring production by Scott Mathews. In 2006, he produced tracks for American Music—The Hightone Records Story and Guitar Hot Shots, released on Hightone Records. Also in 2006, he was nominated for another Grammy in the songwriting category for his work with The Robert Cray Band.

How to Contact "No phone calls or publishing submissions, please." Submit demo CD by mail or an mp3 by email. "Unsolicited submissions are often the best ones and readily accepted. Include SASE if e-mail is not an option. Also include your e-mail address on your demo CD." Responds in 2 months.

Music Mostly **rock/pop**, **alternative** and **singer/songwriters of all styles**. Produced 4 tracks on *Anthology (Best of)*, recorded by John Hiatt (rock/pop), released 2001 on Hip-O. Has produced Elvis Costello, Roy Orbison, Rosanne Cash, Jerry Garcia, Huey Lewis, and many more. Has recorded records with everyone from Barbra Streisand to John Lee Hooker, including Keith Richards, George Harrison, Mick Jagger, Van Morrison, Bonnie Raitt, and Eric Clapton to name but a few.

Tips "These days if you are not independent, you are dependent. The new artists that are coming up and achieving success in the music industry are the ones that prove they have a vision and can make incredible records without the huge financial commitment of a major label. When an emerging artist makes great product for the genre they are in, they are in the driver's seat to be able to make a fair and equitable deal for distribution, be it with a major or independent label. My philosophy is to go where you are loved. The truth is, a smaller label that is completely dedicated to you and shares your vision may help your career far more than a huge label that will not keep you around if you don't sell millions of units. I feel too much pressure is put on the emerging artist when they have to pay hundreds of thousands of dollars back to the label in order to see their first royalty check, We all know those records can be made for a fraction of that cost without compromising quality or commercial appeal.

"I still believe in potential and our company is in business to back up that belief. It is up to us as record makers/visionaries to take that potential into the studio and come out with music that can compete with anything else on the market. Discovering, developing and producing artists that can sustain long careers is our main focus at Hit or Myth Productions. We are proud to be associated with so many legendary and timeless artists and our track record speaks for itself. If you love making music, don't let anyone dim that light. We look forward to hearing from you. (Please check out www.ScottMathews.com for more info, and also www.allmusic.com-keyword; Scott Mathews.) Accept no substitutes!"

☑ MEGA TRUTH RECORDS

P.O. Box 4988, Culver City CA 90231. E-mail: jonbare@aol.com. Web site: www.jonbare.net. **Contact:** Jon Bare, CEO. Record producer and record company. Estab. 1994. Produces 2 CDs/year. Fee negotiable.

How to Contact Submit demo package by mail. Unsolicited submissions are OK. Prefers CD. "We specialize in recording world-class virtuoso musicians and bands with top players." Does not return material. Responds in 2 weeks only if interested.

Music Mostly **rock**, **blues** and **country rock**; also **swing**, **dance** and **instrumental**. Produced Party Platter recorded by Hula Monsters (swing); and Killer Whales, Shredzilla and Orcastra (by Jon Bare and the Killer Whales) (rock), all on Mega Truth Records. Other artists include The Rich Harper Blues Band, Aeon Dream & the Dream Machine and Techno Dudes.

Tips "Create a unique sound that blends great vocals and virtuoso musicianship with a beat that makes us want to get up and dance."

⚏ ☑ MONTICANA PRODUCTIONS

P.O. Box 702, Snowdon Station, Montreal QC H3X 3X8 Canada. **Contact:** David Leonard, executive producer. Record producer, music publisher (Montina Music) and record company (Monticana Records). Estab. 1963. Fee derived from sales royalty when song or artist is recorded.

● Also see the listings for Monticana Records in the Record Companies section and Montina Music in the Music Publishers section of this book.

How to Contact Submit demo package by mail. Unsolicited submissions are OK. Prefers CD with maximum 4 songs. "Demos should be as tightly produced as a master." Include SASE.

Music Mostly **top 40**; also **bluegrass**, **blues**, **country**, **dance-oriented**, **easy listening**, **folk**, **gospel**, **jazz**, **MOR**, **progressive**, **R&B**, **rock** and **soul**.

Tips "Work creatively and believe passionately in what you do and aspire to be. Success comes to those who persevere, have talent, develop their craft and network."

☑ ☑ MUSTROCK PRODUCTIONZ WORLDWIDE

E-mail: recordmode@hotmail.com. President: Ivan "Doc" Rodriguez. Record producer and recording/mixing/mastering engineer. Estab. 1987. Produces various singles and CDs/year. Fee derived from sales royalty and advance paymnt when song or artist is recorded. *" We are not a record company. We provide services for a fee—we do not sign or represent artists. We are a work-for-hire company."*

How to Contact *E-mail first and obtain permission to submit.* Prefers mp3, CD, DVD and lyric sheet. Does not return material. Responds in 2 months. "Unless booking our services, only opinion will be given."

Music Mostly **hip-hop**, **R&B** and **pop**; also **soul**, **ballads** and **soundtracks**. Produced "Poor Georgie" (by MC Lyte/DJ DOC), recorded by MC Lyte on Atlantic Records (rap). Other artists include Caron Wheeler, The Hit Squad, The Awesome II, Black Steel Music, Underated Productions, EPMD, Redman, Dr. Dre & Ed-Lover, Das-EFX, Biz Markie, BDP, Eric B & Rakim, The Fugees, The Bushwackass, Shai and Pudgee, Alisha Keys, 50 cent, Tiro de Garcia, etc.

Tips "Services provided include ProTools production (pre/post/co), digital tracking, mixing, remixing, live show tapes, jingles, etc. For additinal credits, go to www.allmusic.com, type 'Ivan Doc Rodriguez' under 'artist' and enter, or send e-mail."

☐ NEU ELECTRO PRODUCTIONS

P.O. Box 1582, Bridgeview IL 60455. (630)257-6289. E-mail: neuelectro@email.com. Web site: www.neuelectro.com. **Contact:** Bob Neumann, owner. Record producer and record company. Estab. 1984. Produces 16 singles, 16 12" singles, 20 LPs and 4 CDs/year. Fee derived from outright fee from record company or recording artist.

How to Contact Submit demo package by mail. Unsolicited submissions are OK. Prefers CD with 3 songs and lyric sheet or lead sheet. "Provide accurate contact phone numbers and addresses, promo packages and photos." Include SASE for reply. Responds in 2 weeks. "A production fee estimate will be returned to artist."

Music Mostly **dance**, **house**, **techno**, **rap** and **rock**; also **experimental**, **New Age** and **top 40**. Produced "Juicy" (single), written and recorded by Juicy Black on Dark Planet International Records (house); "Make Me Smile" (single), written and recorded by Roz Baker (house); *Reactovate-6* (album by Bob Neumann), recorded by Beatbox-D on N.E.P. Records (dance); and *Sands of Time* (album), recorded by Bob Neumann (New Age). Other artists include Skid Marx and The Deviants.

☑ NEW EXPERIENCE RECORDS/FAZE 4 RECORDS

P.O. Box 683, Lima OH 45802. E-mail: just_chilling_2002@yahoo.com. Web site: www.faze4records.com. **Contact:** A&R Department. Music Publisher: James L. Milligan Jr. Record producer, music publisher (A New Rap Jam Publishing/ASCAP), management firm (Creative Star Management) and record company (New Experience Records, Grand-Slam Records and Pump It Up Records). Estab. 1989. Produces 15-20 12" singles, 2 LPs, 3 EPs and 2-5 CDs/year. Fee derived from sales royalty when song or artist is recorded or outright fee from record company, "depending on services required."

- Also see the listings for A New Rap Jam Publishing in the Music Publishers section of this book.

How to Contact Write first to arrange personal interview. Address material to A&R Dept. or Talent Coordinator. Prefers CD with a minimum of 3 songs and lyric or lead sheet (if available). "If tapes are to be returned, proper postage should be enclosed and all tapes and letters should have SASE for faster reply." Responds in 6-8 weeks.

Music Mostly **pop**, **R&B** and **rap**; also **gospel**, **contemporary gospel** and **rock**. Produced "The Son of God" (single by James Milligan/Anthony Milligan/Melvin Milligan) from *The Final Chapter* (album), recorded by T.M.C. Milligan Conection (R&B, Gospel), released 2002 on New Experience/

Record Producers

Pump It Up Records. Other artists include Dion Mikel, Paulette Mikel, Melvin Milligan and Venesta Compton.

Tips "Do your homework on the music business. Be aware of all the new sampling laws. There are too many sound alikes. Be yourself. I look for what is different, vocal ability, voice range and sound stage presence, etc. Be on the look out for our new blues label Rough Edge Records/Rough Edge Entertainment. Blues material is now being reviewed. Send your best studio recorded material. Also be aware of the new sampling laws and the New Digital downloading laws. People are being jailed and fined for recording music that has not been paid for. Do your homework. We have also signed Diamond Sound Productions, located in Fresno, CA and Ground Breakers Records. Now we can better serve our customers on the East and West Coast. You can also visit our Web site at www.faze4records.com for further information on our services. We are also seeking artists and groups singers from the '60s, '70s, and '80s who would like to be re-signed. Please contact us. Please state your intentions when submitting your material and contact information. We have had submissions from artists who could have received a possible record deal from one of our labels, but we had no contact information. Once again, do your homework, please. Good luck!"

☐ PHILLY BREAKDOWN RECORDING CO.

216 W. Hortter St., Philadelphia PA 19119. (215)848-6725. E-mail: mattcozar@juno.com. **Contact:** Matthew Childs, president. Music Director: Charles Nesbit. Record producer, music publisher (Philly Breakdown/BMI) and record company. Estab. 1974. Produces 3 singles and 2 LPs/year. Fee derived from sales royalty when song or artist is recorded.

How to Contact *Contact first and obtain permission to submit.* Prefers CD with 4 songs and lead sheet. Does not return material. Responds in 2 months.

Music Mostly **R&B**, **hip-hop**, and **pop**; also **jazz**, **gospel**, and **ballads**. Produced "Lonely River" (single by Clarence Patterson/M. Childs) from *Lonely River* (album), recorded by Gloria Clark; and *Taps* (album), recorded by H Factor, both released 2001 on Philly Breakdown. Other artists include Leroy Christy, Gloria Clark, Jerry Walker, Nina Bundy, Mark Adam, Emmit King, Betty Carol, The H Factor, and Four Buddies.

Tips "If you fail, just learn from your past experience and keep on trying, until you get it done right. Never give up."

☐ JIM PIERCE

Dept. SM, 101 Hurt Rd., Hendersonville TN 37075. E-mail: jim@jimpierce.net. Web site: www.jimpierce.net. **Contact:** Jim Pierce, president. Record producer, music publisher (Strawboss Music/BMI) and record company (Round Robin Records). Estab. 1974. Fee derived from sales royalty or outright fee from recording artist. "Artists pay me in advance for my services." Has had over 200 chart records to date.

How to Contact *E-mail first and obtain permission to submit.* Prefers CD with 3 songs and lyric sheet. Does not return material. Responds only if interested. "All submissions should include their contact phone number and/or e-mail address."

Music Mostly **contemporary and traditional country**, **pop** and **gospel**. Have produced projects with George Jones, Waylon Jennings, Willie Nelson, Tommy Cash, Johnny Cash, Jimmy C. Newman, Bobby Helms, Sammi Smith, Charlie Louvin, Lynn Anderson, Melba Montgomery, and many others.

Tips "We use the same musicians as the hit records being played on mainstream country radio. Industry is seeking good singers who can write songs. Viewing our Web site is highly recommended."

☐ REEL ADVENTURES

9 Peggy Lane, Salem NH 03079. (603)898-7097. Web site: www.reeladventures1.homestead.com. **Contact:** Rick Asmega, chief engineer/producer. Record producer. Estab. 1972. Produces 100 12″

singles, 200 LPs, 5 EPs and 40 CDs/year. Fee derived from sales royalty when song or artist is recorded, or outright fee from recording artist or record company.

How to Contact Submit demo package by mail. Unsolicited submissions are OK. Prefers CD. Include SASE. Responds in 6 weeks.

Music Mostly **pop**, **funk**, and **country**; also **blues**, **Christian reggae**, and **rock**. Produced *Funky Broadway* (album), recorded by Chris Hicks; *Testafye* (album), recorded by Jay Williams; and "Acoustical Climate" (single by John G.). Other artists include Nicole Hajj, The Bolz, Second Sinni, Larry Sterling, Broken Men, Melvin Crockett, Fred Vigeant, Monster Mash, Carl Armand, Cool Blue Sky, Ransome, Backtrax, Push, Too Cool for Humans, and Burn Alley.

◻ RN'D DISTRIBUTION, LLC

(formerly RN'D Productions), P.O. Box 540102, Houston TX 77254-0102. (713)521-2616, ext. 10. Fax: (713)529-4914. E-mail: AandR@aol.com. Web site: www.rnddistribution.com. **Contact:** Byron Gates, A&R director. National Sales Director: Ramon Smith. Record producer, record company (Albatross Records), distributor (labels distributed include Albatross Records, TDA Music and Ball In' Records) and music publisher (Ryedale Publishing). Estab. 1986. Produces 25 singles, 20 LPs, 4 EPs and 21 CDs/year.

How to Contact Submit demo package by mail. Unsolicited submissions are OK. Prefers CD with 4 songs and lyric sheet. Does not return material. Responds in 1 month.

Music All types.

☑ ◻ RUSTRON MUSIC PRODUCTIONS

1156 Park Lane, West Palm Beach FL 33417-5957. (561)686-1354. E-mail: rmp_wmp@bellsouth.net. **Contact:** Sheelah Adams, office administrator. Executive Director: Rusty Gordon. Director of A&R: Ron Caruso. Assistant A&R Director: Kevin Reeves. Record producer, record company, manager and music publisher (Rustron Music Publishers/BMI and Whimsong Publishing/ASCAP). Estab. 1970. Produces 10 CDs/year. Fee derived from sales royalty when song or artist is recorded or outright fee from record company. "This branch office reviews all material submitted for the home office in Connecticut."

* Also see the listings for Rustron Music Publishers in the Music Publishers section and Rustron Music Productions in the Record Companies and Managers & Booking Agents sections of this book.

How to Contact *Songwriters may write, call or e-mail first to discuss your submission.* We prefer you e-mail a request for current submission guidelines. Include a SASE or International Response Coupon (IRC) if requesting guidelines or other information by snail-mail. All correspondence should include SASE or International Response Coupon (IRC), no exceptions. Submit CD or cassette demo by snail-mail. Prefers CD with up to 15 songs. We will do a "body of work" ' review for multiple CDs that were produced to sell at performing songwriter's gigs. 1-3 songs on cassette tape submissions. Include 8½ × 11 typed lyric sheets, 1 sheet per song. Also include cover letter clearly explaining your reason for submitting. Tell us about you and if you are a freelance or performing songwriter. Do you create songs with collaborators? Songs for single-song marketing should be 3-3½ minutes long or less and must be commercially viable and carefully crafted with definitive verse melody. New Age fusion or World Music Instrumentals 3-10 minutes each, 1 hour maximum for all songs. Responds in 4 months.

Music Mostly **mainstream**, **progressive country**, **pop** (ballads, blues, theatrical, cabaret), **soft rock**, **folk/rock**, and **adult contemporary electric-acoustic**; also **R&B**, **New Age/world music instrumental fusions**, **children's music**, **women's music**, **African or Native American synthesis**, **reggae**, and **light jazz**. Produced "White House Worries" (single) from *Whitehouse Worries* (album), written and recorded by The Ramifications (progressive country-folk/socio-political-topical), released 2007 on Rustron Records; "Sanibel-Captiva and the Gulf of Mexico" (single—historical

Record Producers

song) from *Song of Longboat Key* (album), recorded by Florida Rank & File (Florida folk); "Take the High Road" (single) from *Voting for Democracy* (album), recorded by The Panama City Pioneers (progressive-political-folk), released 2007 on Whimsong Records. Other artists include Haze Coates, Star Smiley, Jayne Margo-Reby, Stacie Jubal, Deb Criss, Robin Plitt, Boomslang Swampsinger.

Tips "Be open to developing your own unique style. Write well-crafted songs with unpredictable concepts, strong hooks and definitive verse melodies. New Age and World Music composers: evolve your themes and use multiculturally diverse instruments to embellish your compositions/arrangements. Don't be predictable. Experiment with instrumental fusion with jazz and/or classical themes, pop themes and international styles. Don't overproduce your demos or drown the vocals. Craft songs carefully for single-song marketing. On a 10 song album, 9 songs can be eclectic/loosely crafted, it takes only 1 carefully crafted 'radio-ready'song, with the right arrangement to get your album the exposure it needs."

◘ STEVE SATKOWSKI RECORDINGS

P.O. Box 3403, Stuart FL 34995. (772)225-3128. Web site: www.clearsoulproductions.com/stevesat kowski.html. Engineer/producer: Steven Satkowski. Record producer, recording engineer, management firm and record company. Estab. 1980. Produces 20 CDs/year. Fee derived from outright fee from recording artist or record company.

How to Contact Submit demo by mail. Unsolicited submissions are OK. Prefers CD or cassette. Does not return material. Responds in 2 weeks.

Music Mostly **classical**, **jazz** and **big band**. Produced recordings for National Public Radio and affiliates. Engineered recordings for Steve Howe, Patrick Moraz, Kenny G, and Michael Bolton.

ℕ ◙ SHU'BABY MONTEZ MUSIC

P.O. Box 28816, Philadelphia PA 19151. (215)473-5527. E-mail: schubaby@verizon.net. Web site: http://www.smm.indiegroup.com. **Contact:** Shubaby, owner. Record producer. Estab. 1986. Produces 5 Cds and 8 singles/year. Fee derived from outright fee from record company.

• Also see the listing for Shu'Baby Montez Music in the Music Publishers section of this book.

How to Contact Submit demo CD by mail. Unsolicited submissions are OK. Prefers CD with 4 songs and lyric sheet. Include SASE. Responds in 5 weeks.

Music Mostly **R&B**, **hip-hop** and **funk**. Produced "Worst of Luck" and "Down for Me" (singles by Shubaby Schuler/Mushy), recorded by Mushy; "You're Amazing," recorded by Kenny Lee on Urban Logic Records; "Promise Not to Bluff," recorded by Marlaina Valentine on Urban Logic Records, all released in 2007.

Tips "Be on time with all projects."

▨ ◘ SILVER BOW PRODUCTIONS

556 Amess St., New Westminster BC V3L 4A9 Canada. (604)523-9309. Fax: (604)523-9310. E-mail: saddlestone@shaw.ca. Web site: www.saddlestone.net. **Contact:** Candice James, Rex Howard, Grant Lucas—A&R. Record producers. Estab. 1986. Produces 16 singles, and 6 CDs/year. Fee derived from outright fee from recording artist.

• Also see the listings for Saddlestone Publishing in the Music Publishers section and Silver Bow Management in the Managers & Booking Agents section of this book.

How to Contact Prefers CD or cassette with 2 songs and lyric sheet. Does not return material. Responds in 6 weeks.

Music Mostly **country**, **pop**, and **rock**; also **gospel**, **blues** and **jazz**. Produced *Fragile-Handle With Care* (album), recorded by Razzy Bailey on SOA Records (country); *High Society* (album), written and recorded by Darrell Meyers (country); and *Man I Am* (album), written and recorded by Stang Giles (country crossover), both released 2000 on Saddlestone Records. Other artists include Rex Howard, Gerry King, Joe Lonsdale, Barb Farrell, Dorrie Alexander, Peter James, Matt Audette and Cordel James.

◼ ⊘ SOUL CANDY PRODUCTIONS
176-B Woodridge Crescent, Ottawa ON K2B 7S9 Canada. (613)820-5715. Fax: (613)820-8736. E-mail: jshakka@hotmail.com. Web site: www.jonesshakka.com. **Contact:** Jon E. Shakka, CEO. Record producer. Estab. 1988. Produces 1 album/year. Fee derived from sales royalty when song or artist is recorded.
How to Contact *Does not accept unsolicited submissions.*
Music Mostly **funk**, **rap** and **house music**; also **pop**, **ballads** and **funk-rock**. Produced *I'm My Brother's Keeper* (album), recorded by The Jon E. Shakka Project (funk rap), released 2001 on Poku Records. Other artists include Uncut Records, Double F, little rabbit, and LY.

◼ SOUND ARTS RECORDING STUDIO
8377 Westview Dr., Houston TX 77055. (713)464-GOLD. E-mail: sarsjef@aol.com. Web site: www.soundartsrecording.com. **Contact:** Jeff Wells, president. Record producer and music publisher (Earthscream Music). Estab. 1974. Produces 12 singles and 3 CDs/year. Fee derived from sales royalty when song or artist is recorded.
• Also see the listings for Earthscream Music Publishing in the Music Publishers section and Surface Records in the Record Companies section of this book.
How to Contact Submit demo by mail. Unsolicited submissions are OK. Prefers CD with 2-5 songs and lyric sheet. Does not return material. Responds in 6 weeks.
Music Mostly **pop/rock**, **country** and **blues**. Produced Texas Johnny Brown (album), written and recorded by Texas Johnny Brown on Quality (blues); and "Sheryl Crow" (single), recorded by Dr. Jeff and the Painkillers. Other artists include Tim Nichols, Perfect Strangers, B.B. Watson, Jinkies, Joe "King" Carasco (on Surface Records), Mark May (on Icehouse Records), The Barbara Pennington Band (on Earth Records), Tempest, Attitcus Finch, Tony Vega Band (on Red Onion Records), Saliva (Island Records), Earl Gillian, Blue October (Universal Records), and The Wiggles.

☑ ◯ SOUND WORKS ENTERTAINMENT PRODUCTIONS INC.
P.O. Box 7624, Charlottesville VA 22906. (434)242-2411. E-mail: mike@musicjones.com. Web site: www.musicjones.com. **Contact:** Michael E. Jones, president. Record producer, record company (Sound Works Records) and music publisher (Sound Works Music). Estab. 1989. Produces 16 singles, 2 LPs and 20 CDs/year. Fee derived from sales royalty when song or artist is recorded or outright fee from recording artist or record company.
How to Contact Submit demo package by mail. Unsolicited submissions are OK. Prefers cassette with 3-6 songs and lyric sheet. "Please include short bio and statement of goals and objectives." Does not return material. Responds in 6 weeks.
Music Mostly **country**, **folk** and **pop**; also **rock**. Produced "Lonelyville," and "Alabama Slammer" (singles), both written and recorded by Wake Eastman; and "Good Looking Loser" (single), written and recorded by Renee Rubach, all on Sound Works Records (country). Other artists include Matt Dorman, Steve Gilmore, The Tackroom Boys, The Las Vegas Philharmonic, and J.C. Clark.
Tips "Put your ego on hold. Don't take criticism personally. Advice is meant to help you grow and improve your skills as an artist/songwriter. Be professional and business-like in all your dealings."

☑ ◐ SPHERE GROUP ONE
795 Waterside Dr., Marco Island FL 34145. (239)398-6800. Fax: (239)394-9881. E-mail: spheregroupone@att.net. **Contact:** Tony Zarrella, president. Talent Manager: Janice Salvatore. Record producer, artist development and management firm. Produces 5-6 singles and 3 CDs/year. Estab. 1986.
How to Contact Submit CD/video by mail. Unsolicited submissions are OK. Prefers CD or DVD with 3-5 songs and lyric sheets. "Must include: photos, press, résumé, goals and specifics of project submitted, etc." Does not return material.
Music Mostly **pop/rock (mainstream)**, **progressive/rock**, **New Age** and **crossover country/pop**;

Record Producers

Record Producers

also **film soundtracks**. Produced "Rock to the Rescue," "Sunset At Night," "Double Trouble," "Take This Heart," "It's Our Love," and "You and I" (singles by T. Zarrella), recorded by 4 of Hearts (pop/rock) on Sphere Records and/or various labels. Other associated artists include Frontier 9, Oona Falcon, Myth, Survivor, and Wicked Lester/Kiss.

Tips "Take direction, have faith in yourself, producer and manager. Currently seeking artists/ groups incorporating various styles into a focused mainstream product. Groups with a following are a plus. Artist development is our expertise and we listen! In the pocket, exceptional songs, experienced performers necessary."

STUART AUDIO SERVICES

134 Mosher Rd., Gorham ME 04038. (207)892-0960. E-mail: js@stuartaudio.com. Web site: www.st uartaudio.com. **Contact:** John A. Stuart, producer/owner. Record producer and music publisher. Estab. 1979. Produces 5-8 CDs/year. Fee derived from sales royalty when song or artist is recorded, outright fee from recording artist or record company, or demo and consulting fees.

How to Contact *Write or call first and obtain permission to submit or to arrange a personal interview.* Prefers CD with 4 songs and lyric sheet. Include SASE. Responds in 2 months.

Music Mostly **alternative folk-rock**, **rock** and **country**; also **contemporary Christian**, **children's** and **unusual**. Produced *One of a Kind* (by various artists), recorded by Elizabeth Boss on Bosco Records (folk); *Toad Motel*, written and recorded by Rick Charrette on Fine Point Records (children's); and *Holiday Portrait*, recorded by USM Chamber Singers on U.S.M. (chorale). Other artists include Noel Paul Stookey, Beavis & Butthead (Mike Judge), Don Campbell, Jim Newton and John Angus.

STUDIO SEVEN

417 N. Virginia, Oklahoma City OK 73106. (405)236-0643. Fax: (405)236-0686. E-mail: cope@okla. net. **Contact:** Dave Copenhaver, producer. Record producer, record company (Lunacy Records) and music publisher (Lunasong Music). Estab. 1990. Produces 10 LPs and CDs/year. Fee is derived from sales royalty when song or artist is recorded or outright fee from recording artist or record company. "All projects are on a customized basis."

How to Contact *Contact first and obtain permission to submit.* Prefers CD or cassette with lyric sheet. Include SASE. Responds in 6 weeks.

Music Mostly **rock**, **jazz-blues**, **country**, and **Native American**. Produced *Hear Me* (album), recorded by Albert Aguilar, released 2006 on Lunacy Records; *The Shoe* (album), recorded by Curt Shoemaker, released 2006 on Lunacy Records; *The Road Takes the Blame* (album), recorded by Joe Merrick, released 2007 on Lunacy Records; "American Born" (single), recorded by Jeff Fenholt, released 2006; "Divinely Intoxicated" (single), recorded by Stephanie Musser, released 2006 on Passio Productions. Other artists Hinder, Megan Myers, Tessa Newman, Morris McCraven, Natchez, Ronnie & The Imods.

SWIFT RIVER PRODUCTIONS

P.O. Box 231, Gladeville TN 37071. (615)316-9479. E-mail: office@swiftrivermusic.com. Web site: www.swiftrivermusic.com. **Contact:** Andy May, producer/owner. Record producer and record company. Estab. 1979. Produces 40 singles and 4 CDs/year. Fee paid by artist or artist's management. Works with recording client to come up with budget for individual project. Provides world-class backing musicians and thorough pre-studio preparation as needed.

How to Contact *Write or call first and obtain permission to submit.* "Let us know your background, present goals and reason for contacting us so we can tell if we are able to help you. Demo should be clear and well thought out. Vocal plus guitar or piano is fine." Does not return material. Responds in up to 1 month.

Music Mostly **country**, **singer/songwriter**, **Americana** and **roots (folk, acoustic, bluegrass and rock)**; also **instrumental**. Produced *Everett Lilly & Everybody and His Brother* (album), recorded by Everett Lilly (bluegrass/classic country), released 2007; *Sweet Coyote Guitar* (album), recorded by Moe Dixon (singer-songwriter/guitar & vocals), released 2006; *Natick, There's Talk About a Fence and Look What Thoughts Will Do* (albums), by Rick Lee (folk/Americana); *Second Wind* (album), by Bill Mulroney (contemporary folk/Americana); *Dreamin' the Blues* (album), by Henry May (blues guitar); *Flyin' Fast* (album), by Brycen Fast (country), released 2003 on Swift River.

Tips "I'm interested in artists who are accomplished, self-motivated, and able to accept direction. I'm looking for music that is intelligent, creative and in some way contributes something positive. We are a production house; we accept song submissions from our production clients only. Please refer to www.swiftrivermusic.com for more information and to hear our projects."

VALTEC PRODUCTIONS

P.O. Box 6018, Santa Maria CA 93456. (805)928-8559. Web site: www.valtec.net. **Contact:** Joe Valenta, producer. Record producer. Estab. 1986. Produces 20 singles and 10 CDs/year. Fee derived from sales royalty when song or artist is recorded.

How to Contact Submit demo by mail. Unsolicited submissions are OK. Prefers CD or DVD with 3 songs and lyric or lead sheet. Send photo. Does not return material (kept on file for 2 years). Responds in 6 weeks.

Music Mostly **country**, **Christian**, **pop/AC** and **rock**.

THE WEISMAN PRODUCTION GROUP

449 N. Vista St., Los Angeles CA 90036. (323)653-0693. E-mail: parlirec@aol.com. **Contact:** Ben Weisman, owner. Record producer and music publisher (Audio Music Publishers). Estab. 1965. Produces 10 singles/year. Fee derived from sales royalty when song or artist is recorded.

- Also see the listings for Audio Music Publishers and Queen Esther Music Publishers in the Music Publishers section of this book.

How to Contact Submit demo CD by mail. Unsolicited submissions are OK. Prefers CD with 3-10 songs and lyric sheet. Include SASE. "Mention Songwriter's Market. Please make return envelope the same size as the envelopes you send material in, otherwise we cannot send everything back. Just send CD." Responds in 6 weeks.

Music Mostly **R&B**, **soul**, **dance**, and **top 40/pop**; also **gospel** and **blues**.

WESTWIRES RECORDING USA

(formerly Westwires Digital USA), 1042 Club Ave., Allentown PA 18109. (610)435-1924. E-mail: info@westwires.com. Web site: www.westwires.com. **Contact:** Wayne Becker, owner/producer. Record producer and production company. Fee derived from outright fee from record company or artist retainer.

How to Contact *Contact via e-mail for permission to submit.* "No phone calls, please." Submit demo by mail or mp3 by e-mail. Unsolicited submissions are OK. Prefers mp3 with lyrics in MS Word or Adobe PDF file format, or CD, DVD, or VHS videocassette with 3 songs and lyric sheet. Does not return material. Responds in 1 month.

Music Mostly **rock**, **R&B**, **dance**, **alternative**, **folk** and **eclectic**. Produced Ye Ren (Dimala Records), Weston (Universal/Mojo), Zakk Wylde (Spitfire Records). Other artists include Ryan Asher, Paul Rogers, Anne Le Baron, and Gary Hassay

Tips "We are interested in singer/songwriters and alternative artists living in the mid-Atlantic area. Must have steady gig schedule and established fan base."

FRANK WILLSON

P.O. Box 2297, Universal City TX 78148. (210)653-3989. E-mail: bswr18@wmconnect.com. Web site: www.bsw-records.com. **Contact:** Frank Willson, producer. Record producer, management firm (Universal Music Marketing) and record company (BSW Records/Universal Music Records).

Estab. 1987. Produces 20-25 albums/year. Fee derived from sales royalty when song or artist is recorded.

● Also see the listings for BSW Records in the Music Publishers and Record Companies sections and Universal Music Marketing in the Managers & Booking Agents section of this book.

How to Contact Submit demo package by mail. Unsolicited submissions are OK. Prefers CD with 3-4 songs and lyric sheets. Include SASE. Responds in 1 month.

Music Mostly **country**, **blues**, **jazz** and **soft rock**. Other artists include Candee Land, Dan Kimmel, Brad Lee, John Wayne, Sonny Marshall, Bobby Mountain and Crea Beal. "Visit our Web site for an up-to-date listing of artists."

◑ WLM MUSIC/RECORDING

2808 Cammie St., Durham NC 27705-2020. (919)471-3086. Fax: (919)471-4326. E-mail: wlm-musicr ecording@nc.rr.com or wlm-band@nc.rr.com. **Contact:** Watts Lee Mangum, owner. Record producer. Estab. 1980. Fee derived from outright fee from recording artist. "In some cases, an advance payment requested for demo production."

How to Contact Submit demo by mail. Unsolicited submissions are OK. Prefers CD with 2-4 songs and lyric or lead sheet (if possible). Include SASE. Responds in 6 months.

Music Mostly **country**, **country/rock** and **blues/rock**; also **pop**, **rock**, **blues**, **gospel** and **bluegrass**. Produced "911," and "Petals of an Orchid" (singles), both written and recorded by Johnny Scoggins (country); and "Renew the Love" (single by Judy Evans), recorded by Bernie Evans (country), all on Independent. Other artists include Southern Breeze Band and Heart Breakers Band.

◑ WORLD RECORDS

5798 Deer Trail Dr., Traverse City MI 49684. E-mail: jack@worldrec.org. Web site: www.worldrec.o rg. **Contact:** Jack Conners, producer. Record producer, engineer/technician and record company (World Records). Estab. 1984. Produces 1 CD/year. Fee derived from outright fee from recording artist.

How to Contact *Write first and obtain permission to submit.* Prefers CD with 1 or 2 songs. Include SASE. Responds in 6 weeks.

Music Mostly **classical**, **folk**, and **jazz**. Produced *Mahler, Orff, Collins* (album), recorded by Traverse Symphony Orchestra (classical), released 2006; *Reflections on Schubert* (album) recorded by Michael Coonrod (classical), released 2007. Other artists include Jeff Haas and The Camerata Singers.

Ⓝ ◑ ZIG PRODUCTIONS

P.O. Box 707, Hermitage TN 37076.(615)889-7105. E-mail: zig@zigworld.com. Web site: www.zig world.com. **Contact:** Billy Herzig or Wendy Mazur. Record producer. Music publisher (Thistle Hill/ BMI). Estab. 1998. "Occasionally I produce a single that is recorded separate from a full CD project." Produces 6-10 albums. Fee derived from sales royalty when song or artist is recorded and/or outright fee from recording artist. "Sometimes there are investors."

How to Contact Submit a demo by mail. Unsolicited submissions are OK. We do not return submissions.Responds only if interested.

Music Mostly **country**, **Americana**, and **rock**; also **pop**, **r&b**, and **alternative**. Produced "Ask Me to Stay" (single by King Cone/Josh McDaniel) from *Gallery*, recorded by King Cone (Texas country/ Americana). released 2007 on King Cone; "A Cure for Awkward Silence" (single), recorded by Tyler Stock (acoustic rock), released 2007 on Payday Records; "Take Me Back" (single) from *Peace, Love & Crabs*, written and recorded by Deanna Dove (folk-rock), released 2007 on Island Girl. Also produced Robbins & Jones (country), Jordan Mycoskie (country), Carla Rhodes (comedy), Four Higher (alternative), Charis Thorsell (country), Shane Mallory (country), Rachel Rodriguez (blues-rock), Jessy Daumen (country), Frankie Moreno (rock/r&b), Shawna Russell (country), and many others.

ADDITIONAL RECORD PRODUCERS

The following companies are also record producers, but their listings are found in other sections of the book. Read the listings for submission information.

Record Producers

Managers & Booking Agents

Before submitting to a manager or booking agent, be sure you know exactly what you need. If you're looking for someone to help you with performance opportunities, the booking agency is the one to contact. They can help you book shows either in your local area or throughout the country. If you're looking for someone to help guide your career, you need to contact a management firm. Some management firms may also handle booking; however, it may be in your best interest to look for a separate booking agency. A manager should be your manager—not your agent, publisher, lawyer or accountant.

MANAGERS

Of all the music industry players surrounding successful artists, managers are usually the people closest to the artists themselves. The artist manager can be a valuable contact, both for the songwriter trying to get songs to a particular artist and for the songwriter/performer. A manager and his connections can be invaluable in securing the right publishing deal or recording contract if the writer is also an artist. Getting songs to an artist's manager is yet another way to get your songs recorded, since the manager may play a large part in deciding what material his client uses. For the performer seeking management, a successful manager should be thought of as the foundation for a successful career.

The relationship between a manager and his client relies on mutual trust. A manager works as the liaison between you and the rest of the music industry, and he must know exactly what you want out of your career in order to help you achieve your goals. His handling of publicity, promotion and finances, as well as the contacts he has within the industry, can make or break your career. You should never be afraid to ask questions about any aspect of the relationship between you and a prospective manager.

Always remember that a manager works *for the artist*. A good manager is able to communicate his opinions to you without reservation, and should be willing to explain any confusing terminology or discuss plans with you before taking action. A manager needs to be able to communicate successfully with all segments of the music industry in order to get his client the best deals possible. He needs to be able to work with booking agents, publishers, lawyers and record companies.

Keep in mind that you are both working together toward a common goal: success for you and your songs. Talent, originality, professionalism and a drive to succeed are qualities that will attract a manager to an artist—and a songwriter.

BOOKING AGENTS

The function of the booking agent is to find performance venues for their clients. They usually represent many more acts than a manager does, and have less contact with their acts. A booking agent charges a commission for his services, as does a manager. Managers usually ask for a 15-20% commission on an act's earnings; booking agents usually charge around 10%. In the area of managers and booking agents, more successful acts can negotiate lower percentage deals than the ones set forth above.

SUBMITTING MATERIAL TO MANAGERS & BOOKING AGENTS

The firms listed in this section have provided information about the types of music they work with and the types of acts they represent. You'll want to refer to the Category Index on page 382 to find out which companies deal with the type of music you write, and the Geographic Index at the back of the book to help you locate companies near where you live. Then determine whether they are open to your level of experience (see A Sample Listing Decoded on page 11). Each listing also contains submission requirements and information about what items to include in a press kit and will also specify whether the company is a management firm or a booking agency. Remember that your submission represents you as an artist, and should be as organized and professional as possible.

Icons

For More Info

For more instructional information on the listings in this book, including explanations of symbols (N ✓ ✗ ⚘ ✿ 🌐 ◯ ◯ ◯ ⊘), read the article *Songwriter's Market: How Do I Use It?* on page 7.

ADDITIONAL MANAGERS & BOOKING AGENTS

There are **more managers & booking agents** located in other sections of the book! On page 256 use the list of Additional Managers & Booking Agents to find listings within other sections who are also managers/booking agents.

Managers & Agents

☒ ☑ A&A MERSIER TRUCKING ENTERTAINMENT

P.O. Box 12024, Fort Wayne IN 46862-2024. (260)348-2883. Fax: (260)747-1688. **Contact:** Leonard Mersier, owner. Management firm. Estab. 2001. Represents local and regional individual artists and groups; currently handles 6 acts. Recieves 10-20% commission. Reviews material for acts.

How to Contact "Call or submit demo." Prefers CD/CDR. Press kit should include a demo with at least 3-5 songs, cover lyric sheet and a photo. Does not return material. Responds only if interested.

Music Mostly **R&B**, **rap**, and **gospel**; also **jazz**, **blues**, and **hip-hop**. Does not want heavy metal, rock or country. Works primarily with the Elite Untouchables and Too Real. Other acts include Nathan Johnson (R&B singer), Richard Harris (rap artist) and Melinda Silva (R&B, rap singer.)

Tips "Keep your dreams alive, believe in yourself, know who you are and never give up because we won't let you."

☑ AIR TIGHT MANAGEMENT

115 West Rd., P.O. Box 113, Winchester Center CT 06094. (860)738-9139. Fax: (860)738-9135. E-mail: mainoffice@airtightmanagement.com. Web site: www.airtightmanagement.com. **Contact:** Jack Forchette, president. Management firm. Estab. 1969. Represents individual artists, groups or songwriters from anywhere; currently handles 8 acts. Receives 15-20% commission. Reviews material for acts.

How to Contact *Write e-mail first and obtain permission to submit.* Prefers CD or VHS videocassette. If seeking management, press kit should include photos, bio and recorded material. "Follow up with a fax or e-mail, not a phone call." Does not return material. Responds in 1 month.

Music Mostly **rock**, **country** and **jazz**. Current acts include P.J. Loughran (singer/songwriter), Johnny Colla (songwriter/producer, and guitarist/songwriter for Huey Lewis and the News), Jason Scheff (lead singer/songwriter for the group "Chicago"), Gary Burr (Nashville songwriter/producer), Nathan East (singer/songwriter/bassist—Eric Clapton, Michael Jackson, Madonna, 4-Play and others), Rocco Prestia (legendary R&B musician, "Tower of Power" bassist), Steve Oliver (contemporary jazz/pop songwriter/guitarist/vocalist, recording artist), Kal David (blues), Warren Hill (saxophonist/recording artist), and Harvey Mason (percussionist/composer).

☒ ☑ ALERT MUSIC INC.

51 Hillsview Ave., Toronto ON M6P 1J4 Canada. (416)364-4200. Fax: (416)364-8632. E-mail: contact@alertmusic.com. Web site: www.alertmusic.com. **Contact:** W. Tom Berry, president. Management firm, record company and recording artist. Represents local and regional individual artists and groups; currently handles 5 acts. Reviews material for acts.

How to Contact *Write first and obtain permission to submit.* Prefers CD. If seeking management, press kit should include finished CD, photo, press clippings and bio. Include SASE.

Music All types. Works primarily with bands and singer/songwriters. Current acts include Holly Cole (jazz vocalist), Kim Mitchell (rock singer/songwriter), Michael Kaeshammer (pianist/singer), and Roxanne Potvin (blues, singer/songwriter).

☑ ☑ ALL STAR MANAGEMENT

3142 Rainier Ave., Columbus OH 43231-3145. (614)794-2102. Fax: (614)794-2103. E-mail: jisimpson_3498@yahoo.com. **Contact:** John or Mary Simpson, owners. Management firm. Estab. 1980. Represents individual artists, groups and songwriters from anywhere; currently handles 2 acts. Receives 20% commission. Reviews material for acts.

How to Contact Submit demo package by mail. Unsolicited submissions are OK. Prefers CD with 3 songs and lyric or lead sheet. If seeking management, press kit should include CD and/or video with 3 songs, bio, 8×10 photo or any information or articles written about yourself or group, and video if you have one. Does not return material. Responds in 2 months.

Music Mostly **country** and **pop rock**. Works primarily with bands and singers/songwriters. Current acts include Debbie Robins (singer/songwriter, Christian contemporary), and Leon Seiter (country singer/songwriter).

☑ MICHAEL ALLEN ENTERTAINMENT DEVELOPMENT
P.O. Box 111510, Nashville TN 37222. (615)754-0059. E-mail: gmichaelallen@comcast.net. Web site: www.gmichaelallen.com. **Contact:** Michael Allen. Management firm and public relations. Represents individual artists, groups and songwriters; currently handles 2 acts. Receives 15-25% commission. Reviews material for acts.
How to Contact Submit demo package by mail. Unsolicited submissions are OK. Prefers CD/DVD with 3 songs and lyric or lead sheets. If seeking management, press kit should include photo, bio, press clippings, letter and CD/DVD. Include SASE. Responds in 3 months.
Music Mostly **country** and **pop**; also **rock** and **gospel**. Works primarily with vocalists and bands. Currently doing public relations for Sheri Pedigo, Amy Jordyn, Roadmark, and Randy Roberts.

☑ ☐ AMERICAN BANDS MANAGEMENT
3300 South Gessner, Suite 207, Houston TX 77063. (713)785-3700. Fax: (713)785-4641. E-mail: johnblomstrom@aol.com. President: John Blomstrom . Sr. Vice President: Cheryl Byrd. Management firm. Estab. 1973. Represents groups from anywhere; currently handles 3 acts. Receives 15-25% commission. Reviews material for acts.
How to Contact Submit demo package by mail prior to making phone contact. Unsolicited submissions are OK. Prefers cassette or CD. If seeking management, press kit should include cover letter, bio, photo, demo tape/CD, press clippings, video, resume and professional references with names and numbers. Does not return material. Responds in 1 month.
Music Mostly **rock (all forms)** and **modern country**. Works primarily with bands. Current acts include Captain Pink (Motown), Vince Vance & the Valiants (show band) and Rachel (guitarist/singer/modern folk).

☒ ☑ ANGEL GOMEZ MUSIC
21742 Nowlin Ave., Dearborn MI 48124. (313)274-7000. Fax: (313)274-9255. E-mail: angelgomezmusic@aol.com. Web site: www.angelgomezmusic.com. **Contact:** Angel Gomez, president. Management firm. Estab. 1979. Represents local and international individual artists, groups and songwriters; currently handles 3 acts. Receives 15-20% commission. Reviews material for acts.
How to Contact *Write first and obtain permission to submit.* Prefers CD/CDR or DVD of performance with 3-5 songs. If seeking management, include photo, tape/CD, bio, cover letter, press clippings and itinerary of dates. Does not return material. Responds in 2 months.
Music Mostly **rock**, **pop** and **top 40**; also **funk**. Works primarily with individual artists, groups and songwriters. Current artists include Kat McAllister (pop T-40), The Rev. Right Time and the First Cuzins of Funk (new funk) and Bridge (rock).

☑ ☑ BILL ANGELINI ENTERPRISES/BOOKYOUREVENT.COM
(formerly Management Plus), P.O. Box 132, Seguin TX 78155. (210)226-8450. Fax: (210)223-3251. E-mail: bill@bookyourevent.com. Web site: www.bookyourevent.com. **Contact:** Bill Angelini, owner. Management firm and booking agency. Estab. 1980. Represents individual artists and groups from anywhere; currently handles 6 acts. Receives 10-15% commission. Reviews material for acts.
How to Contact Submit demo package by mail. Unsolicited submissions are OK. Prefers CD, VHS videocassette and bio. If seeking management, press kit should include pictures, bio, résumé and discography. Does not return material. Responds in 1 month.
Music Mostly **Latin American**, **Tejano** and **international**; also **Norteno** and **country**. Current acts include Jay Perez (Tejano), Ram Herrera (Tejano), Michael Salgado (Tejano), Flaco Jimenez (Tex-Mex), Electric Cowboys (tex-mex), Los Palominos (Tejano), and Grupo Vida (Tejano).

✒ APODACA PROMOTIONS INC.

717 E. Tidwell Rd., Houston TX 77022. (713)691-6677. Fax: (713)692-9298. E-mail: houston@apoda capromotions.com. Web site: www.apodacapromotions.com. Manager: Domingo A. Barrera. Management firm, booking agency, music publisher (Huina Publishing, Co. Inc.). Estab. 1991. Represents songwriters and groups from anywhere; currently handles 40 acts. Receives 15% commission. Reviews material for acts.

How to Contact Submit demo package by mail. Unsolicited submissions are OK. Prefers CD and lyric and lead sheet. Include SASE. Responds in 2 months.

Music Mostly **international** and **Hispanic**; also **rock**. Works primarily with bands and songwriters. Current acts include Bobby Pulido (Tex-Mex music) Kubia Kings, Alicia Billarreal, Conjunto Atardecer, Bobby Pulido, El Poder Del Norte, Jenniffer Pena, and Ninelconde.

✒ ARTIST REPRESENTATION AND MANAGEMENT

1257 Arcade St., St. Paul MN 55106. (651)483-8754. Fax: (651)776-6338. E-mail: ra@armentertainm ent.com. Web site: www.armentertainment.com. **Contact:** Roger Anderson, agent/manager. Management firm and booking agency. Estab. 1983. Represents artists from anywhere; currently handles 10 acts. Receives 15% commission. Reviews material for acts.

How to Contact Submit CD and video by mail. Unsolicited submissions are OK. Please include minimum 3 songs. If seeking management, references, current schedule, bio, photo, press clippings should also be included. "Priority is placed on original artists with product who are currently touring." Does not return material. Responds only if interested within 30 days.

Music Mostly **melodic rock**. Current acts include Warrant, Firehouse, Jesse Lang, Scarlet Haze, Head East, Frank Hannon of Tesla, LA Guns, Dokken, and Bret Michaels of Poison.

✒ BACCHUS GROUP PRODUCTIONS, LTD.

5701 N. Sheridan Rd., Suite 8-U, Chicago IL 60660. (773)334-1532. E-mail: bacchusgrp@uron.cc. Web site: www.BacchusGroup.com. **Contact:** D. Maximilian, Managing Director and Executive Producer. Director of Marketing: M. Margarida Rainho. Management firm and record producer (D. Maximilian). Estab. 1990. Represents individual artists or groups from anywhere; currently handles 9 acts. Receives 15-25% commission. Reviews material for acts.

How to Contact *Call or e-mail for permission to submit. Does not accept unsolicited submissions.*

Music Mostly **pop**, **R&B/soul**, and **jazz**; also **Latin** and **world beat**. Works primarily with singer/ songwriters, composers, arrangers, bands and orchestras. "Visit our Web site for current acts."

ⓃⒷ BACKSTREET BOOKING

700 West Pete Rose Way, Cincinnati OH 45203. (513)542-9544. Fax: (513)542-9545. E-mail: info@b ackstreetbooking.com. Web site: www.backstreetbooking.com. **Contact:** James Sfarnas, president. Booking agency. Estab. 1992. Represents individual artists and groups from anywhere; currently handles 30 acts. Receives 10-15% commission. Reviews material for acts.

How to Contact *Call first and obtain permission to submit.* Accepts only signed acts with product available nationally.

Music Mostly **niche-oriented music** and **rock**. Current acts include Acumen (progressive rock group), Niacin (fusion), Mike Keneally Band (progressive rock), Cab (jazz fusion), Alex Skolnick Trio (progressive jazz), Johnny Combs—The Man in Black (Johnny Cash tribute), and The Van Dells (rock).

Tips "Build a base on your own."

✒ BARNARD MANAGEMENT SERVICES (BMS)

228 Main St., Suite 3, Venice CA 90291. (310)399-8886. Fax: (310)450-0470. E-mail: bms@barnardu s.com. **Contact:** Russell Barnard, president. Management firm. Estab. 1979. Represents artists,

groups and songwriters; currently handles 2 acts. Receives 10-20% commission. Reviews material for acts.

How to Contact *Write first and obtain permission to submit.* Prefers CD with 3-10 songs and lead sheet. Artists may submit DVD (15-30 minutes) by permission only. If seeking management, press kit should include cover letter, bio, photo, demo tape/CD, lyric sheets, press clippings, video and résumé. Does not return material. Responds in 2 months.

Music Mostly **country crossover**, **blues**, **country**, **R&B**, **rock** and **soul**. Current acts include Mark Shipper (songwriter/author) and Sally Rose (R&B band).

Tips "Semi-produced demos are of little value. Either save the time and money by submitting material 'in the raw,' or do a finished production version."

☑ BIG J PRODUCTIONS

2516 S. Sugar Ridge, Laplace LA 70068. (504)652-2645. **Contact:** Frankie Jay, agent. Booking agency. Estab. 1968. Represents individual artists, groups and songwriters; currently handles over 50 acts. Receives 15-25% commission. Reviews material for acts.

How to Contact *Call first and obtain permission to submit (office hours Monday-Friday: noon-5 pm).* Prefers cassette or VHS videocassette with 3-6 songs and lyric or lead sheet. "It would be best for an artist to lip-sync to a prerecorded track. The object is for someone to see how an artist would perform more than simply assessing song content." Artists seeking management should include pictures, biography, tape or CD and video. Does not return material. Responds in 2 weeks.

Music Mostly **rock**, **pop** and **R&B**. Works primarily with groups with self-contained songwriters. Current acts include Zebra (original rock group), Crowbar (heavy metal) and Kyper (original dance).

☑ ☑ BLANK & BLANK

116 West Market St., 1st Floor, Rear, West Chester PA 19382. (610)692-9300. Fax: (610)692-9301. **Contact:** E. Robert Blank, manager. Management firm. Represents individual artists and groups. Reviews material for acts.

How to Contact *Contact first and obtain permission to submit.* Prefers CD, DVD, or videocassette. If seeking management, press kit should include cover letter, demo tape/CD and video. Does not return material.

☑ THE BLUE CAT AGENCY

E-mail: bluecat_agency@yahoo.com. Web site: www.geocities.com/bluecat_agency. **Contact:** Karen Kindig, owner/agent. Management firm and booking agency. Estab. 1989. Represents individual artists and/or groups from anywhere; currently handles 2 acts. Receives 10-15% commission. Reviews material for acts.

How to Contact *E-mail only for permission to submit.* Prefers cassette or CD. If seeking management, press kit should include, CD or tape, bio, press clippings and photo. SASE. Responds in 2 months.

Music Mostly **rock/pop** "en espanol" and **jazz/latin jazz**. Works primarily with bands (established performers only). Current acts include Kai Eckhardt, Alejandro Santos, Ania Paz, Gabriel Rosati.

☑ BOUQUET-ORCHID ENTERPRISES

P.O. Box 1335, Norcross GA 30091. (770)339-9088. **Contact:** Bill Bohannon, president. Management firm, booking agency, music publisher (Orchid Publishing/BMI) and record company (Bouquet Records). Represents individuals and groups; currently handles 3 acts. Receives 10-15% commission. Reviews material for acts.

• Also see the listing for Orchid Publishing in the Music Publishers section of this book.

How to Contact Submit demo package by mail. Unsolicited submissions are OK. Prefers cassette, CD or videocassette with 3-5 songs, song list and lyric sheet. Include brief résumé. If seeking management, press kit should include current photograph, 2-3 media clippings, description of act, and background information on act. Include SASE. Responds in 1 month.

Music Mostly **country**, **rock** and **top 40/pop**; also **gospel** and R&B. Works primarily with vocalists and groups. Current acts include Susan Spencer, Jamey Wells, Adam Day and the Bandoleers.

☐ BREAD & BUTTER PRODUCTIONS

P.O. Box 1539, Wimberley TX 78676. (512)301-7117. E-mail: sgladson@gmail.com. **Contact:** Steve Gladson, managing partner. Management firm and booking agency. Estab. 1969. Represents individual artists, songwriters and groups from anywhere; currently handles 6 acts. Receives 10-20% commission. Reviews material for acts.

How to Contact Submit demo package by mail. Unsolicited submissions OK. Prefers cassette, videocassette or CD and lyric sheet. If seeking management, press kit should include cover letter, demo tape/CD, lyric sheets, press clippings, video, résumé, picture and bio. Does not return material. Responds in 1 month.

Music Mostly **alternative rock**, **country** and **R&B**; also **classic rock**, **folk** and **Americana**. Works primarily with singer/songwriters and original bands. Current acts include Lou Cabaza (songwriter/producer/manager), Duck Soup (band) and Gaylan Ladd (songwriter/singer).

Tips ''Remember why you are in this biz. The art comes first.''

☑ BROTHERS MANAGEMENT ASSOCIATES

141 Dunbar Ave., Fords NJ 08863. (732)738-0880. Fax: (732)738-0970. E-mail: bmaent@yahoo.com. Web site: www.bmaent.com. **Contact:** Allen A. Faucera, president. Management firm and booking agency. Estab. 1972. Represents artists, groups and songwriters; currently handles 25 acts. Receives 15-20% commission. Reviews material for acts.

How to Contact *Write first and obtain permission to submit.* Prefers CD or DVD with 3-6 songs and lyric sheets. Include photographs and résumé. If seeking management, include photo, bio, tape and return envelope in press kit. Include SASE. Responds in 2 months.

Music Mostly **pop**, **rock**, **MOR** and **R&B**. Works primarily with vocalists and established groups. Current acts include Nils Lofgren and Danny Federici.

Tips ''Submit very commercial material—make demo of high quality.''

☑ CIRCUIT RIDER TALENT & MANAGEMENT CO.

123 Walton Ferry Rd., Hendersonville TN 37075. (615)824-1947. Fax: (615)264-0462. E-mail: dotwool@bellsouth.net. **Contact:** Linda S. Dotson, president. Consultation firm, booking agency and music publisher (Channel Music, Cordial Music, Dotson & Dotson Music Publishers, Shalin Music Co.). Represents individual artists, songwriters and actors; currently handles 10 acts. Works with a large number of recording artists, songwriters, actors, producers. (Includes the late multi-Grammy-winning producer/writer Skip Scarborough.) Receives 10-15% commission (union rates). Reviews material for acts (free of charge).

How to Contact *Write or call first and obtain permission to submit.* Prefers cassette or videocassette with 3 songs and lyric sheet. If seeking consultation, press kit should include bio, cover letter, résumé, lyric sheets if original songs, photo and tape with 3 songs. Videocassettes required of artist's submissions. Include SASE. Responds in 2 months.

Music Mostly **Latin blues**, **pop**, **country** and **gospel**; also **R&B** and **comedy**. Works primarily with vocalists, special concerts, movies and TV. Current acts include Razzy Bailey (award winning blues artist/writer), Clint Walker (actor/recording artist), Ben Colder (comedy/novelty), and Freddy Weller (formerly Paul Revere & The Raiders/hit songwriter).

Tips ''Artists, have your act together. Have a full press kit, videos and be professional. Attitudes

Managers & Agents

are a big factor in my agreeing to work with you (no egotists). This is a business, and we will be building your career.''

◧ CLASS ACT PRODUCTIONS/MANAGEMENT

P.O. Box 55252, Sherman Oaks CA 91413. (818)980-1039. E-mail: pkimmel@gr8gizmo.com. **Contact:** Peter Kimmel, president. Management firm. Estab. 1985. Currently handles 2 acts. Receives 20% commission. Reviews material for acts.

How to Contact Submit demo package by mail. Unsolicited submissions are OK. Include CD, cover letter, bio, and lyric sheets (essential) in press kit. Include SASE. Responds in 1 month.

Music All styles. Current acts include Terpsichore (cyber dance/pop), Don Cameron (pop/rock).

Tips ''We also operate Sound Image Video www.soundimagevideo.com (video production company).''

◖ CLOCKWORK ENTERTAINMENT MANAGEMENT AGENCY

227 Concord St., Haverhill MA 01830. (978)373-5677. E-mail: wjm227@hotmail.com. **Contact:** William J. Macek, esq., entertainment attorney, president. Management firm. Represents groups and songwriters throughout New England with mastered product who are looking for label deals and licensing in US and internationally. Fee is negotiated individually; currently handles multiple acts. Commissions vary. Reviews material for acts.

How to Contact Submit demo package by mail. Unsolicited submissions are OK. Prefers CD or cassette with 3-12 songs. ''Also submit promotion and cover letter with interesting facts about yourself.'' If seeking management, press kit should include cover letter, tape or CD, photo, bio and press clippings. Include SASE. Responds in 1 month.

Music Mostly **rock (all types)** and **top 40/pop**. Works primarily with bar bands and original acts.

☑ ◖ CLOUSHER PRODUCTIONS

P.O. Box 1191, Mechanicsburg PA 17055. (717)766-7644. Fax: (717)766-1490. E-mail: cpinfo@msn.com. Web site: www.clousherentertainment.com. **Contact:** Fred Clousher, owner. Booking agency and production company. Estab. 1972. Represents groups from anywhere; currently handles over 100 acts.

How to Contact Submit demo package by mail. Unsolicited submissions are OK. Prefers VHS videocassette or DVD. If seeking management, press kit should include press clippings, testimonials, credits, glossies, video demo tape, references, cover letter, résumé and bio. Does not return material. ''Performer should check back with us!''

Music Mostly **country**, **old rock** and **ethnic** (German, Hawaiian, etc.); also **dance bands** (regional) and **classical musicians**. ''We work mostly with country, old time R&R, regional variety dance bands, tribute acts, and all types of variety acts.'' Current acts include Jasmine Morgan (country/pop vocalist), Robin Right (country vocalist) and Royal Hawaiians (ethnic Hawaiian group).

Tips ''The songwriters we work with are entertainers themselves, which is the aspect we deal with. They usually have bands or do some sort of show, either with tracks or live music. We engage them for stage shows, dances, strolling, etc. We DO NOT review songs you've written, publish music, or submit performers to recording companies for contracts. We strictly set up live performances for them.''

◖ CONCEPT 2000 INC.

P.O. Box 2950, Columbus OH 43216-2950. (614)276-2000. Fax: (614)275-0163. E-mail: info2k@concept2k.com. Web site: www.concept2k.com. **Florida office:** P.O. Box 2070, Largo FL 33779-2070. (727)585-2922. Fax: (727)585-3835. **Contact:** Brian Wallace, president. Management firm and booking agency. Estab. 1981. Represents international individual artists, groups and songwriters; currently handles 4 acts. Receives 20% commission. Reviews material for acts.

How to Contact Submit demo by mail. Unsolicited submissions are OK. Prefers cassette with 4 songs. If seeking management, include demo tape, press clips, photo and bio. Does not return material. Responds in 2 weeks.

Music Mostly **country**, **gospel** and **pop**; also **jazz**, **R&B** and **soul**. Current acts include Bryan Hitch (contemporary gospel), Shades of Grey (R&B/soul), Dwight Lenox (show group) and Gene Walker (jazz).

Tips "Send quality songs with lyric sheets. Production quality is not necessary."

▣ CONCERTED EFFORTS, INC./FOGGY DAY MUSIC

P.O. Box 600099, Newtonville MA 02460. (617)969-0810. Fax: (617)969-6761. Web site: www.conc ertedefforts.com. Owner: Paul Kahn. Management firm, booking agency and music publisher (Foggy Day Music). Represents individual artists, groups and songwriters from anywhere. Commission varies. Reviews material for acts.

How to Contact Submit demo package by mail. Unsolicited submissions are OK "but call first!" Prefers CD, will accept cassette, with lyric sheet. "No management submissions." Does not return material.

Music Mostly **folk**, **country**, and **rock**; also **world music**, **zydeco**, and **blues**. Current acts include Luther Johnson (blues singer), Holmes Brothers, Roseanne Cash and Orchestra Baobab.

Tips "Simple recorded demo is OK, with lyrics."

☑ ▣ COUNTRYWIDE PRODUCERS

2466 Wildon Dr., York PA 17403. (717)741-2658. E-mail: cwpent@wmconnect.com. **Contact:** Bob Englar, president. Booking agency. Represents individuals and groups; currently handles 8 acts. Receives 15% commission. Reviews material for acts.

How to Contact Query or submit demo package by mail. Unsolicited submissions are OK. If seeking management, press kit should include photo and demo tape. Include SASE. Responds in 1 week.

Music Bluegrass, **blues**, **classical**, and **country**; also **folk**, **gospel**, **polka**, **rock (light),** and **top 40/pop**. Works primarily with show bands. Current acts include The Walls of Time (bluegrass), Shilha Ridge (bluegrass) and Iron Ridge (bluegrass).

☐ STEPHEN COX PROMOTIONS & MANAGEMENT

6708 Mammoth Ave., Van Nuys CA 91405. (818)377-4530. Fax: (818)782-5305. E-mail: stephencox @earthlink.net. **Contact:** Stephen Cox, president. Management firm. Estab. 1993. Represents individual artists, groups or songwriters from anywhere; currently handles 5 acts. Receives 15% commission. Reviews material for acts.

How to Contact *Call first and obtain permission to submit.* Prefers CD. If seeking management, press kit should include biographies, performance history and radio play. "Include a clear definition of goals in a thoughtful presentation." Include SASE. Responds in 2 weeks.

Music Mostly **rock**, **New Age/world** and **alternative**; also **blues**, **folk** and **progressive**. Works primarily with bands. Current acts include Joe Sherbanee (jazz), Val Ewell & Pulse (blues rock), Paul Micich & Mitch Espe (New Age/jazz), Covet (metal) and Jill Cohn (folk rock).

Tips "Establish goals based on research, experience and keep learning about the music business. Start the business as though it will always be you as an independent. Establish a foundation before considering alternative commitments. We aim to educate and consult to a level that gives an artist the freedom of choice to choose whether to go to the majors etc., or retain independence. Remember, promote, promote and promote some more. Always be nice to people, treat them as you would wish to be treated."

☐ D&R ENTERTAINMENT

302 Tanglewood Dr., Broken Bow OK 74728. Phone/fax: (580)584-9429. **Contact:** Don Walton, president. Management firm. Estab. 1985. Represents individual artists from anywhere; currently

handles 2 acts. Receives 15% commission. Reviews material for acts. Also reviews for other country singers.

How to Contact Submit demo package by mail. Unsolicited submissions are OK. Prefers CD, cassette, or videocassette, with lyric and lead sheet. If seeking management, press kit should include brief background of artist, videotape of performance, cover letter, resume, photo, press clippings, and cassette or CD. "Indicate whether you have any financial or prospective financial backing." Does not return material. Responds in 3 months.

Music Mostly **contemporary Christian**; also **country** and **pop**. Works primarily with young beginning singers. Current acts include Kristi Reed (positive country) and Thomas Wells (contemporary Christian).

Tips "I need songs (country) that would fit a young adult singer. In other words no drinking, cheating, marrying songs. A pretty tough choice. Also Christian contemporary songs."

DAS COMMUNICATIONS, LTD.

83 Riverside Dr., New York NY 10024. (212)877-0400. Fax: (212)595-0176. Management firm. Estab. 1975. Represents individual artists, groups and producers from anywhere; currently handles 25 acts. Receives 20% commission.

How to Contact *Does not accept unsolicited submissions.*

Music Mostly **rock**, **pop**, **R&B**, **alternative** and **hip-hop**. Current acts include Joan Osborne (rock), Wyclef Jean (hip-hop), Black Eyed Peas (hip-hop), John Legend (R&B), Spin Doctors (rock), The Bacon Brothers (rock).

DCA PRODUCTIONS

676 9th Ave., #252A, New York NY 10036. (212)245-2063. Fax: (212)245-2367. Web site: www.dcaproductions.com. **Contact:** Suzanne Perotta, office manager. President: Daniel Abrahamsen. Vice President: Geraldine Abrahamsen. Management firm. Estab. 1975. Represents individual artists, groups and songwriters from anywhere; currently handles 14 acts.

How to Contact If seeking management, press kit should include cover letter, bio, photo, demo tape/CD and video. Prefers cassette or DVD with 2 songs. "All materials are reviewed and kept on file for future consideration. Does not return material. We respond only if interested."

Music Mostly **acoustic**, **rock** and **mainstream**; also **cabaret** and **theme**. Works primarily with acoustic singer/songwriters, top 40 or rock bands. Current acts include Andjam (soulful R&B), Lorna Bracewell (singer/songwriter), Lisa Bouchelle (singer/songwriter), Gabrielle (singer/songwriter), and 1910 Fruitgum Company (oldies band). Visit our Web site for a current roster of acts.

Tips "Please do not call for a review of material."

✓ THE EDWARD DE MILES COMPANY

10573 W. Pico Blvd., #352, Los Angeles CA 90064-2348. Phone: (310)948-9652. Fax: (310)474-7705. E-mail: info@edmsahara.com. Web site: www.edmsahara.com. **Contact:** Edward de Miles, president. Management firm, booking agency, entertainment/sports promoter and TV/radio broadcast producer. Estab. 1984. Represents film, television, radio and musical artists; currently handles 15 acts. Receives 10-20% commission. Reviews material for acts. Regional operations in Chicago, Dallas, Houston and Nashville through marketing representatives. Licensed A.F. of M. booking agent.

- Also see listings for Edward De Miles in the Music Publishers and Record Producers sections, and Sahara Records and Filmworks Entertainment in the Record Companies section of this book.

How to Contact *Does not accept unsolicited materials.* Prefers CD with 3-5 songs, 8×10 b&w photo, bio and lyric sheet. "Copyright all material before submitting." If seeking management, include cover letter, bio, demo CD with 3-5 songs, 8×10 b&w photo, lyric sheet, press clippings and video if available in press kit. Include SASE. Does not return material. Responds in 1 month.

Music Mostly **country, dance, R&B/soul, rock, top 40/pop** and **urban contemporary**; also looking for material for **television, radio and film** productions. Works primarily with dance bands and vocalists. Current acts include Steve Lynn (R&B/dance), Multiple Choice (rap) and Devon Edwards (jazz).

Tips "Performers need to be well prepared with their presentations (equipment, showmanship a must)."

N ⚡ ☑ DIVINE INDUSTRIES

(formerly Gangland Artists), Unit 191, 101-1001 W. Broadway, Vancouver BC V6H 4E4 Canada. Fax: (604)737-3602. E-mail: divine@divineindustries.com. Web site: www.divineindustries.com. **Contact:** Allen Moy. Management firm, production house and music publisher. Estab. 1985. Represents artists and songwriters; currently handles 5 acts. Reviews material for acts.

How to Contact *Write first and obtain permission to submit.* Prefers CD or MP3 with lyric sheet. "Videos are not entirely necessary for our company. It is certainly a nice touch. If you feel your audio cassette is strong—send the video upon later request. Something wildly creative and individual will grab our attention." Does not return material. Responds in 2 months.

Music Rock, pop, and **roots**. Works primarily with rock/left-of-center folk show bands. Current acts include 54-40 (rock/pop), Tom Wilson (folk rock), Chin (roots), Ridley Bent, Barney Bentall, John Mann (of Spirit of the West).

N ☑ COL. BUSTER DOSS PRESENTS

341 Billy Goat Hill Rd., Winchester TN 37398. (931)649-2577. Fax: (615)649-2732. E-mail: cbd@vall net.com. Web site: www.stardustcountrymusic.com. **Contact:** Col. Buster Doss, producer. Management firm, booking agency, record company (Stardust Records), record producer and music publisher (Buster Doss Music/BMI). Estab. 1959. Represents individual artists, groups, songwriters and shows; currently handles 14 acts. Receives 15% commission. Reviews material for acts.

How to Contact *Write first and obtain permission to submit.* Prefers cassette with 2-4 songs and lyric sheet. If seeking management, press kit should include demo, photos, video if available and bio. Include SASE. Responds back on day received.

Music Mostly **country, gospel** and **progressive**. Works primarily with show and dance bands, single acts and package shows. Current acts include "Rooster" Quantrell, Linda Wunder, The Border Raiders, "Bronco" Buck Cody, Jerri Arnold, Julie Taylor, Cindy Lee, John Hamilton, Brant Miller, Troy Cooker, and Tennessee Bill Foster.

☑ ◯ JOHN ECKERT ENTERTAINMENT CONSULTANTS

(formerly Pro Talent Consultants), 7723 Cora Dr., Lucerne CA 95458. (707)349-1809 or (310)367-5448 (Mar Vista/Beverly Hills, CA). E-mail: pro_talent_artists@yahoo.com. **Contact:** John Eckert, coordinator. Management firm and booking agency. Estab. 1979. Represents individual artists and groups; currently handles 12 acts. Receives 15% commission. Reviews material for acts.

How to Contact Submit demo package by mail. Unsolicited submissions are OK. "We prefer CD (4 songs). Submit videocassette with live performance only." If seeking management, press kit should include an 8×10 photo, a cassette or CD of at least 4-6 songs, a bio on group/artist, references, cover letter, press clippings, video and business card, or a phone number with address. Does not return material. Responds in 5 weeks.

Music Mostly **country, country/pop** and **rock**. Works primarily with vocalists, show bands, dance bands, and bar bands. Current acts include Ronny and the Daytonas (pop/rock-top 40 band), The Royal Guardsmen (pop/rock/top 40), Gary Lewis & the Playboys (top 40), Question Mark and the Mysterians (top 40 band), and Andy Pratt (vocalist).

Managers & Agents

☒ ◯ THE ELLIS INTERNATIONAL TALENT AGENCY

5617 W. Melvina, Milwaukee WI 53216. (414)444-3385. **Contact:** Darnell Ellis, CEO/president. Management firm, booking agency, music publisher (Ellis Island Music/ASCAP) record company (Safire Records) and record producer (Darnell Ellis). Estab. 1997. Represents individual artists, groups and songwriters from anywhere—*emphasis on female acts*; currently handles 2 acts. Receives 15-20% commission. Reviews material for acts.

 • Also see the listing for Safire Records in the Record Companies section of this book.

How to Contact Submit demo by mail. Unsolicited submissions are OK. Prefers CD or DVD with 4-6 songs and press kit. If seeking management, press kit should include cassette tape or CD with 4-6 songs (demo), 8×10 photo, video tape and reviews. Does not return material. Responds in 6 weeks. "We will respond only if we are interested."

Music Mostly **country**, **pop**, **mainstream pop**, **rock** (all styles)—*emphasis on female acts*— and anything else except rap and hip-hop. Works primarily with singers, singer/songwriters, songwriters and bands. Current acts include Tracy Beck (acoustic, roots, blues, alt. country, pop, swing).

◯ SCOTT EVANS PRODUCTIONS

P.O. Box 814028, Hollywood FL 33081-4028. (954)963-4449. E-mail: evansprod@aol.com. Web site: www.theentertainmentmall.com. **Contact:** Ted Jones, new artists, or Jeanne K., Internet marketing and sales. Management firm and booking agency. Estab. 1979. Represents local, regional or international individual artists, groups, songwriters, comedians, novelty acts and dancers; currently handles over 200 acts. Receives 10-50% commission. Reviews material for acts.

How to Contact New artists can make submissions through the 'auditions' link located on the Web site. Unsolicited submissions are OK. "Please be sure that all submissions are copyrighted and not your original copy as we do not return material."

Music Mostly **pop**, **R&B** and **Broadway**. Deals with "all types of entertainers; no limitations." Current acts include Scott Evans and Company (variety song and dance), Dorit Zinger (female vocalist), Jeff Geist, Actors Repertory Theatre, Entertainment Express, Perfect Parties, Joy Deco (dance act), Flashback 2000 Revue (musical song and dance), Everybody Salsa (Latin song and dance) and Around the World (international song and dance).

Tips "Submit a neat, well put together, organized press kit."

◯ EXCLESISA BOOKING AGENCY

716 Windward Rd., Jackson MS 39206. (601)366-0220. E-mail: exclesis@bellsouth.net. Web site: www.exclesisa-booking.com. **Contact:** Roy and Esther Wooten, booking managers/owners. Booking agency. Estab. 1989. Represents groups from anywhere; currently handles 9 acts. Receives 15% commission. Reviews material for acts.

How to Contact *Call first and obtain permission to submit.* Submit demo package by mail. Unsolicited submissions are OK. Prefers CD or videocassette. If seeking management, press kit should include CD or cassette, videocassette, pictures, address and telephone contact ,and bio. Does not return material. Responds in 2 months.

Music Gospel only. Current acts include The Canton Spirituals, Darrell McFadden & The Disciples, The Jackson Southernaires, Slim & The Supreme Angels, The Pilgrim Jubilees, Spencer Taylor & the Highway Q'cs, The Annointed Jackson Singers, The Southern Sons, Jewel & Converted, and Ms. B & Tha' Band.

Tips "Make sure your demo is clear with a good sound so the agent can make a good judgement."

☒ ◯ S.L. FELDMAN & ASSOCIATES

1505 W. Second Ave. #200, Vancouver BC V6H 3Y4 Canada. (604)734-5945. Fax: (604)732-0922. E-mail: feldman@slfa.com. Web site: www.slfa.com. Booking agency and artist management firm. Estab. 1970. Agency represents mostly Canadian artists and groups; currently handles over 200 acts.

How to Contact *Write or call first to obtain permission to submit a demo.* Prefers CD, photo and bio. If seeking management, contact Watchdog for consideration and include video in press kit. SAE and IRC. Responds in 2 months.

Music Current acts include Elvis Costello, The Chieftains, Joni Mitchell, Diana Krall, Norah Jones, Susan Tedeschi, Ry Cooder, Sissel, Sondre Lerche, Jesse Cook, Pink Martini, and Melody Gardot.

🌐 FRED T. FENCHEL ENTERTAINMENT AGENCY

2104 S. Jefferson Avenue, Mason City IA 50401. (641)423-4177. Fax: (641)423-8662. **Contact:** Fred T. Fenchel, president. Booking agency. Estab. 1964. Represents local and international individual artists and groups; currently handles up to 10 acts. Receives 20% commission.

How to Contact Submit demo by mail. Unsolicited submissions are OK. Prefers cassette or videocassette. Does not return material. Responds in 3 weeks.

Music Mostly **country**, **pop** and some **gospel**. Works primarily with dance bands and show groups; "artists we can use on club dates, fairs, etc." Current acts include New Odyssey (comedy & music), Nerness Family (family, variety music) and The Buck Hollow Band (duo, huge variety of music). "We deal primarily with established name acts with recording contracts, or those with a label and starting into popularity."

Tips "Be honest. Don't submit unless your act is exceptional rather than just starting out, amateurish and with lyrics that are written under the pretense of coming from qualified writers."

🔝 🌐 B.C. FIEDLER MANAGEMENT

53 Seton Park Rd., Toronto ON M3C 3Z8 Canada. (416)421-4421. Fax: (416)421-0442. E-mail: info@bcfiedler.com. **Contact:** B.C. Fiedler. Management firm, music publisher (B.C. Fiedler Publishing) and record company (Sleeping Giant Music Inc.). Estab. 1964. Represents individual artists, groups and songwriters from anywhere; currently handles 3 acts. Receives 20-25% or consultant fees. Reviews material for acts.

How to Contact *Call first and obtain permission to submit.* Prefers CD or VHS videocassette with 3 songs and lyric sheet. If seeking management, press kit should include bio, list of concerts performed in past 2 years including name of venue, repertoire, reviews and photos. Does not return material. Responds in 2 months.

Music Mostly **classical/crossover**, **voice** and **pop**. Works primarily with classical/crossover ensembles, instrumental soloists, operatic voice and pop singer/songwriters. Current acts include Liona Boyd (classical guitar) and Pavlo (instrumental).

Tips "Invest in demo production using best quality voice and instrumentalists. If you write songs, hire the vocal talent to best represent your work. Submit CD and lyrics. Artists should follow up 6-8 weeks after submission."

🌐 🌐 FIRST TIME MANAGEMENT

Sovereign House, 12 Trewartha Rd., Praa Sands-Penzance, Cornwall TR20 9ST England (01736)762826. Fax: (01736)763328. E-mail: panamus@aol.com. Web site: www.songwriters-guild .co.uk. **Contact:** Roderick G. Jones, managing director. Management firm, record company (Rainy Day Records, Mohock Records, Pure Gold Records) and music publisher (Panama Music Library, Melody First Music Library, Eventide Music Library, Musik' Image Music Library, Promo Sonor International Muisc Library, Caribbean Music Library, ADN Creation Music Library, Piano Bar Music Library, Corelia Music Library, PSI Music Library, First Time Music (Publishing U.K.) U.K.— registered members of The Mechanical Copyright Protection Society (MCPS) and The Performing Right Society (PRS)). Estab. 1986. Represents local, regional and international individual aritsts, groups, composers and songwriters. Receives 15-25% commission. Reviews material for acts.

● Also see the listings for First Time Music (Publishing) in the Music Publishers section of this book.

How to Contact Submit demo package by mail. Unsolicited submissions are OK. Prefers CD with 3 songs and lyric sheets. If seeking management, press kit should include cover letter, bio, photo, demo tape/CD, press clippings and anything relevant to make an impression. Does not return material. Responds in 1 month.

Music All styles. Works primarily with songwriters, composers, DJ remixers, rappers, vocalists, groups and choirs. Current acts include Willow (pop), Animal Cruelty (indie/heavy thrash), Bram Stoker (gothic rock group), Kevin Kendle (New Age) Peter Arnold (folk/roots), and David Jones (urban/R&B)).

Tips ''Become a member of the Guild of International Songwriters and Composers (www.songwriters-guild.co.uk). Keep everything as professional as possible. Be patient and dedicated to your aims and objectives.''

☑ FREESTYLE ENTERTAINMENT

(formerly Biscuit Productions Inc.), 3315 E. Russell Rd., Suite A4-117, Las Vegas NV 89120. (888)271-0468. Web site: www.freestyleLLC.com. President: Steve Walker. Management firm. Estab. 1989. Represents individual artists and groups from anywhere; currently handles 3 acts. Receives 20% commission. Reviews material for acts.

How to Contact Submit demo package by mail. Prefers cassette or VHS videocassette. Does not return material. Responds in 2 months.

Music Mostly **rap**, **R&B** and **dance**; also **pop** and **alternative**. Current acts include Jamariah, Biscuit, and Brand X.

☑ BILL HALL ENTERTAINMENT & EVENTS

138 Frog Hollow Rd., Churchville PA 18966-1031. (215)357-5189. Fax: (215)357-0320. E-mail: Billhallevents@verizon.net. **Contact:** William B. Hall III, owner/president. Booking agency and production company. Represents individuals and groups; currently handles 20-25 acts. Receives 15% commission. Reviews material for acts.

How to Contact Submit demo package by mail. Unsolicited submissions are OK. Prefers CD, cassette, or videocassette of performance with 2-3 songs ''and photos, promo material, and CD, record, or tape. We need quality material, preferably before a 'live' audience.'' Does not return material. Responds only if interested.

Music Marching band, **circus** and novelty. Works primarily with ''unusual or novelty attractions in musical line, preferably those that appeal to family groups.'' Current acts include Fralinger and Polish-American Philadelphia Championship Mummers String Bands (marching and concert group), ''Mr. Polynesian'' Show Band and Hawaiian Revue (ethnic group), the ''Phillies Whiz Kids Band'' of Philadelphia Phillies Baseball team, Mummermania Musical Quartet, Philadelphia German Brass Band (concert band), Vogelgesang Circus Calliope, Kromer's Carousel Band Organ, Reilly Raiders Drum & Bugle Corps, Hoebel Steam Calliope, Caesar Rodney Brass Band, Rohe Calliope, Philadelphia Police & Fire Pipes Band, Larry Rothbard's Circus Band, Tim Laushey Pep & Dance Band, Larry Stout (show organist/keyboard player), and Jersey Surf Drum & Bugle Corp.

Tips ''Please send whatever helps us to most effectively market the attraction and/or artist. Provide something that gives you a clear edge over others in your field!''

☐ HARDISON INTERNATIONAL ENTERTAINMENT CORPORATION

P.O. Box 1732, Knoxville TN 37901-1732. (865)688-8680. E-mail: dennishardinson@bellsouth.net. Web site: www.myspace.com/hardison_music07. **Contact:** Dennis K. Hardison, CEO/founder. **Detroit Office:** P.O. Box 28277, Detroit MI 48228-9998. **Contact:** Sylvia Tuggle. Management firm, booking agency, music publisher (Denlatrin Music), record company (Denlatrin Records) and record producer. Estab. 1984. Represents individual artists from anywhere; currently handles 3 acts. Receives 20% commission. Reviews material for acts.

• This company has promoted acts including New Edition, Freddie Jackson, M.C. Lyte and Kool Moe Dee.

How to Contact Submit demo package by mail. Unsolicited submissions are OK. Prefers CD or cassette with 3 songs. If seeking management, press kit should include bio, promo picture and CD. Does not return material. Responds in 6 weeks to the best material.

Music Mostly **R&B**, **hip-hop** and **rap**. Current acts include Dynamo (hip-hop), Shorti (R&B singer/former original member of female group Blaque) and Triniti (record producer, Public Enemy, Dynamo, among others, current engineer for Chuck D).

Tips ''We respond to the hottest material, so make it hot!''

⦿ M. HARRELL & ASSOCIATES
5444 Carolina, Merrillville IN 46410. (219)887-8814. Fax: (480)345-2255. E-mail: mhmkbmgs95@h otmail.com. **Contact:** Mary Harrell, owner. Booking agency. Estab. 1984. Represents individual artists, groups, songwriters, all talents—fashion, dancers, etc.; currently handles 30-40 acts. Receives 10-20% commission. Reviews material for acts.

How to Contact *Call first and obtain permission to submit.* Submit demo by mail. Prefers CD or videocassette with 2-3 songs. Send résumé, bio, photo, demo tape/CD and press clippings. ''Keep it brief and current.'' Does not return material. Responds in 1 month.

Music All types, **country**, **R&B**, **jazz**, **gospel**, **Big Band**, **light rock** and **reggae**. Current acts include Many B (showact), Michael Essany (celebrity talk show host), Bill Shelton & 11th Avenue ('50s rock & roll), Bang (R&B/jazz) and Julian Michael (singer-songwriter/pop).

Tips ''The bands listed can and do tour in the U.S. and Europe (variety, mostly R&B, jazz and top 40) as well as the Chicagoland area. They get steady work and repeat business, because they are good and beat their competition.''

◻ HOT STEAMING COFFEE FILMS
7522 Ave. T, #1, Brooklyn NY 11234. E-mail: enigpublus@aol.com. **Contact:** David K., personal manager. Management firm. Estab. 1997. Represents individual artists, groups and (rarely) songwriters; currently does not represent any act. Receives 12-25% commission.

How to Contact ''E-mail for permission to submit, include a description of the type of material you have. Do not submit anything via mail, in person, or e-mail without WRITTEN PERMISSON via e-mail. If approved for submission, mail a CD with original songs and include lyric sheets. If mailing a press Kit, Press kit should include CD, cover letter, bio, photo, all lyrics with songs.'' **Does not return material and will not be held liable in any manner for any loss of submitted material. NO DROP OFFS.** Responds in 1 month. ''We will contact artist if interested.'' Include e-mail address and phone number for reply. Do not e-mail mp3 files! Songs must be copyrighted to submit.

Music Commercial (Top 40) rock AND female Pop only. No other kinds of music. I am looking for one GREAT artist to work with exclusively. Someone with a commercial Look/Sound (i.e., Britney Spears, Avril Lavigne, Christina Aguilera) and/or great musical ability (i.e., Beck, Bob Dylan)'' Works with original, solo artists and groups.

Tips ''I am dedicated to artists I believe in. I act strictly as a personal manager which means I help them choose songs, submit songs, find a publisher, and/or a record company. Prefer artists who write and perform their own songs. I am currently seeking material. CDs accepted. NO cassette tapes. NO mp3 files. Young male/female artists considered for development (ages 16-28) DO NOT CONTACT ME IF YOU ARE BEYOND THE AGE RANGE I SEEK! HINT: I am interested in poetic, melodic rock or a hot female pop artist with fresh hooks and commercial looks. Someone looking to express a social or political conscience in their music is a big PLUS.''

⦿ INTERNATIONAL ENTERTAINMENT BUREAU
3612 N. Washington Blvd., Indianapolis IN 46205-3592. (317)926-7566. E-mail: ieb@prodigy.net. Booking agency. Estab. 1972. Represents individual artists and groups from anywhere; currently handles 157 acts. Receives 20% commission.

How to Contact *No unsolicited submissions.*

Music Mostly **rock**, **country**, and **A/C**; also **jazz**, **nostalgia**, and **ethnic**. Works primarily with bands, comedians and speakers. Current acts include Five Easy Pieces (A/C), Scott Greeson (country), and Cool City Swing Band (variety).

J & V MANAGEMENT

143 W. Elmwood, Caro MI 48723. (989)673-2889. **Contact:** John Timko, manager/publisher. Management firm, booking agency and music publisher. Represents local, regional or international individual artists, groups and songwriters. Receives 10% commission. Reviews material for acts.

How to Contact *Write first and obtain permission to submit.* Prefers CD or cassette with 3 songs maximum and lyric sheet. If seeking management, include short reference bio, cover letter and résumé in press kit. Include SASE. Responds in 2 months.

Music Mostly **country**. Works primarily with songwriters/vocalists and dance bands. Current acts include John Patrick (country artist/songwriter) and Brandi Ewald (contemporary).

JANA JAE ENTERPRISES

P.O. Box 35726, Tulsa OK 74153. (918)786-8896. Fax: (918)786-8897. E-mail: janajae@janajae.com. Web site: www.janajae.com. **Contact:** Kathleen Pixley, agent. Booking agency, music publisher (Jana Jae Publishing/BMI) and record company (Lark Record Productions, Inc.). Estab. 1979. Represents individual artists and songwriters; currently handles 12 acts. Receives 15% commission. Reviews material for acts.

- Also see the listings for Jana Jae Music in the Music Publishers section, Lark Record Productions in the Record Companies section and Lark Talent & Advertising in the Record Producers section of this book.

How to Contact Submit demo by mail. Unsolicited submissions are OK. Prefers CD or videocassette of performance. If seeking management, press kit should include cover letter, bio, photo, demo tape/CD, lyric sheets and press clippings. Does not return material.

Music Mostly **country**, **classical** and **jazz instrumentals**; also **pop**. Works with vocalists, show and concert bands, solo instrumentalists. Represents Jana Jae (country singer/fiddle player), Matt Greif (classical guitarist), Sydni (solo singer) and Hotwire (country show band).

KENDALL WEST AGENCY

P.O. Box 173776, Arlington TX 76003-3776. (817)468-7800. E-mail: kendallwestagency@adelphia.net. **Contact:** Michelle Vellucci. Booking agency and television producer. Estab. 1994. Represents individual artists and groups from anywhere. Receives 10% commission. Reviews material for acts.

How to Contact *Write first and obtain permission to submit or write to arrange personal interview.* Prefers CD with 5 songs and lead sheet. If seeking management, press kit should include bio, photo, cover letter, CD and resume. Include SASE. Responds in 1 month.

Music Mostly **country**, **blues/jazz**, and **rock**; also **trios**, **dance** and **individuals**. Works primarily with bands. Current acts include Chris & the Roughnecks (Texas music), Shawna Russell (southern rock), Ty England (country), and Jaz-Vil (jazz/blues).

KITCHEN SYNC

8530 Holloway Dr. #328, West Hollywood CA 90069-2475. (310)855-1631. Fax: (310)657-7197. E-mail: ldg@anet.net. **Contact:** Laura Grover. Music production manager. Estab. 1990. Represents individual artists, groups and songwriters from anywhere. Reviews material for acts.

- Kitchen Sync primarily manages the production of music.

How to Contact *Write first and obtain permission to submit.* Prefers DVD with 3 songs and lyric sheet. If seeking management, press kit should include cover letter, resume, bio, press clippings, discography and photo. Include SASE. Responds in 1 month.

Music Mostly **pop/rock**, **country** and **R&B**. Works primarily with producers and singer/songwriters.

Tips "Have a clear artistic mission statement and career goals. I'm mostly interested in overseeing/managing production of material, i.e., creating budgets and mapping out recording plan, booking studios, vendors, etc."

◙ BOB KNIGHT AGENCY

185 Clinton Ave., Staten Island NY 10301. (718)448-8420. **Contact:** Bob Knight, president. Management firm, booking agency, music publisher and royalty collection firm. Estab. 1971. Represents artists, groups and songwriters; currently handles 7 acts. Receives 10-20% commission. Reviews material for acts and for submission to record companies and producers.

How to Contact Submit demo by mail. Unsolicited submissions are OK. Prefers cassette, CD, DVD, or videocassette (if available) with 5 songs and lead sheet "with bio and references." If seeking management, press kit should include bio, DVD, videocassette, CD, or audio cassette, as well as photo. Include SASE. Responds in 2 months.

Music Mostly **top 40/pop**; also **easy listening**, **MOR**, **R&B**, **soul**, **rock** (**nostalgia '50s and '60s**), **alternative**, **country**, and **country/pop**. Works primarily with recording and name groups and artists—'50s, '60s and '70s acts, bands, high energy dance and show groups. Current acts include Delfonics (R&B nostalgia), B.T. Express (R&B), Brass Construction (R&B), Main Ingredient (R&B), Denny Carmella's Review, Denny Carmella's Booty Shack, Carl Thomas (R&B), Santa Esmeralda starring Leroy Gomez (disco), Motown Magic (R&B/tribute), and Skyy (funk/R&B).

Tips "We're seeking artists and groups with completed albums/demos. Also seeking male and female solo artists with powerful and dynamic voice—top 40, pop, R&B, and rock, country, and opera for recording and live performances."

☑ ○ KUPER PERSONAL MANAGEMENT/RECOVERY RECORDINGS

P.O. Box 66274, Houston TX 77266. (713)527-0202. Fax: (713)520-5791. E-mail: recovery@wt.net. Web site: www.recoveryrecordings.com. **Contact:** Koop Kuper, owner. Management firm, music publisher (Kuper-Lam Music/BMI, Uvula Music/BMI, and Meauxtown Music/ASCAP) and record label (Recovery Recordings). Estab. 1979/2002. Represents individual artists, groups and songwriters from Texas; currently handles 5 acts. Receives 20% commission. Reviews material for acts.

How to Contact Submit demo package by mail. Unsolicited submissions are OK. Prefers CD. If seeking management, press kit should include cover letter, press clippings, photo, bio (1 page) tearsheets (reviews, etc.) and demo CD. Does not return material. Responds in 2 months.

Music Mostly **singer/songwriters**, **triple AAA**, **roots rock**, and **Americana**. Works primarily with self-contained and self-produced artists. Current acts include Philip Rodriguez (singer/songwriter), David Rodriguez (singer/songwriter), Def Squad Texas (hip-hop). U.S. Representative for the following Dutch groups: The Watchman (Dutch singer/songwriter), and The Very Girls (Dutch vocal duo).

Tips "Create a market value for yourself, produce your own master tapes, and create a cost-effective situation."

◙ LARI-JON PROMOTIONS

P.O. Box 216, Rising City NE 68658. (402)542-2336. **Contact:** Larry Good, owner. Management firm, music publisher (Lari-Jon Publishing Co./BMI) and record company (Lari-Jon Records). Represents individual artists, groups and songwriters; currently handles 3 acts. Receives 15% commission. Reviews material for acts.

How to Contact Submit demo tape by mail. Unsolicited submissions are OK. Prefers CD with 5 songs and lyric sheet. If seeking management, press kit should include 8×10 photos, cassette, videocassette and bio sheet. Include SASE. Responds in 2 months.

Music Mostly **country**, **gospel** and **'50s rock**. Works primarily with dance and show bands. Represents Kent Thompson (singer), Nebraskaland 'Opry (family type country show), and Brenda Allen (singer and comedienne).

◨ LEVINSON ENTERTAINMENT VENTURES INTERNATIONAL, INC.

1440 Veteran Ave., Suite 650, Los Angeles CA 90024. (323)663-6940. E-mail: leviinc@aol.com. President: Bob Levinson. **Contact:** Jed Leland, Jr. Management firm. Estab. 1978. Represents national individual artists, groups and songwriters; currently handles 4 acts. Receives 15-25% commission. Reviews material for acts.

How to Contact *Write first and obtain permission to submit.* Prefers CD, DVD, cassette, or VHS videocassette with 6 songs and lead sheet. If seeking management, press kit should include bio, pictures and press clips. Include SASE. Responds in 1 month.

Music Mostly **rock**, **MOR**, **R&B** and **country**. Works primarily with rock bands and vocalists.

Tips "Should be a working band, self-contained and, preferably, performing original material."

☑ ◨ RICK LEVY MANAGEMENT

4250 A1AS, D-11, St. Augustine FL 32080. (904)806-0817. Fax: (904)460-1226. E-mail: rick@ricklevy.com. Web site: www.ricklevy.com. **Contact:** Rick Levy, president. Management firm, music publisher (Flying Governor Music/BMI) and record company (Luxury Records). Estab. 1985. Represents local, regional or international individual artists and groups; currently handles 5 acts. Receives 15-20% commission. Reviews material for acts.

How to Contact *Write or call first and obtain permission to submit.* Prefers CD or DVD with 3 songs and lyric sheet. If seeking management, press kit should include cover letter, bio, demo tape/CD, DVD demo, photo and press clippings. Include SASE. Responds in 2 weeks.

Music Mostly **R&B** (no rap), **pop**, **country** and **oldies**; also **children's** and **educational videos** for schools. Current acts include Jay & the Techniques ('60s hit group), The Original Box Tops ('60s), The Limits (pop), Freddy Cannon ('60s), The Fallin Bones (Blues/rock), Tommy Roe ('60s), The Bushwhackers (country), and Sticky Fingers (North America's #1 Rolling Stones tribute band).

Tips "If you don't have 200% passion and committment, don't bother. Be sure to contact only companies that deal with your type of music."

◻ LOGGINS PROMOTION

26239 Senator Ave., Harbor City CA 90710. (310)325-2800. Fax: (310)427-7333. E-mail: promo@logginspromotion.com. Web site: www.logginspromotion.com. **Contact:** Paul Loggins, CEO. Management firm and radio promotion. Represents individual artists, groups and songwriters from anywhere; currently handles 6 acts. Receives 20% commission. Reviews material for acts.

How to Contact If seeking management, press kit should include picture, short bio, cover letter, press clippings and CD (preferred). "Mark on CD which cut you, as the artist, feel is the strongest." Does not return material. Responds in 2 weeks.

Music Mostly **adult**, **top 40** and **AAA**; also **urban**, **rap**, **alternative**, **college**, **smooth jazz** and **Americana**. Works primarily with bands and solo artists.

◨ MANAGEMENT BY JAFFE

68 Ridgewood Ave., Glen Ridge, NJ 07028. (973)743-1075. Fax: (973)743-1075. E-mail: jerjaf@aol.com. President: Jerry Jaffe. Management firm. Estab. 1987. Represents individual artists and groups from anywhere; currently handles 2 acts. Receives 20% commission. Reviews material for acts "rarely." Reviews for representation "sometimes."

How to Contact *Write or call first to arrange personal interview.* Prefers CD or cassette and videocassette with 3-4 songs and lyric sheet. Does not return material. Responds in 2 months.

Music Mostly **rock/alternative**, **pop** and **Hot AC**. Works primarily with groups and singers/song-writers. Current acts include Joe McIntrye (pop) and others.

Tips "If you are influenced by Jesus & Mary Chain, please e-mail. Create some kind of 'buzz' first."

⚡ 🖉 THE MANAGEMENT TRUST LTD.

411 Queen St. W, 3rd Floor, Toronto ON M5V 2A5 Canada. (416)979-7070. Fax: (416)979-0505. E-mail: mail@mgmtrust.ca. Web site: www.mgmtrust.ca. Manager: Jake Gold. Manager: R.J. Guha. General Manager: Shelley Stertz. Management firm. Estab. 1986. Represents individual artists and/or groups; currently handles 8 acts.

How to Contact Submit demo package by mail (Attn: A&R Dept.). Unsolicited submissions are OK. If seeking management, press kit should include CD, bio, cover letter, photo and press clippings. Does not return material. Responds in 2 months.

Music All types. Current acts include Sass Jordan (rock), Brian Byrne (folk rock), The Populars (rock), The Salads (rock), onlyforward (rock), Dearly Beloved (rock/alt), Chris Koster (rock), The Cliks (rock), Billy Klippert (rock), Bobnoxious (rock), The Pursuit of Happiness (rock), and Public (rock).

◻ RICK MARTIN PRODUCTIONS

125 Fieldpoint Road, Greenwich CT 06830. E-mail: rick@easywaysystems.com. Web site: www.ric kmartinproductions.com and www.myspace.com/rickmartinproductions/songwriter. **Contact:** Rick Martin, president. Personal manager and independent producer. Held the Office of Secretary of the National Conference of Personal Managers for 22 years. Represents vocalists; currently produces pop and country crossover music artists in private project studio and looking for a female vocalist in the general area of Greenwich, CT for production project. Receives 15% commission as a personal manager and/or customary production and publishing distributions.

How to Contact Please e-mail for initial contact or submit 2-3 songs and picture.

Music Top 40 and **country crossover**.

Tips "Your demo does not have to be professionally produced to submit to producers, publishers, or managers. In other words, save your money. It's really not important what you've done. It's what you can do now that counts."

🖉 PHIL MAYO & COMPANY

P.O. Box 304, Bomoseen VT 05732. (802)468-2554. Fax: (802)468-2554. E-mail: pmcamgphil@aol.c om. **Contact:** Phil Mayo, President. Management firm and record company (AMG Records). Estab. 1981. Represents individual artists, groups and songwriters from anywhere; currently handles 4 acts. Receives 15-20% commission. Reviews material for acts.

How to Contact *Contact first and obtain permission to submit.* Prefers CD with 3 songs (professinally recorded) and lyric or lead sheet. If seeking management, include bio, photo and lyric sheet in press kit. Does not return material. Responds in 2 months.

Music Mostly **contemporary Christian pop**. Current and past acts have included John Hall, Guy Burlage, Jonell Mosser, Pam Buckland, Orleans, Gary Nicholson, and Jon Pousette-Dart.

Ⓝ 🖉 MAZUR ENTERTAINMENT/MAZUR PUBLIC RELATIONS

P.O. Box 2425, Trenton NJ 08607. (609)890-4550. Fax: (609)890-4556. E-mail: michael@mazurpr.c om. Web site: www.mazurpr.com. **Contact:** Michael Mazur. Management and PR firm. Estab. 1994. Represents groups from anywhere; currently handles 30 acts. Commission varies. Reviews material for acts.

How to Contact Submit demo by mail. Unsolicited submissions are OK. Prefers CD with 2 songs. If seeking management send music and press kit. Include SASE. "We try to reply." Responds in 1 month.

Music All types. Current acts include international and national artists. See Web site.

☑ MEDIA MANAGEMENT

P.O. Box 3773, San Rafael CA 94912-3773. (415)898-7474. Fax: (415)898-9191. E-mail: mediamanag ement9@aol.com. **Contact:** Eugene, proprietor. Management firm. Estab. 1990. Represents international individual artists, groups and songwriters; currently handles 5 acts. Receives 15% commission. Reviews material for acts.

How to Contact Submit demo by mail. Unsolicited submissions are OK. Prefers CD or DVD with lyric sheet. If seeking management, include lyric sheets, demo tape, photo and bio. Does not return material.

Music. R&B, **blues**, **rock**, **country**, and **pop**. Works primarily with songwriting performers/bands. Current acts include The John Lee Hooker Estate—management consultant, (blues); Peter Walker—management, (world folk guitar virtuoso); Dawn McvCoy—management, (country), Greg Anton/ ZERO II (rock).

Tips "Write great radio-friendly songs with great musical and lyrical hooks."

☑ MEGA MUSIC PRODUCTIONS

16950 North Bay Road, Suite 1706, Sunny Isle, FL 33160. (305)604-9666. E-mail: marco@megamusi cevents.com. Web site: www.MegaMusicEvents.com. Contact: Marco Carvajal, general manager. Management firm, booking agency and record producer. "We are also an online record company, and we can provide digital distribution for your music to be sold on the Internet." Represents individual artists and groups from anywhere; currently handles 10 acts. Receives 25-35% commission. Reviews material for acts.

How to Contact *"We ONLY accept online submissions.* Please e-mail Web site or songs and pictures. DO NOT send materials via regular mail. Online only, please."

Music Mostly **pop**, **rock**, **dance**, **Latin**, and **world music**. Works primarily with bands and singers.

Tips "Create a good Web site. If you don't have one, we can help you create one."

[N] □ MERRI-WEBB PRODUCTIONS

P.O. Box 5474, Stockton CA 95205. (209)948-8186. Fax: (209)942-2163. Web site: www.makingmus ic4u.com. **Contact:** Kristy Ledford, A&R coordinator. Management firm, music publisher (Kaupp's & Robert Publishing Co./BMI) and record company (Kaupp Records). Represents regional (California) individual artists, groups and songwriters; currently handles 13 acts. Receives 10-15% commission. Reviews material for acts.

> • Also see the listing for Kaupp & Robert Publishing Company in the Music Publishers section and Kaupp Records in the Record Companies section of the book.

How to Contact *Write first and obtain permission to submit or to arrange personal interview.* Prefers cassette or VHS videocassette with 3 songs maximum and lyric sheet. Include SASE. Responds in 3 months.

Music Mostly **country**, **A/C rock** and **R&B**; also **pop**, **rock** and **gospel**. Works primarily with vocalists, bands and songwriters. Current acts include Bruce Bolin (rock/pop singer), Nanci Lynn (country/pop singer) and Rick Webb (country/pop singer).

□ MIDCOAST, INC.

1002 Jones Rd., Hendersonville TN 37075. (615)400-4664. E-mail: mid-co@ix.netcom.com. Managing Director: Bruce Andrew Bossert. Management firm and music publisher (MidCoast, Inc./BMI). Estab. 1984. Represents individual artists, groups and songwriters; currently handles 2 acts. Reviews material for acts.

How to Contact Submit demo package by mail. Unsolicited submissions are OK. Prefers CD, cassette, VHS videocassette or DAT with 2-4 songs and lyric sheet. If seeking management, press kit should include cover letter, "short" bio, tape, video, photo, press clippings and announcements of any performances in Nashville area. Does not return material. Responds in 6 weeks if interested.

Music Mostly **rock**, **pop** and **country**. Works primarily with original rock and country bands and artists. Current acts include Room 101 (alternative rock).

☑ ☑ MONTEREY PENINSULA ARTISTS/PARADIGM

124 12th Ave. S., Suite 410, Nashville TN 37203. (615)251-4400. Fax: (615)251-4401. Web site: www.MontereyPeninsulaArtists.com. Booking agency. Represents individual artists, groups from anywhere; currently handles 37 acts. Receives 10% commission. Reviews material for acts.

How to Contact *Write or call first to arrange personal interview.*

Music Mostly **country**. Current acts include Lyle Lovett, Ricky Skaggs, Junior Brown, Toby Keith, Travis Tritt, Montgomery Gentry, The Del McCoury Band, Grand Funk Railroad, Kasey Chambers, Robert Earl Keen, Shooter Jennings, and Uncle Kracker.

N ⊕ ◖ MUSIC MARKETING & PROMOTIONS

Post Office Kendenup 6323, South Perth 6951 Australia. (618)9851-4311. Fax: (618)9851-4225. E-mail: mmp@global.net.au. Web site: www.global.net.au/~mmp/. **Contact:** Eddie Robertson. Booking agency. Estab. 1991. Represents individual artists and/or groups; currently handles 50 acts. Receives 20% commission. Reviews material for acts.

How to Contact *Write first and obtain permission to submit.* Unsolicited submissions are OK. Prefers cassette or videocassette with photo, information on style and bio. If seeking management, press kit should include photos, bio, cover letter, press clippings, video, demo, lyric sheets and any other useful information. Does not return material. Responds in 1 month.

Music Mostly **top 40/pop**, **jazz** and **'60s-'90s**; also **reggae** and **blues**. Works primarily with show bands and solo performers. Current acts include Faces (dance band), Peace Love & All That Stuff (retro band), and Soul Corporation (soul).

Tips ''Send as much information as possible. If you do not receive a call after four to five weeks, follow up with letter or phone call.''

☑ NOTEWORTHY PRODUCTIONS

124½ Archwood Ave., Annapolis MD 21401. (410)268-8232. Fax: (410)268-2167. E-mail: mcshane @mcnote.com. Web site: www.mcnote.com. **Contact:** McShane Glover, president. Management firm and booking agency. Estab. 1985. Represents individual artists, groups and songwriters from everywhere; currently handles 6 acts. Receives 15-20% commission. Reviews material for acts.

How to Contact *Write first and obtain permission to submit.* Prefers CD/CDR with lyric sheet. If seeking management, press kit should include CD, photo, bio, venues played and press clippings (preferably reviews). ''Follow up with a phone call 3-5 weeks after submission.'' Does not return material. Responds in 2 months.

Music Mostly **Americana**, **folk**, and **Celtic**. Works primarily with performing singer/songwriters. Current acts include Seamus Kennedy (Celtic/contemporary), and the Rev. Billy C. Wirty (blues).

☑ ◖ PM MUSIC GROUP, INC.

(formerly Precision Management), 957 W. Marietta St. NW, Suite D, Atlanta GA 30318. (800)275-5336, ext. 0381042. E-mail: precisionmanagement@netzero.com. Web site: www.pmmusicgroup.com. **Contact:** St. Paul Williams, operations director. Management firm and music publisher (Mytrell/BMI). Estab. 1990. Represents individual artists and/or groups and songwriters from anywhere; currently handles 3 acts. Receives 20% commission. Reviews material for acts.

How to Contact Submit demo package by mail. Unsolicited submissions are OK. Prefers cassette or VHS videocassette with 3-4 songs and lyric sheet. If seeking management, press kit should include photo, bio, demo tape/CD, lyric sheets, press clippings and all relevant press information. Include SASE. Responds in 6 weeks.

Music Mostly **R&B**, **rap** and **gospel**; also **all types**.

☑ PRESTIGE MANAGEMENT

8600 Wilbur Ave., Northridge CA 91324. (818)993-3030. Fax: (818)993-4151. E-mail: prestige@gte. net. **Contact:** Waddell Solomon, vice president. Management firm. Estab. 1987. Represents individual artists, groups and songwriters from anywhere; currently handles 2 acts. Receives 15% commission. Reviews material for acts.

How to Contact Submit demo by mail. Unsolicited submissions are OK. Prefers CD with 3 songs, photo/bio and lyric sheet. If seeking management, press kit should include photos, bio, recent show dates and recent show reviews. Does not return material. Responds in 1 month.

Music Mostly **pop rock**, **hard rock**, **alternative rock**; also **R&B** and **AAA**. Works primarily with pop/rock bands with strong songs and live shows; also songwriters for film/TV projects. Current acts include Busted, McFly, and V.

☑ ☑ PRIME TIME ENTERTAINMENT

2388 Research Dr., Livermore CA 94550. (408)289-9333. Fax: (925)905-3813. E-mail: artistmanager @aol.com. Web stie:www.primetimeentertainment.com. Owner: Jim Douglas. Management firm and booking agency. Estab. 1988. Represents individual artists, groups and songwriters from anywhere. Receives 10-20% commission. Reviews material for acts.

How to Contact Submit demo package by mail. Unsolicited submissions are OK. Prefers CD with 3-5 songs. If seeking management, press kit should include 8×10 photo, reviews and CDs/tapes. Include SASE. Responds in 1 month.

Music Mostly **jazz**, **country** and **alternative**; also **ethnic**. Artists include Grant Geissman (fusion/ jazz), Jody Watley (R&B), Ray Parker, Jr. (jazz/R&B), and Craig Chaquico (jazz).

Tips "It's all about the song."

☑ RAINBOW TALENT AGENCY

146 Round Pond Lane, Rochester NY 14626. (585)723-3334. Fax: (585)720-6172. E-mail: rtalent@fr ontiernet.net. **Contact:** Carl Labate, President. Management firm and booking agency. Represents artists and groups; currently handles 6 acts. Receives 15-20% commission.

How to Contact Submit demo package by mail. Unsolicited submissions are OK. Prefers CD with minimum 3 songs. May send DVD if available; "a still photo and bio of the act; if you are a performer, it would be advantageous to show yourself or the group performing live. Theme videos are not helpful." If seeking management, include photos, bio, markets established, CD/DVD. Does not return material. Responds in 1 month.

Music Mostly **blues**, **rock**, and **R&B**. Works primarily with touring bands and recording artists. Current acts include Kristin Mainhart (alt light rock); Classic Albums Live (classic rock symphony); Mike Zale (singer-songwriter/recording artist), and Spanky Haschmann Swing Orchestra (high energy swing).

Tips "My main interest is with groups or performers that are currently touring and have some product. And are at least 50% percent original. Strictly songwriters should apply elsewhere."

☐ RASPBERRY JAM MUSIC

(formerly Endangered Species Artist Management), 4 Berachah Ave., South Nyack NY 10960-4202. (845)353-4001. Fax: (845)353-4332. E-mail: muzik@verizon.net. Web site: www.musicandamerica .com or www.anyamusic.com. President: Fred Porter. Vice President: Suzanne Buckley. Management firm. Estab. 1979. Represents individual artists, groups and songwriters from anywhere; currently handles 3 acts. Receives 20% commission. Reviews material for acts.

How to Contact *Call first and obtain permission to submit.* Prefers CD with 3 or more songs and lyric sheet. "Please include a demo of your music, a clear, recent photograph as well as any current press, if any. A cover letter indicating at what stage in your career you are and expectations for your future. Please label the cassette and/or CD with your name and address as well as the song titles.'' If seeking management, press kit should include cover letter, bio, photo, demo/CD, lyric sheet and press clippings. Include SASE. Responds in 6 weeks.

Music Mostly **pop**, **rock** and **world**; also **Latin/heavy metal**, **R&B**, **jazz** and **instrumental**. Current acts include Jason Wilson & Tabarruk (pop/reggae, nominated for Juno award 2001), and Anya (teen singer).

Tips ''Listen to everything, classical to country, old to contemporary, to develop an understanding of many writing styles. Write with many other partners to keep the creativity fresh. Don't feel your style will be ruined by taking a class or a writing seminar. We all process moods and images differently. This leads to uniqueness in the music.''

☑ ◻ REIGN MUSIC AND MEDIA, LLC

(formerly Bassline Entertainment, Inc.), P.O. Box 2394, New York NY 10185. E-mail: talent@reignm m.com. Web site: www.reignmm.com. **Contact:** Talent Relations Dept. Multi-media/Artist Development firm. Estab. 1993 as Bassline Entertainment. Represents local and regional vocalists, producers, and songwriters. Receives 20-25% commission. Reviews material for acts.

How to Contact Submit demo package by mail. Unsolicited submissions are OK. Prefers CD, mp3, or video. If seeking management, press kit should include cover letter, press clippings and/or reviews, bio, demo (in appropriate format), picture and accurate contact telephone number. Include SASE. Responds in 3 weeks.

Music Mostly **pop**, **R&B**, **club/dance** and **hip-hop/rap**; some **Latin**. Works primarily with singer/ songwriters, producers, rappers and bands. Current acts include Stress (hip hop), Mood Swing (R&B/pop), and Critical (rap/hip-hop).

☑ RIOHCAT MUSIC

P.O. Box 764, Hendersonville TN 37077-0764. (615)824-9313. Fax: (615)824-0797. E-mail: tachoir@ bellsouth.net. Web site: www.tachoir.com. **Contact:** Robert Kayne, manager. Management firm, booking agency, record company (Avita Records) and music publisher. Estab. 1975. Represents individual artists and groups; currently handles 4 acts. Receives 15-20% commission.

 • Also see the listing for Avita Records in the Record Companies section of this book.

How to Contact *Contact first and obtain permission to submit.* Prefers CD and lead sheet. If seeking management, press kit should include cover letter, bio, photo, demo tape/CD and press clippings. Does not return material. Responds in 6 weeks.

Music Mostly **contemporary jazz** and **fusion**. Works primarily with jazz ensembles. Current acts include Group Tachoir (jazz), Tachoir/Manakas Duo (jazz) and Jerry Tachoir (jazz vibraphone artist).

☑ A.F. RISAVY, INC.

1312 Vandalia, Collinsville IL 62234. (618)345-6700. Fax: (618)345-2004. E-mail: swingcitymusic@ ameritech.net. Web site: www.swingcitymusic.com. **Contact:** Art Risavy, president. Management firm and booking agency. Divisions include Artco Enterprises, Golden Eagle Records, Swing City Music and Swing City Sound. Estab. 1960. Represents artists, groups and songwriters; currently handles 35 acts. Receives 10% commission. Reviews material for acts.

How to Contact Submit demo by mail. Unsolicited submissions are OK. Prefers CD/CDR, cassette or VHS videocassette with 2-6 songs and lyric sheet. If seeking management, press kit should include pictures, bio and VHS videocassette. Include SASE. Responds in 3 weeks.

Music Mostly **rock**, **country**, **MOR** and **top 40**.

☑ CHARLES R. ROTHSCHILD PRODUCTIONS INC.

330 E. 48th St., New York NY 10017. (212)421-0592. **Contact:** Charles R. Rothschild, president. Booking agency. Estab. 1971. Represents individual artists, groups and songwriters from anywhere; currently handles 25 acts. Receives 25% commission. Reviews material for acts.

How to Contact *Call first and obtain permission to submit.* Prefers cassette, CD or VHS videocassette with 1 song and lyric and lead sheet. If seeking management, include cassette, photo, bio and reviews. Include SASE. Responds in 6 weeks.

Music Mostly **rock**, **pop**, **family** and **folk**; also **country** and **jazz**. Current acts include Richie Havens (folk singer), Leo Kottke (guitarist/composer), Emmylou Harris (country songwriter), Tom Chapin (kids' performer and folksinger) and John Forster (satirist).

☐ RUSTRON/WHIMSONG MUSIC PRODUCTIONS

Send all artist song submissions to: 1156 Park Lane, West Palm Beach FL 33417-5957. (561)686-1354. E-mail: RMP_WMP@bellsouth.net. **Contact:** Sheelah Adams, office administrator. Main Office in Connecticut. ("Main office does not review artist submissions—only South Florida Branch office does." Executive Director: Rusty Gordon. Artist Consultants: Rusty Gordon and Davilyn Whims. Composition Management: Ron Caruso. Management firm, booking agency, music publisher (Rustron Music Publishers/BMI and Whimsong Publishing/ASCAP), record company and record producer. Estab. 1970. Represents individuals, groups and songwriters; currently handles 20 acts. Receives 10-30% commission. Reviews material for acts.

* Also see listings for Rustron Music in the Music Publishers, Record Companies and Record Producers sections of this book.

How to Contact *Call to discuss submission.* Send CD or cassette with 10-15 songs (CD produced to sell at gigs with up to 15 songs on each CD preferred). Provide $8^{1}/_{2} \times 11$ typed lyric sheets for every song in the submission. If seeking management, send press kit including: cover letter, bio, demo CD(s), typed lyric sheets and press clippings. "SASE or International Reply Coupon (IRC)required for all correspondence." Responds in 4 months.

Music Mostly **adult contemporaryelectric-acoustic**, **blues (country folk/urban, Southern)**, **country (rock, blues, progressive)**, **easy listening**, **Cabaret**, **soft rock & pop (ballads)**, **women's music**, **R&B**, **folk/rock**; also **New Age instrumentals** and **New Age folk fusion**. Current acts include Jayne Margo-Reby (folk rock), Star Smiley (country), Robin Plitt (historical folk), Boomslang Swampsinger (Florida folk), Continental Divide (topical folk), Tracie Mitchell & Ivory Coast (folk rock/blues), Florida Rank & File (socio-political/folk/world music).

Tips "Carefully mix demo, don't drown the vocals, 10-15 songs in a submission. Prefer a for-sale CD made to sell at gigs with up to 15 songs on each. Send photo if artist is seeking marketing and/or production assistance. Very strong hooks, definitive verse melody, evolved concepts, unique and unpredictable themes. Flesh out a performing sound and style. The presentation should be unique to the artist. Stage presence a must!"

☑ SA'MALL MANAGEMENT

P.O. Box 261488, Encino CA 91426. (310)317-0322. Fax: (818)506-8534. E-mail: samusa@aol.com. Web site: www.pplentertainmentgroup.com. **Contact:** Ted Steele, vice president of talent. Management firm, music publisher (Pollybyrd Publications) and record company (PPL Entertainment Group). Estab. 1990. Represents individual artists, groups and songwriters worldwide; currently handles 10 acts. Receives 10-25% commission. Reviews material for acts.

* Also see the listings for Pollybyrd Publications Limited and Zettitalia Music International in the Music Publishers section and PPL Entertainment Group in the Record Companies section of this book.

How to Contact *E-mail first and obtain permission to submit.* "Only professional full-time artists who tour and have a fan base need apply. No weekend warriors, please." Prefers CD or cassette. If seeking management, press kit should include picture, bio and tape. Include SASE. Responds in 2 months.

Music All types. Current acts include Riki Hendrix (rock), Buddy Wright (blues), Fhyne, Suzette Cuseo, The Band AKA, LeJenz, B.D. Fuoco, Juz-cuz and Donato.

☑ ◖ SAFFYRE MANAGEMENT
1215 S. Lake St., Unit #D, Burbank CA 91502. (818)842-4368. E-mail: ebsaffyre@yahoo.com. **Contact**: Esta G. Bernstein, president. Management firm. Estab. 1990. Represents individual artists, groups and songwriters from anywhere; currently handles 2 acts. Receives 15% commission.
How to Contact *Call first and obtain permission to submit.* If seeking management, press kit should include cover letter, bio, photo, cassette with 3-4 songs and lyric sheets. Does not return material. Responds in 2 weeks only if interested.
Music Alternative/modern rock and **top 40**. ''We work only with bands and solo artists who write their own material; our main objective is to obtain recording deals and contracts, while advising our artists on their careers and business relationships.''

◖ SANDALPHON MANAGEMENT
P.O. Box 29110, Portland OR 97296. (503)957-3929. E-mail: jackrabbit01@sprintpcs.com. **Contact:** Ruth Otey, president. Management firm, music publisher (Sandalphon Music Publishing/BMI), and record company (Sandalphon Records). Estab. 2005. Represents individual artists, groups, songwriters; works with individual artists and groups from anywhere. Currently handles 0 acts. Receives negotiable commission. Reviews material for acts.
How to Contact Submit demo by mail. Unsolicited submissions are OK. Prefers cassette or CD with 1-5 songs and lyric sheet, cover letter. ''Include name, address, and contact information.'' Include SASE or SAE and IRC for outside the United States. Responds in 1 month.
Music Mostly **rock**, **country**, and **alternative**; also **pop**, **gospel**, and **blues**. ''We are looking for singers, bands, and singer/songwriters who are original but would be current in today's music markets. We help singers, bands, and singer-songwriters achieve their personal career goals.''
Tips ''Submit material you feel best represents you, your voice, your songs, or your band. Fresh and original songs and style are a plus. We are a West Coast management company looking for singers, bands, and singer-songwriters who are ready for the next level. We are looking for those with talent who are capable of being national and international contenders.''

◪ ◉ SERGE ENTERTAINMENT GROUP
P.O. Box 2760, Acworth GA 30102. (678)445-0006. Fax: (678)494-9289. E-mail: sergeent@aol.com. Web site: www.serge.org. **Contact:** Sandy Serge, president. Management and PR firm and song publishers. Estab. 1987. Represents individual artists, groups, songwriters from anywhere; currently handles 20 acts. Receives 20% commission for management. Monthly fee required for PR acts.
How to Contact *E-mail first for permission to submit.* Submit demo package by mail. Unsolicited submissions are OK. Prefers CD or cassette with 4 songs and lyric sheet. If seeking management, press kit should include 8×10 photo, bio, cover letter, lyric sheets, max of 4 press clips, VHS videocassette, performance schedule and CD. ''All information submitted must include name, address and phone number on each item.'' Does not return material. Responds in 6 weeks if interested.
Music Mostly **rock**, **pop** and **country**; also **New Age**. Works primarily with singer/songwriters and bands. Current acts include David McBee (rock), Erik Norlander (prog rock), and Mark Paul Smith (country).

Ⓝ ◪ ◉ SIEGEL ENTERTAINMENT LTD.
1736 W. 2nd Ave., Vancouver BC V6J 1H6 Canada. (604)736-3896. Fax: (604)736-3464. E-mail: siegelent@telus.net. **Contact:** Robert Siegel, president. Management firm and booking agency. Estab. 1975. Represents individual artists, groups and songwriters from anywhere; currently handles more than 100 acts (for bookings). Receives 15-20% commission. Reviews material for acts.
How to Contact *Does not accept unsolicited submissions. E-mail or write for permission to submit.* Does not return material. Responds in 1 month.

Music Mostly **rock**, **pop**, and **country**; also **specialty** and **children's**. Current acts include Johnny Ferreira & The Swing Machine, Lee Aaron, Kenny Blues Boss Wayne (boogie) and Tim Brecht (pop/children's).

⬛◻ SILVER BOW MANAGEMENT
556 Amess St., New Westminster BC V3L 4A9 Canada. (604)523-9309. Fax: (604)523-9310. E-mail: saddlestone@shaw.ca. Web site: www.saddlestone.net. President: Grant Lucas. CEO: Candice James. Management firm, music publisher (Saddlestone Publishing, Silver Bow Publishing), record company (Saddlestone Records) and record producer (Silver Bow Productions, Krazy Cat Productions). Estab. 1988. Represents individual artists, groups, songwriters from anywhere; currently handles 8 acts. Receives standard commission. Reviews material for acts.
  • Also see the listings for Saddlestone Publishing in the Music Publishers section and Silver Bow Productions in the Record Producers section of this book.
How to Contact Submit demo package by mail. Unsolicited submissions are OK. Prefers cassette with 3 songs and lyric sheet. If seeking management, press kit should include 8×10 photo, bio, cover letter, demo tape or CD with lyric sheets, press clippings, video, résumé and current itinerary. "Visuals are everything—submit accordingly." Does not return material. Responds in 2 months.
Music Mostly **country**, **pop** and **rock**; also **R&B**, **Christian** and **alternative**. Works primarily with bands, vocalists and singer/songwriters. Current acts include Darrell Meyers (country singer/songwriter), Nite Moves (variety band), Mark Vance (country/pop), and Stan Giles (country).

◻ T. SKORMAN PRODUCTIONS, INC.
5156 S. Orange Ave., Orlando FL 32809. (407)895-3000. Fax: (407)895-1422. E-mail: ted@tskorman .com. Web site: www.talentagency.com. **Contact:** Ted Skorman, president. Management firm and booking agency. Estab. 1983. Represents groups; currently handles 40 acts. Receives 10-25% commission. Reviews material for acts.
How to Contact *E-mail first for permission to submit.* Prefers CD with 2 songs, or videocassette of no more than 6 minutes. "Live performance—no trick shots or editing tricks. We want to be able to view act as if we were there for a live show." If seeking management, press kit should include cover letter, bio, photo and demo CD or video. Does not return material. Responds only if interested.
Music Mostly **top 40**, **dance**, **pop**, and **country**. Works primarily with high-energy dance acts, recording acts, and top 40 bands. Current acts include Steph Carse (pop).
Tips "We have many pop recording acts and are looking for commercial material for their next albums."

◻ GARY SMELTZER PRODUCTIONS
603 W. 13th #2A, Austin TX 78701. (512)478-6020. Fax: (512)478-8979. E-mail: gsptalent@aol.com. Web site: www.GarySmeltzerProductions.com. **Contact:** Gary Smeltzer, president. Management firm and booking agency. Estab. 1967. Represents individual artists and groups from anywhere. Currently handles 20 acts. "We book about 100 different bands each year—none are exclusive." Receives 20% commission. Reviews material for acts.
How to Contact Submit demo package by mail. Unsolicited submissions are OK. Prefers CD or DVD. If seeking management, press kit should include cover letter, résumé, CD/DVD, bio, picture, lyric sheets, press clippings and video. Does not return material. Responds in 1 month.
Music Mostly **alternative**, **R&B** and **country**. Current acts include Ro Tel & the Hot Tomatoes (nostalgic '60s showband).
Tips "We prefer performing songwriters who can gig their music as a solo or group."

◼◻ SOUTHEASTERN ATTRACTIONS
1025 23rd St. South, Suite 302, Birmingham AL 35205. (205)942-6600. Fax: (205)942-7700. E-mail: staff@seattractions.com. Web site: www.seattractions.com. **Contact:** Agent. Booking agency.

Estab. 1967. Represents groups from anywhere; currently handles 200 acts. Receives 20% commission.

How to Contact Submit demo package by mail. Unsolicited submissions are OK. Prefers CD or DVD. Does not return material. Responds in 2 months.

Music Mostley **rock**, **alternative**, **oldies**, **country** and **dance**. Works primarily with bands. Current acts include Leaderdog (rock), Undergrounders (variety to contemporary), Style Band (Motown/dance), The Connection (Motown/dance), Rollin in the Hay(bluegrass).

☑ SPHERE GROUP ONE

795 Waterside Drive, Marco Island FL 34145. (239)398-6800. Fax: (239)394-9881. E-mail: spheregro upone@att.net. President: Tony Zarrella. Talent Manager: Jon Zarrella. Management firm and record producer. Estab. 1987. Represents individual artists and groups from anywhere; currently handles 5 acts. Receives commission.

How to Contact Submit CD or DVD by mail or e-mail. Unsolicited submissions are OK. Prefers CD or video with 3-5 songs. All submissions must include cover letter, lyric sheets, tape/CD, photo, bio and all press. "Due to large number of submissions we can only respond to those artists which we may consider working with." Does not return material

Music Crossover, **pop/rock**, **pop/country**, and **New Age**; also **R&B**. Works primarily with bands and solo singer/songwriters. Current acts include 4 of Hearts (pop/rock), Frontier 9 (pop/rock), Viewpoint (experimental) and Bombay Green (hybrid pop).

Tips "Develop and create your own style, focus on goals and work as a team and maintain good chemistry with all artists and business relationships."

☐ ST. JOHN ARTISTS

P.O. Box 619, Neenah WI 54957-0619. (920)722-2222. Fax: (920)725-2405. E-mail: jon@stjohn-artists.com. Web site: www.stjohn-artists.com/. **Contact:** Jon St. John and Gary Coquoz, agents. Booking agency. Estab. 1968. Represents local and regional individual artists and groups; currently handles 20 acts. Receives 15-20% commission. Reviews material for acts.

How to Contact *Call first and obtain permission to submit.* Prefers CD or DVD. If seeking management, press kit should include cover letter, bio, photo, demo tape/CD, video and résumé. Include SASE.

Music Mostly **rock** and **MOR**. Current acts include Tribute (variety/pop/country), Boogie & the Yo-Yo's ('60s to 2000s), Vic Ferrari (Top 40 80's-2000's), Little Vito and the Torpedoes(variety 50's-2000's), Center Stage Variety Show Band (variety 60's-2000's) and Da Yoopers (musical comedy/novelty).

☑ STAIRCASE PROMOTION

P.O. Box 211, East Prairie MO 63845. (573)649-2211. **Contact:** Tommy Loomas, president. Vice President: Joe Silver. Management firm, music publisher (Lineage Publishing) and record company (Capstan Record Production). Estab. 1975. Represents individual artists and groups from anywhere; currently handles 6 acts. Receives 25% commission. Reviews material for acts.

- Also see the listings for Lineage Publishing Co. in the Music Publishers section and Capstan Record Production in the Record Companies section of this book.

How to Contact Submit demo by mail. Unsolicited submissions are OK. Prefers cassette with 3 songs and lyric sheet. If seeking management, press kit should include bio, photo, audio cassette and/or video and press reviews, if any. "Be as professional as you can." Include SASE. Responds in 2 months.

Music Mostly **country**, **pop** and **easy listening**; also **rock**, **gospel** and **alternative**. Current acts include Skidrow Joe (country comedian, on Capstan Records), Vicarie Arcoleo (pop singer, on Treasure Coast Records) and Scarlett Britoni (pop singer on Octagon Records).

☑ STARKRAVIN' MANAGEMENT

20501 Ventura Blvd., 217, Woodland Hills CA 91364. (818)587-6801. Fax: (818)587-6802. E-mail: bcmclane@aol.com. Web site: www.benmclane.com. **Contact:** B.C. McLane, Esq. Management and law firm. Estab. 1994. Represents individual artists, groups and songwriters. Receives 20% commission (management); $250/hour as attorney.

How to Contact Submit demo package by mail. Unsolicited submissions are OK. Prefers cassette. Does not return material. Responds in 1 month if interested.

Music Mostly **rock**, **pop** and **R&B**. Works primarily with bands.

☑ T.L.C. BOOKING AGENCY

37311 N. Valley Rd., Chattaroy WA 99003. (509)292-2201. Fax: (509)292-2205. E-mail: tlcagent@ix. netcom.com. Web site: www.tlcagency.com. **Contact:** Tom or Carrie Lapsansky, agent/owners. Booking agency. Estab. 1970. Represents individual artists and groups from anywhere; currently handles 17 acts. Receives 10-15% commission. Reviews material for acts.

How to Contact *Call first and obtain permission to submit.* Prefers CD with 3-4 songs. Does not return material. Responds in 3 weeks.

Music Mostly **rock**, **country** and **variety**; also **comedians** and **magicians**. Works primarily with bands, singles and duos. Current acts include Nobody Famous (variety/classic rock), Mr. Happy (rock), Mad Rush (rock), Dixie Dandies (dixieland), and The Charm (variety/top 40).

☑ ☑ TWENTIETH CENTURY PROMOTIONS

86 River Ave., Waiwick RI 02888. Phone/fax: (401)467-1832. **Contact:** Gil Morse, president. Management firm, booking agency and record producer (20th Century). Estab. 1972. Represents individual artists and groups from anywhere; currently handles 9 acts. Receives 15% commission. Reviews material for acts.

How to Contact *Call first and obtain permission to submit or to arrange personal interview.* Prefers CD or cassette. If seeking management, press kit should include photo and bio. Does not return material. Responds in 3 weeks.

Music Mostly **country** and **blues**. Works primarily with individuals and groups. Current acts include Robbin Lynn, and Charlie Brown's Costars.

Tips "Don't give up."

Ⓝ ☑ UMBRELLA ARTISTS MANAGEMENT, INC.

2612 Erie Ave., P.O. Box 8369, Cincinnati OH 45208. (513)871-1500. Fax: (513)871-1510. E-mail: shertzman@cinci.rr.com. Web site: www.stanhertzman.com. **Contact:** Stan Hertzman, president. Management firm. Represents artists and groups for specific circumstances.

How to Contact *E-mail or phone specific need.*

Music Mostly **progressive**, **rock** and **top 40/pop**. Works with contemporary/progressive pop/rock artists and writers on a per project basis.

☑ ◯ UNIVERSAL MUSIC MARKETING

P.O. Box 2297, Universal City TX 78148. (210)653-3989. E-mail: bswrl8@wmconnect.net. Web site: www.bsw-records.com. **Contact:** Frank Willson, president. Management firm, record company (BSW Records), booking agency, music publisher and record producer (Frank Wilson). Estab. 1987. Represents individual artists and groups from anywhere; currently handles 12 acts. Receives 15% commission. Reviews material for acts.

- Also see the listings for BSW Records in the Music Publishers and Record Companies sections and Frank Wilson in the Record Producers section of this book.

How to Contact Submit demo package by mail. Unsolicited submissions are OK. Prefers CD or DVD with 3 songs and lyric sheet. If seeking management, include tape/CD, bio, photo and current activities. Include SASE. Responds in 6 weeks.

Music Mostly **country** and **light rock**; also **blues** and **jazz**. Works primarily with vocalists, singer/songwriters and bands. Current acts include Candee Land, Darlene Austin, Larry Butler, John Wayne, Sonny Marshall, Bobby Mountain, Crea Beal and Butch Martin (country). "Visit our Web site for an up-to-date listing of current acts."

◪ RICHARD VARRASSO MANAGEMENT

P.O. Box 387, Fremont CA 94537. (510)792-8910. Fax: (510)792-0891. E-mail: richard@varrasso.com. Web site: www.big7records.com. CEO: Richard Varrasso. A&R: Saul Vigil. Management firm. Estab. 1976. Represents individual artists, groups and songwriters from anywhere; currently handles several acts. Receives 10-20% commission. Reviews material for acts.

How to Contact Submit demo package by mail. Unsolicited submissions are OK. Prefers CD. If seeking management, press kit should include photos, bios, cover letter, CD, lyric sheets, press clippings, video, résumé and contact numbers. Good kits stand out. Does not return material. Responds in 2 months.

Music Mostly **rock**, **blues**, and **young country**. Works primarily with concert headliners and singers. Current acts include Gary Cambra of the Tubes, Tim Murphy, Heat, Johnny Gunn, Famous Hits Band featuring Rich Varrasso, Alameda Allstars (Greg Allman's backup band), Richie Barron of HWY2000, and Greg Douglass (songwriter).

◪ WILLIAM F. WAGNER AGENCY

14343 Addison St. #221, Sherman Oaks CA 91423. (818)905-1033. **Contact:** Bill Wagner, owner. Management firm and record producer (Bill Wagner). Estab. 1957. Represents individual artists and groups from anywhere; currently handles 2 acts. Receives 15% commission. Reviews materials for acts.

How to Contact Submit demo tape or CD by mail. Unsolicited submissions are OK. Prefers cassette or CD with 5 songs and lead sheet. If seeking management, press kit should include cover letter, bio, picture, tape or CD with 5 songs. "If SASE and/or return postage are included, I will reply in 30 days."

Music Mostly **jazz**, **contemporary pop** and **contemporary country**; also **classical**, **MOR** and **film and TV background**. Works primarily with singers, with or without band, big bands and smaller instrumental groups. Current acts include Page Cavanaugh (jazz/pop/contemporary/pianist), Sandy Graham (jazz singer), Brant Vogel (country singer and backing group), and Hector King (Spanish/English-language crossover artist/singer-songwriter).

Tips "Indicate in first submission what artists you are writing for, by name if possible. Don't send material blindly. Be sure all material is properly copyrighted. Be sure package shows 'all material herein copyrighted' on outside."

☑ ◪ CHERYL K. WARNER PRODUCTIONS

P.O. Box 179, Hermitage TN 37076. Phone: (615)429-7849. E-mail: cherylkwarner@comcast.net. Web site: www.cherylkwarner.com. **Contact:** Cheryl K. Warner and Associates. Recording and stage production, music consulting, music publisher, record label. Estab. 1988. Currently works with 2 acts. Reviews material for acts.

How to Contact Submit demo package by mail. Unsolicited submissions are OK. Prefers CD or DVD, but will accept cassette with 3 best songs, lyric or lead sheet, bio and picture. Press kit should include CD, DVD, video/audio cassette with up-to-date bio, cover letter, lyric sheets, press clippings, and picture. Does not return material. Responds in 6 weeks if interested.

Music Mostly **country/traditional and contemporary**, **Christian/gospel** and **A/C/pop**. Works primarily with singer/songwriters and bands with original and versatile style. Current acts include Cheryl K. Warner (recording artist/entertainer) and Cheryl K. Warner Band (support/studio).

◙ WEMUS ENTERTAINMENT

2006 Seaboard, Suite 400, Midland TX 79705. (432)689-3687. Fax: (432)687-0930. E-mail: wemus@ aol.com. Web site: www.wemus.com. **Contact:** Dennis Grubb, president. Management firm, booking agency and music publisher (Wemus Music, Inc.). Estab. 1983. Represents local and regional individual artists and groups; currently handles 4 acts. Receives 15-25% commission. Reviews material for acts.

How to Contact Submit demo package by mail. Unsolicited submissions are OK. Prefers CD, cassette, DVD or VHS videocassette with 3-5 songs and lyric sheet. If seeking management, press kit should include glossy head and full body shots and extensive biography. "Make sure address, phone number and possible fax number is included in the packet, or a business card." Does not return material. Responds in 1 month if interested.

Music Mostly **country**. Current acts include The Image (variety), The Big Time (variety), The Pictures (variety) and Pryce Conner.

Tips "We preview and try to place good songs with national artists who are in need of good materials. We have a very tough qualification process and are very selective in forwarding materials to artists and their management."

Ⓝ ◪ ◯ WINTERLAND ENTERTAINMENT MANAGEMENT & PUBLISHING

(formerly T.J. Booker Ltd.), P.O. Box 969, Rossland BC VOG 1YO Canada. (250)362-7795. E-mail: winterland@netidea.com. **Contact:** Tom Jones, owner. Management firm, booking agency and music publisher. Estab. 1976. Represents individual artists, groups and songwriters from anywhere; currently handles 6 acts. Receives 15% commission. Reviews material for acts.

How to Contact Submit demo package by mail. Unsolicited submissions are OK. Prefers CD, cassette or videocassette with 3 songs. If seeking management, include demo tape or CD, picture, cover letter and bio in press kit. Does not return material. Responds in 1 month.

Music Mostly **MOR**, **crossover**, **rock**, **pop**, and **country**. Works primarily with vocalists, show bands, dance bands, and bar bands. Current acts include Kirk Orr (folk/country), Mike Hamilton (rock/blues) and Larry Hayton (rock/blues).

◯ RICHARD WOOD ARTIST MANAGEMENT

69 North Randall Ave., Staten Island NY 10301. (718)981-0641. Fax: (718)273-0797. **Contact:** Richard Wood. Management firm. Estab. 1974. Represents musical groups. Receives 20% commission. Reviews material for acts.

How to Contact Submit demo package by mail. Unsolicited submissions are OK. If seeking management, press kit should include demo tape, photo, cover letter and résumé. Include SASE. Responds in 1 month.

Music Mostly **dance**, **R&B** and **top 40/pop**; also **MOR**. Works primarily with "high energy" show bands and bar bands.

◙ WORLD WIDE MANAGEMENT

P.O. Box 536, Bronxville NY 10708. Fax: (914)337-5309 **Contact:** Steve Rosenfeld, managing director, or Marcy Drexler, director. Management firm and music publisher (Neighborhood Music/ASCAP). Estab. 1971. Represents artists, groups, songwriters and actors; currently handles 5 acts. Receives 15-20% commission. Reviews material for acts.

How to Contact *Write first and obtain permission to submit.* Prefers CD, cassette or videocassette of performance with 3-4 songs. If seeking management, press kit should include cover letter, bio, reviews, press clippings, CD or cassette with lyrics and photo. Does not return material. Responds in 1 month.

Music Mostly **contemporary pop**, **folk**, **folk/rock** and **New Age**; also **A/C**, **rock**, **jazz**, **bluegrass**, **blues**, **country** and **R&B**. Works primarily with self-contained bands and vocalists. Current acts include Aztec Two-Step, Marshall Crenshaw, Oz Noy Trio featuring Anton Fig and Will Lee, Keith Reid, and The Outset Band.

◘ WORLDSOUND, LLC

17837 1st Ave. South Suite 3, Seattle WA 98148. (206)444-0300. Fax: (206)244-0066. E-mail: music @worldsound.com. Web site: www.worldsound.com. **Contact:** Warren Wyatt, A&R manager. Management firm. Estab. 1976. Represents individual artists, groups and songwriters from anywhere; currently handles 8 acts. Receives 20% commission. Reviews material for acts.

How to Contact "Online, send us an e-mail containing a link to your Web site where your songs can be heard and the lyrics are available—PLEASE DO NOT E-MAIL SONG FILES! By regular mail, unsolicited submissions are OK." Prefers CD with 2-10 songs and lyric sheet. "If seeking management, please send an e-mail with a link to your Web site—your site should contain song samples, band biography, photos, video (if available), press and demo reviews. By mail, please send the materials listed above and include SASE." Responds in 1 month.

Music Mostly **rock**, **pop**, and **world**; also **heavy metal**, **hard rock**, and **top 40**. Works primarily with pop/rock/world artists. Current acts include Makana (world music), Treble (pop), La Neo (contemporary/Hawaiian), and Keith Olsen (music producer).

Tips "Always submit new songs/material, even if you have sent material that was previously rejected; the music biz is always changing."

◘ ZANE MANAGEMENT, INC.

1650 Market St., One Liberty Place, 21st Floor, Philadelphia PA 19103. (215)575-3803. Fax: (215)575-3801. E-mail: lzr@braverlaw.com. Web site: www.zanemanagement.com. **Contact:** Lloyd Z. Remick, Esq., president. Entertainment/sports consultants and managers. Represents artists, songwriters, producers and athletes; currently handles 7 acts. Receives 10-15% commission.

How to Contact Submit demo tape by mail. Unsolicited submissions are OK. Prefers CD and lyric sheet. If seeking management, press kit should include cover letter, bio, photo, demo tape and video. Does not return material. Responds in 3 weeks.

Music Mostly **dance**, **easy listening**, **folk**, **jazz (fusion)**, **MOR**, **rock (hard and country)**, **soul** and **top 40/pop**. Current acts include Bunny Sigler (disco/funk), Peter Nero and Philly Pops (conductor), Cast in Bronze (rock group), Pieces of a Dream (jazz/crossover), Don't Look Down (rock/pop), Christian Josi (pop-swing), Bishop David Evans (gospel), Kevin Roth (children's music), and Rosie Carlino (standards/pop).

◘ D. ZIRILLI MANAGEMENT

P.O. Box 255, Cupertino CA 95015-0255. (408)257-2533. Fax: (408)252-8938. E-mail: donzirilli@aol .com. Web site: www.zirilli.com Owner: Don Zirilli. Management firm. Estab. 1965. Represents groups from anywhere; currently handles 1 act. Receives 20% commission or does fee-based consulting. Varies by project. Reviews material for acts.

How to Contact Submit demo package by mail. Unsolicited submissions are OK. Prefers CD, DAT, videocassette or DVD. If seeking management, press kit should include video. Does not return material. Responds in 2 weeks.

Music Mostly **rock**, **surf** and **MOR**. Current acts include Papa Doo Run Run (band).

Tips "Less is more."

ADDITIONAL MANAGERS & BOOKING AGENTS

The following companies are also managers/booking agents, but their listings are found in other sections of the book. Read the listings for submission information.

D
Deep South Entertainment 173
Diamond Entertainment, Joel 210

H
His Power Productions and Publishing 129

K
Kaupps & Robert Publishing Co. 132

L
Lucifer Records, Inc. 180

M
Modal Music, Inc.™ 184

P
Panama Music Group of Companies, The 186

S
Satkowski Recordings, Steve 218

T
Third Wave Productions Ltd. 196
Twin Towers Publishing Co. 151

Music Firms

Advertising, Audiovisual & Commercial

It's happened a million times—you hear a jingle on the radio or television and can't get it out of your head. That's the work of a successful jingle writer, writing songs to catch your attention and make you aware of the product being advertised. But the field of commercial music consists of more than just memorable jingles. It also includes background music that many companies use in videos for corporate and educational presentations, as well as films and TV shows.

SUBMITTING MATERIAL

More than any other market listed in this book, the commercial music market expects composers to have made an investment in the recording of their material before submitting. A sparse, piano/vocal demo won't work here; when dealing with commercial music firms, especially audiovisual firms and music libraries, high quality production is important. Your demo may be kept on file at one of these companies until a need for it arises, and it may be used or sold as you sent it. Therefore, your demo tape or reel must be as fully produced as possible.

The presentation package that goes along with your demo must be just as professional. A list of your credits should be a part of your submission, to give the company an idea of your experience in this field. If you have no experience, look to local television and radio stations to get your start. Don't expect to be paid for many of your first jobs in the commercial music field; it's more important to get the credits and exposure that can lead to higher-paying jobs.

Commercial music and jingle writing can be a lucrative field for the composer/songwriter with a gift for writing catchy melodies and the ability to write in many different music styles. It's a very competitive field, so it pays to have a professional presentation package that makes your work stand out.

Three different segments of the commercial music world are listed here: advertising agencies, audiovisual firms and commercial music houses/music libraries. Each looks for a different type of music, so read these descriptions carefully to see where the music you write fits in.

ADVERTISING AGENCIES

Ad agencies work on assignment as their clients' needs arise. Through consultation and input from the creative staff, ad agencies seek jingles and music to stimulate the consumer to identify with a product or service.

When contacting ad agencies, keep in mind they are searching for music that can capture and then hold an audience's attention. Most jingles are short, with a strong, memorable hook. When an ad agency listens to a demo, it is not necessarily looking for a finished product so much as for an indication of creativity and diversity. Many composers put together a reel of excerpts of work from previous projects, or short pieces of music that show they can write in a variety of styles.

AUDIOVISUAL FIRMS

Audiovisual firms create a variety of products, from film and video shows for sales meetings, corporate gatherings and educational markets, to motion pictures and TV shows. With the increase of home video use, how-to videos are a big market for audiovisual firms, as are spoken word educational videos. All of these products need music to accompany them. For your quick reference, companies working to place music in movies and TV shows (excluding commercials) have a ▧ preceding their listing (also see the Film & TV Index on page 389 for a complete list of these companies).

Like ad agencies, audiovisual firms look for versatile, well-rounded songwriters. When submitting demos to these firms, you need to demonstrate your versatility in writing specialized background music and themes. Listings for companies will tell what facet(s) of the audiovisual field they are involved in and what types of clients they serve. Your demo tape should also be as professional and fully produced as possible; audiovisual firms often seek demo tapes that can be put on file for future use when the need arises.

COMMERCIAL MUSIC HOUSES & MUSIC LIBRARIES

Commercial music houses are companies contracted (either by an ad agency or the advertiser) to compose custom jingles. Since they are neither an ad agency nor an audiovisual firm, their main concern is music. They use a lot of it, too—some composed by inhouse songwriters and some contributed by outside, freelance writers.

Music libraries are different in that their music is not custom composed for a specific client. Their job is to provide a collection of instrumental music in many different styles that, for an annual fee or on a per-use basis, the customer can use however he chooses.

In the following listings, commercial music houses and music libraries, which are usually the most open to works by new composers, are identified as such by **bold** typeface.

The commercial music market is similar to most other businesses in one aspect: experience is important. Until you develop a list of credits, pay for your work may not be high. Don't pass up opportunities if a job is non- or low-paying. These assignments will add to your list of credits, make you contacts in the field, and improve your marketability.

Money and rights

Many of the companies listed in this section pay by the job, but there may be some situations where the company asks you to sign a contract that will specify royalty payments. If this happens, research the contract thoroughly, and know exactly what is expected of you and how much you'll be paid.

Depending on the particular job and the company, you may be asked to sell one-time rights or all rights. One-time rights involve using your material for one presentation only. All rights means the buyer can use your work any way he chooses, as many times as he likes. Be sure you know exactly what you're giving up, and how the company may use your music in the future.

In the commercial world, many of the big advertising agencies have their own publishing companies where writers assign their compositions. In these situations, writers sign contracts whereby they do receive performance and mechanical royalties when applicable.

ADDITIONAL LISTINGS

For additional names and addresses of ad agencies that may use jingles and/or commercial music, refer to the *Standard Directory of Advertising Agencies* (National Register Publishing).

For a list of audiovisual firms, check out the latest edition of *AV Marketplace* (R.R. Bowker). Both these books may be found at your local library. To contact companies in your area, see the Geographic Index at the back of this book.

THE AD AGENCY

P.O. Box 470572, San Francisco CA 94147. **Contact:** Michael Carden, creative director. **Advertising agency and jingle/commercial music production house.** Clients include business, industry and retail. Estab. 1971. Uses the services of music houses, independent songwriter/composers and lyricists for scoring of commercials, background music for video production, and jingles for commercials. Commissions 20 composers and 15 lyricists/year. Pays by the job or by the hour. Buys all or one-time rights.

How to Contact Submit demo tape of previous work. Prefers cassette with 5-8 songs and lyric sheet. Include SASE. Responds in 3 weeks.

Music Uses variety of musical styles for commercials, promotion, TV, video presentations.

Tips "Our clients and our needs change frequently."

ADVERTEL, INC.

P.O. Box 18053, Pittsburgh PA 15236-0053. (412)344-4700. Fax: (412)344-4712. E-mail: pberan@advertel.com. Web site: www.advertel.com. **Contact:** Paul Beran, president/CEO. **Telephonic/Internet production company.** Clients include small and multi-national companies. Estab. 1983. Uses the services of music houses and independent songwriters/composers for scoring of instrumentals (all varieties) and telephonic production. Commissions 3-4 composers/year. Pay varies. Buys all rights and phone exclusive rights.

How to Contact Submit demo of previous work. Prefers CD. "Most compositions are 2 minutes strung together in 6, 12, 18 minute length productions." Does not return material; prefers to keep on file. Responds "right away if submission fills an immediate need."

Music Uses all varieties, including unusual; mostly subdued music beds. Radio-type production used exclusively in telephone and Internet applications.

Tips "Go for volume. We have continuous need for all varieties of music in two minute lengths."

COMMUNICATIONS FOR LEARNING

395 Massachusetts Ave., Arlington MA 02474. (781)641-2350. E-mail: comlearn@thecia.net. Web site: www.communicationsforlearning.com. **Contact:** Jonathan L. Barkan, executive producer/director. Video, multimedia, exhibit and graphic design firm. Clients include multi-nationals, industry, government, institutions, local, national and international nonprofits. Uses services of music houses and independent songwriters/composers as theme and background music for videos and multimedia. Commissions 1-2 composers/year. Pays $2,000-5,000/job and one-time fees. Rights purchased varies.

How to Contact Submit demo and work available for useage. Prefers CD to Web links. Does not return material; prefers to keep on file. "For each job we consider our entire collection." Responds in 3 months.

Music Uses all styles of music for all sorts of assignments.

Tips "Please don't call. Just send your best material available for library use on CD. We'll be in touch if a piece works and negotiate a price. Make certain your name and contact information are on the CD itself, not only on the cover letter."

▨ ENTERTAINMENT PRODUCTIONS, INC.

2118 Wilshire Blvd. 744, Santa Monica CA 90403. (310)456-3143. Fax: (310)456-8950. **Contact:** Anne Bell, Music Director. Producer: Edward Coe. **Motion picture and television production**

company. Clients include motion picture and TV distributors. Estab. 1972. Uses the services of music houses and songwriters for scores, production numbers, background and theme music for films and TV and jingles for promotion of films. Commissions/year vary. Pays by the job or by royalty. Buys motion picture, video and allied rights.

How to Contact Query with résumé of credits. Demo should show flexibility of composition skills. "Demo records/tapes sent at own risk—returned if SASE included." Responds by letter within 1 month, "but only if SASE is included."

Tips "Have résumé on file. Develop self-contained capability."

ℕ K&R ALL MEDIA PRODUCTIONS LLC

(formerly K&R's Recording Studios), 28533 Greenfield, Southfield MI 48076. (248)557-8276. E-mail: recordav@knr.net. Web site: www.knr.net. **Contact:** Ken Glaza. Scoring service and **jingle/commercial music production house**. Clients include commercial and industrial firms. Services include sound for pictures (music, dialogue). Uses the services of independent songwriters/composers and lyricists for scoring of film and video, commercials and industrials and jingles and commercials for radio and TV. Commissions 1 composer/month. Pays by the job. Buys all rights.

How to Contact Submit demo tape of previous work. Prefers CD or VHS videocassette with 5-7 short pieces. "We rack your tape for client to judge." Does not return material.

Tips "Keep samples short. Show me what you can do in five minutes. Go to knr.net 'free samples' and listen to the sensitivity expressed in emotional music." Current projects: Proof and D12 soundtracks.

KEN-DEL PRODUCTIONS INC.

First State Production Center, 1500 First State Blvd., Wilmington DE 19804-3596. (302)999-1111. Estab. 1950. **Contact:** Edwin Kennedy, A&R manager. Clients include publishers, industrial firms and advertising agencies, how-to's and radio/TV. Uses services of songwriters for radio/TV commercials, jingles and multimedia. Pays by the job. Buys all rights.

How to Contact "Submit all inquiries and demos in any format to general manager." Does not return material. Will keep on file for 3 years. Generally responds in 1 month or less.

LAPRIORE VIDEOGRAPHY

67 Millbrook St. Ste. 114, Worcester MA 01606. (508)755-9010. E-mail: peter@lapriorevideo.com. Web site: www.lapriorevideo.com. **Contact:** Peter Lapriore, owner/producer. **Video production company.** Clients include corporations, retail stores, educational and sports. Estab. 1985. Uses the services of music houses, independent songwriters/composers for background music for marketing, training, educational videos and TV commercials and for scoring video. "We also own several music libraries." Commissions 2 composers/year. Pays $150-1,000/job. Buys all or one-time rights.

How to Contact Submit demo of previous work. Prefers CD, or DVD with 5 songs and lyric sheet. Does not return material; prefers to keep on file. Responds in 3 weeks.

Music Uses slow, medium, up-tempo, jazz and classical for marketing, educational films and commercials.

Tips "Be very creative and willing to work on all size budgets."

ℕ NOVUS

121 E. 24th St., 12 Floor, New York NY 10010. (212)487-1377. Fax: (212)505-3300. E-mail: novuscom@aol.com. **Contact:** Robert Antonik, president/creative director. Marketing and communications company. Clients include corporations and interactive media. Estab. 1986. Uses the services of music houses, independent songwriters/composers and lyricists for scoring, background music for documentaries, commercials, multimedia applications, Web site, film shorts, and commercials for radio and TV. Commissions 2 composers and 4 lyricists/year. Pay varies per job. Buys one-time rights.

How to Contact *Write first to arrange personal interview.* Query with résumé. Submit demo of work. Prefers CD with 2-3 songs. "We prefer to keep submitted material on file, but will return material if SASE is enclosed. Responds in 6 weeks.

Music Uses **all styles** for a variety of different assignments.

Tips "Always present your best and don't add quantity to your demo. Novus is a creative marketing and communications company. We work with various public relations, artists managements and legal advisors. We create multimedia events to album packaging and promotion."

N OMNI COMMUNICATIONS

Dept. SM, P.O. Box 302, Carmel IN 46082-0302. (317)846-2345. E-mail: omni@omniproductions.com. Web site: www.omniproductions.com. President: W. H. Long. Creative Director: S.M. Long. Production Manager: Jim Mullet. Television production and audiovisual firm. Estab. 1978. Serves industrial, commercial and educational clients. Uses the services of music houses and songwriters for scoring of films and television productions, CD-ROMs and Internet streams; background music for voice overs; lyricists for original music and themes. Pays by the job. Buys all rights.

How to Contact Submit demo tape of previous work. Prefers CD or DVD. Does not return material. Responds in 2 weeks.

Music Varies with each and every project; from classical, contemporary to commercial industrial.

Tips "Submit good demo tape with examples of your range to command the attention of our producers."

QUALLY & COMPANY INC.

2 E. Oak, Suite 2903, Chicago IL 60611. (312)280-1898. **Contact:** Michael Iva, creative director. **Advertising agency.** Uses the services of music houses, independent songwriters/composers and lyricists for scoring, background music and jingles for radio and TV commercials. Commissions 2-4 composers and 2-4 lyricists/year. Pays by the job. Buys various rights depending on deal.

How to Contact Submit demo CD of previous work or query with résumé of credits. Include SASE, but prefers to keep material on file. Responds in 2 weeks.

Music Uses all kinds of music for commercials.

▲ TRF PRODUCTION MUSIC LIBRARIES

Dept. SM, 747 Chestnut Ridge Rd., Chestnut Ridge NY 10977. (845)356-0800. Fax: (845)356-0895. E-mail: info@trfmusic.com. Web site: www.trfmusic.com. **Contact:** Anne Marie Russo. **Music/ sound effect libraries.** Estab. 1931. Uses the services of independent composers for all categories of production music for television, film and other media. Pays 50% royalty.

* Also see the listing for Alpha Music Inc. in the Music Publishers section of this book.

How to Contact Submit demo CD of new compositions. Prefers CD with 3-7 pieces. Can send audio cassette, DAT or CD with up to 12 tracks. Submissions are not returnable. Responds in 2 to 3 months after receipt.

Music Primarily interested in **acoustic instrumental** music suitable for use as production music, which is theme and background music for TV, film and AV/multimedia.

N ▲ UTOPIAN EMPIRE CREATIVEWORKS

P.O. Box 9, Traverse City MI 49685 or P.O. Box 499, Kapa 'a (Kaua'i) HI 96746. (231)943-5050 or (231)943-4000. E-mail: creativeworks@utopianempire.com. Web site: www.UtopianEmpire.com. **Contact:** Ms. M'Lynn Hartwell, president. Web design, multimedia firm and motion picture/video production company. Primarily serves commercial, industrial and nonprofit clients. We provide the following services: advertising, marketing, design/packaging, distribution and booking. Uses services of music houses, independent songwriters/composers for jingles and scoring of and background music for multi-image/multimedia, film and video. Negotiates pay. Buys all or one-time rights.

How to Contact Submit CD of previous work, demonstrating composition skills or query with resume of credits. Prefers CD or good quality cassette. Does not return material; prefers to keep on file. Responds only if interested.

Music Uses mostly industrial/commercial themes.

Ⓝ VIDEO I-D, INC.

Dept. SM, 105 Muller Rd., Washington IL 61571. (309)444-4323. Fax: (309)444-4333. E-mail: videoi d@videoid.com. Web site: www.VideoID.com. **Contact:** Gwen Wagner, manager, operations. Post production/teleproductions. Clients include law enforcement, industrial and business. Estab. 1977. Uses the services of music houses and independent songwriters/composers for background music for video productions. Pays per job. Buys one-time rights.

How to Contact Submit demo of previous work. Prefers CD or VHS videocassette with 5 songs and lyric sheet. Does not return material. Responds in 1 month.

Play Producers
& Publishers

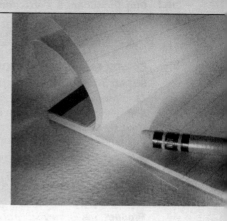

Finding a theater company willing to invest in a new production can be frustrating for an unknown playwright. But whether you write the plays, compose the music or pen the lyrics, it is important to remember not only where to start but how to start. Theater in the U.S. is a hierarchy, with Broadway, Off Broadway and Off Off Broadway being pretty much off limits to all but the Stephen Sondheims of the world.

Aspiring theater writers would do best to train their sights on nonprofit regional and community theaters to get started. The encouraging news is there is a great number of local theater companies throughout the U.S. with experimental artistic directors who are looking for new works to produce, and many are included in this section. This section covers two segments of the industry: theater companies and dinner theaters are listed under Play Producers (beginning on page 264), and publishers of musical theater works are listed under the Play Publishers heading (beginning on page 269). All these markets are actively seeking new works of all types for their stages or publications.

BREAKING IN

Starting locally will allow you to research each company carefully and learn about their past performances, the type of musicals they present, and the kinds of material they're looking for. When you find theaters you think may be interested in your work, attend as many performances as possible, so you know exactly what type of material each theater presents. Or volunteer to work at a theater, whether it be moving sets or selling tickets. This will give you valuable insight into the day-to-day workings of a theater and the creation of a new show. On a national level, you will find prestigious organizations offering workshops and apprenticeships covering every subject from arts administration to directing to costuming. But it could be more helpful to look into professional internships at theaters and attend theater workshops in your area. The more knowledgeable you are about the workings of a particular company or theater, the easier it will be to tailor your work to fit its style and the more responsive they will be to you and your work. (See the Workshops & Conferences section on page 325 for more information.) As a composer for the stage, you need to know as much as possible about a theater and how it works, its history and the different roles played by the people involved in it. Flexibility is the key to successful productions, and knowing how a theater works will only help you in cooperating and collaborating with the director, producer, technical people and actors.

If you're a playwright looking to have his play published in book form or in theater publications, see the listings under the Play Publishers section (page 269). To find play producers and publishers in your area, consult the Geographic Index at the back of this book.

PLAY PRODUCERS

☑ ARKANSAS REPERTORY THEATRE

601 Main, P.O. Box 110, Little Rock AR 72201. (501)378-0445. Web site: www.therep.org. **Contact:** Brad Mooy. Play producer. Estab. 1976. Produces 6-10 plays and musicals/year. "We perform in a 354-seat house and also have a 99-seat 2nd stage." Pays 5-10% royalty or $75-150 per performance.
How to Contact Query with synopsis, character breakdown and set description. Include SASE. Responds in 6 months.
Musical Theater "Small casts are preferred, comedy or drama and prefer shows to run 1:45 to 2 hours maximum. Simple is better; small is better, but we do produce complex shows. We aren't interested in children's pieces, puppet shows or mime. We always like to receive a tape of the music with the book."
Productions *Disney's Beauty & the Beast*, by Woolverton/Ashman/Rice/Menken (musical retelling of the myth); *Crowns*, by Taylor/Cunningham/Marberry (on the significance of African-American women's hats); and *A Chorus Line*, by Kirkwood/Hamlisch/Kleban (auditions).
Tips "Include a good cassette of your music, sung well, with the script."

◫ CIRCA '21 DINNER PLAYHOUSE

Dept. SM, P.O. Box 3784, Rock Island IL 61204-3784. (309)786-2667, ext. 303. Fax: (309)786-4119. E-mail: dpjh@circa21.com. Web site: www.circa21.com. **Contact:** Dennis Hitchcock, producer. Play producer. Estab. 1977. Produces 1-2 plays and 4-5 musicals (1 new musical)/year. Plays produced for a general audience. Three children's works/year, concurrent with major productions. Payment is negotiable.
How to Contact Query with synopsis, character breakdown and set description or submit complete manuscript, score and tape of songs. Include SASE. Responds in 3 months.
Musical Theater "We produce both full length and one act children's musicals. Folk or fairy tale themes. Works that do not condescend to a young audience yet are appropriate for entire family. We're also seeking full-length, small cast musicals suitable for a broad audience." Would also consider original music for use in a play being developed.
Productions *A Closer Walk with Patsy Cline*, *Swingtime Canteen*, *Forever Plaid* and *Lost Highway*.
Tips "Small, upbeat, tourable musicals (like *Pump Boys*) and bright musically-sharp children's productions (like those produced by Prince Street Players) work best. Keep an open mind. Stretch to encompass a musical variety—different keys, rhythms, musical ideas and textures."

THE DIRECTORS COMPANY

311 W. 43rd St., Suite 307, New York NY 10036. (212)246-5877. E-mail: directorscompany@aol.com. Web site: http://mysite.verizon.net/directorscompany. **Contact:** Katherine Heberling, company manager. Artistic/Producing Director: Michael Parva. Play producer. Estab. 1980. Produces 1-2 new musicals/year. Performance space is a 99-seat theatre located in the heart of Manhattan's Theatre District. "It is beautifully equipped with dressing rooms, box office and reception area in the lobby." Pays negotiable rate.
How to Contact Query first. Include SASE. Responds in 1 year.
Musical Theater "The Harold Prince Musical Theatre Program develops new musicals by incorporating the director in the early stages of collaboration. The program seeks cutting edge material that works to break boundaries in music theatre. We produce workshops or developmental productions. The emphasis is on the material, not on production values, therefore, we do not limit cast sizes. However, there are limits on props and production values." No children's musicals or reviews.
Productions *Jubilee*, by Kelly Dupuis/Marc Smollin (an absurdly magical exploration of fate, family, and fish); *Tales of Tinseltown* (reading), by Michael Colby/Paul Katz (a sardonic parody of 1930s

Hollywood); and *Nightmare Alley* (reading), by Jonathan Brielle (about a drifter in 1932 looking for a way to begin a life in hard times).

ⓃFOOLS COMPANY, INC.

P.O. Box 413, Times Square Station, New York NY 10108. E-mail: foolsco@nyc.rr.com. **Contact:** Jill Russell, executive director. Collaborative new and experimental works producer. Estab. 1970. Produces 1 play and 1 musical (1 new musicals) depending on available funding. "Audience is comprised of hip, younger New Yorkers. Plays are performed at various venues in NYC." Pay is negotiable.

How to Contact Query first by e-mail. Include SASE.

Musical Theater "We seek new and unusual, contemporary and experimental material. We would like small, easy-to-tour productions. Nothing classical, folkloric or previously produced." Would also consider working with composers in collaboration or original music for use in plays being developed.

Productions Recent: *Rug Burn*; *Cathleen's Corsage* (alternative performance); and *Blunt Passage* (original drama).

Tips "Come work in NYC!"

ⓃNEW YORK STATE THEATRE INSTITUTE

37 First St., Troy NY 12180. (518)274-3200. E-mail: pbs@capital.net. Web site: www.nysti.org. **Contact:** Patricia Di Benedetto Snyder, producing artistic director. Play producer. Produces 5 plays (1 new musical)/year. Plays performed for student audiences grades K-12, family audiences and adult audiences. Theater seats 900 with full stage. Pay negotiable.

How to Contact Query with synopsis, character breakdown, set description and tape of songs. Include SASE. *Do not send ms unless invited.* Responds in 6 weeks for synopsis, 4 months for ms.

Musical Theater Looking for "intelligent and well-written book with substance, a score that enhances and supplements the book and is musically well-crafted and theatrical." Length: up to 2 hours. Could be play with music, musical comedy, musical drama. Excellence and substance in material is essential. Cast could be up to 20; orchestra size up to 8.

Productions *A Tale of Cinderella*, by W.A. Frankonis/Will Severin/George David Weiss (adaptation of fairy tale); *The Silver Skates*, by Lanie Robertson/Byron Janis/George David Weiss (adaptation of book); *The Snow Queen*, by Adrian Mitchell/Richard Peaslee (adaptation of fairy tale); and *Magna Carta*, by Ed Lange/Will Severin/George David Weiss (new musical drama).

Tips "There is a great need for musicals that are well-written with intelligence and substance which are suitable for family audiences."

ⓃNORTH SHORE MUSIC THEATRE

P.O. Box 62, Beverly MA 01915. (978)232-7200. Fax: (978)921-6351. Web site: www.nsmt.org. **Contact:** John La Rock, producer. Play producer. Estab. 1955. Produces 1 Shakespearian play and 7 musicals (1 new musical)/year. General audiences. Performance space is an 1,500-seat arena theatre, 120-seat workshop. Pays royalty (all done via individual commission agreements).

How to Contact Submit synopsis and CD of songs. Include SASE. Responds within 6 months.

Musical Theater Prefers full-length adult pieces not necessarily arena-theatre oriented. Cast sizes from 1-30; orchestra's from 1-16.

Productions *Tom Jones*, by Paul Leigh, George Stiles; *I Sent A Letter to My Love*, by Melissa Manchester and Jeffrey Sweet; *Just So*, by Anthony Drewe & George Stiles (musical based on Rudyard Kipling's fables); *Letters from 'Nam*, by Paris Barclay (Vietnam War experience as told through letters from GI's); and *Friendship of the Sea*, by Michael Wartofsky & Kathleen Cahill (New England maritime adventure musical).

Tips "Keep at it!"

THE OPEN EYE THEATER

P.O. Box 959, 1000 Main St., Margaretville NY 12455. E-mail: openeye@catskill.net. Web site: www.theopeneye.org. **Contact:** Amie Brockway, producing artistic director. Play producer. Estab. 1972. Produces approximately 3 full length or 3 new plays for multi-generational audiences. Pays on a fee basis.

How to Contact Query first. "A manuscript will be accepted and read only if it is a play for all ages and is: 1) Submitted by a recognized literary agent; 2) Requested or recommended by a staff or company member; or 3) Recommended by a professional colleague with whose work we are familiar. Playwrights may submit a one-page letter of inquiry including a very brief plot synopsis. Please enclose a self-addressed (but not stamped) envelope. We will reply only if we want you to submit the script (within several months)."

Musical Theater "The Open Eye Theater is a not-for-profit professional company working in a community context. Through the development, production and performance of plays for all ages, artists and audiences are challenged and given the opportunity to grow in the arts. In residence, on tour, and in the classroom, The Open Eye Theater strives to stimulate, educate, entertain, inspire and serve as a creative resource."

Productions *Freddy, the King of Detectives*, by Sandra Fenichel Asher, music by Robert Cucinotta; *Twelfth Night or What You Will*, by William Shakespeare, music by Michael Anthony Worden; *The Wide Awake Princess*, adapted by David Paterson from the novel by Katherine Paterson, with music and lyrics by Steve Liebman; and *Pixies, Kings and Magical Things*, by Hans Christian Anderson, adapted by Ric Aver (four children's tales).

PLAYHOUSE ON THE SQUARE

51 S. Cooper, Memphis TN 38104. (901)725-0776. Fax: (901)272-7530. **Contact:** Jackie Nichols, executive producer. Play producer. Produces 12 plays and 4 musicals/year. Plays are produced in a 260-seat proscenium resident theater. Pays $500 for outright purchase.

How to Contact Submit complete manuscript, score and tape of songs. Unsolicited submissions OK. Include SASE. Responds in 6 months.

Musical Theater Seeking "any subject matter—adult and children's material. Small cast preferred. Stage is 26' deep by 43' wide with no fly system."

Productions *Children of Eden*; and *Tommy*, by The Who.

☑ PRIMARY STAGES

307 West 38th St., Suite 1510, New York NY 10018. (212)840-9705. Fax: (212)840-9725. E-mail: info@primarystages.com. Web site: www.primarystages.com. **Contact:** Michelle Bossy, associate artistic director. Play producer. Estab. 1984. Produces 4-5 plays/year. "New York theater-going audience representing a broad cross-section, in terms of age, ethnicity, and economic backgrounds. 199-seat, Off-Broadway theater."

How to Contact Query first with synopsis, character breakdown, set description and tape. "No unsolicited scripts accepted. Submissions by agents only." Include SASE. Responds in up to 8 months.

Musical Theater "We are looking for work of heightened theatricality, that challenges realism— musical plays that go beyond film and televisions standard fare. We are looking for small cast shows under 6 characters total, with limited sets. We are interested in original works, that have not been produced in New York."

Productions *I Sent a Letter to My Love*, by Melissa Manchester/Jeffrey Sweet; *Nightmare Alley*, by Jonathan Brielle; *Call the Children Home*, by Mildred Kayden and Thomas Babe; *Adrift in Macao*, by Christopher Durang and Peter Melnick.

☑ PRINCE MUSIC THEATER

100 S. Broad St., Suite 650, Philadelphia PA 19110. (215)972-1000. Fax: (215)972-1020. E-mail: info@princemusictheater.org. Web site: www.princemusictheater.org. **Contact:** Marjorie Samoff, president and producing director. Play producer. Estab. 1984. Produces 4-5 musicals/year. "Our average audience member is in their mid-40s. We perform to ethnically diverse houses."

How to Contact Submit two-page synopsis with tape or CD of 4 songs. Include SASE. "May include complete script, but be aware that response is at least 10 months."

Music "We seek musicals ranging from the traditional to the experimental. Topics can range. Musical styles can vary from folk pop through opera. Orchestra generally limited to a maximum of 9 pieces; cast size maximum of 10-12."

Musical Theater 2006-2007 Season: *From Tha Hip*, by Clyde Evans, Jr; *Always: The Love Story of Irving Berlin*, conceived by Mark Nadler and KT Sullivan; *A Swell Party: R.S.V.P. Cole Porter*, conceived by Mark Nadler and KT Sullivan; *Annie Get Your Gun*, by Herbert & Dorothy Fields/Irving Berlin; *Stormy Weather: Imagining Lena Horne*, by Sharleen Cooper Cohen; *Tiny Dancer*, by Paul Scott Goodman/Miriam Gordon; *Hair*, Gerome Ragni & James Rado/Galt MacDermot.

Tips "We only produce pieces that are music/lyric driven, not merely plays with music."

Ⓝ SECOND STAGE THEATRE

307 W. 43rd St., New York NY 10036. (212)787-8302. Fax: (212)397-7066. **Contact:** Christopher Burney, associate artistic director. Play producer. Estab. 1979. Produces 4 plays and 1 musical (1 new musical)/year. Plays are performed in a small, 108-seat Off Broadway House. Pays per performance.

How to Contact Query with synopsis, character breakdown, set description, tape of 5 songs (no more). No unsolicited manuscripts. Include SASE. Responds in 6 months.

Musical Theater "We are looking for innovative, unconventional musicals that deal with sociopolitical themes."

Productions *Saturday Night*, by Stephen Sondheim; *Little Fish*, by Michael John LaChiusa; *Crowns*, by Regina Taylor (music-gospel traditional); and The 25th Annual Putnam County Spelling Bee, by Rachel Sheinkin and William Finn (musical).

Tips "Submit through agent; have strong references; always submit the best of your material in small quantities: 5 outstanding songs are better than 10 mediocre ones."

☑ SHAKESPEARE SANTA CRUZ

Theater Arts Center, U.C.S.C., 1156 High Street, Santa Cruz CA 95064. (831)459-5810. E-mail: iago@ucsc.edu. Web site: www.shakespearesantacruz.org. **Contact:** Paul Whitworth, artistic director. Play producer. Estab. 1982. Produces 4 plays/year. Performance spaces are an outdoor redwood grove; and an indoor 540-seat thrust. Pay is negotiable.

How to Contact Query first. Include SASE. Responds in 2 months.

Musical Theater "Shakespeare Santa Cruz produces musicals in its Winter Holiday Season (Oct-Dec). We are also interested in composers' original music for pre-existing plays—including songs, for example, for Shakespeare's plays."

Productions *Cinderella*, by Kate Hawley (book and lyrics) and Gregg Coffin (composer); and *Gretel and Hansel*, by Kate Hawley (book and lyrics) and composer Craig Bohmler; *The Princess and the Pea*, by Kate Hawley (book and lyrics) and composer Adam Wernick.

Tips "Always contact us before sending material."

THE TEN-MINUTE MUSICALS PROJECT

P.O. Box 461194, West Hollywood CA 90046. E-mail: info@tenminutemusicals.org. Web site: www .tenminutemusicals.org. **Contact:** Michael Koppy, producer. Play producer. Estab. 1987. All pieces are new musicals. Pays $250 advance.

How to Contact Submit complete manuscript, score and tape of songs. Include SASE. Responds in 3 months.

Musical Theater Seeks complete short stage musicals of 8-15 minutes in length. Maximum cast: 9. "No parodies—original music only."

Productions Away to Pago Pago, by Jack Feldman/Barry Manilow/John PiRoman/Bruce Sussman; The Bottle Imp, by Kenneth Vega (from the story of the same title by Robert Louis Stevenson); and The Furnished Room, by Saragail Katzman (from the story of the same title by O. Henry), and many others.

Tips "Start with a solid story—either an adaptation or an original idea—but with a solid beginning, middle and end (probably with a plot twist at the climax). We caution that it will surely take much time and effort to create a quality work. (Occasionally a clearly talented and capable writer and composer seem to have almost 'dashed' something off, under the misperception that inspiration can carry the day in this format. Works selected in previous rounds all clearly evince that considerable deliberation and craft were invested.) We're seeking short contemporary musical theater material, in the style of what might be found on Broadway, Off-Broadway or the West End. Think of shows like Candide or Little Shop of Horrors, pop operas like Sweeney Todd or Chess, or chamber musicals like Once on this Island or Falsettos. (Even small accessible operas like The Telephone or Trouble in Tahiti are possible models.) All have solid plots, and all rely on sung material to advance them. Of primary importance is to start with a strong story, even if it means postponing work on music and lyrics until the dramatic foundation is complete."

☑ THUNDER BAY THEATRE

400 N. Second Ave., Alpena MI 49707. (989)354-2267. Web site: www.thunderbaytheatre.com. Artistic Director: Tim Bennett. Play producer. Estab. 1967. Produces 12 plays and 6 musicals (1 new musical)/year. Performance space is thrust/proscenium stage. Pays variable royalty or per performance.

How to Contact Submit complete manuscript, score and tape of songs. Include SASE. Responds in 3 months.

Musical Theater Small cast. Not equipped for large sets. Considers original background music for use in a play being developed or for use in a pre-existing play.

Productions 2006 Musicals: *Nunsense*; *Stand By Your Man: The Tammy Wynette Story*; *Grease*; *You're a Good Man, Charlie Brown*.

☑ WEST END ARTISTS

% St. Luke's Theatre, 308 West 46th St., New York NY 10036. (212)947-3499. Fax: (212)265-4074. **West Coast:** 18034 Ventura Blvd. #291, Encino CA 91316. (818)623-0040. Fax: (818)623-0202. E-mail: egaynes@aol.com. **Contact:** Pamela Hall, associate artistic director. Artistic Director: Edmund Gaynes. Play producer. Estab. 1983. "We operate St. Luke's Theatre, Actors Temple Theatre, and Theatres at 45 Bleecker St. in New York City, and Whitmore-Lindley Theatre Center in Los Angeles." Produces 5 plays and 3 new musicals/year. Audience "covers a broad spectrum, from general public to heavy theater/film/TV industry crowds. Pays 6% royalty.

How to Contact Submit complete manuscript, score and tape of songs. Include SASE. Responds in 3 months.

Musical Theater "Prefer small-cast musicals and revues. Full length preferred. Interested in children's shows also." Cast size: "Maximum 12; exceptional material with larger casts will be considered."

Productions Off-Broadway: *Picon Pie*—one year run (2004-05); *Trolls*—six month run (2005).

Tips "If you feel every word or note you have written is sacred and chiseled in stone and are unwilling to work collaboratively with a professional director, don't bother to submit."

Ⓝ WINGS THEATRE CO.

154 Christopher St., New York NY 10014. (212)627-2960. Fax: (212)462-0024. E-mail: jcorrick@win gstheatre.com. Web site: www.wingstheatre.com. **Contact:** Laura Kleeman, literary manager. Artistic Director: Jeffrey Corrick. Play producer. Estab. 1987. Produces 3-5 plays and 3-5 musicals/year. Performance space is a 74-seat O.O.B. proscenium; repertoire includes a New Musicals Series, a gay-play series—we produce musicals in both series. Pays $100 for limited rights to produce against 6% of gross box office receipts.

How to Contact Submit complete manuscript, CD or tape of songs (score is not essential). Include SASE. Responds in 1 year.

Musical Theater "Eclectic. Entertaining. Enlightening. This is an O.O.B. theater. Funds are limited." Does not wish to see "movies posing as plays. Television theater."

Productions *Scott & Zelda*, by Dave Bates (The Fitzgeralds); *Cowboys*, by Clint Jefferies (gay western spoof); and *The Three Musketeers*, by Clint Jefferies (musical adaptation).

Tips "Book needs to have a well-developed plot line and interesting, fully-realized characters. We place emphasis on well-written scripts, as opposed to shows which rely exclusively on the quality of the music to carry the show. Also be patient—we often hold onto plays for a full year before making a final decision."

Ⓝ WOMEN'S PROJECT AND PRODUCTIONS

55 West End Ave., New York NY 10023. (212)765-1706. Fax: (212)765-2024. Web site: www.wome nsproject.org. **Contact:** Megan E. Carter, associate artistic director. Producing Artistic Director: Julie Crosby. Estab. 1978. Produces 3 plays/year. Pays by outright purchase.

How to Contact *Agented submissions only.*

Musical Theater "We usually prefer a small to medium cast. We produce few musicals and produce women playwrights."

Productions *Ladies*, by Eve Ensler (homelessness); *O Pioneers!*, by Darrah Cloud (adapted from Willa Cather's novel); and *Frida: The Story of Frida Kahlo*, by Hilary Blecher/Migdalia Cruz (biography of Frida Kahlo).

Tips "Resist sending early drafts of work."

PLAY PUBLISHERS

ARAN PRESS

1036 S. Fifth St., Louisville KY 40203. (502)568-6622. Fax: (502)561-1124. E-mail: aranpres@aye.n et. Web site: http://members.aye.net/~aranpres. **Contact:** Tom Eagan, editor/publisher. Play publisher. Estab. 1983. Publishes 5-10 plays and 1-2 musicals/year. Professional, college/university, community, summer stock and dinner theater audience. Pays 50% production royalty or 10% book royalty.

How to Contact Submit manuscript, score and tape of songs. Include SASE. Responds in 2 weeks.

Musical Theater "The musical should include a small cast, simple set for professional, community, college, university, summer stock and dinner theater production."

Publications *Whiskey & Wheaties*, by Bruce Feld; *Who Says Life is Fair*, by Mike Willis; and *Burning Bridges*, by Stephen Avery.

BAKER'S PLAYS

P.O. Box 699222, Quincy MA 02269-9222. (617)745-0805. Fax: (617)745-9891. E-mail: info@bakers plays.com. Web site: www.bakersplays.com. **Contact:** Associate Editor. Play publisher. Estab. 1845. Publishes 15-22 plays and 0-3 new musicals/year. Plays are used by children's theaters, junior and senior high schools, colleges and community theaters. Pays negotiated book and production royalty.

● See the listing for Baker's Plays High School Playwriting Contest in the Contests & Awards section.

How to Contact Submit complete manuscript, score and cassette tape of songs. Include SASE. Responds in 4 months.

Musical Theater "Seeking musicals for teen production and children's theater production. We prefer large cast, contemporary musicals which are easy to stage and produce. Plot your shows strongly, keep your scenery and staging simple, your musical numbers and choreography easily explained and blocked out. Music must be camera-ready." Would consider original music for use in a play being developed or in a pre-existing play.

Productions *Oedipus/A New Magical Comedy* , by Bob Johnson.

Tips "As we publish musicals that can be produced by high school theater departments with high school talent, the writer should know if their play can be done on the high school stage. I recommend that the writer go to performances of original high school musicals whenever possible."

CONTEMPORARY DRAMA SERVICE

885 Elkton Dr., Colorado Springs CO 80907. (719)594-4422. E-mail: merpcds@aol.com. Web site: www.contemporarydrama.com. **Contact:** Arthur Zapel, associate editor. Play publisher. Estab. 1979. Publishes 40-50 plays and 4-6 new musicals/year. "We publish for young children and teens in mainstream Christian churches and for teens and college level in the secular market. Our musicals are performed in churches, schools and colleges." Pays 10-50% book and performance royalty.

How to Contact *Query first* then submit complete manuscript, score and tape of songs. Include SASE. Responds in 1 month.

Musical Theater "For churches we publish musical programs for children and teens to perform at Easter, Christmas or some special occasion. Our school musicals are for teens to perform as class plays or special entertainments. Cast size may vary from 15-25 depending on use. We prefer more parts for girls than boys. Music must be written in the vocal range of teens. Staging should be relatively simple but may vary as needed. We are not interested in elementary school material. Elementary level is OK for church music but not public school elementary. Music must have full piano accompaniment and be professionally scored for camera-ready publication."

Publications *Lucky, Lucky Hudson and the 12th Street Gang*, by Tim Kelly, book, and Bill Francoeur, music and lyrics (spoof of old time gangster movies); *Is There A Doctor in the House?*, by Tim Kelly, book, and Bill Francoeur, music and lyrics (adapted from Moliere comedy); and *Jitterbug Juliet*, by Mark Dissette, book, and Bill Francoeur, music and lyrics (spoof of *Romeo and Juliet*).

Tips "Familiarize yourself with our market. Send $1 postage for catalog. Try to determine what would fit in, yet still be unique."

THE DRAMATIC PUBLISHING COMPANY

311 Washington St., Woodstock IL 60098. (815)338-7170. E-mail: plays@dramaticpublishing.com. Web site: dramaticpublishing.com. **Contact:** Music Editor. Play publisher. Publishes 35 plays and 3-5 musicals/year. Estab. 1885. Plays used by professional and community theaters, schools and colleges. Pays negotiable royalty.

How to Contact Submit complete manuscript, score and tape of songs. Include SASE. Responds in 3 months.

Musical Theater Seeking "children's musicals not over 1¼ hours, and adult musicals with 2 act format. No adaptations for which the rights to use the original work have not been cleared. If directed toward high school market, large casts with many female roles are preferred. For professional, stock and community theater small casts are better. Cost of producing a play is always a factor to consider in regard to costumes, scenery and special effects." Would also consider original music for use in a pre-existing play, "if we or the composer hold the rights to the non-musical work."

Play Producers

Publications *The Little Prince*, by Rick Cummins/John Scoullar; *Hans Brinker*, by Gayle Hudson/ Bobbe Bramson; and *Bubbe Meises, Bubbe Stories*, by Ellen Gould/Holly Gewandter (all are full-length family musicals).

Tips "A complete score, ready to go is highly recommended. Tuneful songs which stand on their own are a must. Good subject matter which has wide appeal is always best but not required."

ELDRIDGE PUBLISHING CO., INC.

P.O. Box 14367, Tallahassee FL 32317. (800)HI-STAGE. E-mail: info@histage.com. Web site: www. histage.com. **Contact:** Susan Shore, musical editor. Play publisher. Estab. 1906. Publishes 50 plays and 1-2 musicals/year. Seeking "large cast musicals which appeal to students. We like variety and originality in the music, easy staging and costuming. Also looking for children's theater musicals which have smaller casts and are easy to tour. We serve the school market (6th grade through 12th); and church market (Christmas musicals)." Pays 50% royalty and 10% copy sales in school market.

How to Contact Submit manuscript, score or lead sheets and CD of songs. Include SASE. Responds in 1 month.

Publications *The Bard is Back*, by Stephen Murray ("a high school's production of Romeo & Juliet is a disaster!"); and *Boogie-Woogie Bugle Girls*, book by Craig Sodaro, music and lyrics by Stephen Murray (WWII themed musical).

Tips "We're always looking for talented composers but not through individual songs. We're only interested in complete school or church musicals. Lead sheets, CDs tape and script are best way to submit. Let us see your work!"

THE FREELANCE PRESS

P.O. Box 548, Dover MA 02030. (508)785-8250. E-mail: info@freelancepress.org. Web site: www.fr eelancepress.org. Managing Editor: Narcissa Campion. Play publisher. Estab. 1979. Publishes up to 3 new musicals/year. "Pieces are primarily to be acted by elementary/middle school to high school students (9th and 10th grades); large casts (approximately 30); plays are produced by schools and children's theaters." Pays 10% of purchase price of script or score, 50% of collected royalty.

How to Contact Query first. Include SASE. Responds in 6 months.

Musical Theater "We publish previously produced musicals and plays to be acted by children in the primary grades through high school. Plays are for large casts (approximately 30 actors and speaking parts) and run between 45 minutes to 1 hour and 15 minutes. Subject matter should be contemporary issues (sibling rivalry, friendship, etc.) or adaptations of classic literature for children (*Syrano de Bergerac, Rip Van Winkle, Pied Piper, Treasure Island*, etc.). We do not accept any plays written for adults to perform for children."

Publications *Tortoise vs. Hare*, by Stephen Murray (modern version of classic); *Tumbleweed*, by Sebastian Stuart (sleepy time western town turned upside down); and *Mything Links*, by Sam Abel (interweaving of Greek myths with a great pop score).

Tips "We enjoy receiving material that does not condescend to children. They are capable of understanding many current issues, playing complex characters, handling unconventional material, and singing difficult music."

SAMUEL FRENCH, INC.

45 W. 25th St., New York NY 10010. (212)206-8990. Fax: (212)206-1429. Web site: www.samuelfre nch.com. Hollywood office: 7623 Sunset Blvd., Hollywood CA 90046. (323)876-0570. Fax: (323)876-6822. President: Leon Embry. **Contact:** Roxane Heinze-Bradshaw, associate editor. Play publisher. Estab. 1830. Publishes 40-50 plays and 2-4 new musicals/year. Amateur and professional theaters.

How to Contact *Query first.* Include SASE. Responds in 10 weeks.

Musical Theater "We publish primarily successful musicals from the NYC, London and regional stage."

Publications *Under the Bridge*, by Kathie Lee Gifford—lyrics/book, and David Pomeranz-music (Christmas/family story); *Sweet Smell of Success*, by Marvin Hamlisch—music, Craig Carnelia—lyrics, and John Guare—book (Hollywood scandal); *Don't Hug Me*, by Phil Olson—book/lyrics, and Paul Olson—music (love and karaoke in a northern Minnesota bar).

HEUER PUBLISHING CO.

P.O. Box 248, Cedar Rapids IA 52406. Main Office: 211 First Ave., SE Suite 200, Cedar Rapids IA 52401. 1-800-950-7529. E-mail: editor@hitplays.com. Web site: www.hitplays.com. Publisher: C. Emmett McMullen. Play publisher. Estab. 1928. Publishes plays, musicals, operas/operettas and guides (choreography, costume, production/staging) for amateur and professional markets, including junior and senior high schools, college/university and community theatres. Focus includes comedy, drama, fantasy, mystery and holiday. Pays by percentage royalty or outright purchase. Pays by outright purchase or percentage royalty.

How to Contact Query with musical CD/tape or submit complete manuscript and score. Include SASE. Responds in 2 months.

Musical Theater ''We prefer one, two or three act comedies or mystery-comedies with a large number of characters.''

Publications *Happily Ever After*, by Allen Koepke (musical fairytale); *Brave Buckaroo*, by Renee J. Clark (musical melodrama); and *Pirate Island*, by Martin Follose (musical comedy).

Tips ''We are willing to review single-song submissions as cornerstone piece for commissioned works. Special interest focus in multicultural, historic, classic literature, teen issues, and biographies.''

PIONEER DRAMA SERVICE

P.O. Box 4267, Englewood CO 80155. 1-800-333-7262. Fax: (303)779-4315. Web site: www.pioneer drama.com. **Contact:** Lori Conary, assistant editor. Play publisher. Estab. 1963. ''Plays are performed by junior high and high school drama departments, church youth groups, college and university theaters, semi-professional and professional children's theaters, parks and recreation departments.'' Playwrights paid 50% royalty (10% sales).

How to Contact Query with character breakdown, synopsis and set description. Include SASE. Responds in 6 months.

Musical Theater ''We seek full length children's musicals, high school musicals and one act children's musicals to be performed by children, secondary school students, and/or adults. We want musicals easy to perform, simple sets, many female roles and very few solos. Must be appropriate for educational market. We are not interested in profanity, themes with exclusively adult interest, sex, drinking, smoking, etc. Several of our full-length plays are being converted to musicals. We edit them, then contract with someone to write the music and lyrics.''

Publications *The Stories of Scheherazade*, book by Susan Pargmon, music and lyrics by Bill Francoeur (musical *Arabian Nights*); *Hubba Hubba: The 1940s Hollywood Movie Musical*, by Gene Casey and Jan Casey (tribute to the 1940s Hollywood movie musical); and *Cinderella's Glass Slipper*, book by Vera Morris, music and lyrics by Bill Francoeur (musical fairy tale).

Tips ''Research and learn about our company. Our Web site and catalog provide an incredible amount of information.''

PLAYERS PRESS, INC.

P.O. Box 1132, Studio City CA 91614. Associate Editor: Karen Flathers. Vice President: Robert W. Gordon. Play publisher, music book publisher, educational publisher. Estab. 1965. Publishes 20-70 plays and 1-3 new musicals/year. Plays are used primarily by general audience and children. Pays variable royalty and variable amount/performance.

How to Contact Query first. Include SASE. Responds in 3-6 months (3 weeks on queries).

Musical Theater "We will consider all submitted works. Presently musicals for adults and high schools are in demand. When cast size can be flexible (describe how it can be done in your work) it sells better."

Publications *The Revolution Machine*, by Donna Marie Swajéoki (American Revolution musical); *The Best of Times*, by Steven Porter (musical adaptation of *A Tale of Two Cities*); *Peter n' the Wolf*, by William-Alan Landes (musical theatre version of the famed Russian Classic by the same name).

Tips "For plays and musicals, have your work produced at least twice. Be present for rehearsals and work with competent people. Then submit material asked for in good clear copy with good audio tapes."

Classical Performing Arts

F inding an audience is critical to the composer of orchestral music. Fortunately, baby boomers are swelling the ranks of classical music audiences and bringing with them a taste for fresh, innovative music. So the climate is fair for composers seeking their first performance.

Finding a performance venue is particularly important because once a composer has his work performed for an audience and establishes himself as a talented newcomer, it can lead to more performances and commissions for new works.

BEFORE YOU SUBMIT

Be aware that most classical music organizations are nonprofit groups, and don't have a large budget for acquiring new works. It takes a lot of time and money to put together an orchestral performance of a new composition, therefore these groups are quite selective when choosing new works to perform. Don't be disappointed if the payment offered by these groups is small or even non-existent. What you gain is the chance to have your music performed for an appreciative audience. Also realize that many classical groups are understaffed, so it may take longer than expected to hear back on your submission. It pays to be patient, and employ diplomacy, tact and timing in your follow-up.

In this section you will find listings for classical performing arts organizations throughout the U.S. But if you have no prior performances to your credit, it's a good idea to begin with a small chamber orchestra, for example. Smaller symphony and chamber orchestras are usually more inclined to experiment with new works. A local university or conservatory of music, where you may already have contacts, is a great place to start.

All of the groups listed in this section are interested in hearing new works from contemporary classical composers. Pay close attention to the music needs of each group, and when you find one you feel might be interested in your music, follow submission guidelines carefully. To locate classical performing arts groups in your area, consult the Geographic Index at the back of this book.

ACADIANA SYMPHONY ORCHESTRA

P.O. Box 53632, Lafayette LA 70505. (337)232-4277. Fax: (337)237-4712. E-mail: information@acad ianasymphony.org. Web site: www.acadianasymphony.org. **Contact:** Geraldine Hubbel, executive director. Symphony orchestra. Estab. 1984. Members are amateurs and professionals. Performs 20 concerts/year, including 1 new work. Commissions 1 new work/year. Performs in 2,230-seat hall with "wonderful acoustics." Pays "according to the type of composition."
How to Contact Call first. Does not return material. Responds in 2 months.
Music Full orchestra: 10 minutes at most. Reduced orchestra, educational pieces: short, up to 5 minutes.
Performances Quincy Hilliard's *Universal Covenant* (orchestral suite); James Hanna's *In Memoriam* (strings/elegy); and Gregory Danner's *A New Beginning* (full orchestra fanfare).

ADRIAN SYMPHONY ORCHESTRA

110 S. Madison St., Adrian MI 49221. (517)264-3121. Fax: (517)264-3833. E-mail: aso@lni.net. Web site: www.aso.org. **Contact:** John Dodson, music director. Symphony orchestra and chamber music ensemble. Estab. 1981. Members are professionals. Performs 25 concerts/year including new works. 1,200 seat hall—"Rural city with remarkably active cultural life." Pays $200-1,000 for performance.
How to Contact Query first. Does not return material. Responds in 6 months.
Music Chamber ensemble to full orchestra. "Limited rehearsal time dictates difficulty of pieces selected." Does not wish to see "rock music or country—not at this time."
Performances Michael Pratt's *Dancing on the Wall* (orchestral—some aleatoric); Sir Peter Maxwell Davies' *Orkney Wedding* (orchestral); and Gwyneth Walker's *Fanfare, Interlude, Finale* (orchestral).

N AMERICAN OPERA MUSICAL THEATRE CO.

400 W. 43rd St. #19D, New York NY 10036. (212)594-1839. Fax: (646)290-8471. E-mail: aomtc@mi ndspring.com. Web site: www.americanoperaco.com. **Contact:** Diana Corto, artistic director. Opera and musical theatre producing/presenting organization. Estab. 1995. Members are professionals with varying degrees of experience. Performs 2 operas, many concerts/year and 1 musical theatre production each year. Audience is sophisticated and knowledgeable about music and theatre. "We rent performance spaces in New York, or are either sponsored by a presenter, or are paid performance fees for opera and concerts."
How to Contact "We are only accepting photos and resumes at this time—no CDs or DVDs."
Music "Must be vocal (for opera or for music theatre). Cast should not exceed 10. Orchestration should not exceed 30, smaller groups preferred. No rock 'n' roll, brassy pop."
Performances Puccini's *La Boheme*; Verdi's *Rigoletto*; *The Jewel Box*; *Iolanta*; *La Molinara* and *The World Goes Round*.

AMHERST SAXOPHONE QUARTET

64 Roycroft Blvd., Amherst NY 14226. (716)839-9716. E-mail: steve@caramaxstudio.com. Web site: www.amherstsaxophonequartet.buffalo.edu. **Contact:** Steve Rosenthal, director. Chamber music ensemble. Estab. 1978. Performs 80 concerts/year including 10-20 new works. Commissions 1-2 composers or new works/year. "We are a touring ensemble." Payment varies.
How to Contact Query first. Include SASE. Responds in 1 month.
Music "Music for soprano, alto, tenor and baritone (low A) saxophone. We are interested in great music of many styles. Level of difficulty is commensurate with full-time touring ensembles."
Performances Lukas Foss's *Saxophone Quartet* (new music); David Stock's *Sax Appeal* (new music); and Chan Ka Nin's *Saxophone Quartet* (new music).
Tips "Professionally copied parts help! Write what you truly want to write."

Classical Arts

☑ ANDERSON SYMPHONY ORCHESTRA

P.O. Box 741, Anderson IN 46015. (765)644-2111. Fax: (765)644-7703. E-mail: aso@andersonsymp hony.org. Web site: www.andersonsymphony.org. **Contact:** Dr. Richard Sowers, conductor. Executive Director: George W. Vinson. Symphony orchestra. Estab. 1967. Members are professionals. Performs 7 concerts/year. Performs for typical mid-western audience in a 1,500-seat restored Paramount Theatre. Pay negotiable.

How to Contact Query first. Include SASE. Responds in several months.

Music "Shorter lengths better; concerti OK; difficulty level: mod high; limited by typically 3 full service rehearsals."

☑ ARCADY

P.O. Box 955, Simcoe ON N3Y 5B3 Canada. (519)428-3185. E-mail: info@arcady.ca. Web site: www.arcady.ca. **Contact:** Ronald Beckett, director. Professional chorus and orchestra. Members are professionals, university music majors and recent graduates from throughout Ontario. "Arcady forms the bridge between the student and the professional performing career." Performs 12 concerts/year including 1 new works. Pay negotiable.

How to Contact Submit complete score and tape of piece(s). Does not return material. Responds in 3 months.

Music "Compositions appropriate for ensemble accustomed to performance of chamber works, accompanied or unaccompanied, with independence of parts. Specialize in repertoire of 17th, 18th and 20th centuries. Number of singers does not exceed 30. Orchestra is limited to strings, supported by a professional quartet. No popular, commercial or show music."

Performances Ronald Beckett's *I Am. . .* (opera); Ronald Beckett's *John* (opera); and David Lenson's *Prologue to Dido and Aeneas* (masque).

Tips "Arcady is a touring ensemble experienced with both concert and stage performance."

ATLANTA POPS ORCHESTRA

P.O. Box 15037, Atlanta GA 30333. (404)636-0020. E-mail: ladkmusic@aol.com. Web site: www.atl antapops.com. **Contact:** Leonard Altieri, general manager. Pops orchestra. Estab. 1945. Members are professionals. Performs 5-10 concerts/year. Concerts are performed for audiences of 5,000-10,000, "all ages, all types." Composers are not paid; concerts are free to the public.

How to Contact Call to request permission to submit. Then send cassette, and score or music, if requested. Include SASE. Responds "as soon as possible."

Performances Vincent Montana, Jr.'s *Magic Bird of Fire*; Louis Alter's *Manhattan Serenade*; and Nelson Riddle's *It's Alright With Me*.

Tips "My concerts are pops concerts—no deep classics."

AUREUS QUARTET

22 Lois Ave., Demarest NJ 07627-2220. (201)767-8704. E-mail: AureusQuartet@aol.com. **Contact:** James J. Seiler, artistic director. Vocal ensemble (a cappella). Estab. 1979. Members are professionals. Performs 75 concerts/year, including 12 new works. Commissions 5 composers or new works/year. Pay varies for outright purchase.

How to Contact Query first. Include SASE. Responds in 2 months.

Music "We perform anything from pop to classic—mixed repertoire so anything goes. Some pieces can be scored for orchestras as we do pops concerts. Up to now, we've only worked with a quartet. Could be expanded if the right piece came along. Level of difficulty—no piece has ever been too hard." Does not wish to see electronic or sacred pieces. "Electronic pieces would be hard to program. Sacred pieces not performed much. Classical/jazz arrangements of old standards are great! Unusual Christmas arrangements are most welcome!"

Tips "We perform for a very diverse audience. Luscious, four part writing that can showcase well-trained voices is a must. Also, clever arrangements of old hits from '50s through '60s are sure bets. (Some pieces could take optional accompaniment).''

BILLINGS SYMPHONY
201 N. Broadway., Suite 350, Billings MT 59101-1936. (406)252-3610. Fax: (406)252-3353. E-mail: symphony@billingssymphony.org. Web site: www.billingssymphony.org. **Contact:** Dr. Uri Barnea, music director. Symphony orchestra, orchestra and chorale. Estab. 1950. Members are professionals and amateurs. Performs 12-15 concerts/year, including 6-7 new works. Traditional audience. Performs at Alberta Bair Theater (capacity 1,416). Pays by outright purchase (or rental).
How to Contact Query first. Include SASE. Responds in 2 weeks.
Music Any style. Traditional notation preferred.
Performances Jim Cockey's *Symphony No. 2 (Parmly's Dream)* (symphony orchestra with chorus and soloists); Ilse-Mari Lee's *Cello Concerto* (concerto for cello solo and orchestra); and Jim Beckel's *Christmas Fanfare* (brass and percussion).
Tips ''Write what you feel (be honest) and sharpen your compositional and craftsmanship skills.''

BIRMINGHAM-BLOOMFIELD SYMPHONY ORCHESTRA
1592 Buckingham, Birmingham MI 48009. (248)645-2276. Fax: (248)645-2276, *51. Web site: www .bbso.org. **Contact:** Charles Greenwell, music director and conductor. Conductor Laureate: Felix Resnick. President and Executive Director: Carla Lamphere. Symphony orchestra. Estab. 1975. Members are professionals. Performs 5 concerts including 1 new work/year. Commissions 1 composer or new work/year ''with grants.'' Performs for middle-to-upper class audience at Temple Beth El's Sanctuary. Pays per performance ''depending upon grant received.''
How to Contact *Query first.* Does not return material. Responds in 6 months.
Music ''We are a symphony orchestra but also play pops. Usually 3 works on program (2 hrs.) Orchestra size 65-75. If pianist is involved, they must rent piano.''
Performances Brian Belanger's *Tuskegee Airmen Suite* (symphonic full orchestra); Larry Nazer & Friend's *Music from ''Warm'' CD* (jazz with full orchestra) ; and Mark Gottlieb's *Violin Concerto for Orchestra* (new world premiere, 2006).

THE BOSTON PHILHARMONIC
295 Huntington Ave., #210, Boston MA 02115. (617)236-0999. Fax: (617)236-8613. E-mail: office@ bostonphil.org. Web site: www.bostonphil.org. **Music Director:** Benjamin Zander. Symphony orchestra. Estab. 1979. Members are professionals, amateurs and students. Performs 2 concerts/year. Audience is ages 30-70. Performs at New England Conservatory's Jordan Hall, Boston's Symphony Hall and Sanders Theatre in Cambridge. Both Jordan Hall and Sanders Theatre are small (approximately 1,100 seats) and very intimate.
How to Contact *Does not accept new music at this time.*
Music Full orchestra only.
Performances Dutilleuxs' *Tout un monde lointain* for cello and orchestra (symphonic); Bernstein's *Fancy Free* (symphonic/jazzy); Copland's *El Salon Mexico* (symphonic); Gershwin's *Rhapsody in Blue*; Shostakovitch's *Symphony No. 10*; Harbison's *Concerto for Oboe*; Holst's *The Planet Suite*; Schwantner's *New Morning for the World*; Berg's *Seven Early Songs*; and Ive's *The Unanswered Question*.

BRAVO! L.A.
16823 Liggett St., North Hills CA 91343. (818)892-8737. Fax: (818)892-1227. E-mail: musicalmenace @earthlink.net and info@bravo-la.com. Web site: www.bravo-la.com. **Contact:** Cellist Dr. Janice Foy, director. An umbrella organization of recording/touring musicians, formed in 1994. Includes the following musical ensembles: Celllissimo! L.A. (cello ensemble); Interstellar Strings (expand-

Classical Arts

able string group with optional piano); Mesto Chamber Players; the New American Quartet (string quartet); The Ascending Wave (harp, soprano, cello or harp/cello duo); Cellissimo! L.A. (cello ensemble); Musical Combustion (harp, flute, cello); I Musicanti (singer, piano and cello); and the Sierra Chamber Players (piano with strings or mixed ensemble). Performs concerts throughout the year. "We take care of PR. There is also grant money the composer can apply for."

How to Contact Submit complete score and tape of piece(s). Include SASE. Responds in a few months.

Music "Classical, Romantic, Baroque, Popular (including new arrangements done by Shelly Cohen, from the 'Tonight Show Band'), ethnic (including gypsy) and contemporary works (commissioned as well). The New American Quartet has a recording project which features music of Mozart's *Eine Kleine Nachtmusik*, Borodin's *Nocturne*, a Puccini Opera Suite (S. Cohen), Strauss' *Blue Danube Waltz*, *Trepak* of Tschaikovsky, *'El Choclo'* (Argentinian tango), *Csardas!* and arrangements of Cole Porter, Broadway show tunes and popular classics."

Performances Joe Giarrusso's *Rhapsody for Cello and Piano* (concert piece modern romantic); Joe Giarrusso's *Cello Sonata* (concert piece); and the upcoming world premiere of Larry Mumford's *Concerto Rhapsody for Cello & Orchestra, with Middle Eastern Instruments*.

Tips "Please be open to criticism/suggestions about your music and try to appeal to mixed audiences. We also look for innovative techniques, mixed styles or entertaining approaches, such as classical jazz or Bach and pop, or ethnic mixes. There are four CD's currently available for purchase online for $20 each. There are also sound clips on the Web site."

◪ CANADIAN OPERA COMPANY

227 Front St. E., Toronto ON M5A 1E8 Canada. (416)363-6671. Fax: (416)363-5584. E-mail: ensembl e@coc.ca. Web site: www.coc.ca. **Contact:** Sandra J. Gavinchuk, music administrator. Opera company. Estab. 1950. Members are professionals. 50-55 performances, including a minimum of 1 new work/year. Pays by contract.

How to Contact Submit complete score and tapes of vocal and/or operatic works. "Vocal works please." Include SASE. Responds in 5 weeks.

Music Vocal works, operatic in nature. "Do not submit works which are not for voice. Ask for requirements for the Composers-In-Residence program."

Performances Dean Burry's *Brothers Grimm* (children's opera, 50 minutes long); Paul Ruders' *Handmaid's Tale* (full length opera, 2 acts, epilogue); Dean Burry's Isis and the Seven Scorpions (45-minute opera for children); Berg's *Wozzek*; James Rolfe's *Swoon* (work title for forthcoming work).

Tips "We have a Composers-In-Residence program which is open to Canadian composers or landed immigrants."

CANTATA ACADEMY CHORALE

P.O. Box 1958, Royal Oak MI 48068-1958. (248)358-9868. **Contact:** Phillip O'Jibway, business manager. Music Director: Dr. Michael Mitchell, music director. Vocal ensemble. Estab. 1961. Members are professionals. Performs 10-12 concerts/year including 1-3 new works. "We perform in churches and small auditoriums throughout the Metro Detroit area for audiences of about 500 people." Pays variable rate for outright purchase.

How to Contact Submit complete score. Include SASE. Responds in 3 months.

Music Four-part a cappella and keyboard accompanied works, two and three-part works for men's or women's voices. Some small instrumental ensemble accompaniments acceptable. Work must be suitable for forty voice choir. No works requiring orchestra or large ensemble accompaniment. No pop.

Performances Libby Larsen's *Missa Gaia: Mass for the Earth* (SATB, string quartet, oboe, percussion, 4-hand piano); Dede Duson's *To Those Who See* (SATB, SSA); and Sarah Hopkins' *Past Life*

Melodies (SATB with Harmonic Overtone Singing); Eric Whiteacre *Five Hebrew Love Songs*; Robert Convery's *Songs of the Children*.
Tips "Be patient. Would prefer to look at several different samples of work at one time."

CARMEL SYMPHONY ORCHESTRA

P.O. Box 761, Carmel IN 46082-0761. (317)844-9717. Fax: (317)844-9916. E-mail: cso@carmelsymp hony.org. Web site: www.carmelsymphony.org. **Contact:** Allen Davis, executive director. Symphony orchestra. Estab. 1976. Members are professionals and amateurs. Performs 15 concerts/ year, including 1-2 new works. Audience is "40% senior citizens, 85% white." Performs in a 1,500-seat high school performing arts center. Pay is negotiable.
How to Contact Query first. Include SASE. Responds in 3 months.
Music "Full orchestra works, 10-20 minutes in length. Can be geared toward 'children's' or 'Masterworks' programs. 65-70 piece orchestra, medium difficulty."
Performances Jim Beckel's *Glass Bead Game* (full orchestra); Percy Grainger's *Molly on the Shore* (full orchestra); and Frank Glover's *Impressions of New England* (full orchestra and jazz quartet).

CONNECTICUT CHORAL ARTISTS/CONCORA

52 Main St., New Britain CT 06051. (860)224-7500. Web site: www.concora.org. **Contact:** Jane Penfield, executive director. Richard Coffey, artistic director. Professional concert choir, also an 18-voice ensemble dedicated to contemporary a cappella works. Estab. 1974. Members are professionals. Performs 15 concerts/year, including 3-5 new works. "Mixed audience in terms of age and background; performs in various halls and churches in the region." Payment "depends upon underwriting we can obtain for the project."
How to Contact Query first. "No unsolicited submissions accepted." Include SASE. Responds in 1 year.
Music Seeking "works for mixed chorus of 36 singers; unaccompanied or with keyboard and/or small instrumental ensemble; text sacred or secular/any language; prefers suites or cyclical works, total time not exceeding 15 minutes. Performance spaces and budgets prohibit large instrumental ensembles. Works suited for 750-seat halls are preferable. Substantial organ or piano parts acceptable. Scores should be very legible in every way."
Performances Don McCullough's *Holocaust Contata* (choral with narration); Robert Cohen's *Sprig of Lilac: Peter Quince at the Clavier* (choral); Greg Bartholomew's *The 21st Century: A Girl Born in Afghanistan* (choral).
Tips "Use conventional notation and be sure manuscript is legible in every way. Recognize and respect the vocal range of each vocal part. Work should have an identifiable rhythmic structure."

DUO CLASICO

4 Essex St., Clifton NJ 07014. (973)655-4379. E-mail: wittend@mail.montclair.edu. Web site: www. davidwitten.com. **Contact:** David Witten. Chamber music ensemble. Estab. 1986. Members are professionals. Performs 16 concerts/year including 4 new works. Commissions 1 composer or new work/year. Performs in small recital halls. Pays 10% royalty.
How to Contact Query first. Include SASE. Responds in 6 weeks.
Music "We welcome scores for flute solo, piano solo or duo. Particular interest in Latin American composers."
Performances Diego Luzuriaga's *La Muchica* (modern, with extended techniques); Robert Starer's *Yizkor & Anima Aeterna* (rhythmic); and Piazzolla's *Etudes Tanguistiques* (solo flute).
Tips "Extended techniques, or with tape, are fine!"

ⓝ GREATER GRAND FORKS SYMPHONY ORCHESTRA

3350 Campus Rd., Mail Stop 7084, Grand Forks ND 58202-7084. (701)777-3359. Fax: (701)777-3320. E-mail: ggfso@und.edu. Web site: www.ggfso.org. **Contact:** James Hannon, music director.

Symphony orchestra. Estab. 1908. Members are professionals and/or amateurs. Performs 6 concerts/year. "New works are presented in 2-4 of our programs." Audience is "a mix of ages and musical experience. In 1997-98 we moved into a renovated, 420-seat theater." Pay is negotiable, depending on licensing agreements.

How to Contact Submit complete score or complete score and tape of pieces. Include SASE. Responds in 6 months.

Music "Style is open, instrumentation the limiting factor. Music can be scored for an ensemble up to but not exceeding: 3,2,3,2/4,3,3,1/3 perc./strings. Rehearsal time limited to 3 hours for new works."

Performances Michael Harwood's *Amusement Park Suite* (orchestra); Randall Davidson's *Mexico Bolivar Tango* (chamber orchestra); and John Corigliano's *Voyage* (flute and orchestra); Linda Tutas Haugen's *Fable of Old Turtle* (saxophone concerto); Michael Wittgraf's *Landmarks*; Joan Tower's *Made in America*.

HEARTLAND MEN'S CHORUS

P.O. Box 32374, Kansas City MO 64171-5374. (816)931-3338. Fax: (816)531-1367. E-mail: hmc@hmckc.org. Web site: www.hmckc.org. **Contact:** Joseph Nadeau, artistic director. Men's chorus. Estab. 1986. Members are professionals and amateurs. Performs 3 concerts/year; 9-10 are new works. Commissions 1 composer or new works/year. Performs for a diverse audience at the Folly Theater (1,100 seats). Pay is negotiable.

How to Contact Query first. Include SASE. Responds in 2 months.

Music "Interested in works for male chorus (ttbb). Must be suitable for performance by a gay male chorus. We will consider any orchestration, or a cappella."

Performances Mark Hayes' *Two Flutes Playing* (commissioned song cycle); Alan Shorter's *Country Angel Christmas* (commissioned chidren's musical); Kevin Robinson's *Life is a Cabaret: The Music of Kander and Ebb* (commissioned musical).

Tips "Find a text that relates to the contemporary gay experience, something that will touch peoples' lives."

HERMANN SONS GERMAN BAND

P.O. Box 162, Medina TX 78055. (830)589-2268. E-mail: herbert@festmusik.com. Web site: www.festmusik.com. **Contact:** Herbert Bilhartz, music director. Community band with German instrumentation. Estab. 1990. Members are both professionals and amateurs. Performs 4 concerts/year including 2 new works. Commissions no new composers or new works/year. Performs for "mostly older people who like German polkas, waltzes and marches. We normally play only published arrangements from Germany."

How to Contact Query first; then submit full set of parts and score, condensed or full. Include SASE. Responds in 6 weeks.

Music "We like European-style polkas or waltzes (Viennese or Missouri tempo), either original or arrangements of public domain tunes. Arrangements of traditional American folk tunes in this genre would be especially welcome. Also, polkas or waltzes featuring one or two solo instruments (from instrumentation below) would be great. OK for solo parts to be technically demanding. Although we have no funds to commission works, we will provide you with a cassette recording of our performance. Also, we would assist composers in submitting works to band music publishers in Germany for possible publication. Polkas and waltzes generally follow this format: Intro; 1st strain repeated; 2nd strain repeated; DS to 1 strain; Trio: Intro; 32 bar strain; 'break-up' strain; Trio DS. Much like military march form. Instrumentation: Fl/Picc, 3 clars in Bb, 2 Fluegelhorns in Bb; 3 Tpts in Bb, 2 or 4 Hns in F or Eb, 2 Baritones (melody/countermelody parts; 1 in Bb TC, 1 in BC), 2 Baritones in Bb TC (rhythm parts), 3 Trombones, 2 Tubas (in octaves, mostly), Drum set, Timpani optional. We don't use saxes, but a German publisher would want 4-5 sax parts. Parts should be medium to medium difficult. All brass parts should be considered one player to the part; woodwinds, two to the part. No concert type pieces; no modern popular or rock styles. However, a 'theme and variations' form with contrasting jazz, rock, country, modern variations would be clever, and our fans might go for such a piece (as might a German publisher).''

Performances New music performed in 2005: Stefan Rundel's *Mein Gluecksstern ("My Lucky Star").*

Tips ''German town bands love to play American tunes. There are many thousands of these bands over there and competition among band music publishers in Germany is keen. Few Americans are aware of this potential market, so few American arrangers get published over there. Simple harmony is best for this style, but good counterpoint helps a lot. Make use of the dark quality of the Fluegelhorns and the bright, fanfare quality of the trumpets. Give the two baritones (one in TC and one in BC) plenty of exposed melodic material. Keep them in harmony with each other (3rds and 6ths), unlike American band arrangements, which have only one Baritone line. If you want to write a piece in this style, give me a call, and I will send you some sample scores to give you a better idea.''

HERSHEY SYMPHONY ORCHESTRA

P.O. Box 93, Hershey PA 17033. (800)533-3088. E-mail: drdackow@aol.com. **Contact:** Dr. Sandra Dackow, music director. Symphony orchestra. Estab. 1969. Members are professionals and amateurs. Performs 8 concerts/year, including 1-3 new works. Commissions ''possibly 1-2'' composers or new works/year. Audience is family and friends of community theater. Performance space is a 1,900 seat grand old movie theater. Pays commission fee.

How to Contact Submit complete score and tape of piece(s). Include SASE. Responds in 3 months.

Music ''Symphonic works of various lengths and types which can be performed by a non-professional orchestra. We are flexible but like to involve all our players.''

Performances Paul W. Whear's *Celtic Christmas Carol* (orchestra/bell choir) and Linda Robbins Coleman's *In Good King Charlie's Golden Days* (overture).

Tips ''Please lay out rehearsal numbers/letter and rests according to phrases and other logical musical divisions rather than in groups of ten measures, etc., which is very unmusical and wastes time and causes a surprising number of problems. Also, please do not send a score written in concert pitch; use the usual transpositions so that the conductor sees what the players see; rehearsal is much more effective this way. Cross cue all important solos; this helps in rehearsal where instruments may be missing.''

N HUDSON VALLEY PHILHARMONIC

35 Market St., Poughkeepise NY 12601. (845)473-5288. Fax: (845)473-4259. E-mail: slamarca@bardavon.org. Web site: www.bardavon.org. **Contact:** Stephen LaMarca, production manager. Symphony orchestra. Estab. 1969. Members are professionals. Performs 20 concerts/year including 1 new work. ''Classical subscription concerts for all ages; Pops concerts for all ages; New Wave concerts—crossover projects with a rock 'n' roll artist performing with an orchestra. HVP performs in three main theatres which are concert auditoriums with stages and professional lighting and sound.'' Pay is negotiable.

How to Contact Query first. Include SASE. Responds only if interested.

Music ''HVP is open to serious classical music, pop music and rock 'n' roll crossover projects. Desired length of work between 10-20 minutes. Orchestrations can be varied by should always include strings. There is no limit to difficulty since our musicians are professional. The ideal number of musicians to write for would include up to a Brahms-size orchestra 2222, 4231, T, 2P, piano, harp, strings.''

Performances Joan Tower's *Island Rhythms* (serious classical work); Bill Vanaver's *P'nai El* (symphony work with dance); and Joseph Bertolozzi's *Serenade* (light classical, pop work).

Tips "Don't get locked into doing very traditional orchestrations or styles. Our music director is interested in fresh, creative formats. He is an orchestrator as well and can offer good advice on what works well. Songwriters who are into crossover projects should definitely submit works. Over the past four years, HVP has done concerts featuring the works of Natalie Merchant, John Cale, Sterling Morrison, Richie Havens, and R. Carlos Naka (Native American flute player), all reorchestrated by our music director for small orchestra with the artist."

N KENTUCKY OPERA

101 S. Eighth St. at Main, Louisville KY 40202. (502)584-4500. Fax: (502)584-7484. E-mail: info@ky opera.org. Web site: www.kyopera.org. **Contact:** Alise Oliver, artistic administration. Opera. Estab. 1952. Members are professionals. Performs 3 main stage/year. Performs at Whitney Hall, The Kentucky Center for the Arts, seating is 2,400; Bomhard Theatre, The Kentucky Center for the Arts, 620; Brown Theatre, 1,400. Pays by royalty, outright purchase or per performance.
How to Contact *Write or call first before submitting. No unsolicited submissions.* Submit complete score. Include SASE. Responds in 6 months.
Music Seeks opera—1 to 3 acts with orchestrations. No limitations.
Performances *Turandot*; *Il Trovatore*; and *Dialogues of the Carmelites*.

LITHOPOLIS AREA FINE ARTS ASSOCIATION

3825 Cedar Hill Rd., Canal Winchester OH 43110-8929. (614)837-8925. Web site: www.cwda.net/ LAFAA/. **Contact:** Virginia E. Heffner, assistant series director. Performing Arts Series. Estab. 1973. Members are professionals and amateurs. Performs 6-7 concerts/year. "Our audience consists of couples and families 30-80 in age. Their tastes run from classical, folk, ethnic, big band, pop and jazz. Our hall is acoustically excellent and seats 400. It was designed as a lecture-recital hall in 1925." Composers "may apply for Ohio Arts Council Grant under the New Works category." Pays straight fee to ASCAP.
How to Contact *Query first.* Include SASE. Responds in 3 weeks.
Music "We prefer that a composer is also the performer and works in conjunction with another artist, so they could be one of the performers on our series. Piece should be musically pleasant and not too dissonant. It should be scored for small vocal or instrumental ensemble. Dance ensembles have difficulty with 15' high 15' deep and 27' wide stage. We do not want avant-garde or obscene dance routines. No ballet (space problem). We're interested in something historical—national or Ohio emphasis would be nice. Small ensembles or solo format is fine."
Performances Patsy Ford Simms' *Holiday Gloria* (Christmas SSA vocal); Andrew Carter's *A Maiden Most Gentle* (Christmas SSA vocal); and Luigi Zaninelli's *Alleluia, Silent Night* (Christmas SSA vocal).
Tips "Call in December of 2007 or January 2008 for queries about our 2007-2008 season. We do a varied program. We don't commission artists. Contemporary music is used by some of our artist or groups. By contacting these artists, you could offer your work for inclusion in their program."

N THE MIRECOURT TRIO

50 Orchard St., Jamaica Plain MA 02130. (617)524-2495. E-mail: tkingcello@aol.com. **Contact:** Terry King. Chamber music ensemble; violin, cello, piano. Estab. 1973. Members are professionals. Performs 2-4 concerts/year including 1 new work. Commissions 1 composer or new work/year. Concerts are performed for university, concert series, schools, societies and "general chamber music audiences of 100-1,500." Pays for outright purchase, percentage royalty or per performance.
How to Contact Query first. Include SASE. Responds in 6 months.
Music Seeks "music of short to moderate duration (5-20 minutes) that entertains, yet is not derivative or cliched. Orchestration should be basically piano, violin, cello, occasionally adding voice or instrument. We do not wish to see academic or experimental works."

Performances Otto Leuning's *Solo Sonata* (solo cello); Lukas Foss's *Three American Pieces* (cello, piano premiere); and Coolidge's *Dialectic No. 1* for piano trio.

Tips "Submit works that engage the audience or relate to them, that reward the players as well."

ORCHESTRA SEATTLE/SEATTLE CHAMBER SINGERS

P.O. Box 15825, Seattle WA 98115. (206)682-5208. E-mail: osscs@osscs.org. Web site: www.osscs. org. **Contact:** Andrew Danilchik, librarian. Symphony orchestra, chamber music ensemble and community chorus. Estab. 1969. Members are amateurs and professionals. Performs 8 concerts/ year including 2-3 new works. Commissions 1-2 composers or new works/year. "Our audience is made up of both experienced and novice classical music patrons. The median age is 45 with an equal number of males and females in the upper income range. Most concerts now held in Benaroya Hall."

How to Contact Query first. Include SASE. Responds in 1 year.

Performances Robert Kechley's *Trumpet Concerto* (classical concerto); Carol Sams's *Earthmakers* (oratorio); and Murl Allen Sanders's *Accordion Concerto* (classical concerto).

PICCOLO OPERA COMPANY INC.

24 Del Rio Blvd., Boca Raton FL 33432-4734. (800)282-3161. Fax: (561)394-0520. E-mail: leejon51@ msn.com. **Contact:** Lee Merrill, executive assistant. Traveling opera company. Estab. 1962. Members are professionals. Performs 1-50 concerts/year including 1-2 new works. Commissions 0-1 composer or new work/year. Operas are performed for a mixed audience of children and adults. Pays by performance or outright purchase. Operas in English.

How to Contact *Query first.* Include SASE.

Music "Musical theater pieces, lasting about one hour, for adults to perform for adults and/or youngsters. Performers are mature singers with experience. The cast should have few performers (up to 10), no chorus or ballet, accompanied by piano or local orchestra. Skeletal scenery. All in English."

Performances Menotti's *The Telephone*; Mozart's *Cosi Fan Tutte*; and Puccini's *La Boheme* (repertoire of more than 22 productions).

SINGING BOYS OF PENNSYLVANIA

P.O. Box 206, Wind Gap PA 18091. (610)759-6002. Fax: (570)223-2748. **Contact:** K. Bernard Schade, Ed. D., director. Vocal ensemble. Estab. 1970. Members are professional children. Performs 100 concerts/year including 3-5 new works. "We attract general audiences: family, senior citizens, churches, concert associations, university concert series and schools." Pays $300-3,000 for outright purchase.

How to Contact *Query first.* Does not return material. Responds in 3 weeks.

Music "We want music for commercials, voices in the SSA or SSAA ranges, sacred works or arrangements of American folk music with accompaniment. Our range of voices are from G below middle C to A (13th above middle C). Reading ability of choir is good but works which require a lot of work with little possibility of more than one performance are of little value. We sing very few popular songs except for special events. We perform music by composers who are well-known and works by living composers who are writing in traditional choral forms. Works which have a full orchestral score are of interest. The orchestration should be fairly light, so as not to cover the voices. Works for Christmas have more value than some other, since we perform with orchestras on an annual basis."

Performances Don Locklair's *The Columbus Madrigals* (opera).

Tips "It must be appropriate music and words for children. We do not deal in pop music. Folk music, classics and sacred are acceptable."

SOLI DEO GLORIA CANTORUM

3402 Woolworth Ave., Omaha NE 68105. (402)341-4111. E-mail: cantorum@berkey.com. Web site: www.berkey.com. **Contact:** Almeda Berkey, music director. Professional choir. Estab. 1988. Members are professionals. Performs 5-7 concerts/year; several are new works. Commissions 1-2 new works/year. Performance space: "cathedral, symphony hall, smaller intimate recital halls as well." Payment is "dependent upon composition and composer."

How to Contact Submit complete score and tape of piece(s). Include SASE. Responds in 2 months.

Music "Chamber music mixed with topical programming (e.g., all Celtic or all Hispanic programs, etc.). Generally a cappella compositions from very short to extended range (6-18 minutes) or multi-movements. Concerts are of a formal length (approx. 75 minutes) with 5 rehearsals. Difficulty must be balanced within program in order to adequately prepare in a limited rehearsal time. 28 singers. Not seeking orchestral pieces, due to limited budget."

Performances Jackson Berkey's *Native Am Ambience* (eclectic/classical); John Rutter's *Hymn to the Creator of Light* (classical); and Arvo Part's *Te Deum* (multi-choir/chant-based classical).

▧ ST. LOUIS CHAMBER CHORUS

P.O. Box 11558, Clayton MO 63105. (636)458-4343. E-mail: maltworm@inlink.com. Web site: www.chamberchorus.org. **Contact:** Philip Barnes, artistic director. Vocal ensemble, chamber music ensemble. Estab. 1956. Members are professionals and amateurs. Performs 6 concerts/year including 5-10 new works. Commissions 3-4 new works/year. Audience is "diverse and interested in unaccompanied choral work and outstanding architectural/acoustic venues." Performances take place at various auditoria noted for their excellent acoustics—churches, synagogues, schools and university halls. Pays by arrangement.

How to Contact Query first. Does not return material. "Panel of 'readers' submit report to Artistic Director. Responds in 3 months. 'General Advice' leaflet available on request."

Music "*Only a cappella writing!* No contemporary 'popular' works; historical editions welcomed. No improvisatory works. Our programs are tailored for specific acoustics—composers should indicate their preference."

Performances Sir Richard Rodney Bennett's *A Contemplation Upon Flowers* (a cappella madrigal); Ned Rorem's *Ode to Man* (a cappella chorus for mixed voices); and Sasha Johnson Manning's *Requiem* (a cappella oratorio).

Tips "We only consider a cappella works which can be produced in five rehearsals. Therefore pieces of great complexity or duration are discouraged. Our seasons are planned 2-3 years ahead, so much lead time is required for programming a new work. We will accept hand-written manuscript, but we prefer typeset music."

SUSQUEHANNA SYMPHONY ORCHESTRA

P.O. Box 485, Forest Hill MD 21050. (410)838-6465. E-mail: sheldon.bair@ssorchestra.org. Web site: www.ssorchestra.org. **Contact:** Sheldon Bair, music director. Symphony orchestra. Estab. 1978. Members are amateurs. Performs 6 concerts/year including 1-2 new works. Composers paid depending on the circumstances. "We perform in 1 hall, 600 seats with fine acoustics. Our audience encompasses all ages."

How to Contact Query first. Include SASE. Responds in 3 or more months.

Music "We desire works for large orchestra, any length, in a 'conservative 20th and 21st century' style. Seek fine music for large orchestra. We are a community orchestra, so the music must be within our grasp. Violin I to 7th position by step only; Violin II—stay within 5th position; English horn and harp are OK. Full orchestra pieces preferred."

Performances Derek Bourgeois' *Trombone Concerto*; Gwyneth Walker's *The Magic Oboe*; Johan de Meij's *Symphony No. 1 "Lord of the Rings"*; Karen Amrhein's *Christmas Mirror*; and Deborah Teason's *Steelband Concerto: Trinity*.

TOURING CONCERT OPERA CO. INC.

228 E. 80th, New York NY 10021. (212)988-2542. Fax: (518)851-6778. E-mail: tcoc@mhonline.net. **Contact:** Anne DeFigols, director. Opera company. Estab. 1971. Members are professionals. Performs 30 concerts/year including 1 new work. Payment varies.

How to Contact Submit complete score and tape of piece(s). Does not return material. Response time varies.

Music "Operas or similar with small casts."

Tips "We are a touring company which travels all over the world. Therefore, operas with casts that are not large and simple but effective sets are the most practical."

VANCOUVER CHAMBER CHOIR

1254 W. Seventh Ave., Vancouver BC V6H 1B6 Canada. E-mail: info@vancouverchamberchoir.com. Web site: www.vancouverchamberchoir.com. **Contact:** Jon Washburn, artistic director. Vocal ensemble. Members are professionals. Performs 40 concerts/year including 5-8 new works. Commissions 2-4 composers or new works/year. Pays SOCAN royalty or negotiated fee for commissions.

How to Contact Submit complete score and tape of piece(s). Does not return material. Responds in 6 months if possible.

Music Seeks "choral works of all types for small chorus, with or without accompaniment and/or soloists. Concert music only. Choir made up of 20 singers. Large or unusual instrumental accompaniments are less likely to be appropriate. No pop music."

Performances The VCC has commissioned and premiered over 200 new works by Canadian and international composers, including Alice Parker's *That Sturdy Vine* (cantata for chorus, soloists and orchestra); R. Murray Schafer's *Magic Songs* (SATB a cappella); and Jon Washburn's *A Stephen Foster Medley* (SSAATTBB/piano).

Tips "We are looking for choral music that is performable yet innovative, and which has the potential to become 'standard repertoire.' Although we perform much new music, only a small portion of the many scores which are submitted can be utilized."

ⓝ ⓒ VANCOUVER YOUTH SYMPHONY ORCHESTRA SOCIETY

3214 West 10th Ave., Vancouver BC V6K 2L2 Canada. (604)737-0714. Fax: (604)737-0739. E-mail: vyso@telus.net. Web site: www.vyso.web.com. **Music Directors:** Roger Cole (artistic director and senior orchestra conductor), Jim Zhang (intermediate orchestra director), and Margerita Kress (debut and junior string orchestra director). Youth orchestra. "There are four divisions consisting of musicians ranging in age from 8-22 years old." Estab. 1930. Members are amateurs. Performs 6-8 concerts/year. Performs 10-15 concerts/year in various lower mainland venues.

How to Contact *Contact first by e-mail and obtain permission to submit.*

Music "The Senior Orchestra performs standard symphonic repertoire. Programs usually consist of an overture, a major symphony and perhaps a concerto or shorter work. The Christmas concert and tour programs are often lighter works. Extensive and varied repertoire is performed by all divisions. Please contact the VYSO for more information."

ⓒ WHEATON SYMPHONY ORCHESTRA

344 Spring Ave., Glen Ellyn IL 60137. (630)858-5552. Fax: (630)790-9703. E-mail: dmattob@aol.com. **Contact:** Don Mattison, manager. Symphony orchestra. Estab. 1959. Members are professionals and amateurs. Performs 6 concerts/year including a varying number of new works. "No pay for performance but can probably record your piece."

How to Contact Query first. Include SASE. Responds in 1 month.

Music "This is a good amateur orchestra that wants pieces in a traditional idiom. Large scale works for orchestra only. No avant garde, 12-tone or atonal material. Pieces should be 20 minutes or less and must be prepared in 3 rehearsals. Instrumentation needed for woodwinds in 3s, full brass 4-3-3-1, 4 percussion and strings—full-instrumentation only. Selections for full orchestra only. No pay for reading your piece, but we will record it at our expense.''

Performances Richard Williams's *Symphony in G Minor* (4 movement symphony); Dennis Johnson's *Must Jesus Bear the Cross Alone, Azon* (traditional); and Michael Diemer's *Skating* (traditional style).

Contests & Awards

Participating in contests is a great way to gain exposure for your music. Prizes vary from contest to contest, from cash to musical merchandise to studio time, and even publishing and recording deals. For musical theater and classical composers, the prize may be a performance of your work. Even if you don't win, valuable contacts can be made through contests. Many times, contests are judged by music publishers and other industry professionals, so your music may find its way into the hands of key industry people who can help further your career.

HOW TO SELECT A CONTEST

It's important to remember when entering any contest to do proper research before signing anything or sending any money. We have confidence in the contests listed in *Songwriter's Market*, but it pays to read the fine print. First, be sure you understand the contest rules and stipulations once you receive the entry forms and guidelines. Then you need to weigh what you will gain against what they're asking you to give up. If a publishing or recording contract is the only prize a contest is offering, you may want to think twice before entering. Basically, the company sponsoring the contest is asking you to pay a fee for them to listen to your song under the guise of a contest, something a legitimate publisher or record company would not do. For those contests offering studio time, musical equipment or cash prizes, you need to decide if the entry fee you're paying is worth the chance to win such prizes.

Be wary of exorbitant entry fees, and if you have any doubts whatsoever as to the legitimacy of a contest, it's best to stay away. Songwriters need to approach a contest, award or grant in the same manner as they would a record or publishing company. Make your submission as professional as possible; follow directions and submit material exactly as stated on the entry form.

Contests in this section encompass all types of music and levels of competition. Read each listing carefully and contact them if the contest interests you. Many contests now have Web sites that offer additional information and even entry forms you can print. Be sure to read the rules carefully and be sure you understand exactly what a contest is offering before entering.

AGO/ECS PUBLISHING AWARD IN CHORAL COMPOSITION

American Guild of Organists, 475 Riverside Dr., Suite 1260, New York NY 10115. (212)870-2310. Fax: (212)870-2163. E-mail: info@agohq.org. Web site: www.agohq.org. **Contact:** Karen A. Rich, competitions coordinator. Biannual award.

Requirements Composers are invited to submit a work for SATB choir and organ in which the organ plays a significant and independent role. Work submitted must be unpublished and approximately 3.5 to 5 minutes in length. There is no age restriction. Deadline: TBA, "but usually late fall in even numbered years." Application information on the Web site.

Awards $2,000 cash prize, publication by ECS Publishing and premier performance at the AGO National Convention.

ALEA III INTERNATIONAL COMPOSITION PRIZE

855 Commonwealth Ave., Boston MA 02215. (617)353-3340. E-mail: kalogeras@earthlink.com. Web site: www.aleaiii.com. For composers. Annual award.

Purpose To promote and encourage young composers in the composition of new music.

Requirements Composers born after January 1, 1978 may participate; 1 composition per composer. Works may be for solo voice or instrument or for chamber ensemble up to 15 members lasting between 6 and 15 minutes. Available instruments are: one flute (doubling piccolo or alto), one oboe (doubling English horn), one clarinet (doubling bass clarinet), one bassoon, one horn, one trumpet, one trombone, one tuba, two percussion players, one harp, one keyboard player, one guitar, two violins, one viola, one cello, one bass, tape and one voice. "One of the 15 performers could play an unusual, exotic or rare instrument, or be a specialized vocalist. For more info and guidelines, please refer to our Web site." All works must be unpublished and must not have been publicly performed or broadcast, in whole or in part or in any other version before the announcement of the prize in late September or early October of 2008. Works that have won other awards are not eligible. Deadline: March 15 2008. Send for application. Submitted work required with application. "Real name should not appear on score; a nom de plume should be signed instead. Sealed envelope with entry form should be attached to each score."

Awards ALEA III International Composition Prize: $2,500. Awarded once annually. Between 6-8 finalists are chosen and their works are performed in a competition concert by the ALEA III contemporary music ensemble. At the end of the concert, one piece will be selected to receive the prize. One grand prize winner is selected by a panel of judges.

Tips "Emphasis placed on works written in 20th century compositional idioms."

☑ AMERICAN SONGWRITER LYRIC CONTEST

1303 16th Avenue S., 2nd Floor, Nashville TN 37212. (615)321-6096. Fax: (615)321-6097. E-mail: info@americansongwriter.com. Web site: www.americansongwriter.com. **Contact:** Matt Shearon. Estab. 1984. For songwriters and composers. Award for each bimonthly issue of American Songwriter magazine, plus grand prize winner at year-end.

Purpose To promote and encourage the craft of lyric writing.

Requirements Lyrics must be typed and a check for $10 (per entry) must be enclosed. Deadlines: January 22, March 23, May 23, July 24, September 25, November 16. Send along with official entry form found on our Web site, or submit online through sonicbids.com. Lyrics only, no cassettes. "If you enter two or more lyrics, you automatically receive a 1-year subscription to *American Songwriter* magazine (Canada: 3 or more; Other Countries: 4 or more)."

Awards A DX1 Martin guitar valued at $700 to bi-monthly contest winner. Grand prize winner receives airfare to Nashville and a demo session; and top 5 winning lyrics reprinted in each magazine, and 12 Honorable Mentions. One entrant interviewed each issue. Also: Grand Prize Winner gets to choose his/her "Dream Co-Writing Session" with either Bobby Braddock ("He Stopped

Loving Her Today") or Kent Blazy ("If Tomorrow Never Comes"). Lyrics judged by independent A&R, PRO representatives, songwriters, publishers, and *American Songwriter* staff.

Tips "You do not have to be a subscriber to enter or win. You may submit as many entries as you like. All genres of music accepted."

ARTISTS' FELLOWSHIPS

New York Foundation for the Arts, 155 Avenue of Americas, 14th Floor, New York NY 10013. (212)366-6900. Fax: (212)366-1778. E-mail: nyfaafp@nyfa.org. Web site: www.nyfa.org. To receive an application, or contact the fellowship's department, call: (212)366-6900, ext. 217. **Contact:** Penelope Dannenberg, director of programs. For songwriters, composers and musical playwrights. Annual award, but each category funded biennially. Estab. 1984.

Purpose "Artists' Fellowships are $7,000 grants awarded by the New York Foundation for the Arts to individual originating artists living in New York State. The Foundation is committed to supporting artists from all over New York State at all stages of their professional careers. Fellows may use the grant according to their own needs; it should not be confused with project support."

Requirements Must be 18 years of age or older; resident of New York State for 2 years prior to application; and cannot be enrolled in any graduate or undergraduate degree program. Applications will be available in July. Deadline: October. Samples of work are required with application. 1 or 2 original compositions on separate audiotapes or audio CDs and at least 2 copies of corresponding scores or fully harmonized lead sheets.

Awards All Artists' Fellowships awards are for $7,000. Payment of $6,300 upon verification of NY State residency, and remainder upon completion of a mutually agreed upon public service activity. Nonrenewable. "Fellowships are awarded on the basis of the quality of work submitted. Applications are reviewed by a panel of 5 composers representing the aesthetic, ethnic, sexual and geographic diversity within New York State. The panelists change each year and review all allowable material submitted."

Tips "Please note that musical playwrights may submit only if they write the music for their plays—librettists must submit in our playwriting category."

BILLBOARD SONG CONTEST

P.O. Box 470306, Tulsa OK 74147. (918)827-6529. Fax: (918)827-6533. E-mail: mark@jimhalsey.com. Web site: www.billboardsongcontest.com. **Contact:** Mark Furnas, Director. Estab. 1988. For songwriters, composers and performing artists. Annual international contest.

Purpose "To reward deserving songwriters and performers for their talent."

Requirements Entry fee: $30.

Awards To be announced. For entry forms and additional information send SASE to the above address or visit Web site.

Tips "Participants should understand popular music structure."

THE BLANK THEATRE COMPANY YOUNG PLAYWRIGHTS FESTIVAL

1301 Lucile Ave., Los Angeles CA 90026. (323)662-7734. Fax: (323)661-3903. E-mail: info@theblank.com. Web site: www.youngplaywrights.com. Estab. 1993. For both musical and non-musical playwrights. Annual award.

Purpose "To give young playwrights an opportunity to learn more about playwriting and to give them a chance to have their work mentored, developed, and presented by professional artists."

Requirements Playwrights must be 19 years old or younger on March 15, 2008. Send legible, original plays of any length and on any subject (co-written plays are acceptable provided all co-writers meet eligibility requirements). Submissions must be postmarked by March 15 and must include a cover sheet with the playwright's name, date of birth, school (if any), home address, home phone number, e-mail address and production history. Pages must be numbered and submit-

Contests & Awards

ted unbound (unstapled). For musicals, a tape or CD of a selection from the score should be submitted with the script. Manuscripts will not be returned. Please do not send originals. Semi-finalists and winners will be contacted in May.

Awards Winning playwrights receive a workshop presentation of their work.

BUSH ARTIST FELLOWS PROGRAM

E-900 First National Bank Bldg., 332 Minnesota St., St. Paul MN 55101. (651)227-5222. E-mail: kpolley@bushfound.org. Web site: www.bushfoundation.org. **Contact:** Kathi Polley, program assistant. Estab. 1976. For songwriters, composers and musical playwrights. Applications in music composition are accepted in even-numbered years.

Purpose "To provide artists with significant financial support that enables them to further their work and their contribution to their communities."

Requirements Applicant must be U.S. Citizens or Permanent Residents AND a Minnesota, North Dakota, South Dakota or western Wisconsin resident for 12 of preceeding 36 months, 25 years or older, not a student. Deadline: late October. Send for application. Audio work samples required with application. "Music composition applications will not be taken again until the fall of 2006. Applications will be taken in the fall of 2006 in the following areas: music composition, scriptworks (screenwriting and playwriting), literature (creative non-fiction, fiction, poetry) and film/video.

Awards Fellowships: $48,000 stipend for a period of 12-24 months. "Five years after completion of preceding fellowship, one may apply again." Applications are judged by peer review panels.

THE CLW MUSIC AWARD/LIAISON

"E-mail for entry." E-mail: bej@india.com. Web site: www.clwma.5u.com. **Contact:** Holly Nigelson or Brenda Jackson, owners/partners (for information and an application). Estab. 2002. For Songwriters and Composers.

Purpose "To aid or further the careers of independent musicians, eligible enrolled music students and certain Native/African/Asian/American Organizations musically.

Requirements "Each song entered must be an original work. The songs may have multiple writers, but only one name need be on the application. The performer or performers must be the writers of the material submitted and must be the same individuals who are attend the Awards. Division of the prizes to any co-writers shall be the responsibility of the person named on the entry form as the leader of the Band or Group. No song previously recorded and released through national or any other type of distribution in any country will be eligible to win. Each entry must consist of: 1) A CD or audiocassette containing 1 song, which shall be 5 minutes in length or less. The side with the entry shall be cued to the beginning of the song and it shall be named or marked so. Failure to maintain this regulation shall result in disqualification; 2) The entry form must be signed in ink, in any color, no roller balls, felt tips, Magic Markers, or anything similar shall be accepted. Any non-legible entry forms shall be disqualified. All signatures must be the originals, and shall be verified; 3) If there are any lyrics included with a song, a lyric sheet must be typed or laser printed, no hand written or ink jet printed lyric sheets shall be accepted. Lyrics must have an English translation lyric sheet also, if applicable. Instrumental music shall not require either; 4) The entry fee of $30, payable by money order, Personal or Business check or Credit Card. Entry fees are not refundable. No solo entries or a-cappella entries shall be accepted. *Employees Family, friends, Affiliates and Associates of this contest are not eligible to win the Contest. Do not send Cash and if you use a major Credit Card, an additional $1.50 will be charged to your account!* There are 5 preliminary rounds of Judging and the Contest Final rounds. 1 Finalist from each category will be selected as a Finalist and 5 Finalists with the highest point totals from the rest of the field will be chosen as Finalists also. After Judging, the 15 Finalists shall be notified by mail and will be sent the proper affidavits, which must be returned not more than 40 Business Days after the date on the Congratulatory letter each shall receive. Any fraudulent or inaccurate information shall result in disqualification and an alternate winner shall be selected. Any printed or recorded submissions shall not be returned. Each contestant must be age 15 or older. Any Winners under the age of 21 shall require a parent or guardian present for the administering of prizes. In the instances where any entrants are younger than age 21, the parent or guardian must also sign the entry form. Winners shall be determined 3 months after the close of submissions for the current contest. The odds for winning the overall CLW Music Award are, at maximum, 12,000 to 1 based upon a person making 1 entry, of the 12,000 required to start the Judging round. The format of this contest does not allow these odds to be greater. If a person enters more than 1 recording, the odds for winning increase accordingly, if the entries are in the same contest. A person can enter more than once in any category but a separate fee is required for each entry. If a contestant does not make the finals they may enter a future contest if they choose to. If a contestant finishes in Third Place or lower and finishes no higher by replacing any finalists that may be disqualified by some means, that contestant may enter a future contest if they choose to. The CLW Music Award and Aubusson Music Publishing are not responsible for any late, lost, damaged or mishandled entries. The contest is open to all Amateur persons in the world who have not earned more than $5,000 from music royalties in the last 2 years. This rule shall apply to an individual or all members of a group or band collectively. If it is found that an entrant violates these requirements, the entrant shall be prosecuted for fraud, and in addition, any amount of winnings shall be returned and the contestant will be disqualified, with another winner being selected in place of the fraudulent one. 15 finalists will perform their entry song, or songs at the finals and be Judged. Those entrants who finish 3rd Place or lower and no higher, are eligible to enter again in the next contest. There are a total of 15 rounds of judging and the results remain unknown to everyone until the presentations. The Awards ceremony will be taped for Broadcast at a later date.

Awards Prizes: 1 CLW Music Award Winner, who will receive $30,000 cash and a Publishing Award; 1 Grand Prize Winner, who will receive $15,000 in cash and a Publishing Award; 1 First Prize Winner, who will receive $7,500 cash and a Publishing Award; 1 Second Prize Winner, who will receive $5,000 cash and a Publishing Award; 1 Third Prize Winner, who will receive $2,500 in cash only; 1 Fourth Prize Winner, who will receive $1,500 cash; 1 Honorary Native American Music Award; 1 Honorary Asian American Music Award; and 1 Honorary African-American Music Award. There will also be 5 Runners Up with the Runners Up each receiving $1,000 cash. No substitutions for any prizes can, or will be, made.

Tips ''DO NOT PHOTOCOPY YOUR ENTRY FORM FOR SOMEONE ELSE, they must have their own contestant serial number on their application. Photocopies are only for you in other categories. Make sure you read the rules and prepare your recording properly. Judging has been configured so that all types of music DO have the same chance of winning this contest. Make sure that you can perform your song live and be prepared to come to do so.''

☑ CMT/NSAI ANNUAL SONG CONTEST

1710 Roy Acuff Place, Nashville TN 37203. (615)256-3354. Fax: (615)256-0034. E-mail: songcontest @nashvillesongwriters.com. Web site: www.nashvillesongwriters.com. **Contact:** Deanie Williams, director. Annual award for songwriters.

Purpose ''A chance for aspiring songwriters to be heard by music industry decision makers. Winners are flown to Nashville for a recording session and an appointment with Music Row executives.''

Requirements Entry fee: $45 for one entry; $60 for 2. In order to be eligible contestants must not be receiving income from any work submitted—original material only. Submissions must include both lyrics and melody. Deadline is different each year; check Web site or send for application. Samples are required with application in the format of cassette or CD.

Awards Varies from year to year; check Web site.

Contests & Awards

COLUMBIA ENTERTAINMENT COMPANY'S JACKIE WHITE MEMORIAL PLAYWRITING CONTEST

309 Parkade Blvd., Columbia MO 65202. (573)874-5628. Web site: www.cectheatre.org. **Contact:** Betsy Phillips, contest director, CEC contest. For musical playwrights. Annual award.

Purpose "We are looking for top-notch scripts suitable for family audiences with 7 or more fully-developed roles."

Requirements "May be adaptations or plays with original story lines and cannot have been previously published. Please write or call for complete rules." Send SASE or visit Web site for application; then send scripts to address above. Full-length play, neatly typed. No name on title page, but name, address and name of play on a 3×5 index card and lead sheets, as well as tape of musical numbers. $20 entry fee.

Awards $500 1st Prize. Play may or may not be produced at discretion of CEC. "The judging committee is taken from members of Columbia Entertainment Company's Executive and Advisory boards, and from theater school parents. Readings by up to eight members, with at least three readings of all entries, and winning entries being read by entire committee. All plays will receive a written evaluation."

Tips "We especially like plays that deal with current day problems and concerns. However, if the play is good enough, any suitable subject matter is fine."

ℕ COMPOSERS GUILD ANNUAL COMPOSITION CONTEST

P.O. Box 586, Farmington UT 84025-0586. (801)451-2275. **Contact:** Ruth B. Gatrell, president. Estab. 1963. For songwriters, musical playwrights and composers. Annual award.

- Also see the Composers Guild listing in the Organizations section of this book.

Purpose "To stimulate musical composition and help composers through judge's comments on each composition submitted. Composers can broaden their creative skills by entering different categories. Categories: Arrangements (original in public domain or with composer's permission); music for children; choral; instrumental; jazz/New Age; keyboard; orchestra/band; popular (all types); vocal solo; young composer (18 or under on August 31)."

Requirements Score and/or cassette or CD. Entry fee: $20 for work 7 minutes or more in length (may include multimovements on compositions), $15 for work less than 7 minutes. Dues are $25/year. Member entry fees: $10 for work 7 minutes or more, $5 less than 7 minutes. Deadline: August 31. Send or call for application.

Awards Award of Excellence $500; 1st Prize in each category except Award of Excellence category $100; 2nd Prize in each category $50; 3rd Prize in each category $25; Honorable Mention certificates. Judge has a doctorate in music, plus compositions published and performed (usually has vast teaching experience). Same judge never used in successive years.

Tips "Submit good clear copies of score. Have cassette cued up. Only one composition per cassette/CD (each entry requires separate cassette/CD). No composer names to appear on score or cassette/CD. Enter as many categories and compositions as you wish. Separate entry fee for each. One check can cover all entries and dues."

CRS NATIONAL COMPOSERS COMPETITION

724 Winchester Rd., Broomall PA 19008. (610)544-5920. E-mail: crsnews@verizon.net. Web site: www.crsnews.org. **Contact:** Caroline Hunt, administrative assistant. Senior Representative: Jack Shusterman. Estab. 1981. For songwriters, composers and performing artists. College faculty and gifted artists. Annual award.

Requirements For composers, songwriters, performing artists and ensembles. The work submitted must be non-published (prior to acceptance) and not commercially recorded on any label. The work submitted must not exceed nine performers. Each composer may submit one work for each application submitted. (Taped performances are additionally encouraged.) Composition must not exceed twenty-five minutes in length. CRS reserves the right not to accept a First Prize Winner. Write with SASE for application or visit Web site. Add $3.50 for postage and handling. Deadline: December 10. Must send a detailed résumé with application form available on our Web page under "Events" category. Samples of work required with application. Send score and parts with optional CD or DAT. Application fee: $50.

Awards 1st Prize: Commercial recording grant. Applications are judged by panel of judges determined each year.

CUNNINGHAM COMMISSION FOR YOUTH THEATRE

(formerly Cunningham Prize for Playwriting), The Theatre School at DePaul University, 2135 N. Kenmore Ave., Chicago IL 60614. (773)325-7938. Fax: (773)325-7920. E-mail: lgoetsch@depaul.edu. Web site: http://theatreschool.depaul.edu. **Contact:** Lara Goetsch, director of marketing/public relations. Estab. 1990. For playwrights. Annual award.

Purpose "The purpose of the Commission is to encourage the writing of dramatic works for young audiences that affirm the centrality of religion, broadly defined, and the human quest for meaning, truth, and community. The Theatre School intends to produce the plays created through this commission in its award-winning Chicago Playworks for Families and Young Audiences series at the historic Merle Reskin Theatre. Each year Chicago Playworks productions are seen by 35,000 students and families from throughout the Chicago area."

Requirements "Candidates for the commission must be writers whose residence is in the Chicago area, defined as within 100 miles of the Loop. Playwrights who have won the award within the last five years are not eligible. Deadline: annually by December 1. Candidates should submit a résumé, a 20 page sample of their work, and a brief statement about their interest in the commission. The submission should not include a proposal for a project the playwright would complete if awarded the commission. The writing sample may be from a play of any genre for any audience."

Awards $5,000. "Winners will be notified by May 1. The Selection Committee is chaired by the Dean of The Theatre School and is composed of members of the Cunningham Commission advisory committee and faculty of The Theatre School."

DELTA OMICRON INTERNATIONAL COMPOSITION COMPETITION

12297 W. Tennessee Place, Lakewood CO 80228. (303)989-2871. E-mail: rbzdx@webtv.net. Web site: www.delta-omicron.org. **Composition Competition Chair:** Judith L. Eidson. For composers. Triennial award.

Purpose "To encourage composers worldwide to continually add to our wonderful heritage of musical creativity instrumentally and/or vocally."

Requirements People from college age on (or someone younger who is enrolled in college). Work must be unpublished and unperformed in public. "View our Web site (www.delta-omicron.org) for specific submission guidelines such as instrument selection and deadline Click on 'Composition Competition' on homepage." Manuscripts should be legibly written in ink or processed, signed with *nom de plume,* and free from any marks that would identify the composer to the judges. Entry fee: $25 per composition. Send for application. Composition is required with application. A total of three copies of composition are required, one for each judge. Music copies should *not* be spiral bound.

Awards 1st Place: $1,000 and world premiere at Delta Omicron Triennial Conference. Judged by 2-3 judges (performers, conductors, and/or composers).

EUROPEAN INTERNATIONAL COMPETITION FOR COMPOSERS/IBLA FOUNDATION

226 East 2nd St., Loft 1B, New York NY 10009. (212)387-0111. E-mail: iblanyc@aol.com. Web site: www.ibla.org. **Contact:** Mr. Michael Yasenak, executive director. Chairman: Dr. S. Moltisanti. Estab. 1995. For songwriters and composers. Annual award.

Purpose "To promote the winners' career through exposure, publicity, recordings with Athena Records and nationwide distribution with the Empire Group."

Requirements Deadline: April 30. Send for application. Music score and/or recording of one work are required with application. Application fee is refunded if not admitted into the program.

Awards Winners are presented in concerts in Europe-Japan, USA.

FULBRIGHT SCHOLAR PROGRAM, COUNCIL FOR INTERNATIONAL EXCHANGE OF SCHOLARS

3007 Tilden St. NW, Suite 5L, Washington DC 20008-3009. (202)686-7877. E-mail: scholars@cies.ii e.org. Web site: www.cies.org. Estab. 1946. For composers and academics. Annual award.

Purpose "Awards for university lecturing and advanced research abroad are offered annually in virtually all academic disciplines including musical composition."

Requirements "U.S. citizenship at time of application; M.F.A., Ph.D. or equivalent professional qualifications; for lecturing awards, university teaching experience (some awards are for profession-als non-academic)." Applications become available in March each year, for grants to be taken up 1½ years later. Application deadlines: August 1, all world areas. Write or call for application. Samples of work are required with application.

Awards "Benefits vary by country, but generally include round-trip travel for the grantee and for most full academic-year awards, one dependent; stipend in U.S. dollars and/or local currency; in many countries, tuition allowance for school age children; and book and baggage allowance. Grant duration ranges from 3 months-1 academic year."

HARVEY GAUL COMPOSITION CONTEST

The Pittsburgh New Music Ensemble, Inc., P.O. Box 99476, Pittsburgh PA 15233. E-mail: pnme@pn me.org. Web site: www.pnme.org. **Contact:** Jeffrey Nytch, DMA, managing director. For compos-ers. Biennial.

Purpose Objective is to encourage composition of new music.

Requirements "Must be citizen of the US. Please submit score and recording, if available (CDs only) of a representative instrumental score." Deadline: September 30, 2008. Send SASE for application or download from www.pnme.org. Samples of work are required with application. Entry fee: $20.

Awards Harvey Gaul Composition Contest: $6,000. Winner will receive commission for new work to be premiered by the PNME.

GRASSY HILL KERRVILLE NEW FOLK COMPETITION

(formerly New Folk Concerts For Emerging Songwriters), P.O. Box 291466, Kerrville TX 78029. (830)257-3600. Fax: (830)257-8680. E-mail: info@kerrville-music.com. Web site: www.kerrvillefol kfestival.com. **Contact:** Dalis Allen, producer. For songwriters. Annual award.

• Also see the listing for Kerrville Folk Festival in the Workshops section of this book.

Purpose "To provide an opportunity for emerging songwriters to be heard and rewarded for excel-lence."

Requirements Songwriter enters 2 original songs burned to CD (*cassettes no longer accepted*), or uploaded to SonicBids, with entry fee; no more than one submission may be entered; 6-8 minutes total for 2 songs. Application online, no lyric sheets or press material needed. Submissions accepted between December 1-March 15 or first 800 entries received prior to that date. Call or e-mail to request rules. Entry fee: $20.

Awards New Folk Award Winner. 32 finalists invited to sing the 2 songs entered during The Kerrville Folk Festival in May. 6 writers are chosen as award winners. Each of the 6 receives a cash award of $450 or more and performs at a winner's concert during the Kerrville Folk Festival in June. Initial round of entries judged by the Festival Producer. 32 finalists judged by panel of 3 performer/ songwriters.

Tips "Do not allow instrumental accompaniment to drown out lyric content. Don't enter without complete copy of the rules. Former winners and finalists include Lyle Lovett, Nanci Griffith, Hal Ketchum, John Gorka, David Wilcox, Lucinda Williams and Robert Earl Keen, Tish Hinojosa, Carrie Newcomer, Jimmy Lafave, etc."

GREAT AMERICAN SONG CONTEST

PMB 135, 6327-C SW Capitol Hill Hwy., Portland OR 97239-1937. E-mail: info@GreatAmericanSong .com. Web site: www.GreatAmericanSong.com. **Contact:** Carla Starrett, event coordinator. Estab. 1998. For songwriters, composers and lyricists. Annual award.

- Also see the listing for Songwriters Resource Network in the Organizations section of this book.

Purpose To help songwriters get their songs heard by music-industry professionals; to generate educational and networking opportunities for participating songwriters; to help songwriters open doors in the music business.

Requirements Entry fee: $25. "Annual deadline. Check our Web site for details or send SASE along with your mailed request for information."

Awards Winners receive a mix of cash awards and prizes. The focus of the contest is on networking and educational opportunities. (All participants receive detailed evaluations of their songs by industry professionals.) Songs are judged by knowledgeable music-industry professionals, including prominent hit songwriters, producers and publishers.

Tips "Focus should be on the song. The quality of the demo isn't important. Judges will be looking for good songwriting talent. They will base their evaluations on the song—not the quality of the recording or the voice performance."

HENRICO THEATRE COMPANY ONE-ACT PLAYWRITING COMPETITION

P.O. Box 27032, Richmond VA 23273. (804)501-5115. Fax: (804)501-5284. E-mail: per22@co.henric o.va.us. **Contact:** Amy A. Perdue, cultural arts coordinator. Cultural Arts Assistant: Elaine Payne. For musical playwrights, songwriters, composers and performing artists. Annual award.

Purpose Original one-act musicals for a community theater organization.

Requirements "Only one-act plays or musicals will be considered. The manuscript should be a one-act original (not an adaptation), unpublished, and unproduced, free of royalty and copyright restrictions. Scripts with smaller casts and simpler sets may be given preference. Controversial themes and excessive language should be avoided. Standard play script form should be used. All plays will be judged anonymously; therefore, there should be two title pages; the first must contain the play's title and the author's complete address and telephone number. The second title page must contain only the play's title. The playwright must submit two excellent quality copies. Receipt of all scripts will be acknowledged by mail. Scripts will be returned if SASE is included. No scripts will be returned until after the winner is announced. The HTC does not assume responsibility for loss, damage or return of scripts. All reasonable care will be taken." Deadline: July 1st. Send for application first.

Awards 1st Prize $300; 2nd Prize $200; 3rd Prize $200.

HOLTKAMP-AGO AWARD IN ORGAN COMPOSITION

American Guild of Organists, 475 Riverside Dr., Suite 1260, New York NY 10115. (212)870-2310. Fax: (212)870-2163. E-mail: info@agohq.org. Web site: www.agohq.org. **Contact:** Karen A. Rich, competitions coordinator. For composers and performing artists. Biennial award.

Requirements Organ solo, no longer than 8 minutes in duration. Specifics vary from year to year. Deadline: TBA, but usually early spring of odd-numbered year. Go to the Web site for application.

Award $2,000 provided by the Holtkamp Organ Company; publication by Hinshaw Music Inc.; performance at the biennial National Convention of the American Guild of Organists.

⃞N ⃞ IAMA (INTERNATIONAL ACOUSTIC MUSIC AWARDS)

2881 E. Oakland Park Blvd, Suite 414, Fort Lauderdale, FL 33306. (954)537-3127. **Contact:** Jessica Brandon, artist relations. Established 2004. E-mail: info@inacoustic.com. Web site: http://www.in acoustic.com. For singer-songwriters, musicians, performing musicians in the acoustic genre.

Purpose "The purpose is to promote the excellence in Acoustic music performance and songwriting." Genres include: Folk, Alternative, Bluegrass, etc.

Requirements Visit Web site for entry form and details. "All songs submitted must be original. There must be at least an acoustic instrument (voice) in any song. Electric and Electronic instruments, along with loops is allowed but acoustic instruments (or voice) must be clearly heard in all songs submitted. Contestants may enter as many songs in as many categories as desired but each entry requires a separate CD, entry form, lyric sheet and entry fee. CDs and lyrics will not be returned. Winners will be chosen by a Blue Ribbon Judging Committee comprised of music industry professionals including A&R managers from record labels, publishers and producers. Entries are judged equally on music performance, production, originality, lyrics, melody and composition. Songs may be in any language. Winners will be notified by e-mail and must sign and return an affidavit confirming that winner's song is original and he/she holds rights to the song. Entry fee: $35/entry.

Awards Prizes: Overall Grand Prize receives $11,000.00 worth of merchandise, First Prizes in all categories win $900.00 worth of merchandise and services, Runner-Up prizes in all categories receive $600.00 worth of merchandise and services. All first prizes and runner-up winners will receive a track on IAMA compilation CD which goes out to radio stations.

Tips "Judging is based on music performance, music production, songwriting and originality/artistry."

KATE NEAL KINLEY MEMORIAL FELLOWSHIP

University of Illinois, College of Fine and Applied Arts, 608 E. Lorado Taft Dr. #100, Champaign IL 61820. (217)333-1661. Web site: www.faa.uiuc.edu. **Contact:** Dr. Kathleen F. Conlin, chair. Estab. 1931. For students of architecture, art or music. Annual award.

Purpose The advancement of study in the fine arts.

Requirements "The Fellowship will be awarded upon the basis of unusual promise in the fine arts. Open to college graduates whose principal or major studies have been in the fields of architecture, art or music." Write or call for fall deadline. Send for application or call. Samples of work are required with application.

Awards "Two or three major Fellowships which yield the sum of $7,500 each which is to be used by the recipients toward defraying the expenses of advanced study of the fine arts in America or abroad." Good for 1 year. Grant is nonrenewable.

L.A. DESIGNERS' THEATRE MUSIC AWARDS

P.O. Box 1883, Studio City CA 91614-0883. (323)650-9600. Fax: (323)654-3210. E-mail: ladesigners @juno.com. Artistic Director: Richard Niederberg. For songwriters, composers, performing artists, musical playwrights and rights holders of music.

Purpose To produce new musicals, operettas, opera-boufes and plays with music, as well as new dance pieces with new music scores.

Requirements Submit nonreturnable cassette, tape, CD or any other medium by first or 4th class mail. "We prefer proposals to scripts." Acceptance: continuous. Submit nonreturnable materials with cover letter. No application form or fee is necessary.

Awards Music is commissioned for a particular project. Amounts are negotiable. Applications judged by our artistic staff.

Tips "Make the material 'classic, yet commercial' and easy to record/re-record/edit. Make sure rights are totally free of all 'strings,' 'understandings,' 'promises,' etc. ASCAP/BMI/SESAC registration is OK, as long as 'grand' or 'performing rights' are available."

THE JOHN LENNON SONGWRITING CONTEST

180 Brighton Rd., Suite 801, Clifton NJ 07012. E-mail: info@jlsc.com. Web site: www.jlsc.com. Estab. 1996. For songwriters. Open year-round.

Purpose "The purpose of the John Lennon Songwriting Contest is to promote the art of songwriting by assisting in the discovery of new talent as well as providing more established songwriters with an opportunity to advance their careers."

Requirements Each entry must consist of the following: completed and signed application; audio cassette, CD or mp3 containing one song only, 5 minutes or less in length; lyric sheet typed or printed legibly (English translation is required when applicable); $30 entry fee. Deadline: December 15, 2006. Applications can be found in various music-oriented magazines and on our Web site. Prospective entrants can send for an application or contact the contest via e-mail at info@jlsc.com.

Awards Entries are accepted in the following 12 categories: rock, country, jazz, pop, world, gospel/inspirational, R&B, hip-hop, Latin, electronic, folk and children's music. Winners will receive EMI Publishing Contracts, Studio Equipment from Brian Moore Guitars, Roland, Edirol and Audio Technica, 1,000 CDs in full color with premium 6-panel Digipaks courtesy of Discmakers, and gift certificates from Musiciansfriend.com. One entrant wil be chosen to TOUR and PERFORM for one week on Warped Tour '06. One Lennon Award winning song will be named "Maxell Song of the Year" and take home an additional $20,000 in cash courtesy of the Maxell Corporation.

MAXIM MAZUMDAR NEW PLAY COMPETITION

One Curtain Up Alley, Buffalo NY 14202-1911. (716)852-2600. Fax: (716)852-2266. E-mail: newplays@alleyway.com. Web site: www.alleyway.com. **Contact:** Literary Manager. For musical playwrights. Annual award.

Purpose Alleyway Theatre is dedicated to the development and production of new works. Winners of the competition will receive production and royalties.

Requirements Unproduced full-length work not less than 90 minutes long with cast limit of 10 and unit or simple set, or unproduced one-act work less than 15 minutes long with cast limit of 6 and simple set; prefers work with unconventional setting that explores the boundaries of theatricality; limit of 1 submission in each category; guidelines available online, no entry form. $25 playwright entry fee. Script, resume, SASE optional. CD or cassette mandatory. Deadline: July 1.

Awards Production for full-length play or musical with royalty and travel and housing determined on a yearly basis; and production for one-act play or musical.

Tips "Entries may be of any style, but preference will be given to those scripts which take place in unconventional settings and explore the boundaries of theatricality. No more than ten performers is a definite, unchangeable requirement."

MID-ATLANTIC SONG CONTEST

Songwriters' Association of Washington, PMB 106-137, 4200 Wisconsin Ave., NW, Washington DC 20016. (301)654-8434. E-mail: masc@saw.org. Web site: www.saw.org. For songwriters and composers. Estab. 1982. Annual award.

• Also see the listing for Songwriters Association of Washington in the Organizations section.

Purpose This is one of the longest-running contests in the nation; SAW has organized twenty contests since 1982. The competition is designed to afford rising songwriters in a wide variety of genres the opportunity to receive awards and exposure in an environment of peer competition.

Requirements Amateur status is important. Applicants should request a brochure/application using the contact information above. Rules and procedures are clearly explained in that brochure. Cassette or CD and 3 copies of the lyrics are to be submitted with an application form and fee for each entry.

Beginning this year, online enteries will also be accepted. Reduced entry fees are offered to members of Songwriters' Association of Washington; membership can be arranged simultaneously with entering. Multie-song discounts are also offered. Applications are mailed out and posted on their Web site around June 1; the submission deadline is usually sometime in mid-August; awards are typically announced late in the fall.

Awards The two best songs in each of ten categories win prize packages donated by the contest's corporate sponsors: Writer's Digest Books, BMI, Oasis CD Manufacturing, Omega Recording Studios, TAXI, Mary Cliff and Sonic Bids. Winning songwriters are invited to perform in Washington, DC at the Awards Ceremony Gala, and the twenty winning songs are included on a compilation CD. The best song in each category is eligible for three grand cash prizes. Certificates are awarded to other entries meriting honorable mention.

Tips "Enter the song in the most appropriate category. Make the sound recording the best it can be (even though judges are asked to focus on melody and lyric and not on production.) Avoid clichés, extended introductions, and long instrumental solos."

THELONIOUS MONK INTERNATIONAL JAZZ COMPOSERS COMPETITION

(Sponsored by BMI) Thelonious Monk Institute of Jazz, 5225 Wisconsin Ave. NW, #605, Washington DC 20015. (202)364-7272. Fax: (202)364-0176. E-mail: lebrown@tmonkinst.org. Web site: www.monkinstitute.org. **Contact:** Leonard Brown, program director. Estab. 1993. For songwriters and composers. Annual award.

Purpose The award is given to an aspiring jazz composer who best demonstrates originality, creativity and excellence in jazz composition.

Requirements Deadline: July 17. Send for application. Submission must include application form, resume of musical experience, CD or cassette, entry, four copies of the full score, and a photo. The composition features a different instrument each year. Entry fee: $35.

Awards $10,000. Applications are judged by panel of jazz musicians. "The Institute will provide piano, bass, guitar, drum set, tenor saxophone, and trumpet for the final performance. The winner will be responsible for the costs of any different instrumentation included in the composition."

NACUSA YOUNG COMPOSERS' COMPETITION

Box 49256 Barrington Station, Los Angeles CA 90049. (310)838-4465. E-mail: nacusa@music-usa.org. Web site: www.music-usa.org/nacusa. **Contact:** Daniel Kessner, president, NACUSA. Estab. 1978. For composers. Annual award.

- Also see the National Association of Composers/USA (NACUSA) listing in the Organization section.

Purpose To encourage the composition of new American concert hall music.

Requirements Entry fee: $20 (membership fee). Deadline: October 30. Send for application. Samples are not required.

Awards 1st Prize: $400; 2nd Prize: $100; and possible Los Angeles performances. Applications are judged by a committee of experienced NACUSA composer members.

SAMMY NESTICO AWARD/USAF BAND AIRMEN OF NOTE

201 McChord St., Bolling AFB, Washington DC 20032-0202. (202)767-1756. Fax: (202)767-0686. E-mail: alan.baylock@bolling.af.mil. **Contact:** Alan Baylock, master sergeant. Estab. 1995. For composers. Annual award.

Purpose To carry on the tradition of excellence of Sammy Nestico's writing through jazz composition. The winner will have their composition performed by the USAF Airmen of Note, have it professionally recorded and receive a $1,000 follow up commission for a second work.

Requirements Unpublished work for jazz ensemble instrumentation (5,4,4,4) style, form and length are unrestricted. Deadline: October 2, 2006. Send for application. Samples of work are required with full score and set of parts (or CD recording).

Awards Performance by the USAF Band Airmen of Note; expense paid travel to Washington, DC for the performance; professionally produced recording of the winning composition; and $1,000 follow up commission for second work. Applications are judged by panel of musicians.

PLAYHOUSE ON THE SQUARE NEW PLAY COMPETITION
51 S. Cooper, Memphis TN 38104. (901)725-0776. **Contact:** Jackie Nichols, executive director. For musical playwrights. Annual award. Estab. 1983.
Requirements Send script, tape and SASE. "Playwrights from the South will be given preference." Open to full-length, unproduced plays. Musicals must be fully arranged for piano when received. Deadline: April 1.
Awards Grants may be renewed. Applications judged by 3 readers.

PORTLAND SONGWRITERS ASSOCIATION ANNUAL SONGWRITING COMPETITION
P.O. Box 42389, Portland OR 97242. (503)914-1000. E-mail: info@portlandsongwriters.org. Web site: www.portlandsongwriters.org. Estab. 1991. For songwriters and composers. Annual award.
Purpose To provide opportunities for songwriters to improve their skills in the art and craft of songwriting, to connect our performing songwriters with the public through PSA sponsored venues and to create a presence and an avenue of approach for members' songs to be heard by industry professionals.
Requirements For information, send SASE. All amateur songwriters may enter. Deadline: December 1, 2007 postmark. Entry fee: $15 members; $20 nonmembers.
Awards Multiple awards totaling $1,000 in prizes. All songs will be reviewed by at least three qualified judges, including industry pros. Finalists may have their songs reviewed by celebrity judges.

PULITZER PRIZE IN MUSIC
709 Journalism Building, Columbia University, New York NY 10027. (212)854-3841. Fax: (212)854-3342. E-mail: pulitzer@www.pulitzer.org. Web site: www.pulitzer.org. **Contact:** Music Secretary. For composers and musical playwrights. Annual award.
Requirements "For distinguished musical composition by an American that has had its first performance or recording in the United States during the year." Entries should reflect current creative activity. Works that receive their American premiere between January 16, 2006 and January 15, 2007 are eligible. A public performance or the public release of a recording shall constitute a premiere. Deadline: January 15. Samples of work are required with application, biography and photograph of composer, date and place of performance, score or manuscript and recording of the work, entry form and $50 entry fee.
Awards "One award: $10,000. Applications are judged first by a nominating jury, then by the Pulitzer Prize Board."

ROCKY MOUNTAIN FOLKS FESTIVAL SONGWRITER SHOWCASE
Planet Bluegrass, ATTN: Songwriter Showcase, P.O. Box 769, Lyons CO 80540. (800)624-2422 or (303)823-0848. Fax: (303)823-0849. E-mail: emily@bluegrass.com. Web site: www.bluegrass.com. **Contact:** Steve Szymanski, director. Estab. 1993. For songwriters, composers and performers. Annual award.
Purpose Award based on having the best song and performance.
Requirements Deadline: June 30. Finalists notified by July 14. Rules available on Web site. Samples of work are required with application. Send CD or cassette with $10/song entry fee. Can now submit online: www.sonicbids.com/rockymountainfolk06. Contestants cannot be signed to a major label or publishing deal. No backup musicians allowed.
Awards 1st Place is a 2006 Festival Main Stage set, custom Hayes Guitar, $100, and a free one song

drumoverdubs (http://www.drumoverdubs.com) certificate (valued at $300); 2nd Place is $500 and a Baby Taylor Guitar; 3rd Place is $400 and a Baby Taylor Guitar; 4th Place is $300; 5th Place is $200; 6th to 10th Place is $100 each. Each finalist will also receive a complimentary three-day Folks Festival pass that includes onsite camping, and a Songwriter In The Round slot during the Festival on our workshop stage.

RICHARD RODGERS AWARDS

American Academy of Arts and Letters, 633 W. 155th St., New York NY 10032. (212)368-5900. **Contact:** Jane Bolster, coordinator. Estab. 1978. Deadline: November 1, 2007. "The Richard Rodgers Awards subsidize staged reading, studio productions, and full productions by nonprofit theaters in New York City of works by composers and writers who are not already established in the field of musical theater. The awards are only for musicals—songs by themselves are not eligible. The authors must be citizens or permanent residents of the United States." Guidelines for this award may be obtained by sending a SASE to above address or download from www.artsandletters.org.

ROME PRIZE COMPETITION FELLOWSHIP

American Academy in Rome, 7 E. 60th St., New York NY 10022-1001. (212)751-7200. Fax: (212)751-7220. E-mail: info@aarome.org. Web site: www.aarome.org. **Contact:** Programs Department. For composers. Annual award.

Purpose "Rome Prize Competition winners pursue independent projects."

Requirements "Applicants for 11-month fellowships must hold a bachelor's degree in music, musical composition or its equivalent." Deadline: November 1. Entry fee: $25. Application guidelines are available through the Academy's Web site.

Awards "Up to two fellowships are awarded annually. Fellowship stipend is $23,000 for 11-months, and includes room and board, and a study or studio at Academy facilities in Rome. In all cases, excellence is the primary criterion for selection, based on the quality of the materials submitted. Winners are announced in mid-April."

TELLURIDE TROUBADOUR CONTEST

Planet Bluegrass, ATTN: Troubadour Competition, P.O. Box 769, Lyons CO 80540. (303)823-0848 or (800)624-2422. Fax: (303)823-0849. E-mail: emily@bluegrass.com. Web site: www.bluegrass.com. **Contact:** Steve Szymanski, director. Estab. 1991. For songwriters, composers and performers. Annual award.

Purpose Award based on having best song and performance.

Requirements Deadline: must be postmarked by April 28; notified May 12, if selected. Rules available on Web site. Send cassette or CD and $10/song entry fee (limit of 2 songs). Can now submit music online at www.sonicbids.com/telluride2006. Contestants cannot be signed to a major label or publishing deal. No backup musicians allowed.

Awards 1st: custom Shanti Guitar, $200 and Festival Main Stage Set; 2nd: $400, "Limo" portable amplifier, and Little Martin guitar; 3rd: $300 and Little Martin guitar; 4th: $200 and Little Martin guitar; 5th: $100 and Baby Taylor guitar. Applications judged by panel of judges.

THE TEN-MINUTE MUSICALS PROJECT

P.O. Box 461194, West Hollywood CA 90046. Web site: www.tenminutemusicals.org. **Contact:** Michael Koppy, producer. For songwriters, composers and musical playwrights. Annual award.

Purpose "We are building a full-length stage musical comprised of complete short musicals, each of which play for between 8-14 minutes. Award is $250 for each work chosen for development towards inclusion in the project, plus a share of royalties when produced."

Requirements Deadline: August 31. Write for guidelines. Final submission should include script, cassette or CD, and lead sheets.

Awards $250 for each work selected. "Works should have complete stories, with a definite beginning, middle and end."

☑ U.S.-JAPAN CREATIVE ARTISTS EXCHANGE FELLOWSHIP PROGRAM

Japan-U.S. Friendship Commission, 1201 15th St. NW, Suite 330, Washington DC 20005. (202)653-9800. Fax: (202)653-9802. E-mail: jusfc@jusfc.gov. Web site: www.jusfc.gov. **Contact:** Margaret Mihori, assistant executive director. Estab. 1980. For all creative artists. Annual award.

Purpose "For artists to go as seekers, as cultural visionaries, and as living liaisons to the traditional and contemporary life of Japan."

Requirements "Artists' works must exemplify the best in U.S. arts." Deadline: Feb. 1, 2008. Send for application and guidelines. Applications available via Internet. Samples of work are required with application. Requires 2 pieces on CD or DVD.

Awards Five artists are awarded a 5 month residency anywhere in Japan. Awards monthly stipend for living expenses, housing and professional support services; up to $6,000 for pre-departure costs, including such items as language training and economy class roundtrip airfare, plus 600,000 yen for monthly living expenses, housing allowance, and professional support services, as well as other arts professionals with expertise in Japanese culture.

Tips "Applicants should anticipate a highly rigorous review of their artistry and should have compelling reasons for wanting to work in Japan."

☑ U.S.A. SONGWRITING COMPETITION

2881 E. Oakland Park Blvd., Suite 414, Ft. Lauderdale FL 33306. (954)537-3127. Fax: (954)537-9690. E-mail: info@songwriting.net. Web site: www.songwriting.net. **Contact:** Contest Manager. Estab. 1994. For songwriters, composers, performing artists and lyricists. Annual award.

Purpose "To honor good songwriters/composers all over the world, especially the unknown ones."

Requirements Open to professional and beginner songwriters. No limit on entries. Each entry must include an entry fee, a cassette tape of song(s) and lyric sheet(s). Judged by music industry representatives. Past judges have included record label representatives and publishers from Arista Records, EMI and Warner/Chappell. Deadline: To be announced. Entry fee: To be announced. Send SASE with request or e-mail for entry forms at any time. Samples of work are not required.

Awards Prizes include cash and merchandise in 15 different categories: pop, rock, country, Latin, R&B, gospel, folk, jazz, "lyrics only" category, instrumental and many others.

Tips "Judging is based on lyrics, originality, melody and overall composition. CD-quality production is great but not a consideration in judging."

☑ UNISONG INTERNATIONAL SONG CONTEST

6520 Platt Ave., #729, West Hills CA 91307-3218. (213)673-4067. E-mail: info@unisong.com. Web site: www.unisong.com. Founders: Alan Roy Scott and David Stark. Estab. 1997. For songwriters (composers and lyricists) and performers. Annual songwriting contest.

Purpose "Unisong was created by songwriters for songwriters."

Requirements Open for entries from October until April. 18 categories cover most song genres, including Lyrics Only and a recently added Performance category. Professional critiques available. Download entry form from Web site or enter directly online. You may also request an entry form by phone or e-mail. CDs or cassettes are accepted by mail. Entries also accepted via MP3.

Awards Over $70,000 in cash and prizes. Grand Prize winner receives an all expenses paid writing and performing retreat to their choice of Costa Rica, Ireland, Crete, Sweden, Denmark, Spain, Iceland, Big Sur, or New Zealand to collaborate with other writers & artists from around the world. There's also an additional "Winner of the Month" contest-within-the-contest, "People's Choice" Award, and Discmakers Winners Compilation CD. Songs judged on song quality above all, not just demo.

Tips "Please make sure your song is professionally presented. Make sure lyrics are typed or printed clearly. Print your personal information clearly. Enter your song in the most appropriate categories, or we can choose them for you for an additional fee."

Y.E.S. FESTIVAL OF NEW PLAYS

Northern Kentucky University Dept. of Theatre, FA-205, Highland Heights KY 41099-1007. (859)572-6303. Fax: (859)572-6057. E-mail: forman@nku.edu. **Contact:** Sandra Forman, project director. Estab. 1983. For musical playwrights. Biennial award (odd numbered years).

Purpose "The festival seeks to encourage new playwrights and develop new plays and musicals. Three plays or musicals are given full productions."

Requirements "No entry fee. Submit a script with a completed entry form. Musicals should be submitted with a piano/conductor's score and/or a vocal parts score. Scripts may be submitted May 1 through Sept. 30, 2008, for the New Play Festival occuring April 2009. Send SASE for application."

Awards Three awards of $500. "The winners are brought to NKU at our expense to view late rehearsals and opening night." Submissions are judged by a panel of readers.

Tips "Plays/musicals which have heavy demands for mature actors are not as likely to be selected as an equally good script with roles for 18-30 year olds."

Organizations

One of the first places a beginning songwriter should look for guidance and support is a songwriting organization. Offering encouragement, instruction, contacts and feedback, these groups of professional and amateur songwriters can help an aspiring songwriter hone the skills needed to compete in the ever-changing music industry.

The type of organization you choose to join depends on what you want to get out of it. Local groups can offer a friendly, supportive environment where you can work on your songs and have them critiqued in a constructive way by other songwriters. They're also great places to meet collaborators. Larger, national organizations can give you access to music business professionals and other songwriters across the country.

Most of the organizations listed in this book are non-profit groups with membership open to specific groups of people—songwriters, musicians, classical composers, etc. They can be local groups with a membership of less than 100 people, or large national organizations with thousands of members from all over the country. In addition to regular meetings, most organizations occasionally sponsor events such as seminars and workshops to which music industry personnel are invited to talk about the business, and perhaps listen to and critique demo tapes.

Check the following listings, bulletin boards at local music stores and your local newspapers for area organizations. If you are unable to locate an organization within an easy distance of your home, you may want to consider joining one of the national groups. These groups, based in New York, Los Angeles and Nashville, keep their members involved and informed through newsletters, regional workshops and large yearly conferences. They can help a writer who feels isolated in his hometown get his music heard by professionals in the major music centers.

In the following listings, organizations describe their purpose and activities, as well as how much it costs to join. Before joining any organization, consider what they have to offer and how becoming a member will benefit you. To locate organizations close to home, see the Geographic Index at the back of this book.

Resources

AARON ENTERPRISES SONGWRITERS GROUP

4411 Red Gate Dr., Disputanta VA 23842. (804)733-5908. **Contact:** Cham Laughlin, founder. Estab. 1997. "Songwriters of all ages, all styles and all skill levels are welcome to join. Applicants must have an interest in songwriting—music writing, lyric writing or co-writing. The main purpose of this organization is to educate songwriters about the business of songwriting, the art and craft of songwriting, lyric writing and structure, musical composition, song structure or arranging and professional presentation of your songs." Offers newsletter, evaluation services, seminars, discounts on demos and leads to publishers. Applications accepted year-round. Membership fee: $25/year with discounts for multiple years.

Tips "Networking is a very important part of this business. Members are offered a large amount of information and that information is explained to them through free seminars, the newsletter or one-on-one phone consultations to ensure the best possible support network for their songwriting careers."

☑ ACADEMY OF COUNTRY MUSIC

5500 Balboa Blvd., #200, Encino CA 91316. (818)788-8000. Fax: (818)877-0999. E-mail: info@acmcountry.com. Web site: www.acmcountry.com. **Contact:** Bob Romeo, executive director. Estab. 1964. Serves country music industry professionals. Eligibility for professional members is limited to those individuals who derive some portion of their income directly from country music. Each member is classified by one of the following categories: artist/entertainer, club/venue operator, musician, on-air personality, manager, talent agent, composer, music publisher, public relations, publications, radio, TV/motion picture, record company, talent buyer or affiliated (general). The purpose of ACM is to promote and enhance the image of country music. The Academy is involved year-round in activities important to the country music community. Some of these activities include charity fund-raisers, participation in country music seminars, talent contests, artist showcases, assistance to producers in placing country music on television and in motion pictures and backing legislation that benefits the interests of the country music community. The ACM is governed by directors and run by officers elected annually. Applications are accepted throughout the year. Membership is $75/year.

ALL SONGWRITERS NETWORK (ASN)

(formerly American Songwriters Network), Dept A95, Box 23912, Ft. Lauderdale FL 33307. (954)537-3463. E-mail: asn@tiac.net. Web site: http://home.tiac.net/~asn. **Contact:** Network Manager. Estab. 1995. Serves "professional level songwriters/composers with monthly music industry leads tipsheet. The tipsheet includes the most current listing of producers, A&R managers, record labels, entertainment attorneys, agents and publishing companies looking for specific material for their projects/albums. Any songwriter from any part of the country or world can be a member of this organization. The purpose of this organization is to foster a better professional community by helping members to place their songs." Membership fee: $140/year.

Tips "Please send SASE or e-mail for application form."

☑ AMERICAN COMPOSERS FORUM

332 Minnesota St., Suite E-145, St. Paul MN 55101. (651)251-2824. Fax: (651)291-7978. Web site: www.composersforum.org. **Contact:** Wendy Collins, member services manager. Estab. 1973. "The American Composers Forum links communities with composers and performers, encouraging the making, playing and enjoyment of new music. Building two-way relationships between artists and the public, the Forum develops programs that educate today's and tomorrow's audiences, energize composers' and performers' careers, stimulate entrepreneurship and collaboration, promote musical creativity, and serve as models of effective support for the arts. Programs include residencies,

fellowships, commissions, producing and performance opportunities, a recording assistance program and a widely-distributed recording label. The Forum's members, more than 1,200 strong, live in 49 states and 16 countries; membership is open to all." Membership dues: Regular (U.S.): $55; Student/Senior (U.S.): $35; Regular (Outside U.S.): $65; Student/Senior (Outside U.S.): $45.

AMERICAN MUSIC CENTER, INC.

30 W. 26th St., Suite 1001, New York NY 10010-2011. (212)366-5260. Fax: (212)366-5265. E-mail: center@amc.net. Web site: www.amc.net. **Contact:** Membership Department. The American Music Center, founded by a consortium led by Aaron Copland in 1939, is the first-ever national service and information center for new classical music and jazz by American composers. The Center has a variety of innovative new programs and services, including a montly Internet magazine (www.newmusicbox .org) for new American music, online databases of contemporary ensembles and ongoing opportunities for composers, an online catalog of new music for educators specifically targeted to young audiences, a series of professional development workshops, and an online listening library (www.ne wmusicjukebox.org). Each month, AMC provides its over 2,500 members with a listing of opportunities including calls for scores, competitions, and other new music performance information. Each year, AMC's Information Services Department fields thousands of requests concerning composers, performers, data, funding, and support programs. The AMC Collection at the New York Public Library for the Performing Arts presently includes over 60,000 scores and recordings, many unavailable elsewhere. "AMC also continues to administer several grant programs: the Aaron Copland Fund for Music; the Henry Cowell Performance Incentive Fund; and its own programs Live Music for Dance and the Composer Assistance Program." Members also receive a link their Web sites on www.amc.n et. The American Music Center is not-for-profit and has an annual membership fee.

AMERICAN SOCIETY OF COMPOSERS, AUTHORS AND PUBLISHERS (ASCAP)

One Lincoln Plaza, New York NY 10023. (212)621-6000 (administration); (212)621-6240 (membership). E-mail: info@ascap.com. Web site: www.ascap.com. President and Chairman of the Board: Marilyn Bergman. CEO: John LoFrumento. Executive Vice President/Membership: Todd Brabec. **Contact:** Member Services at (800)95-ASCAP. **Regional offices—West Coast:** 7920 Sunset Blvd., 3rd Floor, Los Angeles CA 90046, (323)883-1000; **Nashville:** 2 Music Square W., Nashville TN 37203, (615)742-5000; **Chicago:** 1608 N. Milwaukee Ave., Suite 1007, Chicago IL 60647, (773)394-4286; **Atlanta:** PMB 400-541 10th St. NW, Atlanta GA 30318, (404)351-1224; **Florida:** 420 Lincoln Rd., Suite 385, Miami Beach FL 33139, (305)673-3446; **United Kingdom:** 8 Cork St., London W1S 3LJ England, 011-44-207-439-0909; **Puerto Rico:** 654 Ave. Munoz Rivera, IBM Plaza Suite 1101 B, Hato Rey, Puerto Rico 00918, (787)281-0782. ASCAP is a membership association of over 240,000 composers, lyricists, songwriters, and music publishers, whose function is to protect the rights of its members by licensing and collecting royalties for the nondramatic public performance of their copyrighted works. ASCAP licensees include radio, television, cable, live concert promoters, bars, restaurants, symphony orchestras, new media, and other users of music. ASCAP is the leading performing rights society in the world. All revenues, less operating expenses, are distributed to members (about 86 cents of each dollar). ASCAP was the first US performing rights organization to distribute royalties from the Internet. Founded in 1914, ASCAP is the only society created and owned by writers and publishers. The ASCAP Board of Directors consists of 12 writers and 12 publishers, elected by the membership. ASCAP's Member Card provides exclusive benefits geared towards working music professionals. Among the benefits are health, musical instrument and equipment, tour and studio liability, term life and long term care insurance, discounts on musical instruments, equipment and supplies, access to a credit union, and much more. ASCAP hosts a wide array of showcases and workshops throughout the year, and offers grants, special awards, and networking opportunities in a variety of genres. Visit their Web site listed above for more information.

■ ASSOCIATION DES PROFESSIONEL.LE.S DE LA CHANSON ET DE LA MUSIQUE

292 Montreal Rd, Suite 200, ON K1L 6B7 Canada. (613)745-5642. Fax: (613)745-9715. E-mail: info-apcm@rogers.com. Web site: www.apcm.ca. **Contact:** Jean-Emmanuel Simiand, agent de communication. Director: Lucie Mailloux. Estab. 1989. Members are French Canadian singers and musicians. Members must be French singing and may have a CD to be distributed. Purpose is to gather French speaking artists (outside of Quebec, mainly in Ontario) to distribute their material, other workshops, instructions, lectures, etc. Offers instruction, newsletter, lectures, workshops, and distribution. Applications accepted year-round. Membership fee: $60 (Canadian).

ASSOCIATION OF INDEPENDENT MUSIC PUBLISHERS

Los Angeles Chapter: P.O. Box 69473, Los Angeles CA 90069. (818)771-7301. New York line: (212)391-2532. E-mail: LAinfo@aimp.org or NYinfo@aimp.org. Web site: www.aimp.org. Estab. 1977. Purpose is to educate members on new developments in the music publishing industry and to provide networking opportunities. Offers monthly panels and networking events. Applications accepted year-round. Membership fee: NY: $75/year; LA: $65/year.

■ AUSTIN SONGWRITERS GROUP

P.O. Box 2578, Austin TX 78768. (512)203-1972. E-mail: info@austinsongwritersgroup.com. Web site: www.austinsongwritersgroup.com. **Contact:** Lee Duffy, president. Vice President: Brent Allen. Estab. 1986. Serves all ages and all levels, from just beginning to advanced. Perspective members should have an interest in the field of songwriting, whether it be for profit or hobby. The main purpose of this organization is "to educate members in the craft and business of songwriting; to provide resources for growth and advancement in the area of songwriting; and to provide opportunities for performance and contact with the music industry." The primary benefit of membership to a songwriter is "exposure to music industry professionals, which increases contacts and furthers the songwriter's education in both craft and business aspects." Offers competitions, instruction, lectures, library, newsletter, performance opportunities, evaluation services, workshops and "contact with music industry professionals through special guest speakers at meetings, plus our yearly 'Austin Songwriters Conference,' which includes instruction, song evaluations, and song pitching direct to those pros currently seeking material for their artists, publishing companies, etc." Applications accepted year-round. Membership fee: $40/year.

Tips "Our newsletter is top-quality—packed with helpful information on all aspects of songwriting—craft, business, recording and producing tips, and industry networking opportunities."

■ BALTIMORE SONGWRITERS ASSOCIATION

P.O. Box 22496, Baltimore MD 21203. (410)813-4039. E-mail: info@baltimoresongwriters.org. Web site: www.baltimoresongwriters.org. **Contact:** Karyn Oliver, president. Estab. 1997. "The BSA is an inclusive organization with all ages, skill levels and genres of music welcome." Offers instruction, newsletter, lectures, workshops, performance opportunities, music publishing. Applications accepted year-round; membership not limited to location or musical status. Membership fee: $25.

Tips "We are trying to build a musical community that is more supportive and less competitive. We are dedicated to helping songwriters grow and become better in their craft."

THE BLACK ROCK COALITION

P.O. Box 1054, Cooper Station, New York NY 10276. (212)713-5097. E-mail: ldavis@blackrockcoalition.org. Web site: www.blackrockcoalition.org. **Contact:** LaRonda Davis, president. Estab. 1985. Serves musicians, songwriters—male and female ages 18-40 (average). Also engineers, entertainment attorneys and producers. Looking for members who are "mature and serious about music as an artist or activist willing to help fellow musicians. The BRC independently produces, promotes and distributes Black alternative music acts as a collective and supportive voice for such musicians within the music and record business. The main purpose of this organization is to produce, promote and distribute the full spectrum of black music along with educating the public on what black music is. The BRC is now soliciting recorded music by bands and individuals for Black Rock Coalition Records. Please send copyrighted and original material only." Offers instruction, newsletter, lectures, free seminars and workshops, monthly membership meeting, quarterly magazine, performing opportunities, evaluation services, business advice, full roster of all members. Applications accepted year-round. Bands must submit a tape, bio with picture and a self-addressed, stamped envelope before sending their membership fee. Membership fee: $25 per individual/$100 per band.

BROADCAST MUSIC, INC. (BMI)

320 W. 57th St., New York NY 10019. (212)586-2000. E-mail: newyork@bmi.com. Web site: www.bmi.com. **Los Angeles:** 8730 Sunset Blvd., Los Angeles CA 90069. (310)659-9109. E-mail: losangeles @bmi.com. **Nashville:** 10 Music Square East, Nashville TN 37203. (615)401-2000. E-mail: nashville @bmi.com. **Miami:** 5201 Blue Lagoon Dr., Suite 310, Miami FL 33126. (305)266-3636. E-mail: miami@bmi.com. **Atlanta:** Tower Place 100, 3340 Peachtree Rd., NE, Suite 570, Atlanta GA 30326. (404)261-5151. E-mail: atlanta@bmi.com. **Puerto Rico:** MCS Plaza, Suite 206, 255 Ponce De Leon Ave., San Juan PR 00917. (787)754-6490. **United Kingdom:** 84 Harley House, Marylebone Rd., London NW1 5HN United Kingdom. 011-44-207-486-2036. E-mail: london@bmi.com. President and CEO: Del R. Bryant. Senior Vice Presidents, New York: Phillip Graham, Writer/Publisher Relations; Alison Smith, Performing Rights. Vice Presidents: New York: Charlie Feldman; Los Angeles: Barbara Cane and Doreen Ringer Ross; Nashville: Paul Corbin; Miami: Diane J. Almodovar; Atlanta: Catherine Brewton. Senior Executive, London: Brandon Bakshi. BMI is a performing rights organization representing approximately 300,000 songwriters, composers and music publishers in all genres of music, including pop, rock, country, R&B, rap, jazz, Latin, gospel and contemporary classical. "Applicants must have written a musical composition, alone or in collaboration with other writers, which is commercially published, recorded or otherwise likely to be performed." Purpose: BMI acts on behalf of its songwriters, composers and music publishers by insuring payment for performance of their works through the collection of licensing fees from radio stations, Internet outlets, broadcast and cable TV stations, hotels, nightclubs, aerobics centers and other users of music. This income is distributed to the writers and publishers in the form of royalty payments, based on how the music is used. BMI also undertakes intensive lobbying efforts in Washington D.C. on behalf of its affiliates, seeking to protect their performing rights through the enactment of new legislation and enforcement of current copyright law. In addition, BMI helps aspiring songwriters develop their skills through various workshops, seminars and competitions it sponsors throughout the country. Applications accepted year-round. There is no membership fee for songwriters; a one-time fee of $150 is required to affiliate an individually-owned publishing company; $250 for partnerships, corporations and limited-liability companies. "Visit our Web site for specific contacts, e-mail addresses and additional membership information."

CALIFORNIA LAWYERS FOR THE ARTS

Fort Mason Center, Building C, Room 255, San Francisco CA 94123. (415)775-7200. Fax: (415)775-1143. E-mail: cla@calawyersforthearts.org. Web site: www.calawyersforthearts.org. **Southern California:** 1641 18th St., Santa Monica CA 90404. (310)998-5590. Fax: (310)998-5594. E-mail: usercla @aol.com. **Sacramento Office:** 1127 11th St., Suite 214, Sacramento CA 95814. (916)442-6210. Fax: (916)442-6281. E-mail: clasacto@aol.com. **Oakland Office:** 1212 Broadway St., Suite 834, Oakland CA 94612. (510)444-6351. Fax: (510)444-6352. E-mail: oakcla@there.net. **Contact:** Alma Robinson, executive director. Systems Coordinator: Josie Porter. Estab. 1974. "For artists of all disciplines, skill levels, and ages, supporting individuals and organizations, and arts organizations. Artists of all disciplines are welcome, whether professionals or amateurs. We also welcome groups and individuals who support the arts. We work most closely with the California arts community.

Our mission is to establish a bridge between the legal and arts communities so that artists and art groups may handle their creative activities with greater business and legal competence; the legal profession will be more aware of issues affecting the arts community; and the law will become more responsive to the arts community." Offers newsletter, lectures, library, workshops, mediation service, attorney referral service, housing referrals, publications and advocacy. Membership fee: $20 for senior citizens and full-time students; $25 for working artists; $40 for general individual; $60 for panel attorney; $100 to $1,000 for patrons. Organizations: $50 for small organizations (budget under $100,000); $90 for large organizations (budget of $100,000 or more); $100 to $1,000 for corporate sponsors.

CANADA COUNCIL FOR THE ARTS/CONSEIL DES ARTS DU CANADA
350 Albert St., P.O. Box 1047, Ottawa ON K1P 5V8 Canada. (613)566-4414, ext. 5060. E-mail: info@canadacouncil.ca. Web site: www.canadacouncil.ca. **Contact:** Lise Rochon, information officers. Estab. 1957. An independent agency that fosters and promotes the arts in Canada by providing grants and services to professional artists including songwriters and musicians. "Individual artists must be Canadian citizens or permanent residents of Canada, and must have completed basic training and/or have the recognition as professionals within their fields. The Canada Council offers grants to professional musicians to pursue their individual artistic development and creation. There are specific deadline dates for the various programs of assistance. Visit our Web site at www.canada council.ca/music for more details."

CANADIAN ACADEMY OF RECORDING ARTS & SCIENCES (CARAS)
345 Adelaide Street West, 2nd Floor, Toronto, ON M5V 1R5 (416)485-3135. Fax: (416)485-4978. E-mail: info@carasonline.ca. Web site: www.junoawards.ca. **Contact:** Meghan McCabe, office coordinator. President: Melanie Berry. Manager, Awards and Events: Leisa Peacock. Manager, Marketing and Communications: Tammy Kitchener. Membership is open to all employees (including support staff) in broadcasting and record companies, as well as producers, personal managers, recording artists, recording engineers, arrangers, composers, music publishers, album designers, promoters, talent and booking agents, record retailers, rack jobbers, distributors, recording studios and other music industry related professions (on approval). Applicants must be affiliated with the Canadian recording industry. Offers newsletter, nomination and voting privileges for Juno Awards and discount tickets to Juno Awards show. "CARAS strives to foster the development of the Canadian music and recording industries and to contribute toward higher artistic standards." Applications accepted year-round. Membership fee is $50/year (Canadian) + GST = $53.00. Applications accepted from individuals only, not from companies or organizations.

CANADIAN COUNTRY MUSIC ASSOCIATION (CCMA)
626 King Street West, Suite 203, Toronto ON MV5 1M7 Canada. (416)947-1331. Fax: (416)947-5924. E-mail: country@ccma.org. Web site: www.ccma.org. **Contact:** Brandi Mills, communications & marketing. Estab. 1976. Members are artists, songwriters, musicians, producers, radio station personnel, managers, booking agents and others. Offers newsletter, workshops, performance opportunities and the CCMA awards every September. "Through our newsletters and conventions we offer a means of meeting and associating with artists and others in the industry. The CCMA is a federally chartered, nonprofit organization, dedicated to the promotion and development of Canadian country music throughout Canada and the world and to providing a unity of purpose for the Canadian country music industry." See Web site for membership information and benefits.

CANADIAN MUSICAL REPRODUCTION RIGHTS AGENCY LTD.
56 Wellesley St. W, #320, Toronto ON M5S 2S3 Canada. (416)926-1966. Fax: (416)926-7521. E-mail: inquiries@cmrra.ca. Web site: www.cmrra.ca. **Contact:** Michael Mackie, membership ser-

Resources

vices. Estab. 1975. Members are music copyright owners, music publishers, sub-publishers and administrators. Representation by CMRRA is open to any person, firm or corporation anywhere in the world, which owns and/or administers one or more copyrighted musical works. CMRRA is a music licensing agency—Canada's largest—which represents music copyright owners, publishers and administrators for the purpose of mechanical and synchronization licensing in Canada. Offers mechanical and synchronization licensing. Applications accepted year-round.

CENTRAL CAROLINA SONGWRITERS ASSOCIATION (CCSA)

6016 Silkwater Court, Raleigh, NC 27610. (919) 662-7176. E-mail: ccsa_raleigh@yahoo.com. Web site: www.ccsa-raleigh.com. **Contact:** Dawn Williams, President. Founder: Shantel Davis. Established in 1995, CCSA welcomes songwriters of all experience levels from beginner to professional within the local RDU/Triad/Eastern area of North Carolina to join our group. Our members' musical background varies, covering a wide array of musical genres. CCSA meets monthly in Raleigh, NC. We are unable to accept applications from incarcerated persons or those who do not reside in the local area as our group's primary focus is on songwriters who are able to attend the monthly meetings—to ensure members get the best value for their yearly dues. CCSA strives to provide each songwriter and musician a resourceful organization where members grow musically by networking and sharing with one another. Offers yearly newsletter, some workshops, critiques at the monthly meetings, and ability to network with fellow members. Applications are accepted year round. Dues are $12/year (pro-rated for new members at $1/month by date of application) with annual renewal each January.

☑ CENTRAL OREGON SONGWRITERS ASSOCIATION

782 SW Rimrock Way, Redmond OR 97756. (541)548-6306. E-mail: administrator@centraloregonm usic.com. Web site: www.centraloregonmusic.com. President: Matt Engle. Estab. 1993. "Our members range in age from their 20s into their 80s. Membership includes aspiring beginners, accomplished singer/songwriter performing artists and all in between. Anyone with an interest in songwriting (any style) is invited to and welcome at COSA. COSA is a nonprofit organization to promote, educate and motivate members in the skills of writing, marketing and improving their craft." Offers competitions, instruction, newsletter, lectures, library, workshops, performance opportunities, songwriters round, awards, evaluation services and collaboration. Applications accepted year-round. Membership fee is $25.

THE COLLEGE MUSIC SOCIETY

312 E. Pine St., Missoula MT 59802. (406)721-9616. Fax: (406)721-9419. E-mail: cms@music.org. Web site: www.music.org. Estab. 1959. Serves college, university and conservatory professors, as well as independent musicians. "The College Music Society is a consortium of college, conservatory, university and independent musicians and scholars interested in all disciplines of music. Its mission is to promote music teaching and learning, musical creativity and expression, research and dialogue, and diversity and interdisciplinary interaction." Offers journal, newsletter, lectures, workshops, performance opportunities, job listing service, databases of organizations and institutions, music faculty and mailing lists. Applications accepted year-round. Membership fee: $60 (regular dues), $30 (student dues), $30 (retiree dues).

🅽 COMPOSERS GUILD

40 N. 100 West, P.O. Box 586, Farmington UT 84025-0586. (801)451-2275. **Contact:** Ruth Gatrell, president. Estab. 1963.
  • Also see the listing for the Composers Guild Annual Composition Contest in the Contests and Awards section of this book.
Serves all ages, including children. Musical skill varies from beginners to professionals. An interest

in composing is the only requirement. The purpose of this organization is to "help composers in every way possible through classes, workshops and symposiums, concerts, composition contests and association with others of similar interests." Offers competitions, instruction, lectures, newsletter, performance opportunities, evaluation services and workshops. Applications accepted year-round. Membership fee is $25/year. Associate memberships for child, spouse, parent, grandchild or grandparent of member: $15. "Holds four concerts/year. See our listing in the Contests & Awards section for details."

CONNECTICUT SONGWRITERS ASSOCIATION
P.O. Box 511, Mystic CT 06355. E-mail: info@ctsongs.com. Web site: www.ctsongs.com. **Contact:** Bill Pere, Executive Director. Associate Director: Kay Pere. "We are an educational, nonprofit organization dedicated to improving the art and craft of original music. Founded in 1979, CSA has had almost 2,000 active members and has become one of the best known and respected songwriters' associations in the country. Membership in the CSA admits you to 12-18 seminars/workshops/song critique sessions per year at multiple locations in Connecticut. Out-of-state members may mail in songs for free critiques at our meetings. Noted professionals deal with all aspects of the craft and business of music including lyric writing, music theory, music technology, arrangement and production, legal and business aspects, performance techniques, song analysis and recording techniques. CSA offers song screening sessions for members (songs which are voted on by a panel). Songs that 'pass' are then eligible for inclusion on the CSA sampler anthology CD series. Fifteen compilation recordings have been released so far are for sale at local retail outlets and are given to speakers and prospective buyers. CS is well connected in both the independent music scene, and the traditional music industry. CSA also offers showcases and concerts which are open to the public and designed to give artists a venue for performing their original material for an attentive, listening audience. CSA benefits help local soup kitchens, group homes, hospice, world hunger, libraries, nature centers, community centers and more. CSA shows encompass ballads to bluegrass and Bach to rock. Our monthly newsletter, *Connecticut Songsmith*, offers free classified advertising for members, and has been edited and published by Bill Pere since 1980. Annual dues: $40; senior citizen and full time students $30; organizations $80. Memberships are tax-deductible as business expenses or as charitable contributions to the extent allowed by law."

☑ COUNTRY MUSIC ASSOCIATION OF TEXAS
P.O. Box 549, Troy TX 76579. (254)760-5214. Fax: (254)778-3009. **Contact:** Bud Fisher, founder/executive director. Estab. 1989. Open to songwriters, singers, pickers, fans and other professionals of all ages from all over the world. Members are interested in country music, especially traditional, classics. Purpose is to promote traditional and independent country music. Offers performance opportunities and evaluation services. Applications accepted year-round. Membership fee: $35.00/year.
Tips "Membership has grown to over 4,000 fans, musicians and songwriters, making it one of the largest state organizations in America. We hold numerous functions throughout the year and we have helped many local recording artists chart their releases nationwide and in Europe. Texas country music is hot!"

DALLAS SONGWRITERS ASSOCIATION
Sammons Center for the Arts, 3630 Harry Hines, Box 20, Dallas TX 75219. (214)750-0916. E-mail: info@dallassongwriters.org. Web site: www.dallassongwriters.org. **Contact:** Dave Dalton, membership director. President: Alex Townes. Founding President Emeritis: Barbara McMillen. Estab. 1986. Serves songwriters and lyricists of Dallas/Ft. Worth metroplex. Members are adults ages 18-65, Dallas/Ft. Worth area songwriters/lyricists who are or aspire to be professionals. Purpose is to provide songwriters an opportunity to meet other songwriters, share information, find co-writers

and support each other through group discussions at monthly meetings; to provide songwriters an opportunity to have their songs heard and critiqued by peers and professionals by playing cassettes and providing an open mike at monthly meetings and open mics, showcases, and festival stages, and by offering contests judged by publishers; to provide songwriters opportunities to meet other music business professionals by inviting guest speakers to monthly meetings and workshops; and to provide songwriters opportunities to learn more about the craft of songwriting and the business of music by presenting mini-workshops at each monthly meeting. "We offer a chance for the songwriter to learn from peers and industry professionals and an opportunity to belong to a supportive group environment to encourage the individual to continue his/her songwriting endeavors." Offers competitions (including the Annual Song Contest with over $5,000 in prizes, and the Quarterly Lyric Contest), field trips, instruction, lectures, newsletter, performance opportunities, social outings, workshops and seminars. "Our members are eligible for discounts at several local music stores and seminars." Applications accepted year-round. Membership fee: $55. "When inquiring by phone, please leave complete mailing address and phone number where you can be reached day and night."

THE DRAMATISTS GUILD OF AMERICA, INC.
(formerly The Dramatists Guild, Inc.), 1501 Broadway, Suite 701, New York NY 10036. (212)398-9366. Fax: (212)944-0420. E-mail: membership@dramatistsguild.com. Web site: www.dramatistsguild.com. **Contact:** Joshua Levine, director of membership. "For over three-quarters of a century, The Dramatists Guild has been the professional association of playwrights, composers and lyricists, with more than 6,000 members across the country. All theater writers, whether produced or not, are eligible for Associate membership ($95/year); those who are engaged in a drama-related field but are not a playwright are eligible for Subscribing membership ($25/year); students enrolled in writing degree programs at colleges or universities are eligible for Student membership ($35/year); writers who have been produced on Broadway, Off-Broadway or on the main stage of a LORT theater are eligible for Active membership ($150/year). The Guild offers its members the following activities and services: use of the Guild's contracts (including the Approved Production Contract for Broadway, the Off-Broadway contract, the LORT contract, the collaboration agreements for both musicals and drama, the 99 Seat Theatre Plan contract, the Small Theatre contract, commissioning agreements, and the Underlying Rights Agreements contract; advice on all theatrical contracts including Broadway, Off-Broadway, regional, showcase, Equity-waiver, dinner theater and collaboration contracts); a nationwide toll-free number for all members with business or contract questions or problems; advice and information on a wide spectrum of issues affecting writers; free and/or discounted ticket service; symposia led by experienced professionals in major cities nationwide; access to health insurance programs; and a spacious meeting room which can accommodate up to 50 people for readings and auditions on a rental basis. The Guild's publications are: *The Dramatist*, a bimonthly journal containing articles on all aspects of the theater (which includes *The Dramatists Guild Newsletter*, with announcements of all Guild activities and current information of interest to dramatists); and an annual resource directory with up-to-date information on agents, publishers, grants, producers, playwriting contests, conferences and workshops, and an interactive Web site that brings our community of writers together to exchange ideas and share information.

THE FIELD
161 Sixth Ave., New York NY 10013. (212)691-6969. Fax: (212)255-2053. E-mail: info@thefield.org. Web site: www.thefield.org. Contact: any staff member. Estab. 1986. "The Field gives independent performing artists the tools to develop and sustain their creative and professional lives, while allowing the public to have immediate, direct access to a remarkable range of contemporary artwork. The organization was started by eight emerging artists who shared common roots in contemporary dance and theater. Meeting regularly, these artists created a structure to help each other

improve their artwork, and counter the isolation that often comes with the territory of an artistic career. The Field offers a comprehensive series of edcuational programs, resources, and services. Artists can participate in a broad array of programs and services including art development workshops, performance opportunities, career management training and development, fundraising consultations, fiscal sponsorship, a Resource Center, and artist residencies. The Field's goal is to help artists develop their best artwork by deepening the artistic process and finding effective ways to bring that art into the marketplace. Most Field programs cost between $35 and $150, and tickets to our performance events are $10. In addition, since 1992, The Field has coordinated a network of satellite sites in Atlanta, Chicago, Houston, Miami, Philadelphia, Phoenix, Rochester (NY), Salt Lake City, San Francisco, Seattle, Tucson, Richmond (VA), and Washington. The Field is the only organization in New York that provides comprehensive programming for independent performing artists on a completely non-exclusive basis. Programs are open to artists from all disciplines, aesthetic viewpoints, and levels of development.'' Offers workshops and performance opportunities on a seasonal basis. Applications accepted year-round. Membership fee: $100/year.

Tips ''The Field's resource center is an artist-focused library/computer lab where artists can access office equipment and work in a quiet and supportive environment. Located at The Field's office, the Resource Center offers fund-raising resources and hands-on assistance, including databases such as the Foundation Directory Online, computer workstations, and a library of books, journals, and information directories. One-on-one assistance and consultations are also available to guide users through grant writing and other fund-raising endeavors. GoTour (www.gotour.org) is a free Web site offering independent artists the resources they need to take their show on the road. Visitors log on for free and access a national arts network where they can search for venues, network with artists nationwide, find media contacts, read advice from other artists and arts professionals, add information on their local arts community, post tour anecdotes, and list concert informaton and classified ads.''

FILM MUSIC NETWORK
5777 West Century Blvd., Suite 1550, Los Angeles CA 90045. 1-800-774-3700. E-mail: info@filmmusic.net. Web site: www.filmmusicworld.com or www.filmmusic.net. President/Founder: Mark Northam. NY Chapter Manager: Beth Krakower.

FORT WORTH SONGWRITERS ASSOCIATION
P.O. Box 162443, Fort Worth TX 76161. (817)654-5400. E-mail: info@fwsa.com. Web site: www.fwsa.com. President: Judy Boots. Vice-Presidents: Rick Tate and John Terry. Secretary: Lynda Timmons Elvington. Treasurer: Rick Tate. Estab. 1992. Members are ages 18-83, beginners up to and including published writers. Interests cover gospel, country, western swing, rock, pop, bluegrass and blues. Purpose is to allow songwriters to become more proficient at songwriting; to provide an opportunity for their efforts to be performed before a live audience; to provide songwriters an opportunity to meet co-writers. ''We provide our members free critiques of their efforts. We provide a monthly newsletter outlining current happenings in the business of songwriting. We offer competitions and mini workshops with guest speakers from the music industry. We promote a weekly open 'mic' for singers of original material, and hold invitational songwriter showcase events a various times throughout the year. Each year, we hold a Christmas Song Contest, judged by independent music industry professionals. We also offer free web pages for members or links to member Web sites.'' Applications accepted year-round. Membership fee: $35.

THE GUILD OF INTERNATIONAL SONGWRITERS & COMPOSERS
Sovereign House, 12 Trewartha Road, Praa Sands, Penzance, Cornwall TR20 9ST England. (01736)762826. Fax: (01736)763328. E-mail: songmag@aol.comWeb site: www.songwriters-guild.com. General Secretary: Carole Jones. The Guild of international songwriters & Composers is an

international music industry organisation based in England in the United Kingdom. Guild members are songwriters, composers, lyricists, poets, performing songwriters, musicians, music publishers, studio owners, managers, independent record companies, music industry personnel, etc., from many countries throughout the world. The Guild of International Songwriters & Composers has been publishing *Songwriting and Composing Magazine* since 1986, which is issued free to all Guild members throughout their membership. The Guild of International Songwriters and Composers offers advice, guidance, assistance, copyright protection service , information, encouragement, contact information, Intellectual property/copyright protection of members works through the Guild's Copyright Registration Centre along with other free services and more to Guild members with regard to helping members achieve their aims, ambitions, progression and advancement in respect to the many different aspects of the music industry. Information, advice and services available to Guild members throughout their membership includes assistance, advice and help on many matters and issues relating to the music industry in general. Annual membership fees: are £48 for UK residents and £55 for the rest of the world. For further information please visit the Guild's Web site at: www.songwriters-guild.co.uk.

HAWAI'I SONGWRITERS ASSOCIATION

P.O. Box 10248, Honolulu HI 96816. (808)988-6878. Fax: (808)988-6236. E-mail: stanrubens@aol.com. Web site: www.stanrubens.com. **Contact:** Stan Rubens, secretary. Estab. 1972. "We have two classes of membership: Professional (must have had at least one song commercially published and for sale to general public) and Regular (any one who wants to join and share in our activities). Both classes can vote equally, but only Professional members can hold office. Must be 18 years old to join. Our members include musicians, entertainers and record producers. Membership is world-wide and open to all varieties of music, not just ethnic Hawaiian. President, Stan Rubens, has published 4 albums." Offers competitions, instruction, monthly newsletter, lectures, workshops, performance opportunities and evaluation services. Applications accepted year-round. Membership fee: $24. Stan Rubens teaches Songwriting at McKinley High, Adult education.

INTERNATIONAL BLUEGRASS MUSIC ASSOCIATION (IBMA)

2 Music Circle South, Suite 100, Nashville TN 37203. 1(888)GET-IBMA. Fax: (615)256-0450. E-mail: info@ibma.org. Web site: www.ibma.org. Member Services: Jill Snider. Estab. 1985. Serves songwriters, musicians and professionals in bluegrass music. "IBMA is a trade association composed of people and organizations involved professionally and semi-professionally in the bluegrass music industry, including performers, agents, songwriters, music publishers, promoters, print and broadcast media, local associations, recording manufacturers and distributors. Voting members must be currently or formerly involved in the bluegrass industry as full or part-time professionals. A songwriter attempting to become professionally involved in our field would be eligible. Our mission statement reads: "IBMA: Working together for high standards of professionalism, a greater appreciation for our music, and the success of the world-wide bluegrass music community." IBMA publishes a bimonthly International Bluegrass, holds an annual trade show/convention with a songwriters showcase in the fall, represents our field outside the bluegrass music community, and compiles and disseminates databases of bluegrass related resources and organizations. Market research on the bluegrass consumer is available and we offer Bluegrass in the Schools information and matching grants. The primary value in this organization for a songwriter is having current information about the bluegrass music field and contacts with other songwriters, publishers, musicians and record companies." Offers workshops, liability insurance, rental car discounts, consultation and databases of record companies, radio stations, press, organizations and gigs. Applications accepted year-round. Membership fee: for a non-voting patron $40/year; for an individual voting professional $70/year; for an organizational voting professional $200/year.

INTERNATIONAL SONGWRITERS ASSOCIATION LTD.

P.O. Box 46, Limerick City, Ireland. E-mail: jliddane@songwriter.iol.ie. Web site: www.songwriter. co.uk. Contact: Anna M. Sinden, membership department. Serves songwriters and music publishers. "The ISA headquarters is in Limerick City, Ireland, and from there it provides its members with assessment services, copyright services, legal and other advisory services and an investigations service, plus a magazine for one yearly fee. Our members are songwriters in more than 50 countries worldwide, of all ages. There are no qualifications, but applicants under 18 are not accepted. We provide information and assistance to professional or semi-professional songwriters. Our publication, *Songwriter*, which was founded in 1967, features detailed exclusive interviews with songwriters and music publishers, as well as directory information of value to writers." Offers competitions, instruction, library, newsletter and a weekly e-mail newsletter *Songwriter Newswire*. Applications accepted year-round. Membership fee for European writers is £19.95; for non-European writers, US $30.

JUST PLAIN FOLKS MUSIC ORGANIZATION

5327 Kit Dr., Indianapolis IN 46237. (317)513-6557. E-mail: info@jpfolks.com. Web site: www.jpfol ks.com. **Contact:** Brian Austin Whitney (brian@jpfolks.com), founder or Linda Berger (linda@jpfol ks.com), projects director. Estab. 1998. "Just Plain Folks is among the world's largest Music Organizations. Our members cover nearly every musical style and professional field, from songwriters, artists, publishers, producers, record labels, entertainment attorneys, publicists and PR experts, performing rights organization staffers, live and recording engineers, educators, music students, musical instrument manufacturers, TV, Radio and Print Media and almost every major Internet Music entity. Representing all 50 US States and over 100 countries worldwide, we have members of all ages, musical styles and levels of success, including winners and nominees of every major music industry award, as well as those just starting out. A complete demographics listing of our group is available on our Web site. Whether you are a #1 hit songwriter or artist, or the newest kid on the block, you are welcome to join. Membership does require an active e-mail account." The purpose of this organization is "to share wisdom, ideas and experiences with others who have been there, and to help educate those who have yet to make the journey. Just Plain Folks provides its members with a friendly networking and support community that uses the power of the Internet and combines it with good old-fashioned human interaction. We help promote our members ready for success and educate those still learning." Offers special programs to members, including:

- *Just Plain Notes Newsletter:* Members receive our frequent e-mail newsletters full of expert info on how to succeed in the music business, profiles of members successes and advice, opportunities to develop your career and tons of first-person networking contacts to help you along the way. (Note: we send this out 2-3 times/month via e-mail only.)
- *Just Plain Mentors:* We have some of the friendliest expert educators, writers, artists and industry folks in the business who volunteer their time as part of our Mentor Staff. Included are John and JoAnn Braheny, Jason Blume, Harriet Schock, Pat and Pete Luboff, Derek Sivers, Jodi Krangle, Steve Seskin, Alan O'Day, Walter Egan, Sara Light, Danny Arena, Barbara Cloyd, Michael Laskow, Anne Leighton, Mark Keefner, Valerie DeLaCruz, Karen Angela Moore, Ben McLane, Jack Perricone, Pat Pattison, Mark Baxter, Harold Payne, Joey Arreguin, John Beland, Susan Gibson, Art Twain, Diane Rapaport, Nancy Moran, Fett, Mike Dunbar, R. Chris Murphy, Bobby Borg, Paul Reisler, and many others.
- *JPFolks.com Web site:* Our home page serves as your pathway to the resources and members of the group worldwide. With message boards, lyric feedback forums, featured members music, member profiles, member contact listings, member links pages, chapter homepages, demographics information, our Internet radio station and all the back issues of our newsletter, "Just Plain Notes."
- *Roadtrips:* We regularly tour the US and Canada, hosting showcases, workshops and friendly

member gatherings in each city we visit. We provide opportunities for all our members, at all levels and welcome everyone to our events. Most events are free of charge.

• *Chapters:* Just Plain Folks has over 100 active local chapters around the world run by local member volunteer coordinators. Each chapter is unique but many host monthly networking gatherings, showcases, educational workshops and community service events. To join a chapter, or start one in your city, please visit the chapter section of the jpfolks.com Web site for a current list of chapters and guidelines.

• *Music Awards:* Just Plain Folks has one of the largest and most diverse Member Music Awards programs in the world. The most recent awards involved over 25,000 albums and 350,000 songs in over 50 genres. Music Award nominees and winners receive featured performance slots at showcases around the world throughout the year. Current submission instructions can be found on the Web site in the Awards section.

Membership requests are accepted year-round. "To become a member, simply send an e-mail to join@jpfolks.com with the words 'I Want To Join Just Plain Folks.' In the e-mail, include your name, address, Web site (if applicable) and phone number for our files." There are currently no membership fees.

Tips "Our motto is 'We're All In This Together!'"

☑ THE LAS VEGAS SONGWRITERS ASSOCIATION

P.O. Box 42683, Las Vegas NV 89116-0683. (702)223-7255. E-mail: writeon4011@earthlink.net. Web site: www.lasvegassongwriters.com. **Contact:** Betty Kay Miller, president. Estab. 1980. "We are an educational, nonprofit organization dedicated to improving the art and craft of the songwriter. We want members who are serious about their craft. We want our members to respect their craft and to treat it as a business. Members must be at least 18 years of age. We offer quarterly newsletters, monthly information meetings, workshops three times a month and quarterly seminars with professionals in the music business. We provide support and encouragement to both new and more experienced songwriters. We critique each song or lyric that's presented during workshops, we make suggestions on changes—if needed. We help turn amateur writers into professionals. Several of our songwriters have had their songs recorded on both independent and major labels." Dues: $30/year.

LOS ANGELES MUSIC NETWORK

P.O. Box 2446, Toluca Lake CA 91610-2446. (818)769-6095. E-mail: info@lamn.com. Web site: www.lamn.com. **Contact:** Tess Taylor, president. Estab. 1988. "Connections. Facts. Career advancement. All that is available with your membership in the Los Angeles Music Network (LAMN). Our emphasis is on sharing knowledge and information, giving you access to top professionals and promoting career development. LAMN is an association of music industry professionals, i.e., artists, singers, songwriters, and people who work in various aspects of the music industry with an emphasis on the creative. Members are ambitious and interested in advancing their careers. LAMN promotes career advancement, communication and continuing education among music industry professionals and top executives. LAMN sponsors industry events and educational panels held bimonthly at venues in the Los Angeles area, and now in other major music hubs around the country (New York, Las Vegas, Chicago).Monthly LAMN Jams are extremely popular among our members: the 'anti-American Idol' singer-songwriter contest gives artists an opportunity to perform in front of industry experts and receive instant feedback to their music, lyrics and performance. As a result of the exposure, Tim agan won the Esquire songwriting contest. This paired him with multi-platinum songwriter and recording artist John Mayer, with whom Fagan co-wrote 'Deeper.' Publisher Robert Walls has pitched music from LAMN performers to hit TV shows like *The OC* and *Gray's Anatomy*, and the upcoming flick *The Devil Wears Prada*. Other performers have received offers including publishing deals and studio gigs." Offers instruction, newsletter, lectures, seminars, music industry job listings, career counseling, resume publishing, mentor network, résumé resource guide and many professional networking opportunities. See our Web site for current job listings and a calendar of upcoming events. Applications accepted year-round. Annual membership fee is $110 (subject to change without notice).

LOUISIANA SONGWRITERS ASSOCIATION

P.O. Box 80425, Baton Rouge LA 70898-0425. (504)443-5390. E-mail: zimshah@aol.com. Web site: www.lasongwriters.org. **Contact:** Connie Zimmermann, membership coordinator. Serves songwriters. "LSA was organized to educate songwriters in all areas of their trade, and promote the art of songwriting in Louisiana. LSA is honored to have a growing number of songwriters from other states join LSA and fellowship with us. LSA membership is open to people interested in songwriting, regardless of age, musical ability, musical preference, ethnic background, etc. At this time we are operating as an Internet-only Yahoo Group where we share info, gigs, opportunities, etc. At this time we are not holding regular meetings, although we do meet for various functions periodically. Please visit our group at http://launch.groups.yahoo.com/group/louisianasongwriters/. We do not at this time require any dues for membership participation."

☒ MANITOBA AUDIO RECORDING INDUSTRY ASSOCIATION (MARIA)

1-376 Donald St., Winnipeg MB R3B 2J2 Canada. (204)942-8650. Fax: (204)942-6083. E-mail: info@ manitobamusic.com. Web site: www.manitobamusic.com. **Contact:** Rachel Stone, associate coordinator. Estab. 1987. Organization consists of "songwriters, producers, agents, musicians, managers, retailers, publicists, radio, talent buyers, media, record labels, etc. (no age limit, no skill level minimum). Must have interest in the future of Manitoba's sound recording industry." The main purpose of MARIA is to foster growth in all areas of the Manitoba music industry primarily through education, promotion and lobbying. Offers newsletter, lectures, directory of Manitoba's music industry, workshops and performance opportunities; also presents demo critiquing sessions and comprehensive member discount program featuring a host of participating Manitoba businesses. MARIA is also involved with the Prairie Music Weekend festival, conference and awards show. Applications accepted year-round. Membership fee: $50 (Canadian funds).

MEET THE COMPOSER

75 Ninth Ave, 3R Suite C, New York NY 10011. (212)645-6949. Fax: (212)645-9669. E-mail: mtc@m eetthecomposer.org. Web site: www.meetthecomposer.org. Estab. 1974. "Meet The Composer serves composers working in all styles of music, at every career stage, through a variety of grant programs and information resources. A nonprofit organization, Meet The Composer raises money from foundations, corporations, individual patrons and government sources and designs programs that support all genres of music—from folk, ethnic, jazz, electronic, symphonic, and chamber to choral, music theater, opera and dance. Meet The Composer awards grants for composer fees to non-profit organizations that perform, present, or commission original works. This is not a membership organization; all composers are eligible for support. Meet The Composer was founded in 1974 to increase artistic and financial opportunities for composers by fostering the creation, performance, dissemination, and appreciation of their music." Offers grant programs and information services. Deadlines vary for each grant program.

MEMPHIS SONGWRITERS' ASSOCIATION

4728 Spottswood, #191, Memphis TN 38117-4815. (901)577-0906. E-mail: admin@memphissongwr iters.org. Web site: www.memphissongwriters.org. **Contact:** Phillip Beasley, MSA president. Estab. 1973. "MSA is a nonprofit songwriters organization serving songwriters nationally. Our mission is to dedicate our services to promote, advance, and help songwriters in the composition of music, lyrics and songs; to work for better conditions in our profession; and to secure and protect the rights of MSA songwriters. We also supply copyright forms. We offer critique sessions for writers at our monthly meetings. We also have monthly open mic songwriters night to encourage creativity, networking and co-writing. We host an annual songwriter's seminar and an annual songwriter's showcase, as well as a bi-monthly guest speaker series, which provide education, competition and entertainment for the songwriter. In addition, our members receive a bimonthly newsletter to keep them informed of MSA activities, demo services and opportunities in the songwriting field.'' Annual fee: $50; Student/Senior: $35.

☑ MINNESOTA ASSOCIATION OF SONGWRITERS
P.O. Box 4262, Saint Paul MN 55104. E-mail: info@mnsongwriters.org. Web site: www.mnsongwrit ers.org. ''Includes a wide variety of members, ranging in age from 18 to 80; type of music is very diverse ranging from alternative rock to contemporary Christian; skill levels range from beginning songwriters to writers with recorded and published material. Main requirement is an interest in songwriting. Although most members come from the Minneapolis-St. Paul area, others come in from surrounding cities, nearby Wisconsin, and other parts of the country. Some members are fulltime musicians, but most represent a wide variety of occupations. MAS is a nonprofit community of songwriters which informs, educates, inspires and assists its members in the art and business of songwriting.'' Offers instruction, newsletter, lectures, workshops, performance opportunities and evaluation services. Applications accepted year-round. Membership fee: Individual: $25; Business: $65.

Tips ''Members are kept current on resources and opportunities. Original works are played at meetings and are critiqued by involved members. Through this process, writers hone their skills and gain experience and confidence in submitting their works to others.''

☑ ☒ MUSIC BC—PACIFIC MUSIC INDUSTRY ASSOCIATION
#501-425 Carrall St., Vancouver BC V6B 6E3 Canada. (604)873-1914. 1-888-866-8570 (Toll Free in BC). Fax: (604)873-9686. E-mail: info@musicbc.org. Web site: www.musicbc.org. Estab. 1990. Music BC(PMIA) is a non-profit society that supports and promotes the spirit, development, and growth of the BC music community provincially, nationally, and internationally. Music BC provides education, resources, advocacy, opportunities for funding, and a forum for communication. Visit Web site for membership benefits.

MUSICIANS CONTACT
P.O. Box 788, Woodland Hills CA 91365. (818)888-7879. E-mail: muscontact@aol.com. Web site: www.musicianscontact.com. **Contact:** Sterling Howard, president. Estab. 1969. ''The primary source of paying jobs for musicians and vocalists nationwide. Job opportunities are posted daily on the Internet. Also offers exposure to the music industry for solo artists and complete acts seeking representation.''

NASHVILLE SONGWRITERS ASSOCIATION INTERNATIONAL (NSAI)
1710 Roy Acuff Place, Nashville TN 37203. (615)256-3354 or (800)321-6008. Fax: (615)256-0034. E-mail: nsai@nashvillesongwriters.com. Web site: www.nashvillesongwriters.com. Executive Director: Barton Herbison. Purpose: a not-for-profit service organization for both aspiring and professional songwriters in all fields of music. Membership: Spans the United States and several foreign countries. Songwriters may apply in one of four annual categories: Active ($150 U.S/$100 International—for songwriters who have at least one song contractually signed to a publisher affiliated with ASCAP, BMI or SESAC); Associate ($150 U.S/$100 International—for songwriters who are not yet published or for anyone wishing to support songwriters); Student ($100 U.S/$100 International—for full-time college students or for students of an accredited senior high school); Professional ($100—for songwriters who derive their primary source of income from songwriting or who

are generally recognized as such by the professional songwriting community). Membership benefits: music industry information and advice, song evaluations by mail, quarterly newsletter, access to industry professionals through weekly Nashville workshop and several annual events, regional workshops, use of office facilities, discounts on books and discounts on NSAI's three annual events. There are also "branch" workshops of NSAI. Workshops must meet certain standards and are accountable to NSAI. Interested coordinators may apply to NSAI.

- Also see the listing for NSAI Songwriters Symposium (formerly NSAI Spring Symposium) in the Workshops section of this book.

THE NATIONAL ASSOCIATION OF COMPOSERS/USA (NACUSA)

P.O. Box 49256, Barrington Station, Los Angeles CA 90049. E-mail: nacusa@music-usa.org. Web site: www.music-usa.org/nacusa. **Contact:** Daniel Kessner, president. Estab. 1932. Serves songwriters, musicians and classical composers. "We are of most value to the concert hall composer. Members are serious music composers of all ages and from all parts of the country, who have a real interest in composing, performing, and listening to modern concert hall music. The main purpose of our organization is to perform, publish, broadcast and write news about composers of serious concert hall music—mostly chamber and solo pieces. Composers may achieve national notice of their work through our newsletter and concerts, and the fairly rare feeling of supporting a non-commercial music enterprise dedicated to raising the musical and social position of the serious composer." Offers competitions, lectures, performance opportunities, library and newsletter. Applications accepted year-round. Membership fee: National (regular): $25; National (students/seniors): $15.

- Also see the listing for NACUSA Young Composers' Competition in the Contests section of this book.

Tips "99% of the money earned in music is earned, or so it seems, by popular songwriters who might feel they owe the art of music something, and this is one way they might help support that art. It's a chance to foster fraternal solidarity with their less prosperous, but wonderfully interesting classical colleagues at a time when the very existence of serious art seems to be questioned by the general populace."

OKLAHOMA SONGWRITERS & COMPOSERS ASSOCIATION

105 S. Glenn English, Cordell OK 73632. Web site: www.oksongwriters.com. **Contact:** Ann Wilson Hardin, treasurer/membership. Estab. 1983. Serves songwriters, musicians, professional writers and amateur writers. "A nonprofit, all-volunteer organization providing educational and networking opportunities for songwriters, lyricists, composers and performing musicians. All styles of music. We sponsor major workshops, open-mic nights, demo critiques and the OSCA Newsletter. Throughout the year we sponsor contests and original music showcases." Applications accepted year-round. Membership fee: $20 for new members, $10 for renewal. Applications may be made through our Web site.

☑ OPERA AMERICA

330 Seventh Ave., 16th Floor, New York NY 10001. (212)796-8620. Fax: (212)796-8631. E-mail: frontdesk@operaamerica.org. Web site: www.operaamerica.org. **Contact:** Rebecca Ackerman, membership manager. Estab. 1970. Members are composers, librettists, musicians, singers, and opera/music theater producers. Offers conferences, workshops, and seminars for artists. Publishes online database of opera/music theater companies in the US and Canada, database of opportunities for performing and creative artists, online directory of opera and musical performances world-wide and US, and an online directory of new works created and being developed by current-day composers and librettists, to encourage the performance of new works. Applications accepted year-round. Publishes quarterly magazine and a variety of electronic newsletters. Membership fee is on a sliding scale by membership level.

OUTMUSIC

P.O. Box 376, Old Chelsea Station, New York NY 10113-0376. (212)330-9197. E-mail: info@outmusi
c.com. Web site: www.outmusic.com. **Contact:** Ed Mannix, communications director. Estab. 1990.
"OUTMUSIC is comprised of gay men, lesbians, bisexuals and transgenders. They represent all
different musical styles from rock to classical. Many are writers of original material. We are open
to all levels of accomplishment—professional, amateur, and interested industry people. The only
requirement for membership is an interest in the growth and visibility of music and lyrics created
by the LGBT community. We supply our members with support and networking opportunities. In
addition, we help to encourage artists to bring their work 'OUT' into the world." Offers newsletter,
lectures, workshops, performance opportunities, networking, industry leads and monthly open
mics. Sponsors Outmusic Awards. Applications accepted year-round. For membership information
go to www.outmusic.com.
Tips "OUTMUSIC has spawned *The Gay Music Guide*, The Gay and Lesbian American Music Awards
(GLAMA), several compilation albums and many independent recording projects."

PACIFIC NORTHWEST SONGWRITERS ASSOCIATION

P.O. Box 98564, Seattle WA 98198. (206)824-1568. E-mail: pnsapals@hotmail.com. " PNSA is a
nonprofit organization, serving the songwriters of the Puget Sound area since 1977. Members have
had songs recorded by national artists on singles, albums, videos and network television specials.
Several have released their own albums and the group has done an album together. For only $45
per year, PNSA offers monthly workshops, a quarterly newsletter and direct contact with national
artists, publishers, producers and record companies. New members are welcome and good times
are guaranteed. And remember, the world always needs another great song!"

☑ PITTSBURGH SONGWRITERS ASSOCIATION

523 Scenery Dr., Elizabeth PA 15037. (412)751-9584. E-mail: vstragand@aol.com. Web site: www.p
ittsburghsongwritersassociation.com. **Contact:** Van Stragand, president. Estab. 1983. "We are a
non-profit organization dedicated to helping its members develop and market their songs. Writers
of any age and experience level welcome. Current members are from 20s to 50s. All musical styles
and interests are welcome. Our organization wants to serve as a source of quality material for
publishers and other industry professionals. We assist members in developing their songs and their
professional approach. We provide meetings, showcases, collaboration opportunities, instruction,
industry guests, library and social outings. Annual dues: $25. We have no initiation fee. Prospective
members are invited to attend two free meetings. Interested parties please call Van Stragand at
(412)751-9584."

SAN DIEGO SONGWRITERS GUILD

3368 Governor Dr., Suite F-326, San Diego CA 92122. E-mail: sdsongwriters@hotmail.com. Web
site: www.sdsongwriters.org. **Contact:** Joseph Carmel, membership/correspondence. Estab. 1982.
"Members range from their early 20s to senior citizens with a variety of skill levels. Several members
perform and work full time in music. Many are published and have songs recorded. Some are getting
major artist record cuts. Most members are from San Diego county. New writers are encouraged to
participate and meet others. All musical styles are represented." The purpose of this organization
is to "serve the needs of songwriters and artists, especially helping them in the business and craft
of songwriting through industry guest appearances." Offers competitions, newsletter, workshops,
performance opportunities, discounts on services offered by fellow members, in-person song
pitches and evaluations by publishers, producers and A&R executives. Applications accepted year-
round. Membership dues: $55 full; $30 student; $125 corporate sponsorship. Meeting admission
for non-members: $20 (may be applied toward membership if joining within 30 days).
Tips "Members benefit most from participation in meetings and concerts. Generally, one major

meeting held monthly on a Monday evening, at the Doubletree Hotel, Hazard Center, San Diego. E-mail for meeting details. Can join at meetings."

SESAC INC.

152 W. 57th St., 57th Floor, New York NY 10019. (212)586-3450. Fax: (212)489-5699. Web site: www.sesac.com. **Nashville:** 55 Music Square East, Nashville TN 37203. (615)320-0055. Fax: (615)329-9627; **Los Angeles:** 501 Santa Monica Blvd., Suite 450, Santa Monica CA 90401. (310)393-9671. Fax: (310)393-6497; **London:** 67 Upper Berkeley St., London WIH 7QX United Kingdom. (020)76169284. **Contact:** Tim Fink, associate vice president writer/publisher relations. Chief Operating Officer: Pat Collins. Coordinator-Writer/Publisher Relations: Diana Akin. SESAC is a selective organization taking pride in having a repertory based on quality rather than quantity. Serves writers and publishers in all types of music who have their works performed by radio, television, nightclubs, cable TV, etc. Purpose of organization is to collect and distribute performance royalties to all active affiliates. As a SESAC affiliate, the individual may obtain equipment insurance at competitive rates. Tapes are reviewed upon invitation by the Writer/Publisher Relations dept.

SOCAN (SOCIETY OF COMPOSERS, AUTHORS AND MUSIC PUBLISHERS OF CANADA)

Head Office: 41 Valleybrook Dr., Toronto ON M3B 2S6 Canada. English Information Center: (866)(307)6226. French Information Center: (866) (800)55-SOCAN. Fax: (416)445-7108. Web site: www.socan.ca. CEO: Andre LeBel. Vice President Member Relations & General Manager, West Coast Division: Kent Sturgeon. Vice President Member Services: Jeff King. Director, Member Relations: Lynne Foster. "SOCAN is the Canadian copyright collective for the communication and performance of musical works. We administer these rights on behalf of our members (composers, lyricists, songwriters, and their publishers) and those of affiliated international organizations by licensing this use of their music in Canada. The fees collected are distributed as royalties to our members and to affiliated organizations throughout the world. We also distribute royalties received from those organizations to our members for the use of their music worldwide. SOCAN has offices in Toronto, Montreal, Vancouver, Edmonton, and Dartmouth."

SOCIETY OF COMPOSERS & LYRICISTS

400 S. Beverly Dr., Suite 214, Beverly Hills CA 90212. (310)281-2812. Fax: (310)284-4861. E-mail: execdir@thescl.com. Web site: www.thescl.com. The professional nonprofit trade organization for members actively engaged in writing music/lyrics for films, TV, and/or video games, or are students of film composition or songwriting for film. Primary mission is to advance the interests of the film and TV music community. Offers an award-winning quarterly publication, educational seminars, screenings, special member-only events, and other member benefits. Applications accepted year-round. Membership fee: $135 Full Membership (composers, lyricists, songwriters—film/TV music credits must be submitted); $85 Associate/Student Membership for composers, lyricists, songwriters without credits only; $135 Sponsor/Special Friend Membership (music editors, music supervisors, music attorneys, agents, etc.).

SODRAC INC.

759 Square Victoria, Suite 420, Montreal QC H2Y 2J7 Canada. (514)845-3268. Fax: (514)845-3401. E-mail: sodrac@sodrac.ca. Web site: www.sodrac.ca. **Contact:** Sébastien Croteau, membership department (author, composer and publisher) orFrançois Dell' Aniello, visual arts and crafts department (visual artist and rights owner). Estab. 1985. "SODRAC is a reproduction rights collective society facilitating since 1985 the clearing of rights on musical and artistic works based on the Copyright Board of Canada tariffs or through collective agreements concluded with any users and is responsible for the distribution of royalties to its national and international members. The Society

counts over 5,000 Canadian members and represents musical repertoire originating from nearly 100 foreign countries and manages the right of over 25,000 Canadian and foreign visual artists. SODRAC is the only reproduction rights society in Canada where both songwriters and music publishers are represented, equally and directly.'' Serves those with an interest in songwriting and music publishing no matter what their age or skill level is. ''Members must have written or published at least one musical work that has been reproduced on an audio (CD, cassette, or LP) or audio-visual support (TV, DVD, video), or published five musical works that have been recorded and used for commercial purposes. The new member will benefit from a society working to secure his reproduction rights (mechanicals) and broadcast mechanicals.'' Applications accepted year-round.

Ⓝ SONGWRITERS & LYRICISTS CLUB
E-mail: makinsonrobert@hotmail.com. Contact: Robert Makinson, founder/director. Estab. 1984.
- The Songwriters & Lyricists Club is not currently taking on new members. Offers booklet titled *Songwriters & Lyricists Handbook*, available on Amazon.com.

Tips ''Plan and achieve realistic goals. We specialize in classical, folk, country, inspirational, and humorous novelty songs and lyrics.''

SONGWRITERS AND POETS CRITIQUE
P.O. Box 21065, Columbus OH 43221. E-mail: leeann@SongwritersCritique.com. Web site: www.songwriterscritique.com. **Contact:** LeeAnn Pretzman, secretary. Estab. 1985. Serves songwriters, musicians, poets, lyricists and performers. Meets second and fourth Friday of every month to discuss club events and critique one another's work. Offers seminars and workshops with professionals in the music industry. ''We critique mail-in submissions from long-distance members. Our goal is to provide support and opportunity to anyone interested in creating songs or poetry.'' Applications are accepted year-round. Annual dues: $30.

SONGWRITERS ASSOCIATION OF WASHINGTON
PMB 106-137, 4200 Wisconsin Ave. NW, Washington DC 20016. (301)654-8434. E-mail: membership@SAW.org. Web site: www.SAW.org. Estab. 1979. ''SAW is a nonprofit organization operated by a volunteer board of directors. It is committed to providing its members opportunities to learn more about the art of songwriting, to learn more about the music business, to perform in public, and to connect with fellow songwriters. SAW sponsors various events to achieve these goals: workshops, open mics, songwriter exchanges, and showcases. In addition, SAW organizes the Mid-Atlantic Song Contest open to entrants nationwide each year; ''the competition in 2003 was the twentieth contest SAW has adjudicated since 1982.'' (Contest information masc@saw.org). As well as maintaining a Web site, SAW publishes *SAW Notes*, a bimonthly newsletter for members containing information on upcoming local events, member news, contest information, and articles of interest. Joint introductory membership with the Washington Area Music Association is available at a savings. Use the contact information above for membership inquiries.

THE SONGWRITERS GUILD OF AMERICA (SGA)
1560 Broadway, Suite #1306, New York NY 10036. (212)768-7902. Fax: (212)768-9048. E-mail: ny@songwritersguild.com. Web site: www.songwritersguild.com. **New York Office:** 1560 Broadway, Suite #408, New York, NY 10036; **Los Angeles Office:** 6430 Sunset Blvd., Suite 705, Hollywood CA 90028, (323)462-1108. Fax: (323)462-5430. E-mail: la@songwritersguild.com. **Nashville Office:** 209 10th Ave. S., Suite 534, Nashville TN 37203. (615)742-9945. Fax: (615)742-9948. E-mail: nash@songwritersguild.com. **SGA Administration:** 1500 Harbor Blvd., Wechawken NJ 07086. (201)867-7603. Fax:(201)867-7535. E-mail: corporate@songwritersguild.com.
- Also see the listings for The Songwriters Guild Foundation in the Workshops & Conferences section.

President: Rick Carnes. Executive Director: Lewis M. Bachman. East Coast Project Manager: Mark Saxon. West Coast Project Manager: Aaron Lynn. Central Project Manager: Evan Shoemke. Estab. 1931. "The Songwriters Guild of America (SGA) is a voluntary songwriter association run by and for songwriters. It is devoted exclusively to providing songwriters with the services and activities they need to succeed in the business of music. The preamble to the SGA constitution charges the board to take such lawful actions as will advance, promote and benefit the profession. Services of SGA cover every aspect of songwriting including the creative, administrative and financial." A full member must be a published songwriter. An associate member is any unpublished songwriter with a desire to learn more about the business and craft of songwriting. The third class of membership comprises estates of deceased writers. The Guild contract is considered to be the best available in the industry, having the greatest number of built-in protections for the songwriter. The Guild's Royalty Collection Plan makes certain that prompt and accurate payments are made to writers. The ongoing Audit Program makes periodic checks of publishers' books. For the self-publisher, the Catalogue Administration Program (CAP) relieves a writer of the paperwork of publishing for a fee lower than the prevailing industry rates. The Copyright Renewal Service informs members a year in advance of a song's renewal date. Other services include workshops in New York and Los Angeles, free Ask-A-Pro sessions with industry pros, critique sessions, collaborator service and newsletters. In addition, the Guild reviews your songwriter contract on request (Guild or otherwise); fights to strengthen songwriters' rights and to increase writers' royalties by supporting legislation which directly affects copyright; offers a group medical and life insurance plan; issues news bulletins with essential information for songwriters; provides a songwriter collaboration service for younger writers; financially evaluates catalogues of copyrights in connection with possible sale and estate planning; operates an estates administration service; and maintains a nonprofit educational foundation (The Songwriters Guild Foundation)."

SONGWRITERS OF WISCONSIN INTERNATIONAL

P.O. Box 1027, Neenah WI 54957-1027. (920)725-5129. E-mail: sowi@new.rr.com. Web site: www. SongwritersOfWisconsin.org. **Contact:** Tony Ansems, president. Workshops Coordinator: Mike Heath. Estab. 1983. Serves songwriters. "Membership is open to songwriters writing all styles of music. Residency in Wisconsin is recommended but not required. Members are encouraged to bring tapes and lyric sheets of their songs to the meetings, but it is not required. We are striving to improve the craft of songwriting in Wisconsin. Living in Wisconsin, a songwriter would be close to any of the workshops and showcases offered each month at different towns. The primary value of membership for a songwriter is in sharing ideas with other songwriters, being critiqued and helping other songwriters." Offers competitions (contest entry deadline: May 15), field trips, instruction, lectures, newsletter, performance opportunities, social outings, workshops and critique sessions. Applications accepted year-round. Membership dues: $30/year.

Tips "Critique meetings every last Thursday of each month, January through October, 7 p.m.-10 p.m. at The Country Inn & Suites, 355 N. Fox River Dr., Appleton WI."

SPNM—PROMOTING NEW MUSIC

St. Margarets House, 4th Floor, 18-20 Southwark St., London SE1 1TJ United Kingdom. 020 7407 1640. Fax: 020 7403 7652. E-mail: spnm@spnm.org.uk. Web site: www.spnm.org.uk. Executive Director: Abigail Pogson. Administrator: Katy Kirk. Estab. 1943. "All ages and backgrounds are welcome, with a common interest in the innovative and unexplored. We enable new composers to hear their works performed by top-class professionals in quality venues." Offers magazine, lectures, workshops, special offers and concerts. Annual selection procedure, deadline September 30. "From contemporary jazz, classical and popular music to that written for film, dance and other creative media, SPNM is one of the main advocates of new music in Britain today. Through its eclectic program of concerts, workshops, education projects and collaborations and through its publications, new notes, spnm brings new music in all guises to many, many people.'' Other calls for specific events throughout year. Membership fee: Ordinary: £25; Concessions: £10; Friend: £35. **Tips** ''Most calls for pieces are restricted to those living and/or studying in UK/Ireland, or to British composers living overseas.''

TEXAS MUSIC OFFICE

P.O. Box 13246, Austin TX 78711. (512)463-6666. Fax: (512)463-4114. E-mail: music@governor.sta te.tx.us. Web site: www.governor.state.tx.us/music. **Contact:** Casey Monahan, director. Estab. 1990. ''The main purpose of the Texas Music Office is to promote the Texas music industry and Texas music, and to assist music professionals around the world with information about the Texas market. The Texas Music Office serves as a clearinghouse for Texas music industry information using their seven databases: Texas Music Industry (7,150 Texas music businesses in 94 music business categories); Texas Music Events (915 Texas music events); Texas Talent Register (7,050 Texas recording artists); Texas Radio Stations (837 Texas stations); U.S. Record Labels; Classical Texas (detailed information for all classical music organizations in Texas); and International (450 foreign businesses interested in Texas music). Provides referrals to Texas music businesses, talent and events in order to attract new business to Texas and/or to encourage Texas businesses and individuals to keep music business in-state. Serves as a liaison between music businesses and other government offices and agencies. Publicizes significant developments within the Texas music industry.'' Publishes the Texas Music Industry Directory (see the Publications of Interest section for more information).

▓ TORONTO MUSICIANS' ASSOCIATION

15 Gervais Dr., Suite 500, Toronto ON M3C 1Y8 Canada. (416)421-1020. Fax: (416)421-7011. E-mail: info@torontomusicians.org. Web site: www.torontomusicians.org. Executive Director: Bill Skolnick. Estab. 1887. Serves musicians—*All* musical styles, background, areas of the industry. ''Must be a Canadian citizen, show proof of immigration status, or have a valid work permit for an extended period of time.'' The purpose of this organization is ''to unite musicians into one organization, in order that they may, individually and collectively, secure, maintain and profit from improved economic, working and artistic conditions.'' Offers newsletter. Applications accepted year-round. Joining fee: $225 (Canadian); student fee: $100 (Canadian). Student must have proof of school enrollment.

VOLUNTEER LAWYERS FOR THE ARTS

1 E. 53rd St., 6th Floor, New York NY 10022. (212)319-ARTS (2787), ext. 1 (Monday-Friday 9:30-12 and 1-4 EST). Fax: (212)752-6575. E-mail: vlany@vlany.org. Web site: www.vlany.org. **Contact:** Elena M. Paul, esq., executive director. Estab. 1969. Serves songwriters, musicians and all performing, visual, literary and fine arts artists and groups. Offers legal assistance and representation to eligible individual artists and arts organizations who cannot afford private counsel and a mediation service. VLA sells publications on arts-related issues and offers educational conferences, lectures, seminars and workshops. In addition, there are affiliates nationwide who assist local arts organizations and artists. Call for information.

WASHINGTON AREA MUSIC ASSOCIATION

6263 Occoquan Forest Drive, Manassas VA 20112. (202)338-1134. Fax: (703)393-1028. E-mail: dcmusic@wamadc.com. Web site: www.wamadc.com. **Contact:** Mike Schreibman, president. Estab. 1985. Serves songwriters, musicians and performers, managers, club owners and entertainment lawyers; ''all those with an interest in the Washington music scene.'' The organization is designed to promote the Washington music scene and increase its visibility. Its primary value to members is its seminars and networking opportunities. Offers lectures, newsletter, performance opportunities and workshops. WAMA sponsors the annual Washington Music Awards (The Wammies) and The Crosstown Jam or annual showcase of more than 300 artists at 60 venues in the DC area. Applications accepted year-round. Annual dues: $35 for one year; $60 for two years.

WEST COAST SONGWRITERS

(formerly Northern California Songwriters Association), 1724 Laurel St., Suite 120, San Carlos CA 94070. (650)654-3966. E-mail: ian@westcoastsongwriters.org. Web site: www.westcoastsongwrite rs.org. **Contact:** Ian Crombie, executive director. Serves songwriters and musicians. Estab. 1979. "Our 1,200 members are lyricists and composers from ages 16-80, from beginners to professional songwriters. No eligibility requirements. Our purpose is to provide the education and opportunities that will support our writers in creating and marketing outstanding songs. WCS provides support and direction through local networking and input from Los Angeles and Nashville music industry leaders, as well as valuable marketing opportunities. Most songwriters need some form of collaboration, and by being a member they are exposed to other writers, ideas, critiquing, etc." Offers annual West Coast Songwriters Conference, "the largest event of its kind in northern California. This 2-day event held the second hand in September features 16 seminars, 50 screening sessions (over 1,200 songs listened to by industry professionals) and a sunset concert with hit songwriters performing their songs." Also offers monthly visits from major publishers, songwriting classes, competitions, seminars conducted by hit songwriters ("we sell audio tapes of our seminars—list of tapes available on request"), mail-in song-screening service for members who cannot attend due to time or location, a monthly e-newsletter, monthly performance opportunities and workshops. Applications accepted year-round. Dues: $40/year, student; $75/year, regular membership; $150/year, pro-membership; $250/year, contributing membership.

Tips "WCS's functions draw local talent and nationally recognized names together. This is of a tremendous value to writers outside a major music center. We are developing a strong songwriting community in Northern and Southern California. We serve the San Jose, Monterey Bay, East Bay, San Francisco, Los Angeles, and Sacramento areas and we have the support of some outstanding writers and publishers from both Los Angeles and Nashville. They provide us with invaluable direction and inspiration."

Workshops & Conferences

F or a songwriter just starting out, conferences and workshops can provide valuable learning opportunities. At conferences, songwriters can have their songs evaluated, hear suggestions for further improvement and receive feedback from music business experts. They are also excellent places to make valuable industry contacts. Workshops can help a songwriter improve his craft and learn more about the business of songwriting. They may involve classes on songwriting and the business, as well as lectures and seminars by industry professionals.

Each year, hundreds of workshops and conferences take place all over the country. Songwriters can choose from small regional workshops held in someone's living room to large national conferences such as South by Southwest in Austin, Texas, which hosts more than 6,000 industry people, songwriters and performers. Many songwriting organizations—national and local—host workshops that offer instruction on just about every songwriting topic imaginable, from lyric writing and marketing strategy to contract negotiation. Conferences provide songwriters the chance to meet one on one with publishing and record company professionals and give performers the chance to showcase their work for a live audience (usually consisting of industry people) during the conference. There are conferences and workshops that address almost every type of music, offering programs for songwriters, performers, musical playwrights and much more.

This section includes national and local workshops and conferences with a brief description of what they offer, when they are held and how much they cost to attend. Write or call any that interest you for further information. To find out what workshops or conferences take place in specific parts of the country, see the Geographic Index at the end of this book.

Get the Most From a Conference

BEFORE YOU GO:

- **Save money.** Sign up early for a conference and take advantage of the early registration fee. Don't put off making hotel reservations either—the conference will usually have a block of rooms reserved at a discounted price.

- **Become familiar with all the pre-conference literature.** Study the maps of the area, especially the locations of the rooms in which your meetings/events are scheduled.

- **Make a list of three to five objectives you'd like to obtain,** e.g., what you want to learn more about, what you want to improve on, how many new contacts you want to make.

AT THE CONFERENCE

- **Budget your time.** Label a map so you know where, when and how to get to each session. Note what you want to do most. Then, schedule time for demo critiques if they are offered.

- **Don't be afraid to explore new areas.** You are there to learn. Pick one or two sessions you wouldn't typically attend. Keep your mind open to new ideas and advice.

- **Allow time for mingling.** Some the best information is given after the sessions. Find out "frank truths" and inside scoops. Asking people what they've learned at the conference will trigger a conversation that may branch into areas you want to know more about, but won't hear from the speakers.

- **Attend panels.** Panels consist of a group of industry professionals who have the capability to further your career. If you're new to the business you can learn so much straight from the horse's mouth. Even if you're a veteran, you can brush up on your knowledge or even learn something new. Whatever your experience, the panelist's presence is an open invitation to approach him with a question during the panel or with a handshake afterwards.

- **Collect everything:** especially informational materials and business cards. Make notes about the personalities of the people you meet to later remind you who to contact and who to avoid.

AFTER THE CONFERENCE:

- **Evaluate.** Write down the answers to these questions: Would I attend again? What were the pluses and minuses, e.g., speakers, location, food, topics, cost, lodging? What do I want to remember for next year? What should I try to do next time? Who would I like to meet?

- **Write a thank-you letter** to someone who has been particularly helpful. They'll remember you when you later solicit a submission.

APPEL FARM ARTS AND MUSIC FESTIVAL

P.O. Box 888, Elmer NJ 08318. (856)358-2472. Fax: (856)358-6513. E-mail: perform@appelfarm.org. Web site: www.appelfarm.org. **Contact:** Sean Timmons, artistic director. Estab Festival: 1989; Series: 1970. "Our annual open air festival is the highlight of our year-round Performing Arts Series which was established to bring high quality arts programs to the people of South Jersey. Festival includes acoustic and folk music, blues, etc." Past performers have included Indigo Girls, John Prine, Ani DiFranco, Randy Newman, Jackson Browne, Mary Chapin Carpenter, David Gray, Nanci Griffith and Shawn Colvin. In addition, our Country Music concerts have featured Toby Keith, Joe Diffie, Ricky Van Shelton, Doug Stone and others. Programs for songwriters and musicians include performance opportunities as part of Festival and Performing Arts Series. Programs for musical playwrights also include performance opportunities as part of Performing Arts Series. Festival is a one-day event held in June, and Performing Arts Series is held year-round. Both are held at the Appel Farm Arts and Music Center, a 176-acre farm in Southern New Jersey. Up to 20 songwriters/musicians participate in each event. Participants are songwriters, individual vocalists, bands, ensembles, vocal groups, composers, individual instrumentalists and dance/mime/movement. Participants are selected by CD submissions. Applicants should send a press packet, CD and biographical information. Application materials accepted year round. Faculty opportunities are available as part of residential Summer Arts Program for children, July/August.

N ARCADY MUSIC FESTIVAL

P.O. Box 780, Bar Harbor ME 04609. E-mail: arcady@arcady.org. Web site: www.arcady.org. **Contact:** Dean Stein, artistic executive director. Estab. 1980. Promotes classical chamber music, and other musical events, including master classes, fiddle festival and a youth competition in Maine. Offers programs for performers. In-school programs and workshops take place year-round in several towns in Eastern Maine. 30-50 professional, individual instrumentalists participate each year. Performers selected by invitation. "Sometimes we premiere new music by songwriters but usually at request of visiting musician."

ASCAP MUSICAL THEATRE WORKSHOP

1 Lincoln Plaza, New York NY 10023. (212)621-6234. Fax: (212)621-6558. E-mail: mkerker@ascap.com. Web site: www.ascap.com. **Contact:** Michael A. Kerker, director of musical theatre. Estab. 1981. Workshop is for musical theatre composers and lyricists only. Its purpose is to nurture and develop new musicals for the theatre. Offers programs for songwriters. Offers programs annually, usually April through May. Event took place in New York City. Four musical works are selected. Others are invited to audit the workshop. Participants are amateur and professional songwriters, composers and musical playwrights. Participants are selected by demo CD submission. Deadline: mid-March. Also available: the annual ASCAP/Disney Musical Theatre Workshop in Los Angeles. It takes place in January and February. Deadline is late November. Details similar to New York workshop as above.

ASCAP WEST COAST/LESTER SILL SONGWRITER'S WORKSHOP

7920 Sunset Blvd., 3rd Floor, Los Angeles CA 90046. (323)883-1000. Fax: (323)883-1049. E-mail: info@ascap.com. Web site: www.ascap.com. Estab. 1963. Annual workshop for advanced songwriters sponsored by the ASCAP Foundation. Re-named in 1995 to honor ASCAP's late Board member and industry pioneer Lester Sill, the workshop takes place over a four-week period and features prominent guest speakers from various facets of the music business. Workshop dates and deadlines vary from year to year; refer to www.ascap.com for updated info. Applicants must submit two songs on a CD (cassette tapes not accepted), lyrics, brief bio and short explanation as to why they would like to participate. Limited number of participants are selected each year.

BMI-LEHMAN ENGEL MUSICAL THEATRE WORKSHOP

320 W. 57th St., New York NY 10019. (212)586-2000. E-mail: musicaltheatre@bmi.com. Web site: www.bmi.com. **Contact:** Jean Banks, senior director of musical theatre. Estab. 1961. "BMI is a music licensing company which collects royalties for affiliated writers. We have departments to help writers in jazz, concert, Latin, pop and musical theater writing." Offers programs "to musical theater composers, lyricists and librettists. The BMI-Lehman Engel Musical Theatre Workshops were formed in an effort to refresh and stimulate professional writers, as well as to encourage and develop new creative talent for the musical theater." Each workshop meets 1 afternoon a week for 2 hours at BMI, New York. Participants are professional songwriters, composers and playwrights. "BMI-Lehman Engel Musical Theatre Workshop Showcase presents the best of the workshop to producers, agents, record and publishing company execs, press and directors for possible option and production." Call for application. Tape and lyrics of 3 compositions required with application. "BMI also sponsors a jazz composers workshop. For more information call Raette Johnson at (212)830-8337."

⚡ ✅ CANADIAN MUSIC WEEK

5355 Vail Court, Mississauga ON L5M 6G9 Canada. (905)858-4747. Fax: (905)858-4848. E-mail: festival@cmw.net. Web site: www.cmw.net. Contact: Phil Klygo, festival coordinator. Estab. 1985. Offers annual programs for songwriters, composers and performers. Event takes place mid-March in Toronto. 100,000 public, 300 bands and 1,200 delegates participate in each event. Participants are amateur and professional songwriters, vocalists, composers, bands and instrumentalists. Participants are selected by submitting demonstration tape. Send for application and more information. Concerts take place in 25 clubs and 5 concert halls, and 3 days of seminars and exhibits are provided. Fee: $375 (Canadian).

CUTTING EDGE MUSIC BUSINESS CONFERENCE

1524 N. Claiborne Ave., New Orleans LA 70116. (504)945-1800. Fax: (504)945-1873. E-mail: cut_ed ge@bellsouth.net. Web site: www.jass.com/cuttingedge. Executive Producer: Eric L. Cager. Showcase Producer: Nathaniel Franklin. Estab. 1993. "The conference is a five-day international conference which covers the business and educational aspects of the music industry. As part of the conference, the New Works showcase features over 200 bands and artists from around the country and Canada in showcases of original music. All music genres are represented." Offers programs for songwriters and performers. "Bands and artists should submit material for consideration of entry into the New Works showcase." Event takes place during August in New Orleans. 1,000 songwriters/musicians participate in each event. Participants are songwriters, vocalists and bands. Send for application. Deadline: June 1. "The Music Business Institute offers a month-long series of free educational workshops for those involved in the music industry. The workshops take place each October. Further information is available via our Web site."

PETER DAVIDSON'S WRITER'S SEMINAR

P.O. Box 497, Arnolds Park IA 51331. (712)332-9329. E-mail: peterdavidson@mchsi.com. **Contact:** Peter Davidson, seminar presenter. Estab. 1985. "Peter Davidson's Writer's Seminar is for persons interested in writing all sorts of materials, including songs. Emphasis is placed on developing salable ideas, locating potential markets for your work, copyrighting, etc. The seminar is not specifically for writers of songs, but is very valuable to them, nevertheless." Offers programs year-round. One-day seminar, 9:00 a.m.-4:00 p.m. Event takes place on various college campuses. In even-numbered years offers seminars in Minnesota, Iowa, Nebraska, South Dakota, Kansas, Colorado and Wyoming. In odd-numbered years offers seminars in Minnesota, Iowa, Nebraska, South Dakota, Missouri, Illinois, Arkansas and Tennessee. Anyone can participate. Send SASE for schedule. Deadline: day of the seminar. Fee: $45 to $59. "All seminars are held on college campuses in college facilities—various colleges sponsor and promote the seminars."

Resources

FOLK ALLIANCE ANNUAL CONFERENCE

962 Wayne Ave., Suite 902, Silver Spring MD 20910. (301)588-8185. Fax: (301)588-8186. E-mail: fa@folk.org. Web site: www.folk.org. **Contact:** Tony Ziselberger, membership services director. Estab. 1989. Conference/workshop topics change each year. Conference takes place mid-February and lasts 4 days at a different location each year. 2,000 attendees include artists, agents, arts administrators, print/broadcast media, folklorists, folk societies, merchandisers, presenters, festivals, recording companies, etc. Artists wishing to showcase should contact the office for a showcase application form. Closing date for application is May 31. Application fee is $20 for 2005 conference. Additional costs vary from year to year. Housing is separate for the event, scheduled for Feb. 16-19, 2006 in Austin, TX.

- Also see the listing for The Folk Alliance in the Organizations section of this book.

I WRITE THE SONGS

2221 Justin Rd., Suite 119-142, Flower Mound TX 75028. (972)317-2760. Fax: (972)317-4737. E-mail: info@iwritethesongs.com. Web site: www.iwritethesongs.com. **Contact:** Sarah Marshall, administrative director. Estab. 1996.

- Mary Dawson recently released a new book entitled *How to Get Somewhere in the Music Business from Nowhere with Nothing*, which answers 25 years of questions she has received from aspiring songwriters. For more information on the book, visit www.fromnowherewithnothing.com.

"I Write the Songs" is an on-the-air songwriting seminar. It is an Internet radio talk show especially created to inspire and instruct aspiring songwriters in all genres of commercial music. A detailed description of the program and its hosts, Mary Dawson and Sharon Braxton, can be found on the Web site. The Web site address will also link you to the broadcasts — both current shows and archived—where you can hear programs covering INSTRUCTION on the craft and business of songwriting; INTERVIEWS with famous and 'soon-to-be-famous' songwriters; STORIES BEHIND THE HITS; and CRITIQUES of original songs submitted by listeners. "I Write the Songs" offers frequent contests and competitions. All aspiring songwriters earning less than $5,000 annually from song royalties are eligible. To be considered for an "I Write the Songs" Critique show, demos may be sbmitted on cassette or CD with typed lyric sheet. Does not return material. Featured songs are selected at random. Writers whose songs are selected for a show will receive a CD copy of the program on which their song is critiqued. Mary Dawson conducts songwriting seminars across the country and internationally.

☑ INDEPENDENT MUSIC CONFERENCE

InterMixx.com, Inc., 304 Main Ave., PMB 287, Norwalk CT 06851. (203)606 4649. E-mail: info@gopmc.com. Web site: www.gopmc.com. Executive Director: Noel Ramos. Estab. 1992. "The purpose of the IMC is to bring together rock, hip hop and acoustic music for of panels and showcases. Offers programs for songwriters, composers and performers. 250 showcases at 20 clubs around the city. Also offer a DJ cutting contest." Held annually at the Sheraton Society Hill Hotel in Philadelphia in September. 3,000 amateur and professional songwriters, composers, individual vocalists, bands, individual instrumentalists, attorneys, managers, agents, publishers, A&R, promotions, club owners, etc. participate each year. Send for application.

KERRVILLE FOLK FESTIVAL

Kerrville Festivals, Inc., P.O. Box 291466, Kerrville TX 78029. (830)257-3600. E-mail: info@kerrville-music.com. Web site: www.kerrvillefolkfestival.com. **Contact:** Dalis Allen, producer. Estab. 1972. Hosts 3-day songwriters' school, a 4-day music business school and New Folk concert competition sponsored by *Performing Songwriter* magazine. Festival produced in late spring and late summer. Spring festival lasts 18 days and is held outdoors at Quiet Valley Ranch. 110 or more songwriters participate. Performers are professional songwriters and bands. Participants selected by submitting demo, by invitation only. Send cassette, or CD, promotional material and list of upcoming appearances. "Songwriter and music schools include lunch, experienced professional instructors, camping on ranch and concerts. Rustic facilities. Food available at reasonable cost. Audition materials accepted at above address. These three-day and four-day seminars include noon meals, handouts and camping on the ranch. Usually held during Kerrville Folk Festival, first and second week in June. Write or check the Web site for contest rules, schools and seminars information, and festival schedules. Also establishing a Phoenix Fund to provide assistance to ill or injured singer/songwriters who find themselves in distress."

- Also see the listing for New Folk Concerts For Emerging Songwriters in the Contests & Awards section of this book.

LAMB'S RETREAT FOR SONGWRITERS

Presented by SPRINGFED ARTS, a nonprofit organization, P.O. Box 304, Royal Oak MI 48068-0304. (248)589-1594. Fax: (248)589-3913. E-mail: johndlamb@ameritech.net. Web site: www.springfed. org. **Contact:** John D. Lamb, director. Estab. 1995. Offers programs for songwriters on annual basis; November 1-4, 2007 and November 8-11, 2007 at The Birchwood Inn, Harbor Springs, MI. 60 songwriters/musicians participate in each event. Participants are amateur and professional songwriters. Anyone can participate. Send for registration or e-mail. Deadline: two weeks before event begins. Fee: $275-495, includes all meals. Facilities are single/double occupancy lodging with private baths; 2 conference rooms and hospitality lodge. Offers song assignments, songwriting workshops, song swaps, open mic and one-on-one mentoring. Faculty are noted songwriters, such as Michael Smith, Chuck Brodsky, Tom Prasada Rao, and Corinne West. Partial scholarships may be available by writing: Blissfest Music Organization, %Jim Gillespie, P.O. Box 441, Harbor Springs, MI 49740. Deadline: 2 weeks before event.

MANCHESTER MUSIC FESTIVAL

P.O. Box 33, Manchester VT 05254. (802)362-1956 or (800)639-5868. Fax: (802)362-0711. E-mail: info@ManchesterMusicFestival.org. Web site: www.mmfvt.org. **Contact:** Robyn Madison, managing director. Estab. 1974. Offers classical music education and performances. Summer program for young professional musicians offered in tandem with a professional concert series in the mountains of Manchester VT. Up to 23 young professionals, age 18 and up, are selected by audition for the Young Artists Program, which provides instruction, performance and teaching opportunities, with full scholarship for all participants. Printable application available on Web site. Application fee: $40. Commissioning opportunities for new music, and performance opportunities for professional chamber ensembles and soloists for both summer and fall/winter concert series. "Celebrating 28 years of fine music."

MUSIC BUSINESS SOLUTIONS/CAREER BUILDING WORKSHOPS

P.O. Box 230266, Boston MA 02123-0266. (888)655-8335. E-mail: peter@mbsolutions.com. Web site: www.mbsolutions.com. **Contact:** Peter Spellman, director. Estab. 1991. Workshop titles include "Discovering Your Music Career Niche," "How to Release an Independent Record" and "Promoting and Marketing Music in the 21st Century." Offers programs for music entrepreneurs, songwriters, musical playwrights, composers and performers. Offers programs year-round, annually and bi-annually. Event takes place at various colleges, recording studios, hotels, conferences. 10-100 songwriters/musicians participate in each event. Participants are both amateur and professional songwriters, vocalists, music business professionals, composers, bands, musical playwrights and instrumentalists. Anyone can participate. Fee: varies. "Music Business Solutions offers a number of other services and programs for both songwriters and musicians including: private music career counseling, business plan development and internet marketing; publication of *Music Biz*

Insight: Power Reading for Busy Music Professionals, a bimonthly e-zine chock full of music management and marketing tips and resources. Free subscription with e-mail address."

✔ NEMO MUSIC SHOWCASE & CONFERENCE

312 Stuart St. 4th Floor, Boston MA 02116. (617)348-2899. Fax: (617)348-2830. E-mail: kristin@ne moboston.com. Web site: www.nemoboston.com. **Contact:** Kristin Bredimus, conference &festival director. Estab. 1996. Music showcase and conference, featuring the Boston Music Awards and 3 days/nights of a conference with trade show and more than 200 nightly showcases in Boston. Offers showcases for songwriters. Offers programs annually. Event takes place in October. 1,500 songwriters/musicians participate at conference; 3,000 at awards show; 20,000 at showcases. Participants are professional songwriters, vocalists, composers, bands and instrumentalists. Participants are selected by invitation. Send for application or visit Web site.

⬙ NORTH BY NORTHEAST MUSIC FESTIVAL AND CONFERENCE (NXNE)

189 Church St., Lower Level, Toronto ON M5B 1Y7 Canada. (416)863-6963. Fax: (416)863-0828. E-mail: info@nxne.com. Web site: www.nxne.com. **Contact:** Travis Bird, festival manager or Gillian Zulauf, conference and panel coordinator. Estab. 1995. "Our festival takes place mid-June at over 30 venues across downtown Toronto, drawing over 2,000 conference delegates, 450 bands and 50,000 music fans. Musical genres include everything from folk to funk, roots to rock, polka to punk and all points in between, bringing exceptional new talent, media front-runners, music business heavies and music fans from all over the world to Toronto." Participants include emerging and established songwriters, vocalists, composers, bands and instrumentalists. Festival performers are selected by submitting a CD and accompanying press kit or applying through sonicbids.com. Application forms are available by Web site or by calling the office. Submission period each year is from November 1 to the third weekend in January. Submissions "early bird" fee: $25. Conference registration fee: $175-300. "Our conference is held at the deluxe Holiday Inn on King and the program includes mentor sessions—15-minute one-on-one opportunities for songwriters and composers to ask questions of industry experts, roundtables, panel discussions, keynote speakers, etc. North By Northeast 2007 will be held June 7-10."

NSAI SONG CAMPS

1710 Roy Acuff Place, Nashville TN 37023. 1-800-321-6008 or (615)256-3354. Fax: (615)256-0034. E-mail: songcamps@nashvillesongwriters.com. Web site: www.nashvillesongwriters.com. **Contact:** Deanie Williams, NSAI Events Director. Estab. 1992. Offers programs strictly for songwriters. Event held 4 times/year in Nashville. "We provide most meals and lodging is available. We also present an amazing evening of music presented by the faculty." Camps are 3 days long, with 36-112 participants, depending on the camp. "There are different levels of camps, some having preferred prerequisites. Each camp varies. Please call, e-mail or refer to Web site. It really isn't about the genre of music, but the quality of the song itself. Song Camp strives to strengthen the writer's vision and skills, therefore producing the better song. Song Camp is known as 'boot camp' for songwriters. It is guaranteed to catapult you forward in your writing! Participants are all aspiring songwriters led by a pro faculty. We do accept lyricists only and composers only with the hopes of expanding their scope." Participants are selected through submission of 2 songs with lyric sheet. Song Camp is open to NSAI members, although anyone can apply and upon acceptance join the organization. There is no formal application form. See Web site for membership and event information.

• Also see the listing for Nashville Songwriters Association International (NSAI) in the Organizations section of this book.

NSAI SONGWRITERS SONGPOSIUM

1710 Roy Acuff Place, Nashville TN 37203. (615)256-3354 OR 1-800-321-6008. Fax: (615)256-0034. E-mail: events@NashvilleSongwriters.com. Web site: www.nashvillesongwriters.com. Covers "all types of music. Participants take part in publisher evaluations, as well as large group sessions with different guest speakers." Offers annual programs for songwriters. Event takes place in April in downtown Nashville. 300 amateur songwriters/musicians participate in each event. Send for application.

☒ ORFORD FESTIVAL

Orford Arts Centre, 3165 Chemim DuParc, Orford QC J1X 7A2 Canada. (819)843-9871 or 1-800-567-6155. Fax: (819)843-7274. E-mail: centre@arts-orford.org. Web site: www.arts-orford.org. **Contact:** Anne-Marie Dubois, registrar/information manager. Artistic Coordinator: Nicolas Bélanger. Estab. 1951. "Each year, the Orford Arts Centre produces up to 35 concerts in the context of its Music Festival. It receives artists from all over the world in classical and chamber music." Offers master classes for music students, young professional classical musicians and chamber music ensembles. New offerings include master classes for all instruments,voice, and opera. Master classes last 2 months and take place at Orford Arts Centre from the end of June to the middle of August. 350 students participate each year. Participants are selected by demo tape submissions. Send for application. Closing date for application is mid to late March. Check our Web site for specific dates and deadlines. Scholarships for qualified students.

THE SONGWRITERS GUILD FOUNDATION

6430 Sunset Blvd., Suite 705, Hollywood CA 90028. (323)462-1108. Fax: (323)462-5430. E-mail: la@songwritersguild.com. Web site: www.songwritersguild.com. West Coast Regional Director: B. Aaron Meza. Assistant West Coast Regional Director: Eric Moromisato. Nashville office: 1222 16th Ave., S, Nashville TN 37212. (615)329-1782. Fax: (615)329-2623. Southern Regional Director: Rundi Ream. Assistant Southern Regional Director: Evan Shoemake. E-mail: sganash@aol.com. New York office: 200 W. 72nd Street, New York NY 10023. (212)768-7902. Fax: (212)768-9048. National Projects Director: George Wurzbach. Offers a series of workshops with discounts to members. "There is a charge for each songwriting class. Charges vary depending on the class. SGA members receive discounts! Also, the Re-write workshop and Ask-A-Pro/Song Critique are free!"

• Also see the Songwriters Guild of America listing in the Organizations section.

Ask-a-Pro/Song Critique (Hollywood and Nashville offices) SGA members are given the opportunity to present their songs and receive constructive feedback from industry professionals. A great chance to meet industry people, make contacts, ask questions and get your song heard! Free to SGA members. Reservations required. Call for schedule. Free.

Phil Swan Song Styles/Songwriting Workshops (Hollywood and Nashville offices) This 8-week workshop taught by Phil Swann, Dreamworks SKG staff writer is perfect for those writers who want to become better songwriters in the country, pop, and rock genres as well as more savvy the changing marketplaces. Fee.

Special Seminars and Workshops Other special seminars have been presented by such industry professionals as Dale Kawashima, John Braheny and Dr. George Gamez. Fee.

Building a Songwriting Career A 3-day workshop for songwriters, musicians and recording artists, etc. to help them discover how they can establish a career in the exciting world of songwriting. Features SGA professional songwriters and music business executives in panel discussions about intellectual property, creativity, the craft and business of songwriting and more. Fee.

Re-Write Workshop (Hollywood office) Conducted by Michael Allen. Songwriters will have the chance to have their songs critiqued by their peers with an occasional guest critique. Free.

Harriet Schock Songwriting Workshop (Hollywood office) A 10-week course consisting of nine lessons which help create a solid foundation for writing songs effortlessly. Fee.

Jai Josefs Writing Music for Hit Songs (Hollywood office) This 10-week course will show songwriters how to integrate the latest chord progressions, melodies, and grooves from all styles of music into their writing.

Song Critique New York's oldest ongoing song critique. Guild songwriters are invited to either perform their song live or present a cassette demo for feedback. A Guild moderator is on hand to direct comments. Nonmembers may attend and offer comments. Free.

Street Smarts (New York office) Street Smarts is a 3-hour orientation session for new SGA members. It introduces the basics in areas such as: contracts, copyrights, royalties, song marketing and more. The session is free to members and is scheduled whenever there is a minimum of 8 participants.

Pro-Shop For each of 6 sessions an active publisher, producer or A&R person is invited to personally screen material from professional Guild writers. Participation is limited to 10 writers, and audit of 1 session. Audition of material is required. Coordinator is producer/musician/award winning singer, Ann Johns Ruckert. Fee; $75 (SGA members only).

SGA Week Held in spring/summer of each year, this is a week of scheduled events and seminars of interest to songwriters at each of SGA's regional offices. Events include workshops, seminars and showcases. For schedule and details contact the SGA office beginning several weeks prior to SGA Week.

SOUTH BY SOUTHWEST MUSIC CONFERENCE (SXSW)

SXSW Headquarters, P.O. Box 4999, Austin TX 78765. (512)467-7979. Fax: (512)451-0754. E-mail: sxsw@sxsw.com. Web site: www.sxsw.com. **Contact:** Conference Organizer. **Europe:** Cill Ruan, 7 Ard na Croise, Thurles, Co. Tipperary Ireland. Phone: 353-504-26488. Fax: 353-504-26787. E-mail: una@sxsw.com. **Contact:** Una Johnston. **Asia:** Meijidori Bldg. 403, 2-3-21 Kabuki-cho Shinjuku-ku, Tokyo 160-0021 Japan. Phone: +82 3-5292-5551. Fax: +82 3-5292-5552. E-mail: info@sxsw-asia.com. **Contact:** Hiroshi Asada. **Australia/New Zealand/Hawaii:** 20 Hordern St., Newtown NSW 2042 Australia. Phone: 61-2-9557-7766. Fax: 61-2-9557-7788. E-mail: tripp@sxsw.om. **Contact:** Phil Tripp. Estab. 1987. South by Southwest (SXSW) is a private company based in Austin, Texas, with a year-round staff of professionals dedicated to building and delivering conference and festival events for entertainment and related media industry professionals. Since 1987, SXSW has produced the internationally-recognized music and media conference and festival (SXSW). As the entertainment business adjusted to issues of future growth and development, in 1993, SXSW added conferences and festivals for the film industry (SXSW Film) as well as for the blossoming interactive media (SXSW Interactive Festival). Now three industry events converge in Austin during a Texas-sized week, mirroring the ever increasing convergence of entertainment/media outlets. The next SXSW Music Conference and Festival will be held March 12-16, 2008 at the Austin Convention Center in Austin, TX. Offers panel discussions, "Crash Course" educational seminars and nighttime showcases. SXSW Music seeks out speakers who have developed unique ways to create and sell music. With our Wednesday Crash Courses and introductory panels, the basics will be covered in plain English. From Thursday through Saturday, the conference includes over fifty sessions including a panel of label heads discussing strategy, interviews with notable artists, topical discussions, demo listening sessions and the mentor program. And when the sun goes down, a multitude of performances by musicians and songwriters from across the country and around the world populate the SXSW Music Festival, held in venues in central Austin." Write, e-mail or visit Web site for dates and registration instructions.

Tips "Go to the Web site in early-September to apply for showcase consideraton. SXSW is also involved in North by Northeast (NXNE), held in Toronto, Canada in late Spring."

THE SWANNANOA GATHERING—CONTEMPORARY FOLK WEEK

Warren Wilson College, P.O. Box 9000, Asheville NC 28815-9000. E-mail: gathering@warren-wilson.edu. Web site: www.swangathering.com. Director: Jim Magill. "For anyone who ever wanted to make music for an audience, we offer a comprehensive week in artist development, including classes in Songwriting—with a special concentration in melody writing and commercial songwriting—Performance, Sound & Recording, and Vocal Coaching, along with daily panel discussions of other business matters such as promotion, agents and managers, logistics of touring, etc.'' 2007 staff include Ellis Paul, Tom Paxton, Cliff Eberhardt, Christine Kane, Brooks Williams, Tom Kimmel, Kate Campbell, Billy Jonas, Andrea Stolpe, Alan Rowoth, Siobhan Quinn, and Ray Chesna. For a brochure or other info contact The Swannanoa Gathering at the phone number/address above. Tuition: $417. Takes place last week in July. Housing (including all meals): $317. Annual program of The Swannanoa Gathering Folk Arts Workshops.

THE TEN-MINUTE MUSICALS PROJECT

P.O. Box 461194, West Hollywood CA 90046. E-mail: info@tenminutemusicals.org. Web site: www .tenminutemusicals.org. **Contact:** Michael Koppy, producer. Estab. 1986. Promotes short complete stage musicals. Offers programs for songwriters, composers and musical playwrights. ''Works selected are generally included in full-length 'anthology musical'—11 of the first 16 selected works are now in the show Stories 1.0, for instance.'' Awards a $250 royalty advance for each work selected. Participants are amateur and professional songwriters, composers and musical playwrights. Participants are selected by demonstration tape or CD, script, lead sheets. Send for application or visit Web site. Deadline: August 31st annually.

TUNESMITH PRO—The Next Step . . .

E-mail: info@tunesmith.net. Web site: www.tunesmith.net. **Contact:** Nancy Cassidy, Tunesmith.-net and Tunesmith PRO owner. Estab. 2001. Offers an annual ''Write with a Pro'' song competition. The 2007 Competition was won by the songwriting team of Loewen, Cantwell, and Pearson with a song titled ''Love Drives a Fast Car'' . Pros that participated were Kerry Kurt Phillips, Jeremy Spillman, Bobby Terry, Tony Ramey and Brad Martin. David Norris was named 2007 Tunesmith Songwriter of the Year and a song penned by Norris, Grimes, and Dooley titled ''Jesus Left the Building'' was named 2007 Tunesmith Song of the Year. Tunesmith is proud to be associated with Dennis Management, 1002 18th Avenue South, Nashville TN, offering management services to Texas Artist, Jarrod Birmingham www.jarrodbirmingham.com and Nashville recording artist Tammy Cassidy www.myspace.com/tammycassidymusic. Tunesmith is looking for the best uncut songwriters available to take part in the song competition and become members of the NEW Tunesmith PRO, in addition to Tunesmith's main Web site. E-mail or visit our Web site for updates www.tunesmith.net.

UNDERCURRENTS

P.O. Box 94040, Cleveland OH 44101-6040. (440)331-0700. E-mail: music@undercurrents.com. Web site: www.undercurrents.com. **Contact:** John Latimer, president. Estab. 1989. A music, event and art marketing and promotion network with online and offline exposure featuring music showcases, seminars, trade shows, networking forums. Ongoing programs and performances for songwriters, composers, and performers. Participants are selected by EPK, demo, biography and photo. Register at www.undercurrents.com.

WEST COAST SONGWRITERS CONFERENCE

(formerly Northern California Songwriters Association Conference), 1724 Laurel St., Suite 120, San Carlos CA 94070. (650)654-3966 or (800)FOR-SONG. Fax: (650)654-2156. E-mail: info@westcoasts ongwriters.org. Web site: www.westcoastsongwriters.org. **Contact:** Ian Crombie, executive director. Estab. 1980. ''Conference offers opportunity and education. 16 seminars, 50 song screening sessions (1,500 songs reviewed), performance showcases, one on one sessions and concerts.'' Offers programs for lyricists, songwriters, composers and performers. ''During the year we have competitive open mics. Winners go into the playoffs. Winners of the playoffs perform at the sunset concert at the conference." Event takes place second weekend in September at Foothill College, Los Altos Hills CA. Over 500 songwriters/musicians participate in this event. Participants are songwriters, composers, musical playwrights, vocalists, bands, instrumentalists and those interested in a career in the music business. Send for application. Deadline: September 1. Fee: $110-315. "See our listing in the Organizations section."

WINTER MUSIC CONFERENCE INC.
3450 NE 12 Terrace, Ft. Lauderdale FL 33334. (954)563-4444. Fax: (954)563-1599. E-mail: info@win termusicconference.com. Web site: www.wintermusicconference.com. President: Margo Possenti. Estab. 1985. Features educational seminars and showcases for dance, hip hop, alternative and rap. Offers programs for songwriters and performers. Offers programs annually. Event takes place March of each year in Miami FL. 3,000 songwriters/musicians participate in each event. Participants are amateur and professional songwriters, composers, musical playwrights, vocalists, bands and instrumentalists. Participants are selected by submitting demo tape. Send SASE, visit Web site or call for application. Deadline: February. Event held at either nightclubs or hotel with complete staging, lights and sound.

Retreats & Colonies

This section provides information on retreats and artists' colonies. These are places for creatives, including songwriters, to find solitude and spend concentrated time focusing on their work. While a residency at a colony may offer participation in seminars, critiques or performances, the atmosphere of a colony or retreat is much more relaxed than that of a conference or workshop. Also, a songwriter's stay at a colony is typically anywhere from one to twelve weeks (sometimes longer), while time spent at a conference may only run from one to fourteen days.

Like conferences and workshops, however, artists' colonies and retreats span a wide range. Yaddo, perhaps the most well-known colony, limits its residencies to artists "working at a professional level in their field, as determined by a judging panel of professionals in the field." The Brevard Music Center offers residencies only to those involved in classical music. Despite different focuses, all artists' colonies and retreats have one thing in common: They are places where you may work undisturbed, usually in nature-oriented, secluded settings.

SELECTING A COLONY OR RETREAT

When selecting a colony or retreat, the primary consideration for many songwriters is cost, and you'll discover that arrangements vary greatly. Some colonies provide residencies as well as stipends for personal expenses. Some suggest donations of a certain amount. Still others offer residencies for substantial sums but have financial assistance available.

When investigating the various options, consider meal and housing arrangements and your family obligations. Some colonies provide meals for residents, while others require residents to pay for meals. Some colonies house artists in one main building; others provide separate cottages. A few have provisions for spouses and families. Others prohibit families altogether.

Overall, residencies at colonies and retreats are competitive. Since only a handful of spots are available at each place, you often must apply months in advance for the time period you desire. A number of locations are open year-round, and you may find planning to go during the "off-season" lessens your competition. Other colonies, however, are only available during certain months. In any case, be prepared to include a sample of your best work with your application. Also, know what project you'll work on while in residence and have alternative projects in mind in case the first one doesn't work out once you're there.

Each listing in this section details fee requirements, meal and housing arrangements, and space and time availability, as well as the retreat's surroundings, facilities and special activities. Of course, before making a final decision, send a SASE to the colonies or retreats that interest you to receive their most up-to-date details. Costs, application requirements and deadlines are particularly subject to change.

MUSICIAN'S RESOURCE

For other listings of songwriter-friendly colonies, see *Musician's Resource* (available from Watson-Guptill Publications, 770 Broadway, New York NY 10003, 1-800-278-8477, info@watsonguptill.com), which not only provides information about conferences, workshops and academic programs but also residencies and retreats. Also check the Publications of Interest section in this book for newsletters and other periodicals providing this information.

☑ BREVARD MUSIC CENTER

P.O. Box 312, 349 Andante Ln., Brevard NC 28712. (828)862-2140. Fax: (828)884-2036. E-mail: bmc@brevardmusic.org. Web site: www.brevardmusic.org. **Contact:** Dorothy Knowles, admissions coordinator. Estab. 1936. Offers 6-week residencies from June through the first week of August. Open to professional and student composers, pianists, vocalists, collaborative pianists and instrumentalists of classical music. A 2-week jazz workshop is offered in June. Accommodates 400 at one time. Personal living quarters include cabins. Offers rehearsal, teaching and practice cabins.
Costs $4,100 for tuition, room and board. Scholarships are available.
Requirements Call for application forms and guidelines. $50 application fee. Participants are selected by audition or demonstration tape and then by invitation. There are 80 different audition sites throughout the US.

Ⓝ BYRDCLIFFE ARTS COLONY

34 Tinker St., Woodstock NY 12498. (845)679-2079. Fax: (845)679-4529. E-mail: wguild@ulster.net. Web site: www.woodstockguild.org. **Contact:** Carla T. Smith, executive director. Estab. 1991. Offers 1-month residencies June-September. Open to composers, writers and visual artists. Accommodates 10 at one time. Personal living quarters include single rooms, shared baths and kitchen facilities. Offers separate private studio space. Composers must provide their own keyboard with headphone. Activities include open studio, readings, followed by pot luck dinner once a month. The Woodstock Guild, parent organization, offers music and dance performances, gallery exhibits and book signings.
Costs $300/month. Residents are responsible for own meals and transportation.
Requirements Deadline: March 1. Send SASE for application forms and guidelines. Accepts inquiries via fax or e-mail. $35 application fee. Submit a score of at least 10 minutes with 2 references, résumé and application.

DORSET COLONY HOUSE

P.O. Box 510, Dorset VT 05251-0510. (802)867-2223. Fax: (802)867-0144. E-mail: dorsetcolony@hotmail.com. Web site: www.dorsetcolony.org. **Contact:** John Nassivera, executive director. Estab. 1980. Offers up to 1-month residencies September-November and April-May. Open to writers, composers, directors, designers and collaborators of the theatre. Accommodates 9 at one time. Personal living quarters include single rooms with desks with shared bath and shared kitchen facilities.
Costs $230/week and $800/month. Meals not included. Transportation is residents' responsibility.
Requirements Send SASE for application forms and guidelines. Accepts inquiries via fax or e-mail. Submit letter with requested dates, description of project and résumé of productions.

⊕ THE TYRONE GUTHRIE CENTRE

Annaghmakerrig, Newbliss, County Monaghan, Ireland. (353)(047)54003. Fax: (353)(047)54380. E-mail: info@tyroneguthrie.ie. Web site: www.tyroneguthrie.ie. **Contact:** Program Director. Estab. 1981. Offers year-round residencies. Artists may stay for anything from 1 week to 3 months in the Big House, or for up to 6 months at a time in one of the 5 self-catering houses in the old farmyard. Open to artists of all disciplines. Accommodates 15 at one time. Personal living quarters include bedroom with bathroom en suite. Offers a variety of workspaces. There is a music room for composers and musicians, a photographic darkroom and a number of studios for visual artists. At certain times of the year it is possible, by special arrangement, to accommodate groups of artists, symposiums, master classes, workshops and other collaborations.

Costs Artists who are not Irish residents must pay €650 per week, all found, for a residency in the Big House and €325 per week (plus gas and electricity costs) for one of the self-catering farmyard houses. To qualify for a residency, it is necessary to show evidence of a significant level of achievement in the relevant field.

Requirements Send SAE and IRC for application forms and guidelines. Accepts inquiries via fax or e-mail. Fill in application form with cv to be reviewed by the board members at regular meetings.

THE HAMBIDGE CENTER

Attn: Residency Director, P.O. Box 339, Rabun Gap GA 30568. (706)746-5718. Fax: (706)746-9933 E-mail: residents@hambidge.org. Web site: www.hambidge.org. **Contact:** Rosemary Magee, residency chair. Estab. 1934 (Center); 1988 (residency). Offers 2-week to 2-month residencies year round. Open to all artists. Accommodates 8 at one time. Personal living quarters include a private cottage with kitchen, bath, and living/studio space. Offers composer/musical studio equipped with piano. Activities include communal dinners February through December and nightly or periodic sharing of works-in-progress.

Costs $150/week.

Requirements Send SASE for application forms and guidelines, or available on Web site. Accepts inquiries via fax and e-mail. Application fee: $30. Deadlines: January 15, April 15, and September 15.

ISLE ROYALE NATIONAL PARK ARTIST-IN-RESIDENCE PROGRAM

800 E. Lakeshore Dr., Houghton MI 49931. (906)482-0984. Fax: (906)482-8753. E-mail: ISRO_Parkin fo@nps.gov. Web site: www.nps.gov/ISRO/. **Contact:** Greg Blust, coordinator. Estab. 1991. Offers 2-3 week residencies from mid-June to mid-September. Open to all art forms. Accommodates 1 artist with 1 companion at one time. Personal living quarters include cabin with shared outhouse. A canoe is provided for transportation. Offers a guest house at the site that can be used as a studio. The artist is asked to contribute a piece of work representative of their stay at Isle Royale, to be used by the park in an appropriate manner. During their residency, artists will be asked to share their experience (1 presentation per week of residency, about 1 hour/week) with the public by demonstration, talk, or other means.

Requirements Deadline: postmarked February 16, 2007. Send for application forms and guidelines. Accepts inquiries via fax or e-mail. A panel of professionals from various disciplines, and park representatives will choose the finalists. The selection is based on artistic integrity, ability to reside in a wilderness environment, a willingness to donate a finished piece of work inspired on the island, and the artist's ability to relate and interpret the park through their work.

N KALANI OCEANSIDE RETREAT

RR 2 Box 4500, Pahoa-Beach Road HI 96778-9724. (808)965-7828. Fax: (808)965-0527. E-mail: kalani@kalani.com. Web site: www.kalani.com. **Contact:** Richard Koob, director. Estab. 1980. Offers 2-week to 2-month residencies. Open to all artists who can verify professional accomplishments. Accommodates 120 at one time. Personal living quarters include private cottage or lodge room with private or shared bath. Full (3 meals/day) dining service. Offers shared studio/library spaces. Activities include opportunity to share works in progress, ongoing yoga, hula and other classes; beach, thermal springs, Volcanos National Park nearby; olympic pool/spa on 120-acre facility.

Cost $58-230/night lodging with stipend, including 3 meals/day. Transportation by rental car from $35/day, Kalani service $55/trip, or taxi $80/trip.
Requirements Accepts inquiries via fax or e-mail.

THE MACDOWELL COLONY

100 High St., Peterborough NH 03458. (603)924-3886. Fax: (603)924-9142. E-mail: admissions@ma cdowellcolony.org. Web site: www.macdowellcolony.org. **Contact:** Admissions Director. Estab. 1907. Offers year-round residencies of up to 8 weeks. Open to writers, composers, film/video makers, visual artists, architects and interdisciplinary artists. Personal living quarters include single rooms with shared baths. Offers private studios on 450-acre grounds.
Cost None (contributions accepted).
Requirements Visit Web site for application forms and guidelines (which include work sample requirements). Application deadline: January 15, April 15 and September 15.

NORTHWOOD UNIVERSITY ALDEN B. DOW CREATIVITY CENTER

4000 Whiting Dr., Midland MI 48640. (989)837-4478. E-mail: creativity@northwood.edu. Web site: www.northwood.edu/abd. **Contact** Nancy Barker, executive director. Estab. 1979. Offers 10-week summer residencies (mid-June through mid-August). Fellowship Residency is open to individuals in all fields (the arts, humanities or sciences, etc.) who have innovative, creative projects to pursue. Accommodates 3 at one time. Each Fellow is given a furnished apartment on campus, kitchen, bath and large living room. Fellows' apartments serve as their work space as well as their living quarters unless special needs are requested.
Cost $10 application fee. Room and board is provided plus a $750 stipend to be used toward project costs or personal needs. ''We look for projects which are innovative, creative, unique. We ask the applicant to set accomplishable goals for the 10-week residency.''
Requirements Send for application information and guidelines. Accepts inquiries via e-mail. Applicants submit 2-page typed description of their project; cover page with name, address, phone numbers plus summary (30 words or less) of project; support materials must be submitted via e-mail—will not accept tapes, CDs, or slides by postal mail; personal résumé; facilities or equipment needed; and $10 application fee. Application deadline: December 31 (postmarked).

N SITKA CENTER FOR ART & ECOLOGY

P.O. Box 65, Otis OR 97368-0065. (541)994-5485. Fax: (541)994-8024. E-mail: info@sitkacenter.org. Web site: www.sitkacenter.org. **Contact:** Laura Young, program manager. Estab. 1971. Offers 4-month residencies in October through January or February through May; shorter residencies are available upon arrangement. Open to emerging, mid-career, or professional artists and naturalists. Residences include 3 living quarters, each self-contained with a sleeping area, kitchen and bathroom. Offers 4 studios. Workshops or presentations are encouraged; an exhibition/presentation to share residents' works is held in January and May.
Cost Residency and housing provided. The resident is asked to provide some form of community service on behalf of Sitka.
Requirements *Applications due by April 21 for a Fall or Spring residency.* Send completed application with résumé, 2 letters of recommendation, work samples and SASE.

VIRGINIA CENTER FOR THE CREATIVE ARTS

154 San Angelo Dr., Amherst VA 24521. (434)946-7236. Fax: (434)946-7239. E-mail: vcca@vcca.c om. Web site: www.vcca.com. **Contact:** Sheila Gulley Pleasants, director of artists' services. Estab. 1971. Offers residencies year-round, typical residency lasts 2 weeks to 2 months. Open to originating artists: composers, writers and visual artists. Accommodates 22 at one time. Personal living quarters include 20 single rooms, 2 double rooms, bathrooms shared with one other person. All meals are

served. Kitchens for fellows' use available at studios and residence. Activities include trips in the VCCA van twice a week into town. Fellows share their work regularly. Four studios have pianos.
Cost No transportation costs are covered. Artists are accepted at the VCCA without consideration for their financial situation. The actual cost of a residency at the Virginia Center is $120 per day per Fellow. "We ask Fellows to contribute according to their ability. Suggested daily contribution is $30."
Requirements Send SASE for application form or download from Web site. Applications are reviewed by a panel of judges. Application fee: $25. Deadline: May 15 for October-January residency; September 15 for February-May residency; January 15 for June-September residency.

State &
Provincial
Grants

A rts councils in the United States and Canada provide assistance to artists (including poets) in the form of fellowships or grants. These grants can be substantial and confer prestige upon recipients; however, **only state or province residents are eligible**. Because deadlines and available support vary annually, query first (with a SASE) or check Web sites for guidelines.

UNITED STATES ARTS AGENCIES

Alabama State Council on the Arts, 201 Monroe St., Montgomery AL 36130-1800. (334)242-4076. E-mail: staff@arts.alabama.gov. Web site: www.arts.state.al.us.

Alaska State Council on the Arts, 411 W. Fourth Ave., Suite 1-E, Anchorage AK 99501-2343. (907)269-6610 or (888)278-7424. E-mail: aksca_info@eed.state.ak.us. Web site: www.eed. state.ak.us/aksca.

Arizona Commission on the Arts, 417 W. Roosevelt St., Phoenix AZ 85003-1326. (602)771-6501. E-mail: info@azarts.gov. Web site: www.azarts.gov.

Arkansas Arts Council, 1500 Tower Bldg., 323 Center St., Little Rock AR 72201. (501)324-9766. E-mail: info@arkansasarts.com. Web site: www.arkansasarts.com.

California Arts Council, 1300 I St., Suite 930, Sacramento CA 95814. (916)322-6555. E-mail: info@caartscouncil.com. Web site: www.cac.ca.gov.

Colorado Council on the Arts, 1625 Broadway, Suite 2700, Denver CO 80202. (303)892-3802. E-mail: online form. Web site: www.coloarts.state.co.us.

Connecticut Commission on Culture & Tourism, Arts Division, One Financial Plaza, 755 Main St., Hartford CT 06103. (860)256-2800. Web site: www.cultureandtourism.org.

Delaware Division of the Arts, Carvel State Office Bldg., 4th Floor, 820 N. French St., Wilmington DE 19801. (302)577-8278 (New Castle Co.) or (302)739-5304 (Kent or Sussex Counties). E-mail: delarts@state.de.us. Web site: www.artsdel.org.

District of Columbia Commission on the Arts & Humanities, 410 Eighth St. NW, 5th Floor, Washington DC 20004. (202)724-5613. E-mail: cah@dc.gov. Web site: http://dcarts .dc.gov.

Florida Arts Council, Division of Cultural Affairs, R.A. Gray Building, Third Floor, 500 S. Bronough St., Tallahassee FL 32399-0250. (850)245-6470. E-mail: info@florida-arts.org. Web site: www.florida-arts.org.

Georgia Council for the Arts, 260 14th St., Suite 401, Atlanta GA 30318. (404)685-2787. E-mail: gaarts@gaarts.org. Web site: www.gaarts.org.

Guam Council on the Arts & Humanities Agency, P.O. Box 2950, Hagatna GU 96932. (671)646-2781. Web site: www.guam.net.

Hawaii State Foundation on Culture & the Arts, 2500 S. Hotel St., 2nd Floor, Honolulu HI 96813. (808)586-0300. E-mail: ken.hamilton@hawaii.gov. Web site: www.state.hi.us/sfca.

Idaho Commission on the Arts, 2410 N. Old Penitentiary Rd., Boise ID 83712. (208)334-2119 or (800)278-3863. E-mail: info@arts.idaho.gov. Web site: www.arts.idaho.gov.

Illinois Arts Council, James R. Thompson Center, 100 W. Randolph, Suite 10-500, Chicago IL 60601. (312)814-6750. E-mail: iac.info@illinois.gov. Web site: www.state.il.us/agency/iac.

Indiana Arts Commission, 150 W. Market St., Suite 618, Indianapolis IN 46204. (317)232-1268. E-mail: IndianaArtsCommission@iac.in.gov. Web site: www.in.gov/arts.

Iowa Arts Council, 600 E. Locust, Des Moines IA 50319-0290. (515)281-6412. Web site: www.iowaartscouncil.org.

Kansas Arts Commission, 700 SW Jackson, Suite 1004, Topeka KS 66603-3761. (785)296-3335. E-mail: KAC@arts.state.ks.us. Web site: http://arts.state.ks.us.

Kentucky Arts Council, 21st Floor, Capital Plaza Tower, 500 Mero St., Frankfort KY 40601-1987. (502)564-3757 or (888)833-2787. E-mail: kyarts@ky.gov. Web site: http://artscouncil.ky.gov.

Louisiana Division of the Arts, Capitol Annex Bldg., 1051 N. 3rd St., 4th Floor, Room #420, Baton Rouge LA 70804. (225)342-8180. Web site: www.crt.state.la.us/arts.

Maine Arts Commission, 193 State St., 25 State House Station, Augusta ME 04333-0025. (207)287-2724. E-mail: MaineArts.info@maine.gov. Web site: www.mainearts.com.

Maryland State Arts Council, 175 W. Ostend St., Suite E, Baltimore MD 21230. (410)767-6555. E-mail: msac@msac.org. Web site: www.msac.org.

Massachusetts Cultural Council, 10 St. James Ave., 3rd Floor, Boston MA 02116-3803. (617)727-3668. E-mail: mcc@art.state.ma.us. Web site: www.massculturalcouncil.org.

Michigan Council for Arts & Cultural Affairs, 702 W. Kalamazoo St., P.O. Box 30705, Lansing MI 48909-8205. (517)241-4011. E-mail: artsinfo@michigan.gov. Web site: www.michigan.gov/hal/0,1607,7-160-17445_19272---,00.html.

Minnesota State Arts Board, Park Square Court, 400 Sibley St., Suite 200, St. Paul MN 55101-1928. (651)215-1600 or (800)866-2787. E-mail: msab@arts.state.mn.us. Web site: www.arts.state.mn.us.

Mississippi Arts Commission, 501 N. West St., Suite 701B, Woolfolk Bldg., Jackson MS 39201. (601)359-6030. Web site: www.arts.state.ms.us.

Missouri Arts Council, 815 Olive St., Suite 16, St. Louis MO 63101-1503. (314)340-6845 or (866)407-4752. E-mail: moarts@ded.mo.gov. Web site: www.missouriartscouncil.org.

Montana Arts Council, 316 N. Park Ave., Suite 252, Helena MT 59620-2201. (406)444-6430. E-mail: mac@mt.gov. Web site: www.art.state.mt.us.

National Assembly of State Arts Agencies, 1029 Vermont Ave. NW, 2nd Floor, Washington DC 20005. (202)347-6352. E-mail: nasaa@nasaa-arts.org. Web site: www.nasaa-arts.org.

Nebraska Arts Council, 1004 Farnam St., Plaza Level, Omaha NE 68102. (402)595-2122 or (800)341-4067. Web site: www.nebraskaartscouncil.org.

Nevada Arts Council, 716 N. Carson St., Suite A, Carson City NV 89701. (775)687-6680. E-mail: online form. Web site: http://dmla.clan.lib.nv.us/docs/arts.

New Hampshire State Council on the Arts, 2½ Beacon St., 2nd Floor, Concord NH 03301-4974. (603)271-2789. Web site: www.nh.gov/nharts.

New Jersey State Council on the Arts, 225 W. State St., P.O. Box 306, Trenton NJ 08625. (609)292-6130. Web site: www.njartscouncil.org.

New Mexico Arts, Dept. of Cultural Affairs, P.O. Box 1450, Santa Fe NM 87504-1450. (505)827-6490 or (800)879-4278. Web site: www.nmarts.org.

New York State Council on the Arts, 175 Varick St., New York NY 10014. (212)627-4455. Web site: www.nysca.org.

North Carolina Arts Council, 109 East Jones St., Cultural Resources Building, Raleigh NC 27601. (919)807-6500. E-mail: ncarts@ncmail.net. Web site: www.ncarts.org.

North Dakota Council on the Arts, 1600 E. Century Ave., Suite 6, Bismarck ND 58503. (701)328-7590. E-mail: comserv@state.nd.us. Web site: www.state.nd.us/arts.

Commonwealth Council for Arts and Culture (Northern Mariana Islands), P.O. Box 5553, CHRB, Saipan MP 96950. (670)322-9982 or (670)322-9983. E-mail: galaidi@vzpacifica.net. Web site: www.geocities.com/ccacarts/ccacwebsite.html.

Ohio Arts Council, 727 E. Main St., Columbus OH 43205-1796. (614)466-2613. Web site: www.oac.state.oh.us.

Oklahoma Arts Council, Jim Thorpe Building, 2101 N. Lincoln Blvd., Suite 640, Oklahoma City OK 73105. (405)521-2931. E-mail: okarts@arts.ok.gov. Web site: www.arts.state.ok.us.

Oregon Arts Commission, 775 Summer St. NE, Suite 200, Salem OR 97301-1280. (503)986-0082. E-mail: oregon.artscomm@state.or.us. Web site: www.oregonartscommission.org.

Pennsylvania Council on the Arts, 216 Finance Bldg., Harrisburg PA 17120. (717)787-6883. Web site: www.pacouncilonthearts.org.

Institute of Puerto Rican Culture, P.O. Box 9024184, San Juan PR 00902-4184. (787)724-0700. E-mail: www@icp.gobierno.pr. Web site: www.icp.gobierno.pr.

Rhode Island State Council on the Arts, One Capitol Hill, Third Floor, Providence RI 02908. (401)222-3880. E-mail: info@arts.ri.gov. Web site: www.arts.ri.gov.

American Samoa Council on Culture, Arts and Humanities, P.O. Box 1540, Office of the Governor, Pago Pago AS 96799. (684)633-4347. Web site: www.prel.org/programs/pcahe/PTG/terr-asamoa1.html.

South Carolina Arts Commission, 1800 Gervais St., Columbia SC 29201. (803)734-8696. E-mail: info@arts.state.sc.us. Web site: www.southcarolinaarts.com.

South Dakota Arts Council, 711 E. Wells Ave., Pierre SD 57501-3369. (605)773-3301. E-mail: sdac@state.sd.us. Web site: www.artscouncil.sd.gov.

Tennessee Arts Commission, 401 Charlotte Ave., Nashville TN 37243-0780. (615)741-1701. Web site: www.arts.state.tn.us.

Texas Commission on the Arts, E.O. Thompson Office Building, 920 Colorado, Suite 501, Austin TX 78701. (512)463-5535. E-mail: front.desk@arts.state.tx.us. Web site: www.arts.state.tx.us.

Utah Arts Council, 617 E. South Temple, Salt Lake City UT 84102-1177. (801)236-7555. Web site: http://arts.utah.gov.

Vermont Arts Council, 136 State St., Drawer 33, Montpelier VT 05633-6001. (802)828-3291. E-mail: online form. Web site: www.vermontartscouncil.org.

Virgin Islands Council on the Arts, 5070 Norre Gade, St. Thomas VI 00802-6872. (340)774-5984. Web site: http://vicouncilonarts.org.

Virginia Commission for the Arts, Lewis House, 223 Governor St., 2nd Floor, Richmond VA 23219. (804)225-3132. E-mail: arts@arts.virginia.gov. Web site: www.arts.state.va.us.

Washington State Arts Commission, 711 Capitol Way S., Suite 600, P.O. Box 42675, Olympia WA 98504-2675. (360)753-3860. E-mail: info@arts.wa.gov. Web site: www.arts.wa.gov.

West Virginia Commission on the Arts, The Cultural Center, Capitol Complex, 1900 Kanawha Blvd. E., Charleston WV 25305-0300. (304)558-0220. Web site: www.wvculture.org/arts.

Wisconsin Arts Board, 101 E. Wilson St., 1st Floor, Madison WI 53702. (608)266-0190. E-mail: artsboard@arts.state.wi.us. Web site: www.arts.state.wi.us.

Wyoming Arts Council, 2320 Capitol Ave., Cheyenne WY 82002. (307)777-7742. E-mail: ebratt@state.wy.us. Web site: http://wyoarts.state.wy.us.

CANADIAN PROVINCES ARTS AGENCIES

Alberta Foundation for the Arts, 10708 - 105 Ave., Edmonton AB T5H 0A1. (780)427-9968. Web site: www.cd.gov.ab.ca/all_about_us/commissions/arts.

British Columbia Arts Council, P.O. Box 9819, Stn. Prov. Govt., Victoria BC V8W 9W3. (250)356-1718. E-mail: BCArtsCouncil@gov.bc.ca. Web site: www.bcartscouncil.ca.

The Canada Council for the Arts, 350 Albert St., P.O. Box 1047, Ottawa ON K1P 5V8. (613)566-4414 or (800)263-5588 (within Canada). Web site: www.canadacouncil.ca.

Manitoba Arts Council, 525-93 Lombard Ave., Winnipeg MB R3B 3B1. (204)945-2237 or (866)994-2787 (in Manitoba). E-mail: info@artscouncil.mb.ca. Web site: www.artscouncil.mb.ca.

New Brunswick Arts Board (NBAB), 634 Queen St., Suite 300, Fredericton NB E3B 1C2. (506)444-4444 or (866)460-2787. Web site: www.artsnb.ca.

Newfoundland & Labrador Arts Council, P.O. Box 98, St. John's NL A1C 5H5. (709)726-2212 or (866)726-2212. E-mail: nlacmail@nfld.net. Web site: www.nlac.nf.ca.

Nova Scotia Department of Tourism, Culture, and Heritage, Culture Division, 1800 Argyle St., Suite 601, P.O. Box 456, Halifax NS B3J 2R5. (902)424-4510. E-mail: cultaffs@gov.ns.ca. Web site: www.gov.ns.ca/dtc/culture.

Ontario Arts Council, 151 Bloor St. W., 5th Floor, Toronto ON M5S 1T6. (416)961-1660 or (800)387-0058 (in Ontario). E-mail: info@arts.on.ca. Web site: www.arts.on.ca.

Prince Edward Island Council of the Arts, 115 Richmond St., Charlottetown PE C1A 1H7. (902)368-4410 or (888)734-2784. E-mail: info@peiartscouncil.com. Web site: www.peiart scouncil.com.

Québec Council for Arts & Literature, 79 boul. René-Lévesque Est, 3e étage, Québec QC G1R 5N5. (418)643-1707 or (800)897-1707. E-mail: info@calq.gouv.qc.ca. Web site: www.calq. gouv.qc.ca.

The Saskatchewan Arts Board, 2135 Broad St., Regina SK S4P 1Y6. (306)787-4056 or (800)667-7526 (Saskatchewan only). E-mail: sab@artsboard.sk.ca. Web site: www.artsbo ard.sk.ca.

Yukon Arts Section, Cultural Services Branch, Dept. of Tourism & Culture, Government of Yukon, Box 2703 (L-3), Whitehorse YT Y1A 2C6. (867)667-8589 or (800)661-0408 (in Yukon). E-mail: arts@gov.yk.ca. Web site: www.btc.gov.yk.ca/cultural/arts.

Publications of Interest

Knowledge about the music industry is essential for both creative and business success. Staying informed requires keeping up with constantly changing information. Updates on the evolving trends in the music business are available to you in the form of music magazines, music trade papers and books. There is a publication aimed at almost every type of musician, songwriter and music fan, from the most technical knowledge of amplification systems to gossip about your favorite singer. These publications can enlighten and inspire you and provide information vital in helping you become a more well-rounded, educated, and, ultimately, successful musical artist.

This section lists all types of magazines and books you may find interesting. From songwriters' newsletters and glossy music magazines to tip sheets and how-to books, there should be something listed here that you'll enjoy and benefit from.

PERIODICALS

The Album Network, 110 West Spazier, Burbank CA 91502. (818)842-2600. Web site: www. musicbiz.com. *Weekly music industry trade magazine.*

American Songwriter Magazine, 50 Music Square W., Suite 604, Nashville TN 37203-3227. (615)321-6096. E-mail: info@americansongwriter.com. Web site: www.americansongwriter.com. *Bimonthly publication for and about songwriters.*

Back Stage East, 770 Broadway, 4th Floor, New York NY 10003. (646)654-5700.

Back Stage West, 5055 Wilshire Blvd., Los Angeles CA 90036. (323)525-2358 or (800)745-8922. Web site: www.backstage.com. *Weekly East and West Coast performing artist trade papers.*

Bass Player, P.O. Box 57324, Boulder CO 80323-7324. (800)234-1831. E-mail: bassplayer@neodata.com. Web site: www.bassplayer.com. *Monthly magazine for bass players with lessons, interviews, articles, and transcriptions.*

Billboard, 1515 Broadway, New York NY 10036. (800)745-8922. E-mail: bbstore@billboard.com. Web site: www.billboard.com. *Weekly industry trade magazine.*

Canadian Musician, 23 Hannover Dr., Suite 7, St. Catharines, Ontario L2W 1A3 Canada. (877)746-4692. Web site: www.canadianmusician.com. *Bimonthly publication for amateur and professional Canadian musicians.*

Chart, 200-41 Britain St., Toronto, Ontario M5A 1R7 Canada. (416)363-3101. E-mail: chart@c hartnet.com. Web site: www.chartattack.com. *Monthly magazine covering the Canadian and international music scenes.*

CMJ New Music Report/CMJ New Music Monthly, 151 W. 25th St., 12 Floor, New York NY 10001. (917)606-1908. Web site: www.cmj.com. *Weekly college radio and alternative music tip sheet.*

Country Line Magazine, 16150 S. IH-35, Buda TX 78610. (512)295-8400. E-mail: editor@cou ntrylinemagazine.com. Web site: www.countrylinemagazine.com. *Monthly Texas-only country music cowboy and lifestyle magazine.*

Daily Variety, 5700 Wilshire Blvd., Suite 120, Los Angeles CA 90036. (323)857-6600. Web site: www.variety.com. *Daily entertainment trade newspaper.*

Dramalogue, 1456 N. Gordon, Hollywood CA 90028. Web site: www.dramalogue.com. *L.A.-based entertainment newspaper with an emphasis on theatre and cabaret.*

The Dramatist, 1501 Broadway, Suite 701, New York NY 10036. (212)398-9366. Fax: (212)944-0420. Web site: www.dramaguild.com. *The quarterly journal of the Dramatists Guild, the professional association of playwrights, composers and lyricists.*

Entertainment Law & Finance, New York Law Publishing Co., 345 Park Ave. S., 8th Floor, New York NY 10010. (212)545-6174. *Monthly newsletter covering music industry contracts, lawsuit filings, court rulings and legislation.*

Exclaim!, 7-B Pleasant Blvd., Suite 966, Toronto, Ontario M4T 1K2 Canada. (416)535-9735. E-mail: exclaim@exclaim.ca. Web site: http://exclaim.ca. *Canadian music monthly covering all genres of non-mainstream music.*

Fast Forward, Disc Makers, 7905 N. Rt. 130, Pennsauken NJ 08110-1402. (800)468-9353. Web site: www.discmakers.com/music/ffwd. *Quarterly newsletter featuring companies and products for performing and recording artists in the independent music industry.*

Guitar Player, 1601 W. 23rd St., Suite 200, Lawrence KS 60046-0127. (800)289-9839. Web site: www.guitarplayer.com. *Monthly guitar magazine with transcriptions, columns, and interviews, including occasional articles on songwriting.*

Hits Magazine, 14958 Ventura Blvd., Sherman Oaks CA 91403. (818)501-7900. Web site: www.hitsmagazine.com. *Weekly music industry trade publication.*

Jazztimes, 8737 Colesville Rd., 9th Floor, Silver Spring MD 20910-3921. (301)588-4114. Web site: www.jazztimes.com. *10 issues/year magazine covering the American jazz scene.*

The Leads Sheet, Allegheny Music Works, 1611 Menoher Blvd., Johnstown PA 15905. (814)255-4007. Web site: www.alleghenymusicworks.com. *Monthly tip sheet.*

Music Business International Magazine, 460 Park Ave., S. of 9th, New York NY 10116. (212)378-0406. *Bimonthly magazine for senior executives in the music industry.*

Music Connection Magazine, 16130 Ventura Blvd., Suite 540, Encino CA 91436. (818)795-0101. E-mail: contactMC@musicconnection.com. Web site: www.musicconnection.com. *Biweekly music industry trade publication.*

Music Morsels, P.O. Box 2760, Acworth GA 30102. (678)445-0006. Fax: (678)494-9269. E-mail: SergeEnt@aol.com. Web site: www.serge.org/musicmorsels.htm. *Monthly songwriting publication.*

Music Row Magazine, 1231 17th Ave. S, Nashville TN 37212. (615)321-3617. E-mail: info@ musicrow.com. Web site: www.musicrow.com. *Biweekly Nashville industry publication.*

Offbeat Magazine, OffBeat Publications, 421 Frenchman St., Suite 200, New Orleans LA 70116. (504)944-4300. E-mail: offbeat@offbeat.com. Web site: www.offbeat.com. *Monthly magazine covering Louisiana music and artists.*

The Performing Songwriter, P.O. Box 40931, Nashville TN 37204. (800)883-7664. E-mail: order @performingsongwriter.com. Web site: www.performingsongwriter.com. *Bimonthly songwriters' magazine.*

Radio and Records, 2049 Century Park East, 41st Floor, Los Angeles CA 90067. (310)553-4330. Fax: (310)203-9763. E-mail: subscribe@radioandrecords.com. Web site: www.radio andrecords.com. *Weekly newspaper covering the radio and record industries.*

Radir, Radio Mall, 2412 Unity Ave. N., Dept. WEB, Minneapolis MN 55422. (800)759-4561. E-mail: info@bbhsoftware.com. Web site: www.bbhsoftware.com. *Quarterly radio station database on disk.*

Sing Out!, P.O. Box 5460, Bethlehem PA 18015. (888)SING-OUT. Fax: (610)865-5129. E-mail: info@singout.org. Web site: www.singout.org. *Quarterly folk music magazine.*

Songcasting, 15445 Ventura Blvd. #260, Sherman Oaks CA 91403. (818)377-4084. *Monthly tip sheet.*

Songlink International, 23 Belsize Crescent, London NW3 5QY England. Web site: www.son glink.com. *10 issues/year newsletter including details of recording artists looking for songs; contact details for industry sources; also news and features on the music business.*

Variety, 5700 Wilshire Blvd., Suite 120, Los Angeles CA 90036. (323)857-6600. Fax: (323)857-0494. Web site: www.variety.com. *Weekly entertainment trade newspaper.*

Words and Music, 41 Valleybrook Dr., Don Mills, Ontario M3B 2S6 Canada. (416)445-8700. Web site: www.socan.ca. *Monthly songwriters' magazine.*

BOOKS & DIRECTORIES

101 Songwriting Wrongs & How to Right Them, by Pat & Pete Luboff, Writer's Digest Books, 4700 E. Galbraith Rd., Cincinnati OH 45236. (800)448-0915. Web site: www.writers digest.com.

The A&R Registry, by Ritch Esra, SRS Publishing, 7510 Sunset Blvd. #1041, Los Angeles CA 90046-3418. (800)377-7411 or (800)552-7411. E-mail: musicregistry@compuserve.com.

Attention: A&R, by Teri Muench and Susan Pomerantz, Alfred Publishing Co. Inc., P.O. Box 10003, Van Nuys CA 91410-0003. (818)892-2452. Web site: www.alfredpub.com.

The Billboard Guide to Music Publicity, revised edition, by Jim Pettigrew, Jr., Billboard Books, 1695 Oak St., Lakewood NJ 08701. (800)344-7119.

Breakin' Into Nashville, by Jennifer Ember Pierce, Madison Books, University Press of America, 4501 Forbes Rd., Suite 200, Lanham MD 20706. (800)462-6420.

CMJ Directory, 151 W. 25th St., 12th Floor, New York NY 10001. (917)606-1908. Web site: www.cmj.com.

Contracts for the Music industry, P.O. Box 952063, Lake Mary FL 32795-2063. (407)834-8555. E-mail: info@songwriterproducts.com. Web site: www.songwriterproducts.com. *Book and computer software of a variety of music contracts.*

The Craft and Business of Songwriting, by John Braheny, Writer's Digest Books, 4700 E. Galbraith Rd., Cincinnati OH 45236. (800)448-0915. Web site: www.writersdigest.com.

The Craft of Lyric Writing, by Sheila Davis, Writer's Digest Books, 4700 E. Galbraith Rd., Cincinnati OH 45236. (800)448-0915. Web site: www.writersdigest.com.

Creating Melodies, by Dick Weissman, Writer's Digest Books, 4700 E. Galbraith Rd., Cincinnati OH 45236. (800)448-0915. Web site: www.writersdigest.com.

Directory of Independent Music Distributors, by Jason Ojalvo, Disc Makers, 7905 N. Rt. 130, Pennsauken NJ 08110. (800)468-9353. E-mail: discman@discmakers.com. Web site: www.discmakers.com.

Easy Tools for Composing, by Charles Segal, Segal's Publications, 16 Grace Rd., Newton MA 02159. (617)969-6196.

FILM/TV MUSIC GUIDE, by Ritch Esra, SRS Publishing, 7510 Sunset Blvd. #1041, Los Angeles CA 90046-3418. (800)552-7411. E-mail: musicregistry@compuserve.com or srspubl@aol.com. Web site: www.musicregistry.com.

Finding Fans & Selling CDs, by Veronique Berry and Jason Ojalvo, Disk Makers, 7905 N. Rt. 130, Pennsauken NJ 08110-1402. (800)468-9353. E-mail: discman@diskmakers.com. Web site: www.discmakers.com.

Guide to Independent Music Publicity, by Veronique Berry, Disc Makers, 7905 N. Rt. 130, Pennsauken NJ 08110-1402. (800)468-9353. E-mail: discman@discmakers.com.

Guide to Master Tape Preparation, by Dave Moyssiadis, Disk Makers, 7905 N. Rt. 130, Pennsauken NJ 08110-1402. (800)468-9353. E-mail: discman@discmakers.com.

Hollywood Creative Directory, 3000 W. Olympic Blvd. #2525, Santa Monica CA 90404. (800)815-0503. Web site: www.hcdonline.com. *Lists producers in film and TV.*

The Hollywood Reporter Blu-Book Production Directory, 5055 Wilshire Blvd., Los Angeles CA 90036. (323)525-2150. Web site: www.hollywoodreporter.com.

Hot Tips for the Home Recording Studio, by Hank Linderman, Writer's Digest Books, 4700 E. Galbraith Rd., Cincinnati OH 45236. (800)448-0915. Web site: www.writersdigest.com.

How to Get Somewhere in the Music Business from Nowhere with Nothing, by Mary Dawson, CQK Books, % CQK Music Group, 2221 Justin Rd., Suite 119-142, Flower Mound TX 75028. (972)317-2720. Fax: (972)317-4737. Web site: www.FromNowhereWithNothing.com.

How to Promote Your Music Successfully on the Internet, by David Nevue, Midnight Rain Productions, P.O. Box 21831, Eugene OR 97402. Web site: www.rainmusic.com.

How to Write Songs on Guitar: A Guitar-Playing and Songwriting Course, by Rikky Rooksby, Backbeat Books, 600 Harrison St., San Francisco CA 94107. (415)947-6615. E-mail: books@musicplayer.com. Web site: www.backbeatbooks.com.

How You Can Break Into the Music Business, by Marty Garrett, Lonesome Wind Corporation, P.O. Box 2143, Broken Arrow OK 74013-2143. (800)210-4416.

Louisiana Music Directory, OffBeat, Inc., 421 Frenchmen St., Suite 200, New Orleans LA 70116. (504)944-4300. Web site: www.offbeat.com.

Lydian Chromatic Concept of Tonal Organization, Volume One: The Art and Science of Tonal Gravity, by George Russell, Concept Publishing Company, 258 Harvard St., #296,

Brookline MA 02446-2904. E-mail: lydconcept@aol.com. Web site: www.lydianchromatic concept.com

Melody in Songwriting, by Jack Perricone, Berklee Press, 1140 Boylston St., Boston MA 02215. (617)747-2146. E-mail: info@berkleepress.com. Web site: www.berkleepress.com.

Melody: How to Write Great Tunes, by Rikky Rooksby, Backbeat Books, 600 Harrison St., San Francisco CA 94107. (415)947-6115. E-mail: books@musicplayer.com. Web site: www.backbeatbooks.com.

Music Attorney Legal & Business Affairs Registry, by Ritch Esra and Steve Trumbull, SRS Publishing, 7510 Sunset Blvd. #1041, Los Angeles CA 90046-3418. (800)552-7411. E-mail: musicregistry@compuserve.com or srspubl@aol.com.

Music Directory Canada, seventh edition, Norris-Whitney Communications Inc., 23 Hannover Dr., Suite 7, St. Catherines, Ontario L2W 1A3 Canada. (877)RING-NWC. E-mail: mail@nor.com. Web site: http://nor.com.

Music Law: How to Run Your Band's Business, by Richard Stin, Nolo Press, 950 Parker St., Berkeley CA 94710-9867. (510)549-1976. Web site: www.nolo.com.

Music, Money and Success: The Insider's Guide to the Music Industry, by Jeffrey Brabec and Todd Brabec, Schirmer Books, 1633 Broadway, New York NY 10019.

The Music Publisher Registry, by Ritch Esra, SRS Publishing, 7510 Sunset Blvd. #1041, Los Angeles CA 90046-3418. (800)552-7411. E-mail: musicregistry@compuserve.com or srspubl@aol.com.

Music Publishing: A Songwriter's Guide, revised edition, by Randy Poe, Writer's Digest Books, 4700 E. Galbraith Rd., Cincinnati OH 45236. (800)448-0915. Web site: www.writers digest.com.

The Musician's Guide to Making & Selling Your Own CDs & Cassettes, by Jana Stanfield, Writer's Digest Books, 4700 E. Galbraith Rd., Cincinnati OH 45236. (800)448-0915. Web site: www.writersdigest.com.

Musicians' Phone Book, The Los Angeles Music Industry Directory, Get Yourself Some Publishing, 28336 Simsalido Ave., Canyon Country CA 91351. (805)299-2405. E-mail: mpb@earthlink.net. Web site: www.musiciansphonebook.com.

Nashville Music Business Directory, by Mark Dreyer, NMBD Publishing, 9 Music Square S., Suite 210, Nashville TN 37203. (615)826-4141. E-mail: nmbd@nashvilleconnection.com. Web site: www.nashvilleconnection.com.

Nashville's Unwritten Rules: Inside the Business of the Country Music Machine, by Dan Daley, Overlook Press, One Overlook Dr., Woodstock NY 12498. (845)679-6838. E-mail: overlook@netstep.net.

National Directory of Independent Record Distributors, P.O. Box 452063, Lake Mary FL 32795-2063. (407)834-8555. E-mail: info@songwriterproducts.com. Web site: www.song writerproducts.com.

The Official Country Music Directory, ICMA Music Directory, P.O. Box 271238, Nashville TN 37227.

Performance Magazine Guides, 1203 Lake St., Suite 200, Fort Worth TX 76102-4504. (817)338-9444. E-mail: sales@performancemagazine.com. Web site: www.performance magazine.com.

Radio Stations of America: A National Directory, P.O. Box 452063, Lake Mary FL 32795-2063. (407)834-8555. E-mail: info@songwriterproducts.com. Web site: www.songwriterproducts.com.

The Real Deal—How to Get Signed to a Record Label from A to Z, by Daylle Deanna Schwartz, Billboard Books, 1695 Oak St., Lakewood NJ 08701. (800)344-7119.

Recording Industry Sourcebook, Music Books Plus, P.O. Box 670, 240 Portage Rd., Lewiston NY 14092. (800)265-8481. Web site: www.musicbooksplus.com.

Reharmonization Techniques, by Randy Felts, Berklee Press, 1140 Boylston St., Boston MA 02215. (617)747-2146. E-mail: info@berkleepress.com. Web site: www.berkleepress.com.

The Songwriters Idea Book, by Sheila Davis, Writer's Digest Books, 4700 E. Galbraith Rd., Cincinnati OH 45236. (800)448-0915. Web site: www.writersdigest.com.

Songwriter's Market Guide to Song & Demo Submission Formats, Writer's Digest Books, 4700 E. Galbraith Rd., Cincinnati OH 45236. (800)448-0915. Web site: www.writersdigest.com.

Songwriter's Playground—Innovative Exercises in Creative Songwriting, by Barbara L. Jordan, Creative Music Marketing, 1085 Commonwealth Ave., Suite 323, Boston MA 02215. (617)926-8766.

The Songwriter's Workshop: Harmony, by Jimmy Kachulis, Berklee Press, 1140 Boylston St., Boston MA 02215. (617)747-2146. E-mail: info@berkleepress.com. Web site: www.berkleepress.com.

The Songwriter's Workshop: Melody, by Jimmy Kachulis, Berklee Press, 1140 Boylston St., Boston MA 02215. (617)747-2146. E-mail: info@berkleepress.com. Web site: www.berkleepress.com.

Songwriting and the Creative Process, by Steve Gillette, Sing Out! Publications, P.O. Box 5640, Bethlehem PA 18015-0253. (888)SING-OUT. E-mail: singout@libertynet.org. Web site: www.singout.org/sopubs.html.

Songwriting: Essential Guide to Lyric Form and Structure, by Pat Pattison, Berklee Press, 1140 Boylston St., Boston MA 02215. (617)747-2146. E-mail: info@berkleepress.com. Web site: www.www.berkleepress.com.

Songwriting: Essential Guide to Rhyming, by Pat Pattison, Berklee Press, 1140 Boylston St., Boston MA 02215. (617)747-2146. E-mail: info@berkleepress.com. Web site: www.berkleepress.com.

The Songwriting Sourcebook: How to Turn Chords Into Great Songs, by Rikky Rooksby, Backbeat Books, 600 Harrison St., San Francisco CA 94107. (415)947-6615. E-mail: books@musicplayer.com. Web site: www.backbeatbooks.com.

The Soul of the Writer, by Susan Tucker with Linda Lee Strother, Journey Publishing, P.O. Box 92411, Nashville TN 37209. (615)952-4894. Web site: www.journeypublishing.com.

Successful Lyric Writing, by Sheila Davis, Writer's Digest Books, 4700 E. Galbraith Rd., Cincinnati OH 45236. (800)448-0915. Web site: www.writersdigest.com.

This Business of Music Marketing and Promotion, by Tad Lathrop and Jim Pettigrew, Jr., Billboard Books, Watson-Guptill Publications, 770 Broadway, New York NY 10003. E-mail: info@watsonguptill.com.

Resources

Tim Sweeney's Guide to Releasing Independent Records, by Tim Sweeney, TSA Books, 31805 Highway 79 S., Temecula CA 92592. (909)303-9506. E-mail: info@tsamusic.com. Web site: www.tsamusic.com.

Tim Sweeney's Guide to Succeeding at Music Conventions, by Tim Sweeney, TSA Books, 31805 Highway 79 S., Temecula CA 92592. (909)303-9506. Web site: www.tsamusic.com.

Texas Music Industry Directory, Texas Music Office, Office of the Governor, P.O. Box 13246, Austin TX 78711. (512)463-6666. E-mail: music@governor.state.tx.us. Web site: www.governor.state.tx.us/music.

Tunesmith: Inside the Art of Songwriting, by Jimmy Webb, Hyperion, 77 W. 66th St., 11th Floor, New York NY 10023. (800)759-0190.

Volunteer Lawyers for the Arts Guide to Copyright for Musicians and Composers, One E. 53rd St., 6th Floor, New York NY 10022. (212)319-2787.

Writing Better Lyrics, by Pat Pattison, Writer's Digest Books, 4700 E. Galbraith Rd., Cincinnati OH 45236. (800)448-0915. Web site: www.writersdigest.com.

Writing Music for Hit Songs, by Jai Josefs, Schirmer Trade Books, 257 Park Ave. S., New York NY 10010. (212)254-2100.

The Yellow Pages of Rock, The Album Network, 120 N. Victory Blvd., Burbank CA 91502. (800)222-4382. Fax: (818)955-9048. E-mail: ypinfo@yprock.com.

Web Sites of Interest

The Internet provides a wealth of information for songwriters and performers, and the number of sites devoted to music grows each day. Below is a list of some Web sites that can offer you information, links to other music sites, contact with other songwriters and places to showcase your songs. Since the online world is changing and expanding at such a rapid pace, this is hardly a comprehensive list. But it gives you a place to start on your journey through the Internet to search for opportunities to get your music heard.

About.com Musicians' Exchange: http://musicians.about.com
Site featuring headlines and articles of interest to independent musicians, as well as numerous links.

American Music Center: www.amc.net
Classical/jazz archives, includes a list of composer organizations and contacts.

American Society of Composers, Authors and Publishers (ASCAP): www.ascap.com
Database of performed works in ASCAP's repertoire. Also includes songwriter, performer and publisher information, ASCAP membership information and industry news.

American Songwriter Magazine Homepage: www.americansongwriter.com
This is the official homepage for _American Songwriter Magazine_, featuring an online article archive, e-mail newsletter, and links.

Backstage Commerce: www.backstagecommerce.com
Offers secure online ordering support to artist Web sites for a commission.

The Bandit A&R Newsletter: www.banditnewsletter.com
Offers newsletter to help musicians target demos and press kits to labels, publishers, managers and production companies actively looking for new talent.

Bandname.com: www.bandname.com
Online band name registry and archive, as well as digital storefront services and classifieds.

Bathtubmusic.com: www.bathtubmusic.com
Online distributor of independent music.

Beaird Music Group Demos: www.beairdmusicgroup.com
Nashville demo service with samples and testimonial by _6 Steps to Songwriting Success_ author Jason Blume.

Berklee School of Music: www.berkleemusic.com
Offers online instruction, including a certificate program in songwriting.

Billboard.com: www.billboard.com
Music industry news and searchable online database of music companies by subscription.

The Blues Foundation: www.blues.org
Information on the foundation, its membership and events.

Jason Blume Hompage: www.jasonblume.com
This is the official homepage for *6 Steps to Songwriting Success* and *This Business of Songwriting* author Jason Blume. Offers articles and song critique services.

John Braheny Homepage: www.johnbraheny.com
John Braheny is the author of *The Craft and Business of Songwriting*, and his site features articles, interviews, and a blog with commentary on business and creative issues.

Broadcast Music, Inc. (BMI): www.bmi.com
Offers lists of song titles, songwriters and publishers of the BMI repertoire. Also includes BMI membership information, and general information on songwriting and licensing.

The Buzz Factor: www.thebuzzfactor.com
Offers press kit evaluation, press release writing, guerrilla music marketing, tips and weekly newsletter.

CDBABY: www.cdbaby.com
An online CD store dedicated solely to independent music.

CDFreedom: www.cdfreedom.com
Online CD store for independent musicians.

Center for the Promotion of Contemporary Composers (CPCC): www.under.org/cpcc
Web site for the Center for the Promotion of Contemporary Composers.

Chorus America: www.chorusamerica.org
The Web site of Chorus America, a national service organization for professional and volunteer choruses, including job listings and professional development information.

Cat Cohen's Homepage: www.catcohen.com
Homepage for singer-songwriter/producer Cat Cohen, author of *Songwriting for your Original Act* and contributor to John Braheny's *Craft & Business of Songwriting*. Offers ''Anatomy of a Hit'' hit song analysis columns, as well as songwriters' workshops.

Creative Musicians Coalition (CMC): www.aimcmc.com
Web site of the CMC, an international organization dedicated to the advancement of independent musicians, links to artists, and tips and techniques for musicians.

Custom Drum Tracks: www.realdrumstudio.com
Demo services by drummer/producer Pat Bautz, featuring custom drum tracks recorded and delivered online.

Dino's Demos: www.dinosdemos.com
Nashville song demo service with samples available online.

Film Music Network: www.filmmusicworld.com or www.filmmusic.net
Offers new about the fim music world, as well as educational and networking opportunities and an e-mail newsletter.

Fourfront Media and Music: www.knab.com
This site by music industry consultant Christopher Knab offers in-depth information on product development, promotion, publicity and performance.

Frank's Nashville Demos: www.nashville-songdemo.com
Nashville song demo service with sample demos available online.

Robin Frederick Homepage: www.robinfrederick.com
Official Web site for songwriting instructor Robin Frederick, offering articles and information on courses.

FromNowhereWithNothing.com: www.fromnowherewithnothing.com
Web site for Mary Dawson's new book about breaking into the music business, *How to Get Somewhere in the Music Business from Nowhere with Nothing.*

Garageband.com: www.garageband.com
Online music hosting site where bands can post music and profiles, and then be critiqued by online listeners and industry insiders.

Getsigned.com: www.getsigned.com
Interviews with industry executives, how-to business information and more.

Government Liaison Services: www.trademarkinfo.com
An intellectual property research firm. Offers a variety of trademark searches.

Guitar Nine Records: www.guitar9.com
Offers articles on songwriting, music theory, guitar techniques, etc.

Guitar Principles: www.guitarprinciples.com
Homepage for guitar teacher Jamie Andreas, offering instructional books, free newsletter, and message boards.

Harmony Central: www.harmony-central.com
Online musicians community with in-depth reviews of just about every piece of music equipment imaginable.

Harry Fox Agency: www.harryfox.com
Offers a comprehensive FAQ about licensing songs for use in recording, performance and film.

Independent Distribution Network: www.idnmusic.com/
Web site of independent bands distributing their music, with advice on everything from starting a band to finding labels.

Independent Songwriter Web Magazine: www.independentsongwriter.com
Independent music reviews, classifieds, message board and chat sessions.

Indie-Music.com: http://indie-music.com
Full of how-to articles, record label directory, radio links and venue listing.

International Songwriters Association (ISA): www.songwriter.co.uk
Homepage for *Songwriter Magazine*, offering articles and newsletter.

Jazz Composers Collective: www.jazzcollective.com
Industry information on composers, projects, recordings, concerts and events.

Jazz Corner: www.jazzcorner.com
Web site for musicians and organizations featuring links to 70 Web sites for jazz musicians and organizations, and the Speakeasy, an interactive conference area.

Just Plain Folks: www.jpfolks.com or www.justplainfolks.org
Online songwriting organization featuring messageboards, lyric feedback forums, member profiles, featured members' music, contact listings, chapter homepages, and an Internet radio station. (See the Just Plain Folks listing in the Organizations section).

Kathode Ray Music: www.kathoderaymusic.com
Specializes in marketing and promotion consultation.

Li'l Hank's Guide for Songwriters in L.A.: www.halsguide.com
Web site for songwriters with information on clubs, publishers, books, etc. as well as links to other songwriting sites.

Los Angeles Goes Underground: http://lagu.somaweb.org
Web site dedicated to underground rock bands from Los Angeles and Hollywood.

Pat & Pete Luboff Homepage: www.writesongs.com
This is the official Web site for *101 Songwriting Wrongs & How to Right Them* authors Pat & Pete Luboff. Offers information on workshops, consultation services, articles, useful links, and a collaboration agreement template for songwriters to download and use.

Lyrical Line: www.lyricalline.com
Offers places to market your songs, critique service, industry news and more.

LyricIdeas.com: www.lyricideas.com
Offers songwriting prompts, themes, and creative techniques for songwriting.

Lyricist.com: www.lyricist.com
Jeff Mallet's songwriter site offering contests, tips and job opportunities in the music industry.

MI2N (THE MUSIC INDUSTRY NEWS NETWORK): www.mi2n.com
Offers news on happenings in the music industry and career postings.

The Muse's Muse: www.musesmuse.com
Classifieds, catalog of lyric samples, songwriting articles, organizations, and chat room.

Music Books Plus: www.musicbooksplus.com
Online bookstore dedicated to music books on every imaginable music-related topic. Offers a free e-mail newsletter.

Music Publishers Association: www.mpa.org
Provides a copyright resource center, directory of member publishers and information on the organization.

Music Yellow Pages: www.musicyellowpages.com
Phone book listings of music-related businesses.

The Musicians Guide Through the Legal Jungle: www.legaljungleguide.com/resource.htm
Offers articles on copyright law, music publishing and talent agents.

MySpace.com: www.myspace.com
Social networking site featuring music Web pages for musicians and songwriters.

Nashville Songwriters Association International (NSAI): www.nashvillesongwriters.com
Official NSAI homepage offers news, links, online membership registration, and message board for members.

National Association of Composers USA (NACUSA): www.music-usa.org/nacusa
Web site of the organization dedicated to promotion and performance of new music by Americans, featuring a young composers' competition, concert schedule, job opportunities and more.

National Music Publishers Association: www.nmpa.org
The organization's online site with information about copyright, legislation and other concerns of the music publishing world.

Online Rock: www.onlinerock.com
Offers e-mail, marketing and free webpage services. Also features articles, chat rooms, links, etc.

Opera America: www.operaamerica.org
Web site of Opera America, featuring information on advocacy and awareness programs, publications, conference schedules and more.

Outersound: www.outersound.com
Information on finding a recording studio, educating yourself in the music industry, and a list of music magazines to advertise in or get reviewed by.

PerformerMag: www.performermag.com
Offers articles, music industry news, classifieds, and reviews.

***Performing Songwriter Magazine* Homepage:** www.performingsongwriter.com
This is the official homepage for *Performing Songwriter Magazine*, featuring articles and links.

Pamela Philips-Oland Homepage: www.pamoland.com
This the official site for *The Art of Writing Great Lyrics* and *The Art of Writing Love Songs* author Pamela Philips-Oland. Offers lyric critique service and a blog on various topics of interest to songwriters.

Pollack's Beatles Analysis: www.icce.rug.nl/ ~ soundscapes/DATABASES/AWP/awp-notes_on.shtml
In their time, the Beatles rewrote the book on pop songwriting, and this Web site is a treasure trove of insights into how the Beatles' songwriting worked.

Public Domain Music: www.pdinfo.com
Articles on public domain works and copyright, including public domain song lists, research resources, tips and a FAQ.

PUMP AUDIO: www.pumpaudio.com
License music for film and TV on a non-exclusive basis.

RecordingProject.com: www.recordingproject.com
Site dedicated to recording enthusiasts, both professional and beginning/amateur. Features discussion boards and extensive articles on tracking, mixing, effects, etc.

Record-Producer.com: www.record-producer.com
Extensive site dedicated to audio engineering and record production. Offers a free newsletter, online instruction, and e-books on various aspects of record production and audio engineering.

Rhythm Net: www.rhythmnet.com
Online CD store for independent musicians.

SESAC Inc.: www.sesac.com
Includes SESAC performing rights organization information, songwriter profiles, organization news, licensing information and links to other sites.

Soma FM: www.somafm.com
Internet underground/alterative radio with nine stations broadcasting from San Francisco.

Song Shark: www.geocities.com/songshark
Web site of information on known song sharks.

Songcatalog.com: www.songcatalog.com
Online song catalog database for licensing.

SongConsultant.com: www.songconsultant.com
Song consultations by Nashville songwriter/producer/publisher Dude McLean.

Songlink: www.songlink.com
Offers opportunities to pitch songs to music publishers for specific recording projects, also industry news.

SongRamp.com: www.songramp.com
Online songwriting organization with message boards, blogs, news, and streaming music channels.

Songsalive!: www.songsalive.org
Online songwriters organization and community.

Songscope.com: www.songscope.com
Online song catalog database for pitching and licensing.

Songwriter101.com: www.songwriter101.com
Offers articles, music industry news, and message boards.

SongwriterDemo.com: www.songwriterdemo.com
Song demo studio based in Nashville.

The Songwriters Connection: www.songwritersconnection.com
Offers articles, song critiques, workshops, seminars, and one-on-one consultations with *The Secrets of Songwriting* author Sarah Tucker.

Songwriter's Guild of America (SGA): www.songwritersguild.com
Offers industry news, member services information, newsletters, contract reviews and more.

Songwriter's Resource Network: www.songwritersresourcenetwork.com
Online information and services designed especially for songwriters.

The Songwriters Studio: www.thesongwritersstudio.com
Nashville demo service operated by producer Steven Cooper.

SongwriterUniverse.com: www.songwriteruniverse.com
Features articles, interviews, song evaluations, consultations, streaming music channels, a monthly contest, message boards, and links.

The Songwriting Education Resource: www.craftofsongwriting.com
An educational site for Nashville songwriters offering discussion boards, articles, and links.

Resources

SongU.com: www.songu.com
Offers online songwriting courses, networking opportunities, e-mail newsletter, and opportunities to pitch songs to industry professionals.

Sonic Bids: www.sonicbids.com
Features an online press kit template with photos, bio, music samples, and a date calendar.

StarPolish: www.starpolish.com
Features articles and interviews on the music industry.

SummerSongs Songwriting Camps: www.summersongs.com
Offers songwriting camp information and online registration.

Tagworld.com: www.tagworld.com
Social networking site similar to MySpace where bands and singer-songwriters can post songs, build a fanbase, and network.

TAXI: www.taxi.com
Independent A&R vehicle that shops demos to A&R professionals.

United States Copyright Office: http://www.copyright.gov
The homepage for the U.S. copyright office, offering information on registering songs.

The Velvet Rope: www.velvetrope.com
Famous/infamous online music industry message board.

Weirdomusic.com: www.weirdomusic.com
Online music magazine with articles, reviews, downloads, and links to Internet radio shows.

Yahoo!: www.yahoo.com/Entertainment/Music/
Use this search engine to retrieve over 20,000 music listings.

Resources

RESOURCES

Glossary

A cappella. Choral singing without accompaniment.

AAA form. A song form in which every verse has the same melody; often used for songs that tell a story.

AABA, ABAB. A commonly used song pattern consisting of two verses, a bridge and a verse, or a repeated pattern of verse and bridge, where the verses are musically the same.

A&R Director. Record company executive in charge of the Artists and Repertoire Department who is responsible for finding and developing new artists and matching songs with artists.

A/C. Adult contemporary music.

Advance. Money paid to the songwriter or recording artist, which is then recouped before regular royalty payment begins. Sometimes called ''up front'' money, advances are deducted from royalties.

AFIM. Association for Independent Music (formerly NAIRD). Organization for independent record companies, distributors, retailers, manufacturers, etc.

AFM. American Federation of Musicians. A union for musicians and arrangers.

AFTRA. American Federation of Television and Radio Artists. A union for performers.

AIMP. Association of Independent Music Publishers.

Airplay. The radio broadcast of a recording.

AOR. Album-Oriented Rock. A radio format that primarily plays selections from rock albums as opposed to hit singles.

Arrangement. An adaptation of a composition for a recording or performance, with consideration for the melody, harmony, instrumentation, tempo, style, etc.

ASCAP. American Society of Composers, Authors and Publishers. A performing rights society. (See the Organizations section.)

Assignment. Transfer of rights of a song from writer to publisher.

Audio Visual Index (AVI). A database containing title and production information for cue sheets which are available from a performing rights organization. Currently, BMI, ASCAP, SOCAN, PRS, APRA and SACEM contribute their cue sheet listings to the AVI.

Audiovisual. Refers to presentations that use audio backup for visual material.

Background music. Music used that creates mood and supports the spoken dialogue of a radio program or visual action of an audiovisual work. Not feature or theme music.

b&w. Black and white.

Bed. Prerecorded music used as background material in commercials. In rap music, often refers to the sampled and looped drums and music over which the rapper performs.

Black box. Theater without fixed stage or seating arrangements, capable of a variety of formations. Usually a small space, often attached to a major theater complex, used for workshops or experimental works calling for small casts and limited sets.

BMI. Broadcast Music, Inc. A performing rights society. (See the Organizations section.)

Booking agent. Person who schedules performances for entertainers.

Bootlegging. Unauthorized recording and selling of a song.

Business manager. Person who handles the financial aspects of artistic careers.

Buzz. Attention an act generates through the media and word of mouth.

b/w. Backed with. Usually refers to the B-side of a single.

C&W. Country and western.

Catalog. The collected songs of one writer, or all songs handled by one publisher.

CD. Compact Disc (see below).

CD-R. A recordable CD.

CD-ROM. Compact Disc-Read Only Memory. A computer information storage medium capable of holding enormous amounts of data. Information on a CD-ROM cannot be deleted. A computer user must have a CD-ROM drive to access a CD-ROM.

Chamber music. Any music suitable for performance in a small audience area or chamber.

Chamber orchestra. A miniature orchestra usually containing one instrument per part.

Chart. The written arrangement of a song.

Charts. The trade magazines' lists of the best-selling records.

CHR. Comtemporary Hit Radio. Top 40 pop music.

Collaboration. Two or more artists, writers, etc., working together on a single project; for instance, a playwright and a songwriter creating a musical together.

Compact disc. A small disc (about 4.7 inches in diameter) holding digitally encoded music that is read by a laser beam in a CD player.

Composers. The men and women who create musical compositions for motion pictures and other audio visual works, or the creators of classical music composition.

Co-publish. Two or more parties own publishing rights to the same song.

Copyright. The exclusive legal right giving the creator of a work the power to control the publishing, reproduction and selling of the work. Although a song is technically copyrighted at the time it is written, the best legal protection of that copyright comes through registering the copyright with the Library of Congress.

Copyright infringement. Unauthorized use of a copyrighted song or portions thereof.

Cover recording. A new version of a previously recorded song.

Crossover. A song that becomes popular in two or more musical categories (e.g., country and pop).

Cut. Any finished recording; a selection from a LP. Also to record.

DAT. Digital Audio Tape. A professional and consumer audio cassette format for recording and playing back digitally-encoded material. DAT cassettes are approximately one-third smaller than conventional audio cassettes.

DCC. Digital Compact Cassette. A consumer audio cassette format for recording and playing back digitally-encoded tape. DCC tapes are the same size as analog cassettes.

Demo. A recording of a song submitted as a demonstration of a writer's or artist's skills.

Derivative work. A work derived from another work, such as a translation, musical arrangement, sound recording, or motion picture version.

Distributor. Wholesale marketing agent responsible for getting records from manufacturers to retailers.

Donut. A jingle with singing at the beginning and end and instrumental background in the middle. Ad copy is recorded over the middle section.

E-mail. Electronic mail. Computer address where a company or individual can be reached via modem.

Engineer. A specially-trained individual who operates recording studio equipment.

Enhanced CD. General term for an audio CD that also contains multimedia computer information. It is playable in both standard CD players and CD-ROM drives.

EP. Extended play record or cassette containing more selections than a standard single, but fewer than a standard album.

EPK. Electronic press kit. Usually contains photos, sound files, bio information, reviews, tour dates, etc. posted online. Sonicbids.com is a popular EPK hosting Web site.

Final mix. The art of combining all the various sounds that take place during the recording session into a two-track stereo or mono tape. Reflects the total product and all of the energies and talents the artist, producer and engineer have put into the project.

Fly space. The area above a stage from which set pieces are lowered and raised during a performance.

Folio. A softcover collection of printed music prepared for sale.

Following. A fan base committed to going to gigs and buying albums.

Foreign rights societies. Performing rights societies other than domestic which have reciprocal agreements with ASCAP and BMI for the collection of royalties accrued by foreign radio and television airplay and other public performance of the writer members of the above groups.

Harry Fox Agency. Organization that collects mechanical royalties.

Grammy. Music industry awards presented by the National Academy of Recording Arts and Sciences.

Hip-hop. A dance oriented musical style derived from a combination of disco, rap and R&B.

Hit. A song or record that achieves top 40 status.

Hook. A memorable ''catch'' phrase or melody line that is repeated in a song.

House. Dance music created by remixing samples from other songs.

Hypertext. Words or groups of words in an electronic document that are linked to other text, such as a definition or a related document. Hypertext can also be linked to illustrations.

Indie. An independent record label, music publisher or producer.

Infringement. A violation of the exclusive rights granted by the copyright law to a copyright owner.

Internet. A worldwide network of computers that offers access to a wide variety of electronic resources.

ips. Inches per second; a speed designation for tape recording.

IRC. International reply coupon, necessary for the return of materials sent out of the country. Available at most post offices.

Jingle. Usually a short verse set to music designed as a commercial message.

Lead sheet. Written version (melody, chord symbols and lyric) of a song.

Leader. Plastic (non-recordable) tape at the beginning and between songs for ease in selection.

Libretto. The text of an opera or any long choral work. The booklet containing such text.

Listing. Block of information in this book about a specific company.

LP. Designation for long-playing record played at $33\frac{1}{3}$ rpm.

Lyric sheet. A typed or written copy of a song's lyrics.

Market. A potential song or music buyer; also a demographic division of the record-buying public.

Master. Edited and mixed tape used in the production of records; the best or original copy of a recording from which copies are made.

MD. MiniDisc. A 2.5 inch disk for recording and playing back digitally-encoded music.

Mechanical right. The right to profit from the physical reproduction of a song.

Mechanical royalty. Money earned from record, tape and CD sales.

MIDI. Musical instrument digital interface. Universal standard interface that allows musical instruments to communicate with each other and computers.

Mini Disc. (See MD above.)

Mix. To blend a multi-track recording into the desired balance of sound, usually to a 2-track stereo master.

Modem. MOdulator/DEModulator. A computer device used to send data from one computer to another via telephone line.

MOR. Middle of the road. Easy-listening popular music.

MP3. File format of a relatively small size that stores audio files on a computer. Music saved in a MP3 format can be played only with a MP3 player (which can be downloaded onto a computer).

Ms. Manuscript.

Multimedia. Computers and software capable of integrating text, sound, photographic-quality images, animation and video.

Music bed. (See **Bed** above.)

Music jobber. A wholesale distributor of printed music.

Music library. A business that purchases canned music, which can then be bought by producers of radio and TV commercials, films, videos and audiovisual productions to use however they wish.

Music publisher. A company that evaluates songs for commercial potential, finds artists to record them, finds other uses (such as TV or film) for the songs, collects income generated by the songs and protects copyrights from infringement.

Music Row. An area of Nashville, TN, encompassing Sixteenth, Seventeeth and Eighteenth avenues where most of the major publishing houses, recording studios, mastering labs, songwriters, singers, promoters, etc. practice their trade.

NARAS. National Academy of Recording Arts and Sciences.

The National Academy of Songwriters (NAS). The largest U.S. songwriters' association. (See the Organizations section.)

Needle-drop. Refers to a type of music library. A needledrop music library is a licensed library that allows producers to borrow music on a rate schedule. The price depends on how the music will be used.

Network. A group of computers electronically linked to share information and resources.

NMPA. National Music Publishers Association.

One-off. A deal between songwriter and publisher which includes only one song or project at a time. No future involvement is implicated. Many times a single song contract accompanies a one-off deal.

One-stop. A wholesale distributor of who sells small quantities of records to ''mom and pop'' record stores, retailers and jukebox operators.

Operetta. Light, humorous, satiric plot or poem, set to cheerful light music with occasional spoken dialogue.

Overdub. To record an additional part (vocal or instrumental) onto a basic multi-track recording.

Parody. A satirical imitation of a literary or musical work. Permission from the owner of the copyright is generally required before commercial exploitation of a parody.

Payola. Dishonest payment to broadcasters in exchange for airplay.

Performing rights. A specific right granted by U.S. copyright law protecting a composition from being publicly performed without the owner's permission.

Performing rights organization. An organization that collects income from the public performance of songs written by its members and then proportionally distributes this income to the individual copyright holder based on the number of performances of each song.

Personal manager. A person who represents artists to develop and enhance their careers. Personal managers may negotiate contracts, hire and dismiss other agencies and personnel relating to the artist's career, review material, help with artist promotions and perform many services.

Piracy. The unauthorized reproduction and selling of printed or recorded music.

Pitch. To attempt to solicit interest for a song by audition.

Playlist. List of songs a radio station will play.

Points. A negotiable percentage paid to producers and artists for records sold.

Producer. Person who supervises every aspect of a recording project.

Production company. Company specializing in producing jingle packages for advertising agencies. May also refer to companies specializing in audiovisual programs.

Professional manager. Member of a music publisher's staff who screens submitted material and tries to get the company's catalog of songs recorded.

Proscenium. Permanent architectural arch in a theater that separates the stage from the audience.

Public domain. Any composition with an expired, lapsed or invalid copyright, and therefore belonging to everyone.

Purchase license. Fee paid for music used from a stock music library.

Query. A letter of inquiry to an industry professional soliciting his interest.

R&B. Rhythm and blues.

Rack Jobber. Distributors who lease floor space from department stores and put in racks of albums.

Rate. The percentage of royalty as specified by contract.

Release. Any record issued by a record company.

Residuals. In advertising or television, payments to singers and musicians for use of a performance.

RIAA. Recording Industry Association of America.

Royalty. Percentage of money earned from the sale of records or use of a song.

RPM. Revolutions per minute. Refers to phonograph turntable speed.

SAE. Self-addressed envelope (with no postage attached).

SASE. Self-addressed stamped envelope.

SATB. The abbreviation for parts in choral music, meaning Soprano, Alto, Tenor and Bass.

Score. A complete arrangement of all the notes and parts of a composition (vocal or instrumental) written out on staves. A full score, or orchestral score, depicts every orchestral part on a separate staff and is used by a conductor.

Self-contained. A band or recording act that writes all their own material.

SESAC. A performing rights organization, originally the Society of European Stage Authors and Composers. (See the Organizations section.)

SFX. Sound effects.

Shop. To pitch songs to a number of companies or publishers.

Single. 45 rpm record with only one song per side. A 12″ single refers to a long version of one song on a 12″ disc, usually used for dance music.

Ska. Fast tempo dance music influenced primarily by reggae and punk, usually featuring horns, saxophone and bass.

SOCAN. Society of Composers, Authors and Music Publishers of Canada. A Canadian performing rights organization. (See the Organizations section.)

Solicited. Songs or materials that have been requested.

Song plugger. A songwriter representative whose main responsibility is promoting uncut songs to music publishers, record companies, artists and producers.

Song shark. Person who deals with songwriters deceptively for his own profit.

SoundScan. A company that collates the register tapes of reporting stores to track the actual number of albums sold at the retail level.

Soundtrack. The audio, including music and narration, of a film, videotape or audiovisual program.

Space stage. Open stage that features lighting and, perhaps, projected scenery.

Split publishing. To divide publishing rights between two or more publishers.

Staff songwriter. A songwriter who has an exclusive agreement with a publisher.

Statutory royalty rate. The maximum payment for mechanical rights guaranteed by law that a record company may pay the songwriter and his publisher for each record or tape sold.

Subpublishing. Certain rights granted by a U.S. publisher to a foreign publisher in exchange for promoting the U.S. catalog in his territory.

Synchronization. Technique of timing a musical soundtrack to action on film or video.

Take. Either an attempt to record a vocal or instrument part, or an acceptable recording of a performance.

Tejano. A musical form begun in the late 1970s by regional bands in south Texas, its style reflects a blended Mexican-American culture. Incorporates elements of rock, country, R&B and jazz, and often features accordion and 12-string guitar.

Thrust stage. Stage with audience on three sides and a stagehouse or wall on the fourth side.

Top 40. The first 40 songs on the pop music charts at any given time. Also refers to a style of music which emulates that heard on the current top 40.

Track. Divisions of a recording tape (e.g., 24-track tape) that can be individually recorded in the studio, then mixed into a finished master.

Trades. Publications covering the music industry.

12″ Single. A 12-inch record containing one or more remixes of a song, originally intended for dance club play.

Unsolicited. Songs or materials that were not requested and are not expected.

VHS. ½″ videocassette format.

Vocal score. An arrangement of vocal music detailing all vocal parts, and condensing all accompanying instrumental music into one piano part.

Web site. An address on the World Wide Web that can be accessed by computer modem. It may contain text, graphics and sound.

Wing space. The offstage area surrounding the playing stage in a theater, unseen by the audience, where sets and props are hidden, actors wait for cues, and stagehands prepare to chance sets.

World music. A general music category which includes most musical forms originating outside the U.S. and Europe, including reggae and calypso. World music finds its roots primarily in the Caribbean, Latin America, Africa and the south Pacific.

World Wide Web (WWW). An Internet resource that utilizes hypertext to access information. It also supports formatted text, illustrations and sounds, depending on the user's computer capabilities.

Category
Indexes

The Category Indexes are a good place to begin searching for a markets. They break down the listings by section (music publishers, record companies, etc.) and by the type of music they are interested in. For example, if you write country songs, and are looking for a publisher to pitch them, go to the Music Publishers heading and then check the companies listed under the Country subheading. The music categories cover a wide range of variations within each genre, so be sure to read each listing thoroughly to make sure your own unique take on that genre is a good match. Some listings do not appear in these indexes because they did not cite a specific preference. Listings that were very specific, or whose music descriptions don't quite fit into these categories also do not appear. (Category listings for **Music Publishers** begin on this page, **Record Companies** on page 373, **Record Producers** on page 378 and **Managers & Booking Agents** begin on page 382.)

MUSIC PUBLISHERS

Adult Contemporary (also easy listening, middle of the road, AAA, ballads, etc.)

R&B (also soul, black, urban, etc.)

World Music (also reggae, ethnic, calypso, international, world beat, etc.)

RECORD COMPANIES

Adult Contemporary (also easy listening, middle of the road, AAA, ballads, etc.)

World Music (also reggae, ethnic, calypso, international, world beat, etc.)

RECORD PRODUCERS

Adult Contemporary (also easy listening, middle of the road, AAA, ballads, etc.)

Alternative (also modern rock, punk, college rock, new wave, hardcore, new music, industrial, ska, indie rock, garage, etc.)

Blues

New Age (also ambient)

Novelty (also comedy, humor, etc.)

Pop (also top 40, top 100, popular, chart hits, etc.)

World Music (also reggae, ethnic, calypso, international, world beat, etc.)

Openness to Submissions Index

Use this index to find companies open to your level of experience. It is recommended to use this index in conjunction with the Category Indexes found on page 366. Once you have compiled a list of companies open to your experience and music, read the information in these listings, paying close attention to the **How to Contact** subhead. (Also see A Sample Listing Decoded on page 11.)

◐ PREFERS EXPERIENCED, BUT OPEN TO BEGINNERS
Music Publishers

Openness Index

◖ OPEN TO PREVIOUSLY PUBLISHED/WELL-ESTABLISHED

Music Publishers

Record Companies

Film & TV Index

This index lists companies who place music in motion pictures and TV shows (excluding commercials). To learn more about their film/TV experience, read the information under **Film & TV** in their listings. It is recommended to use this index in conjunction with the Openness to Submissions Index beginning on page 389.

Geographic Index

This Geographic Index will help you locate companies by state, as well as those in countries outside of the U.S. It is recommended to use this index in conjunction with the Openness to Submissions Index on page 389. Once you find the names of companies in this index you are interested in, check the listings within each section for addresses, phone numbers, contact names and submission details.

Geographic Index

General Index

Use this index to locate specific markets and resources. Also, we list companies that appeared in the 2007 edition of *Songwriter's Market*, but do not appear this year, Instead of page numbers beside these markets you will find two-letter codes in parenthesis that explain why these markets no longer appear. The codes are (**ED**)—Editorial Decision, (**NS**)—Not Accepting Submissions, (**NR**)—No (or late) Response to Listing Request, (**OB**)—Out of Business, (**RR**)—Removed by Listing's Request, (**UC**)—Unable to Contact.

Songwriter's Market
Feedback

If you have a suggestion for improving *Songwriter's Market*, or would like to take part in a reader survey we conduct from time to time, please make a photocopy of this form (or cut it out of the book), fill it out, and return it to:

Songwriter's Market Feedback
4700 East Galbraith Road
Cincinnati, OH 45236
Fax: (513) 531-2686

◯ **Yes!** I'm willing to fill out a short survey by mail or online to provide feedback on *Songwriter's Market* or other books on songwriting.

◯ **Yes!** I have a suggestion to improve *Songwriter's Market* (attach a second sheet if more room is necessary):

_____
_____
_____
_____
_____
_____
_____
_____

Name: _____
Address: _____
City: _____ State: _____ Zip: _____
Phone: _____ Fax: _____
E-mail: _____ Web site: _____

I am a

◯ songwriter
◯ performing songwriter
◯ musician
◯ other: _____